Mastering

British Politics

Macmillan Master Series

Mastering

British Politics

Third edition

F. N. Forman
and
N. D. J. Baldwin

MACMILLAN

First edition 1985 reprinted four times
Second edition 1991 reprinted four times
Third edition 1996

Published by
MACMILLAN PRESS LTD
Houndmills, Basingstoke, Hampshire RG21 6XS
and London
Companies and representatives
throughout the world

ISBN 0–333–61626–X

A catalogue record for this book is available
from the British Library.

10   9   8   7   6   5   4   3   2   1
05   04   03   02   01   00   99   95   97   96

Typeset by Tek-Art, Croydon, Surrey.

Printed in Great Britain by Biddles Ltd, Guildford and King's Lynn

To the memory of
J. F. R. F. and D. A. M. B.

Contents

List of Figures

Preface

This book is a general introduction to the British system of government and politics. It is an attempt to convey clear information about every significant aspect of the subject and to facilitate an understanding of the British political system and contemporary British politics.

Britain and the world have changed considerably since the second edition was published in 1991. Sterling has left the Exchange Rate Mechanism of the European Monetary System. Financial markets have demonstrated their awesome power in a world of unimpeded capital movements. There has been a notable increase in the influence of the mass media and in Britain relations between the media and the party in office have been unusually hostile. The role of the judiciary and the courts at national and European level has grown largely at the expense of national Governments and Parliaments. More generally, the British nation-state – like its counterparts on the Continent of Europe – has had its traditionally dominant position eroded both by the growing competence and jurisdiction of the European Union and by the insistent claims and pressures from the 'nations' and localities within its own borders.

Perhaps most significant of all, British society and social attitudes have changed since the era of Margaret Thatcher in that ideas of community and partnership have come back into fashion with powerful, but as yet uncertain, effects upon both the process and the outcome of British politics. Equally, there is evidence of growing public cynicism, sometimes bordering upon contempt, for what happens in Whitehall and Westminster as well as a noticeable preference for local or private action.

One of the clear consequences of these developments has been to place constitutional issues firmly back upon the British political agenda after a period of about two decades when economic and social questions seemed more pressing. Another consequence has been the unavoidable need to conduct any sensible analysis of the British political system within its European and global contexts. Insular perspectives and analysis are no longer particularly useful or instructive in a world of global media and global markets.

Within the compass of a single volume it is not possible to provide a detailed description and analysis of all the topics covered. Readers who wish to delve more deeply into any particular aspect of the British political system should refer to the suggestions for further reading at the end of each chapter.

Part I deals with the political and electoral context within which the process of British politics takes place. *Chapter 1* considers British political culture, which is defined as the historical, cultural and attitudinal setting within which British political institutions have to function. *Chapter 2* discusses the evolving constitution by describing the key characteristics and analysing some of the leading interpretations of constitutional developments in Britain. *Chapter 3* describes the electoral system and assesses its strengths and weaknesses in the eyes of academics and politicians alike. *Chapter 4* deals with voting behaviour by identifying the most significant groups in the electorate, the main influences upon voting and some continuing uncertainties about the future.

Part II considers the sources of power, pressure and opinion within the British political system. *Chapter 5* deals principally with the two main political parties by considering their ideological principles, political functions, national organisation and constituency activities. *Chapter 6* reviews the main functions, organisation and power of pressure groups, and analyses the nature and extent of their involvement in the political process. *Chapter 7* looks at the increasingly significant role of the media, and assesses the nature and extent of their influence upon the political system. *Chapter 8* considers public opinion by seeking to explain its formation, sources and effects upon British politics.

Part III describes the history, activity and significance of the traditional institutions which constitute Parliament in Britain. *Chapter 9* reviews the powers and functions of the Monarchy, the ways in which it is financed, and its troubled relations with the media and the public. *Chapter 10* on the House of Lords touches upon the history of the institution before dealing with its composition, powers and functions, as well as the various proposals for reform. *Chapter 11* describes the composition, powers and functions of the House of Commons before briefly reviewing the progress of reform.

Part IV deals with the main components of central Government in Britain. *Chapter 12* examines the machinery of Cabinet government before going on to analyse the power of the Prime Minister and the role of the Cabinet. *Chapter 13* describes the structure and work of Departments, considers the role of Ministers and reviews some of the key problems of central Government. *Chapter 14* deals with the civil service by describing its composition and functions, reviewing the key issues and methods of control, and examining the executive Agencies and their implications for the future of the civil service in Britain.

Part V is concerned with the other public institutions in the British political system. *Chapter 15* deals with the public sector, notably the problems which have been posed by the public corporations in the past and the issues which have been raised more recently by the theory and practice of privatisation. It also focuses upon some topical issues raised by non-departmental public bodies and other forms of largely unaccountable public administration. *Chapter 16* describes the structure and composition, powers and functions of local government before going on to consider the vexed relations between central and local government and the various attempts by the centre to achieve greater control over the localities. It also considers some of the implications for all forms of sub-national government of current proposals for constitutional reform. *Chapter 17* considers the legal system, but concentrates especially upon the changing relationship between citizens and the state, the role of the police and the impact of administrative law. It also makes reference to the growing influence of European law upon the British legal system.

Part VI considers some broader and more philosophical issues relating to Britain's changing role in Europe, the process and outcome of policy and decision making, and the nature and limits of democracy in Britain. *Chapter 18* looks at the increasingly complex and significant impact of the European Union upon the course of politics in Britain. *Chapter 19* deals with the process of policy and decision making in British central Government by identifying the main stages in the process and analysing some of the key aspects and possible improvements. *Chapter 20* concludes the book with a few synoptic observations about the essence of British Parliamentary democracy.

As in previous editions, many people have helped in the preparation and development of the text. We would particularly like to thank Suzannah Tipple for her constant encouragement and support, and Keith Povey for his editorial assistance. We must record our gratitude to those who have read and commented upon various chapters in this third edition: Charles Anson, Mary Baber, Sir Robin Butler, Lord Lawson, Lord Merlyn Rees, Richard Mottram, Sir Patrick Nairne, Professor Philip Norton, Chris Pond, Professor Rod Rhodes, Peter Riddell, Michael Welsh and David Willetts. Our thanks are also due to the excellent staff in the Library of the House of Commons who were courteous and helpful as usual.

Any insights achieved in this edition – and indeed in earlier editions – owe a great deal to those mentioned and to many others too numerous to list on this occasion. Any errors of fact or opinion are, of course, entirely our responsibility.

London and Wroxton   F.N. FORMAN
December 1995   N.D.J. BALDWIN

Acknowledgements

The authors and publishers wish to thank the following for permission to use copyright material: The Economist for Fig. 9.4 from *The Economist*, 25 January 1992. Copyright © The Economist 1992; Financial Times for Fig. 18.1 from *Financial Times*, 9 December 1994; Guardian News Service Ltd for Fig. 16.3 from *The Guardian*, 3 May 1994; The Controller of Her Majesty's Copyright Office for Crown copyright material; The Independent for Figs. 15.4 and 16.4 from *The Independent*, 14 May 1995, 29 March 1995; Times Newspapers Ltd for Fig. 4.1, graphic, 'How Britain Voted: Region by Region', *The Sunday Times*, 12 April 1992, Fig. 4.3, table, 'Portrait of the Electorate', *The Sunday Times*, 12 April 1992, Fig. 4.5, graphic, 'How 11.1 Million Voters Changed Their Mind', *The Sunday Times*, 12 April 1992, and Fig. 5.1, 'What the Parties Stand for', *The Sunday Times*, 15 March 1992. Copyright © Times Newspapers Ltd 1992; and Fig 9.3, table, 'The Royal Family's Working Year', *The Times*, 1 January 1994. Copyright © Times Newspapers Ltd 1994. Every effort has been made to trace all the copyright-holders, but if any have been inadvertently overlooked the publishers will be pleased to make the necessary arrangement at the first opportunity.

PART 1

The Political and Electoral Context

1 British political culture

Any book on British politics has to begin with a chapter on British political culture, since this is the context within which British politics take place. The term 'political culture' is taken to mean the historical, cultural and attitudinal setting within which British political institutions have to function.[1] It is not easy to generalise about British political culture, but it is possible to identify some key characteristics which influence both the process and the outcome of politics in Britain.

1.1 Key characteristics

The key characteristics of British political culture can be stated quite simply, but they need to be qualified and refined if they are to be useful to students of British politics. It has often been said that politics in Britain are influenced by the notable continuity of Britain's national history, the unitary nature of the state, the underlying cohesion of the society, and the degree of political agreement on fundamental issues. Traditionally, there has been considerable moderation in the policies pursued by successive Governments of all parties and this has been matched by a considerable degree of public detachment from the process of politics, except, of course, at election times and on other occasions when political crises or scandals heighten media and public interest.

General statements of this kind have often been made and sometimes in a rather complacent tone. Yet it would be unwise to accept them at face value and it would be well to examine the extent to which they now accord with the evidence available today.

Historical continuity

There has been notable continuity in Britain's national history and the country is one of the oldest nation states in Europe. Such continuity is symbolised by some of its national institutions, such as the Monarchy and the two Houses of Parliament, which date back at least to medieval times (see Chapters 9, 10 and 11 for further details). Although there have also been some notable discontinuities in Britain's national history, such as the Civil War and the Interregnum in the mid-seventeenth century, the country has not been invaded successfully against the popular will since 1066, and the only successful revolution since the Civil War was the political *coup* of 1688 when James II fled the throne and William and Mary were invited by Parliament from Holland to take his place. This continuity applies to a greater or lesser extent to all parts of the United Kingdom.

In the case of *Wales*, the Welsh have been living in the same kingdom as the English since the fourteenth century English conquests. The link was later reinforced and personified by the victory of Henry Tudor (a Welshman) at the battle of Bosworth Field in 1485, and subsequently ratified by Act of Parliament in 1536 at the behest of his son Henry VIII.

In the case of *Scotland*, the constitutional bond between the Scots and the English was first established in 1603 when James VI of Scotland succeeded Elizabeth I of England and so became James I of England. The bond was later sealed by the Act of Union in 1707, although what was by then the Hanoverian succession (from Germany) to the throne of the United Kingdom was not secure until the defeat of the Young (Stuart) Pretender in 1745.

In the case of *Ireland*, the troubled relationship between the Irish and the English can be traced back at least to the Anglo-Norman invasion of Ireland in 1169-71. The Act of Union in 1800, which marked the unification of the two countries in one kingdom, was later ruptured by the 1916 Irish national uprising. This led to the partition of Ireland in 1921 and the creation of the six counties of Northern Ireland in 1922 as the last remaining part of the United Kingdom on the island of Ireland.

The result of this long and chequered history is that the British people now live in what is known officially as the United Kingdom of Great Britain and Northern Ireland. However, it will be more convenient in the rest of this book to use the colloquial term 'Britain' to describe the country as a whole. Figure 1.1 is a map of the British Isles showing the boundaries of England, Wales, Scotland and Northern Ireland; as well as the location of some of the principal cities.

Unitary state

One important consequence of Britain's national history is that the people now live in a unitary state – indeed, the most unitary state in the whole of the European Union. This means essentially that the laws passed by Parliament at Westminster apply normally to the entire country and that in nearly all important matters it is correct to speak of the country being governed from London. However, this observation has to be increasingly qualified to take account of Britain's membership of the European Union which in practice has diluted the doctrine of Parliamentary supremacy and the dominance of London. Of course, there is also a well established structure of local government in Britain which can claim a degree of legitimacy, since local Councillors are directly elected by the people in their localities. Yet (as we shall see in Chapter 16) the powers and functions of local government are determined by Parliament at Westminster and have been substantially reduced by successive Conservative Administrations since 1979.

Unlike the situation in the United States or Germany, where there are codified constitutions which define the legal rights and duties of the various levels of government, in the United Kingdom it is Parliament which is legally and constitutionally supreme (except in those matters where European law now prevails) and its writ runs throughout the United Kingdom. Of course (as we shall see in Chapters 17 and 18), the law of the land in cer-

Figure 1.1 Map of the British Isles

tain areas can be interpreted and sometimes modified by judicial decisions in the Courts and, increasingly, by the European Court of Justice as well. Yet in Britain it is still a basic principle that traditionally no institution has been considered on a par with Parliament and it is this which has given force to the idea that Britain is a Parliamentary democracy in a unitary state.

Cultural cohesion

For a long time there has been considerable cultural cohesion in Britain which has been reinforced by the fact that about four fifths of the total population are English and about four fifths live in urban or suburban areas. This means that in many respects the great majority of the British people live similar lives and hold a range of common attitudes based upon broadly common experience. They purchase goods manufactured for a mass market, they use common public services, they earn their living in a number of recognisably standard ways, they spend their leisure time in a range of common pursuits, and they share broadly similar aspirations for themselves and their families. Above all, they are subjected every day to the same influences of the mass media which (especially in the case of television) now do more than anything else to create a sense of shared national experience.

On the other hand, there are some significant cultural variations which derive from a wide range of economic, social, geographical and ethnic factors. For example, the traditional industrial structure in the midlands and the north of the country has been significantly different (until recent times) from the more modern service structure in the south and the east of the country, at any rate outside parts of London. Yet this pattern too has been changing as old industries have declined and sometimes disappeared altogether, while a new and predominantly service economy has grown up to a greater or lesser extent in all parts of the country under the spreading influence of new information technology.

Equally, while in the nation as a whole ethnic minorities make up no more than about one twentieth of the entire population, there are some parts of the large cities – for example, London, Bradford or Leicester – where people from ethnic minorities account for more than one fifth and sometimes as much as one third of the local population. In recent times these demographic developments have led some spokesmen for the Moslem community, for example, to call for the establishment of legal and constitutional arrangements designed to give them special status and a real degree of cultural and religious autonomy within the United Kingdom.

In all parts of the country British society still divides on class lines, although many of the traditional class distinctions based upon the occupation of the male head of household have been rendered increasingly meaningless by changes in the labour market and in the balance of economic power and responsibilities within families.[2] From one point of view it seems that, as people in all classes become more similar in their ways of life and material aspirations, the tendency towards social uniformity could increase. Yet from another point of view this looks less likely, because of the widening disparities of income and wealth between the poorest and the richest sections of society.[3] Indeed, current social developments in Britain and elsewhere suggest that there is a growing gulf between the experience and prospects of the well-off and skilled majority who are in well rewarded and relatively secure economic positions and the disadvantaged and relatively unskilled minority who are either employed in peripheral, part-time and low paid work or are not economically active at all – at any rate in the formal economy.

In future, much will depend upon the extent to which common economic and social aspirations are fulfilled or thwarted by the distribution of the available opportunities between different individuals, different social groups and different parts of the country. It will also depend upon the extent to which nationalist or racialist impulses are stoked up or dampened down, especially for those living in outlying or ethnically distinct parts of the country.

With regard to the various sub-national identities, a small minority of the Welsh are Welsh speaking and attracted by the cause of *Plaid Cymru*, the Welsh Nationalist Party, and their number could grow in future if the Principality appeared to languish or be seriously disadvantaged by London rule. As it happens, there is evidence to suggest that the Welsh economy has grown faster than its English counterpart in recent years thanks, in large part, to the disproportionate share of inward investment from abroad which it has been able to attract.

A somewhat larger minority of the Scots identify with the cause of the *Scottish*

National Party which aspires to full Scottish independence within the European Union. However, mainstream opinion north of the border (which is mostly Labour) seems more disposed towards the idea of devolution to a Scottish National Assembly, as was evident from the success of the multi-party campaign (not including the Scottish Conservatives or the Scottish Nationalists) for a Scottish Constitutional Convention.[4]

In *Northern Ireland*, political circumstances are even more peculiar in that opinion is divided on religious and constitutional lines according to the contrasting attitudes of the Protestant/Unionist and Catholic/Nationalist communities towards the idea of eventual Irish reunification. The hard-line Protestant/Unionists wrap themselves in the Union Jack, but might prefer to have self-government for their part of Ireland free from Westminster control as they did from 1922 to 1972 when they governed themselves from Stormont Castle. The hard-line Catholic/Nationalists, who support *Sinn Fein* (the political wing of the Irish Republican movement in the north), have been prepared to use both the bomb and the ballot in their struggle for reunification with the rest of Ireland. Since the end of 1993 the British and Irish Governments have been working together in a positive effort to advance what has been described as 'the peace process' in Northern Ireland. This initiative by the two Governments was originally prompted by exploratory talks between John Hume, leader of the Social Democratic and Labour Party, and Gerry Adams, leader of Sinn Fein. It was formalised in the Downing Street Declaration signed by John Major and Albert Reynolds on 15 December 1993. It has subsequently been carried forward by the cease-fire announced by the IRA at the end of August 1994, which has brought the first sustained period of peace to the Province for a quarter of a century.

Due allowance must, therefore, be made for all these nationalist and centrifugal forces in the United Kingdom. We should also take account of the growing cultural diversity in British society, which can result, for example, in the existence of primary school classes in such places as Tower Hamlets in London or Handsworth in Birmingham in which white, Anglo-Saxon children are in a tiny minority and English is not the first language for the vast majority of such children when they are at home.

Two kinds of consensus

There is an underlying political consensus in Britain, but it needs to be carefully defined if we are not to get the wrong ideas about it. A clear distinction has to be drawn between consensus on matters of policy and consensus on matters of procedure. We shall therefore deal briefly with each in turn.

Consensus on matters of policy was most marked during the Second World War, when there was a strong national commitment to a united war effort both at home and abroad. In the spheres of economic and social policy this was reflected in the general support given to the goals of the 1942 Beveridge Report which foreshadowed the principal elements in the post-war Welfare State and the 1944 Keynesian White Paper on Employment which established the post-war objective of full employment. Such an approach was adhered to in broad terms by successive Governments, whether Labour or Conservative, for 25 years or so after the war. However, in the later 1960s this consensus began to be called into question during the period of the second Wilson Administration (1966-70) and it was all but abandoned in the early 1970s during the first two years (1970-72) of the Heath Administration.

From the late 1970s until the downfall of Margaret Thatcher in 1990, policy consensus was out of fashion and party politics were polarised at any rate between the dominant elements in the two main parties. However, since the more pragmatic and emollient John Major took over the leadership of the Conservative Party in 1990 and with the emergence of Tony Blair as the elected leader of the 'new' Labour Party in 1994, there have been some signs that British politics may be assuming a more consensual pattern once again, at least in relation to those Thatcherite ideas which have been broadly accepted in all parties. For example, the diminished political role of the trade unions, the preference for home ownership, and the shrinking of the state industrial sector are all aspects of the Thatcherite legacy which seem to have been accepted by the Opposition parties.

It is true that in the early 1990s the Conservative leadership flirted with some older, neo-Victorian policy themes which emphasised the moral dimension of public policy under the rubric of 'Back to Basics', a slogan used by John Major at the 1993 Conservative Party Conference when he and his party needed a theme to distract public attention from the unpopular effects of economic recession. These and other factors have injected new elements of controversy into the political debate about the future of the Welfare State and its impact upon the attitudes and behaviour of the general public. All of this serves to indicate that there is nothing inevitable or permanent about periods of policy consensus or periods of policy conflict in the ebb and flow of British politics.

Consensus on matters of procedure, on the other hand, seems to have survived intact in its traditional form for a much longer period. Ever since the successive extensions of the franchise in the nineteenth and early twentieth centuries (see Chapter 3, pp. 29-30), this kind of consensus has been signified by widespread agreement upon the desirability of using Parliamentary channels for the implementation and ratification of political change. However, certain powerful pressure groups and minority sections of public opinion have occasionally challenged this view – for example, those who backed or took part in the campaigns for non-payment of the 'Poll Tax' in the late 1980s. It has included widespread acceptance of the view that General Election results should be regarded as decisive, provided, of course, the popular ballot produces for the victorious party a clear majority in the House of Commons. It has also included broad agreement upon the undesirability of making extensive constitutional changes unless backed by overwhelming all-party support. Nevertheless, this last point of consensus did not seem to inhibit the Thatcher Government's sustained assault upon the alleged overspending and other shortcomings of local government, and it seems unlikely to deter a future Labour Government from introducing a Scottish Parliament in Edinburgh and a Welsh Assembly in Cardiff.

It should be noted that all such examples of procedural consensus and periodic departures from it need to be seen against the background of the recurrent constitutional controversies which arise in Britain from time to time, especially when national institutions feel threatened by their counterparts at sub-national and supra-national level. Since the mid-1970s there has been a long running argument about the merits or otherwise of devolution to Scotland and Wales, reform of the House of Lords, the use of referenda in a Parliamentary constitution, and the possible introduction of proportional representation in the name of achieving a 'fairer' electoral system. In the late 1980s there were equally fierce debates about the reform of the official secrecy law and the 1989 Labour policy review included a wide range of constitutional reforms, including commitments to a Freedom of Information Act and the creation of regional Assemblies in England. Since the 1992 General Election the Conservative Parliamentary Party has been split, and the Conservative Government has been nearly defeated, by the bitter dispute over the extent of Britain's commitment to the process of European integration. For these and other reasons it is now harder than it used to be to argue that there is a secure procedural consensus in British politics.

1.2 Other significant features

There are a number of other significant features in British political culture which are worth mentioning at this stage. Some are more associated with the period from 1945 to 1979. Others arise from the growing diversity of British society in recent times which has served to reduce its traditional cultural and political cohesion.

Moderation of Governments

It has been traditional to argue that a significant feature of British political culture is the moderation and restraint shown by all Governments.[5] This has been reflected in the fact that, whereas all modern British Governments with a working majority in the House of Commons have had almost unfettered powers of legislation and political decision, they have usually exercised such power in a rather moderate and restrained way. Of course, such an assertion always seems more credible to the supporters than the opponents of any Government. Nevertheless there are some compelling reasons why it has often been borne out in practice, notwithstanding the noticeably more ideological tone and actions of central Government in the 1970s and 1980s.

Such moderation should not be confused with what were identified as middle-of-the-road policies of the kind pursued with conviction and continuity by Labour and Conservative Governments in the first 25 years or so after the Second World War. Rather it should be defined as a clear recognition by nearly all politicians in office that the vast majority of the British people greatly prefer an atmosphere of willing co-operation to unwelcome conflict and are more than likely to cast their votes at elections under the influence of such a preference. An even more fundamental reason for such moderation and restraint is that the economic and political realities of the modern world impose such cautious behaviour upon all Governments, no matter how abrasive or exhilarating the rhetoric may be. In the complex conditions of the interdependent world in which we live and with the growing realisation of our common ecological as well as economic predicament, every Government soon discovers that it can wield relatively little creative power, except on the surface or in the margin of events. Both at home and abroad there are many other influential participants in the political process who can prevent any Government from being able to achieve much more than that. It is in this sense of impaired capacity for taking truly independent and effective action that any modern Government simply has to be moderate and restrained in what it attempts to do.

Public detachment from politics

It has also been said of British political culture that the British people are relatively detached from the process of party politics, put a high value upon the maintenance of political stability, and are not usually keen to face up to the need for radical change, especially if it would affect them directly.[6] This view is reflected in the typically low turn-out at local elections; and the strength of parochial opposition to any larger developments which may be in the wider public interest, but which threaten to disturb 'my back yard'. It is also reflected in the widespread public preference for the quiet life and for 'cultivating one's garden' which finds expression in various social institutions from pubs to fishing clubs that absorb so much of the time and energy of the British people. In these circumstances the idea of active or continuous participation in the process of party politics appeals to no more than small and unusual minorities in the population, although the willingness to defend particular interests or advance particular causes is now a defining characteristic of the modern, media-influenced democracy in Britain.

The British people join a myriad of voluntary organisations according to taste and experience. Indeed, the British are some of the foremost 'joiners' in all the advanced industrial countries. Whether individual citizens are members of the National Trust or the Consumers' Association, the MCC or the RSPCA, they find themselves involved in the process of politics from time to time, even if only in connection with a single issue at a particular time (see Chapter 6, p.103). The point is that most ordinary citizens are not very sanguine about the role or capacity of Government – hence the familiar joke, 'I'm from the Government and I'm here to help you.' The result is that many people have concluded that it is not very sensible to hold high expectations of Government or other public agencies and this has led them to be especially wary of the promises made by politicians at election time. Yet paradoxically such scepticism and even mistrust of Government does not prevent many of the same people, notably those employed in the public sector or competing for positional goods in the political market place, from looking to Government and other public agencies for material advantage or redress of grievances.

As Paul Barker has written, there has been 'an undoubted retreat into the shell of self (or perhaps self plus family)'.[7] Concern with relative advantage or deprivation within narrowly defined reference groups and a determination to protect one's local environment have been more evident than general interest (except when artificially prompted by opinion pollsters) in the competitive performance of the economy or the transcendent issues of war and peace, ecological survival or disaster. The struggle for material satisfaction, or in some cases day-to-day survival, is so all absorbing for most people that few have either the time or the inclination to involve themselves directly in the formal process of party politics. In these circumstances the idea of a conscious political culture has meaning and resonance only for practising politicians, pressure group activists and media or academic pundits. Having said that, however, it is as well to notice that these atypical people seem to have grown in number and influence in recent times.

Social fragmentation

It can be argued that in recent times British society has become more fragmented than it was during the period from 1945 to 1979. There is a good deal of evidence for this, both systematic and anecdotal. In terms of hard economic facts, the gap has widened since 1979 between the richest ten per cent and the poorest ten per cent of the population.[8] The labour market has become significantly more stratified as a result of technological development, more flexible patterns of employment and greater self-confidence among senior managers. This has led to a growing proportion of casual and insecure workers within the labour force, the imposition of many more short term contracts, a dramatic growth of part-time work (especially for women), and a secular trend towards self-employment as more and more firms have shed labour and staff. Even the declining (though preponderant) proportion of core workers still enjoying the full panoply of acquired rights and privileges feel more insecure than they used to in the modern labour market.

In terms of political attitudes, the most resonant observation of the 1980s was Margaret Thatcher's assertion that 'there is no such thing as society'.[9] This summed up in a single phrase the rampant individualism of those years which created a new layer in the property owning democracy, a temporary and unsustainable property boom and a number of new millionaires. In the long recession which followed and in the more sober and cautious 1990s, the prevailing social attitudes are rather different and have become markedly more communitarian. However, the legacy of personal insecurity and social division has remained, nowhere more obviously than in the starkly different career prospects of the minority which has marketable skills, training or tertiary education, and the majority of people in all generations (but especially those over 50) who missed the opportunity to enhance their intellectual capital. In short, there are many who argue – especially, although not exclusively, on the left of British politics – that Britain has become a dramatically more unequal society since 1979 and that this has been too high a price to pay for the new opportunities which have been enjoyed by some people.[10]

1.3 The European context

Although Britain joined the European Community (as it then was called) as long ago as 1973 (see Chapter 18, p. 401), it has only been comparatively recently that Britain's membership of what is now called the European Union has begun really to influence not only how things are done, but what can (and cannot) be done in British politics. The 1972 Treaty of Accession allowed Britain a transition period of five years in most cases within which to adapt its laws and practices to the European model in those areas of policy where European law was applicable. It did not take Harold Wilson and the then Labour Opposition very long to decide that the terms of membership were not good enough and would consequently have to be renegotiated by a future Labour Government. This is precisely what happened when Labour came to power in 1974 and soon after Britain's membership on the basis of Labour's 'renegotiated terms' was approved by a two to one majority in the 1975 Referendum.

By the time that Margaret Thatcher and the Conservatives returned to power in 1979, it had become clear that Britain's net financial contribution to the European Community budget was unacceptably large. Consequently, she and the then Foreign Secretary, Lord Carrington, set out to negotiate special rebate arrangements designed to limit Britain's net contributions in future years. This was an objective which they achieved and for a few years thereafter the British political class seemed to be relatively content (apart from a few die-hard anti-Europeans in both main parties) with the terms and conditions of Britain's membership.

However, the evangelists for the European idea on the Continent (and to a limited extent in Britain) continued to work towards their ultimate goal – the evolution of an ever closer union of European peoples. In the minds of the Founding Fathers and their disciples this has always implied a process of European nation-building which one day would reach fruition with the creation of a European state to complement the constituent states of the European Union. The momentum in this direction was resumed in the 1986 Single European Act which made legislative provision for the creation of a Single Market throughout the European Community. This was a project which appealed to Margaret Thatcher and her senior Conservative colleagues, because it was a tangible expression of market economics on a European scale, Yet it necessarily entailed a pooling of sovereignty by all the member states to an extent which had not been attempted successfully since the 1950 Coal and Steel Community from which Britain stood aside. Thus both the depth and the breadth of European integration, to which Britain committed itself, were very significantly extended at that time.

More recently, Britain's European partners, in what has now become a European Community of fifteen member states, were keen to complement the liberal economics of the Single Market with other measures of common policy in the social and political spheres. At the end of the 1980s they therefore set in motion a programme of further integration which eventually culminated in the 1992 Treaty of Maastricht. At the heart of this new twist in the spiral of European integration was the idea of progress by stages towards European Monetary Union and a single European currency (ECU). This further degree of European integration alarmed John Major and Douglas Hurd, then British Prime Minister and Foreign Secretary respectively. They therefore insisted upon Britain's right to defer a decision on such a step, unless and until a future British Government and a future British Parliament decided to take it. They also negotiated for Britain an opt-out from all the provisions in the so-called Social Chapter of the Treaty – notably those concerning the right of workers to be consulted by their employers through Works Councils and other measures designed to mitigate the social consequences of market forces.

For the purpose of trying to persuade the so-called 'Euro-sceptics' in the House of Commons of the merits of the Maastricht Treaty, Douglas Hurd in particular tended to present it as the 'high-water mark' of the old integrationist philosophy and the birth of a new hybrid approach towards closer European co-operation based upon *international* as well as supranational pillars – in other words, a *confederal* as opposed to a federal approach to the future. Yet once again it seems that the British view of these matters may take insufficient account of the ambition of leading politicians on the Continent to take every available opportunity gradually to construct a real European Union.

The reason for dwelling upon these developments is to emphasise the extent to which Britain's membership of the European Union has influenced, is influencing and will continue to influence the development of British political culture over the years. In recent times the attitudes of many in the British political class (especially in the Conservative Party) have become more querulous and defensive towards the European project. Yet the reality is that Britain is most unlikely ever to quit the European Union, and there is no provision in the European Treaties for the expulsion of a member state – however troublesome or uncooperative it may become. On the other hand, the process of ever closer European integration is driven by private sector interests as well as by leading politicians, and there is evidence that business people, tourists, young people and many others take the existence and the opportunities of the European Union very much for granted. Thus in the longer run the correlation of forces does not necessarily favour the more cautious and sceptical approach of much of the political class in Britain.

1.4 Conclusion

When we consider British political culture, the main need is to distinguish between the cluster of dated myths and stereotypes which still appears in some accounts and the changing political and social realities which must qualify such traditional notions. If we wish to have an up-to-date understanding, it is necessary to realise that many of the traditional values and assumptions of British politics have been called into question by recent developments. For example, when the British economy grew strongly during most of the 1980s, there was little evidence of the values of civic culture which had been identified and admired by American academics visiting Britain in the 1950s and 1960s. A spirit of tolerance and a disposition to compromise were hardly the hallmarks of the Thatcher era and both main parties polarised significantly. In many ways British society became coarser in the 1980s as the British economy grew rapidly and a large number of people began to rise or fall by their own efforts.

Yet British political culture in the 1990s appears to be developing in rather different directions. This is partly due to the obvious differences between Margaret Thatcher 'the warrior' and John Major 'the healer', although it is a nice irony that the latter was elected to the leadership of the Conservative Party in 1990 in the mistaken belief that he was the most Thatcherite of the three candidates (the others being Michael Heseltine and Douglas Hurd). It is partly due to the influence of the so-called 'modernisers' in the Labour Party, who supported first Neil Kinnock, then John Smith and now Tony Blair in their efforts to convince the electorate that the modern Labour Party no longer threatens the interests of the middle class – or seemingly anyone else for that matter.

The most significant explanation, however, may be that after the boom and bust economic cycle of the late 1980s and early 1990s, great swathes of British society (especially those living in London and the South East) have become markedly more debt-averse and risk-averse. The result is that the public mood for the rest of the 1990s and perhaps beyond seems likely to be more cautious and sober than before. If sustained, this is likely to affect many aspects of economic, social and political behaviour; notably by encouraging more people to veer towards co-operation rather than conflict when they have a choice. The quest for equality had its heyday in the immediate post-war period. The quest for liberty reached its apotheosis during the later Thatcher period. It may be that in the mid-1990s the hour of fraternity or community has arrived. If this is so, it seems likely to be true in several different senses, including the growing realisation that people in Britain are living as much in an European and global context as in a British political culture.

Suggested questions

1   What are the key characteristics of British political culture and how have these been influenced by Britain's membership of the European Union?
2   Is the nature of British society conducive to the practice of democratic politics?
3   How has the growing heterogeneity of British society affected British political culture?

Notes

1. See D. Kavanagh: 'Political culture in Great Britain, the decline of the civic culture'; in G. Almond and S. Verba (eds): *The Civic Culture Revisited*, (Boston, Little Brown, 1980), pp. 136-62.
2. For example, many more women now go out to work than in former times and in some households women are now the principal or sole earners.
3. A study by Alissa Goodman and Steven Webb for the Institute for Fiscal Studies, entitled '*For richer, for poorer; the changing distribution of income in the United Kingdom, 1961-91*; showed that the increase in income inequality during the 1980s dwarfed the fluctuations in inequality seen in previous decades. The income share of the poorest tenth of the population fell back from 4.2 per cent in 1961 to 3 per cent in 1991 with most of this fall occurring during the 1980s. By contrast the share of the richest tenth of the population rose from 22 per cent to 25 per cent over the three decades (IFS Commentary No. 42, June 1994).
4. The campaign culminated in the so-called 'Claim of Right' which was signed by representatives of most parties in Scotland (excluding the Conservatives and the Scottish National Party) in Edinburgh at the end of March 1989. It reflected the fact that according to opinion polls at that time about 80 per cent of the Scots wanted to have a Parliament of their own with legislative and tax-raising powers.
5. See R.M. Punnett: *British Government and Politics*; 6th edn (London, Heinemann, 1994).
6. See A.H. Birch: *The British System of Government*; 9th edn (London, Allen and Unwin, 1993).
7. *New Society*, 29 November 1979.
8. See IFS Commentary No. 42.
9. See her long interview with *Woman's Own*, 31 October 1987.
10. See W. Hutton: *The State we're in* (London, Jonathan Cape, 1995), pp. 169-92.

Further reading

Almond, G.A. and Verba, S. (eds), *The Civic Culture Revisited* (Boston: Little, Brown, 1980).
Britain, An Official Handbook (London: HMSO, 1995).
Catterall, P. (ed.), *Contemporary Britain, An Annual Review* (Oxford: Blackwell, 1993).
Dahrendorf, R., *On Britain* (London: BBC, 1982).
Marwick, A., *British Society since 1945* (Harmondsworth: Penguin, 1982).
Morgan, K.O., *The People's Peace, British History 1945-89* (Oxford: OUP, 1990).
Paxman, J., *Friends in High Places: who runs Britain?* (London: Michael Joseph, 1990).
Rubinstein, W., *Capitalism, Culture and Decline in Britain, 1750-1990* (London: Routledge, 1993).
Sampson, A., *The Essential Anatomy of Britain* (London: Hodder and Stoughton, 1992).
Social Trends 25 (London: HMSO, 1995).

2 The evolving constitution

A constitution is usually defined as a body of fundamental principles, rules and conventions according to which a state or other organisation is governed. According to such a definition, Britain has a constitution. Yet as we shall see, it is notably different from the constitutions of most other democratic countries, principally because it is uncodified and relies upon the idea of Parliamentary supremacy.

2.1 Key characteristics

Although the key characteristics of the British constitution can be stated quite simply, they contain some powerful paradoxes and internal contradictions. This is mainly because it is an evolving constitution which is changing and developing all the time. At one time some characteristics may be particularly significant, at another time others, and so on. This makes it an interesting subject to study, but one which is hard to describe in a definitive way.

No codification

The British constitution is unusual in that it is uncodified and has not been assembled at any time into a single consolidated document. This makes it very different not only from the American constitution and those found on the Continent of Europe, but also from those of many Commonwealth countries which were granted their constitutional independence by Britain. Indeed, of all the democratic countries in the world, only Israel is comparable to Britain in having no single consolidated document codifying the way in which its political institutions are supposed to function and setting out the basic rights and duties of its citizens.

Yet in the absence of a single, basic constitutional text, it should not be assumed that Britain has no constitutional documents from which guidance can be derived where there is a need to elucidate the laws and conventions which govern British politics. For example, *Magna Carta*, which was signed by King John at the behest of the barons in 1215, is perhaps Britain's best known constitutional document. It provided in 61 clauses a clear

statement of feudal laws and customs. Many other documents of equal or greater constitutional significance have been drawn up since then.

The Bill of Rights in 1689 put the stamp of Parliamentary approval on the succession of William and Mary to the throne deserted by James II and extended the powers of
Parliament at the expense of the Crown. The Act of Settlement in 1701 was described in
its preamble as 'an Act for the further limitation of the Crown and the better securing of
the rights and liberties of the subject'. The Act of Union with Scotland in 1707 declared
in Article 3 that 'the United Kingdom of Great Britain be represented by one and the
same Parliament to be styled the Parliament of Great Britain'. The Act of Union with
Ireland in 1800 brought about the formation of the United Kingdom of Great Britain and
Ireland – later to be amended to 'Northern Ireland' following Irish partition in 1921.

The Reform Act in 1832 was the first of a series of statutes over the period from then
until modern times which were designed to extend the franchise at Parliamentary elections. The Ballot Act in 1872 introduced secret ballots for all elections to Parliament and
all contested municipal elections. The Local Government Act in 1888 established elected County Councils for the first time in new administrative counties. The Parliament Act
in 1911 regulated the relations between the two Houses of Parliament and confirmed the
legislative supremacy of the House of Commons, while reducing the maximum span of
a Parliament from seven to five years. The Redistribution of Seats Act in 1944 established independent Parliamentary Boundary Commissions to demarcate the constituencies on a fair and regular basis. The Representation of the People Act in 1969 lowered
the voting age from 21 to 18. The European Parliamentary Elections Act in 1978 provided for direct elections every five years to the European Parliament. It is worth noting
that, with the exception of Magna Carta and the Bill of Rights, all the examples given
are drawn from statute law – in other words, Acts of Parliament. This emphasises the
overriding importance of Parliament in Britain's uncodified constitution.

There are, however, many other documentary sources, including judicial proceedings, which clarify Britain's constitution by setting out the rights and duties which subsequently the people have come to take for granted. For example, in Bushell's Case of
1670, Lord Chief Justice Vaughan established the independence of juries. In Sommersett's
Case of 1772, Lord Mansfield recognised the freedom of a former slave from the American
colonies on the grounds of his residence in England and argued that slavery was 'so odi-
ous that nothing can be suffered to support it but positive law'. In Beatty v. Gillbanks of
1882, Justice Field established the principle that a man may not be convicted for a lawful act, even if he knows that it may cause another to commit an unlawful act.

Other sources of guidance on Britain's uncodified constitution include Erskine May,
the classic and constantly up-dated reference book written by successive Clerks of the
Commons on the procedures and privileges of the lower House; and certain learned works
written by eminent constitutional authorities down the ages, such as Blackstone and Bagehot.[1]

Considerable flexibility

Another key characteristic of the British constitution is its considerable flexibility. This
derives partly from the absence of neat constitutional formulae consolidated into a single, authoritative document – in contrast, for example, with the codified constitution of
the French Fifth Republic. However, it is essentially because no Parliament can bind its
successors and any Parliament can undo the legislation of its predecessors that it is dif-

ficult to achieve formal methods of constitutional limitation in Britain. Since Britain joined the European Community in 1973 the fabled flexibility of British constitutional arrangements has begun to be eroded by the gradual impact of European law. Increasingly the rulings of the European Court of Justice determine and codify sections of British law in those areas covered by the various European Treaties to which Britain is a party. In the process British constitutional and legal arrangements are beginning to resemble those on the Continent of Europe.

It is, therefore, apparent from even a cursory study of British history that the traditional flexibility of Britain's constitution has stemmed from the way in which the theoretically absolute and unlimited power of Parliament (in effect the governing majority in the House of Commons) has been severely modified and limited in practice by the weight of political tradition and precedent, the influence of constitutional conventions, and the well established commitment to the rule of law. All these traditional and practical constraints upon the theoretical supremacy of Parliament are now joined by the invasive influence of European law as a function of Britain's membership of the European Union. Together they qualify the traditional precepts and represent the latest stage in the evolution of the British constitution.

Importance of conventions

Another key characteristic of the British constitution is the importance of conventions, in other words established custom and practice. The conventions which have been so powerful in their influence upon constitutional developments in Britain are the product of organic growth over the centuries. They include, for example, the convention that the Monarch should send first for the leader of the largest single party in the House of Commons when it is necessary to form a new Government following a General Election or the fall of a Prime Minister in office; and the convention that Ministers are responsible and can be held to account by Parliament for what does or does not happen in their Departments.

This helps to explain why certain principles not declared in law – such as the Royal prerogative or Ministerial responsibility – have developed so fully over the years. It is also one of the reasons why there are such formidable obstacles to the achievement of deliberate constitutional reform in Britain. Another reason validated by long experience is that it is necessary to secure all-party agreement for such changes, and yet this precondition has rarely been fulfilled. Hence there is a paradoxical quality in Britain's constitutional arrangements which can best be understood only after close study of the way in which its political institutions have evolved over the centuries rather than by reference to any basic constitutional document. This is why we refer to Britain's evolving constitution which reflects the more general development of British politics and society over the centuries.

2.2 Views of the constitution

For schematic purposes we can say that there are really three different views of the constitution in Britain. There is the *classic liberal view*, which is based upon nostalgia for the period when the House of Commons really did hold sway over the Executive. There is the *governmental view*, which is based upon the assumption that the Executive is answerable not so much to Parliament as to the electorate every four or five years at General Elections. There is the *empirical view*, which seeks to take account both of the weakness of Parliament in relation to the Executive and of the Government of the day in relation to all the other limiting forces in the real world both within Britain and abroad.

Classic liberal view

Of the various interpretations of the British constitution which have been put forward over the years, perhaps the most traditional is the classic liberal view which is associated with the writings of Bagehot and Dicey in the nineteenth century.[2] This view holds that the House of Commons is the supreme political institution with the power to make and unmake Governments, pass any laws and resolve the great political issues of the day.

It accords only subsidiary constitutional significance to the Monarchy and the House of Lords. It takes little account of the political parties, pressure groups, the civil service, the media or public opinion. As R.H.S. Crossman pointed out, such a view could only have been valid for the period before any significant extension of the franchise, before the establishment of disciplined political parties with national organisations, and before the development of an impartial meritocratic civil service.[3]

This classic liberal view applied only during a brief era, 1832-67, when the House of Commons really was supreme. During that atypical period no fewer than ten Administrations fell because the House of Commons withdrew its support. By about 1885 the main principles propounded by Bagehot and Dicey were already being eroded or overtaken by new political realities which became steadily more apparent during the last quarter of the nineteenth century. For example, the legislative supremacy of Parliament was gradually overcome by the growing power of the political parties as they sought to appeal to a wider electorate which was extended in successive Reform Bills. The rule of law, which Dicey had identified as a fundamental principle of the constitution, was not necessarily the paramount consideration for all participants in the political process, at any rate for the disadvantaged sections of the community which often appealed to superior notions of natural justice. The importance of conventions meant little to all those who were outside the charmed circle of Parliamentary politics.

In modern conditions students of the British constitution need to make sense of a much more complex and bureaucratic form of democracy in which Parliamentary supremacy is only one important principle among many. The classic liberal view, although still regarded with respect and firmly established among the received ideas of British politics, is no longer particularly instructive as a guide to contemporary politics. It has been rendered rather obsolete by the enormously increased scope of modern Government and by the power of political parties, pressure groups, the media and public opinion. This elitist Parliamentary model of the nineteenth century has had to give way to the claims of a more pluralist and populist kind of democracy in the late twentieth century. The classic liberal view is shown in diagrammatic form in Figure 2.1.

Figure 2.1 Classic view of the Constitution

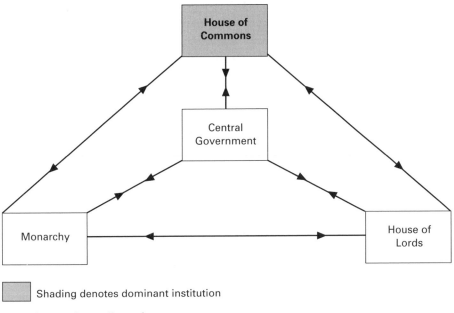

Shading denotes dominant institution

Arrows denote lines of contact

Governmental view

Another well known interpretation of the British constitution may be called the governmental view. This holds that the former power of the Monarch has been passed not to Parliament but to the Prime Minister and Cabinet, subject only to criticism in Parliament and periodic confirmation or rejection by the mass electorate at General Elections. It is a view usually associated with the writings of L. S. Amery and Herbert Morrison.[4] It maintains that the Government has a clear responsibility to govern and that the essential form of political accountability is the responsibility of the governing party to the electorate. Accordingly the role of the Opposition and all back-bench MPs is to act essentially as filters or megaphones between the Government of the day and the electorate. L. S. Amery was succinct when he wrote that 'the combination of responsible leadership by Government with responsible criticism in Parliament is the essence of our constitution'.[5]

Although this view, too, has to be qualified if we are to form an accurate impression of the way in which the British constitution really works, it has more validity than the classic liberal view which is now characterised by sentimentality towards a vanished era of truly Parliamentary government. In the administrative and legislative spheres at any rate modern British Governments have had virtually unlimited power, provided they have had a reliable working majority in the House of Commons and as long as they have been careful to keep their Parliamentary supporters united behind them. Under the terms of the 1911 Parliament Act a Government can retain this power for a maximum term of five years before it is obliged to seek a fresh mandate from the electorate. In view of the notable imbalance of political resources between Government and Opposition, there is some truth in Lord Hailsham's allegation that the British political system is ' an elective dictatorship' tempered only by the minimal restraints of constitutional conventions and the governing party's normal desire to get re-elected.[6] The Governmental view is shown diagrammatically in Figure 2.2.

Figure 2.2   Governmental view of the Constitution

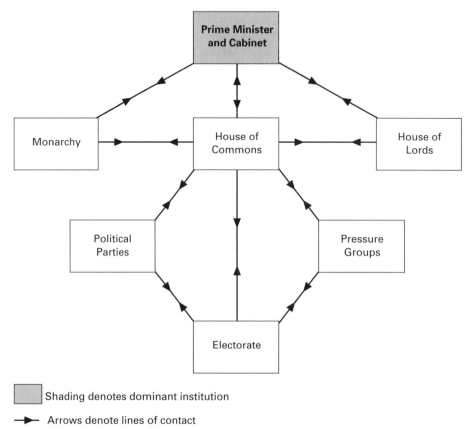

Shading denotes dominant institution

Arrows denote lines of contact

Empirical view

More accurate still in modern conditions is the empirical view of the constitution which emphasises both the weakness of Parliament in relation to the Government of the day and the weakness of the Executive in relation to pressure groups, the media, public opinion and other actors on the national and international scene. It emphasises the way in which a deliberate extension of constitutional power can lead to a decline in effective power, no matter how great the Parliamentary majority or the political momentum of the party in office. This is essentially because, if a Government becomes over-extended in its ambitions or over-loaded in its commitments, it is likely to encounter so many real world obstacles and to create so many political enemies that it is unable to achieve its objectives.

Indeed, a dispassionate reading of British constitutional history leads to the important conclusion that the most abiding political problem has been the gaining and retaining of public consent for the actions of any Government. Stage by stage from the thirteenth century to the present time, Governments in Britain, whether led by the Monarch or by a Prime Minister in Parliament, have had to cede and share power with the other great interests in the land – and nowadays increasingly with their partners in the European Union. Effective government has only been possible with the consent, or at least the tacit acquiescence, of those most directly affected by it or involved with it. Against this background it makes sense to regard successive British Governments as stable rather than strong, and to avoid confusing the concentration of responsibility with the concentration of power. Today public opinion, the influence of the media and the growth of European law are all examples of the powerful forces which condition and limit the exercise of power by any British Government.

Thus the contemporary British constitution is based upon *two key paradoxes*. The first is the limited power of a theoretically supreme Parliament. This reflects the fact that, while Parliament is perfectly capable of passing any law, it is in practice able only to criticise and intermittently control the Government of the day. It also reflects the growing political power and legal competence of the European Union, which has tended to reduce the power of the national Governments within it and hence the national Parliaments which claim to control them. The second is the limited power of the allegedly all-powerful Executive, which reflects the fact that, while a Government with a working majority in the House of Commons can invariably get its way in Whitehall and Westminster, little is achieved if its freedom of manoeuvre is unduly circumscribed by administrative constraints, media influence, interest group pressure or the impact of European law. This

Figure 2.3 Empirical view of the Constitution

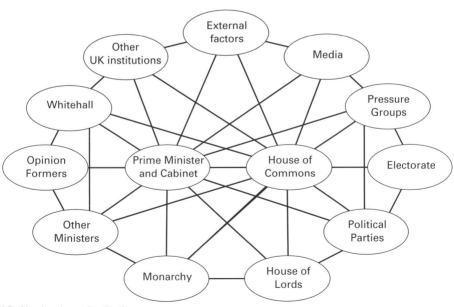

N.B. No dominant institution
Everything influences and is influenced by everything else

complicated network of informal checks and balances means that the evolving constitution continues to develop organically, but provides few constitutional safeguards against the arbitrary exercise of executive power.

Formal limitation of the power of any British Government is now more often sought and found in the rulings of the European Court of Justice or the European Court of Human Rights. On the other hand, informal constraints upon the power of all national Governments are to be observed most clearly these days in the capacity of the global financial markets to discipline any national authorities which lose credibility in the eyes of global investors, and in the enormous new power of the global media corporations. For a diagrammatic representation of this view see Figure 2.3 on the preceding page.

2.3 Pressures for change

Over the years constitutional changes have occurred piecemeal, even haphazardly, in response to the needs of public policy or the dictates of political necessity. No coherent pattern seems to have emerged and there has been no real attempt to co-ordinate the various initiatives which have been taken. Some have argued that there is an emerging constitutional crisis caused most notably by two factors: the challenge to British Parliamentary supremacy posed by the encroachment of European law, and the ever widening gap between the received ideas about Britain's 'unwritten constitution' and contemporary political realities. We shall look briefly at each of these matters in turn. However, before that we must consider the threat posed by the use of referenda to the system of Parliamentary government in Britain.

The use of referenda

The use of referenda in Britain in two celebrated cases in the 1970s produced some of the most notable constitutional developments of modern times.[7] 'Referendum' is defined in the *Concise Oxford Dictionary* (6th edition) as 'the referring of political questions to the electorate for direct decision by general vote'. As such, any referendum is still an unusual device in the British political system which has been dominated for so long by the assumptions and practices of Parliamentary democracy. It sits uneasily with Britain's traditional constitutional arrangements, although it must be added that its apparently satisfactory use on two important occasions in the 1970s testified to the robust flexibility of the British constitution.

In 1975 Britain's membership of the European Community (as the European Union was then called) on the terms 'renegotiated' by the Labour Government was put to a national referendum, mainly because the Labour party was so deeply divided on the issue that it was unable to reach a collective decision which would bind the entire Cabinet, and because it was thought that this device would settle the issue once and for all for both main parties. Indeed, the Wilson Administration was so seriously split on the issue that it was necessary to suspend the normal convention of collective responsibility for the duration of the referendum campaign, so that Cabinet Ministers and others could argue freely against each other in public – something which had not happened since the open agreement to differ in the National Government (made up of both

Labour and Conservatives) in 1931 on the issue of tariff reform.

In 1979 the legislation proposed by the Callaghan Government and passed by Parliament for the devolution of certain legislative powers to Scotland and Wales had to be put to separate referenda in each of those parts of the United Kingdom, because there seemed to be no other way of overcoming the persistent and effective Parliamentary opposition to the legislation from both sides of the House of Commons – but especially from the Government back-benches. As things turned out, the House of Commons passed an amendment to the legislation which insisted that, unless at least 40 per cent of those *entitled to vote* in each relevant part of the country supported the policy, the provisions of the legislation would not be put into effect. This proved to be a sufficient obstacle to the implementation of the legislation, since in neither Scotland nor Wales did as many as 40 per cent of those qualified to vote cast a 'Yes' vote.[8]

These two special cases of Europe and devolution have since been seen by many people as valid precedents for the use of referenda in future, especially when the position taken by a majority in the House of Commons is fiercely opposed by an irreconcilable minority in the governing party or is apparently at odds with the view held by a majority of public opinion – in the latter case, for example, on the emotive issue of capital punishment. In this context there were strong calls for a national referendum on British adherence to the 1992 Maastricht Treaty from Margaret Thatcher and other members of a vociferous all-party campaign against Britain's participation in the latest stage in the process of ever deeper European integration. These calls were resisted by the Major Government which managed to win a crucial vote in the House of Commons on the matter. Nevertheless the issue has not gone away and it is now believed that there may be a political necessity to hold another referendum on Europe to give the general public a chance to ratify or reject the constitutional implications either of the 1996 Inter-Governmental Conference on the implementation of the Maastricht Treaty or of participation in a single European currency if a future British Government and a future British Parliament decided that Britain should join such an arrangement.

The pressures for the use of referenda in these and other cases reflect a number of different factors. In part referenda are now seen as a way of enabling the governing party at any time to reconcile the irreconcilable on portentous issues, such as the nature and extent of Britain's relationship with the other member states of the European Union, where no satisfactory compromise formula seems to be available to the two sides of the argument within each of the main parties. In part the pressure for referenda reflects growing public impatience with the fastidious views of many MPs in all parties who refuse to toe a populist line on a number of emotive issues. In part it is testimony to the diminished status and authority of Parliament in the eyes of a much less deferential public and a largely hostile media. In relation to Britain's seemingly impossible situation within the European Union (where the future project advocated by Britain's partners is unattractive to a majority in Britain, but the model preferred in Britain is not really on offer anywhere else in the European Union), the idea of holding further referenda has naturally appealed most to the politicians in office at any time, whether Labour or Conservative, because such issues seem capable of dividing and possibly destroying either main party in office. The bleak fact is that Government and Parliament in Britain (and indeed in many other representative democracies) now lack the necessary authority to impose such decisions upon the people via the traditional Parliamentary procedures. In short, it crystallises the problem of democratic legitimacy in modern society.

The encroachment of European law

The challenge to British Parliamentary supremacy posed by the encroachment of European law is an issue with the most far-reaching constitutional implications. It has been high-lighted by those in all parties who have opposed Britain's membership of the European Union (or at any rate Britain's deeper integration into the Union), just as it has tended to be played down by those who have favoured Britain's full participation at every stage of the European adventure. Now that Britain has been a member of the European Union for more than two decades, virtually no one is seriously arguing the case for British with-drawal. Yet a growing number of politicians in all parties (especially in the increasing-ly parochial Conservative Party) have been arguing for a redefinition of Britain's relations with her European Union partners along international rather than supranational lines. Indeed, Douglas Hurd and other senior Conservative Ministers argued that the 1992 Treaty of Maastricht was the 'high-water mark' of the supranational tide in Europe and that the alternative of internationalism as the basis for a future European confederation of nation states was, and indeed ought to be, much more prominent on the European agenda.

On the assumption that Britain remains within the European Union, the likely result will be that the supremacy of Parliament at Westminster will become increasingly atten-uated within the United Kingdom as the scope of European law is extended into more areas of British national life. More decisions of political importance will probably be taken at European level by the European institutions in which Britain will have no more than a minority stake, and more of the decisions in the Council of Ministers will proba-bly be taken by qualified majority vote in view of the enormous difficulties of running a Union of 15 or more member states on a basis of unanimity. The so-called 'democra-tic deficit', which recent European developments have revealed, is unlikely to be closed by Westminster and the other national Parliaments, but increasingly by the European Parliament with its growing powers of co-decision with the Council of Ministers. In an effort to staunch this integrationist tide British Conservative Ministers have forcefully put the case for the doctrine of 'subsidiarity' which holds that no decisions should be taken at European level which could more appropriately be taken at national level or below. Yet by no means all Britain's European partners have seen things in this way or have been as determined to safeguard theoretical national sovereignty and actual nation-al responsibility. Whatever the outcome of this titanic struggle between the suprana-tionalists and the internationalists in the European Union, it is clear that it no longer makes sense to consider the British constitution in an exclusively national context.

Other pressures for change

These and other constitutional developments affecting Britain may have been misinter-preted or even misrepresented in some cases. Yet they have encouraged some searching reconsideration of many basic constitutional assumptions in Britain, and strengthened the case for procedural, electoral and constitutional reform.

The advocates of Parliamentary reform have argued – and in December 1994 achieved the agreement of the House of Commons – for further procedural changes at Westminster designed to introduce more sensible hours of working, attract more women and other under-represented groups to stand for Parliament, and somewhat enhance the currently low reputation of all MPs in the eyes of the public.[9] The Liberal Democrats and some others in each of the main parties have campaigned for electoral reform, specifically the introduction of various forms of proportional representation in elections to Westminster. The Labour Party has put forward a very ambitious programme of constitutional reform which would add up to eleven measures, including reform of the House of Lords to deprive hereditary peers of the right to vote in its proceedings, the creation of a Scottish Parliament and a Welsh Assembly, and the possibility of regional assemblies in England (but in this case without fiscal or law-making powers). Leading legal figures and others in the multi-party movement, *Charter 88*, have argued the case for a new constitutional settlement based upon a new Bill of Rights and a codified constitution which would have to be interpreted and protected by a powerful new Supreme Court.[10]

The Conservative Government under Margaret Thatcher pushed through Parliament a wide range of legislation which, while not deliberately designed to bring about constitutional change, had some significant constitutional implications.[11] The 1979-83 Conservative Administration introduced legislation to restrict the already limited autonomy of local government. The 1983-87 Conservative Administration introduced further legislation to curb high spending local authorities and to abolish the Greater London Council and the other Metropolitan County Councils. The 1987-90 Thatcher Administration introduced the highly controversial Community Charge (Poll Tax) into Scotland in 1989 and into England and Wales (but not Northern Ireland) in 1990, along with the Uniform Business Rate which replaced industrial and commercial rates.

Under John Major's leadership since 1990 the sustained Conservative assault upon local government has diminished slightly, although tight financial control by central Government remains an important hallmark of Conservative policy. Between 1990 and 1992 the Community Charge was scrapped and the Council Tax introduced in its place with a greater emphasis upon property values (in 1991) rather than population as the basis for assessment. Michael Heseltine, who returned to the Cabinet in 1990 as Secretary of State for the Environment for a second time, addressed the issue of local government boundaries by establishing the so-called Banham Commission to examine the issue in the various parts of the country. After taking the unusual step of holding postal referenda in the counties where the proposals were most contentious, the Commission recommended the replacement of only 8 counties by all-purpose unitary authorities, thus enabling 31 counties in England to survive – albeit in some cases in geographically truncated form.[12]

Whereas the Conservatives under John Major have become more cautious in their attitude towards local government than they were under Margaret Thatcher, Ministers have demonstrated their continuing radical credentials more clearly in relation to extensive reform of the civil service. The result of this process (discussed more fully in Chapter 14) is that the civil service will have been reduced from over 700,000 in 1979 to under 500,000 by the end of the Parliament elected in 1992 and that at least 100 so-called 'Next Steps' Agencies have been established to deliver public goods and services more efficiently.[13]

Furthermore, from the late 1980s to the present day an issue of more general constitutional importance has been illuminated in a sharper light. This is the political problem posed by the ever widening gap between the received ideas about Britain's uncodified constitution and the contemporary political realities. One manifestation of this has been the multi-party and non-party campaign under the banner of *Charter 88* for comprehensive constitutional reform. This campaign has been based upon a 10-point programme which has called, among other things, for a new Bill of Rights, an independent and reformed judiciary and proportional representation for elections to Parliament at Westminster.[14]

Another manifestation of a more party political character has been the extent of Scottish disgust with all things English and Conservative, which has been evident since the dramatic SNP victory at the Glasgow Govan by-election in November 1988. In the eyes of many Scots this was a clear protest against both English Conservatism and the perceived ineffectiveness of the Scottish Labour Party at Westminster. A good deal of renewed momentum has been achieved by the Scottish National Party and from time to time it has commanded strong support in opinion polls conducted north of the border.[15] These pressures have also given a new sense of urgency to those who have campaigned for the establishment of a Scottish Parliament with its own law-making powers and certainly galvanised most of the other parties into supporting the so-called 'Claim of Right' for Scotland at the multi-party Constitutional Convention which has held in Edinburgh in March 1989.

The other main constitutional issue which has been brought to the fore during John Major's occupancy of 10 Downing Street is the constitutional future of Northern Ireland. The first break-through came in the form of the Downing Street Declaration of 15 December 1993 which was signed by John Major and Albert Reynolds on behalf of the British and Irish Governments. This led to exploratory peace talks both between London and Dublin and between each of the Governments and representatives of the Protestant/Unionist and Catholic/Nationalist communities in Northern Ireland. At the time of writing the fruits of this 'peace process' have been the announcement of a complete ceasefire by the IRA in August 1994 and talks about talks at official level on the Northern Ireland issue. All these developments have served to give the age-old Irish question renewed prominence in British politics and to raise some hopes of finally solving the intractable Irish problem.

2.4 Conclusion

Some years ago Nevil Johnson argued that 'the gap between the theory and the reality of British political institutions and procedures has assumed serious dimensions' and 'the root of the political difficulty is to be found in a refusal to recognise that much of the traditional language of the British constitution . . . has lost its vitality'.[16] This is a point of view which has become all the more persuasive as the British nation-state has been challenged by the European Union from above and by local loyalties, whether nationalist or parochial, from below. In such dynamic conditions the preservation of traditional constitutional forms will become increasingly difficult, and deliberate constitutional change will probably seem increasingly necessary.

The clear conclusion is that constitutional change and reform is nearly always on the agenda of British politics. Sometimes it is there explicitly, because the politicians in office wish to change the constitutional arrangements. Sometimes it is there implicitly, because the policies of a radical Government have important constitutional implications. Sometimes it is forced onto the political agenda by nationalist movements within the United Kingdom or supranational developments within the European Union. In any event it is clear that change is constant, if not always predictable or welcome, in Britain's evolving constitution.

Suggested questions

1 What are the key features of the British constitution?
2 Which view of the British constitution accords best with contemporary political circumstances?
3 What difference is Britain's membership of the European Union likely to make to constitutional arrangements in Britain?

Notes

1. William Blackstone, who was professor of Common Law at Oxford University, published his famous *Commentaries upon the laws of England* between 1765 and 1769. In that work he presented a clear and systematic description of English law in the mid-eighteenth century. Walter Bagehot was equally famous in the nineteenth centry for his great work, *The English Constitution*, which was published in 1867. This set out what he saw as the principles of British Parliamentary democracy at that time.
2. See W. Bagehot, *The English Constitution* (London: Fontana, 1978) and A.V. Dicey, *The Law of the Constitution* (London: Macmillan, 1959).
3. See R.H.S. Crossman's Introduction to W. Bagehot, *The English Constitution*; p. 35.
4. See L.S. Amery, *Thoughts on the Constitution* (Oxford: OUP, 1947), and H. Morrison, *Government and Parliament* (Oxford: OUP, 1959).
5. L.S. Amery, *Thoughts on the Constitution*, p. 32.
6. See Q. Hailsham, *The Dilemma of Democracy* (London: Collins, 1978) for an exposition of this argument.
7. For a fuller discussion of this subject see D.E. Butler and A. Ranney (eds), *Referendums: a comparative study of practice and theory* (Washington, D.C.: American Enterprise Institute, 1978), and V. Bogdanor, *The People and the Party System* (Cambridge: CUP, 1981), pp. 11-93.
8. In the event the vote in Scotland recorded 52 per cent of those who voted in favour and 48 per cent against, while the vote in Wales recorded a mere 20 per cent of those who voted in favour and 80 per cent against. This meant that in the Scottish case only 33 per cent of the qualified electorate voted 'Yes' and in the Welsh case only 12 per cent.
9. See *Hansard*, 19 December 1994, Cols 1456 - 1509, for further details.
10. *Charter 88* was launched in London as a non-party political movement on 29 November 1988. It took the view that fundamental liberties were insufficiently protected by the British constitution, since liberty in Britain was based not so much on a set of rules as a state of mind. It therefore called for a codified constitution, electoral reform, a new Bill of Rights, reform of the House of Lords, reform of the judiciary, and more equitable power sharing between central and local government.
11. For a fuller exposition of this argument see C. Graham and T. Prosser, *Waiving the rules: the constitution under Thatcherism* (Milton Keynes: Open University Press, 1988).
12. See *Financial Times*, 16 December 1994.
13. See Chapter 14, pp. 301-306 for further details.
14. The other seven points recommended in *Charter 88* were: the subjection of executive and prerogative power to the rule of law; the introduction of freedom of information and more open government; the creation of a democratically elected, non-hereditary House of Lords; control of the Executive by a democratically renewed Parliament; legal remedies against the abuse of power by central or local government; a more equitable distribution of power between the

various levels of government; and a written and codified constitution anchored in the principle of universal citizenship.

15. For example, a System Three poll in March 1989 showed that 52 per cent of those questioned in Scotland supported the SNP policy of independence for Scotland within the European Union, while 67 per cent did not believe that the campaign for a Scottish Assembly would succeed in persuading a Conservative Government. More recently, Scottish public opinion seems to have cooled somewhat on the idea of Scottish independence, although it still seems to be preferred to the other options by a narrow margin of the Scottish electorate. For example, in a Market Research Scotland poll published in *Scotland on Sunday* on 12 February 1995, 37 per cent favoured independence, 35 per cent favoured devolution, 19 per cent the unionist *status quo* and 9 per cent were undecided.

16. N. Johnson, *In search of the constitution* (London: Methuen, 1980), p. 26.

Further reading

Benn, T., *Common Sense* (London: Hutchinson, 1993).

Brazier, R., *Constitutional Reform* (Oxford: Clarendon Press, 1991).

Charter 88, Supplement to the Votes and Proceedings (London: House of Commons, 2 December 1988).

Graham, C. and Prosser, T. (eds), *Waiving the rules, the constitution under Thatcherism* (Milton Keynes: Open University Press, 1988).

Hailsham, Q., *On the Constitution* (London: Harper Collins, 1992).

Hennessy, P., *The Hidden Wiring: Unearthing the British Constitution* (London: Victor Gollancz, 1995).

Johnson, N., *In search of the constitution* (London: Methuen, 1980).

Norton, P., *The British Constitution in Flux* (Oxford: Martin Robertson, 1982).

Oliver, D., *Government in the United Kingdom* (Milton Keynes: Open University Press, 1991).

Ranney, A. (ed.), *The referendum device* (Washington, D.C.: American Enterprise Institute, 1981).

Wright, T., *Citizens and Subjects* (London: Routledge, 1994).

③ The electoral system

The electoral system in Britain is the product of historical evolution and development. It began to be put on a democratic basis at the time of *The Great Reform Act of 1832*. This gave the right to vote to an additional half-a-million individuals who had not previously had it, taking the proportion of the enfranchised adult population to 5 per cent. Subsequent Acts carried forward the process of enfranchisement:

1867 *The Representation of the People Act* – which carried forward the principles of the 1832 legislation, increasing the electorate to number almost 2.5 million (13 per cent of the adult population).

1872 *The Ballot Act* – which introduced the principle of secret or confidential voting.

1883 *The Corrupt & Illegal Practices Act* – which made bribery and other corrupt practices at elections criminal offences.

1884 *The Representation of The People Act* – which extended the franchise to householders and tenements and to all those who occupied land or tenements with an annual value of not less than ten pounds. The main effect of this Act was to give the vote to working men in the counties, taking the total number of voters to 5 million, 25 per cent of the adult population.

1885 *The Redistribution of Seats Act* – which introduced the principle of equal electoral districts – equal in terms of numbers of voters – and to a great extent ensured single-member constituencies.

1918 *The Representation of the People Act* – which did away with virtually all restrictions on adult male suffrage and extended the vote to include 8.5 million women over the age of 30, creating an electorate of over 21 million people, or 75 per cent of the adult population.

1928 *The Representation of the People (Equal Franchise) Act* – which placed women on the same basis as their male counterparts, namely enfranchising virtually all those 21 years of age and over, leading to an electorate of 27 million potential voters, 99 per cent of the adult population.

1948 *The Representation of the People Act* – which further extended the principle of 'one person, one vote' by abolishing additional votes for university graduates and for those owning business premises and land in constituencies other than those in which they lived.

1969   *The Representation of the People Act* – which reduced the minimum age of voting from 21 to 18.

1985   *The Representation of the People Act* – which extended the right to vote to British citizens resident abroad for a period of up to five years from leaving the country.

1989   *The Representation of the People Act* – which extended the right to vote to British citizens living abroad to up to twenty years from leaving Britain, a potential electorate of over 2 million, although by the time of the 1992 General Election only 34,454 had registered to vote.

The result of this is that there exists in Britain today a system of universal adult suffrage in which all British nationals – as well as citizens of the Irish Republic and of Commonwealth countries resident in the United Kingdom – aged 18 and over have the right to vote (including those British nationals living overseas and those temporarily on holiday abroad), with the exception of convicted felons, certified lunatics and peers of the realm.

3.1 The system today

At the 1992 General Election, 2948 candidates stood for election to the House of Commons and 43,249,721 people were eligible to vote. The 651 constituencies varied considerably in population and geographical area, although the average electorate in each constituency was approximately 66,500. For example, the Western Isles with the smallest electorate (22,784) was one of the largest in geographical area over (2,000 square miles), whereas the Isle of Wight with the largest electorate (99,838) was geographically confined to quite a small area (147 square miles). The largest constituency was Ross, Cromarty and Skye covering 3,686 square miles (with an electorate of 55,524); the smallest was Chelsea covering only 2.2 square miles (with an electorate of 42,371).

These discrepancies derive mainly from the fact that the population has expanded in some parts of the country, for example, East Anglia and the South West of England – while it has contracted in other parts, such as the inner city areas of London, Birmingham and Liverpool. The Boundary Commissions, which are strictly independent bodies, attempt every 10 to 15 years to rectify the most glaring anomalies. Reports of the Commissions for England, Scotland and Wales were approved by Parliament in 1983; the report for Northern Ireland was approved in 1982. As a result of these, the number of Parliamentary constituencies was increased from 635 to 650 for the General Election of 1983. By 1992, following an interim review, an additional constituency had been added by dividing the Milton Keynes constituency into two. The most recent review was approved by Parliament in 1995, taking the number of Parliamentary constituencies from 651 to 659 for the 1996/97 General Election.

Electoral mechanisms

On election day voters go to the polls to cast their votes in secret by putting 'X' against one name on the ballot paper. Any other mark may produce a spoiled vote which would be judged invalid at the end of the count. The marked ballot papers are folded and deposited by the voters in locked ballot boxes where they remain until the polling stations close at 10.00 p.m. (they open at 7.00 a.m.). The ballot boxes are then transported to a central point in the constituency (often a Town Hall) where the counting of the votes takes place under the supervision of the Acting Returning Officer (normally the Chief Executive of the local authority concerned). The results are declared at varying times depending upon the nature and size of the constituency, usually not less than about three hours after the closing of the polls but sometimes not until the following day.

Since 1948 it has also been permissible to cast postal votes if the voters concerned apply to be put on their constituency postal registers at least two weeks before polling day. Those who qualify for postal votes include people prevented by the nature of their job from voting in person (for example, merchant seamen or long-distance lorry drivers), people who are too sick or handicapped to vote in person, and those who have moved out of the constituency but are still on the electoral register where they used to live, including those living overseas, provided they have not been away for more than twenty years. People away on holiday on polling day also qualify for postal votes or can get a friend or relative to cast a proxy vote for them, provided they complete in advance the necessary formalities specified in the applicable legislation. In the General Election of 1992 about 720,000 postal votes were cast, 2.1 per cent of the total vote. Despite particular efforts in this regard by the parties, this was well down on the 793,000 cast in 1987 (2.4 per cent). Traditionally postal voting has generally been reckoned to favour the Conservative Party because of its superior organisation; in 1992, however, the Labour Party was convinced that some of its gains were due to its more effective efforts to secure the postal vote.[1] Nonetheless, postal votes can only make a decisive difference to a result in very marginal constituencies as in the vast majority of constituencies the number of postal votes only ranges between 500 and 1500.[2]

Individuals who are British citizens, or citizens of another Commonwealth country or of the Irish Republic, may stand as candidates for election to the House of Commons, provided that they are not disqualified from so doing. Those *not* legally entitled to stand include:

1 undischarged bankrupts
2 individuals sentenced to more than one year's imprisonment (until pardon or completion of sentence)[3]
3 certified lunatics
4 members of the House of Lords
5 ordained clergy in the Church of England, the Church of Scotland, the Church of Ireland and the Roman Catholic Church.
6 individuals holding offices stipulated in the House of Commons Disqualification Act, 1975, including civil servants, certain local government officials, judges, members of the regular armed forces and members of the police service.

There is no age limit – either minimum or maximum – for candidates, although Members of Parliament cannot take their seat in the House of Commons until they are 21 years of age. Similarly, there is no residence requirement, either in the constituency concerned or indeed in the country.

In order to be able to stand, an individual must be both nominated and seconded and then supported by a further eight individuals whose names appear on the electoral register in the constituency concerned. In addition, candidates must deposit a sum of £500 with the Returning Officer, a sum which is refunded after the election if they obtain more than 5 per cent of the votes cast. Since 1970 candidates have been allowed to put on the ballot papers not only their names (which appear in alphabetical order), but also a description of their party or political position in not more than six words - for example, 'Conservative'. 'Labour Party candidate', 'Liberal Democrat'.

An example of a ballot paper is provided in Figure 3.1.

Figure 3.1 *Example of a ballot paper*

	VOTE FOR ONE CANDIDATE ONLY	
1	**BURSTOW** (Paul Kenneth Burstow, of 114 Grove Road, Sutton, Surrey Liberal Democrat)	
2	**DUFFY** (James Duffy, of 6 Langley Avenue, Surbiton, Surrey, KT6 6QL Green Party)	
3	**HATCHARD** (Angela Rose Hatchard, of 5 May Tree Walk, Woodley Park, Lancashire, WN8 6UP Natural Law Party Candidate)	
4	**MAITLAND** (Olga Helen Maitland, of 21 Cloudesley Street, London, N1 0HX The Conservative Party Candidate)	
5	**MARTIN** (Geoffrey Clifford Martin, of 284 Gander Green Lane, Sutton, Surrey, SM3 9QF The Labour Party Candidate)	

Reproduced with the kind permission of the Returning Officer of the London Borough of Southwark

Each candidate is restricted by law to a maximum expenditure during the three to five weeks campaign. For the General Election of 1992 this stood at £4330 plus 4.9p for each name on the register of voters in a rural constituency and £4330 plus 3.7p for each name on the register of voters in an urban constituency.[4] This allowed a maximum expenditure – on average – of £7588 in a rural seat and £6790 in an urban seat, although most candidates declare expenses of rather less than the legal maxima.[5] In addition candidates are entitled to post one communication relating to the election to each household in a constituency free of charge, providing it weighs no more than 57 grammes.

With figures such as these it appears that Parliamentary elections are fought 'on the cheap' in Britain as compared with other countries. The main reason is that the serious money is spent by the political parties centrally – £23 million in 1992, £15 million in 1987 and £7.6 million in 1983.[6] Even so, these are not enormous figures for a country with an electorate of more than 43 million. The real explanation is that neither the parties nor the candidates have to spend large sums of money on buying TV time – indeed they are prohibited from doing so – unlike the position in the United States for example.

Each candidate has to have a designated agent who is legally responsible for seeing that all aspects of election law are observed and who, in an extreme case, could be sent to prison if found guilty of electoral malpractice by a court. The agent also serves in most cases as the local campaign manager for the candidate, although this is not part of an agent's legal duties. The bulk of the work in every election campaign is done by voluntary workers who are usually paid-up members of the party, but who may simply be sympathisers with the party cause or with the particular candidate.

First-past-the-post

The British electoral system is commonly described as 'first-past-the-post'. This means that in each constituency the candidate with the largest number of votes wins the seat. Usually this has the effect of turning the largest single minority of votes cast in the nation into a clear majority of seats in the House of Commons for the largest single party. In this way the system has benefited the two leading parties and discriminated against the political fortunes of all other parties, unless their votes are geographically concentrated in a particular part of the country.

This pattern of discrimination has been discernible for years in the British electoral system. At the 14 General Elections since the Second World War no party has ever won even half the votes cast, and often far fewer.[7] Yet the winning party has seldom won fewer than half the seats in the House of Commons. Both the Conservative and Labour parties have benefited from this so-called 'multiplier effect' which can produce a sizeable majority of Parliamentary seats on the basis of a minority of the popular votes cast. For example, the Labour Party enjoyed a positive differential (that is, between the percentage of seats won and votes cast) of 14 per cent in 1945 and 11 per cent in October 1974, while the Conservative Party enjoyed a positive differential of 8 per cent in 1959, 9 per cent in 1979, and 15 per cent in 1987. On the other hand, the Liberal Party has been the most notable victim of the system during the period since 1945. From 1945 to 1979, the Liberal share of the popular vote ranged from 2 per cent in 1951 to 19 per cent in February 1974. Yet the system prevented the Liberals from winning more than 2 per cent of the seats in the Commons even in their most successful attempt, in February 1974. In the 1983 General Election, this multiplier effect worked even more dramatically against the interests of the Alliance of Liberals and Social Democrats which won 25 per cent of the votes cast but only 3 per cent of the seats in the House of Commons. In the 1987 General Election it was virtually the same story with the Alliance winning about 23 per cent of the votes cast, but still getting only 3 per cent of the seats in the House of Commons. In 1992 the Liberal Democrats secured 18 per cent of the vote but only 3 per cent of the representation in the House of Commons. Figure 3.2 demonstrates the multiplier effect at the 1992 General Election.

Figure 3.2 Voting by party in 1992

Party	Number of votes	% of electorate	% of votes cast	% of seats won
Conservative	14,094,156	32.59	41.9	51.6
Labour	11,557,134	26.72	34.4	41.6
Liberal Democrat	5,998,446	13.87	17.8	3.1
Scottish Nationalist (SNP)	629,552	1.46	1.9	0.5
Plaid Cymru (PC)+	156,796	0.36	0.5	0.6
Green+	170,047	0.39	0.5	–
Ulster Unionist (OUP)	271,049	0.62	0.8	1.4
Democratic Unionist (DUP)	103,039	0.23	0.3	0.5
Popular Unionist	19,305	0.04	0.1	0.1
SDLP	184,445	0.43	0.5	0.6
Sinn Fein	78,291	0.18	0.2	–
Others	348,179	0.81	1.1	–
Total	33,610,399	77.70	100	100

+ Plaid Cymru totals include three joint PC/Green candidates.
Note: The total electorate stood at 43,249,721

From this it can be seen that whereas it took 41,946 votes to elect a Conservative MP, it took 42,646 votes to elect a Labour MP and 299,922 votes to elect a Liberal Democrat MP. Plainly, the number of seats won is in no way proportional to the number of votes cast by the electorate. This was brought home particularly clearly in both 1951 and February 1974. In the General Election of 1951, the Labour Party obtained 231,067 more votes (0.8 per cent) than the Conservative Party, but the Conservatives won 26 more seats than Labour. Similarly – although the roles were reversed – in the General Election of February 1974, the Conservative Party secured 225,789 more votes (0.7 per cent) than Labour, but the Labour Party won four more seats than the Conservatives. These results occurred because the votes of one party – the Conservatives in 1951 and Labour in 1974 – happened to be more effectively concentrated in a number of marginal constituencies, thus giving the winning party an edge over the other main party in Parliament. Yet the system has never been arithmetically fair to all parties and it has always had a bias against second or third parties whose votes are not socially or regionally concentrated. Its political merits lie elsewhere, namely in the tendency for most General Elections to produce effective Parliamentary majorities for single-party Governments. This has enabled the electorate to hold the governing party to account for what happens, or fails to happen, during a particular Parliament.

Proportional representation

The characteristics of the British electoral system have led many people, especially supporters of the smaller parties, to argue strongly for the introduction of a system based upon proportional representation.[8] There are a number of variants of the basic idea.

The proposal which has found the most favour over the years is for proportional representation on the basis of a *Single Transferable Vote* in large multi-member constituencies. This would allow the electorate in each constituency to vote for individual candidates in order of preference. To secure election, a candidate would need to obtain a certain quota of votes (established by dividing the total number of valid votes cast by the number of representatives to be returned for the constituency plus one, and then adding one to this total). Thus in a five-member constituency in which 240,000 votes were cast, the number of votes required for the quota (and hence election) would be 40,001:

$$\frac{240,000}{5+1} \ +1 \ = 40,001$$

If five candidates obtain this number of first preference votes, this is the end of the process. If, however, fewer than five reach the quota, a process of transference, or redistribution, takes place. Firstly, the 'excess' votes of the candidates who have gained more votes than the quota are transferred on the basis of second preferences, with the amount by which the votes of such candidates exceed the quota determining the value of the second preference votes. Hence, if a candidate gains 1500 first preference votes and the quota is 1000, a third of the votes has not been used. This candidate's second preference votes are therefore worth one third of a vote each. As a result, if 600 second preference votes went to candidate 'X', candidate 'X' would be allocated an additional 200 votes to add to his total of first preference votes. After the second preference votes of those with more than the quota have been transferred, and if five candidates have not yet obtained the quota, then the candidate with the fewest first preference votes is eliminated and the votes transferred on the basis of second preferences. This process is then continued until enough candidates reach the quota and all seats are filled.

Under this system, every elected candidate could be said to have sufficient votes from the electorate (at least on the basis of second and subsequent preferences) and it would be possible for the voters to vote for individual candidates within the ideological range of any large party. For example, in a safe Conservative constituency the voters might choose two hard-line Conservatives, one moderate Conservative, one Liberal Democrat and one centre-right Labour. In a safe Labour seat, they might equally choose one left-winger and two mainstream supporters of Tony Blair from Labour's ranks, one Liberal Democrat and one moderate Conservative.

This system of proportional representation was recommended by a Speaker's Conference in 1917. It was actually used in some of the multi-member University seats between 1918 and 1948; it was advocated by the Kilbrandon Commission in 1973 as part of the proposals for devolved Assemblies in Scotland and Wales; and it is currently used in Northern Ireland both for elections to the European Parliament and for local government elections. It is also the system used for Parliamentary elections in the Replublic of Ireland. It is estimated by many – certainly if current voting habits continued under a reformed system – that the likely outcome of a General Election fought on the basis of the Single Transferable Vote system would be Coalition Government – a Government made up of more than one political party.

Another variant of proportional representation which has been advocated is based upon the *Additional Member* principle. In this system, which is used in the Federal Republic of Germany, half of the Bundestag (Lower House) members are elected by plurality in single-member constituencies and the other half from party lists drawn up within each Land (state). The voters each have two votes: one for a constituency candidate and one for a regional party list. The former enables the voters to express their first preferences and, if it is in a good area for their party, to secure their first choice for Parliament by direct election. The latter enables the voters to express what amounts to a second preference, usually by voting for the party list of one of the smaller parties in an attempt to ensure that the major opponent of their first preference does not get elected. In other words they cast their second vote for the party they dislike least in an attempt to exclude the party they dislike most. The system can often improve the Parliamentary prospects for the smaller parties (such as the Free Democrats or the Greens) which might not otherwise have enough concentrated voting strength to get any of their candidates elected on a basis of first-past-the-post. It is also qualified by the so-called 5 per cent threshold which prevents parties with less than 5 per cent of the popular vote or three outright victories on the basis of first-past-the-post from securing any representation at all in the Bundestag.

Yet another variant which might well attract all-party support in Britain is based upon the *Two-Ballot System* used in France. This uses single member constituencies, but requires a candidate to win over half the votes cast in order to be elected on the first ballot. Failure to do this triggers a second ballot in which the result is decided by simple plurality, that is to say first-past-the-post. To go forward to the second ballot (if there is no outright winner on the first ballot), candidates require at least 12.5 per cent of the votes cast in the first ballot. This eliminates a great number of candidates from smaller parties or political splinter groups and automatically clarifies the voters' choice at the second ballot. The great advantage of this system is that it ensures majority support at least for those elected on the first ballot. The most commonly recognised disadvantage is that it is capable of producing bipolarised distortions which make it possible for a candidate who came third on the first ballot to triumph on the second because some of the supporters of the candidates who came first or second may find the third placed candidate the least unacceptable of the candidates in the second round. In other words, at the first ballot the voters choose, whereas at the second they eliminate. This system certainly does not avoid the imbalance between votes obtained and seats won identified under the first-past-the-post system - a point underlined by the fact that in the 1981 elections to the French National Assembly, the Socialists secured 62 per cent of the seats on the basis of only 38 per cent of the votes cast.

Two other systems should be noted. Firstly, there is the *Party List System*. Here the whole country could constitute a single constituency. Each party draws up a list of its candidates and the voters vote for the party they prefer. Once the votes have been counted, the parties are allocated seats in proportion to the number of votes they obtained. Hence, if a party gets 25 per cent of the vote, it gets 25 per cent of the seats, with individual candidates securing election according to their position on their party's list. This system is currently in use in Israel, Norway, Portugal and Turkey – in Israel it is used in its 'pure' form; the others use variants on the theme, for example by region and using thresholds. Some countries – for example Belgium, Denmark, Finland, the Netherlands,

Spain and Sweden – use a variation of this system, enabling voters to indicate a preference for candidates on the list. Secondly, there is the *Alternative Vote System* under which candidates contest single-member constituencies and voters mark the candidates in order of preference. If a candidate secures over half the votes cast, the candidate is elected; but if no candidate in a constituency does so, then the candidate with the fewest votes is eliminated and the votes redistributed according to the preferences indicated. This process continues until the support for a candidate passes the 50 per cent threshold. This system is currently in use for elections to the lower house in Australia.

Nearly all the MPs in the minor parties and some MPs in the large parties favour a change to proportional representation in Britain. Yet on present evidence it does not seem likely to be introduced, not least of all because the great majority of MPs in both large parties share a strong vested interest in the present electoral system and therefore oppose any such change in electoral law. Thus, electoral reform is unlikely to occur in Britain unless it is forced upon one or other of the large parties by the imperatives of political bargaining in a future 'hung Parliament', that is to say one in which no single party has an overall majority in the House of Commons. Nevertheless, questions of electoral fairness, concerns about a 'democratic deficit' and a focus on the lack of legitimacy of the first-past-the-post system are likely to remain part of the political and constitutional debate unless and until the current system is changed.

3.2 Criteria of assessment

In a celebrated text written more than 35 years ago W. J. M. Mackenzie suggested four criteria by which an electoral system could be assessed. These were the quality of those elected, the effectiveness of the legislature, the fairness of the electoral results, and the degree of public confidence inspired.[9] It may therefore be convenient to consider the British electoral system in the light of these four, admittedly rather ideal, criteria.

The quality of the MPs

Members of Parliament in Britain are not strictly representative of the general public in that they are usually better educated and financially better off than the electorate as a whole. Of course these general observations should come as no real surprise since similar statements could be made about every national assembly throughout the world, including those in former Communist countries. Yet there remains an utopian bias in some quarters in favour of achieving a more 'representative' House of Commons – by which people usually mean one composed of those more like them!

Taking the House of Commons which was elected in April 1992, we find that 39 per cent of Conservative MPs and 42 per cent of Labour MPs came from what can be described as professional occupations, namely the law, education, medicine, accountancy and so on. In addition, 38 per cent of Conservative MPs and 8 per cent of Labour MPs had an occupational background in business. A further 22 per cent of Conservative MPs and 28 per cent of Labour MPs had their occupational background as political organisers, journalists and so on. Only 1 per cent (four) of Conservative MPs and 22 per cent (59) of Labour MPs could be categorised as manual workers. As far as the Liberal

Democrat MPs were concerned, these categories accounted for 60 per cent, 10 per cent, 30 per cent and 0 per cent respectively.

Among Conservative MPs, 62 per cent had been educated at public school (with 16 per cent of those having been to Eton) and 86 per cent had experienced higher or further education, 45 per cent having been to either Oxford or Cambridge. Among Labour MPs only 14 per cent had received a public school education (and only 5 per cent of those had been to Eton), but 84 per cent had experienced higher or further education, although only 16 per cent had been to either Oxford or Cambridge. Among the Liberal Democrat MPs, 50 per cent had received a public school education (none at Eton), 90 per cent had received further or higher education, and 30 per cent had been to either Oxford or Cambridge.[10] Although the socio-economic differential has narrowed noticeably in recent years, it is nevertheless still apparent that Conservative MPs tend to come from more privileged backgrounds than their Labour and Liberal Democrat counterparts.

Certainly the House of Commons is far from being a microcosm of the population as a whole – a point which is most clearly evidenced by the fact that only 9.2 per cent of MPs elected in 1992 were women, even though women comprised 52 per cent of the total electorate at the time, and by the fact that only 0.9 per cent were from ethnic minorities, even though ethnic minorities comprised 5.9 per cent of the population.

Of course, characteristics such as educational and occupational background are not necessarily signs of quality and in any case the standard of MPs could always be higher. Yet quality is not really a function of the electoral system. It derives much more from the intermittent nature of Parliamentary work, the frustrations of life on the back-benches, the unwillingness of many employers to encourage their employees to stand for Parliament, and the low esteem in which politicians are held by the vast majority of the British people. All these factors may discourage many able people from standing for Parliament or even from entering active politics in the first place. Furthermore, in the front-bench-dominated political system that exists in Britain, no more than about 90 MPs are paid members of any Government and no more than about another 90 are involved in the tasks of front-bench Opposition. Thus the vast majority of MPs in the House of Commons at any time are obliged to busy themselves with other forms of political activity, such as liaising with outside interests or welfare work on behalf of their constituents. This may be appreciated by their contacts and expected by their constituents, but it does not necessarily attract the most talented people into Parliament.

Effectiveness of the legislature

There are many shortcomings in the British legislature, but they should not necessarily be attributed to the workings of the electoral system. One of the familiar charges levelled against the British system is that it makes it all too easy for one or other of the parties to win an overall majority in the Commons which can then be used to push through its partisan legislation, often against rather ineffective Parliamentary opposition and sometimes in defiance of the expressed wishes of the general public. According to this argument, Parliament is actually too effective at churning out partisan, ill-considered legislation and too ineffective at controlling the actions of the Government of the day. If this is so, it is essentially because all MPs not in the Government have little involvement and no responsibility in the formative stages of policy and decision making. It is also because Government back-benchers are inhibited by party loyalty and political self-interest from pursuing continuous public criticism of their own Ministers. Parliamentary control is therefore left largely in the hands of the Opposition, which is usually unable to do more than kick up a fuss about controversial Government decisions or delay the contentious elements in the Government's legislative programme. The system is indeed one in which although the Opposition has its say the Government gets its way, at any rate most of the time.

The British people expect their Members of Parliament to be doughty champions of their interests and unabashed spokesmen for their concerns. This is what they expect from an effective legislature. In practice, constituents are often disappointed to discover that the power of party loyalty usually overrides both more parochial and more altruistic considerations when it comes to votes in the House of Commons.. The argument for this position is effectively that MPs on the Government side are elected principally to support Government policy as set out in the party Manifesto and other relevant documents and can only rarely go against that imperative without undermining what is described as 'the mandate theory' of Government. Thus, those opposed to or critical of the Government's programme may well win the argument, but usually lose the vote at the end of debates in Parliament.

Fairness of the results

It is here that we enter the area of greatest controversy about the British electoral system. While it enables the electorate to choose what is normally a single-party Government every four or five years at General Election time, it does not produce a House of Commons which is anything like an exact reflection of the votes cast for each party. Essentially, it is a system which enables the largest single minority of voters in the national electorate to bring about the return of single-party Government with an overall majority in the House of Commons. There is, in fact, a threshold of between 35 per cent and 40 per cent of the votes cast above which (especially in marginal seats with three or more candidates) a party has a good chance of capturing seats, but below which it is likely to fail to form the Government.

This situation arises because most General Elections in Britain tend to be contests between at least three parties in which the second and third ranking parties frequently split the losing vote between them, thus ensuring that neither has a real chance of defeating the leading party. Obviously there is always the possibility of tactical voting by the supporters of one or other of the losing parties, yet on the whole this has not made much difference to the results (except occasionally at by-elections), since none of the parties can be sure of delivering enough of its supporters to guarantee such an outcome. The same flaw affects the idea of an electoral pact between the various Opposition parties in which all but one of them would stand down in individual constituencies in favour of the party with the best chance of defeating the incumbent.

In the General Election of February 1974 the third party (the Liberals) received more than 6 million votes, a little more than half the votes received by either the Conservative or Labour parties, but won only 14 seats in the House of Commons, less than one twentieth of the seats secured by either of the two main parties. At the same time, and as previously pointed out, the party which won the election (Labour) did so with fewer popular votes than the party which came second in terms of Parliamentary seats (the Conservatives). In the 1983 General Election the discrepancy between votes and seats was even more striking: the Conservative Party secured 61 per cent of the seats on 42.4 per cent of the votes cast, the Labour Party got 32 per cent of the seats on 27.6 per cent of the votes cast, while the Alliance of Liberals and Social Democrats, although receiving 25.4 per cent of the popular vote - just 2.2 per cent less than Labour - won only 3.5 per cent of the seats, 28.5 per cent less than Labour. In the General Election of 1992, despite polling almost 6 million votes (more than half the level of support obtained by the Labour Party), the Liberal Democrats still only obtained 20 seats in the House of Commons, in stark contrast to the 271 seats won by Labour.

Of course, the results could be very different if the potential supporters of third parties, those who abstain from voting and those who are deterred from supporting their first preference for fear of casting wasted votes, were all to vote in accordance with their real political preferences. In that case, there would be a possibility of parties which previously came third coming first in many parts of the country.

The most sensible conclusion is that the British electoral system is likely to remain unfair to third parties, but it is by no means clear that a particular party will always come third. In the scheme of things, fairness is not the prime consideration. The overriding purpose is to elect a Government with a sufficient Parliamentary majority to ensure its authority to govern throughout the period of a normal four or five year Parliament; in essence this means single-party Government.

Public confidence inspired

It is difficult to produce reliable measures of public confidence in something as abstract as an electoral system. One way of assessing it is to note the degree of popular support for electoral reform as measured by opinion polls. This has consistently proved attractive to representative samples of the electorate as a whole.[11] Not that exact parallels can be drawn, but it is nonetheless interesting to point out that when consulted in a referendum in September 1992, the people of New Zealand voted overwhelmingly (84.5 per cent) to end their first-past-the-post electoral system.[12]

Another way of assessing public confidence in the electoral system is to log the performance of the two large parties at successive General Elections. In view of the fact that they are so clearly associated in the public mind with adherence to the existing electoral system, a high level of support for both of them together could also be interpreted as support for the existing rules of the game. Doing this, we find that the proportion of the electorate voting for the Conservative and Labour parties taken together fell consistently from 79 per cent in 1951 to 55 per cent in October 1974. It rose to 62 per cent in 1979, fell back to 51 per cent in 1983, rose again to 55 per cent in 1987 and increased to 59 per cent in 1992. In the General Election of 1992, a sizeable proportion of the electorate (22 per cent) did not vote at all and the Conservative Party won with the support of only 32.5 per cent of the total electorate.[13] In so far as any valid or lasting conclusion can be drawn from this evidence, it can hardly be that the British public has given a massive vote of confidence in the electoral system.

3.3 The debate

Firstly, supporters of the first-past-the-post system argue that the system works well, pointing out that it has led to stable Governments based upon Parliamentary majorities of one party rather than Coalitions, which can be weak and ineffective. Single party Government is said to mean strong, accountable and responsive Government.

Critics of the present system counter this view in a variety of ways. (1) They argue that the system does not work well, pointing to the anomalies already referred to in this chapter as evidence of this. (2) They deny that stability is inherent in the system citing 1950-51, 1964-66, February and October 1974, and the periods 1976-79 and 1994-95 to back this up. (3) They point out that if by 'strong' Government is meant a Government that can force through unpopular legislation – such as the Poll Tax – then perhaps 'weak' Government, a Government that would have to listen to the views and opinions of others, would be no bad thing. (4) They assert that there is no justification for the view that proportional representation necessarily results in weak and unstable Government – citing the examples of Germany and Sweden to support the assertion. (5) They argue that the supporters of first-past-the-post are deluding themselves if they believe the system ensures decisive and strong action on the part of Government, and cite the weakness of John Major's Government at the time of the Parliamentary ratification of the Maastricht Treaty as evidence for their case. (6) They argue that the system encourages adversarial politics – citing the nationalisation, denationalisation, re-nationalisation and privatisation of the steel industry as one example of the damaging consequences of this approach to politics. (7) They point out that the first-past-the-post system is capable of creating Governments which behave like elective dictatorships, but which do so on a minority of the popular vote.

Secondly, supporters of the first-past-the-post system argue that electoral reform would lead to Coalition Government and that this would place disproportionate power in the hands of the minor parties. It would be the minor parties which would dictate the outcome of elections, it would be the minor parties which would exert disproportionate influence on Government policy and it could be the minor parties which would determine the date and the occasion of the subsequent election. In short, the tail would be wagging the dog. To support this assertion they point to the role of the Free Democrats in Germany, a party which has often struggled to get even 10 per cent of the vote and yet has been an essential component of most post-war German Governments.

Those who argue for electoral reform respond by asking why this should be a problem if it ensures effective, successful Government – and cite the 'German Economic Miracle' as evidence of what can be achieved in such circumstances. Besides which, they go on to point out, 'deals' with minor parties are not unknown in the British political system, citing the Lib-Lab Pact of 1977-79 and the Conservative Government's dependence upon the Ulster Unionists at the time of the Maastricht debates in 1992-93. In their view, there is nothing inherently wrong in Coalition Governments, since the main political parties are Coalitions in themselves. In other words, the present system is based upon intra-party coalitions, whereas a reformed system would depend on inter-party Coalitions.

Thirdly, those who argue in favour of the current electoral system caution that any reform could lead to the rise of extremists – citing the rise of the Fascist Right (the Republican Party) in Germany in the early 1990s.

Advocates of reform respond by observing that those who profess to be worried by the danger of Fascism and the extreme Right would do better to consider introducing formal checks and balances into Britain's constitutional arrangements – such as a written constitution, a new Bill of Rights, and electoral reform. Without this there exists a system which allows, even facilitates, Government by a single party, with the support of about two fifths of the popular vote, enjoying predominant power in Westminster. They go on to point out that an electoral system based on proportional representation would be an instrument which more accurately reflected the strength or weakness of the various political tendencies in society. It would follow, therefore, that if racist or extremist sentiment were present, they would be reflected through the electoral system.

Fourthly, supporters of the current electoral arrangements believe that reform would lead to weak Government – citing the example of Italy where there were 54 Governments in the period 1944-1995 and where the politicians have finally turned to the first-past-the-post system as a way out of the troubles associated with their previous proportional system.

Critics of the current British system would respond by observing that Italy has not adopted the first-past-the-post system entirely, but rather a mixed system in which 75 per cent of members of the Chamber of Deputies are elected by first-past-the-post and the remaining 25 per cent under a proportional system designed to ensure representation for those unlikely to win under pure first-past-the-post. They also point out that there have been more individuals in British Cabinets since 1944 than in Italian Cabinets, thus casting doubt upon the relative stability of the British system. Finally, they make the point that what happens in a particular society is generally the product of that society, not of its electoral arrangements.

3.4 Conclusion

The British electoral system has come a long way since Queen Victoria confided to her diary that 'it seems to me a defect in our much famed constitution to have to part with an admirable Government . . . merely on account of the number of votes'.[14] Nowadays, a General Election is usually seen as a public verdict upon the record of the party in Government and the competing attractions of the various Opposition parties. Yet the mass electorate is politically sovereign only on condition that it exercises its sovereignty when invited to do so by the Prime Minister of the day and within the limits of political choice offered by the political parties.

Modern British politics is essentially about the struggle for power between the political parties. Of course, there has always been some ideology in the political rhetoric and the party manifestos. Yet for most of those who reach the top of the political tree the ideological content has often been little more than a necessary part of the political ritual, the tribute which party leaders and others have had to pay to their more zealous followers and supporters, especially when in Opposition. Some would argue that this changed when Margaret Thatcher was Leader of the Conservative Party from 1975 to 1990. Yet the appeal of pragmatism usually trumps ideology if the latter is seen as a threat to a party's chances of gaining or retaining power.

In short, the conduct of elections and the Parliamentary results which ensue are seldom more important than the actual behaviour of the parties either when elected into Government or when released for the self-indulgence of Opposition. While free elections on the basis of universal adult suffrage are an indispensable foundation for the electoral system, it is the quality of party politics between elections and the conduct of every Government in office which counts far more in British Parliamentary democracy.

Suggested questions

1 Describe the working of the British electoral system.
2 To what extent does the British electoral system satisfy the four criteria suggested by W.J.M. Mackenzie?
3 Analyse the arguments for and against a change to proportional representation in Britain.

Notes

1. See D. Butler and D. Kavanagh, *The British General Election of 1992* (London: Macmillan, 1992), pp. 243-44.
2. In the Cambridge constituency at the 1992 General Election the postal vote accounted for 10 per cent of the total vote (5085 votes an increase of 46 per cent over the 2758 postal votes cast in 1987). It was a seat the Labour Party captured on a 6.4 per cent swing with a majority of only 580.
3. This is stipulated in the Representation of the People Act, 1981, and was a direct result of the Bobby Sands case in Northern Ireland.
4. These figures are reviewed annually and increased if needs be in line with inflation. There was no increase in 1993, but in 1994 they were increased to a base of £4642 plus 5.2p per elector in a rural seat and 3.9p per elector in an urban seat. Under the Representation of the People Act, 1989, separate, higher, limits apply in the case of Parliamentary by-elections. In 1994 the basis was £18572 plus 20.8p per elector in a rural constituency and 15.8p per elector in an urban constituency.
5. In 1992 the average expenditure of Conservative candidates was £5840 (80 per cent), of Labour candidates £5090 (71 per cent) and of Liberal Democrat candidates £3169 (43 per cent). As far as victorious candidates were concerned the figures rose to 91 per cent, 84 per cent and 96 per cent respectively. The Conservative agent in the Monmouth constituency faced a ceiling of £7260.78 and returned election expenses amounting to £7260.78. See D. Butler and D. Kavanagh, *The British General Election of 1992*, pp. 44-45.
6. The official expenses – the cost – of the 1992 General Election were something over £42 million (quite apart from the annual cost of the electoral register which was £40 million in 1991-92), and are met by the Government out of the Consolidated Fund. This was a figure only slightly offset by the £450,000 received by the Treasury from lost deposits.
7. 1945, 1950, 1951, 1955, 1959, 1964, 1966, 1970, February 1974, October 1974, 1979, 1983, 1987 and 1992.
8. See V. Bogdanor, *The People and the Party System* (Cambridge: CUP, 1981), pp. 97-258, and V. Bogdanor, *What is Proportional Representation?* (Oxford: Robertson, 1984), for fuller discussion of proportional representation.
9. See W.J.M. Mackenzie, *Free Elections* (London: Allen & Unwin, 1958), pp. 69-71.
10. See D. Butler and D. Kavanagh, *The British General Election of 1992*, pp.211-230.
11. For example, an opinion poll conducted by MORI in September 1994 showed 45 per cent of respondents supporting a change to PR and 23 per cent opposed to such a change : MORI poll conducted 24-26 September 1994 for *The Economist*.
12. See S. Collins, 'Vote for Change Overwhelming', *New Zealand Herald*, 21 September 1992.

13. The statistics on turnout at General Elections depend very much upon the accuracy of the Electoral Register. On average, it has been little more than 90 per cent accurate and even less so in inner city areas where the population is very mobile. In addition, it has been claimed that there has been an increase in the number of unregistered voters in the 1980s and 1990s, possibly to as many as 2 million. In September 1994 a Labour Party report (*The Missing Millions: disenfranchised citizens*) claimed that 20 per cent of people in their early 20s, nearly 25 per cent of black people and 38 per cent of those relying on a private landlord to fill in registration forms, did not appear on the electoral register. Part of the undoubted increase is a direct result of individuals choosing not to register in an attempt to avoid paying the poll tax in the period 1988-92.
14. Quoted in E. Longford, *Victoria R.I.* (London: Weidenfeld & Nicolson, 1964), p. 518.

Further reading

Alderman G., *British Elections: myth and reality* (London: Batsford, 1978).
Bogdanor, V., *The People and the Party System* (London: CUP, 1981).
Bogdanor, V., *What is Proportional Representation?* (Oxford: Robertson, 1984).
Butler, D., *British General Elections Since 1945* (Oxford: Blackwell, 1989).
Butler, D., and Kavanagh, D., *The British General Election of 1992* (London: Macmillan, 1992)
Denver, D., *Elections and Voting Behaviour in Britain* (London: Phillip Allen, 1989).
Finer, S.E. (ed.), *Adversary Politics and Electoral Reform* (London: Anthony Wigram, 1975), *The Report of the Hansard Society Commission on Electoral Reform* (London: Hansard Society, 1976).
King, A. (ed) *Britain at the Polls 1992* (London: Chatham House, 1993).
Lakeman, E., *Power to Elect: the case for proportional Representation* (London: Heinemann, 1982).
Norton, P., 'Does Britain Need Proportional Representation?', in Blackburn, R. (ed.) *Constitutional Studies* (London: Mansell, 1992).
Plant, R. *The Plant Report on Electoral Reform* (The Labour Party/Guardian Newspaper, 1991).
Rawlings, H. F., *Law and the Electoral Process* (London: Sweet & Maxwell, 1988).

4 Voting behaviour

Voting behaviour in Britain since the Second World War (1939-45) has been characterised mainly by the tendency of the electorate at General Elections to divide between two main parties, namely the Conservative Party and the Labour Party. There have been occasions in recent history, however, when the formation of a three-party – or in Wales and especially in Scotland a four-party – system seemed to be imminent. For example, in the early 1970s there was a revival in the fortunes both of the Liberal Party and of the Nationalist parties, with the Liberal Party taking 19.3 per cent and 18.3 per cent of the national vote in the February and October 1974 General Elections respectively, with the Scottish Nationalists receiving 30.4 per cent of the vote in Scotland and Plaid Cymru 10.8 per cent of the vote in Wales in October 1974. Although the talk was of multi-party politics, by 1979 the fortunes of the minor parties had declined.

Similarly, in the early 1980s, following the formation of the Alliance between the Liberals and the newly formed Social Democrats, it looked for a time as though the two party mould of British politics would be broken. Yet in the event this was not to be the case. The Alliance split asunder in the wake of the 1987 General Election, when Dr David Owen and some Social Democrats refused to join the newly formed Liberal Democrats, and the leadership of the Labour Party appeared to rediscover the path of political moderation and common sense. In the 1992 General Election the Liberal Democrats attracted 17.8 per cent of the popular vote nationally and 31.4 per cent in the South West of England (compared with 19.2 per cent for Labour), while the Scottish Nationalists received 21.5 per cent of the Scottish vote (compared with 25.7 per cent for the Conservatives, 39 per cent for Labour and 13.1 per cent for the Liberal Democrats). Nonetheless, the traditional two-party model of voting behaviour seems to have been reasserted, at any rate at General Elections on a nation-wide level – in contrast to local elections or Parliamentary by-elections when other parties have been more successful.

It is perhaps not altogether surprising that this should be so, since the dominance of two main parties (not always the same two parties) has clear antecedents in British political history and has been encouraged by the electoral system (see Chapter 3). In the late eighteenth and early nineteenth centuries there was a struggle for power between the Whigs and the Tories. In the late nineteenth and early twentieth centuries there was a struggle between the Liberals and the Conservatives. During the first few decades of the twentieth century it was uncertain whether or not Labour would displace the Liberals as the main opponent of the Conservatives. However, since the end of the Second World War for many people the effective choice at all General Elections has been between Conservative and Labour parties.

4.1 Groups in the electorate

It is possible to identify many different groups in the British electorate. The lines of political cleavage can be drawn in a number of different ways, according to various criteria. In this section we shall summarise the position according to the most widespread and familiar definitions.

Party loyalists

At General Elections since the Second World War the Conservative and Labour parties have been able to count upon the loyal support of a significant number of core voters, individuals who have supported their party almost regardless of the issues or other factors. Estimates have put the number of core voters at between 6.5 million and 7.5 million for each main party. However, recent surveys have indicated that the proportion of the electorate strongly identifying with and consistently voting for one or other of the two main parties has declined. From the mid-1970s there has also been a significant number of voters who have consistently chosen to support first the Liberal Party and, more recently, the Liberal Democrats. Estimates have put this core Liberal vote at between 1 million and 1.5 million – a marked increase from the 1960s when it was between 0.5 and 0.75 million and indeed from the 1950s when it was as low as 0.25 million voters.

In Scotland and Wales there have been sections of the electorate which have voted consistently for the nationalist parties, the Scottish National Party (SNP) and Plaid Cymru (PC). However, it is hard to ascertain how many of these voters can be considered 'core' supporters, since both the SNP and PC have always attracted substantial and varying protest votes and their electoral fortunes have fluctuated accordingly. At the 1992 General Election together they collected 783,991 votes, only 2.3 per cent of the total vote in the United Kingdom but 21.5 per cent in Scotland and 8.8 per cent in Wales.

Among the electorate in Northern Ireland (785,093 voted at the 1992 General Election), between one half and two thirds have habitually voted for an assortment of Unionist/Protestant candidates (50.3 per cent in 1992), while the votes of the rest of the electorate have gone to the Nationalist/Republican/Catholic candidates, particularly the Social Democratic and Labour Party (SDLP) but also to Sinn Fein, the political wing of the IRA. In 1992 the SDLP received 23.5 per cent of the vote, while Sinn Fein received 10 per cent. In addition there exists the non-sectarian Alliance Party (which received 8.7 per cent of the popular vote in Northern Ireland in 1992), while in 1992 (for the first time for nearly 20 years) the Conservative Party also contested seats in the Province, obtaining 5.7 per cent support.

Floaters and abstainers

The vital group of floating voters has varied in number and in composition at each General

Election since the Second World War. This volatile section of the electorate, which by definition is never made up of exactly the same people from one General Election to the next, seems to have grown in size over the years. Over the period 1959-79 about half the electorate changed its voting behaviour at least once, if we include moves to and from abstention.[1] Over one third of those who voted Labour in 1979 deserted the party in 1983, as did nearly one quarter of those who voted Conservative, thus effectively determining the outcome of the 1983 election. At the 1987 General Election it was the Alliance of Liberals and Social Democrats which suffered most from the floating vote, losing nearly one third of its 1983 vote to other parties or to non-voting. Each of the main parties too suffered from defectors, with the Conservatives losing 23 per cent of their 1983 vote to other parties and abstention and Labour losing 25 per cent in the same way. At the 1992 General Election, of those eligible to vote in both 1987 and 1992, 16 per cent moved from supporting one party to supporting another party and an additional 20 per cent moved to or from abstention. Such floating voters therefore provide the key to electoral victory or defeat at every General Election.

In particular, the floating voters determine the electoral fortunes of the minor parties, since without the benefit of desertions from both main parties it would be difficult for them to collect many extra votes. Of course there is always the possibility that a third party can become one of the two leading parties in Parliament, provided it manages to break through a threshold of about 35 per cent of the votes cast, above which it is likely to win a substantial number of seats in the House of Commons but below which it is likely to languish in frustrating Parliamentary weakness. For example, the 17.8 per cent of the popular vote won by the Liberal Democrats in 1992 secured only 3.0 per cent of the seats in the House of Commons. Nonetheless, it is possible for a third party to make such a breakthrough. After all, it was in just such a manner that the Labour Party gradually displaced the Liberals during the first half of the twentieth century.

As for those who do not vote, for whatever reason, we discover that such people have accounted for between 16 per cent and 28 per cent of the total electorate at General Elections since the Second World War.[2] Since voting is voluntary in Britain, such non-voters can have a vital influence upon the electoral outcome. For example, it has been estimated that differential non-voting had a vital influence upon the results of the 1951 and both the 1974 General Elections. It could have a similarly crucial influence upon any future General Elections.

Social class as a basis for voting

Traditionally one of the most significant cleavages in the British electorate has been based upon class factors of one kind or another. Indeed, in 1967 Peter Pulzer observed that 'class is the basis of British party politics; all else is embellishment and detail'.[3] Yet the meaning of social class has changed and its correlation with voting behaviour has changed accordingly.

At General Elections since the Second World War the Conservative vote has usually consisted of perhaps two thirds of the total middle-class vote and about one third of the total working-class vote, according to the broadest definitions. The Labour vote has usually been made up of perhaps one quarter of the total middle-class vote and more than one half of the total working-class vote, according to the same broad definitions. The minor party votes in England have tended to be even less class-based (which has been part of their electoral problem), and in the other parts of the United Kingdom there has been no overwhelming class bias in the votes of the nationalist parties.

There has always been a significant number of people whose voting behaviour could not easily be explained or predicted on traditional class lines. The most notable example has been that of the working-class Conservatives.[4] Typically, more than one third of all Conservative votes at General Elections since the war have come from working-class people. This means, for example, that at the 1983 General Election there must have been at least four million working-class people who voted Conservative, while at the 1987 General Election the party is estimated to have received as much as 37 per cent of the manual workers' vote – its best achievement among this group at any election since the Second World War. In the General Election of 1992 it is estimated that 46 per cent of the total Conservative vote came from within the working-class, 35 per cent of the working-class casting their votes for Conservative candidates. In view of the bottom-heavy shape of the social structure in Britain, it is evident that the Conservative Party could not be elected to office if it did not manage to attract a sufficient proportion of the working-class vote. Equally, it is clear that the Labour Party was badly damaged by the steady erosion of its working-class base in the 1980s, an erosion that was only partly reversed in 1992 when it still failed to achieve even half the working-class vote and attracted the support of only 46 per cent of trade unionists (30 per cent of whom voted Conservative and 19 per cent Liberal Democrat).

In general, class-based voting of the traditional kind has weakened steadily in Britain over the years since the 1950s and 1960s, notably within the changing working class. In 1959 Labour's share of the vote of manual workers and their families was 40 per cent larger than its share of the vote of white-collar workers and their families. By 1983 the gap had narrowed to 19 per cent. The equivalent figure stood at 20 per cent in 1987 and 19 per cent in 1992. For a considerable period in the 1970s and 1980s the Labour Party lost working-class votes to the Conservatives. For example, at the 1983 General Election there was a swing from Labour to the Conservatives of 2 per cent among skilled manual workers and 4 per cent among semi-skilled and unskilled workers. At the 1987 General Election Labour concentrated upon trying to recover the working-class support which it had lost in 1983 and to some extent it was successful in doing so. It increased its vote among the semi-skilled and unskilled manual workers and their families by 6 per cent, but it continued to lose the votes of skilled workers and their families, where the swing to the Conservatives was more than 2 per cent compared with 1983.[5] In 1992, however, there was a 3.5 per cent swing to Labour among skilled manual workers, which saw support for Labour move ahead of support for the Conservatives in this category.

At the 1983 General Election it was the Alliance which was the main beneficiary of working-class desertions from Labour, since it gathered three times as many such votes as the Conservatives. Yet at the 1987 General Election Labour's fortunes varied as between the traditional and the new working class. It did well among the traditional unskilled manual working class at the expense of the Alliance, whereas among the new skilled working class both Labour and the Alliance lost votes to the Conservatives. While on average between 1945 and 1970 62 per cent of all manual workers had voted Labour, by 1983 Labour support from this quarter had fallen to 38 per cent. At the 1987 General Election its support from this category recovered slightly to stand at 40 per cent, while by 1992 it had further increased to stand at 45 per cent.[6] What we have witnessed is nothing short of the transformation of working-class voting behaviour and this has rightly been described by Ivor Crewe as 'the most significant post-war change in the social basis of British politics'.[7]

The decline of traditional class-based voting in Britain could be attributed partly to the changing nature of the working class and partly to the desertion from Labour of the new skilled working class, especially those in this group who were owner-occupiers living in the south of England. A Gallup survey conducted at the time of the 1983 General Election showed that Labour trailed the Conservatives by 22 per cent among working-class owner-occupiers and by 16 per cent among working-class voters living in the south of England.[8] At the 1987 General Election Labour managed once again to achieve a strong position for itself among the traditional working class (especially those who were trade union members living in Scotland or the north of England), whereas among the new skilled working class it continued to lose support to the Conservatives. By 1992 Labour had recaptured lost ground, but still trailed behind the Conservatives among working-class owner-occupiers (39 per cent to 41 per cent) and among working-class voters in the south of England (38 per cent to 40 per cent).[9] Thus Disraeli's 'two nations' are not only to be found in different classes and different parts of the country, but also within the British working class itself.

Gender and age differences in voting

Two further ways of categorising the electorate are by gender and age.[10] With regard to *gender differences in voting*, Labour have traditionally had a clear lead among male voters at General Elections since the Second World War, scoring a notable 19 per cent advantage over the Conservatives in 1945 and 1966. On the other hand, the Conservatives have traditionally had a clear lead among the female voters, scoring an almost as impressive 12 per cent and 13 per cent advantage over Labour in 1951 and 1955 respectively. At the 1979 General Election the Conservatives managed to maintain their strength among female voters with a 9 per cent lead over Labour, but since it was such a good result for the Conservatives, they also scored a 5 per cent lead over Labour among male voters. At the 1983 General Election this trend was reversed and, unusually, the Conservatives drew more of their support from men than from women. This was mainly because the Alliance made such inroads into the female vote, gaining 28 per cent of female support as compared with the 12 per cent achieved by the Liberals on their own in 1979. At the 1987 General Election all the parties drew their support about equally from men and women. In 1992, once again, more women voted Conservative than did men, while more men voted Labour than did women.[11]

With regard to *age-related differences in voting behaviour*, Labour has traditionally done particularly well among voters under the age of 30, scoring a 28 per cent lead over the Conservatives in 1945, a 17 per cent lead in 1966 and a 16 per cent lead in October 1974. On the other hand, the Conservatives have traditionally done rather well among those in late middle age (50-64), scoring an 18 per cent lead over Labour in 1951, a 14 per cent lead in 1955 and a 13 per cent lead in 1959. The fortunes of the two main parties in the other age groups (30-49 and 65 plus) have been more evenly balanced. Whereas Labour did well among the 30-49 group in 1945 and 1966 with leads over the Conservatives of 16 per cent and 13 per cent respectively, the Conservatives did well among those over 65 in 1955, 1970 and February 1974 with leads over Labour of 9 per cent, 9 per cent and 14 per cent respectively. In 1979 Labour was able to retain a small lead of 1 per cent over the Conservatives among the 18-24 age group, notwithstanding the fact that it trailed the Conservatives by 7 per cent among voters of all ages and by 10 per cent among those aged 35 and over. At both General Elections in the 1980s Conservative voting support increased steadily with age, while Labour continued to do well among younger voters – for example, in 1987 Labour did best among voters in the 18-24 age group in which it secured the support of 40 per cent.[12] This general pattern was repeated in the 1992 General Election, although the Conservatives gained ground amongst the 18-24 age group (up 2 per cent over 1987), while Labour made additional headway among those aged 25-34 (up 5 per cent over 1987) and 35-54 (up 5 per cent over 1987), primarily at the expense of the Liberal Democrats.[13]

Other sectional cleavages

There are, of course, other sectional cleavages in voting behaviour in Britain. In many ways these have become increasingly important over the years as the voters have become more volatile and instrumental in their voting behaviour.

Firstly, there are the *geographical variations in voting behaviour*. At the 1979 General Election the Midlands and the south of England voted strongly for the Conservatives, especially in the new towns and the more prosperous working-class suburbs. On the other hand, South Wales, the north of England and much of Scotland remained largely loyal to the Labour Party.[14] At the 1983 General Election the Conservatives had a 38.6 per cent lead over Labour in the south east of England (excluding London) while Labour had a 5.6 per cent lead over the Conservatives in the north of England; indeed, the Conservatives led Labour in every region except the north of England and in Scotland and Wales. Four years later in 1987 Labour made up some of its lost ground, coming out ahead of the Conservatives in the North West as well as in Yorkshire and Humberside and continuing to be ahead in the North, Scotland and Wales. The Alliance of Liberals and Social Democrats, although falling back slightly compared with 1983, continued to pose the main threat to the Conservatives in certain areas, out-polling the Labour Party in the South West (32.8 per cent as against 16.2 per cent), in the South East excluding London (26.9 per cent against Labour's 16.8 per cent) and in East Anglia (25.8 per cent against Labour's 21.7 per cent).

At the 1992 General Election there were further sharp regional variations in voting behaviour. This can be seen in Figure 4.1 (page 51). From Figure 4.1 it can be seen that the Labour Party increased its vote in every area of Great Britain except in Scotland, where its vote fell by 3.4 per cent. In each other area it rose by between 3.3 per cent (South West) and 7.4 per cent (East Midlands). Once again the party was ahead of the Conservatives in the North, the North West, Yorkshire and Humberside, Scotland and Wales. However, there was an increase in Conservative support in the North, Yorkshire and Humberside and in Scotland, with Scotland demonstrating a 2.5 per cent overall swing to the Conservatives. In all other areas there was a decline in the Conservative vote of between 0.2 per cent (North West) and 3.3 per cent (South West). The North/South divide was again clearly apparent.

The rebuff for the Liberal Democrats was nation-wide. Their vote dropped in every region, from between 6.2 per cent (East Anglia) and 1.6 per cent (South West). If the South West and parts of the South East are excluded, their vote fell by between 6.2 per cent and 4.8 per cent. In many respects they emerged from the election dependent upon the old Liberal Party's base of the rural, peripheral middle-class.

Figure 4.1 How Britain voted in 1992, region by region

How the parties shares changed from 1987

North	% of vote	+/- on '87	1992 Seats +/-
CON	33.4	+1.0	6 -2
LAB	50.6	+4.2	29 +2
LD	15.5	-5.5	1 0

Northern Ireland	% of vote	+/- on '87	1992 Seats +/-
OUP	35.8	-2.0	9 0
DUP	13.6	+1.9	3 0
APNI	9.1	-0.9	0 0
SF	10.3	-1.1	0 -1
SDLP	22.7	+1.6	4 +1
OTHR	8.5	+0.5	1 1

North West	% of vote	+/- on '87	1992 Seats +/-
CON	37.8	-0.2	27 -7
LAB	44.9	+3.7	44 +8
LD	15.8	-4.8	2 -1

West Midlands	% of vote	+/- on '87	1992 Seats +/-
CON	44.8	-0.8	29 -7
LAB	38.8	+5.5	29 +7
LD	15.0	-5.8	0 0

Wales	% of vote	+/- on '87	1992 Seats +/-
CON	28.6	-0.9	6 -2
LAB	49.5	+4.4	27 +3
LD	12.4	-5.5	1 -2
NAT	8.8	+1.5	4 +1

Scotland	% of vote	+/- on '87	1992 Seats +/-
CON	25.7	+1.7	11 +1
LAB	39.0	-3.4	49 -1
LD	13.1	-6.1	9 0
NAT	21.5	+7.5	3 0

Yorks / Humberside	% of vote	+/- on '87	1992 Seats +/-
CON	37.9	+0.5	20 -1
LAB	44.4	+3.7	34 +1
LD	16.8	-4.8	0 0

East Midlands	% of vote	+/- on '87	1992 Seats +/-
CON	46.6	-2.0	28 -3
LAB	37.4	+7.4	14 +3
LD	15.2	-5.8	0 0

East Anglia	% of vote	+/- on '87	1992 Seats +/-
CON	51.0	-1.1	17 -2
LAB	28.0	+6.3	3 +2
LD	19.5	-6.2	0 0

South West	% of vote	+/- on '87	1992 Seats +/-
CON	44.8	-0.8	29 -7
LAB	38.8	+5.5	29 +7
LD	15.0	-5.8	0 0

South East	% of vote	+/- on '87	1992 Seats +/-
CON	44.8	-0.8	29 -7
LAB	38.8	+5.5	29 +7
LD	15.0	-5.8	0 0

Greater London	% of vote	+/- on '87	1992 Seats +/-
CON	45.3	-1.2	48 -10
LAB	37.0	+5.6	35 +10
LD	15.2	-6.1	1 -2

Source: *Sunday Times*, 12 April 1992

The consequences of this territorial disintegration of British politics are quite striking. Although the Labour vote in 1992 rose across the whole of the south and east of England, the party managed to win only an additional 7 seats in these areas (excluding Greater London) and held only 10 seats compared with 161 for the Conservatives. On the other hand, the Conservatives won no seats in the great northern cities of Liverpool, Manchester and Newcastle; only two in Edinburgh, none in Glasgow, and none in Cardiff. The North/South divide in British politics was confirmed once again. (See map on pp 458-59.)

Secondly, there are the *sociological differences in voting behaviour*, of which perhaps the most remarkable in recent years has been the cleavage between the traditional and the new working class. As a stereotype, the former group could be described as those who live in Scotland or the north of England, are Council tenants, trade union members and work in the public sector. Equally, the latter group could be described as those who live in the south and east of England, are owner-occupiers, non-trade-union members and work in the private sector, very often in a self-employed capacity.

At the 1983 General Election Labour led the Alliance by 23 per cent and the Conservatives by 21 per cent among voters who were Council tenants, while the Conservatives had a 19 per cent lead over the Alliance among working-class owner-

Figure 4.2 Profile of the electorate in 1992

% of 1992 voters		1983 vote			1987 vote			1992 vote		
		Con	Lab	L/D	Con	Lab	L/D	Con	Lab	L/D
100	Total	44	28	26	43	32	23	43	35	18
49	Men	42	30	25	43	32	23	41	37	18
51	Women	46	26	27	43	32	23	44	34	18
14	18-24	42	33	32	33	40	21	35	39	19
19	25-34	40	29	29	39	33	25	40	38	18
33	35-54	44	27	27	45	29	24	43	34	19
34	55+	47	27	24	46	31	21	46	34	17
23	Pensioner	51	25	23	47	31	21	48	34	16
19	AB-prof	60	10	28	57	14	26	56	20	22
24	C1-white collar	51	20	27	51	21	26	52	25	19
27	C2-skilled	40	32	26	40	36	22	38	41	17
30	DE-skilled	33	41	24	30	48	20	30	50	15
67	Owner occupier	52	19	28	50	23	25	49	30	19
23	Council tenant	26	47	24	22	56	19	24	55	15
7	Private tenant	41	33	23	39	37	21	33	40	21
7	Men 18-24	41	35	21	42	37	19	39	35	18
7	Women 18-24	42	31	25	31	42	24	30	43	19
9	Men 25-34	37	34	28	41	33	24	40	37	17
10	Women 25-34	42	25	30	37	33	27	40	38	18
16	Men 35-54	42	29	27	42	32	24	40	37	19
17	Women 35-54	46	24	28	47	27	25	46	32	19
17	Men 55+	45	28	25	45	31	23	43	38	17
17	Women 55+	49	26	24	46	32	20	49	32	17
9	Men 65+	50	25	23	47	30	22	44	38	16
9	Women 65+	51	25	23	46	33	20	51	31	17
4	Unemployed (m)	25	49	24	21	56	20	24	52	17
3	Unemployed (f)	32	41	24	23	54	19	26	51	16
17	North (m)	35	39	24	34	42	20	33	46	14
19	North (f)	40	33	25	33	41	22	36	43	15
13	Midlands (m)	43	31	23	46	34	19	44	38	16
13	Midlands (f)	46	27	24	45	29	24	46	36	16
19	South (m)	48	23	28	49	22	28	46	29	22
20	South (f)	51	19	30	51	24	24	50	27	22
	Homeowners									
36	Middle-class	58	12	29	57	15	26	56	21	20
31	Working-class	46	25	27	43	32	23	41	39	17
	Council tenants									
2	Middle-class	32	39	25	28	41	24	34	40	18
21	Working-class	25	49	24	21	58	18	22	58	15
	Trade Unions									
23	Members	31	39	29	30	42	26	30	47	19
15	Men	29	41	28	31	42	25	30	48	18
8	Women	34	34	31	29	41	27	31	44	21
3	18-24	31	34	23	29	46	23	30	42	20
5	25-34	29	37	32	28	47	23	28	49	19
10	35-54	30	40	29	29	40	29	31	45	20
5	55+	32	40	26	36	37	24	33	49	16
10	ABC1	38	27	33	37	30	30	36	36	24
8	C2	27	44	27	28	47	24	27	52	17
5	DE	25	50	24	22	56	19	24	59	13
9	North	26	44	28	25	50	21	25	53	14
6	Midlands	32	40	25	35	39	24	32	49	18
8	South	35	32	32	33	34	32	35	38	26

Taken from an aggregate analysis of 22,727 voters in Great Britain interviewed byt Mori during the election, weighted to the actual outcome. Key: L/D, Liberal Democrat; m, men; f, women.

Source: *Sunday Times*, 12 April 1992

occupiers and a 21 per cent lead over Labour in the same category. Among trade-unionist voters the Conservatives improved their position and came second to Labour with 31 per cent as compared with 39 per cent in that category. Yet the defection of trade-unionist voters was responsible for the biggest drop in any single category of the Labour vote (down by 14 per cent to 39 per cent), while the Alliance increased its support among trade-unionist voters by 12 per cent in line with its general performance in the electorate. Labour's strongest position was among those of the unemployed who decided to vote, with a 24 per cent lead over the Conservatives among the male unemployed and a 9 per cent lead among the female unemployed.

At the 1987 General Election Labour led the Conservatives by 34 per cent and the Alliance by 37 per cent among voters who were Council tenants, while the Conservatives had a 21 per cent lead over Labour and a 19 per cent lead over the Alliance among owner-occupiers in the working class. Among trade-unionist voters Labour improved its position compared with 1983 by establishing a 12 per cent lead over the Conservatives and a 16 per cent lead over the Alliance. Labour also improved its position among the unemployed, taking 56 per cent of the male unemployed vote and 54 per cent of the female unemployed vote, as against 21 and 23 per cent respectively for the Conservatives and 20 and 19 per cent for the Alliance. As far as socio-economic groups were concerned, as in 1983 the Conservatives attracted the votes of an absolute majority in both the AB-professional (57 per cent) and the C1-white collar (51 per cent) categories, and the largest following of any party amongst C2-skilled with 40 per cent as opposed to 36 per cent for Labour and 22 per cent for the Alliance. The Labour Party topped the poll among those classified as DE-skilled – attracting 48 per cent as opposed to 30 per cent for the Conservatives and 20 per cent for the Alliance. Although well behind the Conservatives, the Alliance out-polled the Labour Party in both the AB-professional and C1-white collar categories, securing 25 per cent support in both, in contrast to Labour's 14 per cent and 21 per cent respectively.

At the 1992 General Election the Conservative Party still led Labour among working-class home-owners, but only just (41 per cent to 39 per cent), with the Liberal Democrats way behind on 17 per cent, a drop of 10 per cent since 1983 and 6 per cent since 1987. Among owner-occupiers, Labour had also closed the gap, notwithstanding the fact that it was still substantial at 49 per cent for the Conservative and 30 per cent for Labour (a gap of 19 per cent), whereas the equivalent figures in 1983 had been 52 per cent and 19 per cent (a gap of 33 per cent). Labour's lead among working-class Council tenants was 36 per cent, with 58 per cent to the Conservatives' 22 per cent. Conservative support from trade unionists held steady, but a drop in support from this group for the Liberal Democrats – down to 19 per cent from 26 per cent in 1987 – ensured a rise in support for the Labour Party from 42 to 47 per cent. The Labour Party also secured an absolute majority of support among the unemployed, although there was a drop in the support for both Labour and the Liberal Democrats within this category and a rise in the support given to the Conservative Party. See Figure 4.2 for more detail.

As far as socio-economic classification was concerned, the 1992 result showed the Conservative Party still attracting majority support from among both the AB-professional and C1-white collar groups. Nonetheless, Labour was able to make inroads into both, increasing its support by 6 per cent and 4 per cent respectively. Among C2-skilled voters the Labour Party supplanted the Conservative Party as the recipient of the highest level of support from this group (41 per cent to 38 per cent), while it attracted the support of 50 per cent of those in the DE-skilled category. Support for the Liberal Democrats from both these final categories declined by 5 per cent as compared with 1987.

In short, the British electorate no longer divides neatly into two traditional, class-based voting groups, essentially because British society is no longer like that. The voters have become less easy to categorise in sociological terms and less inclined to adhere to their traditional voting allegiances. In such circumstances predictions of voting behaviour along traditional lines on the basis of a simple split between middle class and working class are unlikely to be accurate in modern conditions. Greater account has now to be taken of the social mobility and the electoral volatility of modern British society.

- *Conservative loyalist*: Man or woman of more than 55, middle class, owner-occupier, living in the south of England and often self-employed.

- *Labour loyalist*: Man or woman of less than 24, manual worker, Council tenant, living in an urban area in the north of England, Scotland or Wales, working in the public sector and a member of a trade union.

- *Liberal Democrat voter*: Man or woman of 25 to 34, middle class, owner-occupier, living in any part of Britain and working in a white collar job in the private or public sector.

Figure 4.3   Profiles of some typical voters

4.2 Main influences on voting

Traditionally it has been argued that there are three main influences on voting behaviour in Britain – political inheritance, self-interest, and the performance of the party in office.[15] Of course, there are other important influences on voting behaviour which cannot be ignored, such as policy and sentiment, image and technique. As we have already observed, other social factors such as occupation, housing tenure, educational attainment, and neighbourhood or peer group pressures, also have an impact. We must therefore take account of a wide variety of influences if we are to form a complete picture.

Political inheritance

The influence of political inheritance means the political attitudes and loyalties which voters derive from their parents and families. On the basis of surveys conducted in the 1960s Butler and Stokes were able to show a high correlation (typically over 75 per cent) between the voting behaviour of one generation and the next within family households.[16] This was not surprising at the time, in view of the well-established fact that the opinions of young people on most issues, whether political or not, tended to accord with those of their parents. Indeed there is still considerable inertia in the party political loyalties of many voters at General Elections, which in most cases reflects the voting habits derived from family inheritance and social surroundings. This can be seen most clearly in the few remaining tight-knit communities, such as the valleys in South Wales, where there is still effectively a one party voting tradition (in this case for the Labour Party) in spite of the fact that modern social and geographical mobility has begun to erode it at the edges.

The key point at recent General Elections has been that it has not always been possible for either of the main parties to turn such traditional loyalties fully into a level of voting support commensurate with their party identifiers in opinion polls. For example, at the 1992 General Election 34 per cent of the electorate claimed to regard themselves as instinctively Labour supporters, and whereas 34.4 per cent of those who voted actually supported Labour candidates, this was the equivalent of only 26.7 per cent of the electorate. [17] This is because the strength of voter commitment to either of the two main parties has become more attenuated over the years as a result of the long-run decline in party political allegiance and participation in Britain as in all other advanced societies. Indeed, this social development has tended to damage the electoral prospects of the Liberal Democrats most of all, since so much of their potential voting support as registered in opinion polls and at by-elections is significantly weaker and more transient than that given to either of the two main parties by their declared supporters.

Self-interest

The influence of self-interest derives very largely from the personal experience, favourable or unfavourable, consistent or contradictory, of millions of individual voters. For example, there is a fortunate minority of people in Britain who are born into well-off families, benefit from a good education, and manage to lead happy and successful lives. In the majority of cases such people have tended to vote Conservative. Equally, there is a large section of the public (typically several million) for whom life is a constant struggle against adverse material conditions. Their lives are characterised by financial insecurity, dependence upon the state and its agencies, and impoverished expectations. In the majority of cases such people have tended to vote Labour, if they have decided to vote at all.

Certainly the 56 per cent of those in the AB-professional group and the 52 per cent categorised as C1-white collar who voted Conservative at the 1992 General Election are likely to have done so principally for reasons of self-interest, although they often describe their reasons for voting in terms of their conception of the national interest – 'what is good for me is good for Britain.' The minority within those groups who voted either Labour or Liberal Democrat were more likely to have done so for ideological or altruistic reasons. Indeed, it is worth noting that at recent General Elections the Labour and Liberal Democrat parties made some noticeable advances among the growing middle-class electorate and that the Liberal Democrats now find their social base among the well educated middle class – hence in their Manifesto pledge in 1992 to earmark a one penny in the pound Income Tax increase to provide additional funding for education, they were playing to their natural supporters. This suggests that self-interest is not always a dominant influence upon voting behaviour – people do not *necessarily* vote with their wallets. Undoubtedly other factors, such as ideology and altruism, apathy and disillusion, play an important part as well.

Government performance

The performance of the party in office might seem to be an influence on voting behaviour too obvious to be worth stating, if it were not for the fact that it emphasises the importance of the growing tendency for many people to vote *instrumentally*. This is the technical term to describe what happens when millions of floating voters effectively strike a bargain with the politicians, whereby they reward the party in office with re-election or punish it with electoral defeat according to their assessment of its period in Government.[18]

This is certainly a view of voting behaviour which is widely held by practising politicians in Britain. It is also supported by the well-established axiom that parties in Government are more likely to *lose* an election than parties in Opposition are to *win* one. Equally, it is clear from the four successive Conservative victories in 1979, 1983, 1987 and 1992 that it was possible for a large British political party to suffer a small, but significant decline in its share of the votes cast and still win each election handsomely – thanks largely to the fragmentation of the non-Conservative vote. Paradoxically, it was possible for a governing party to lose voting support and still win successive General Elections, just as it was possible for one or more of the Opposition parties to gain voting support and still lose quite heavily.

Policy and sentiment

In recent years policy and sentiment have been increasingly important influences upon voting behaviour in Britain. As the voters have become more volatile and instrumental in their attitudes, such factors have begun to weigh at least as heavily as traditional social allegiances.

With regard to *policy-based voting*, Sarlvik and Crewe have shown that more than two thirds of the votes for the three national parties at the 1979 General Election could have been predicated correctly on the basis of the view held by the voters on certain salient policy issues; and the correlation was over 90 per cent for Conservative and Labour voters.[19] They argued that this was a reflection of the fact that over the period 1964-79 there had been a dramatic decline in the level of popular support for three key Labour policies – further nationalisation, the reinforcement of trade-union power, and higher tax-financed spending upon the Welfare State. These policies, which had commanded majority support in 1964 (at any rate among those voters who identified with the Labour Party), received less than 25 per cent support among Labour voters in 1979. Labour had therefore lost a great deal of its earlier policy-based appeal.

Yet nothing remains exactly the same in this area of analysis. After a period in the 1970s and early 1980s when many of Labour's most salient policies were not popular with the electorate (for example, the commitment to higher direct taxation or support for unilateral nuclear disarmament), the party emerged from a period of comprehensive policy review with a range of more moderate and pragmatic policies which seem to have proved attractive to the electorate, at least on the basis of answers to opinion polls. Neil Kinnock (1983-92), John Smith (1992-94) and Tony Blair (1994-) all deliberately sought to lead the Labour Party in a more modern and moderate direction. Tony Benn on behalf of the Left accused the leadership of 'diluting Socialism', declaring that 'the direction of the Labour Party now gives the impression of being superficial in analysis, weak in remedies, defensive in its posture and vague in its approach'.[20] The leadership hit back, with Neil Kinnock declaring that the party had to modernise, asserting that Labour politicians could not face the future with 'their heads in the clouds, ignoring the real world that people and parties and movements have to live in . . . with their heads turned round, gazing longingly at the past, trying to call back yesterday'.[21]

This should remind us that all voters are less inclined than they used to be to vote in accordance with traditional class or family loyalties, and more inclined to vote in the light of which party most closely reflects their own interests and policy preferences. Indeed, evidence adduced by Sarlvik and Crewe suggested that voters' opinions on the policies and performances of each party are twice as likely to explain their voting behaviour as all their social and economic characteristics taken together.[22] A Gallup survey conducted for the BBC at the time of the 1983 General Election also showed that, when the voters preferred the policies of one Party but the leader of another, they decided in favour of the former by about four to one, a tendency which on that occasion worked principally to the advantage of the Conservatives.[23]

Yet in weighing the influence of policy on voting behaviour, it is important to distinguish between those policies which the voters, when questioned by opinion pollsters, may consider to be the best in the abstract or for the sake of the country, and those for which they actually vote in the privacy of the polling booth. At the 1987 General Election the Labour Party would have won if the voters had cast their votes in accordance with their altruistic policy preferences as expressed in answer to opinion polls at the time. The same thing was true at the 1992 General Election. For example, when Gallup asked the question 'Of all the urgent problems facing the country at the present time, when you decided which way to vote, which two issues did you personally consider most important?', 41 per cent of respondents mentioned health, 36 per cent mentioned unemployment, and 23 per cent mentioned education – all issues on which the Labour Party enjoyed a lead as the best party – yet the Conservatives still won the election quite comfortably.[24] Evidently, altruism does not necessarily translate into voting behaviour when the voters are choosing a Government at a General Election. The explanation for this has been provided by Ivor Crewe, who has pointed out that, when answering opinion pollsters, the voters respond altruistically and in the abstract, whereas when actually voting they tend to think much more instrumentally of their personal and family interests.[25]

With regard to *capricious sentiment* as an influence upon voting behaviour, Hilde Himmelweit and others have shown that, 'although in practice both consistency (that is, party loyalty) and ideological thinking (that is, policy considerations) influence the decision to vote, each election is like a new shopping expedition in a situation where new as well as familiar goods are on offer'.[26] This means that evidence from recent General Elections can be interpreted and explained by using a consumer model of voting behaviour. Of course, a great deal depends upon how the voters feel during the period just before and during an election campaign and upon whether the public eventually decides to vote for positive or negative reasons or indeed to vote at all.

At the 1987 General Election, for example, the Conservative Party achieved a landslide majority in Parliament with almost the same share of the votes cast as in 1983. This was because the votes cast for the other national parties were fairly evenly divided between Labour and the Alliance, but even more because more than two thirds of those who (according to opinion polls at the outset of the campaign) had seriously considered voting for the Alliance eventually did *not* do so on polling day, because they came to the conclusion that such action might give victory to whichever of the two main parties they disliked the most.

At the 1992 General Election a Mori survey found that 11 per cent of those who identified themselves as Liberal Democrat supporters a week before polling day switched to vote Conservative on polling day, as did 4 per cent of those who had identified themselves as Labour supporters. In addition 8 per cent of Labour supporters switched to the Liberal Democrats. The reasons for switching support were varied: 29 per cent said they did so because they liked the policies of the party to which they switched; 13 per cent said they did so because they disliked the policies of the other parties; 10 per cent said they did so because they liked the leader of the party to which they switched; and 56 per cent said they did so because they disliked the leaders of the other parties.[27]

Image and technique

Party images and campaign techniques are some of the other significant influences upon voting behaviour in this age of modern mass media. They have been identified by the political communications specialists of all the parties as crucial to electoral success in the modern age.

Party images have been formed in the public mind by the party leaders themselves – for example, Lloyd George as the Welsh Wizard, Winston Churchill as the British bull-dog, Stanley Baldwin as the quintessential English country gentleman, Harold Macmillan as 'Super Mac', James Callaghan as 'jovial gentleman Jim', Margaret Thatcher as the 'Iron Lady'. More recently, we have seen the association of classlessness and geniality with John Major, sympathy and good humour with Neil Kinnock, competence and honesty with John Smith, and vision and modernity with Tony Blair. Party images are also formed by the performance and behaviour of the parties whether in Government or Opposition. The party leaders and their media advisers work hard to preserve or improve their respective images. Indeed, the presentation of policy, if not policy itself, is usually influenced by professional assessments of the image it is likely to convey. Above all, the parties are careful to try to foster an image of unity in their own ranks and of disunity in the ranks of their opponents, since the appearance of disunity is invariably damaging to electoral prospects.

Party images are formed incrementally, even subliminally, over many years by what the parties do or fail to do when in Government and by the way they behave when in Opposition. For example, the Conservative Party undoubtedly benefited at both the 1983 and 1987 General Elections from Margaret Thatcher's acknowledged experience in high office and her resolute public image as someone who stuck to her guns when the going got tough – for instance, at the depth of the recession in the early 1980s, at the time of the Falklands crisis in 1982, and during the Westland affair in 1986. Equally, during the late 1970s and well into the 1980s the Labour Party suffered in the eyes of many people from a poor image which was the product of unconvincing leadership, party in-fighting and internecine ideological struggles. During the 1987 General Election the Labour Party strove very hard and quite effectively to present the party leader, Neil Kinnock, in a favourable and 'presidential' light, impressing many media professionals and party work-ers in the process; but even this was not enough to counter an adverse public image that had taken years to crystallise. Similarly, the Labour Party suffered in the 1992 General Election from Neil Kinnock's lack of credibility as an alternative Prime Minister and from John Smith's unwise decision as Shadow Chancellor to present an alternative tax-raising 'Budget' during the first week of the campaign.

Campaign techniques can also have an important influence upon voting behaviour, especially since many of the floating voters do not make up their minds until the final stages of the campaign. The parties therefore make every effort during the campaign to get as much good media coverage as possible and to present both their leaders and their policies in the most favourable light. Yet, in spite of these often expensive efforts, the actual conduct of the campaign seldom makes a decisive difference to the electoral outcome. For example, although it was widely agreed that the Labour leadership fought a brilliant media campaign in 1987, it seems clear that this had little or no effect upon the battle with the Conservatives for first place, but a considerable effect upon the battle with the Alliance for second place. On the other hand, in the 1992 General Election campaign the Conservatives had some success with their vivid posters (put up on 4500 sites) and newspaper advertising drawing attention to what they described as 'Labour's Double Whammy' – namely, higher taxes and higher prices – and asserting that the average voter would pay over £1000 a year more in tax under a Labour Government. In the case of the minor parties, which in normal times do not get much media attention, effective campaign techniques can be more significant in drawing helpful attention both to their leaders and to their policies – as was shown by the positive impact of the Liberal Leader, Jeremy Thorpe, in the February 1974 General Election.

Other influences on voting

In one of the most authoritative studies of voting behaviour in Britain, Heath, Jowell and Curtice demonstrated the advantages of drawing multi-dimensional maps of the electorate. [28] Using this technique, it is possible to take full account of all the various cleavages in the electorate and go beyond the familiar criteria of social class and electoral geography. A modern list of the other variables should include the influence of neighbourhood, occupation, housing tenure, share ownership, educational attainment, gender, and racial identity. On this last point, for example, it appears from survey data that at the 1992 General Election 79 per cent of ethnic minority voters voted Labour, 10 per cent voted Conservative and 9 per cent voted Liberal Democrat. Although better-off ethnic minority voters are relatively less likely to vote Conservative than their white counterparts (29 per cent against 43 per cent in 1992), it has been predicted that the late 1990s will witness the end of Labour hegemony among ethnic minority voters. [29] Indeed, the Commission for Racial Equality has calculated that as many as 40 Parliamentary constituencies would not be retained by the Labour Party if Asian, Afro-Caribbean and other ethnic minority voters divided their loyalties in the same proportions as white voters. [30]

In short, there is a wide variety of influences upon voting behaviour in Britain. The traditional influences – that is, political inheritance, self-interest, and the performance of the party in office – are still of fundamental importance. Yet the more ephemeral influences (for instance, policy and sentiment, image and technique) have made themselves increasingly felt in recent years and have assumed a growing importance as the voters have shown more volatility in their voting behaviour and as General Election campaigns have become more presidential both in style and in content. The use of such modern techniques emphasises the manipulative aspects of modern party politics and reminds us of the influence of the mass media. Yet in spite of such new developments, it is clear that British electoral politics have not been completely Americanised, not least because of the tight legal limits upon the amount which each Parliamentary candidate may spend on election expenses during the rather brief General Election campaigns in Britain, and the fact that it is impossible for the parties under British electoral law to purchase broadcasting time on the electronic media.

4.3 Continuing uncertainties

There are some continuing uncertainties which are likely to have a significant influence upon the outcome of future General Elections in Britain. Will the voters be more or less concerned with issues of policy? Will the Conservative vote grow or decline among the new working class? Will a substantial part of the middle class continue to vote Labour or Liberal Democrat? Will men and women come to have less differentiated political leanings? Will ethnic minority voters continue to divide their loyalties differently from their white counterparts? Will the electorate become more or less volatile in its voting behaviour? Will the Liberal Democrats and the Nationalists continue to attract sizeable levels of support, or will they suffer significant defections? Will voting turn-out at General Elections grow or decline? To what extent will there be signs of political alienation? Whatever the difficulties, it is worth exploring some of these important questions.

Instrumental or expressive voting

There was a time in the late 1950s and early 1960s when some observers proclaimed the end of ideology in Britain and other advanced Western countries. [31] More recently, however, ideology and policy considerations have become once again a significant influence upon voting behaviour. This is consistent with the evidence for so-called *instrumental voting*, whereby voters assess the policies, attitudes and images of the various parties and then cast their votes in the light of their own interests.

From the late 1970s and throughout the 1980s it seems that the positions taken by the different parties on the main issues of policy had a significant effect upon voting behaviour at General Elections. This was brought about partly by the continuing fragmentation of the traditional working class, which created a rootless, upwardly mobile group whose voting behaviour was particularly susceptible to instrumental appeals from the politicians to their particular interests. It was also a reflection of the increasing sophistication of all those voters who regarded their decisions at General Elections as really another form of consumer choice. For such people, as long as there appeared to be an attractive political product on offer, a significant number of them measured its claims against not only their own policy preferences but also their assessment of their own interests. In such a political beauty contest between the parties, the voters' perceptions of political issues and of their own interests in relation to party policies have a significant effect upon election results.

On the other hand, there is considerable evidence in support of the so called *expressive interpretation of voting* – that is to say, the tendency of many in the electorate to vote in accordance with the norms and values of the principal social group to which they belong. According to this theory of voting behaviour, many of the preferences which are expressed in opinion polls by reference to voter predilections for particular party policies are actually little more than rationalisations of more basic interests or a cover for a dominant social identification. In other words, if voting behaviour is determined principally by social identity, then one need only look at the changing class proportions within society to be able to forecast likely outcomes.

Conservatives and the fragmented working class

It is striking that, in spite of presiding over the two worst economic recessions since the Second World War, namely in 1980-82 and 1990-92, the Conservative Party still retains the support of a significant number of working-class voters. This support is critically dependent upon its ability to maintain an image of integrity and a reputation for competence in office, something which was severely dented during the early and mid-1990s. It also depends upon the image of the party in the eyes of the so-called authoritarian working class – that is, those working-class voters who are attracted by whichever party takes the toughest line on issues, such as law and order, immigration, trade-union reform and defence. In that respect the Conservatives probably retain a small relative advantage over the other parties because of their legislative action and rhetoric over a long period of time. Nonetheless, the headway made by Tony Blair on the law-and-order issue when Shadow Home Secretary clearly showed that the Conservative Party could not afford to take such support for granted.

Provided that the Conservative Party can restore its claim to competence, focus on its experience in office, and deliver a renewed sense of economic well-being by the time of the next election, it is likely that the self-interest of at least some of the working class (notably those whom Brian Walden described as 'strivers') will deliver to the party a substantial vote. In 1979 the Conservatives benefited from widespread revulsion at the trade union excesses during the so called 'Winter of Discontent'. In 1983 they benefited from the patriotic appeal of victory in the Falklands and from a divided Opposition. In 1987 they benefited from a rising tide of prosperity and a divided Opposition. In 1992 they benefited from a new leader, the absence of the Poll Tax, an electorate still reluctant to trust the Labour Party, and once again a divided Opposition. It is hard to see how they will be quite so fortunate in future elections, but in order to have a good chance of winning again, they will need to retain a good part of the working-class vote which they won in 1979, 1983, 1987 and 1992.

Labour and the fragmented middle class

It is worth noting that, over the last decade and more, even when the Labour Party has fared badly at General Elections, its middle-class voting support has held up rather well. There is no complete explanation for this and no certainty that it will continue to be true in future. It may partly be explained by Labour's strong support among white-collar workers in the public sector – for example, teachers and health service workers. It could even be strengthened if Labour managed to broaden its appeal to encompass more issues of concern to the growing middle-class electorate, such as law and order, the quality of public services, protection of the environment, and greater economic opportunities for women. In recent times there has been real evidence of Labour's ability to do this.

Of course, another explanation for this phenomenon is simply that, as the electorate as a whole becomes more middle-class, so Labour voters are likely to become more middle-class as they move up the economic and social ladder. Even though their improved material circumstances and middle-class life-style might be thought to be more consistent with voting Conservative, such voters remain loyal to their social origins and principles and so vote Labour.

Gender differences in voting

In so far as women usually live longer than men and Conservative voting behaviour is usually more prevalent later in life, it is likely that many women will have a tendency to vote Conservative. Yet recent evidence on this issue now points to virtual equality of voting preferences between the sexes for each of the large political parties.

On the one hand, the traditional model of family life, with the wife and mother staying at home at least while the children are young, suggests that some women are likely to remain relatively insulated from the pro-Labour voting pressures which have been characteristic of at least the highly unionised sectors of employment. Even when married women return to work, many of them take part-time employment in the service sector, so that their jobs can be compatible with their continuing family responsibilities. Once again this does not make it in any way certain that they will develop Labour voting habits.

On the other hand, at the 1987 General Election the Conservative Party got the same proportion of its votes from men as from women (as indeed did both the Labour Party and the Alliance of Liberals and Social Democrats), a result which flew in the face of the traditional assumption that the party does better among female voters. There were a number of plausible explanations as to why this occurred. *Firstly*, there was the fact that some women did not like Margaret Thatcher's forceful style of politics. *Secondly*, there was the fact that on several key issues of the campaign – for example, unemployment, the health service, and the quality of education – many women found the Conservative Party unconvincing, unattractive or both. *Thirdly*, there was the fact that women of all ages, especially middle-class women of child-bearing age, were often attracted by the style and approach of the Alliance leaders, David Owen and David Steel. Perhaps the most obvious explanation was that 'Thatcherism' had a strong appeal to many male voters, especially those in the upwardly mobile working class.

Nonetheless, analysis of the 1992 General Election result once again showed women more likely to vote Conservative than men, by 44 per cent to 41 per cent, with evidence that the replacement of Margaret Thatcher by John Major was a significant contributor to this state of affairs. Quite which factors will come to the fore to influence gender preferences at future General Elections is difficult to predict. It does seem, however, that the Conservative Party no longer enjoys an automatic, natural advantage among women voters.

Electoral volatility

There is no way of knowing for certain whether or not the British electorate will become more volatile in future. However, there have been signs of considerable volatility over the past two decades and it seems likely that the trend will continue in the future.

At the 1992 General Election there was further evidence of electoral volatility to add to the body of evidence provided by analysis of elections since the mid-1970s. For example, it has been estimated that in the four weeks of the campaign as many as 11.1 million voters changed their minds, some of them more than once, with much of the initial flow being away from the 'don't knows' towards Labour and the Liberal Democrats. Similarly, it has been estimated that 21 per cent of the electorate decided how they would cast their vote in the final week of the campaign. During this last week 12 per cent of Labour's supporters shifted their allegiance, while nearly 20 per cent of Liberal Democrat

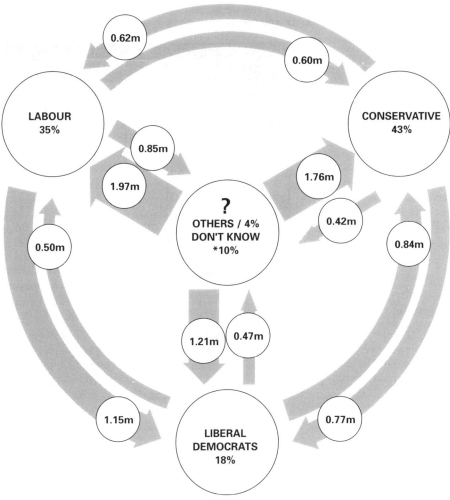

Figure 4.4 Electoral volatility in 1992

Width of arrows represents number of voters
*Percentages represent standing of the parties after reallocating the don't knows

Net voter movement during campaign

	Conservative	Labour	Liberal Democrat	Others / Don't know
	+3.20M	+3.09M	+3.13M	+1.74M
	-1.81M	-2.60M	-1.81M	-4.94M
NET	+1.39M	+0.49M	+1.32M	+3.20M

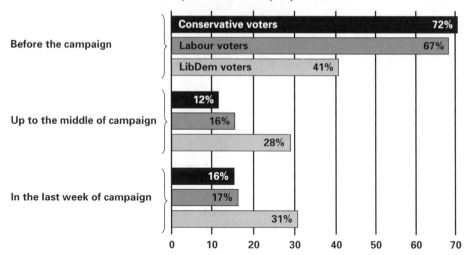

Figure 4.4 continued

THE DECISION
Q. When did you decide which party to vote for?

Source: Mori, *The Sunday Times*, 12 April 1992

supporters deserted the party. The Conservative vote was much steadier, and towards the end was swollen by defecting Liberal Democrats. Of those who ended up voting Liberal Democrat, only 41 per cent had made up their minds to do so before the campaign got underway, against 72 per cent of Conservatives and 67 per cent of Labour voters. By the middle of the campaign the Liberal Democrats had persuaded another 28 per cent of their eventual voters to back them, but as many as 30 per cent of Liberal Democrat voters made up their minds to support the party only in the last week of the campaign; indeed, 12 per cent decided to do so only in the last 24 hours. The volatility of the electorate during the 1992 General Election campaign is shown in Figure 4.4.

In future the impact of electoral volatility will depend upon the net effect of a number of different factors. It is likely that increased volatility will be encouraged by the relative weakening of traditional associations between class and party, the growing tendency for voters to cast their votes instrumentally, the advent of capricious 'consumer' voting, and the unsettling influence of the media on the opinion polls and voting behaviour. On the other hand, volatility could decrease if there were to be a general recognition of the futility of casting votes for smaller parties or a sustained secular trend towards a sea-change in voting behaviour of the kind which can occur in Britain once every 20 years or so. Only time will tell.

Participation or alienation

If political participation is measured simply in terms of the turn-out at General Elections since the Second World War, we can see that it has fluctuated between a high point of 84 per cent in 1950 and a low point of 73 per cent in 1970, with an average of 76.6 per cent over the entire period. In 1970 and 1983 for seasonal reasons (both elections were held in June, when many people were on holiday) and in October 1974 for reasons directly connected with public alienation from the political process (two General Elections in one year) the number of those not voting rivalled or exceeded the number of those who voted for the party which came second. Given that the two-party struggle has been a dominant characteristic of the British political system since the war, these facts could be interpreted as signs of real alienation from the political process.

It is also reasonable to argue that such signs of disenchantment with the two large parties are not necessarily signs of dissatisfaction with the electoral system or alienation from the entire political process. Indeed, it is worth remembering that many individual party candidates regularly get more than 50 per cent of the votes cast in their own constituencies. Yet there can be no escape from the fact that the struggle for power between the two leading parties has been the dominant characteristic of the British political system since the Second World War, so perhaps the conclusion is justified.

There are ebbs and flows in the tide of support for the two main parties. In 1951 they secured between them 96.8 per cent of the popular vote. This declined gradually to 87.5 per cent in 1964, rose to 89.8 per cent in 1966 and stood at 89.4 per cent in 1970. It fell sharply to 74.9 per cent in February 1974 and 75.0 per cent in October 1974. It rose again in 1979 to 80.9 per cent, but fell again in 1983 to 70.0 per cent. Since that time it has gradually increased to 73.1 per cent in 1987 and 76.3 per cent in 1992. It remains to be seen whether this reassertion of the 'traditional' duopoly will continue at the expenses of the smaller parties or whether the tide can again be reversed by the minor parties. On this point it should perhaps be noted that in 1992 the combined Conservative and Labour share of the vote was still lower than at any General Election between 1929 and February 1974. Thus, as Curtice and Steed observed, any conclusion that the 1992 Election heralded a return to two-party politics was premature to say the least.[32]

4.4 Conclusion

In conclusion, it can be said that the main influences upon voting behaviour in Britain are political inheritance, self-interest, and the performance of the party in office. Nevertheless these are often subjective influences which can depend upon the conclusions which individual voters draw from their own experience and observation of the political scene. From a more objective point of view, it seems clear that social class, economic occupation, housing tenure, educational attainment and geographical location are among the most important influences upon the way people cast their votes at General Elections. Furthermore, the voters do not cast their votes in a vacuum. They go to the polls (or decide not to bother) after weeks and months of verbal bombardment by the politicians and the media as well as assiduous attention from the opinion pollsters. All these various forces help to form the views of the voters, whose voting behaviour has become more volatile and even capricious in consequence.

There is still some validity in the view of Jean Blondel, who wrote years ago that, 'the simple division between working and middle class . . . contributes to the clearest cleavage in British political attitudes and voting behaviour'.[33] Yet such a statement no longer tells us all we need to know about voting behaviour in Britain in the 1990s. This is because the traditional working class has become significantly smaller while the middle class has grown, in each case as a function of changing patterns of employment. Such social changes ought to favour the Conservatives, although current opinion poll evidence (in 1994/95) suggests that the Labour Party will do well in spite of its apparent structural handicap. Whatever happens in the minds of the voters, it is well to remember that there are few, if any, certainties in voting behaviour.

Suggested questions

1   What are the main divisions in the British electorate?
2   Which are the most significant influences upon voting behaviour in Britain?
3   Is social class still a decisive factor in determining the outcome of elections in Britain?

Notes

1. B. Sarlvik and I. Crewe, *Decade of Dealignment* (London: CUP, 1983), p. 66.
2. Since about 6 per cent of the names on the Electoral Register are redundant (i.e. dead, double-counted, emigrated etc.), the true level of non-voting is somewhat lower than the usual figures suggest.
3. P. Pulzer, *Political Representation and Elections in Britain* (London: Macmillan, 1967), p.98.
4. For a fuller discussion of this subject see R. T. McKenzie and A. Silver, *Angels in Marble* (London: Heinemann, 1968), and J.H. Goldthorpe, *Social Mobility and Class Structure in Modern Britain* (Oxford: Clarendon Press, 1980).
5. See I. Crewe, 'A new class of politics', in *The Guardian*, 15 June 1987.
6. See Mori poll, *The Sunday Times*, 12 April 1992.
7. *The Guardian*, 13 June 1983.
8. *Ibid.*
9. See Mori poll, *The Sunday Times*, 12 April 1992 and Gallup Post Election Survey 10-11 April 1992.
10. The evidence on differences in voting behaviour by gender and age has been written up in successive Nuffield Election Studies since 1950. The figures given here are derived from those studies.
11. See Mori poll, *The Sunday Times*, 12 April 1992.
12. See the Gallup Survey commissioned by the BBC and published in *The Guardian*, 15 June 1987.
13. See Mori poll, *The Sunday Times*, 12 April 1992.
14. For detailed breakdown of regional variations in voting behaviour see successive *Times Guides to the House of Commons* which are published after each General Election.
15. See, for example, A.H. Birch, *The British System of Government*, 8th edn (London: Allen & Unwin, 1990), pp. 78-82.
16. See D.E. Butler and D. Stokes, *Political Change in Britain*, 2nd edn (London: Macmillan, 1974, pp. 48-66).
17. See A. Heath, R. Jowell, J. Curtice with B. Taylor, *Labour's Last Chance? The 1992 Election and Beyond* (Aldershot: Dartmouth, 1994).
18. See A. Heath *et al.*, *How Britain Votes* (Oxford: Pergamon Press, 1985).
19. See B. Sarlvik and I. Crewe, *Decade of Dealignment*, pp. 247-344.
20. Tony Benn, *The Guardian*, 11 April 1988.
21. Neil Kinnock, *The Sunday Times*, 12 June 1988.
22. See B. Sarlvik and I. Crewe, *Decade of Dealignment*, p. 113.
23. *The Guardian*, 14 June 1983.
24. See D. Kavanagh, 'Spirals of Silence', *The Guardian*, 21 April 1992.

25. *The Guardian*, 16 June 1987.
26. H. T. Himmelweit *et al., How Voters Decide* (London: Academic Press, 1981), p. 14.
27. See R. Worcester, 'Don't blame the opinion pollsters', *The Times*, 13 April 1992.
28. See A. Heath *et al., How Britain Votes*, pp. 170-75.
29. Patrick Edwards, Director, Greater London Action for Racial Equality. Cited in *The Guardian*, 6 August 1994.
30. See 'Connections', Commission for Racial Equality, August 1994.
31. See, for example, D. Bell, *The End of Ideology*, revised edition (London: Collier Macmillan, 1965).
32. J. Curtice and M. Steed in D. E. Butler and D. Kavanagh, *The British General Election of 1992* (London: Macmillan, 1992), p. 322.
33. J. Blondel, *Voters, Parties and Leaders* (Harmondsworth: Penguin, 1974), p. 86.

Further reading

Butler, D. E., and Jowett, P., *Party Strategies in Britain: a study of the 1984 European elections* (London Macmillan, 1985).
Butler, D. E., and Kavanagh, D., *The British General Election of 1992* (London: Macmillan, 1992).
Franklin, M., *The Decline of Class Voting in Britain* (London: University Press, 1985).
Goldthorpe, J. H., *Social Mobility and Class Structure in Modern Britain* (Oxford: Clarendon Press, 1980).
Heath, A., *et al., Understanding Political Change: the British voter 1964-1987* (Oxford: Pergamon Press, 1991).
Heath, A. *et al., How Britain Votes* (Oxford: Pergamon Press, 1985).
Himmelweit. H. T., *et al., How Voters Decide* (London: Academic Press, 1981).
Miller. W. L., *et al., How Voters Change* (Oxford: Clarendon Press, 1990).
Robertson. D., *Class and the British Electorate* (Oxford: Martin Robertson, 1983).
Rose. E., and McAlister, I., *Voters Begin to Choose* (London: Sage, 1986).
Sarlvik. B., and Crewe, I., *Decade of Dealignment* (London: University Press, 1983).
Scarborough, E., *Political Ideology and Voting* (Oxford: Clarendon Press, 1984).

PART 2

Sources of Power, Pressure and Opinion

5) The political parties

In Britain there is a system of party government – government by and through political parties. Parties are at the very centre of the system: national, organised, disciplined political parties. The rise of parties changed the nature of elections, altered the relationship between Members of Parliament and their constituents, determined the position of Prime Minister and Cabinet and transformed the House of Commons. As a result political parties have a dominant influence upon the whole nature of the British political system.

5.1 Origins and historical development

Although groups identified as either Whigs or Tories could be found in Parliament as early as the seventeenth century, parties in the modern sense only appeared in the nineteenth century as a direct consequence of Parliamentary reform. Due to successive extensions of the franchise (see Chapter 3), factions or groups within the House of Commons were increasingly obliged to organise outside Parliament in an attempt to secure the necessary voter support at elections.

The 1832 Reform Act led to the creation of a number of 'societies' whose function it was to arrange for the registration of voters sympathetic to their cause. The Tories established a central organisation to co-ordinate their efforts in this regard in 1832, and were followed two years later by the Whigs. However, it was the consequences of the 1867 Representation of the People Act which triggered the creation of parties in their modern form. The 1867 Act created a larger electorate, too large to deal with effectively in the traditional ways of personal influence, bribery, intimidation, and so on. Consequently, national party organisations were created through which widespread electoral support could be mobilised – seeking to secure the election of 'our' party and the defeat of 'their' party, with politics becoming a matter of 'us' against 'them'. Thus the National Union of Conservative Associations was established in 1867 and the National Liberal Federation ten years later in 1877. The age of nationally organised and relatively disciplined political parties had arrived in Britain.

Against this background it is easy to see that British politics is party politics which takes place in what is, fundamentally, a two-party system. In this chapter, therefore, we shall focus principally upon the Conservative and Labour parties, as they have been the two most significant political forces in Britain, at any rate since the Second World War. Beyond them we shall look at the smaller parties, whether those with an aspiration throughout Britain – such as the Liberal Democrats – or those with a more geographically limited vocation, such as the nationalist parties in Scotland and Wales. We shall also consider briefly the parties in Northern Ireland and the fringe parties in the rest of the United Kingdom – the Greens, the British National Party and so on.

At the outset it is worth trying to offer a common definition which can be applied to every political party to a greater or lesser extent. In the eighteenth century Edmund Burke defined a political party as 'a body of men united for promoting by their joint endeavours the national interest upon some particular principle in which they are all agreed'.[1] Today, however, there are difficulties with such a definition, not least because it places such an emphasis upon agreements freely entered into between relatively independent individuals – an emphasis which no longer reflects the realities of modern British politics. Political parties in Britain, as elsewhere in the democratic world, are nowadays more like organised coalitions, each containing a wide spectrum of ideology, principle, opinion and belief. As a result, a rather better definition of a political party in modern conditions might be: 'an organised and relatively disciplined group of people who freely combine to advance a set of political attitudes or beliefs with a view to translating them via success at elections into administrative decisions or legislative actions'. In other words, all parties try to influence and a few aspire to win the democratic power of Government.

5.2 Ideological principles

Since the Second World War it has been the Conservative and Labour Parties which have dominated the British political scene. They have brought to British politics two distinct ideological traditions within which their respective political principles have been advanced in the light of circumstances prevailing at the time.

The Conservative Party

The Conservative tradition stresses the importance of strong government, in the sense that Conservatives believe that a Government should act with determination and self-confidence based upon the democratic legitimacy which it derives from its Parliamentary majority in the House of Commons. Conservatives have traditionally been suspicious of political ideology of an imperative or all embracing kind, although during Margaret Thatcher's period as Leader (1975-90) many observers doubted the validity of such a proposition. In the opinion of Samuel Beer, the ideas of independent authority for the Executive, class rule by those deemed best equipped to govern, pragmatic decisions of a non-ideological character and strong determined government were all discernible in Conservative political thought for a long time.[2]

Occasionally in the course of its long history the Conservative Party has been swept along on the wave of some particular ideology, but such periods have not usually lasted or brought enduring political success. Joseph Chamberlain, a refugee from the Liberal Party, did not get very far with his campaign for tariff reform during the early years of the twentieth century. Edward Heath felt obliged to reverse the radical free market policies on which he and his colleagues had entered office in 1970. Yet, even though a conscious political ideology does not seem to belong in the Conservative tradition, the party appeared much more ideological in the 1980s – certainly in its free-market rhetoric and occasionally in its actions. This reflected the influence of what was then called the New Right upon Conservative thinking. Pressure groups outside Parliament, such as the Institute of Economic Affairs and the Adam Smith Institute, and factions within Parliament, such as the self-styled *No Turning Back Group* of radical Conservative back-benchers, combined to push the party's policy and decision-making in a markedly more right-wing direction and to give extra political impetus to the Thatcherite revolution.

In present circumstances the Conservative Party stands for a free economy and a strong state.[3] This implies the maintenance of sound money (sometimes called 'monetarism'); the control of public expenditure; the diminution of the public sector via the policy of privatisation; the reduction of tax rates on income; the pursuit of a range of 'supply side' reforms, such as legislative curbs on trade-union power, Council house sales to sitting tenants, and various forms of economic deregulation; greater freedom of choice for consumers, parents, and patients; a more selective approach towards social security and unemployment benefit; the reform and deliberate weakening of local government; the reduction and reform of the civil service; a tough approach towards law and order; strict controls on immigration; the maintenance of the nation's defences against terrorism and external military threats; and what could be regarded as an unsentimental, even nationalistic, attitude towards British membership of the European Union.

The party has also made a point, even a fetish, of trying to preserve party unity (or at least the appearance of unity), since it is well aware of the political disadvantages of obvious disunity. Nevertheless, this has not prevented the conduct of a bitter (though often coded) argument between the Thatcherites and the non-Thatcherites about the pace and scale of supply side reform (such as privatisation) nor has it prevented frequent outbreaks of internecine strife within the party about the nature and extent of Britain's commitment to the future development of the European Union during the 1990s. The former argument has largely been resolved in favour of the Thatcherites, since most of the prominent 'Wets' were sacked or retired from the Cabinet by the end of the 1980s and the rest of the party came to recognise the force of three successive General Election victories under the leadership of Margaret Thatcher. The latter argument remains unresolved following the Parliamentary ratification of the 1992 Maastricht Treaty and at the time of writing it looks as though only a commitment by John Major to put the result of the 1996 Inter-Governmental Conference to a referendum in Britain will be able to hold the Conservative Parliamentary Party together on the European issue.

During Margaret Thatcher's period as leader of the party (1975-90), the emphasis in Conservative rhetoric was put increasingly on the paramount importance of individual attitudes and behaviour in response to material incentives and legislative penalties. Leading party spokesmen were at pains to emphasise the comparatively limited role of the state and other public agencies, but equally to stress that the law should be clearly defined and strongly enforced in those areas in which state power could legitimately be exercised. There were also sustained attempts to reward individual success and to penalise failure, whether in education, work or life in general. Above all, the Conservatives sought to persuade people not to look to the Government for salvation, but to take responsibility for themselves and their families.

Under John Major's leadership of the party since November 1990, a more emollient style of leadership and a less exclusive approach to politics has been developed. Nonetheless, there has also been considerable continuity of policy, especially in respect of the party's commitments to sound money, reducing the size of the public sector and concentrating social security on those who need it most. Under John Major the Conservatives have presented a less ideological and more pragmatic profile. The slogans and ideas most closely associated with John Major's period as Prime Minister include his declared wish to create 'a nation at ease with itself'; the concept of 'the Citizens Charter' designed to make the providers of public services more responsive to the needs and expectations of citizens as customers and consumers; the aspiration that Britain should be 'at the heart of Europe' (but without any commitment to federation); and what turned into a rather counter-productive call to get 'back to basics' in such areas as education and law and order. John Major's critics in the media and in his own party have accused him both of having insufficient political conviction and of failing to demonstrate real leadership qualities. In these respects unfavourable contrasts have been drawn with his predecessor, notwithstanding the fact that he was chosen to succeed Margaret Thatcher in 1990 very largely because he was thought to be different in style and character.

The Labour Party

From the outset, and certainly ever since the party constitution was adopted in 1918, the Labour tradition was based upon a commitment to the ideology of Socialism. Yet from the beginning the importance of ideology was balanced to some extent by the more pragmatic outlook of the Fabians and Christian Socialists. It was also tempered by trade-union scepticism towards some socialist principles. Nevertheless, as Samuel Beer observed, 'if the implication of sudden and violent change is extracted . . . it is correct to say that the meaning of Socialism to the Labour Party was a commitment to ultimate social revolution'.[4] To the Labour Party this always meant more than a commitment to the public ownership of the means of production, distribution and exchange, as laid down originally in Clause IV of the party constitution. It also meant a commitment to a form of moral collectivism which drew upon the reserves of fellowship and fraternity traditionally associated with the trade union movement.

The Socialist tradition continued in the modern Labour Party. For example, the October 1974 Labour Manifesto contained a clear commitment to 'an irreversible shift in the balance of wealth and power' in favour of working people. The fact that the Labour Party, when in office, has not always acted in a particularly Socialist way has merely engendered disillusion and recrimination among its more zealous members. It was for this reason that the party swung markedly to the Left following defeat at the 1979 General Election. Many activists in the constituency Labour parties gave strong support to the campaign of Tony Benn and others on the Left of the Party in favour of constitutional changes within the Labour movement designed to make Labour MPs more accountable to the ideological elements in the constituency parties and to diminish the more cautious influence of the Parliamentary leadership upon Labour policy. As a result the Left was able to secure radical alterations to the party constitution in 1981, alterations which provided for the mandatory reselection of sitting MPs and election of the Leader and Deputy Leader of the party by an electoral college made up of the trade unions (40 per cent), the Parliamentary Labour Party (PLP) (30 per cent) and the constituency parties (30 per cent).

During this period the position of the Left within the party was strengthened by the election of Michael Foot as Leader and by the decision of a number of Labour MPs to join the newly formed Social Democratic Party. Labour's Manifesto for the 1983 General Election was the most Left-wing in its history and as such was described at the time by one critic in the party as 'the longest suicide note in history'.

Within days of the election defeat Michael Foot resigned the leadership of the party and after four months of campaigning Neil Kinnock, another leading Left-winger but politically more realistic and about 30 years younger, was elected to succeed him. He accepted the proposition that the party's chances of returning to power would be determined largely by its ability to formulate credible and coherent policies that were neither a source of intra-party strife nor repugnant to the electorate at large. To this end the decision was taken to concentrate less on policy and more on campaigning, the leadership being determined to rebuild the party with a more modern image and more moderate policies. It was for this reason that Labour policy commitments to withdraw Britain from the European Community, to re-nationalise privatised industries, and to repeal aspects of Conservative industrial relations legislation were abandoned or toned down, although the commitment to nuclear disarmament remained.

Following yet another electoral defeat for the party at the 1987 General Election, Neil Kinnock and his fellow 'modernisers' realised that in order to have a chance of defeating the Conservatives in future, it was necessary further to modernise both the party's internal structures and its policies. In attempting to achieve these objectives, they followed three courses of action.

Firstly, they introduced a wider franchise for the selection and reselection of party candidates in order to stop small groups of hardline activists dominating the process and to make constituency parties more representative of ordinary Labour supporters and the party more attractive to the voters. *Secondly*, they restructured the National Executive Committee (NEC) to give the Shadow Cabinet and the PLP more power and the NEC and the Party Conference less power for similar reasons. *Thirdly*, they initiated a wide ranging policy review designed to produce a set of modern policies for the 1990s which would improve Labour's chances of returning to office.

The Policy Review was overwhelmingly endorsed at the 1989 Labour Conference. Having dropped the Socialist policies which were perceived as having made Labour unelectable, Neil Kinnock felt able to declare that the party was 'fit for Government'. Undoubtedly the party was more united than it had been for many years and it had become a more formidable contender for power than it had been for a considerable time. Although the Policy Review did not offer a completely new definition of Labour's ideological principles for the 1990s, it did convey to the British electorate the symbolically important fact that the party had modernised its stance and abandoned old-fashioned Socialism.

Following yet another defeat for the Labour Party at the 1992 General Election, Neil Kinnock resigned as Leader and John Smith was elected in his place. The new Leader, who was also a 'moderniser', immediately decided to build upon the reforms of his predecessor by pledging to abolish trade-union block votes within the Labour movement and to introduce the principle of 'one member one vote' into the party's own decision making. After a fierce and often passionate debate at the 1993 Labour Conference, delegates voted in favour of One Member One Vote (OMOV) for the selection of Parliamentary candidates, reform of the system for electing the Leader and Deputy Leader, and the abolition of the union block vote in Party Conference decisions. In short, although the party remained the political voice of the trade unions, the relationship between the two was put upon a modern and politically acceptable basis of individual membership and voluntary participation.

Thus by the time of John Smith's untimely death in May 1994 and the election of Tony Blair as his successor in July 1994, the Labour Party had moved a very long way from the old-fashioned Socialism for which it had stood – at least rhetorically – in the 1970s and early 1980s. Indeed, Tony Blair has seemed so moderate and pragmatic on some issues – such as education and law and order – that it has seemed possible sometimes that Labour might position itself to the Right of the Conservatives on particular issues where majority public opinion seems to hold such a position. However, Tony Blair has been careful to say that Labour's redefinition of its policy has not altered its traditional commitment to social justice. Rather it has balanced that commitment with honest recognition of the new economic and political realities both in Britain and world-wide. Labour rhetoric now includes frequent references to '*partnership*' between the public and private sectors of the economy, '*fairness*' in taxation and social security arrangements, and '*democracy*' in relation to health and education and the oversight of extra-governmental organisations.

In view of the dynamics of policy development within the Labour Party, it is difficult to give a definitive description of exactly where the party stands on the main political issues at the time of writing. In general, however, it seems that the party favours the use of the tax and social security systems for more significant redistribution of income and wealth from the better off to the poor; higher public spending upon the National Health Service, pensions, education, and social security; more purposeful intervention in industrial and regional policy by a strengthened Department of Trade and Industry; the repeal of some of the Conservative trade union legislation and its replacement with a new charter or workers' rights; the reversal or alteration of many of the Conservative education reforms, for example by restoring to local authority control Grant Maintained Schools and City Technology Colleges; the strengthening of the Scottish and Welsh economies by the establishment of elected Assemblies in each of those parts of the United Kingdom, matched eventually by the creation of new English regional assemblies; the reform of the House of Lords and procedural changes in the House of Commons; closer co-operation with Britain's partners in the European Union in supporting interventionist and redistributive policies at European level; and an apparent willingness to retain Britain's nuclear deterrent until such time as it might be abandoned in the context of multilateral nuclear disarmament.

Following a long series of electoral defeats, Labour has made a significant shift towards a more moderate and pragmatic policy stance. Three successive Labour Leaders since Michael Foot have sought to maximise the party's chances of returning to power and have clearly believed that this could not be achieved on the basis of old-style Socialism. The party's willingness to accept some of the economic and social changes made by the Conservatives during the 1980s is somewhat reminiscent of Conservative willingness in the late 1940s to accept many of the changes made by the post-war Labour Government. In each case the principal Opposition party recognised that there had been a sea change in the conventional wisdom and assumptions of British politics which it had to accept if it were to persuade the voters of its suitability for office.

The Labour Party's shift towards pragmatism and moderation has been particularly noticeable on some sensitive and important issues, such as trade union reform and wider home ownership; but it has become increasingly evident right across the board. For example, mainstream Labour attitudes on public ownership, taxation and consumer rights have become more cautious and less doctrinaire than they used to be, and Tony Blair and John Prescott (his Deputy) have even persuaded the party to accept a new, more modern definition of Clause IV of the 1918 party constitution. In short, Neil Kinnock, John Smith, and Tony Blair have seemed determined to let no ideological shibboleths stand in the way of the return to power of a modern and voter-friendly Labour Party on a modern and pragmatic platform.

The Liberal Democrats

The Liberal Democrats were formally launched on 3 March 1988, under the slogan 'The New Choice – The Best Future', born out of the decision by the old Liberal Party and the Social Democratic Party (SDP) to merge their two separate parties – previously co-operating as *the Alliance* – into a single entity. Under their newly elected leader, Paddy Ashdown, the party sought to establish a distinctive political profile. In doing so, it identified four pillars of policy: *firstly*, investing in the future by allocating more public funds to education, health and the nation's technological base: *secondly*, modernising and defending democracy by developing a new concept of citizenship: *thirdly*, developing a more ambitious environmental policy; and, *fourthly*, laying great stress upon Britain's international vocation and responsibilities. Within its new concept of citizenship, the party was strongly committed to the achievement of a fairer voting system; devolution of power to Assemblies in Scotland, Wales and the regions of England; greater power for individuals at their place of work; the introduction of legislation guaranteeing freedom of information; and a new Bill of Rights. Above all, they advocated a less divisive and more decentralised approach to solving the continuing problems of British politics within the context of the European Union, to which they showed more commitment than either of the two main parties.

For the Liberal Democrats the result of the 1992 General Election was a bitter blow, not so much because of long-held expectations of major gains – the party had consistently been in single figures in the polls for much of the time since its formation – but because of the perceived success of their campaign. With only 17.8 per cent of the votes cast and just 20 MPs, every part of their pre-election strategy had come to nothing; no hung Parliament, no sign of Labour collapse despite the shock of four defeats in a row, no real evidence of electoral advance by the party, save, perhaps, in the South West of England. As for the declared strategy of replacing Labour as the Centre Left alternative to the Conservatives, it was very much a case of back to the drawing board.

Figure 5.1   Party policies at the 1992 General Election

The Issues	Conservative	Labour	Liberal Democrat
Taxation	Continue tax cuts, ambition of 20% basic rate; inheritance tax only for very rich; 40% rate on estates over £500,000; seek one tax free account for every saver; council tax, revalue homes every three years.	Top rate 50% earnings threshold 'well over' £30,000; reverse last week's budget changes, abolisyh 9% national insurance contributions; new tax on unearned income (pensioners exempt).	Add 1p to basic rate if necessary; increase tax thresholds; abolish mortgage relief for new borrowers, replace with 'housing cost relief'.

Figure 5.1 continued

The Issues	Conservative	Labour	Liberal Democrat
Industry	Privatise British coal, BR; require trade unionists to opt in annually to trade unions; individuals to sue unlawful strikers in public sector; protection for workerson personal contracts through industrial tribunal.	National economic assessment, dual budget-spending announcement; National Investment Bank, private capital for public projects; tax incentives for investors.	Combine Monopolies and Mergers Commission with OFT, power to break up privatised monopolies; BT break-up; more private rail service; new restrictive practices act.
Health	Extend opt-out hospitals, fund holding G.P.s; increase spending extra £2.7 billion next year; two-year maximum waiting time for patients; performance league tables; private treatment if NHS inadequate.	End GP fund-holding, opt-out hospitals to health authorities; Department of Health and Community Care (re-named); right to smoke free environment at work; free eye tests and dental checks.	End GP fund-holding, NHS trusts; more freedom for doctors to refer patients to chosen hospitals; free eye and dental checks; salaried GPs, accredited specialists.
Education	Extend city technology colleges, grant-maintained schools, opt-outs; performance-related teachers' pay; teachers, governors to control 80% school budgets by 1994; retain A-level gold standard.	Abolish city technology colleges, grant maintained schools' charitable status, phase out assisted places scheme; reform A-levels.	Return city technology colleges, grant-maintained schools to local authority control; review private schools' charitable status, phase out assisted places scheme; reform A-levels.
Training	Tax relief possible for companies improving training schemes	Skills UK, new organisation to direct training policy; employers to pay 0.5% of payroll on training; right for 16-year-old to stay on at school or traineeship based on National Training Qualifications.	Require working 16 to 19-year-olds to undergo education, training two days per week; return further education colleges to local authorities; adult education fees for fixed periods to key groups.
Defence	Order fourth Tridant, 512 warheads; 6% defence budget over four years; 'options for change' review, cut 116,000 soldiers; retain autonomy, subservient to neither NATO nor European Community.	Cancel fourth Trident order depending on contractual position and cost; no 'first-use' policy for nuclear weapons, end British nuclear testing; Defence Diversification Agency.	Limit warheads on four Trident submarines to same (192) or fewer than Polaris; cut £1 billion (50%) from military research to civil research; 'significant reduction' in armaments.
Law and order	Reorganise police service, nominate police chief for every town; identify potential criminals as young as six; monitor police response, satisfaction with service.	Increase police numbers over lifetime of parliament; body to investigate miscarriages of justice; Sentencing Council for consistency in punishment orders; prisoners' ombudsman.	Extend Court of Appeal powers; regional appeal courts; Judicial Services Commission to nominate judges; public defender to investigate miscarriages of justice; plea-bargaining.

Figure 5.1 continued

The Issues	Conservative	Labour	Liberal Democrat
Environment	Environmental Protection Agency; develop wind, wave, solar power; stabilise carbon dioxide emissions by 2005, phase out CFC emissions by 2000; 'green' taxes; extra green-belt protection.	Appoint 'green minister'; Environmental Protection Esecutive; stablisise then cut CO2 emissions by year 2000;cut VAT on environment-friendly goods; return water companies to public sector.	Energy taxes to cut industrial gases; 'pollution-added tax' on damaging goods; cut carbon dioxide emissions by 30% by 2005, sulphur dioxide emissions by 60% in five years; Environmental Protection Agency.
Social policy	Increase pensions, child benefit annually in line with inflation; improve disablement benefits; unemployed, sickness, income support benefits in line with inflation; cut benefit delays.	Pensions up £5 per week (single), £8 per week (couple), linked to average earnings or prices; flexible retirement age; child benefit up £9.95; minister for children, children's rights commissioner.	Priority increase in pensions, £5 (single), £8 (couple); increase child benefit by £1 per week per child.
Employment	Extend performance-related public sector pay; assist people to join union of their choice, union leaders to disclose salaries, stop abuse of 'check off' of union dues.	Minimum wage, at least half average male earnings (£3.40 an hour), £10,000 fine and three months prison for offending employers; Industrial Court, statutory duty to promote equal treatment.	Cut jobless by 400,000 in year; job creation/training programme costing £3 billion; jobless to improve council homes, other buildings; secondment of redundant exectuvies to small business.
Local government	Replace two-tier system, more unitary locaol authorities; cabinet style councils; performance tables for councils; retain uniform business rate.	Regional tier in England, elected regional government in second term, strategic authority for London elected by PR; Quality Commission, 'customer contracts' for residents, annual satisfaction surveys.	Ombudsman for every council; compensation for sub-standard services; public question times at council meetings, 'neighbourhood committees', uniform business rate replaced by site-value rating.
Housing	Boost homownership to 75%, rent-into-mortgage scheme for council tenants; mortgage-rescue scheme for council tenants, stamp duty relief until August; possibly subsidies for conversions, e.g. flats above shops.	National Housing Bank; phased release council house sale receipts; leaseholders' rights to buy freeholds collectively or extend leases; outlaw 'gazumping'.	Mortgage-to-rent scheme; building societies take ownership, seek rent to get 8% return on capital; support shared ownership; reform housing benefit system, pay claimants in advance of need, lend deposits.
Transport	Continue £12 billion roadbuilding, double trunk road programme over 10 years; BR privatisation white paper; compensation for delayed travellers.	Halt BR privatisation moves; transport safety inspectorate; strengthen passenger watchdogs; halt road schemes not yet out to contract; 'traffic calming', bus-priority schemes, cycle routes.	Increase petrol prices substantially, fuel taxes linked to pollution emissions; phase out vehicle excise duty, 'road pricing'; private rail lines, high-speed link Channel to North and West.

Figure 5.1 continued

The Issues	Conservative	Labour	Liberal Democrat
Arts and Media	Protect 'listed' artworks from export; extra finance for museum purchases; support 'Millennium Fund' to repair national museums and construct new buildings; devolve Arts Council powers.	Ministry for Arts and Media; phase out museum, art gallery charges; ownership of TV companies and newspapers to Monopolities and Mergers Commission; abolish Broadcasting Standards Council.	Ministry for Arts and Communications, arts spending to 1% of GDP; broadcasting act, renew BBC charter responsibilities, abolish Broadcasting Standards Council; lift Sinn Fein broadcasting ban.
Constitution	Categorically opposed to proportional representation and devolution for Scotland, Wales or English regions; streamline Whitehall departments.	Replace Lords with elected second chamber, proportional representation for Scottish assembly, freedom of information act; Commons committee on security service.	PR; incorporate European Convention of Human Rights, move to bill of human rights, written constitution; Senate replaces Lords; home rule for Scotland, Wales; fixed-term parliaments.
Equal opportunities	Opportunity 2000, encourage promotion of talented women and ethnic minorities but against positivediscrimination.	Ministry for Women, cabinet minister; simplify, extend race equality laws; citizenship law to respect 'family life'; strengthen laws on rape and domestic violence.	Wide-ranging initiatives across all policy areas.
Scotland	Oppose devolution or independence but ready to consider higher Westminster profile for Scottish interests; abolish regional authorities; privatise forestry commission and tourist board.	Scottish parliament in Edinburgh in first year, legislative and revenue raising powers, elected by 'additional member' PR, limited power to vary tax, plus contribution from UK taxation.	Home rule for Scotland; Scottish assembly logical consequence of European union; power over all policy except defence, foreign affairs and large-scale economics.
Wales	Oppose devolution or independe but ready to consider high Westminster profiel for Welsh interests; redraw local government map, 23 new all-purpose authorities such as Pembrokeshire.	Directly elected Welsh assembly, single tier 'most - purpose' local authorities; Welsh language act, fair treatment of daily users; Welsh-medium schooling for all families wanting it.	Welsh language act; offer Welsh-medium schooling to all families who want it.
Northern Ireland	Support Anglo-Irish agreement, continue to promote all-party talks suspended in pre-election period.	Review Prevention of Terrorism Act; end strip-searching, plastic bullets; support Anglo-Irish agreement; creation of a united Ireland by consent.	Support Anglo-Irish agreement; reject coalition with Unionists.

Figure 5.1 continued

The Issues	Conservative	Labour	Liberal Democrat
Europe	Minister for European Affairs of cabinet rank-reject imposition of a single currency or European Central Bank removing control of economic policy; retain control of immigration, drugs and anti-terrorist policy.	Support single currency development if there is a 'real convergence' between British and EC economies. Sign Social Charter immediately; develop European environmental charter.	Single European currency, independent central bank, move to narrow band of ERM soon as possible; political integration, Euro citizenship; Rapid Reponse Force, peace-keeping, disaster relief.

Source: *Sunday Times*, 15 March 1992

The Nationalist Parties

The Scottish National Party (SNP) has been motivated principally by the quest for Scottish independence and has therefore been able to encompass a broad ideological spectrum of opinion on nearly all other issues. In recent times most of the party has been able to unite on the basis of left-of-centre opposition to English, Conservative rule from London and Edinburgh, and the aspiration for an independent Scotland within the European Union.

Plaid Cymru, the Welsh Nationalist Party, has an ideology which is based upon its determination to preserve the Welsh language and culture as the foundation of a distinctive Welsh identity within the United Kingdom. The party has both a radical and a moderate wing, with the former being in favour of certain forms of direct action in protest against the English dominance of Wales (for instance on the issues of Welsh water for English cities or English second homes in Wales) and the latter seeming more content to use the traditional channels of Parliamentary influence to advance the Welsh nationalist cause.

Northern Ireland Parties

In Northern Ireland the majority Protestant community is represented at Westminster by various factions of the Unionist cause – the *Ulster Unionist Party* (UUP), the *Democratic Unionist Party* (DUP), the *Ulster Popular Unionists* and the *Independent Unionists*. All of them stand, to a greater or lesser extent, for continued Protestant supremacy and the maintenance of Northern Ireland as an integral part of the United Kingdom. The minority Catholic community is represented mainly by the *Social Democratic and Labour Party* (SDLP), which has campaigned to improve the economic and social conditions of its supporters and which favours closer links between Northern Ireland and the Irish Republic as a step towards eventual Irish unity by consent. A smaller part of the Catholic community gives its support to the much more radical *Sinn Fein*, the political wing of the Irish Republican movement in the north, which campaigns openly for the withdrawal of British troops from Northern Ireland and the subsequent establishment of a united Ireland – a policy which from the late 1960s through into the 1990s they sought to achieve by all means at their disposal, including the use of force. In addition to the Protestant/Unionist and Catholic/Nationalist parties there is the non-sectarian

Alliance Party of Northern Ireland. Launched in 1970, it has not been successful in Westminster elections and attracted only 8.7 per cent of the Northern Ireland vote in 1992.

Many of the Unionists have adopted an increasingly 'garrison' mentality, not least because they came to feel that the constitutional position of Northern Ireland had been placed in jeopardy, firstly by the 1985 Anglo-Irish Agreement between the British Government and the Government of the Irish Republic, secondly by the Downing Street Declaration signed by the British Prime Minister and the Irish Taoiseach on 15 December 1993, and thirdly by the IRA announcement of a 'complete cessation of military operations' at the end of August 1994.

The Fringe Parties

There are many fringe parties in British politics – indeed, a total of 930 candidates (a record number) stood under a minor party or independent label in the General Election of 1992. Some of the smallest, particularly those from the extremes of both Right and Left, wax and wane with bewildering frequency. On the extreme Right, both the *British National Party* (BNP) and the *National Democrats* (formerly the *National Front*) are based upon a white racialist ideology which is heavily tinged with xenophobia and impatience with the democratic methods of Parliamentary politics. On the extreme Left, *the Communist Party of Great Britain* – formed in 1920 – was one of the most unreconstructed and Stalinist parties in the whole of Western Europe, since it strongly opposed any firm Western response to the Soviet military threat and any liberalising tendencies in the Soviet Union or Eastern Europe. However, in 1991, seeking to shed its Stalinist image and to be seen as 'an open democratic party of the new, pluralistic and radical Left', the party re-named itself the *Democratic Left*. Also on the extreme Left are the *Socialist Workers' Party* and the *Workers' Revolutionary Party*, which were distinguishable from the old Communist Party mainly by their attachment to the idea of workers' control in industry and commerce and by their more favourable attitude towards reform in what was the Soviet Union.

In a different category altogether there is the *Green Party*, which stands for an ecological approach to all political issues. Formed as the People's Party in 1973, it became the Ecology Party in 1975 and changed to its current name in 1985. It reached considerable prominence in the late 1980s, riding the wave of a buoyant popular environmentalism which swept across Europe at the time. Indeed, in the 1989 elections to the European Parliament it secured 14.5 per cent of the votes cast (20 per cent in the south east of England), coming second in six seats out of 78 in Britain and third in 61. However, because of internal disputes and structural weaknesses, the re-emergence of the Liberal Democrats, the effects of the recession and the fact that the other parties sought to display their own 'green' credentials; the party proved unable to build on this performance, and in the 1992 General Election its average share of the vote in the 253 seats which it contested was only 1.3 per cent.

In the 1992 General Election the largest number of fringe party candidates – 309 – stood under the label of the *Natural Law Party*, a group whose campaign was designed to promote 'vedic science' espoused by Maharishi Mahesh Yogi as the solution to the world's problems, but which on average obtained only 0.4 per cent of the votes cast. Also on the fringe can be found a selection of 'loonies' – the *Official Monster Raving Loony*

Party, the *Loony Green Giant Party* and others – all individuals who have sought to get involved simply for the fun of it and who have undoubtedly added a touch of colour to British elections.

Most successful of all the fringe parties in the General Election of 1992, securing an average of 1.7 per cent, was the *Liberal Party*, a group of dissident Liberals who had refused to go along with the 1988 merger with the SDP. Indeed, the leader, Michael Meadowcroft, secured 8.3 per cent of the vote and was the only fringe party candidate to save his deposit.

5.3 Political functions

The political parties in Britain perform a range of political functions. Essentially these can be reduced to one primary function and a number of subsidiary functions, all of which contribute to the working of the British political system.

Primary function

The primary function of the main political parties in Britain, as Robert McKenzie made clear, is to sustain competing teams of potential leaders in the House of Commons in order that the electorate as a whole may choose between them at periodic General Elections.[5] Indeed, any attempt by the parties to play a more prominent role in their own right would cut across the chain of responsibility from Cabinet to Parliament to electorate which is fundamental to the British system of Parliamentary democracy. In the British political system constitutional power resides essentially with the Prime Minister and Cabinet, supported by a working majority in the House of Commons. In these circumstances the supreme function of the parties is bound to be the gaining and retaining of public consent for the exercise of such power. Any other conception of their paramount task would be inaccurate and improper, according to the conventional wisdom.

Subsidiary functions

All the parties perform similar subsidiary functions which vary in importance depending upon the particular circumstances of the time. *Firstly*, they encourage public interest and participation in the process of politics. In other words, they provide permanent structures within which individuals and groups can act if they wish to play a part in politics at the local, national or European levels.

Secondly, the parties reflect, moderate and direct into constitutional channels the views and interests of a wide range of sectional groups. Of course, pressure groups have a powerful independent existence in their own right within the political system. Yet the existence of the parties enables and encourages all sectional groups to act in a constitutional manner and leads them to pay more attention to Parliament than might otherwise be the case.

Thirdly, they provide legitimate frameworks for the ventilation, discussion and criticism of political issues. This function has been more prominent in the Labour and Liberal

Democrat parties than in the Conservative Party, because the former believe in the virtues of considerable grass roots influence upon the process of policy making, whereas the latter has traditionally allowed only a very limited role for its activists in this sphere. However, in the 1980s this contrast became somewhat less marked, since Conservative activists felt encouraged by Margaret Thatcher and her like-minded Parliamentary colleagues to make more forcefully known their support for radical policies, especially when such developments appeared to be blocked or delayed by some of the more traditional figures in the Parliamentary party. Consequently, since taking over as Leader in 1990, John Major has had to take account of the Party Conference to a greater extent than any of his predecessors, a fact emphasised at the 1993 Conference when he felt obliged to reduce the pressure on his position as Leader with a direct appeal to the basic instincts of traditional Conservative supporters by calling for a return to core Conservative values. On the other hand, although the annual Conference is theoretically the supreme policy-making body within the Labour movement, its 'decisions' can be heavily influenced and even manipulated by the Parliamentary leadership acting in conjunction with the most powerful affiliated trade unions.

Lastly, and by no means least important, the political parties exist to build up membership, raise money, select candidates and organise political campaigns at local, national and European levels. In the Labour Party the greater part of the money and a large proportion of the membership comes from the affiliated trade unions. In individual constituencies the local trade union branches contribute much of the income for the constituency parties (although on average less than half), while at the national level about 60 per cent of the party's income comes from the trade unions which affiliate to the party varying proportions of their membership. In the Conservative Party, on the other hand, a great part of the money comes from donations made by industry and commerce, although in the constituencies the Conservatives (like Labour) usually manage to raise considerable sums of money through the efforts of their voluntary workers. The Liberal Democrats seek to raise money both locally and nationally in broadly similar ways, except for the fact that they do not rely on official trade union support and their support from business is both more limited and usually more concentrated in certain quarters.

In modern political conditions all parties find it increasingly difficult to keep going financially at a time when the costs of political activity are rising and the membership of political parties is dwindling in a disturbing way. For example, the Conservative Party claimed a membership of 2.8 million in 1953, a figure which had declined to fewer than 750,000 by the middle 1990s. Similarly, although the Labour Party claimed over 1 million members in 1953, this had declined to something under 300,000 towards the end of 1994. The Liberal Democrats claimed a membership of 100,000 in the middle 1990s. As far as the costs of political activity are concerned – as outlined in Chapter 3 – the 1992 General Election campaign cost the parties centrally about £23.2 million, 51.6 per cent more than in 1987. Since the publication of the Houghton Report in 1976, there has been the additional possibility for the parties to receive financial support from public funds in proportion to the votes which they secured at the previous General Election.[6] In theory, this could go a long way towards alleviating the financial problem of the parties, as it has done on the Continent, where a similar, but more generous, approach applies. In practice, it has proved impossible so far to get the necessary all-party agreement to anything more than token financial support for the Leader of the Opposition and a few other senior Opposition figures (including the Leader of the Liberal Democrats). This is mainly because the Conservative Party is ideologically opposed to state aid to political parties, does not wish to discourage the fund-raising efforts of its own voluntary workers and seeks to retain the comparative advantage which it has traditionally derived from voluntary arrangements.

5.4 National organisation

In matters of national party organisation there is a notable contrast between the Conservative Party, which was created from the centre and the top down, and the Labour Party which was created from the grass roots up. The Conservative organisation was originally intended to act as the handmaid of the Parliamentary party, whereas the Labour organisation was conceived as the servant of the National Executive Committee and ultimately the annual Party Conference. Such contrasting origins and traditions have left their mark upon the way in which each of the main parties is organised today. Having said this, however, it should be pointed out that Neil Kinnock, who led the Labour Party between 1983 and 1992, made significant organisational changes in the Labour Party which brought it more under the sway of the Parliamentary leadership, changes which both his successors, John Smith and Tony Blair, have been able to take further.

The Conservative Party

The Conservative Party organisation is under the control of the Party Chairman who is appointed by and responsible to the Leader of the Party. The Party Chairman is normally a trusted colleague of the Party Leader with a seat in the Commons or the Lords and usually a place in the Cabinet as well. It is rare for the Chairman to be at odds with the Leader, but, if that happens, it is the Chairman who has to go.

Conservative Central Office exists to carry out the wishes of the Leader of the Party and to meet the various organisational needs of the party at every level. It is also the head office and central point of co-ordination for the party organisation in the different parts of the country (although the Scottish Conservative Party has its own organisational structure) and thus provides support, material and advice for the Constituency Associations. It includes the Conservative Research Department, which acts as a briefing organisation for the party and a miniature civil service for the Parliamentary leadership when the party is in Opposition.

The Party Conference is organised by the National Union of Conservative Associations, but with the guidance of the Party Chairman and key officials at Central Office. The Conference provides an annual occasion not so much for policy making as for the activists from constituencies all over the country (at least 5000 people in all) to come together for a mixture of social and political purposes, including ritual adulation of the Party Leader on the final day. However, with the decline of deference in British politics, it is no longer wise or easy for the party leadership to ignore the view of the party rank and file. As Richard Kelly has observed in commenting on the modern Tory Conference, 'its bourgeois participants feel sure that they convey the new *vox populi* and are naturally impatient with any leaders who do not listen'.[7]

Between annual Conferences (held every autumn) the National Union continues to function on behalf of the party in the country and helps to maintain cohesion and morale in the constituency Associations. The governing body of the National Union is called the Central Council. Since this consists of about 4000 people and meets only once a year in the spring, it is really a slightly smaller-scale Party Conference. It has an Executive Committee of about 200 people representing all sections of the party which meets five times a year. This in turn elects a General Purposes Committee of about 60 people which makes most of the day-to-day decisions of the National Union, including those related to the agenda and arrangements of the annual Party Conference.

Within the framework of the National Union there are various advisory committees at national level which are often replicated at area and constituency levels as well. These include the Women's National Committee, the Local Government Advisory Committee, the Trade Union Advisory Committee, the Young Conservative National Committee, the Conservative Political Centre National Committee and so on. Yet none of these bodies is much more than a sounding-board for a particular section of party opinion. Nearly all those who are prominent in these hierarchies have to be elected by those below them, although some are co-opted on the basis of their special knowledge or personal contacts. They provide useful frameworks for political discussion within the party (especially the Conservative Political Centre which was designed for this), although there is usually no likelihood of deflecting the party leadership from a particular course of action to which it is strongly committed.

Just occasionally one or other of these bodies within the party has been known to go astray and cause the party leadership considerable embarrassment. One example was the Federation of Conservative Students which was infiltrated by the extreme Right during the early 1980s and as a result became an embarrassment to the party which had to be wound up and replaced by the more docile and amenable Conservative Collegiate Forum which is organised and controlled from Central Office. Furthermore there has been some pressure within the party since the mid-1970s for the Party Chairman to be an elected and not an appointed position. This pressure has been associated with the so-called Charter Movement that got going following the Chelmer Report, which in the 1970s had made recommendations for the reorganisation of the voluntary party along more democratic lines. See Figure 5.2 for a diagram of Conservative Party organisation.

In the House of Commons the party is organised within a framework capped by the 1922 Committee, which was named after a famous meeting of Conservative back-benchers held at the Carlton Club in that year. The Committee is led by its Chairman, who is a senior back-bencher elected annually by back-bench colleagues. It has an influential Executive Committee made up of other senior back-benchers also elected annually by their colleagues. Under its auspices there is a considerable substructure of party back-bench committees each covering an area of policy – for example, finance, industry, agriculture, employment, environment, education, defence, foreign affairs and so on – and each with a slate of officers elected annually by their colleagues. In the House of Lords the party is more loosely organised in the Committee of Conservative and Unionist Peers.

When the party is in Government, such committees can have an influence on policy via the subtle process of *the politics of anticipated reaction*, that is, when Ministers adjust their intended actions in the light of expected or actual responses from the relevant back-bench committees. When the party is in Opposition, such committees are

Figure 5.2 Conservative Party organisation

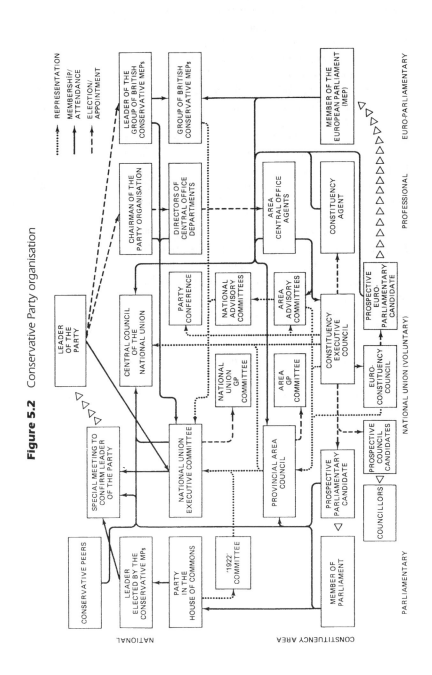

probably more influential and they are certainly busier, since the various shadow spokes-men are appointed chairmen of the relevant committees and their fellow officers from the back-benches can have considerable influence upon the process of party policy mak-ing. In Opposition there has also been a so-called Business Committee which is made up of the officers of the 1922 Committee and the officers of all the various back-bench committees under one rubric. This has served as a broader institutional link between the Shadow Cabinet and the various back-bench subject committees.

As for the position of the Party Leader, before 1965 such a person was said to 'emerge' from a process of informal soundings and consultations within all sections of the party, but principally in the Commons. Since 1965 the choice of Party Leader has resulted from a process of election by all members of the Parliamentary party in the Commons, who are expected to consult each other informally and take account of the views of the party in the Lords, the European Parliament and the country as well. Such elections can take place every year in the autumn. Yet, as long as the Leader maintains the confidence of the Parliamentary party, the contest is merely an annual formality with only one nomi-nation.

Margaret Thatcher secured the leadership in 1975 by challenging the then Leader, Edward Heath, while the party was in Opposition. She remained unchallenged until 1989 when the back-bencher Sir Anthony Meyer challenged her unsuccessfully. The follow-ing year, 1990, Michael Heseltine challenged her and, although obtaining only 152 votes to her 204 on the first ballot, secured enough support under the rules to ensure a second ballot, thus undermining her position to such an extent that she withdrew from the con-test. On the second ballot – which allowed new candidates to enter the contest – John Major came top of the poll with 185 votes and secured the leadership because the other candidates did not press their rights to initiate a third ballot, even though he had not achieved a large enough margin of victory to rule it out. Following considerable media speculation that John Major was to be challenged for the leadership of the party in 1992, 1993 and 1994, and as a direct result of mounting speculation in 1995, John Major him-self resigned as party leader in June 1995, challenging critics to 'put up or shut up'. This brought forth a challenge from John Redwood, but John Major secured re-election on the first, and as a consequence only, ballot. The general point remains, however, that Conservative Party Leaders in office as Prime Minister are not normally challenged, pro-vided they maintain the confidence of their Cabinet colleagues and of the Parliamentary party.

The Labour Party

The Labour Party organisation is under the control of the General Secretary, who is the senior paid official responsible to the National Executive Committee, which is account-able in its turn to the annual Party Conference. In view of the dual hierarchy in the party, the Leader of the Party and senior Parliamentary colleagues can be at odds over matters of policy and procedure with prominent members of the National Executive Committee, who are often back-bench MPs of a more radical disposition elected to the NEC by the constituency Labour Parties.

However, under Neil Kinnock's leadership (1983-92) and thereafter under the lead-ership of both John Smith (1992-94) and Tony Blair (1994-), serious efforts were made by the Parliamentary leadership to regain effective control of the NEC and the party organisation which serves it. This has meant much greater emphasis upon attractive presentation of united Labour policy and much greater influence from the centre than was formerly the case in the Labour movement.

The staff at Labour Party headquarters, including the Research Department, are responsible to the General Secretary. They perform a range of support functions similar to those performed by Conservative Central Office. The Party Chairman, who normally holds office for one year only, is usually the member of the NEC with the longest continuous membership of that body and with responsibility to the party as a whole rather than to the Leader of the Party.

The Labour Party Conference has always been a much more powerful gathering than its Conservative counterpart. Its claim to a real political role is based upon the fact that it is constitutionally and formally the policy-making body of the party, while the party in Parliament is theoretically little more than the Parliamentary arm of the entire Labour movement.[8] The Conference is presided over by the Chairman of the Party, who is assisted by a Conference Arrangements Committee composed of representatives of all the main sections of the Labour movement. Traditionally the Conference was dominated by the block votes of the trade unions. For example, the Transport and General Workers Union had a block vote of about 1.2 million and the Amalgamated Engineering Union had one of about 840,000 votes. By comparison neither the smaller trade unions nor the constituency parties had much voting power at Conference, although they could make their influence felt with extra militancy. The Conference was composed of mandated delegations which were expected to vote in accordance with the decisions previously taken by the organisations which they represented. However, in 1993 the union block vote was abolished with union delegates thenceforth being free to vote independently and with the proportion of union votes falling to 50 per cent of the total. Labour Members of Parliament can attend Conference, but unless they are members of the NEC, they do not usually play a prominent part in the proceedings.

The NEC is the powerful body which claims to act in the name of the entire Labour movement between annual Conferences. It includes representatives of the affiliated trade unions, the constituency parties, the Women's Section, the Young Socialists, other affiliated Socialist societies, together with automatic representation for the Leader, the Deputy Leader and the Party Treasurer. It acts in the name of the Conference and carries on the business of the party from one year to the next. It also has a constitutional claim to a major role in party policy-making and to participation with the Cabinet or Shadow Cabinet in the preparation of the Party Manifesto. There is therefore an inherent tension between it and the leadership of the Parliamentary Party, although in recent years, certainly on the big political issues which really matter, the leadership has usually been able to get its way.

In the House of Commons the Parliamentary Labour Party is led by the Leader, who chairs the Parliamentary Committee (Shadow Cabinet) which is the executive committee of the party in Parliament when it is in Opposition. Since 1970 the weekly meetings of the entire PLP have been chaired by an elected Chairman who is usually a senior backbencher. As in the Conservative Party, back-benchers involve themselves with various subject groups, depending upon their particular policy or constituency interests. In both cases, however, they have relatively little formative influence over the process of policy making.[9] See Figure 5.3 for a diagram of Labour Party organisation.

Figure 5.3 Labour Party organisation

Annual Conference
Elected delegates from Constituency Labour Parties, national trade unions and affiliated organisations; ex officio Labour MPs, peers and European MPs; endorsed candidates; NEC

National Executive Committee
12 union representatives, 7 from constituencies, 5 women, 1 from Socialist Societies, Treasurer, Leader and Deputy Leader – all elected by Conference; plus Labour Party Young Socialists representative

Labour Members of the European Parliament

Regional Council of the Labour Party
There are 11 regional areas. Each holds an annual conference, with representatives from constituency parties. The conference elects a regional executive committee

Parliamentary Labour Party
Labour MPs and Labour members of the House of Lords; headed by the Party Leader and Deputy Leader

County Labour Party Management Committee
(Regional Party Management Committee in Scotland.) Representatives from constituency parties and other organisations in the counties

Local Government Committee
In Greater London only: representatives from the General Committees of every Constituency Labour Party in the borough

District Labour Party Management Committee
Representatives of Constituency Labour Parties, unions and other affiliated groups – where two or more constituencies are involved

Constituency Labour Party General Committee
Elected representatives from branches, women's organisations, Labour Party Young Socialists branches, workplace branches and affiliated organisations in the constituency

Constituency Labour Party Executive Committee
The General Committee elects officers and an Executive Committee to look after the detailed organisation of the constituency party

Labour Party Branches
Every Labour Party member belongs first to his or her branch, which is based on boundaries as decided by the General Committee

Other Labour Party Groups and Affiliated Organisations

Labour Party women's organisations, Young Socialists, workplace branches, trade unions and socialist societies which affiliate locally

In Opposition, the members of the PLP vote every year for those of their colleagues who aspire to places in the Shadow Cabinet. The top 15 are elected and the Leader is then free to distribute the portfolios between them. The junior shadow spokesmen are appointed by the Leader according to the usual criteria of political clout, personal merit and regional or ideological balance. In Government, the Party Leader is, of course, Prime Minister and therefore free to allocate the real Ministerial responsibilities as appropriate, subject to the usual political considerations of ideological and regional balance within the party. However, in particular response to pressure in the early 1980s – when Tony Benn and others on the Hard Left of the party urged that members of a Labour Cabinet should be elected by the PLP rather than appointed by the Prime Minister of the day – provision is now made for all the elected members of the Shadow Cabinet to become members of the Cabinet automatically when the party moves into Government, although not necessarily in the Ministerial posts which they have been shadowing.

From 1922 to 1980 the Leader of the Party was elected exclusively by the PLP. However, after the 1979 General Election, the Hard Left of the party was successful in its long-running campaign to take this power out of the exclusive hands of Labour MPs. Following an agreement at Bishops Stortford in 1981, this power was entrusted to an electoral college in which the three main sections of the Labour movement are represented. Following changes in 1993 the college votes are divided into thirds with individual party members accounting for one third, Labour MPs and MEPs accounting for one third, and trade union members (plus the members of other affiliated organisations) all voting individually accounting for the remaining one third. Candidates for the leadership must be MPs and their nominations must be supported by at least one eighth of the PLP.

Main party contrasts

The organisation of each of the main parties reflects the contrast between the traditionally hierarchic principles of the Conservative Party and the traditionally democratic aspirations of the Labour Party. In the former case, this means that party decisions are normally taken expeditiously and implemented without undue debate or difficulty. In the latter case, it means that the origins of party decisions have often been blurred and the implementation occasionally challenged by some of those involved. In short, the Conservative Party has tended to be more amenable to firm leadership from the top, whereas the Labour Party has often seemed temperamentally and organisationally averse to it. Nonetheless it has been observed that in the post-Thatcher Conservative Party and the post-Kinnock Labour Party these traditional views are no longer wholly accurate; indeed, some might say that the defining characteristics of the two parties have been reversed.

The problem for Labour has been that it has been difficult adequately to control a party which has served a movement which has aspired to be both ideological and democratic, although the ideology of democratic Socialism holds that there is no conflict between these two characteristics. The problems of the Conservatives have been more subtle, but just as real on occasions. In spite of their autocratic style and tradition, the management of the party has been by no means trouble-free. For example, exposure to a hostile Party Conference can be an unpleasant and tricky ordeal for even the most senior and experienced politicians, especially when the representatives have bayed for blood on the more atavistic issues, such as decolonisation in the 1950s, Rhodesia in the 1960s, law and order in the 1980s, and Europe in the 1990s. Indeed, the issue of Europe has come close to destroying the Conservative Parliamentary Party on several occasions in the 1990s.

In the Conservative Party effective power is wielded mainly by the Leader, and to a lesser extent by the other senior Parliamentary figures, in Government or Opposition. The senior figures in the hierarchy of the National Union are soothed with Knighthoods rather than seriously consulted on matters of policy and on the whole the voluntary side of the party knows its place in the scheme of things. Yet even a powerful Conservative Leader cannot afford to ignore party opinion, since the activists can put pressure upon back-benchers who then feel obliged to lobby Ministers or shadow spokesmen as the case may be. It has also been noticeable over the years that Conservative Leaders seem to have been more vulnerable than their Labour counterparts to political 'assassination' when they fail to win General Elections or are directly involved in other events politically calamitous for their party.

In the Labour Party power has always been more diffuse, certainly from the adoption of the party constitution in 1918, since it has been shared between the PLP on the one hand and the affiliated trade unions and constituency parties on the other. This uneasy alliance has been balanced sometimes in favour of the extra-Parliamentary elements and sometimes in favour of the PLP. In the 1970s and early 1980s great efforts were made by the constituency parties to seize a larger share of power, heavily encouraged by Tony Benn who sought to make them his own power-base within the Labour movement, and to strengthen the NEC against the PLP. Power has tended to reside with the Parliamentary leadership more when the party has been in Government and less when it has been in Opposition. A great deal has depended upon the inclinations and ambitions of the leading figures in the movement at different times. Yet, as we have seen in the cases of Neil Kinnock and Tony Blair, if a Labour Leader is determined to assert authority, this can certainly be done, provided there is backing from the most powerful figures in the party. See Figure 5.4 for a diagram of Liberal Democrat Party organisation.

The Liberal Democrats

The organisation of the Liberal Democrats is federal in nature, in that there are autonomous parties in England, Scotland and Wales, each with its own national offices, staff and conferences. The party in England is further sub-divided into 12 regional parties. The Federal Conference, which meets twice a year, is composed of representatives from the constituencies, the Parliamentary Party, associated organisations – such as those representing youth – and the officers of the national organisation. The party's Federal Executive, the Federal Policy Committee and the Federal Conference Committee all report to it. See Figure 5.4 for a diagram of Liberal Democrat Party organisation.

Responsibility for developing and presenting party policy, including the preparation of the General Election Manifesto, is placed upon the Federal Policy Committee. This is composed of the Party Leader, the Party President, five representatives of the party in both Houses of Parliament, three representatives from local authority Councillors, two representatives each from the Scottish and Welsh parties, and 13 members elected by the Federal Conference. Responsibility for directing, co-ordinating and implementing the work of the Federal Party falls to the Federal Executive, a body formed on a similar basis to the Federal Policy Committee. Its tasks include setting up a Finance and Administration Committee to manage the finances and direct the administration of the Federal Party, including its headquarters at 4 Cowley Street, London SW1, and the appointment of a

Figure 5.4 Liberal Democrat Party organisation

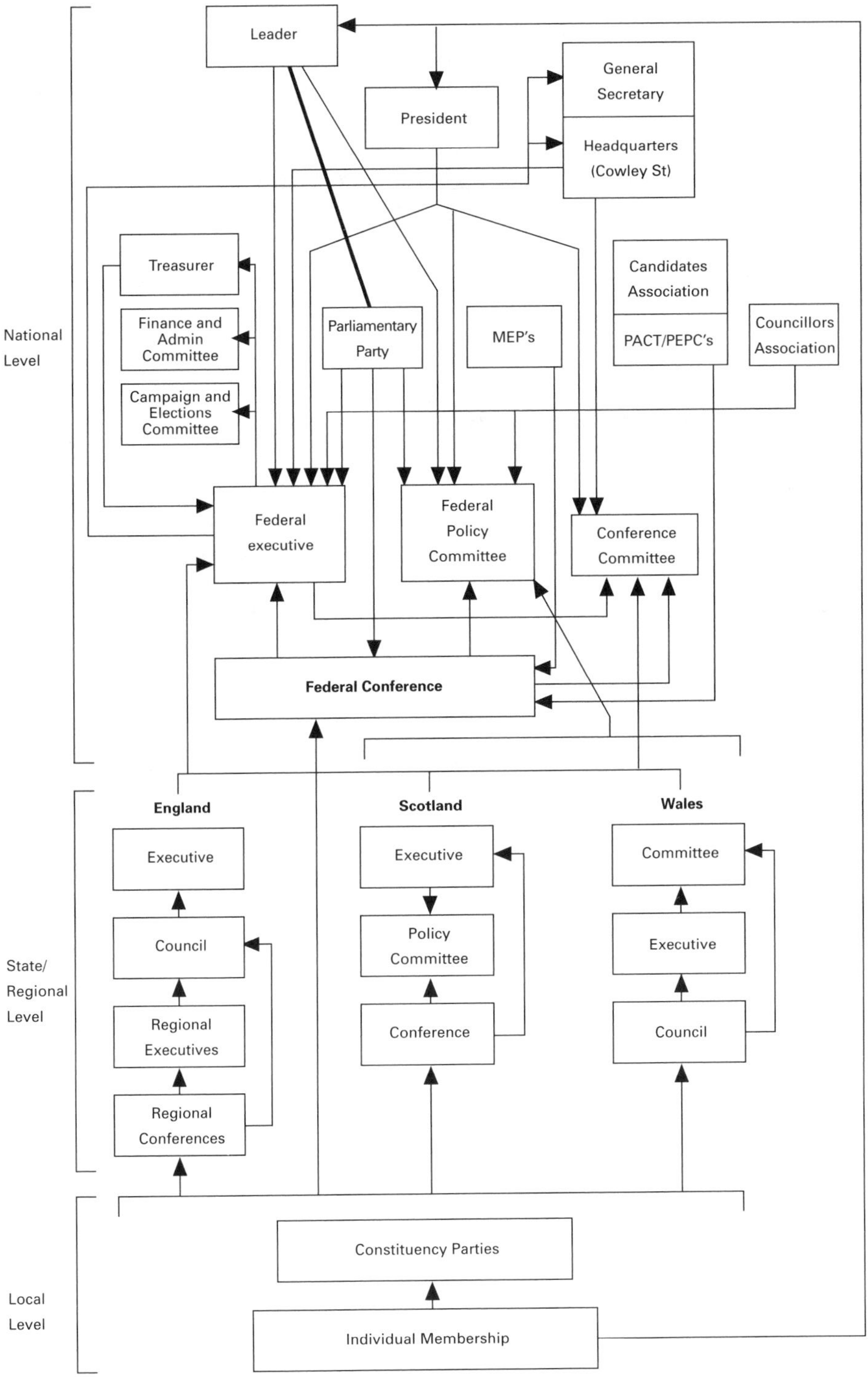

General Secretary. Party headquarters is divided into seven Departments – membership and direct mail, finance, campaigns and elections, policy, conference, party newspaper, and the General Secretary's Department.

Elections for the position of Leader of the Party are held every two years, unless postponed by a vote of two thirds of the Federal Executive. Apart from this, an election can be held either at the Leader's own request or following the loss of the Leader's Parliamentary seat, or a vote of no confidence in the Leader by a majority of Liberal Democrat MPs, or at the request of 75 local parties. Candidates for the leadership have to be an MP, to be proposed and seconded by MPs and to be supported by at least 200 party members in at least 20 local parties or associated organisations. The election of the Leader is carried out on the basis of one member one vote via a postal ballot of the entire party membership.

5.5 Constituency activities

It is when we consider the constituency activities of the parties that we notice more similarities than contrasts, in spite of the wide variety of people who are involved. For example, both of the main parties and the Liberal Democrats have sought to ensure and maintain political activity in all the constituencies, except in Northern Ireland.[10] Nevertheless, all three parties have tended to focus their resources and concentrate their efforts rather more directly than this blanket approach might suggest. In particular, the Liberal Democrats have concentrated their efforts and resources in relatively few constituencies where they already have local support and where their electoral prospects appear to be quite good. Constituency organisations vary in size from a mere handful of members in areas where parties are weak to as many as several thousand in the strongest areas of the large parties. In all cases they exist to serve the campaigning and fundraising purposes of the parties and to enable them to contest local, Parliamentary and European elections.

Financial support

Unlike local party organisations in the United States, constituency parties in Britain try to remain solvent and operational throughout the time between General Elections. They are assisted in doing this by the need to contest local and European elections at regular intervals and occasionally Parliamentary by-elections as well. Yet they rely for their continued existence upon individual and corporate subscriptions and donations made possible by the voluntary efforts and fund-raising activities of the party workers.

In the *Labour Party*, the constituency organisations receive considerable financial support from local trade union branches and in some cases individual MPs are sponsored and financially supported by particular trade unions. In the *Conservative Party*, a considerable portion of the income at constituency level comes from local business and commercial interests, although the bulk of the money is raised from individual subscriptions and voluntary fund-raising activities of all kinds. The *Liberal Democrats* have sought to maintain similar activities at constituency level in order to perform similar political functions, but they often have had to struggle to maintain viable levels of income and support.

Local membership

The active members of the various constituency parties come from many different walks of life. In all parties they tend to hold political views which are more zealous and uncompromising than those of the electorate in general. Indeed, if this were not the case, it is unlikely that many of them would be sufficiently motivated to join in the first place or to remain as paid-up members of their political party.

It is difficult to generalise about the membership of constituency parties, since a wide variety of people become involved in politics at the local level at one time or another. Suffice it to say that the active members of Conservative Constituency Associations often include middle-aged and elderly women, retired people, farmers and their spouses, small businessmen, and local traders. The active members of constituency Labour parties often include men rather than women, people in public-sector trade unions, those involved in cause groups, and a number of more traditional supporters for whom involvement in Labour politics almost runs in the family. The active members of the Liberal Democrats tend to be drawn from a wider cross-section of the population. They include many people who are not usually so closely identified with obvious class interests and some who have not previously been active in party politics at all.

In the final analysis no generalisations about party membership are really satisfactory. All that can be said with any certainty is that the trends over the years have been characterised by a steady erosion of active support for each of the two main parties and by significantly changing social composition in each case. No one knows exactly how many paid-up members there are in either of the large parties (see p. 84). It is also noticeable that over the period since the early 1970s the Conservative Party has become less dominated at constituency level by traditional middle-class people, while the Labour Party in the constituencies has become more middle class than it was before. Such social changes at constituency level have had an important effect upon the character of each of the parties in Parliament. The Conservative Party has moved noticeably 'down market' in its composition and attitudes, while the Labour Party has become less closely associated with the interests and outlook of the traditional working class.

Political power

In so far as members of constituency parties exercise effective political power, they do so mainly through their right to select and, occasionally, de-select Parliamentary and local government candidates. Labour activists have greater power than this, since they also have a share in the electoral college which chooses the Party Leader, while in the Liberal Democrats the Party Leader is essentially elected on the basis of one member one vote. In all the political parties it is accepted that ordinary party members should have some real influence upon the process of policy making, although Conservative MPs have traditionally been wary of according power to their activist supporters.

In the *Conservative Party* the key constituency bodies are the Executive Councils of perhaps 30 to 80 members, composed partly of Association Officers (Chairman, Vice-Chairmen, Treasurer and so on), but mostly of representatives of the various wards or branches in the constituency. In the *Labour Party* the key constituency bodies are the General Management Committees, which are composed in the same sort of way, but which are often somewhat smaller. In such gatherings local party activists can have direct and significant influence upon the political process, especially in the Labour Party with its procedures for sending resolutions to the annual Party Conference where they can become agreed party policy if they secure the necessary two thirds majority. In view of the fact that roughly two thirds of all the seats in the Commons have been considered 'safe' for one or other of the two main parties, the power to select the candidate has often amounted to the ability to determine the choice of the MP in many parts of the country. This has been the real foundation of political power at constituency level and it has had to be taken very seriously by MPs and candidates alike.

Candidate selection

In each of the main parties the candidates for Parliament chosen by the 'selectorates' have tended to be rather different both from the groups which select them and from the electorate as a whole. There has been a tendency over the years for social convergence between the Parliamentary candidates of the two main parties. This has often meant the selection of middle-aged, middle-class white men with families in preference to women, blue-collar workers or people from the ethnic minorities.

However, in recent times it has become increasingly necessary to qualify this over-all description. In the *Conservative Party* there is nowadays a wider variety of candidates for Parliament. Although the privileged origins of some Conservative aspirants remain very noticeable, there has also been a growing number of self-made men and a few women who have managed to fight their way into Parliament. In the *Labour Party* the changes have been even more dramatic in recent years. Nowadays many more Labour candidates are being selected from the ranks of the 'talking classes' in white-collar and public-sector occupations to the exclusion of many of the more traditional types from the old fashioned working class. In the late 1970s and early 1980s this coincided with a marked shift towards more radical attitudes in constituency Labour parties which put a greater emphasis upon the selection of candidates who were eager (or at least prepared) to carry out the wishes of the party activists. Indeed a preference for radical minority activists (whether feminists, blacks or gays) became increasingly evident in the London Labour Party and in some other areas where such people got themselves entrenched in local parties. However, from the middle 1980s the Labour leadership began to take a greater interest in candidate selection and in the 1990s, at the behest of Walworth Road, a growing number of Labour constituency parties practised something akin to positive discrimination in favour of women candidates or those from ethnic minorities, especially at by-elections which attracted more than the usual amount of national media attention.

The position has been rather different as far as the *Liberal Democrats* are concerned. Traditionally the Liberal Party attracted men and women of broadly liberal outlook who wished to see the liberal point of view translated into public policy. However, it did not lay great insistence upon strict adherance to party orthodoxy. This approach has continued in the Liberal Democrats, although it has been tempered by a degree of hard-nosed political realism and a willingness to follow the line laid down by the leadership, both of which characteristics were brought to the party from the former SDP.

While the nature and strength of a candidate's commitment to party ideology seems to have become more important in determining an individual's progress in all parties, it is no longer usually the case that the wealth or family connections of an aspiring candidate have much bearing upon the chances of success at constituency level (although it must be said that there have been a few husband-and-wife or other family combinations in the House of Commons). Since the late 1940s all parties have set low limits on the personal donations which candidates or MPs may make to their constituency parties, so it is no longer possible to purchase a nomination, as it used to be, at any rate in the Conservative Party before the Second World War. Yet some candidates still have a better chance of success than others, especially at by-elections, when the parties wish to take no unnecessary chances, and in the competition for the safest seats.

In the *Labour Party* candidates seeking selection have to be nominated by at least one branch of the constituency party, a process which can often be strongly influenced by the affiliated trade union with the largest representation in the locality. At the national level there are two lists of Parliamentary candidates which are kept at party headquarters in London following endorsement of the names by the NEC. List A is made up of trade union-sponsored candidates and List B of the rest. On the whole those on List A have more success in securing candidatures, although they may not do quite so well in the competition for safe Labour seats. Moreover, some candidates who emerge as 'favourite sons' of their constituency parties do not appear on either of the national lists, but nevertheless are usually endorsed by the NEC if they are selected. In exceptional cases the modern Labour Party has actually limited the range of local choice or even imposed a candidate upon the local party in order to avoid the selection of a candidate believed to be detrimental to the party's chances at a by-election.[11] In the mid-1990s, in a move designed to ensure that more women would be elected to Parliament, positive discrimination in favour of women came to be exercised in candidate selection.

In the *Conservative Party* there is also a list of approved Parliamentary candidates which is kept centrally at party headquarters in London. In order to get on this list aspirants have to go through a complicated process of written submissions and personal interviews, as well as a subsequent assessment process. In some cases these stages can prove more difficult than the later appearance before constituency selection committees. Furthermore each constituency Association has the unfettered right to select anyone it likes, even if the person concerned is not on the centrally approved list of Parliamentary candidates at the time. Once again the situation is often slightly different at by-elections, in that the Area Agent of the party usually takes great care to guide the constituency selection committee towards the choice of someone who is expected to be able to cope with all the extra media publicity that is now associated with modern Parliamentary by-elections.

In the *Liberal Democrats* responsibility for the shortlisting of candidates rests with the executive committee of the local party or a shortlisting sub-committee appointed by it. All candidates must be on the party's list of approved candidates, a process which involves a series of oral and written interviews, tests and submissions. Unless a sitting MP or previous candidate is reselected, the process involves drawing up a shortlist incorporating a specified number of candidates which, subject to there being a sufficient number of applicants, must include at least one member of each sex. Each member of the party in the constituency has a vote in the process and the choice of candidate is determined by proportional representation.

5.6 Conclusion

Political parties are central to the British political system. Indeed, there exists in Britain a system of government by and through political parties. In Britain it is political parties which compete for power and the maintenance of party discipline is a very important factor in determining a party's chances at General Elections.

In Government, the task of the victorious party is three-fold. *Firstly*, its leading members who become Ministers have the responsibility of ensuring that the policies on which they were elected are translated into administrative decisions or legislation as appropriate. *Secondly*, Government Ministers and Whips have to ensure that the Government's measures are supported and carried whenever there are key votes in Parliament. *Thirdly*, leading political figures in the governing party have to propound and defend the merits of Government policy both through the media and in direct contacts with members of the public.

In Opposition, the task of the defeated parties is simpler in that, apart from licking their wounds and sorting out their internal difficulties, their main duties are to criticise and oppose the Government of the day, and to elaborate alternative policies and political stances which can be put before the electorate in the run-up to the following General Election. In this context it is important to note that the second largest party in the House of Commons becomes *the official Opposition* and thus shares with the Governing party the responsibilities of conducting Parliamentary proceedings in an effective and business-like manner, which normally allows the Government of the day to get its way in the end while allowing the Opposition full opportunities to play its constitutional role.

While the two main parties differ quite considerably in their history, ideology and constituency membership, they are more similar in many other respects than some accounts have suggested. When in Opposition, each Party has tended to use distinctive political language and to develop a distinctive political style in order to differentiate itself from the party in Government and often from its own record or behaviour in previous times. When in Government, each party has traditionally behaved in a broadly responsible and moderate way and until the early 1970s each pursued policies which belonged within the framework of the post-war consensus (see Chapter 8).

From the early 1970s a number of significant developments in each of the main parties led them both to depart quite markedly from their previous adherence to the post-war consensus. The Labour Party began to change significantly when in Opposition from 1970 to 1974, as Tony Benn and others on the Left of the party began to denigrate the 1964-70 Labour Government for its failure to be sufficiently Socialist. The Conservative Party began to change when in Opposition from 1974 to 1979 as Sir Keith (later Lord) Joseph and Margaret Thatcher (later Baroness Thatcher) began to redefine the purposes and priorities of Conservatism in contradistinction to the policies pursued during the second half of the 1970-74 Conservative Government. As a consequence of these movements of opinion, the ideological gap between the two parties became wider during most of the 1970s and 1980s.

The position began to change yet again in the late 1980s. One result of winning three General Elections in a row was to make the Conservative Party increasingly radical and self-confident in its Thatcherite beliefs. On the other hand, another consequence of this chain of Conservative victories was to force the Labour Party under successive Leaders since Michael Foot to reconsider and revise many of its previously Socialist policies in a determined and conscious attempt to make its appeal more credible to the mass electorate. The situation changed once again with the downfall of Margaret Thatcher in November 1990 and the election of John Major to the leadership of the Conservative Party in her place. One consequence of the change was to make the Conservative Party itself, as well as the public at large, much less clear about what it stood for or where it was going. Whereas there was a body of doctrine which could be described as 'Thatcherism', and although some of this undoubtedly outlasted Margaret Thatcher's period as Leader, pundits and practitioners alike searched in vain for a coherent set of political principles and beliefs which could legitimately be described as 'Majorism'. When set alongside the fact that the process of revisionism within the Labour Party started by Neil Kinnock continued under John Smith and Tony Blair, some observers have begun to doubt whether there will be much that is authentically either Left or Right of centre on offer to the public from either of the two main parties at the next General Election.

Only the passage of time and the verdict of the electorate will show which of the parties has been successful in the competition for votes. Much will depend upon whether the so-called 'new realism' is a passing fad or a permanent adjustment, changing for good some of the basic values and assumptions of the British people. Much will depend upon whether John Major can improve the electoral fortunes of his party which has plunged to unusually low levels of popularity since September 1992. Similarly, much will depend upon whether Tony Blair can convince the electorate that his party is once again fit for Government in much the same way as Harold Wilson proved able to do in 1963-64. Much will also depend upon events and influences outside the control of politicians, such as the workings of global markets and the practices of global media. Indeed, a durable or definitive conclusion is not possible, since in party politics, as in life, it is the journey and not the arrival which matters.

Suggested questions

1   What are the principal functions of political parties in the British political system?
2   'British politics is party politics.' What factors lie behind such a view?
3   Where does real power lie in the Conservative and Labour parties?

Notes

1. E. Burke, 'Thoughts on the Cause of the Present Discontents' (1770), *Works* vol. I, see G.H. Sabine, *A History of Political Theory,* 3rd edn (London: Harrap, 1968), p. 611.
2. S. Beer, *Modern British Politics* (London: Faber, 1969), p. 247.
3. See A. Gamble, *The Free Economy and the Strong State* (London: Macmillan Education, 1988).
4. S. Beer, *Modern British Politics,* p. 135.
5. See R. T. McKenzie, *British Political Parties,* 2nd edn (London: Heinemann, 1963), p. 645.
6. See the Report of the Committee on Financial Aid to Political Parties, Cmnd 6601 (London: HMSO, 1976).
7. *The Spectator,* 8 October 1988.
8. For further discussion of this subject see L. Minkin, *The Labour Party Conference* (Manchester University Press, 1980).
9. This is because in the Labour Party the NEC shares the policy-making role with the Parliamentary

leadership, while in the Conservative Party policy-making is dominated by the Leader and a few senior Parliamentary colleagues.

10. From the late 1980s there was pressure from grass-roots Conservatives in Northern Ireland to recreate Conservative Associations in the Province which could again be affiliated to the National Union. This idea was approved in principle at the 1989 Conservative Party Conference. As a result Conservative Party candidates contested eleven of the seventeen Parliamentary constituencies in Northern Ireland at the 1992 General Election, securing 5.7 per cent of the votes cast.

11. One of the best examples was when Robert Kilroy-Silk resigned as Member of Parliament for Knowsley North in 1986, having made allegations about Militant infiltration into his constituency party. He was succeeded by George Howarth who was imposed upon the local party by the national hierarchy of the party at Walworth Road in London.

Further reading

Davies, A. J., *To Build a New Jerusalem* (London: Michael Joseph, 1992).

Gamble, A., *The Free Economy and the Strong State* (London: Macmillan Education, 1988).

Ingle, S. *The British Party System*, 2nd edn (Oxford: Basil Blackwell, 1990).

Pelling, H., *A Short History of the Labour Party*, 10th edn (London: Macmillan, 1993).

Riddell, P., *The Thatcher Era and Its Legacy* (Oxford: Basil Blackwell, 1991).

Seldon, A., (ed.), *UK Political Parties since 1945* (Hemel Hempstead: Philip Allan, 1990).

Seldon, A and Ball, S. (ed), *Conservative Century: the Conservative Party since 1900* (London: University Press, 1994).

Shaw, E., *The Labour Party Since 1979: Crisis and Transformation* (London: Routledge, 1994).

Stevenson, J., *Third Party Politics since 1945: Liberals, Alliance and Liberal Democrats* (Oxford: Basil Blackwell, 1993).

Young, H., *One of Us*, revised edition (London: Pan Books, 1990).

6 Pressure groups

In the British context pressure groups have been defined in a number of different ways. W. J. M. Mackenzie defined them as 'organised groups possessing both formal structure and real common interests in so far as they influence the decisions of public bodies'.[1] Moodie and Studdert-Kennedy defined them as 'any organised group which attempts to influence Government'.[2] Samuel Finer defined them as 'organisations . . . trying to influence the policy of public bodies in their own chosen direction, though never themselves prepared to undertake the direct Government of the country'.[3] Peter Shipley defined them as 'an association of individuals joined together by a common interest, belief, activity or purpose that seeks to achieve its objectives, further its interests and enhance its status in relation to other groups, by gaining the approval and co-operation of authority in the form of favourable policies, legislation and conditions.'[4] Thus a pressure group is any group in society which, through political action, seeks to achieve changes which it regards as desirable or to prevent changes which it regards as undesirable.

The expression *'pressure groups'* is a comprehensive term which subsumes both sectional interest groups and more widely based attitudinal cause groups. The former are usually well-established groups advocating or defending a vested interest. The latter can be ephemeral organisations which may decline or disappear when their goals have been achieved, although in modern times they have played an increasingly influential and continuous role in the political process. However, the term presupposes that all pressure groups are *promotional* in the sense that they seek to promote their various objectives in the most effective possible ways. It also implies that they are *irresponsible* in the strict sense that they are not democratically accountable to the general public. It is the political parties which have to accept that form of responsibility and which are vulnerable to the verdict of the electorate at every General Election, and at other elections to a lesser extent as well.

In attempting to achieve their objectives, pressure groups seek access, either directly or indirectly, to the political and governmental systems in order to influence the whole policy-making process. In essence this means seeking to influence the formation, process and administration of policy by means of contacts with Ministers, civil servants, MPs, peers, local authorities, political parties, other groups, the media, the general public and, increasingly, with individuals, institutions and other groups elsewhere in the European Union.

Pressure groups reach into every area of political, economic and social life. Their activity, indeed their active co-operation, is often an essential prerequisite for the smooth working of national Government. According to *group theory*, individual representation is not realistic in modern society, but collective representation can be for people as home owners, car drivers, employers, consumers, teachers, doctors and so on. Consequently, the state does respond to pressure groups through which the interests and opinions of different people can be both expressed and given direction. The 'father' of group theory was Arthur F. Bentley, who wrote in 1908 that it was only through the analysis of group activities that one could achieve a true knowledge of government.[5] For Bentley politics was about groups and their effects on each other and on Government – 'the tool of the strongest groups'. His argument, however, took insufficient account of the impact of political parties and of elections upon policy making, since pressure groups have to function within a framework which is shaped and influenced by both.

Nonetheless, pressure groups are still an important and influential part of the British political system. Traditionally, the British have been an organised people and, in many respects, the nation's history can be seen to have been one of competing sectional interests – competition, for example, between craft and merchant guilds, professional groupings, landowners, factory owners, railway developers and trade unions – all continuously striving to influence, or even dominate, the course of national politics. Equally, British history has seen the continuous pursuit of ideals and causes, as witness, for example, the cause group campaigns to abolish slavery, end child labour, extend the franchise, or improve prison conditions.

6.1 Classification of groups

When looking at pressure groups, it is necessary to make a preliminary distinction between *Interest Groups* (sometimes known as sectional groups) and *Attitude Groups* (sometimes known as cause groups). The former are often defensive in their functions and closely involved with the institutions of central Government. The latter often begin as institutional outsiders, but some of them have attained a degree of prominence which virtually requires their views to be taken into account. In practice, of course, there is considerable overlap between the two types of group and some find a place in both categories.

Interest groups

Interest groups are all those whose basis of association is a common interest, usually economic or vocational. Put simply, they exist to promote the interests of their members. The best example of an interest group would be a trade union, an employers association or a professional association. As far as trade unions are concerned, there are a large number of these bodies in Britain – such as UNISON (an amalgamation of NALGO, NUPE and COHSE, all public service unions) with 1,457,726 members, the TGWU (Transport and General Workers Union) with 949,107 members, the AEEU (Amalgamated Engineering & Electrical Union) with 835,019 members and the MSF (Manufacturing Science & Finance Union) with 516,000 members – as well as the TUC (Trades Union Congress), which is the trade association for 68 independent trade unions with a combined membership in 1995 of 7,303,419; essentially, a union of trade unions.[6]

With regard to employers' associations, there is the CBI (Confederation of British Industry), which exists primarily to ensure that Governments understand the intentions, needs and problems of British business. With a membership of firms, employers' associations and trade associations covering 50 per cent of both the UK's workforce and output, it is the leading 'voice' of business in Britain. Modern rivals for the CBI include the Chambers of Commerce and the Institute of Directors, and there are many more trade associations which speak for different sectors of British industry and commerce. With regard to professional associations, prominent examples would include the Royal College of Nursing which represents nurses, the Law Society for solicitors and the Bar Council for barristers, to name but a few. A vast array of other groups would also be classified as 'interest groups', such as the Society of Authors, the Royal British Legion, the Association of Licensed Taxi Drivers, the Scottish Whisky Association and the AA (Automobile Association).

Attitude groups

Attitude groups are those which seek to achieve objectives based upon shared attitudes or beliefs, rather than common material interests. The activities of such groups are directed towards the advancement of particular causes. For example, there are the groups dedicated to the cause of environmental protection, such as Friends of the Earth (200,000 members), Greenpeace (350,000 members), The National Trust (2.2 million members) and The Council for the Protection of Rural England (45,000 members). There are groups dedicated to prison reform, such as The Howard League for Penal Reform (8000 members and supporters); groups dedicated to electoral reform, such as The Electoral Reform Society (1800 members); and groups dedicated to nuclear disarmament, such as CND – The Campaign for Nuclear Disarmament (45,000 members in 1995).

Many attitude groups seek to do battle on behalf of those who find it difficult or impossible to fight for themselves. Examples would include animal welfare groups, such as the RSPCA – Royal Society for the Prevention of Cruelty to Animals (79,000 members) – and The League Against Cruel Sports (35,000 members and supporters); and child welfare groups, such as The Child Poverty Action Group (almost 7,000 members).[7] There are also a wide range of attitude groups which campaign for moral causes, such as those arguing for or against legal abortion, those arguing for or against smoking, and those which have been involved for and against legal Sunday trading. The examples given are no more than the tip of a very large iceberg. Indeed, no one really knows how many pressure groups there are, although one reputable source lists some 6,300 national and voluntary organisations in Britain.[8] Not all of these would necessarily fall within everyone's definition of a pressure group, but the figure gives some idea of the scale of what is involved, not least because it does not include local organisations.

From this it is apparent that pressure groups differ widely. They can be large or small, permanent or temporary, proactive or reactive, rich or poor, powerful or weak, successful or unsuccessful, or any combination of such possible permutations.

6.2 Main functions

In the contemporary British context pressure groups have a number of main functions. *Firstly*, they act as intermediaries between Government and the public. This is a role which has become more important as the scope and complexity of politics have increased and as it has become more difficult for the political parties on their own to perform all the representative functions. This means that they act as spokesmen and negotiators on behalf of clearly defined sectional interests – for example, the National Farmers' Union on behalf of farmers or the British Medical Association on behalf of doctors. It also means that they help all Governments to develop and implement their policies by entering into detailed consultations on proposals for administrative action or legislation and subsequently by delivering a measure of public consent to the output of the policy and decision making process. For example, Shelter has had considerable influence upon housing legislation over the years, the Child Poverty Action Group has consistently pressed for improvements to help the poor and especially families with children, and the Magistrates' Association is regularly consulted about the development of the criminal law.

Secondly, they act as opponents and critics of Government, especially when the interests of those whom they claim to represent are threatened by Government policy. For example, the British Medical Association was in the forefront of the campaign to resist the Conservative Government's reforms of the National Health Service in the late 1980s and early 1990s, while the Bar Council and the Law Society lobbied heavily against some of the Major Government's proposals for reform of the legal profession. Some people might argue that, in behaving like this, they are duplicating or even usurping the rightful role of the political parties. Yet that would really be an outdated point of view in a modern, pluralist democracy. As Robert McKenzie pointed out long ago, 'the voters undertake to do far more than select their elected representatives; they also insist on their right to advise, cajole and warn them regarding the policies which they should adopt and they do this for the most part through the pressure group system'.[9]

Thirdly, they have acted as extensions or agents of Government. This is a role which has grown in importance whenever the tendency towards corporatism has grown in British society.[10] For example, the British Medical Association had a number of expert and advisory functions under the auspices of the 1946 National Health Service Act. The National Farmers' Union had a number of analogous functions under the auspices of the 1947 and 1957 Agriculture Acts. The Law Society is responsible for administering the system of state-financed legal aid. Perhaps the most familiar example of corporatism, especially under Labour Governments, has been the prominent role played by the CBI and the TUC both as economic interest groups and as virtually obligatory partners with Government in nearly all matters to do with the management of the economy and often much else as well. Examples would include the special employment and training measures which were administered by the Manpower Services Commission set up in 1973, or the regulations made by the Health and Safety Executive under the auspices of the 1974 Health and Safety at Work Act.

Fourthly, they have acted occasionally as substitutes for or outright opponents of Government itself. This is a very rare occurrence in British politics and it is not a role which even the most powerful groups are keen to play, since it can so easily engender a serious and lasting public backlash. If it happens, it is usually the result of either a breakdown of Government authority in certain areas of policy or the deliberate implementation of some form of syndicalism.[11] To some extent the former conditions applied in certain circumstances during the serious trade union disruption of essential public services which took place during the 'winter of discontent' in 1979. The latter conditions applied on a local scale during the time of the Meriden Co-operative in the late 1970s, when the workers themselves took over and ran their own motor cycle factory for a while until market forces and Japanese competition got the better of them.

Fifthly, they act as publicists and purveyors of information in order to promote a particular point of view or defend a particular standpoint. For example, during the 1980s the Campaign for Nuclear Disarmament was very active in its efforts to secure favourable media coverage and publicity for its cause of unilateral nuclear disarmament in Britain as an example to the rest of the world. It sought to do this by organising public meetings, mass demonstrations and other carefully planned media events, as well as by producing a wide range of campaigns material and propaganda. Equally, some environmental groups, such as Friends of the Earth or Greenpeace, have used similar techniques in their successful campaign for environmental improvement, for example the use of returnable bottles, the preservation of rare animal species or the abandonment of the fast-breeder reactor programme in Britain. The Child Poverty Action Group is an unabashed user of publicity as a battering ram for change. As one of its early directors made clear, 'our main aim is to shift Government, not to chat with civil servants – coverage in the media is our strategy'.[12] Equally, from its formation in 1966 the housing group Shelter showed itself to be a most effective publicist of the dreadful housing conditions in which many millions lived and the need for substantial improvement. More recently animal welfare protesters have used publicity to considerable advantage in their campaign against the live animal export trade.

In nearly all cases the most familiar and successful techniques involve staging media events to attract publicity and then further steps to capitalise upon the public attention thus gained by advancing persuasive arguments in suitable supporting material. The publicity techniques may involve an unlikely combination of endorsement by show business personalities and follow-up with detailed and well-researched arguments. Sometimes those concerned even go so far as to undertake difficult or dangerous stunts in order to capture media attention; for example, the Greenpeace campaigns to save whales and seals by sailing small boats into the hunting areas in order to disrupt the activities to which they objected. The media coverage achieved for campaigns of this kind is not an end in itself, but rather a means of getting such issues onto the political agenda and of putting pressure on politicians to take appropriate action. Some other cause groups are essentially defensive. These have included the Wing Airport Resistance Association which helped to prevent the sitting of a third London airport at Cublington in Buckinghamshire, and the M23 Action Group which helped to persuade the Government to drop its plans to extend a motorway through residential Wallington in south London.

Finally, pressure groups offer an alternative career path into public life for those who may not be completely enamoured with conventional party politics. Examples of individuals who attained national prominence through such pressure group activity include Jonathon Porritt through Friends of the Earth; Des Wilson through Shelter and later CLEAR, the Campaign for Lead-Free Air; Frank Field through the Child Poverty Action Group; Joan Ruddock through CND; and Mary Whitehouse through the National Listeners and Viewers Association.

6.3 Channels of influence

There are many channels of influence open to pressure groups through which they can try to achieve their objectives. These channels relate very closely to the various institutional structures through which decisions are taken and to the nature of the British political system itself. As a result, groups in Britain attempt to exert influence through five basic channels – namely directly upon public opinion, indirectly via the choice of candidates for public office, shamelessly via financial contributions to party funds, predictably via pressure during the legislative process, and continuously via expert and technical representations to civil servants in Whitehall.

Firstly, pressure groups attempt to influence public opinion through all the media of mass communication – notably press, television, and radio – and use all the techniques of the public relations industry. The purpose of such pressure is either to persuade the public to act directly – for example, the RSPCA's campaign to persuade shoppers not to buy products from companies that did not meet the animal protection group's criteria for 'cruelty-free' animal testing – or to mobilise them politically and so achieve a group's objectives via effective influence upon Whitehall and Westminster. Obtaining favourable publicity and mobilising public sympathy may not in itself be enough to ensure a permanent solution to the problem identified. For example, in the late 1960s the National Campaign for the Homeless (Shelter) produced publicity of considerable emotional power which aroused widespread public concern, but action by Government to eradicate the problems identified did not ensue. Subsequent research in the early 1990s showed that Britain still had one of the highest rates of homelessness in the European Union.

Secondly, groups can seek to exert influence on the selection of candidates for public office. The most obvious example in this respect is provided by trade union sponsorship of Labour Party candidates. At the time of the 1992 General Election 17 unions sponsored a total of 173 Labour candidates, 143 of whom were subsequently elected. Consequently, 53 per cent of the Parliamentary Labour Party elected in 1992 were trade union sponsored. Some other groups encourage their members, if already involved in a political party, to participate in candidate selection in an attempt to ensure that candidates well disposed to their objectives are selected. Examples of this practice can be found in the groups on either side of the argument over blood sports and country pursuits. The effect, however, is usually only marginal, since it is such an indirect and uncertain method.

Thirdly, groups still make financial contributions to political parties in the hope that their money will buy political influence. Once again the most familiar example is provided by the open and well established financial support by many trade unions to the Labour Party. Yet in recent years greater media and public attention has been paid to the more opaque financial support from certain companies, entrepreneurs and commercial interests to the Conservative Party. These donations constitute a sizeable part of the party's national income – estimates vary, but suggest a figure of at least 50 per cent. The interesting question here is whether and, if so, to what extent such financial support really succeeds in buying effective influence. In trying to reach a sensible conclusion on this, it is worth noting, for example, that when in 1991 British Airways, a long-term contributor to Conservative Party funds, announced that it would no longer do so because of the Government's alleged failure to defend the B.A. interest in the negotiations on international air routes and access to Heathrow, Ministers paid no obvious heed to such shameless pressure from Lord King, the Chairman of the company.

Fourthly, pressure groups seek to exert influence during the passage of legislation through the House of Commons and the House of Lords. They attempt to influence MPs and Peers in a variety of ways. They may, for example deluge Members of either House with letters from the public urging their point of view or arrange for a mass lobby of Parliament which entails large numbers of people seeking to present their views directly to MPs and Peers at Westminster. They can prepare detailed briefs for Parliamentary debates, a tactic used with great effect, for example, by the Haemophilia Society in 1987 when it persuaded a large number of MPs to press the Government to provide special financial help to the 1200 haemophiliacs who had become HIV positive – and hence vulnerable to AIDS – as a result of receiving contaminated blood and plasma in the course of NHS treatment. Many groups maintain close personal contacts with individual MPs and Peers, either directly or through the growing band of professional lobbyists. This practice can both advance the interests of the groups concerned and provide useful information and advice for Members of both Houses of Parliament, especially those in Opposition who do not normally have the benefit of civil service advice.[13]

Finally, groups seek continuously to make expert and technical representations to the civil servants in Whitehall who are there to provide policy and administrative advice to Governments of all political complexions. As the tasks of modern Government have become more technical and complex, the necessity for close liaison between the Whitehall bureaucratic machine and a myriad of pressure groups has increased. The resulting relationship is a two-way affair: pressure groups seek information on decisions which may affect their areas of interest and try to ensure advantageous decisions, while civil servants on behalf of their political masters seek data and expert advice as well as the co-operation of groups in the implementation of policy.

All these different channels of influence for pressure groups are not, of course, mutually exclusive. Very often a group will be engaged, for example, in discussions with a Government Department about a particular legislative proposal while at the same time trying to influence MPs and Peers by mounting a publicity campaign. However, this account does demonstrate, albeit in a rather schematic form, the range of opportunities which pressure groups seek to exploit in the British political system.

6.4 Organisation and power

Pressure groups in Britain are organised in almost as many ways as there are different groups. The pattern of organisation which evolves and the degree of power which can be exerted depend upon a number of different factors. It is therefore worth considering the various aspects in turn.

Nature and scope of membership

When the interests of the membership are material and immediate, a group will usually reflect them and concentrate most of its resources upon defending them by whatever means are available. For example, for many years until the coal dispute of 1984-85, the

National Union of Mineworkers (NUM) proved its ability to exploit both the strength of its organisation and the concentration of its interest as a way of gaining substantial material rewards for its members. The result was that the miners managed to stay consistently at or near the top of the industrial earnings league and all Governments treated them with wary respect. On the other hand, when the interests of the membership are diffuse and varied, it is usually more difficult for a group to exert direct and immediate influence on behalf of its members. For example, the Consumers' Association, which has had a paid-up membership equivalent to a mere 3 per cent of all families in Britain, has been more successful in raising the profile of consumer interests and consumer rights in general than in defending the position of individual consumers. Nevertheless, the high quality and well publicised research done by organisations of this kind can have a considerable impact upon firms and upon Government.

The power of a group depends to a considerable extent upon both the coverage and the cohesion of its membership. If a group has a clear identity and purpose and if it manages to attract into its membership a high proportion of those eligible to join, it can be said to have a good coverage and is likely to be effective in defence of its members' interests. This has been borne out by the British Medical Association (BMA) which over the years has had over 80 per cent of all practising doctors in membership and which showed its political muscle during the late 1980s and early 1990s at the time of considerable public debate about the Government's reforms of the National Health Service (NHS). On the other hand, if a group seeks to represent a wide range of interests, it is likely to have little natural cohesion and to be rather ineffective in defence of its members' interests. For example, neither the TUC, which seeks to represent 68 affiliated trade unions and 7.3 million individual trade unionists, nor the CBI, which seeks to do the same for some 250,000 subscribing companies and employers' and trade associations, has been really effective on behalf of its members, since the need to be inclusive has weakened the cohesion and hence the effectiveness of each organisation. The TUC has had the added problem that the membership of trade unions declined by 40 per cent – more than 4.8 million members – between 1979 and 1994, while the CBI has had the obvious difficulty of trying to represent employers both large and small in both the private and public sectors. For these reasons, among others, neither organisation has been particularly powerful or effective in recent times.

Loyalty of the rank and file

The degree of loyalty shown by the rank and file towards their leaders and spokesmen is another aspect of the relative power or weakness of any group. Certainly such loyalty cannot be taken for granted in an age of greatly diminished deference. However, in most circumstances, the leaders of a pressure group have more scope for initiative if they are in the job for life and not subject to periodic recall or re-election, an advantage long enjoyed by several prominent trade union leaders. It is also the case that the leadership enjoys more latitude if the material interests of the rank and file are not directly threatened by any policy initiatives. For example, Clive Jenkins' advocacy of an embargo on the sale of equipment to South Africa under apartheid was tolerated and even supported as long as the members of his trade union (then called the Association of Technical and Managerial Staff) had no material interest which was threatened by such a stance.

On the other hand, when the activities of pressure group leaders seem likely to prejudice the interests of the ordinary members, the rank and file are quite likely to reject the lead which is given. For example, Clive Jenkins was allowed to indulge in left-wing posturing on virtually any policy issue except the idea of nationalising the banks and insurance companies, since that would have posed a direct threat to the jobs of many of his union's members. Equally, Arthur Scargill, as President of the NUM, was opposed by a majority of his own members when he was precipitate in seeking their endorsement for a political campaign of industrial action against the 1979-83 Conservative Government and succeeded only in splitting his union in 1984-85 when he persuaded his Executive to launch an all-out strike against threatened pit closures without first securing the support of his members in a union ballot. In 1979 the NUM, with a membership of 372,122, was widely regarded as providing the 'shock troops' of the Labour movement. However, by 1994 it could claim only 18,227 members, a fall of 95 per cent; indeed, with British Coal employing only 8000 miners by then, the union's actual membership was probably even lower. Although much of this decline was due to broader factors, such as the general state of the economy and the specific competitiveness of the British coal industry, it is undoubtedly the case that the trade-union leadership – both in style and content – was also a contributory factor, and this serves as a pointer to how *not* to lead a pressure group.

Political leverage

The power of pressure groups also depends upon the degree of political leverage which they can exert. If a group is in a position to exert significant leverage, it can be truly formidable. Such leverage can take the form of an ability to deny to the rest of society the provision of goods or services which the community cannot easily do without and which others are not able to supply. For example, power station workers or air traffic controllers can be in such a position, as can computer operators in the civil service or safety workers in the water industry. Currency speculators and company treasurers can also wield comparable financial power in the money markets which amounts to a form of highly effective political leverage. In 1989 the brewing industry showed its ability to sway the then Conservative Government, partly through its ability to exploit a clever and hard-hitting advertising campaign, partly through an adroit use of political contacts, and partly because many Conservative back-benchers realised the significant part which it played in providing financial support for the party.[14]

This kind of leverage on its own may not be sufficient for the attainment of a pressure group's objectives without the support of other attributes of group power, such as civil service contacts, the ability to use the media effectively and financial or political clout. Yet it can achieve a great deal in a complex, modern society in which such groups can sometimes be in a position to hold the rest of the community to ransom. Only very rarely does it consist in the ability to create completely new balances of power in society which allow one particular group or interest to coerce the rest. On such occasions the Government of the day may have to use the full powers of the modern state – for instance, a massive police presence or even military units – in order to counter one brand of ruthlessness with another. No system of democratic Government can afford to tolerate, still less allow itself to be defeated by, groups using the sort of leverage through violence or coercion which has become all too familiar in parts of the world today.

Certainly some groups have used campaigns of civil disobedience as a way to try and achieve their aims. The Suffragettes were an early example. More recently there was the wide-scale campaign for the non-payment of the Poll Tax, some virulent activity engaged in by the campaign against the Child Support Agency and the port demonstrations coordinated by CIWF (Compassion in World Farming) against the live animal export trade in 1994-95. Other groups have become involved – some intentionally, others unintentionally – in direct action which has involved violence. Examples of this would be the picket-line violence at Grunwick in 1977, at Warrington in 1983, at Wapping in 1987 or during the miners' strike in 1984-85; the inner city riots of the early 1980s, the Poll Tax riot in Trafalgar Square in 1990, and the riot against the Criminal Justice and Public Order Bill in 1994; and the actions of the Animal Liberation Front involving arson attacks in the early 1990s. It is perhaps worth noting that in most cases the use of civil disobedience is effective in advancing the interests of the groups concerned, whereas degeneration into violence is invariable counter-productive.

Civil Service contacts

The strength and frequency of contacts with the civil service is another aspect of the power and influence of groups. As J. J. Richardson and A. G. Jordan have pointed out, 'it is the relationships involved in committees, the policy community of Departments and groups, the practices of co-option and the consensual state which account better for policy outcomes than examinations of party stances, Manifestos or Parliamentary influence'.[15] On the whole established groups prefer to have a continuous, quiet influence upon the process of Government rather than an intermittent and noisy impact based upon the use of media publicity and the staging of public demonstrations. Widely publicised campaigns are something of a last resort for groups which normally succeed in keeping in close touch with the civil service and the rest of the policy-making community. They use their reliable and frequent contacts with Whitehall and the expertise of their own professional staff to influence Ministerial decisions and the detailed content of legislation. In such cases resorting to widely publicised campaigns is almost an admission of failure.

A number of groups secure official representation on advisory committees established within the orbits of Whitehall Departments and in this way are able to support and monitor the detailed aspects of policy implementation. This gives them extra status and recognition in Whitehall, rights of access to Ministers when the need arises and opportunities for consultation and influence not available to others outside the charmed circle of customary consultative arrangements in central Government. For example, the National Farmers' Union (NFU) was deeply involved in the development and application of British agricultural policy from the 1947 Agriculture Act to Britain's entry into the European Community in 1973. Since then it has had to concentrate more on trying to influence the development of the Common Agricultural Policy, principally in representations to the European Commission and European Parliament through the European farmers' organisation, COPA. Equally, in the 1960s and 1970s, the CBI and the TUC both managed to establish the convention that they should be widely and frequently consulted by central Government on all matters of direct interest and concern to them. However, since 1979, neither body has been made so welcome by the Conservative Government, which came to power determined to reduce their status and influence over policy.

Obviously the nature and extent of such consultation has varied from time to time and from Government to Government, depending upon the priorities and objectives of the Ministers concerned. Following the establishment of the National Economic Development Council ('Neddy' in popular parlance) in 1962, it was generally accepted practice that what were called 'the two sides of industry' should be consulted by Government on a frequent and extensive basis. Many of these consultations were formalised within the Neddy framework and took place within a large number of so-called sector working parties. Other contacts took place directly between Whitehall officials and representatives of trade unions and trade associations. Such habitual consultation, which was for many years an important element of the policy and decision making process, has been downgraded by the Conservatives since 1979. For example, in 1987 it was announced that 'Neddy' would meet only four times instead of ten times a year as previously; and in December 1992 'Neddy' was abolished altogether.

However, there have been examples of very close and continuous consultation between privileged interest groups and Government Departments even under recent Conservative Administrations whose Ministerial rhetoric often inveighed against such corporatist contacts. The classic case has probably been the relationship between the Road Transport Federation, the principal lobby group for the road freight interest, and the Department of Transport which, until a shift of policy in 1994, had consistently pushed ahead with the road building programme seemingly in defiance of the Treasury, the competing railway lobby and the general environmental interest. Another example would be the Prison Reform Trust, which has established a niche role despite having neither a large membership nor significant financial resources; the Home Office always consults the Trust when considering policy on prisons.

Publicity value

The publicity value of the causes espoused by different groups is another factor which influences the success or failure of such organisations. For example, the favourable publicity secured by Age Concern in its campaign in the 1970s to get a better financial deal for pensioners was clearly beneficial to that particular cause, although the political priorities of the 1974-79 Labour Government had a lot to do with the outcome as well. Equally, the publicity traditionally secured by the Child Poverty Action Group for poor families with children or by Shelter for the homeless was beneficial to those particular sections of society, at any rate as long as Ministers were either sympathetic to their arguments or embarrassed into action. An example of this last point occurred in 1977 when the then Labour Government was preparing to go back on its previous commitment to introduce a Child Benefit scheme. The Child Poverty Action Group leaked Cabinet minutes to this effect and the resulting protests forced the Government to back-track and introduce the scheme after all. In the early 1980s the Campaign for Lead-Free Air (CLEAR) was able to make considerable headway towards achieving its goal as a result of the publicity arising first from the leaking of a letter from the Government's Chief Medical Officer to the effect that lead in petrol was permanently reducing the IQ of many children, and then from the report of the Royal Commission on Environmental Pollution which confirmed the dangers to children and called for the banning of lead in petrol.

On the other hand, the publicity secured by the Campaign for Nuclear Disarmament in the late 1950s and early 1960s had little effect upon public policy at the time, other than too harden the resolve of the then Conservative Government to oppose such a policy. In general, the publicity gained by a group for its cause depends upon the spirit of the times as much as its technical skill in using the media to its own advantage. Thus the public demonstrations and other media events organised by CND and other 'peace groups' in the early 1980s seem to have had more effect upon public opinion than the Aldermaston marches of the 1950s, although while Margaret Thatcher was Prime Minister they made relatively little headway in influencing the Conservative Government in Britain. Besides which, much of their thunder was stolen by the dramatic disarmament initiatives of Presidents Reagan and Gorbachev.

Financial power

The mere possession of wealth and financial power cannot buy success in pressure group politics, although it obviously helps to pay the bills and to finance the necessary publicity. An examination of the available evidence suggests that not even the most lavishly funded campaigns achieve their objectives simply because they can out-spend their opponents. This may be a tribute to the probity and impartiality of the British civil service or it may reflect the way in which the British party system shields politicians from the full force of group pressures. Whatever the reasons, it is difficult to point to any occasions when money on its own has bought success for a pressure group.

For example, there is no conclusive evidence that the expensive 'Mr Cube' campaign of Tate & Lyle and other sugar producers against the proposed nationalisation of the sugar refining industry in the late 1940s had a decisive influence upon the subsequent decision of the Labour Government not to proceed with such a policy after the 1950 General Election. Indeed the much stronger explanation is that the collapse of Labour's Parliamentary majority, from 146 to 5, made it seem politically imprudent for the Government to proceed further with this particular case of nationalisation. Similarly, there is no conclusive evidence that the fact that the 'Keep Britain In' campaign outspent the 'National Referendum Campaign' (those campaigning for British withdrawal) by ten-to-one (£1,481,583 to £133,630) had a decisive effect upon the way in which the British people voted in the 1975 Referendum on Britain's membership of the European Community. Rather, it appears to have been the coalition of political authority represented by the leading personalities of the pro-European campaign which had the most positive impact upon the result, since their public reputations then compared very favourably with those of the leading personalities on the anti-European side of the argument.[16]

During the long period of Conservative rule since 1979, critics of the Government argued that its health policy was undermined by the financial and political power of the tobacco industry which successfully resisted pressures for a complete ban on all tobacco advertising. Similarly, they argued that its macro-economic policy was distorted by the excessive influence of the property and construction sector which became the most overheated part of the economy in the late 1980s. The former example may provide a valid case study of the financial power of a sectional interest group and its ability to influence Government policy. The latter example is better defined as a case study of how this particular sector of industry and the Ministers who championed it overplayed their hand to the eventual detriment not only of those directly concerned but also the British economy as a whole when the recession hit in the early 1990s.

Voting power

As for the power of groups to deliver votes at elections, twentieth century British history has shown that the pull of party consistently triumphs over the pull of groups. Ever since the emergence of recognisably modern political parties during the last quarter of the nineteenth century, the nature of the British first-past-the-post electoral system and the influence of strong party discipline has left all groups with a poor chance of striking effective political bargains with individual Members of Parliament or Parliamentary candidates. Yet this is not to say that certain influential groups cannot exercise considerable influence upon the parties, especially when the latter are in Opposition and unshielded by civil service advice.

Unlike the situation in the United States, individual politicians in Britain do not have to construct precarious platforms of electoral support by seeking to appeal directly to powerful interest or cause groups in their constituencies. If their party has been in office, they tend to concentrate upon presenting the record of their party in the most favourable light. If their party has been in Opposition, they tend to demonstrate how bad things have been under the stewardship of their opponents and how they could do much better if given the chance. Yet this is not to say that it is ever sensible or prudent for politicians to ignore the pressure of groups which are active or influential in their own constituencies.

Of course, there remains the special case of trade union influence upon the Labour Party.[17] This stems from the fact that the creation of the Labour Party at the end of the nineteenth century was largely the work of the trade unions and ever since then trade-union influence within the wider movement has been significant and occasionally decisive. However, in the 1990s the links between the Labour Party and the trade unions became the focus of considerable debate, and there was even some talk of a 'friendly divorce'. Nonetheless, the connection is one of the defining links in British politics, and although it may change, it is doubtful that it will be ended. Yet no matter how close and crucial the relationship between the Labour Party and the trade unions has been over the years, it would be unwise to generalise from it when assessing the role of other pressure groups in the British political system.

6.5 Involvement in politics

Since the British political system is pluralist, liberal, and democratic, it affords many opportunities for the involvement of pressure groups in the policy- and decision-making process.[18] Indeed, it is impossible fully to describe political activity in Whitehall and Westminster without giving an account of the part played by pressure groups. They have become seemingly inevitable participants in the process of official consultation and as such they contribute to the maintenance of public consent for the acts of Government. Their involvement in the policy- and decision-making process is shown diagrammatically in Figure 6.1.

Policy germination

At the initial stage of policy germination the main role of pressure groups is to identify

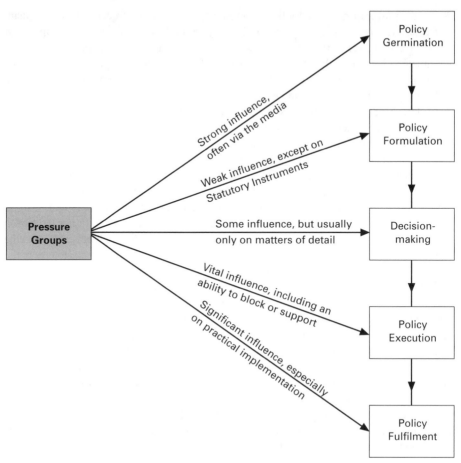

Figure 6.1 Pressure group involvement in politics

Policy Germination

Policy Formulation

Decision-making

Policy Execution

Policy Fulfilment

Pressure Groups

Strong influence, often via the media

Weak influence, except on Statutory Instruments

Some influence, but usually only on matters of detail

Vital influence, including an ability to block or support

Significant influence, especially on practical implementation

problems and to get issues onto the political agenda. This is something which they can do rather well and which they are sometimes even encouraged to do by Ministers. This is because the latter often prefer to appear to be responding to external pressures rather than taking unprompted initiatives. For example, the National Society for Clean Air (previously the Smoke Abatement Society) was to a considerable extent instrumental in getting the problems of air pollution onto the political agenda in the 1950s. It then conducted a sustained campaign of publicity and persuasion which helped to bring about the passage of the Clean Air Act in 1956. Equally, the Institute of Economic Affairs can claim much of the credit for getting the policy of privatisation onto the political agenda in the 1980s, since it had been campaigning for this for years beforehand.

In playing their part at this early stage of the policy- and decision-making process, pressure groups depend very heavily upon their ability to excite the interest of the media. Without such media assistance many of the campaigns would never get off the ground at all. For example, the creation of the Department of the Environment in 1970 was to a considerable extent a political response to the pressure exerted over many years by the Conservation Society and other environmental groups who had wanted their concerns more clearly represented in Whitehall. It was also a response to the growing public interest in environmental matters which later found international expression at the 1972 Stockholm Conference. Equally, in the 1980s and early 1990s, Friends of the Earth, Greenpeace and other environmental pressure groups had a significant influence upon the pace and direction of various 'green' initiatives not only at national level but also at the European and wider international levels as well.

Pressure groups also need to persuade powerful politicians of the good sense and timeliness of their cause. For example, the Road Haulage Association (RHA) worked very closely with leading figures in the Conservative Party when the latter were in Opposition between 1945 and 1951 and was able to persuade them of the case for the denationalisation of its industry. The result of this pressure was seen in the partial denationalisation of the industry by the Conservative Government soon after its victory at the 1951 General Election. Equally the proponents of employee share ownership, such as Job Ownership Ltd, worked hard and continuously during the 1980s and early 1990s to persuade the Conservative Government to giver further legislative backing and tax relief to a cause which chimed in well with Conservative thinking on worker participation and wider share ownership.

When pressure groups wish to get issues onto the political agenda, the most effective approach is usually to persuade officials in the relevant Whitehall Department of the importance of their particular problem or interest and then to follow up with expert and detailed advice on how it might be tackled in ways which would be congruent with the principles of the Government of the day. A notably successful practitioner of this technique was the National Farmers' Union (NFU) which over the years from the 1947 Agriculture Act until British entry into the European Community in 1973 enjoyed an exclusive and almost symbiotic relationship with the Ministry of Agriculture. This relationship influenced the outcome of every annual farm price review and was also credited with having given rise to the 1957 Agriculture Act, which gave the NFU an even more entrenched consultative role. The other principal way of achieving such an objective is for a group to get on a common wavelength with leading figures in the governing party and then provide them with new ideas which can be presented as a logical development of their existing policies. Once again a good example of the effectiveness of this technique is provided by the way in which so called political 'think-tanks', like the Institute of Economic Affairs and the Centre for Policy Studies, managed to play the role of intellectual pathfinders for the free market policies of the Conservatives in the 1980s.

Policy formulation

Pressure groups can also have influence, but not such an important role, at the stage of policy formulation. When a political party is in Opposition, policy formulation is mainly the work of its leading personalities, who are assisted by officials from the party organisation. When a party is in Government, it is mainly the work of civil servants in the Departments concerned. Yet in each case those who formulate policy may well consult pressure groups, provided the latter can be trusted to preserve the necessary confidentiality and are able to supply useful expert advice or information.

The role of groups can be especially significant when policy needs to be formulated as new legislation. For example, the Town and Country Planning Association has made frequent representations over the years and some of its ideas have been incorporated in planning legislation; the Society of Conservative Lawyers had some real influence upon the policy formulated by the Conservative Party in Opposition during the late 1970s and this made a significant contribution to the subsequent British Nationality Act of 1981. There is therefore a role for pressure groups to play at the stage of policy formulation, although it is not usually as prominent as at other stages of the process.

Decision making

In a strict sense pressure groups have no direct involvement at the decision-making stage of the political process, since this is essentially a matter for elected politicians. Yet even such an apparently clear-cut statement does not fully reflect the various ways in which political decisions are actually taken in modern Britain. For example, many Ministerial decisions are really taken by civil servants acting in the name of Ministers, notably in the detailed and complex area of delegated legislation. Groups with the necessary expertise and access to officials can play an influential part in this aspect of decision making. Examples could be found in the close and frequent contacts between the Law Society and the Lord Chancellor's Department, the Local Authority Associations and the Department of the Environment or the British Medical Association and the Department of Health. However, it is necessary to note that the influence of all these groups declined under the Conservative Government of Margaret Thatcher (1979-1990), not least because Ministers were engaged in measures of radical reform affecting each of these vested interests.

Since the introduction of new legislation also involves important decision making of a kind, pressure groups can play an influential part at this stage of the political process as well. For example, the 1982 Criminal Justice Act was influenced at least in important matters of detail by the persistent representations made during the committee stage of the legislative process by groups such as the Magistrates Association and the National Association for the Care and Resettlement of Offenders (NACRO). Equally, the Committee of Vice-Chancellors and Principals (CVCP) waged an effective and successful campaign in 1993-94 to persuade Ministers at the Department for Education to modify their legislative proposals for the reform of student unions by accepting the political goal (however reluctantly), but then offering a more sensible way of implementing the policy in practice. Similarly, the Finance Bills which pass through the House of Commons every year and which contain legislative changes of considerable importance can be influenced in matters of detail by pressure groups with interests to defend or causes to advance. For example, the Institute of Chartered Accountants and other professional bodies were instrumental in persuading Treasury Ministers to drop a clause from the 1994 Finance Bill concerning Inland Revenue rights of access to confidential papers in the possession of accountants and other financial advisers, pending further detailed consultations with the interested bodies designed to refine and improve the measure. In these various ways groups can be involved to some extent at the decision-making stage.

Policy execution

The real test of effective power for all modern Governments is how well they manage to execute their policies. Ministerial decisions or Acts of Parliament are not worth very much if they cannot be implemented in practice, either because of administrative impracticality or because the people who have to execute them decide to withdraw their co-operation.

Formidable delaying power is available to civil servants. If senior civil servants wish to delay the decisions of Ministers, there are many ways in which they can do so. The most gentle technique is simply to go slowly in the administrative implementation of what has already been decided. Another is to support further consultations on the detailed implementation of policy with the groups directly affected. Yet another is to put up their own Minister to argue with Ministerial colleagues that time is not ripe for a decision in the first place. Most drastic of all is the tactic of deliberate non-co-operation, which was used in many parts of the civil service during the long dispute over pay and conditions in 1981. This did temporary damage to the efficiency of Government and led, for exam-ple, to long delays in the collection of some public revenues and the payment of some social security benefits.

The role of groups can also be vital, since their active cooperation or passive acqui-escence is often a condition of the satisfactory execution of policy. For example, in the early 1990s the National Union of Teachers (NUT), the National Association of Schoolmasters/Union of Women Teachers (NAS/UWT) and the Association of Teachers and Lecturers refused to co-operate with the Conservative Government's plans for nation-al curriculum assessment, boycotting the tests involved. It was a course of action that forced the Government to make significant concessions. Similarly, the BMA initially advised its members not to co-operate with the Health Authorities and others in imple-menting the Conservative Government's plans for the reform of the National Health Service in the late 1980s. In all such cases acquiescence in Government policy by the relevant practitioners or workers is an important condition of successful policy execu-tion. Such examples emphasise the key point that one of the main tasks of Ministers is to assess the limits of what is 'politically possible' in a given situation at a given time. In making such assessments, it is clear that the co-operation of the relevant civil servants and interest groups is a distinct advantage and their non-co-operation a serious liability in the execution of policy.

Policy fulfilment

A similar point can be made about the final stage of policy fulfilment. Few policies can be brought to fruition without the active co-operation or at least the passive acquiescence of the groups most directly affected. Ministers and civil servants commit serious mis-takes if they are ever tempted to equate the political process solely with what happens in Whitehall and Westminster. In modern political conditions there are also many exter-nal factors which can influence the success or failure of a given policy. For example, the world-wide commodity price explosion of 1972-73 damaged the counter-inflation policies of the 1970-74 Conservative Government, while the limitations imposed upon national sovereignty by the 1986 Single European Act restricted the Major Administra-tion's room for manoeuvre in negotiating with its European partners in the run-up to the 1992 Treaty of Maastricht. Similarly, in September 1992 the Conservative Government proved unable to sustain its monetary policy in the face of a tidal wave of sterling being sold on the foreign exchanges, and was forced to suspend British membership of the Exchange Rate Mechanism of the European Monetary System by the power of market forces. Such examples inevitably extend the scope of the present discussion beyond the sphere of national politics. Yet it is undeniable that, in what is an increasingly interdependent world, political issues have to be considered in a much wider context if we are to take full account of all the limitations upon the alleged autonomy of national Governments.

Politicians may imagine, especially when they have been in office a long time, that they have become the undisputed masters of the political scene. Yet they always do well to remember that in modern political conditions they need the co-operation of interest groups and the support of other external influences if they are to have a reasonable chance of fulfilling their policies.

6.6 Conclusion

The effectiveness of a pressure group does not depend simply upon its size, its privileged contacts or its financial resources. It depends rather upon a wide variety of internal and external factors. *Internal factors* include size, unity of purpose, leadership quality, organisational competence and financial backing. *External factors* include the nature of the political environment, the strength of other competing groups and the attitudes of the media and the general public. Politicians take all such factors into account when deciding upon the weight and significance to accord to the representation of particular groups.

In Britain support for pressure groups, particularly attitude groups, has burgeoned in the past 35 years, not least because of increasingly widespread disillusion among the public at large with the established political parties. As active participation in party politics has continued its long term decline, this has been matched by an equally impressive growth in pressure group participation. For example, Friends of the Earth increased its membership from 1000 in 1971 to 200,000 in 1977, while the membership of the National Trust is now larger at 2.2 million than any other voluntary organisation in the country and about three times larger than the largest political party (the Conservatives).

In these circumstances there are reasons for regarding the activities of pressure groups as broadly beneficial to the British political system and other reasons for regarding them as rather harmful. *On the positive side*, there are at least four points which can be made. *Firstly*, they can provide the Government of the day with expert information and advice which would not necessarily be available from other sources. *Secondly*, they can provide frameworks for public participation in the political process between General Elections by all who are unwilling or unable to channel their energies through one or other of the political parties. *Thirdly*, they help to define and focus public attention upon issues which may not be ripe for decision but which need nevertheless to be placed on the political agenda. *Fourthly*, they can provide a form of institutional ratification and public consent for the actions of Government which can assist Ministers in the difficult tasks of policy execution and fulfilment.

On the negative side, there are at least four reasons for regarding pressure groups with suspicion if not distaste. *Firstly*, they tend to give too much weight in the political process to the importance of the concurrent majority – that is, the various sectional groups in Britain's pluralist society – to the detriment of the Parliamentary majority – that is, the part of the electorate which voted for the winning party in the House of Commons at the preceding General Election. *Secondly*, they can become accomplices in a system of government which is based upon exclusive, metropolitan circles of policy and decision making and which may act to the detriment of everyone else. *Thirdly*, they have reinforced the tendencies towards corporatism in British society and during the 1970s in particular this worked to the detriment of Parliament and the traditions of British Parliamentary democracy. *Fourthly*, as Douglas Hurd put it in 1986, when reflecting on his experience as Home Secretary, 'the weight of these groups, almost all of them pursuing a legitimate cause, has very substantially increased in recent years and adds greatly not just to the volume of work but also to the difficulty of achieving decisions in the general interest'.[19] Nowhere is this last point more evident than in the case of the "Nimby" (not in my back yard) groups which oppose particular technology and other developments – such as new power stations, motorways or rail links – because of the perceived adverse effects upon their own quality of life at local level, and yet support (or at least take routine advantage) of such developments when sited elsewhere.

Pressure groups have undoubtedly injected considerable vitality into contemporary British politics, providing their members with real access to and influence upon the political system, and the general public with information, advice and ideas which would probably not be forthcoming from modern political parties. Without the activities of pressure groups (aided and abetted by the media), the political process would be heavily stacked in favour of the Government of the day and this would not be good for the health of British democracy.

In conclusion, it is necessary to assess the role of pressure groups in parallel with an assessment of the political parties. Both categories of institution play vital roles of mediation and representation which contribute to the working of the British political system. Whereas pressure groups are not democratically accountable in the way that political parties have to be, they do share common aspirations to reflect and defend the views and interests of their members. In this way they bring a measure of public consent to the working of the political process and help to endow it with a measure of legitimacy which otherwise it might not have. On the other hand, they are increasingly seen by Ministers as 'serpents' which can prevent political decisions being taken in the general interest. Either way, they are among the most significant sources of power, pressure and opinion in the British political system.

Suggested questions

1 What are the main functions of pressure groups in British politics?
2 Which factors make some pressure groups more powerful than others?
3 At what stages in the political process do pressure groups exert their most effective influence?

Notes

1. Quoted in R. Rose (ed.), *Studies in British Politics*, 3rd edn (London: Macmillan, 1976), p. 343.
2. G. C. Moodie and G. Studdert-Kennedy, *Opinions, Publics and Pressure Groups* (London: Allen & Unwin, 1970), p. 60.
3. S. E. Finer, *Anonymous Empire*, revised edition (London; Pall Mall, 1966), p. 3.
4. P. Shipley (ed.), *Directory of Pressure Groups and Representative Associations* (London: Wilton House, 1976), p. 3.
5. A. F. Bentley, *The Process of Government* (Cambridge, Mass.: Harvard University Press 1908)
6. Membership figures are those provided by the Certification Office, Trades Union Congress, September 1994.

7. Membership figures are those of April 1995.
8. G. P. Henderson and S. P. A. Henderson (eds), *Directory of British Associations and Associations in Ireland*, 9th edn (London: CBD Research, 1988).
9. Quoted in R. Kimber and J. J. Richardson (eds), *Pressure Groups in Britain* (London: Dent, 1974), p. 280.
10. '*Corporatism*' is a term which has often been used pejoratively by those who believe that democratic representation should be territorially based upon constituencies rather than functionally based upon the various sectional interests in society. For our purposes here it is taken to mean the tendency in modern British politics for Government to deal directly with the 'social partners' (that is employers and trade unions) to the detriment perhaps of the elected Members of Parliament. See R. K. Middlemass, *Politics in Industrial Society* (London: Deutsch, 1979), for a fuller discussion of this subject.
11. '*Syndicalism*' is a term which was used originally to describe the movement among industrial workers at he end of the nineteenth century (especially in France) of which the primary aim was the transfer of the means of production, distribution and exchange from capitalist owners to groups of workers at factory level. On the British experience of syndicalism see B. Holton, *British Syndicalism, 1900-14* (London: Pluto Press, 1976).
12. Quoted in 'A nation of groupies', *The Economist*, 13 August 1994.
13. See M. Rush (ed.), *Parliament and Pressure Politics* (London: OUP, 1990).
14. See J. Warner, 'The clout of the beerage', *The Independent*, 18 July 1989.
15. J. J. Richardson and A. G. Jordan, *Governing Under Pressure* (Oxford: Martin Robertson, 1979), p. 74.
16. See D. Butler and U. Kitzinger, *The 1975 Referendum* (London: Macmillan, 1976), p. 285.
17. See H. Pelling, *A History of British Trade Unionism* (London: Macmillan, 1963), and H. Pelling, *A Short History of the Labour Party* (London: Macmillan, 1965), for a fuller account of this relationship.
18. See Chapter 19 for a fuller description of the policy and decision-making process in Britain.
19. Lecture to the Royal Institute of Public Administration, 19 September 1986.

Further reading

Brennan, T., *Pressure Groups and the Political System* (London: Longman, 1985).
Byrne, P., *The Campaign for Nuclear Disarmament* (London: Croom Helm, 1988).
Crouch C., and Dore, R. (eds), *Corporatism and Accountability: organised interests in British public life* (Oxford: Clarendon Press, 1990).
Grant, W., *Business and Politics in Politics in Britain*, 2nd edn (London: Macmillan, 1993).
Jordan, A. G. and Richardson, J. J., *Government and Pressure Groups in Britain* (London: OUP, 1987).
Lowe, O. and Goyder, J., *Environmental Groups in Politics* (London: Allen & Unwin, 1983).
Marsh, D., *The New Politics of British Trade Unionism: union power and the Thatcher legacy* (London: Macmillan, 1992).
Mazey, S., and Richardson, J. J. (eds), *Lobbying in the European Community* (London: OUP, 1993).
Middlemass, K., *Power, Competition and the State*, vol. 3: *The End of the Post-War-Era* (London: Macmillan, 1991).
Miller, C., *Lobbying Government* (Oxford: Basil Blackwell, 1987).
Rush, M. (ed.), *Parliament and Pressure Politics* (London: OUP, 1990).
Whiteley, P., and Winyard, S., *Pressure for the Poor: the poverty lobby and policy making* (London: Methuen, 1987).
Wilson, D., *Pressure, the A to Z of Campaigning in Britain* (London: Heinemann, 1984).

7　The Media

In considering the media in Britain, we are concerned with more than neutral channels of communication. We are examining some of the most influential participants in the political system, even though they have no formally recognised place in British constitutional arrangements. For better or worse we live in a mass media age which is characterised by the widespread use (and abuse) of the various channels of communication for a broad range of political and other purposes. Politicians need the media more than ever and seek every opportunity to get their messages across to the public. Equally, those who own or work for the media are not too shy to exert a real influence upon the political process in Britain and all other countries.

7.1 The current situation

The current situation in all parts of the media is particularly dynamic and consequently in a state of flux. The following paragraphs can therefore offer only a snapshot taken at a particular time and the information provided should be seen in that light. In the press, some publications come and go, some change hands, and nearly all have to adapt or modify their appeal in response to technological change or market pressures. The trend towards multi-media companies under multi-national ownership has been growing fast with the result that it is almost a misnomer to refer any longer to 'the British press'. In the electronic media, national boundaries and jurisdictions mean even less and the emergence of huge multi-national media corporations with global reach, such as News International, Reuters or CNN, means that people in Britain and elsewhere are increasingly living in what Marshall McLuhan described many years ago as 'a global village' of instantaneous mass-media communications. The effects of these developments upon politics and culture in Britain, as in other countries, have yet to be fully recognised or understood.

The press

The current situation in the British press is that there are five daily national newspapers of quality, six of the tabloid variety, four Sunday national newspapers of quality, and five of the tabloid variety. There is only one significant evening newspaper in London, *The Evening Standard*, but there are a number of successful daily newspapers in other parts of the country – for example, *The Western Morning News*, *The Yorkshire Post*, *The Manchester Evening News* and *The Glasgow Herald*. There are a number of weekly newspapers which give prominence to political issues – for example, *The Economist*, *The Spectator* or *The New Statesman & Society*. There are also a number of more academic periodicals which specialise in political issues, such as *Political Quarterly*, *Parliamentary Affairs*, *Government and Opposition* and *Public Administration*. Mention should also be made of the communist daily newspaper, *The Morning Star*, the satirical and anti-Establishment periodicals, such as *Private Eye*, and the publications of the political fringe, such as *Militant* and *Socialist Worker* on the far Left or *Spearhead* on the far Right. There is, therefore, a wide variety of political points of view expressed in the British press, although it is worth noting that some of the most widely read publications are not really political at all – for example, *Radio Times*, *Woman's Own* or *Hello!*

Until the 1980s one common denominator for nearly all the British press was the difficulty of making a profit. This was due to old-fashioned management practices and chaotic labour relations, and it brought in its wake increasing concentration of ownership as titles were forced to amalgamate or close. When the national newspapers were based in Fleet Street, virtually every attempt by management to introduce new technology was fiercely and effectively resisted by the powerful print unions. It was only after a new breed of tougher newspaper owners had founded or bought some of the titles, such as Eddy Shah with *Today* and Rupert Murdoch with *The Sun*, that things began to change in a radical way. A number of bitter industrial disputes were fought between the traditional print unions and the new owners when the latter set out to break the trade union stranglehold by moving their production facilities to new lower cost locations in the East End of London, and by introducing the latest technology which enabled journalists to write and produce their own copy with only a minimum requirement for traditional printers' skills. These bitter struggles exemplified both the ingrained resistance to change which had characterised the industry in the past and the inevitability of such change once a determined employer, such as Rupert Murdoch, decided to break ranks with the more traditional newspaper proprietors and to bust the previous, mutually destructive arrangements between employers and trade unions in the industry.

Since that time there has been a new climate of fierce commercial competition in the British newspaper market which has enabled those proprietors with the deepest purse, such as Rupert Murdoch from Australia or Conrad Black from Canada, to put enormous competitive pressure not only on each other but also on their weaker competitors, such as *The Independent*. The rival newspaper and media empires have engaged in fierce price wars designed to secure the largest possible share of what has become a highly competitive market and eventually to eliminate at least the weakest competitors in the various sectors of the market. Against this background it is not surprising to find that only six multi-national companies, dominated in each case by very wealthy individuals or families, own all the mass circulation newspapers in Britain, and that one person – Rupert Murdoch – controls a huge multi-media empire world-wide and owns 37 per cent of the British national press. A table of the various national newspapers with their circulation figures and political leanings is set out in Figure 7.1.

Figure 7.1 Main national newspapers, February 1995

Title and Foundation Date	Publishing Company	Political Leaning	February 1995 Circulation
Broadsheet Dailies			
The Times 1788	News International	Pro-Tory Euro-sceptic	526,000
The Guardian 1821	Guardian Newspapers	'New' Labour	397,000
Daily Telegraph 1855	The Telegraph	Pro-Tory but doubts about John Major	1,244,000
Financial Times 1888	Pearson Group	Business and European newspaper	292,000
The Independent 1986	Newspaper Publishing	Centre-Left	274,000
Tabloid Dailies			
Daily Mail 1896	Associated Newspapers	Pro-Tory, but doubts about John Major	1,802,000
Daily Express 1900	United Newspapers	Pro-Tory	1,350,000
Daily Mirror 1903	Mirror Group	Pro-Labour	2,481,000
The Sun 1969	News International	Chauvinist and populist	4,053,000
Daily Star 1978	United Newspapers	Pro-Tory	744,000
Today 1986	News International	Pro-Labour, but fickle	607,000
Broadsheet Sundays			
The Observer 1791	Guardian Newspapers	Centre-Left	490,000
The Sunday Times 1822	News International	Pro-Tory but radical and republican	1,193,000
Sunday Telegraph 1961	The Telegraph	Pro-Tory Euro-sceptic	644,000
The Independent on Sunday 1990	Newspaper Publishing	Centre-Left	322,000

Figure 7.1 continued

Title and Foundation Date	Publishing Company	Political Leaning	February 1995 Circulation
Tabloid Sundays			
News of the World 1843	News International	Chauvinist and populist	4,785,000
The People 1881	Mirror Group	Pro-Labour	2,018,000
Sunday Express 1918	United Newspapers	Pro-Tory	1,527,000
Sunday Mirror 1963	Mirror Group	Pro-Labour	2,563,000
The Mail on Sunday 1982	Associated Newspapers	Pro-Tory but fickle	1,971,000

The electronic media

In television the situation at the time of writing is that four terrestrial channels provide a national service covering the entire country. There are the two BBC channels with *BBC1* designed to appeal to a mass audience with a mixture of entertainment and news programmes, while *BBC2* puts more emphasis upon its educative role and tries to cater for minority audiences as well. There are the two commercial channels with *ITV* (Channel 3) competing for a mass audience directly with BBC1, while *Channel 4* competes with BBC2 by offering programmes which appeal to a wider range of minority audiences and by acting as a 'publisher' for independent programme makers as well.[1]

The BBC makes and broadcasts most of its own material from a vertically integrated broadcasting organisation employing thousands of journalists, technicians and programme makers. It is financed from the proceeds of an annual licence fee (currently £84.50p a year for a colour television) which is levied by law on all who own a television set. In contrast, commercial television is financed by the proceeds of advertising carried during and between its programmes. Its output is produced by 15 regional programme companies, each with an exclusive franchise for part of the country for an agreed contractual period (usually 10 years). The BBC is run by a Director-General and management team, who are in their turn answerable to the Chairman and Board of BBC Governors chosen on rotation by the Home Secretary of the day, but representing a wide range of backgrounds, opinion and experience. On the other hand, the commercial television companies are answerable to the Independent Television Commission (ITC) which is there to play much the same buffer role as the BBC Board of Governors in relation to any political pressures from the Government of the day. On the BBC, news is gathered by its own correspondents and broadcast by its own producers and technicians; whereas on commercial television the news is gathered by Independent Television News (ITN), a separate non-profit making organisation established for the purpose and jointly owned by the programme companies. See Figure 7.2 for a simplified chronology.

Satellite television has been one of the growth areas of the media in Britain and

Figure 7.2 *The electronic media in Britain: a simplified chronology*

1904 Wireless Telegraphy Act required that all wireless transmitters and receivers be licensed by the Post Office.

1922 British Broadcasting Company established a cartel of radio manufacturers and licensed to broadcast with revenue derived from licence fees payable by wireless users to the Post Office.

1923 Sykes Committee established by the Post Office to consider the collection and distribution of license fees and royalties, and all other aspects of broadcasting.

1925 Crawford Committee established to suggest guidelines for the future of broadcasting.

1927 British Broadcasting Corporation established with John Reith as its first Director-General.

1938 resignation of John Reith as Director-General.

1946 Labour White Paper on broadcasting policy favoured 'some element of competition' in the expanding field of television.

1954 Television Act provided for the establishment of Independent Television, a new commercial TV channel financed from the proceeds of TV advertising, and the Independent Television Authority, a new regulatory body to oversee commercial TV in Britain.

1955 start of Commercial Television broadcasting and of Independent Television News.

1962 Pilkington Committee Report on the future of broadcasting in Britain.

1963 Television Act on broadcasting standards and practice.

1964 BBC 2 launched as a new television channel.

1967 introduction of colour television on BBC 2 and the re-naming of BBC Light Programme, Third Programme and Home Service as Radios 2, 3 and 4.

1969 colour television introduced on BBC 1 and ITV.

1972 Independent Local Radio launched and Independent Television Authority re-named the Independent Broadcasting Authority.

1977 Annan Committee Report on the future of broadcasting.

1981 Broadcasting Complaints Commission brought into operation.

1982 Channel 4, the second commercial TV channel in the UK, began broadcasting.

1984 Sky Channel, the first TV channel in the UK, began broadcasting.

1985 Cable Authority began granting franchises and regulating the new cable services in the UK.

1986 Peacock Report published on the financing of the BBC.

1988 Broadcasting Standards Council brought into operation and the House of Commons agreed to the televising of its proceedings on an experimental basis.

1989 televising of the House of Commons made permanent.

1990 Broadcasting Act created the Independent Television Commission to replace the Independent Broadcasting Authority and the Cable Authority, and to license and regulate all commercial television services.

1991 Radio Authority established to license, regulate and oversee the expansion of commercial radio and to introduce three new national radio channels.

1991 European Broadcasting Directive came into force in the UK, together with the Council of Europe Convention of Trans-frontier Television.

1992 Department of National Heritage created to take over Ministerial responsibility for broadcasting policy from the Home Office.

1995 Conservative proposals on Media Ownership and longer term regulatory issues.

around the world over the past few years. At the time of writing there are 20 satellite channels available in Britain to the 3,400,000 people who currently pay subscriptions for them. These include the *Sky* channels partly owned by Rupert Murdoch; various film, sport and special interest channels; and *CNN*, the world-wide news channel owned by Ted Turner in the United States. There has also been a rapid growth of *cable television* in Britain in the 1990s with an increasing number of people choosing to pay for connection to cable networks, partly because these seem to offer more local services than broadcasting, but mainly because modern cable technology can offer a range of facilities for private households, including telephony, interactive shopping, banking and distance learning.

On radio the BBC has five national channels – Radio 1 to 5 – which each cater for a different segment of the wide range of public interests and tastes. *Radio 1* provides mostly popular music and is aimed very much at a younger audience. *Radio 2* provides middle-of-the-road music programmes and light entertainment of one kind or another. *Radio 3* caters for minority interests of a more high-brow and cultured variety, as well as providing such traditional services as commentaries on Test Match cricket. *Radio 4* provides most of the solid news, information and analysis of arts and current affairs, as well as some high quality drama and popular entertainment. *Radio 5* provides 24-hour sports and news coverage. The *BBC World Service* broadcasts to more than 150 countries around the world and sets a standard of radio reporting and analysis which is widely admired.

Local radio services are provided in Britain from 42 BBC local radio stations, and from 150 commercial local radio stations which are financed – like commercial television – from the proceeds of advertising carried on air during and between the programmes. Local radio of both kinds broadcasts a great deal of popular music and other mass appeal programmes designed to ensure an adequately large audience. Yet it also concentrates to a considerable extent upon covering local and community issues and for these purposes puts considerable emphasis upon public phone-in programmes and other forms of local audience participation. Many would argue that this has been a healthy development which has boosted a sense of community and democracy in parts of the country where previously it was rather lacking.

7.2 The problems of the press

The problems of the press are both internal and external. For the purposes of this chapter, however, we shall be concerned mainly with the ways in which the activity of the press and some of its methods of work cause disquiet, even hostility among politicians and public alike. Most people in Britain are content that there is a free press, but, if there is a common thread of public criticism, it is invariably that the press is too 'free', namely that it may have become too powerful and too invasive of people's privacy. [2] On the other hand, editors and journalists are often more concerned to defend the rights and independence of the 'Fourth Estate' against what they are sometimes inclined to see as tyrannical Ministers and draconian laws. In this age-old struggle between politicians and the press, there has often been a good deal of hypocrisy and double standards on both sides. This has made it hard to get at the truth at any time. Nevertheless the following section attempts to cover the salient issues and perennial problems.

Influence and bias

All the national newspapers have political reporters and commentators who usually take distinctive lines on the political issues of the day. In the popular or tabloid newspapers, however, the main purposes are to entertain the readers and maintain or boost the circulation, so that advertisers do not take their custom elsewhere and profits can be increased. The result of these commercial imperatives is that the coverage of political issues is usually not very extensive and certainly not very subtle. Instead the emphasis is put upon presenting news and opinion in stark and eye-catching ways with the use of dramatic photographs, screaming headlines and vivid language.[3] Indeed, few readers of the tabloid press seem to pay much attention to the political line taken by the newspaper which they habitually read and the political influence of such organs seems to have been exaggerated by journalists and politicians alike. The readers are demonstrably more interested in the sport, scandal and soft pornography which dominate so many pages. The editors clearly know what sells such newspapers and invariably allocate their column inches accordingly.

As a general rule, the influence of the tabloid press seems to vary inversely with the knowledge or interest of its readers. For example, when *The Sun* (which had previously supported the Labour Party) gave strong and unequivocal support to the Conservatives at the 1979 General Election, this appears to have influenced the Conservative voting behaviour of many of its readers at that election, although there were other factors which probably had a greater influence upon the extent to which both skilled and unskilled workers and their families switched to the Conservatives in that watershed election. Equally, the *Daily Mirror*, which has consistently supported the Labour Party at General Elections since the war, seems to have a significant influence upon the voting behaviour of its readers by persuading many of them, if wavering, to remain loyal to their traditional Labour allegiance. Thus it may be that the relatively frivolous nature of such 'newspapers' in normal times and the relative ignorance or lack of interest in politics among their readers actually increase the political influence which they can have if their editors decide to pull out all the stops in favour of a particular political party at election time.

The quality national newspapers devote much more space to political reporting and comment, and certainly they all aspire to influence the political process in their chosen directions. Their influence is usually of a subtle and indirect kind in that they seek to persuade the politicians themselves, civil servants involved in the policy process and the wide variety of other interest groups and opinion formers who are involved directly or indirectly in British politics. Thus well known commentators, such as Samuel Brittan in the *Financial Times*, Peter Riddell in *The Times* and Hugo Young in *The Guardian*, can have real influence from time to time upon the evolving political debate. Similarly, leading articles, political features and even letters to the editor in such newspapers are taken seriously and often carry weight in Whitehall and Westminster. Such columns are rather like a house notice board for the political class and they have some disproportionate impact in view of the elitist and metropolitan character of so much political opinion formation in Britain.

Many on the Left of British politics have argued that there is a persistent bias in the national press in favour of the Conservatives and against the views and interests of the Labour Party. It certainly used to be true that the *Daily Mirror* was the only national daily newspaper which consistently supported the Labour Party as a matter of editorial policy. Apart from its sister paper, the *Sunday Mirror*, all the other national newspapers could be divided essentially between those which were still broadly in favour of policies derived from the post-war consensus (for example, *The Guardian* and *The Observer*) and those which were invariably pro-Conservative (for example, the *Daily Express* and the *Sunday Telegraph*). However, this traditional pattern seems to have been upset since the 1992 General Election and especially since the financial shock and political set-back of 'Black Wednesday' on 16 September 1992 when Britain was forced out of the European Exchange Rate Mechanism by enormous turbulence in the global currency markets. This seriously damaged the political credibility of John Major and the Conservative Government and led subsequently to the sacking of the then Chancellor of the Exchequer, Norman Lamont, in the summer of 1993. It also gave new heart to the so-called Euro-sceptics in the Conservative Parliamentary Party who disliked both Britain's legal obligations to the European Union and any regime of fixed exchange rates.

It remains to be seen whether those in the press who between 1992 and 1995 campaigned so assiduously to remove John Major from 10 Downing Street, did so as a prelude to urging their readers to vote against the Conservatives at the next General Election, or did so in an attempt to hasten John Major's departure and his replacement in advance of the next General Election with another Conservative leader more to their taste whom they could sincerely urge their readers to support in a future General Election; if the latter, it would appear to have failed following John Major's re-election as Conservative Leader in July 1995. None the less, at the time of writing the situation appears fluid and no one can be sure of what line the various newspapers will take when the next General Election takes place.

Privacy and public interest

One of the strongest political and public concerns about the press is the way in which it is seen to invade people's privacy and make some lives miserable as a result of various forms of media intrusion – whether telephone tapping, bugging with directional microphones, photography with telephoto lenses, or intimidatory 'door-stepping' of people in the news. Although the concern is often voiced by and on behalf of politicians, it is a problem which can afflict many other people as well, including members of the Royal family, television personalities, sports stars and a whole range of show business people (most of whom would not make such a lucrative living if they were not so frequently in the public eye). It can also afflict quite ordinary people from time to time, if and when they are involved in some particularly newsworthy event, such as the death of a child, a 'lucky' win on the National Lottery, the loss of a loved one in a terrorist outrage, or some other personal tragedy. In nearly every such case self-righteous editors and investigating journalists seek to justify their actions by claiming that 'the public has a right to know' and that their journalism is 'in the public interest'. Sometimes this may, indeed, be true; but more often the real (unadmitted) explanation is that sensational journalism boosts the circulation of the newspapers which get scoops and hence increases both the advertising revenue and the profits of the media corporations which stand to benefit.

There is no denying the fact that significant numbers of the public are 'interested' in such squalid journalism, since the circulation figures of the newspapers concerned invariably increase dramatically when they serialise a colourful political memoir, such as Alan Clark's *Diaries*, or publish the transcript of sensational revelations about the

Royal family, such as the so-called 'Camillagate Tapes' which purported to record in lurid and highly compromising detail some private telephone conversations between the Prince of Wales and his friend Mrs Camilla Parker Bowles. Nor is there much doubt that many prominent figures in public life benefit – at any rate financially – when they sell their stories to the press, as less prominent people also do when they succumb to the lure of so-called cheque-book journalism.

It is more questionable, however, whether what interests the newspaper-buying public is always 'in the public interest', since such vivid and sensational journalism has manifestly damaged the reputation of the Royal family and has not exactly assisted John Major to govern the country with confidence at a time when an unusually large number of his political colleagues have been exposed by the media in compromising circumstances. Indeed on this last point the attack on *The Guardian* in April 1995 by the then Chief Secretary to the Treasury, Jonathan Aitken – in which he spoke about 'the cancer of bent and twisted journalism' and 'the fight against falsehood and those who peddle it' – was seen by some as an attempt by the Government to halt the debilitating attacks on Ministers over allegations of 'sleaze' which had led to 17 resignations during John Major's premiership. Those who hold a brief for the Fourth Estate will invariably say, when challenged, that members of the Government and all in public life deserve all they get when their indiscretions or wrongdoings are exposed. Yet there was not always such open warfare between journalists and those in public life, as can be seen from the much more discreet way in which journalists and editors declined to report or publish all that they knew to be true of Edward VIII, Harold Macmillan, or President Kennedy. The inescapable conclusion is that the press, like the public, has become much less deferential to politicians and others in public life; and that the competitive pressures upon all editors to 'publish and be damned' are now compelling in a world of intense media competition in which any newspaper which acts 'responsibly' by withholding a sensational story will almost certainly lose ground commercially to one of its rivals which is not so fastidious.

In the contemporary British context, the question has arisen, therefore, as to what – if anything – can or should be done about these problems. In April 1989 the Conservative Government charged the Calcutt Committee with the difficult task of examining the issues and making recommendations on 'what measures (whether legislative or otherwise) are needed to give further protection to individual privacy from the activities of the press and improve recourse against the press for the individual citizen, taking account of existing remedies including the law on defamation and breach of confidence'.[4] At the time of writing the delayed Government response to the Calcutt Report is still awaited. This is likely to take the form of a White Paper with 'green edges' – in other words, one in which the conclusions will be open for further discussion. In any case the key questions in the debate would seem to be: (1) can there be an effective right to privacy; (2) if so, who can claim such a right and to what extent; and (3) how can suitable redress be provided for those who believe that their privacy has been intolerably invaded?

Firstly, everyone should be able to expect a high degree of privacy about those aspects of their lives of which public disclosure could be severely prejudicial to their interests – for example, sensitive information about their medical condition or their tax position. This means that doctors or tax inspectors are usually under a rigorous duty of confidentiality to patients and tax-payers respectively. However, those who *choose* to enter public life or who accept a position of public responsibility cannot reasonably expect so much privacy, at any rate in connection with their public duties. Furthermore, public figures who sound off on issues of personal morality or integrity – as certain politicians have chosen to do in recent years – should not be surprised if this tempts the media to explore their lives for sensational double standards between their public pronouncements and their private practices.

The challenge in this area is to draw a convincing and generally acceptable line between those in public life and everyone else, and then perhaps a further line for those in public life between the 'public' and 'private' aspects of their lives. In practice, the latter distinction has proved almost impossible to sustain, because any journalist exploring a good story will tend to argue that a revelation drawn from the private life of someone normally in the public eye *necessarily* has a bearing upon either that person's fitness to hold public office or the public's ability to put its trust in the person concerned. In such testing circumstances those actively engaged in public life and, regrettably, often their families too are regarded by the media as fair game whenever any newsworthy information is uncovered about them. It is therefore difficult to see how there could be an enforceable statutory right to privacy covering all aspects of people's lives and certainly not for those who have chosen to be in public life.

Secondly, in seeking appropriate means of redress for those whose privacy has been intolerably invaded, a distinction should be drawn between the existing *voluntary* restraints upon the press symbolised by the self-regulation of the Press Complaints Commission and any more exacting forms of press regulation which may be imposed by Parliament in future. At the time of writing the consensus of political opinion in all parties appears to be a sense of caution towards the Calcutt proposal for a new Press Complaints Tribunal with statutory powers to award compensation to individuals and to restrain publication of material in breach of a statutory code of practice by means of injunctions. The possibility of even more draconian penalties, such as withdrawal of licences to publish for varying periods of time depending upon the gravity of the offence, was not recommended by the Calcutt Committee, which was keen to stress in its report that the press should be given one final chance to prove that voluntary self-regulation can be made to work.

In these circumstances it seems likely that the eventual response of Government and Parliament will be a minimalist package composed of a new law against entering private property without consent with the intention of obtaining personal information intended for publication, placing a surveillance device on private property for the same purpose, and taking photographs or making tape recordings of people on private property with a view to identifying them without their consent. Even if such a law were to be passed, it is likely that the press would have a legal defence that it was only seeking 'to expose the commission of any crime or other seriously anti-social conduct', as suggested in the Calcutt Report.

Notwithstanding David Mellor's colourful assertion that the days of press self-regulation were numbered and that the media were 'drinking in the last-chance saloon' it seems unlikely that the Government would add to its woes by introducing new legislation significantly to curtail press freedom, which is what any new law to protect privacy would inevitably entail. Furthermore, the few leading figures in the Fourth Estate who have expressed some sneaking sympathy with the view that excesses by parts of the media have made statutory regulation more likely, have also made the point that it would be easier to countenance new statutory controls if there were already in the background a codified constitution containing fundamental safeguards for freedom of expression (such as the First Amendment to the American constitution) and legislation guaranteeing freedom of information.

Secrecy and censorship

Another important characteristic of the British press is that it has been more inhibited than in most other Western countries by the traditional secrecy of British Government and the restrictive attitudes in Whitehall towards the unauthorised disclosure of official information. Such secretive habits were established years ago and have persisted at least since the 1911 Official Secrets Act which in Section 2 was meant to deter public servants (including Ministers) from communicating and journalists or others from receiving any official information whose disclosure had not been authorised, that is to say deliberately released by Ministers or by senior civil servants acting on their behalf. There has been, of course, a certain Alice in Wonderland quality about this aspect of the law which for years allowed Ministers to authorise their own indiscretions (if it suited their political purposes), but which equally allowed the system to come down like a ton of bricks on any unfortunate participant in the Whitehall or Westminster game caught disseminating or receiving information which Ministers wished to be kept secret. Over the years the effect of this legislation was to discredit the whole idea of official secrecy in Britain without removing the need for occasional, often farcical prosecutions. This bred an understandably cynical response among all journalists and even some public servants.

Thus there was a widespread welcome when the Conservative Government introduced a new Official Secrets Bill in November 1988.[5] This was designed to remove the 'catch-all' provisions in Section 2 of the 1911 Act and replace them with provisions which restrict the application of the criminal law to specific categories of official information – such as defence, security and intelligence, international relations, law and order, and the interception of communications (phone tapping or letter opening). However, it has since become perfectly obvious that the effect of the new law upon the press and the rest of the media is actually more restrictive, although less capricious, than the discredited law which it replaced. It is therefore hard to argue that much, if anything, has been gained for the cause of journalistic freedom.

The same cautious and restrictive attitudes which have inhibited freedom of the press, are evident in the so-called 'D Notice' system which is designed to prevent publication in the press or broadcasting in the electronic media of sensitive defence information by the simple expedient of issuing a private written warning from an official committee consisting of officials and journalists together. While these obscure arrangements have certainly been successful over the years in achieving a degree of self-censorship among those journalists who cover defence and security issues, the opaque nature of the restrictive arrangements and the unpredictability of intervention by the D Notice Committee have bred further cynicism among those most directly affected.

Similarly restrictive attitudes are reflected in the libel and copyright laws in Britain which have also had the effect of inhibiting aggressive and fearless reporting, especially when the subject under journalistic investigation is an individual or a company which has the wealth and self-confidence to use the law to the full. These laws confer extensive powers of prior restraint and hence effective censorship upon those who wish to prevent publication or broadcasting of anything which, their lawyers advise, may be libellous or defamatory by the simple expedient of obtaining a High Court injunction to stop it.

They also permit wealthy or determined individuals to go to Court to obtain 'justice' in libel cases and, if successful in their suits, to secure from juries orders for damages which have been known to reach half a million pounds or more.[6] While there is an obvious need for people to be able to protect themselves from libel or defamation in the media, or even intolerable invasion of privacy as discussed above, it is generally unsatisfactory that only the rich, the powerful and the well-connected seem able to avail themselves of the protection of the law in this way, while the rest of the population is neither adequately protected from journalistic excesses nor sufficiently compensated by journalistic vigilance for the public good.

Freedom of information

Concerted attempts have been made over the years to deal with the problems of secrecy and censorship which affect the British press and other media by introducing proposals designed to promote freedom of information and by pursuing a vigorous pressure group campaign towards this end. In 1978 a report by 'Justice', the British Section of the International Commission of Jurists, recommended a Code of Practice on the disclosure of official information for all Government Departments and other public bodies to be supervised by the Parliamentary Commissioner for Administration (the Ombudsman).[7] At about the same time a Liberal MP, Clement Freud, introduced a Private Member's Bill designed to legislate for freedom of information along the lines of detailed proposals made a year or so earlier by the Outer Circle Policy Unit.[8] Since that time other backbenchers in all parties have tried to introduce legislation along similar lines and in limited areas (for example, environmental information) they have been successful. Yet so far no all-encompassing Freedom of Information Bill has reached the statute book in Britain.

However, both the Labour Party and the Liberal Democrats now favour reforming the law in such a way that a public right of access to official information would be enshrined in statute law and the onus put upon public authorities to satisfy the Courts of any justification for non-disclosure. This principle is the reverse of that contained in existing legislation, which holds that all classified information should remain restricted unless its release has been specifically authorised either by a Minister or by a Court. The reformers have also wanted to give British citizens the right to see their personal files and to establish a reliable register of all official files, except those which involve the security of the state. They have favoured the establishment of some form of appeals procedure against refusal to supply official information and the introduction of a judicial remedy for aggrieved citizens in cases of proven non-compliance with the law. Only certain categories of information – including some defence and security material, information involving commercial confidentiality, and information which must be safeguarded for reasons of privacy – would be exempt from the provisions of such legislation if it were introduced.

Apart from the inherent unwillingness of most Ministers and civil servants to respond positively to such proposals, the main argument used against them has usually been the alleged extra cost to public funds which would be involved in applying such legislation. It is also pointed out that in those countries where such legislation has been implemented – for example, Sweden and the United States – the actual experience has been that pressure groups and commercial interests have made much greater use of it than ordinary people. At bottom the idea provokes the fundamental antipathy of Ministers, civil servants and most other public officials in Britain towards the disclosure of any official information other than that which is unavoidably forced upon them (for example, in public inquiries) or whose release is believed by Ministers to be advantageous to the Government's cause. In these circumstances it is not easy to be confident that any code of practice or even new legislation would do much to change such attitudes in a political and official elite as congenitally secretive as the one in Britain.

The role of the Lobby

A paradoxical aspect of the position of the press in Britain is that, whereas there is so much emphasis upon secrecy and censorship in the formal and legal arrangements, in practice a great deal of information is made available to the press and electronic media on what are called 'Lobby terms'.[9] This practice involves supplying accredited Lobby journalists (that is, those entitled to frequent the Members' Lobby and other restricted parts of the Palace of Westminster) with privileged and unattributable information and comment on the strict understanding that there is no disclosure of sources or direct attribution of comments. The practice has spread beyond the precincts of the Palace of Westminster to every part of Whitehall, so that every Department (and especially 10 Downing Street) has contacts with certain journalists who are the privileged recipients of official information and guidance which is regularly given to them. Indeed, most Ministers and even some officials see it as an important part of their jobs to keep at least a few journalists well informed of what is happening or about to happen in their areas of responsibility. Equally, the journalists concerned find it convenient to take advantage of this form of news management by Government and by Parliament, since it ensures a steady flow of news, gossip and opinion.

This Lobby system has advantages for both the providers and the recipients of such privileged information. For Ministers and officials it can be an effective way of defusing potentially difficult issues through judicious and timely leaks, so that when the information is formally released, much of its adverse publicity impact has been removed. A good example of this technique would be the early leaking of rising unemployment figures or an early indication of bad trade figures, so that the markets do not respond adversely when the figures are formally released. The system is also used to fly kites for new policy initiatives in order to get some idea of how they might be received by the media and the public. Occasionally it is used to pursue in the media policy arguments or personality conflicts which are taking place behind closed doors in Whitehall or Westminster. For example, the Press Office at 10 Downing Street was known to guide journalists towards taking an unfavourable view of Ministers who had incurred Margaret Thatcher's personal displeasure – sometimes to the extent that the Minister concerned learned of his fall from favour more surely from inspired stories in the press than from any face-to-face contact with the Prime Minister.[10]

It is a moot point whether the use of Lobby techniques and indeed the entire Lobby system are really desirable. Some national newspapers have challenged it. For example, *The Independent* and *The Guardian* boycotted the unattributable briefings at 10 Downing Street for a period in the late 1980s and early 1990s, but still kept their Lobby correspondents and made use of information gathered on 'Lobby terms'. Yet the vast majority of political journalists have been prepared to play the game, since it can help them to get a good story and occasionally to increase the circulation of their newspapers. The attractions for politicians are more obvious unless and until the shroud of anonymity is lifted to the embarrassment of those who have been too indiscreet.

7.3 The problems of the electronic media

The problems of the electronic media are both technological and ideological. They are technological in the sense that there are a number of developments in train which, even if Government and Parliament were to take no action, would significantly affect the media environment now and in the future. For example, the technologies of television and telecommunications are fast converging, so that by one means or another the limitations traditionally imposed by broadcasting spectrum scarcity are likely to be overcome or by-passed. This means that a wider range of programmes and services will be made available locally, nationally and internationally; and these services are likely to have improved sound and visual quality. It also means that the range of programme content could be widened as the technology of encryption enables direct payment by subscription to register customer choice in a cost-effective way.

Perhaps most significant of all, with the spread of satellite television and the growth of global media companies, national media frontiers are becoming porous and may even disappear with uncertain consequences for public taste, national culture and regulatory arrangements. Eloquent concern has already been expressed in many quarters about the need to safeguard quality, to prevent excessive concentration of ownership and to work out new regulatory arrangements, increasingly at international level, to match the global reach of the new technologies and the global structure of the largest media companies. So far at least the global media companies seem to be winning.

The problems are ideological in the sense that the present Conservative Government in Britain seems convinced that 'the growth of [media] choice means that a rigid regulatory structure neither can nor should be perpetuated'.[11] This almost *laissez-faire* attitude is in stark contrast to that of the French or Chinese Governments which have been taking both administrative and legislative action to safeguard their respective national cultures against what they see as undesirable external influences upon their societies projected by the global (usually Anglo-Saxon) media. In most cases the approach of the present British Government has been consistent with its overall policy of de-regulation, although it has equally asserted that 'rules will still be needed to safeguard programme standards on such matters as good taste and decency, and to ensure that the unique power of the broadcast media is not abused'.[12] Both the quotations just given are drawn from a single paragraph in the 1988 Broadcasting White Paper and reveal the tensions, not to say contradictions, which have existed in the present Government's policy between the urge to liberalise and the attempt to regulate, however difficult the latter may prove to be in such a rapidly changing, market-led and technologically driven sector.

It is already clear (in 1995) that much of the policy set out in 1988 has been overtaken by events, notably by the fact that terrestrial broadcasting is being challenged and in some cases overtaken by new satellite and cable technologies. The Conservatives in Britain still seem to believe that the circle can be squared by having both less regulation and better regulation – the latter being defined as 'lighter, more flexible, more efficiently administered' regulation. It remains to be seen whether this synthesis of opposites will be effective in practice. Much will depend upon how well the Department of National Heritage (the Department with the regulatory responsibilities for the media in Britain) manages to resist the pressures from elsewhere in Whitehall (notably the Treasury and the Department of Trade and Industry) for a market-driven response to developments in the media. Still more will depend upon actual technological developments in the global market-place which are likely to render ineffective, even obsolete, any national regulations.

The power of television

The power of television has affected many aspects of British life and in the political sphere notably the style and nature of political debate. As Anthony Smith has observed, television has become a well from which society draws many of its common allusions (illusions?) and an important source of social reference points.[13] This means that, in considering the power of television, we need to look not so much at its impact upon voting behaviour (which until recent times appears to have been minimal) as its capacity to influence the way in which the political debate is conducted both between elections and during election campaigns.

In essence political issues are often treated as if they were simply another form of public entertainment and politics as a rather esoteric spectator sport. This has encouraged the tendency for politicians to perform before the people rather than reason with them. The respectable argument for this practice is that it serves to grab and hold the attention of what might otherwise be an uninterested and cynical viewing public. Yet while it may produce a greater public awareness of some political issues, it does not necessarily raise the level of public understanding and may even produce a bias against it.[14]

In so far as television has had a discernible effect upon political allegiance in Britain, it seems to have been one of reinforcement rather than conversion, although the early studies on this subject seemed also to suggest that the direct effects upon voting behaviour were rather slight either way. For example, Trenaman and McQuail in their pioneering study of the 1959 General Election (the first televised campaign in Britain) showed that the main effect of television was simply to increase the store of information and opinion available to the electorate.[15] In a follow-up study of the 1964 General Election, Blumler and McQuail showed that the only other discernible effect was to boost slightly the popularity of the Liberal Party by giving it an abnormal degree of media exposure.[16] In 1981 television coverage of the newly formed Social Democratic Party seemed to have a similar, but temporary effect which assisted it in early by-elections. However, with the notable increase in voter volatility since the mid-1970s, it seems plausible that the impact of television upon elections has become greater than it was when the conventional wisdom on this matter was established.

Nowadays saturation coverage characterises the portrayal of General Election campaigns on television and it seems that the British public may have had enough of it. For example, during the 1987 campaign Gallup Polls discovered that 69 per cent of its samples expected there to be too much political coverage on television (getting in the way of or displacing their favourite regular programmes), while another opinion poll discovered that 27 per cent thought there should be no election coverage at all![17] Certainly the widely held opinion among the psephological experts was that Labour had 'won' the media battle against the Conservatives hands down, but this did not seem to make any difference to the level of support for Labour which was the same on polling day as it had been at the beginning of the campaign. After the 1992 General Election the standard view of the experts was that while television coverage may have shaped the rhythm and pattern of the campaign, it had much less influence upon the final outcome; except that in as much as the campaign had a presidential quality, the Conservatives clearly 'won' with John Major much more credible in the role of Prime Minister than Neil Kinnock could ever be.[18]

One of the most significant effects of television upon British politics has been manifest in the style and methods of political argument and election campaigning. Since the 1964 General Election campaign, the parties have held daily press conferences each morning during the formal campaign period. This development, amplified by the nightly news bulletins on BBC and ITN, has had the effect of focusing public attention upon the party leaders and a few of their most senior colleagues. The emphasis upon a presidential style of campaigning has been increased by the presence of a veritable media circus with the party leaders as they go on tour around the country. All of this has diminished the role and importance of most Parliamentary candidates, except in very marginal seats or at highly publicised by-elections. It has also diminished still further the value of public meetings as a form of political campaigning, although again there are partial exceptions to this rule in some rural constituencies with small cohesive communities and at significant by-elections.

Equally significant in its effect upon British politics has been the tendency for television to personalise, trivialise and sensationalise nearly every political issue. It does this almost unconsciously in that programme producers will tend to prefer staging interviews with the party leaders rather than with other lesser political figures. Indeed, the producers cannot really be more high-minded or restrained than this, since they are in competition with the tabloid press and other parts of the media which are inclined to be sensational in their treatment of all issues. Banner headlines which scream messages such as 'Major on the ropes' or 'Blair miles ahead', set a vivid standard with which television feels obliged to compete. Furthermore, it is thought appropriate to translate the antagonistic conventions of the House of Commons into the television and radio studios, and leading television interviewers, such as Jeremy Paxman or John Humphrys, regard their clashes with the party leaders as a central part of the political ritual in modern politics.

Influence, bias and agenda setting

Just as some on the Left of British politics have been concerned about anti-Labour bias in the national press, so others in all parties have maintained that television is far from being a neutral medium of mass communication. According to this argument, the political effect of television is no longer simply to reinforce existing values and preferences in society, but actually to *set the agenda* of political discussion. Public faith in the impartiality of television news is said to be misplaced on the grounds that true objectivity can never be achieved by those who produce and edit the programmes. The Glasgow Media Group, in particular, has argued that the news is not really 'the news', but an arbitrary selection and presentation of certain information and opinion according to the undeclared criteria and preferences of those who produce and present the programmes.[19] It is interesting that these Left-wing academics are not alone in their suspicion of television decision-makers, but are joined in such feelings by a whole swathe of Right-wing political opinion which is equally convinced that the programme-makers in general and the BBC in particular are out to do them down by innuendo and any other methods which come to hand.

If there really is such a media conspiracy against the politicians, it is worth noting that the sense of paranoia is experienced by Left and Right alike. The counter-argument, which has been put by Martin Harrison and Alastair Hetherington, is essentially that political bias on television is in the eye of the viewer, just as on radio it is in the ear of the listener.[20] Such sceptics have pointed out that everything really depends upon the broadcast material selected for analysis and that in the case of the Glasgow Media Group the academics concerned were essentially displaying their own prejudices. Equally, there are many on the Conservative side of the argument who believe that they have cause to complain about the iconoclastic and even subversive nature of some television programmes. For example, the BBC Panorama programme *Real Lives*, which was screened in 1986, purported to equate the life and motivation of an acknowledged IRA terrorist with that of an Ulster loyalist, thus leaving the viewers with the clear impression that the one was morally indistinguishable from the other. Similarly, the *This Week* programme 'Death on the Rock' analysed the way in which three suspected IRA terrorists were killed on a street in Gibraltar in broad daylight by members of the Special Air Service (SAS) and conducted its analysis in such a provocative and controversial way that there was a considerable political row followed by a highly controversial Coroner's Inquest.

In more recent times Conservative politicians have felt persecuted by the media and convinced that the real agenda of some newspaper editors and programme makers has been to topple John Major, if not to bring about the defeat of the Conservatives at the next General Election. In most cases leading media people reply to such political charges by arguing either that they are simply holding up a mirror to some politically uncomfortable reality or merely pursuing their vocation as investigative journalists or both. In the final analysis most political reporting and editorialising is a matter of taste and judgement rather than right or wrong doing – unless, of course, there is a well-founded suspicion that the law may have been broken. In most cases discipline is imposed by the professionalism of the media people themselves and only in the last resort by the Courts. An example of this 'last resort' occurred in March 1995 when the BBC was forced to abandon plans to screen in Scotland – three days before Local Elections – a *Panorama* interview with John Major after this was challenged in the Courts by both the Labour and Liberal Democrat parties and a judge ruled that the programme breached the strict impartiality rules governing the BBC.

The power of radio

Radio is also a powerful medium which has its effect upon both politics and society in Britain. The programmes broadcast by the BBC on its five national channels serve to entertain, inform and educate the public. Taken together they seek to offer a balanced media output, but one which has moved some distance from the original Reithian objectives for the BBC which were to keep a broadly *equal* balance between entertainment and public education.

The expansion of local radio since the late 1960s has also left its mark upon the development of British popular culture and indeed upon British society as a whole. The BBC now has 38 local radio stations in England, as well as 4 'national' stations covering the non-English parts of the United Kingdom namely Radio Wales, Radio Scotland, Radio Ulster and Radio Cymru (a Welsh language station). However, the BBC's efforts in local radio are now overwhelmed by the 150 commercial radio stations which cover virtually every locality in the United Kingdom. This total includes two national radio stations (Classic FM and Virgin 215), five regional stations, as well as a variety of new cable and satellite services. The Radio Authority receives a constant stream of applications to broadcast from commercial undertakings which seek to take advantage of the additional frequencies which will be released from 1996.

This explosion of local radio in all parts of the country has given a real boost to local consciousness and some of the more colourful local personalities (political and otherwise) have thrived in the new atmosphere which has been created. Apart from heavy doses of popular music and other forms of popular entertainment, the stations tend to broadcast a large number of chat shows, quiz games and phone-in programmes which provide opportunities for members of the public to air their views and prejudices, while politicians and other public figures have extra opportunities to demonstrate their activity and concern. Thus local radio has undoubtedly contributed to the vitality of British life and often it provides the most vivid forum for local political debate. Yet the *raison d'être* of the expansion has been the opportunity for commerical profit.

In the future, radio in Britain will have further opportunities for development and expansion. The commercial sector will benefit from the lighter regulatory regime of the Radio Authority, while the BBC will continue to be responsible for public service broadcasting. There will be less spectrum scarcity and more wave-lengths available for new services, including probably a new tier of community or special interest radio stations which hitherto have tended to broadcast illegally from pirate facilities. All of this means that there will be more opportunities for media entrepreneurs to make money out of commercial radio, more competition for the BBC which may feel obliged to dilute its commitment to the public service ethos in order to retain a significant share of a much larger total radio audience, and new opportunities for pressure and cause groups to peddle their ideas (as happens now in the United States with the so-called media evangelists) in a more pluralist and less regulated media environment. Many of these developments may affect the nature of British politics; all of them will affect the quality of life in Britain.

The impact of new technologies

It is already clear that new technologies are likely to have a very significant impact upon the development of the media in Britain. The availability of more radio frequencies, as well as the growth of satellite, cable and digital transmission of television, will make many more services technically possible whether for a local, national or supranational audience. The main constraint upon the pace and scale of these developments is likely to be the ability to make them commercially viable within a reasonable period rather than any serious doubts about their technical feasibility or their political acceptability.

If everything goes well and the new technologies are developed along the benign lines foreseen by their most enthusiastic proponents, we could see the development of a society which was described by Kenneth Baker, when Minister for Information Technology, as 'better informed . . . more relaxed, less formal, more mobile, less enamoured with structure, more skilled, less ridden with class and social differences, and full of scope for more individuality'.[21] Yet if things go differently and the new technologies are developed overwhelmingly for short-term commercial gain and subsequently perhaps for manipulative purposes either by powerful media corporations or by public authorities at a national or supranational level, then individual freedom could be eroded, social variety could be stifled and totalitarian tendencies could spread.

The likelihood that the traditional distinction between television and telecommunications will be increasingly blurred or even eliminated by technological developments could mean that there will be a larger range of home-based education; new opportunities for tele-working and buying and selling directly from home; and a variety of new consumer services such as electronic mail (Internet) and tele-banking. The progressive introduction of pay-as-you-view television programmes will increasingly limit universal public access to programmes which hitherto have been virtually free goods provided to every household with a television set, assuming only the payment of a very cost effective licence fee. Members of the public are likely to resent having to pay explicitly for mass audience programmes which previously they were able to enjoy 'free' at the time of screening (for example, the FA Cup Final, the Grand National, Trooping the Colour and so on) and even those with minority interests and enthusiasms (for example, opera, ballet or vintage cars) may prefer going to real events or perhaps buying or renting videotapes of the same rather than paying quite substantial subscriptions in order to be able to watch encrypted, live programmes.

Notwithstanding these factors, it is probably too soon to tell what will be the full consequences of these new media technologies upon British society and British politics. Taking a favourable view, it is possible to foresee a future in which a more open and competitive media market can be achieved which will give both viewers and listeners greater choice and greater influence without detriment to the range or quality of the services provided. Taking an unfavourable view, these developments could lead to a waste of scarce resources, the erosion of social diversity and significant damage to the popular culture.

The decision to encourage the development of cable television in Britain can now be seen to have been of considerable significance.[22] Initially the market for cable television and related services in Britain did not expand as rapidly as the Conservative Government had expected. This led the Labour Party in its 1989 Policy Review to commit itself to the promotion of cable technology in Britain on a much more ambitious scale with the prospect of a considerable sum of public money being allocated to finance a new national fibre-optic communications network (now known as an 'information super highway'). Yet as the British economy recovered from the long recession of the early 1990s, the commercial prospects for cable services seemed to improve dramatically. The result is that many (mostly foreign owned) companies have entered this market and more households have been willing to pay for cable television and related services, including telephony, which are often provided as part of the package.

The growth of Direct Broadcasting by Satellite (DBS) has also been impressive after a shaky start during the early years of commercial operation in Britain. In recognition of the high initial development costs of satellite technology, the 1984 Cable and Broadcasting Act provided for the companies concerned a 15 year contract period rather than the 8 year franchises awarded to the cable companies. This apart, the general approach of the Conservative Government has been that the market should determine how far and how fast satellite television develops in Britain. Considerable investment has already been made in this technology in Britain and elsewhere in Europe, which underlines the point that the regulatory arrangements – like the technology – are likely to be further developed on an international or even supranational level.

At present the regulation of high-powered DBS is done by the Cable Authority, whereas the medium powered satellite services are not subject to British regulation at all. If this regulatory gap is to be closed, there are three proposed solutions. Firstly, the regulation of programme content by the Independent Television Commission (ITC) could be extended to cover nearly all satellite services received directly whether from British or foreign satellites. Secondly, foreign satellite services could be monitored in Britain either by the ITC or by the Broadcasting Standards Council (BSC) whose statutory remit is to guard against obscene or grossly offensive material. Thirdly, the British and other Governments could continue to work for international agreement on a Council of Europe Convention on Trans-frontier Broadcasting which would seek to lay down prescribed minimum standards covering both programme content and advertising. Such standards would then be enforced in all the signatory countries through a procedure which would enable the 'receiving state' to take action against any other country which allowed the transmission of offensive services.[23]

It is clear that the extensive commercial development of such technology could have far-reaching implications for traditional ideas of national sovereignty and cultural identity. The British people have already begun to experience the invasive consequences of junk food and tabloid television imported from the United States. Such problems could be even more serious for other Governments, especially in fragile or rootless societies. In the global media village more and more programmes are likely to be standardised and monoglot, purveying mid-Atlantic mediocrity designed to satisfy a global audience. The possible implications for the quality of life in Britain and other countries could be very disturbing.

7.4 The media and politics

There is no doubt that the media have come to play an increasingly important part in the British political system over the last 30 years or so. The journalists, editors, presenters and producers no longer carry conviction if they claim that all they are doing is to reflect what is happening in British politics and society. Indeed, the more thoughtful members of the media professions readily acknowledge their ability to influence the agenda of politics and recognise the tensions which media priorities can create between them and the politicians.

There are really five main points which need to be made about the role of the media in modern British politics. *Firstly*, it is argued by politicians and others in the public eye that the media, and especially television, give a distorted impression of politics and the political world, since bad news is nearly always given precedence over good news, disunity over unity, gossip and speculation over solid reporting and analysis. These media tendencies are usually more noticeable in the tabloid press and television, but even the so-called quality media are not above a little distortion or oversimplification when it suits them. The usual explanation is that the imperatives of the market and the need to compete for fickle public attention require the media to behave in this way. Whether sincerely given or not, it seems that these explanations will become even more valid as the liberalisation of the media market proceeds still further.

As we noted earlier in this chapter, such media distortions can take the form of perceived bias in the reporting of the activities and policies of the political parties. More often, however, the distortion is of a different kind, namely the tendency to personalise and sensationalise complicated political issues for the sake of gaining and retaining the attentions of the public. This was evident, for example, in the tendency of the media to portray the Thatcher Government in presidential terms and to overemphasise the gladiatorial nature of the conflict between the two main parties. It was also evident in the sustained campaign in many parts of the media between 1992 and 1995 to denigrate John Major and to try to force him out of office by presenting his pragmatic approach to politics as the absence of leadership. Of course, the media professionals will reply that this sort of presentation merely reflects political realities, equates with the importance attached to leadership by members of each main party, and has been borne out by the views of the public as expressed in numerous opinion polls. While there is some force in all these pleas in mitigation, it remains an observable fact that a great deal of the media coverage of British politics has oscillated between occasional sycophancy and frequent character assassination.

Secondly, it is argued by political scientists and others that the media have an unrivalled capacity to set the agenda of politics, often in cooperation – it must be said – with energetic campaigning groups. In one sense this is a more weighty point than the first, since it emphasises what can be one of the most constructive roles played by the media in the British political system. The positive result of this can be that public attention is drawn to new or difficult issues which might not otherwise receive the attention which they deserve from the political parties or established sectional interests. Two examples of issues which have been dramatised by the media in this way are the environmental issues of 'green' politics and the wide range of issues which go under the heading of consumer politics. Clearly if the Fourth Estate is doing its proper job in areas of this kind, it is likely to warn the public of impending problems and probe beneath the surface of events in attempts to reveal what is really happening.

Probably the main reason why some people are made uneasy by this aspect of the media is that they may hold the rather old-fashioned view that political parties should be the sole – or at least the principal – organisations with the right to initiate new policies. In reality there is bound to be considerable interplay between the politicians and the media in the process of political agenda-setting, as we shall see in more detail in Chapter 19. This is not because politicians are bereft of new ideas, but rather because (for those in Opposition or on the back-benches) the process of Government policy making is unusually opaque and exclusive.

Thirdly, whenever the party in power at Westminster has a comfortable majority in the House of Commons, those in the media can be tempted to take the view that they have a duty to provide effective opposition, especially if the politicians on the Opposition benches appear temporarily unwilling or unable to do so. Such a view was widely held in media circles during most of the 1980s when the Conservatives had large majorities in the House of Commons and the Labour Party seemed preoccupied with trying to sort out its own problems. In such circumstances there was a real temptation for those in the media to try to fill the gap left by an ineffective and demoralised Opposition. Certainly this was how the situation was seen at the time by many Conservative politicians who have since retained their suspicions of the media during the long period in the 1990s when their party has been deeply unpopular and the Labour Party has greatly risen in public esteem.

Of course, all Governments, when they become deeply unpopular, are tempted to conclude that the media are to blame for their difficulties. This was very evident during the time of the second Wilson Administration (1966-70), especially following the mortal blow to Labour's prestige inflicted by the 1967 devaluation of Sterling – the second time such a thing had happened to a Labour Government since the Second World War. Such attitudes of persecution and paranoia have been equally evident during John Major's period at 10 Downing Street, especially following 'Black Wednesday' on 16 September 1992 when Sterling was forced out of the European Exchange Rate Mechanism and subsequently devalued by 15 per cent. On the other hand, leading figures in the media have had cause from time to time to resent Government attempts to manage the news or manipulate the media for party political purposes. While there can be no final or definitive assessment of this controversy, most neutral observers would probably agree that it is not healthy for a Parliamentary democracy if the media became effectively the real opposition to the Government of the day.

Fourthly, it is argued by some of a traditional disposition that the media in Britain and other modern societies can have a deleterious effect upon the quality of life by producing various forms of cultural pollution. This fear is felt particularly in relation to the possible effects of weakening the regulatory framework within which the media operate and it is reinforced by the evidence of lower cultural standards associated with the tabloid press and equivalent television.

It was clear from the 1988 Broadcasting White Paper and subsequent statements made by Ministers that the Home Office (at the time the responsible Department) fought a strong rearguard action against the liberalising instincts of 10 Downing Street and the Department of Trade and Industry. Yet the outcome, so far as commercial television was concerned, was clearly favourable to the free play of market forces. As the *Financial Times* observed in a critical editorial not long afterwards, 'British broadcasting faces a future in which bottom line considerations will increasingly dictate the contents of programmes.'[24] Set against this, Channel 4 was shielded to some extent from the full force of commercial competition, and the traditional financial framework of the BBC (based upon the annual licence fee) was subsequently safeguarded until 2001.[25]

Notwithstanding these few reassurances for the traditionalists, there remains a real fear in some quarters that the quality of British broadcasting may deteriorate during the transition from the former paternalistic duopoly of the BBC and ITV to a much more open free market constrained by only the lightest regulation. Even the Peacock Committee, whose work provided much of the stimulus for the 1988 White Paper, had emphasised the importance of achieving an appropriate balance between taxation, advertising revenue and viewer subscriptions when constructing a sound financial base for British broadcasting in the future. Yet in spite of this advice, Conservative Ministers approved a future for British broadcasting which is likely to put the new media entrepreneurs very much in the driving seat. Worries are therefore likely to remain that the few remaining islands of real broadcasting quality – such as Radio 3, BBC2 and Channel 4 – may not survive very long in a sea of mass media mediocrity.

Fifthly, strong concern has been expressed in many quarters that heavy concentrations of media ownership could develop unless effective rules are laid down and enforced to prevent such outcomes. In 1989 the then Home Secretary, Douglas Hurd, made it clear to the House of Commons that 'we should regard it as quite unacceptable if British broadcasting were allowed to be dominated by a handful of tycoons or international conglomerates'.[26] The Government therefore promised effective rules to safeguard diversity of ownership and editorial stance, and Ministers made it clear that excessive cross-media holdings would be prevented. Specifically, it was laid down in subordinate legislation that no single media group would be allowed to own two large television or radio franchises and that no British national newspaper group would be allowed to have more than a 20 per cent stake in any satellite company, terrestrial television or radio franchise.[27]

With regard to the enforcement of such rules, Ministers proposed that the Independent Television Commission and the Radio Authority should be given the necessary powers for effective enforcement. These included the ability to set licence conditions in relation to prospective changes in shareholdings, to require changes in a company as a condition of awarding or renewing a licence, and to withdraw licences altogether in the event of false declarations by companies. Taken together, these added up to a formidable range of powers and conditions which provided some reassurance for those who were concerned about rampant commercialism in the media.

However, few knowledgeable observers have been convinced that it will be easy to ensure high quality and diversity of ownership once the free play of market forces takes full effect. Apart from other considerations, it is difficult to argue that regulations should be strictly imposed at a national level in Britain when many of the new technologies can only be effectively regulated at a continental or even a global level. In many ways the idea of national media could become as obsolete as the idea of national capitalism and if so, we shall all have to adjust our traditional assumptions.

In short, in considering the evolving relationship between the media and politics, a great deal depends upon the mixture of interest, temperament and ideology which prevails at any time. In the 1980s Conservative Ministers argued that by giving more power of choice to readers, listeners and viewers, it is possible to engender greater diversity and commercial opportunity without sacrificing quality. Their critics and others of a sceptical disposition have maintained that there is a real danger of the dynamics of fierce commercial competition reducing real consumer choice and diminishing quality. Only time will tell which side of the argument is proved right. It could be that in Britain and other countries we are witnessing an explosion of consumer choice and commercial opportunity, but it could equally be that the Philistines are at the gates.

7.5 Conclusion

We have seen in this chapter how the power of the media in Britain is in one sense greater, but in another sense not so great as it was in previous times – for example, during the heyday of the press barons, Rothermere, Northcliffe and Beaverbrook, in the early part of this century. Today television in particular has a strong influence upon the context and style of British politics, especially during election campaigns. On the other hand, the media do not entirely determine public opinion and they cannot really topple Governments as, it might be argued, they were able to do on certain occasions in the mid-nineteenth century.

Certainly television has an unsettling and pervasive influence upon the British political system. For most politicians it has acted like a lamp to moths with the result that they have often seemed fatally attracted to its light. In many ways radio and television studios have replaced the Chamber of the House of Commons as the principal battle-ground of British politics. This would not matter very much if it were not for the fact that in the minds of the general public television in particular has gained an aura of impartiality and authority not enjoyed to anything like the same extent by the other forms of media. Thus the power, and the responsibility, of television with its ability to influence the political agenda is now an important factor in any modern democracy.

On the positive side of the argument it is worth underlining the fact that television has provided greatly increased scope for communication between opinion formers and decision makers on the one hand and the general public on the other. This is definitely a plus factor in a less deferential and more participatory democracy. Yet even this advantage of the modern media may prove a disappointment if the rapid exploitation of the new commercial opportunities creates more scope for media mediocrity. The existing tendencies towards bias, triviality and sensationalism seem unlikely to disappear, since they are not even generally acknowledged by most of those who work in the media. In these circumstances the onus of proof is on the leading lights of the media to demonstrate that these concerns can be allayed and that the new technologies and commercial opportunities can be developed in ways which will enhance the quality of life and the vitality of British democracy.

With these general considerations in mind, it is possible to summarise the overall contribution of the media to the British political system as (1) the encouragement of a greater awareness of political issues among the general public, and (2) the influencing of the political agenda through media choices of the issues and personalities to be dramatised. The latter is especially significant in the context of pressure group politics where so many different and competing interests vie for the attention of politicians and public alike. It also reminds us that political priorities are often influenced not so much by the intrinsic importance of particular issues as by the nature and extent of the coverage given to them by the media.

Of course, the influence of the media extends well beyond the sphere of party politics, since it has a demonstrable effect upon the values, assumptions, attitudes and behaviour of millions of ordinary people. For example, the media have contributed to the mindless materialism of modern society by reinforcing the widely held assumptions that individual status and social progress should be measured principally in terms of the income people receive and the money they spend. They have also influenced public attitudes towards Government and other public agencies by raising expectations that problems exposed or discussed in the media will therefore be swiftly addressed and solved. More positively, the media have raised the level of public awareness and prompted urgent official responses to many of the problems and injustices of the modern world – for example, environmental degradation or assaults upon human rights in many parts of the world. They can therefore be a force for good as well as harm.

In short, while the media have undoubtedly made it more difficult for Governments to govern by highlighting the flaws and shortcomings in public policy and the politicians responsible for it, and by encouraging a level of public expectations which no Governments have been able to satisfy; they have also communicated a great deal of useful information and opinion to the general public, and probably raised the levels of public consciousness in certain areas in ways which have been beneficial for democracy. In forming conclusions on their role in Britain or any other comparable country, it is as well to remember that in a free society the media are always more likely to be critics than buttresses of those in power, and it is right that this should be so in a pluralist, liberal democracy.

Suggested questions

1 Describe the changing structure and ethos of the media in Britain.
2 How influential is the British press?
3 In what ways do radio and television influence the practices of British politics?

Notes

1. Figures published in the national press for the week ending 26 February 1995, for example, showed that the most popular programmes on BBC 1 and ITV were the soap-operas 'East-Enders' and 'Coronation Street' with more than 16 million viewers in each case. On BBC 2 and Channel 4 there was a wider range of programmes with ratings at lower but nonetheless impressive levels of between 4 million and 6 million viewers - for example, 'Top Gear' and 'Gardeners' World' on BBC 2 and 'The Real Holiday Show' and 'Countdown' on Channel 4.
2. See our discussion of the Calcutt Report on pp. 237-240 below.
3. Among the most famous headlines of recent years have been those which appeared in *The Sun*, such as 'Gotcha' at the time of the sinking of the Argentinian cruiser Belgrano during the 1982 Falklands conflict, and 'Up yours Delors' at the time of maximum conflict between Jacques Delors, President of the European Commission, and the British Conservative Government.
4. Quoted in the Report of the Calcutt Committee on privacy and related matters (London: HMSO, 1990).
5. This later became part of the law of he land as the 1989 Official Secrets Act.
6. For example, in July 1987 Jeffrey Archer (as Lord Archer then was) was awarded £500,000 in damages against *The Star* which had libelled him with allegations about an assignation with a prostitute, and in December 1988 Elton John secured £1 million from *The Sun* in an out-of-court settlement for an alleged libel.
7. *Freedom of Information* (London: Justice, 1978).
8. *An Official Information Act* (London: Outer Circle Policy Unit, 1977).
9. For a fuller discussion of the Lobby system see J. Margach, *The Anatomy of Power* (London: Star, 1981), pp. 125-155.
10. It is now well known that Sir Bernard Ingham, when he was Margaret Thatcher's Press Secretary at 10 Downing Street, organised Lobby briefings in Whitehall to discredit Michael Heseltine at the time of the 1986 Westland Crisis; and that in the same year he fell into the habit of describing John Biffen, then Leader of the House of Commons, to Lobby journalists as 'a semi-detached member of the Cabinet', thus signalling Margaret Thatcher's later decision to sack John Biffen from the Government immediately after the 1987 General Election.
11. See 'Broadcasting in the Nineties – competition, choice and quality', Cmnd 517, November 1988, para 2.5.
12. *Ibid.*
13. A. Smith, *The Politics of Information* (London: Macmillan, 1978), p. 5.
14. This point was well made by John Birt and Peter Jay in *The Times* on 28 February, 30 September and 1 October 1975.
15. See J. Trenaman and D. McQuail, *Television and the Political Image* (London: Methuen, 1961).
16. See J. G. Blumler and D. McQuail, *Television in Politics* (London: Faber, 1968).

17. See M. Harrison on broadcasting in D.E. Butler and D. Kavanagh, *The British General Election of 1987* (London: Macmillan, 1988), p. 139.
18. See D.E. Butler and D. Kavanagh, *The British General Election of 1992* (London: Macmillan, 1992), p. 253.
19. See Glasgow Media Group, *Bad News* (London: Routledge and Kegan Paul, 1981), pp. 12-13.
20. See M. Harrison, *T.V. News, Whose Bias?* (Hermitage, Berkshire: Policy Journals, 1985), and A. Hetherington, *News, newspapers and television* (London: Macmillan, 1985).
21. K. Baker, *Towards an Information Economy*; speech to the British Association for the Advancement of Science, 7 September 1982.
22. See 'The Development of cable services and systems'; Cmnd 8866 (London: HMSO, 1983).
23. See 'Broadcasting in the Nineties'; Cmnd 517, November 1988, Chapter XI.
24. *Financial Times*, 14 June 1989.
25. See 'The future of the B.B.C.'; Cmnd 2621, (London: HMSO, 1994), para 5.10.
26. *Hansard*, 8 February 1989, Col. 1011.
27. In spite of these Government decisions, Ministers in the Thatcher Administration seemed prepared to allow News International to be an exception to the general rule, since the company was permitted to establish Sky Television while retaining its ownership of 37 per cent of the national press in Britain. However, at the time of writing it seems possible that further legislation will be introduced to abolish the 20 per cent limit on the stake that British-based newspaper companies can buy in terrestrial television companies and *vice versa* on the grounds that multi-media companies should now be treated and regulated as single entitles. The limit may also be replaced by a broader measurement of concentration, such as 'share of voice', which would take account of a combination of circulation and ratings, and thus reflect the new realities or multi-media ownership.

Further reading

Curran, J. and Seaton, J., *Power without responsibility*, 3rd edn (London: Routledge, 1991).
Hargreaves, I., *Sharper Vision* (London: Demos, 1994).
Harris, R., *Good and faithful servant* (London: Faber, 1990).
Hetherington A., *News, newspapers and television* (London: Macmillan, 1985).
Ingham B., *Kill the Messenger* (London: Fontana, 1991).
Margach, J., *The Anatomy of Power* (London: Star, 1981).
Negrine, R., *Politics and the mass media in Britain* (London: Routledge, 1989).
Seaton, J. and Pimlott, B., *The Media in British Politics* (Aldershot: Gower, 1987).
Seymour-Ure, C., *The British press and broadcasting since 1945* (Oxford: Blackwell, 1991).

8 Public opinion

The term 'public opinion' has no generally accepted fixed and definite meaning. Certainly the diversity that exists reflects the different views taken at different times by different people, depending upon the society in which they lived and the political outlook which they had. Whereas Jeremy Bentham (1748-1832) defined it as 'a system of law emanating from the body of the people',[1] Robert Peel (1788-1850) defined it as 'that great compound of folly, weakness, prejudice, wrong feeling, right feeling, obstinacy and newspaper paragraphs'.[2] Dean Inge (1860-1954) saw it as 'a vulgar, impertinent, anonymous tyrant'.[3] while Oscar Wilde (1854-1900) described it as 'an attempt to organise the ignorance of the community and to elevate it to the dignity of physical force'.[4]

Nicolas Sebastien Chamfort (1741-1794) asked simply 'How many fools does it take to make a public?'[5] and William Hazlitt (1778-1830) observed that 'there is not a more mean, stupid, dastardly, pitiless, selfish, spiteful, envious, ungrateful animal than the public'.[6] A. V. Dicey (1835-1922) declared public opinion to be 'a mere abstraction', and 'not a power which has any independent existence', defining it simply as 'a general term for the beliefs held by a number of human beings',[7] and more particularly as 'the wishes and ideas as to legislation held by the majority of those citizens who have . . . taken an effective part in public life'.[8] V. O. Key (1908-1963) was perhaps more cynical when he defined it as 'those opinions of private persons which Governments find it prudent to heed'.[9]

In Britain in the nineteenth century public opinion was usually considered to be synonymous with the views of the relatively small number of people who were enfranchised and so able to have effective political influence, at least at election time. Nowadays it is generally accepted that public opinion includes the views and prejudices of all adults, no matter how shallow or fitful or indeed non-existent their involvement in politics.

Broadly speaking, public opinion can be described as what people think ought to be done – or ought not to be done – on a particular issue at a particular time. On those matters which impinge upon the concerns, interests or emotions of the public it is likely that enough individuals will react in the same way for their collective private opinions to constitute a manifestation of public opinion. As a result, public opinion can be seen as being the views expressed by an aggregation of individuals. It is a point of view – an opinion – held in common by a number of people – the public – on issues of social, economic or political significance. Thus, for the purposes of this chapter, public opinion is defined as *the sum of opinions held on social, economic and political issues by the entire popula-tion.* Having said this, however, there are of course many different components of pub-lic opinion which vary from issue to issue and from time to time. As Richard Rose put it, 'there is not a single public with which the Government seeks to communicate; there is a variety of publics distinguishable by their degrees of organisation, their policy pref-erences and their knowledge or interest in political issues'.[10] The composition of public opinion is therefore more akin to a mosaic than to a well-defined or predictable diagram. It is nevertheless possible to show the flow of public opinion in diagrammatic form, and this is done in Figure 8.1.

Figure 8.1   The flow of public opinion

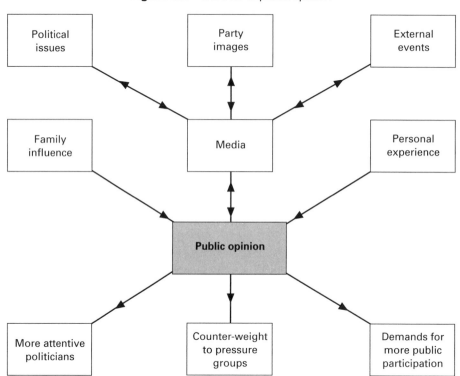

8.1 The formation of opinion

Inheritance and experience

Expert studies have shown that public opinion is formed from a myriad of private opin-ions, whether personal or group opinions. Such private opinions are often formed quite early in life, usually when people first become aware of political issues. They tend to be derived principally from family influence and personal experience, with the pressures from school, work, friends and neighbours all playing a part.

In the 1960s Butler and Stokes wrote an important book in which they demonstrated the strength of *family influence* as a factor in voting behaviour.[11] Although the growth of electoral volatility in the 1970s and 1980s indicated that its significance had declined, young people today still derive many of their attitudes and opinions from their parents and family influence remains one of the more constant factors in the development of every young generation. Of course, there have always been young people who reject the attitudes and opinions of their parents, either as part of a transient adolescent rebellion or as a function of economic and social mobility. Yet on the whole family influence still plays a major part in the formation of opinion.

As for the influence of *personal experience*, it is obvious that this has a significant impact upon the formation of individual opinions. Few people form their opinions on political issues on a basis of detached or altruistic ratiocination, since this is a luxury which is usually available only to those whose material circumstances and educational background allow them to adopt such a Platonic stance. For most people individual opinions are formed in the light of the fortune or misfortune which they experience during the course of their lives, whether at home, at work or at leisure. Indeed, it has been argued that it is the formative experience of young adults which has the most lasting influence upon their opinions later in life. This is known as '*the cohort theory*' of opinion formation and it certainly seemed to fit those who came of age in 1945 as well as those who did so in the late 1950s. Some would argue that the theory is still valid, notably in the tendency during the late 1980s and early 1990s for those in their twenties and thirties to reject old-style Socialism and accept many of the tenets of Thatcherite Conservatism. A cautious conclusion must be that formative experience remains important as an influence upon the formation of opinion, but that the pace and scale of economic and social change in the modern world has generated much greater volatility than in the past.

Issues and images

Opinions are also formed by individual responses to political issues and party images. Traditionally the psephological evidence seemed to suggest that people tend to reconcile their political opinions with their party allegiances, rather than the other way around. In the 1950s and 1960s neither policy nor ideology seemed to mean very much to the average British citizen whose political opinions and voting behaviour appeared to be largely unaffected by such considerations. Yet evidence drawn from the 1970s and 1980s suggests that *political issues* do have an impact upon the formation of public opinion and hence upon voting behaviour. For example, Ivor Crewe concluded that 'it was issues, not organisation or personalities, that won the (1979) election for the Conservatives'.[12] Indeed even those who voted Labour on that occasion often preferred Conservative policies, although evidently not enough to persuade them to align their votes with their policy preferences. For much of the 1980s the nature and extent of trade union power was one of the major issues in the political debate and on the whole its salience worked in favour of the Conservatives who were seen to adopt a consistently tougher stance in relation to the trade unions. The same might be said of the issue of nuclear weapons on which the Labour leadership had, perhaps reluctantly, to concede points to the Conservative position.

Yet, in considering the influence of political issues upon opinion, we need to distinguish between the bread-and-butter issues of daily life (such as inflation, jobs, health, or pensions) upon which most people have strongly held views which influence their voting behaviour, and the more esoteric issues of policy (for example, the control of money supply or theories of nuclear deterrence) upon which some people hold opinions, but which tend not to interest the vast majority. In considering the influence of issues in the latter category, it is as well not to exaggerate the authenticity or originality of the views held by the general public.

Among the more ephemeral considerations which influence the formation of public opinion, *the images* of the parties and especially of their leaders constitute another important factor in modern political conditions. For example, for decades the Conservative Party managed to preserve an image of competence in Government which led many people to support it even when it might not have appeared particularly warm or sympathetic to most of the general public. Several of its leaders – such as Winston Churchill, Harold Macmillan, and Margaret Thatcher – were respected and even occasionally revered for their achievements in office, although they did not necessarily engender feelings of warmth or affection in the hearts and minds of many people. In the mid- and late 1980s, the party's reputation for competence in Government was tarnished by the 1986 Westland Affair, the unwelcome surge in inflation and interest rates, and by the introduction of the Poll Tax. Similarly, under the much criticised leadership of John Major the party's reputation for competence suffered further damage, particularly during the passage of the legislation to align UK law with the 1992 Maastricht Treaty and, more especially, when Britain was forced to leave the European Exchange Rate Mechanism of the European Monetary System in September 1992.

On the other hand, the Labour Party has traditionally had an image of understanding and concern for ordinary people which has helped it to retain the voting loyalties of a large part of the electorate. This achievement was partly a reflection of the positive personal image of several of its leaders – such as Clement Attlee, Hugh Gaitskell, and Harold Wilson – but mainly a tribute to the image of the Party as the Parliamentary vanguard of the entire Labour movement at a time when the latter had authenticity, fraternity and solidarity. From the middle 1970s, however, Labour had more trouble with its image, particularly during the brief period of Michael Foot's leadership in the early 1980s, and it required all the media and presentational skills of Labour image-makers to attempt to recreate and present a positive, modern image for the party. They did so with considerable success, to the extent that by the middle 1990s, under the leadership of Tony Blair, the party appeared new, responsible and distinctly electable.

Notwithstanding the wonders that the image-makers and spin-doctors can perform, it should be borne in mind that it is the performance and credibility of the Government of the day – any Government – which is likely to be decisive in the battle for the hearts and minds of the British people and which mainly determines the outcome of General Elections. In Britain, as in other countries, Governments tend to lose elections rather than Opposition parties to win them.

The power of the media

As we saw in Chapter 7, perhaps the most influential factor in the formation of public opinion in Britain today is the power of the media to reflect, explain or distort the most important political issues and personalities at any time. For example, during the 1980s and into the 1990s most of the tabloid press conducted a ruthless and single-minded campaign to portray the Labour Party as completely beholden to the trade unions and the trade unions as stereotypically mindless and militant. Such a campaign would not have been remotely credible to the general public if certain trade union leaders – for example, Arthur Scargill of the NUM – had not played into the hands of the newspaper proprietors by behaving in a manner which might have been calculated to lend credence to their caricatures. Yet undeniably the public's image of the so-called 'loony Left', whether identified with some of the trade unions or some of the town halls up and down the country, was heavily influenced, even determined, by the columns and pictures in *The Sun*, the *News of the World*, *The Mail on Sunday*, the *Daily Express* and other such newspapers. Conversely these same newspapers and others like them consistently indulged in sycophancy towards Margaret Thatcher in a crude and sustained attempt, one must suppose, to keep the Conservatives in office. By contrast, following the 1992 General Election most of these same newspapers turned viciously against John Major, criticising him mercilessly for what they alleged were his failures of leadership. If the Conservatives lose the 1996/7 General Election, historians will doubtless attribute the outcome at least in part to this improbable switch by the so-called 'Tory press' into the camp of Tony Blair and 'new' Labour.

As for radio and television, the part which these broadcast media play in the formation of public opinion is generally agreed to be more insidious, even manipulative. It consists essentially of helping to set the political agenda by influencing the relative salience of different political issues as they waft in and out of the public's consciousness. It is not so much that influential programmes, like *Today, Panorama* or *News at Ten*, consciously set out to tell the general public what to think about a given politician or political issue; but rather that they set the framework of values, assumptions and information within which the public has to try to make up its own mind. In a world in which real public interest in politics is desultory and attention spans are alarmingly short, this form of media influence is obviously both ephemeral and unpredictable. Indeed it may well be that the influence of the media is greater via mass entertainment programmes, such as *Eastenders, Brookside, Coronation Street* or *The Archers*, than it is via the more serious programmes which are specifically designed to inform and educate the public. In any event we cannot review the various factors which influence the formation of public opinion in Britain today without laying great stress upon the role of the mass media.

8.2 The sources of opinion

Public opinion is an amorphous and infinitely malleable concept. Like information on the electronic superhighway, it will pass on by without being picked up unless the proper receiving apparatus is available, switched on and tuned in. The opinions of the public are communicated to politicians in a variety of ways, although it is perhaps more accurate to say that politicians *perceive* public opinion from a number of different sources. Ten can be identified: General Elections, by-elections, European and local elections, referenda, opinion polls, surveys and enquiries, direct contact with the public, organised groups, political parties and the media, and it is important to look at each of these in turn.

General Elections

Political leaders are continually conscious of the fact that their performance is constantly subjected to evaluation by the public. They are also acutely aware that the decision about whether or not they hold office ultimately depends upon the judgement of the public as expressed at a General Election. The significance of this was witnessed in the political demise of Margaret Thatcher and the rise of John Major, when a party in Government deposed one leader and chose another in order that it should remain – or at least have a better chance of remaining – the party of Government. Just as Harold Macmillan replaced Anthony Eden in 1957 when the party believed that it was staring defeat in the face, so too John Major replaced Margaret Thatcher in 1990.[13] For politicians, nothing concentrates the mind more than the prospect of defeat at the next General Election. The victory of John Major in the July 1995 leadership election was further evidence of this fact.

Also important in this context is the theory of the 'mandate'. The idea here is that at the time of a General Election each political party publishes its programme – its Manifesto – outlining in general terms what it proposes to do and what policies it will pursue, if it were to form the Government. The assumption is that the voters will read the various Manifestos and will make up their minds on how to cast their votes accordingly, based upon their assessment of and support for the policies outlined. This process is then presumed to grant to the newly elected Government the seal of public approval to implement the policies concerned – the public gives a mandate to the Government to act as it said it would do.

In the past there have been instances of General Elections being called specially so that the Government of the day might obtain an electoral mandate on a particular issue. For example, in the two elections of 1910 the Liberal Government under H. H. Asquith sought the backing of the electorate for its 1909 Budget and plans to limit the powers of the House of Lords.[14] Similarly, in 1923 Stanley Baldwin sought to appeal to the people quite specifically for a mandate on the introduction of tariff protection.[15] In October 1931 the National Government, which had come into being in August, went to the country seeking what was described at the time as 'a doctor's mandate', in order to deal with the economic crisis from a position of strength, namely with the support of the public behind it.[16] More recently, in February 1974, Edward Heath, in the midst of an industrial confrontation with the NUM (National Union of Mineworkers), dissolved Parliament more than one year before he needed to in order to secure a new mandate to strengthen the Government's hand in dealing with the industrial conflict and the wider consequences of the 1973-74 world oil crisis.[17]

A problem arises with regard to the concept of the mandate, however, if it is taken to its logical conclusion, namely that a Government can only introduce measures that have previously been placed before the electorate. It is for this reason that Governments have tended to show a rather more wide-ranging understanding of what is entailed, namely that the role of the electorate is to choose the Government not the Government's policies. Hence a Government obtains a general mandate to govern for a maximum period of time (limited to five years by the 1911 Parliament Act) and is less committed to specific policies. As a consequence the doctrine of the mandate cannot be applied too literally or without qualification to allow for changing economic and political circumstances.

In addition it is anyway necessary to question the very basis of the theory, for although the parties lay their policy proposals before the electorate, the extent to which the public studies them, let alone understands them, is doubtful. Besides which, voters are not able to pick and choose, save between parties: Manifestos are set menus; the public cannot vote *à la carte*.

Finally, there is the matter of the ability of the electoral system itself to reflect accurately the wishes of the voters. For example, in the 1951 General Election more people voted Labour than voted Conservative, yet the result produced a Conservative Government. Similarly, in the General Election of February 1974, more people voted Conservative than voted Labour, but the result brought the Labour Party to power. More particularly, no Government since 1935 has secured a majority of the *popular* vote and yet, with only one exception (February 1974), every Government has been backed by a majority in the House of Commons. These matters have been dealt with fully in Chapter 3, so it is not necessary to repeat the arguments here, except to say that, for a variety of reasons, British elections may not produce results which reflect the wishes of the public – indeed the reverse is possible.

By-elections

If in the period between General Elections a Member of Parliament either dies or resigns, a new election – known as a by-election – is held in order to fill the resulting vacancy. By-elections have become ways in which the popularity, or otherwise, of the Government of the day is put to the test, they are fought on national issues and their results are often interpreted as reflecting public opinion as a whole. This is so even though most individual constituencies are far from perfect samples of the country at large, the number of people casting a vote is likely to be no more than 45-55,000, there may be particular factors involved with regard to one or other of the candidates, and there may be issues specific to the area concerned which affect the way people vote. Whether or not by-elections are an accurate reflection of public opinion, politicians certainly take them seriously. For example, in October 1933 a by-election occurred in East Fulham. It was a seat that had been held by the Conservatives in 1931 with a majority of 14,521; it was captured by the Labour candidate on a disarmament platform with a majority of 4840, a massive switch of votes in just two years. The Prime Minister, Stanley Baldwin, took the result as evidence of a pacifist wave sweeping the country and it subsequently influenced his whole approach to the issue of rearmament.[18] Similarly, the Orpington by-election in March 1962 –which saw a Conservative majority over Labour of 14,760 turned into a Liberal majority of 7855 – provided a shock to the then Prime Minister, Harold Macmillan. When on 12 July 1962 the Conservatives were beaten into third place at a subsequent by-election in North-East Leicester, Harold Macmillan responded by carrying through a very extensive Cabinet reshuffle – the so-called 'night of the long knives' in which he dismissed a third of his Cabinet.[19]

On the other hand, there is the case of the Hull North by-election which took place early in 1966. This produced an increased majority for the Labour Party and was undoubtedly an important factor in persuading the Prime Minister, Harold Wilson, to call a General Election – the result of which was the return of the Government with a considerably enhanced majority. Two more examples will suffice. Firstly, the Beaconsfield by-election in May 1982. Although this took place following a series of sensational by-election victories by the Liberals and Social Democrats, the Conservatives held the seat with ease thanks largely to the patriotic surge of support for the governing party associated with its decision at that time to send a British Task Force to the Falkland Islands following the Argentinian invasion in April 1982. Finally, there was the Ribble Valley by-election in March 1991, when a Conservative majority of 19,528 was turned into a Liberal Democrat majority of 4601, although the seat had been the Conservative Party's tenth safest. Described at the time by the victorious candidate as 'the Poll-Tax by-election', it was seen by many as a referendum on the issue. This strengthened the hand of those within the Government who were seeking an alternative to the Poll Tax, enabling them finally to grasp one of the nettles that had so damaged Margaret Thatcher. As a result, the Cabinet agreed the following month to replace the Poll Tax with a new Council Tax which turned out to be a more acceptable alternative.[20]

European and local elections

Just as the results of by-elections are seen as snap-shots of public opinion, so too are the results of European and local elections which often tend to be fought on national issues with the popularity of the national Government of the day being judged in the process. For example, the campaign for the local elections of May 1990 was widely portrayed as being a referendum on the performance of the Conservative Government in general and Margaret Thatcher in particular. In the event, the results were cleverly presented by Kenneth Baker, then Conservative Party Chairman, as nothing like as bad as expected in view of the fact that the party's overall losses were actually less than predicted and the Conservatives had managed to retain control of two of their 'flagship Councils', Wandsworth and Westminster. In this case the Conservative Party may have lost the electoral battle, but it won the propaganda war and the immediate effect was to reduce the pressure on Margaret Thatcher's leadership, at least for a time.

Similarly, the elections to the European Parliament in June 1994 came after a series of electoral setbacks for the Conservative Party – the loss of the Newbury and Christchurch by-elections to the Liberal Democrats in May and July 1993 and widespread losses to the Liberal Democrats in the May 1993 and May 1994 local elections – all of which put considerable pressure on the leadership of the Prime Minister, John Major. The expectation in some quarters was of electoral annihilation for the Conservatives and widespread gains by the Liberal Democrats. As things turned out, however, the results were not as bad as originally feared, not least because the Liberal Democrats did not make widespread gains. The immediate conclusion of many Conservative MPs was that they could breathe more easily and, as a result, back-bench pressure on John Major was temporarily reduced.

Referenda

Britain has only had one *national* referendum since the war. It was held in June 1975 on the issue of whether or not the country should remain in the European Economic Community, and produced, on a turnout of 65 per cent, a majority of almost two to one in favour of Britain's continued membership of the EEC.[21] There have however been three *regional* referenda – one in Northern Ireland in 1973 and one each in Scotland and Wales in 1979. The Northern Ireland referendum was on the question: 'Do you want Northern Ireland to remain part of the United Kingdom?' Over 600,000 people voted, with about 58 per cent of the whole electorate casting its votes in the affirmative.[22]

The referenda in Scotland and Wales were on whether or not to establish Assemblies with devolved powers in both Scotland and Wales. In Wales only 12 per cent of the electorate voted in favour, compared with 47 per cent who voted against. In Scotland 33 per cent of the electorate voted in favour and 31 per cent against. However, because the legislation had stipulated that at least 40 per cent of the electorate in each case would have to give its approval for the legislation to be implemented, the policy of devolution was not put into effect.[23]

The reasons for holding these referenda owed little or nothing to the idea that the people ought to be consulted because of the importance of the issues involved. Rather they were the result – in 1975 – of deep and irreconcilable divisions within the governing party and – in 1979 – of the Parliamentary circumstances in which a minority Labour Government was seeking to legislate on an issue which divided its own back-bench supporters. Similarly, the Northern Ireland referendum can only be understood in the light of the troubled and often tragic history of the Province.

While on the subject of referenda, it is also necessary to point out that just as elections are seen by some as distorting rather than reflecting public opinion, so the same point can be made about referenda, not least because of the difficulty of putting complex issues before the public for a simple 'Yes' or 'No' answer. There is also the traditional view that the use of referenda is contrary to the theory of British Parliamentary democracy. This is a matter to which we shall return later in the chapter.

Finally within this section it is necessary to include a brief account of a number of recent initiatives which have extended the principle of consultation through the use of local votes in a number of areas. For example, the *Housing Act, 1988*, provided for Council tenants to 'choose' a landlord by allowing them to vote to transfer to a Housing Association, trust or private landlord. Similarly, the *Education Act, 1989*, provided for schools to 'opt out' of Local Authority control via an affirmative vote amongst parents. Finally, the Conservative Government in the years since 1979 introduced a whole series of legislative measures of trade union reform, among which the *Trade Union Act, 1984*, stipulated that trade unions should hold secret ballots before taking industrial action.

Public opinion polls

Essentially, public opinion polls are a means by which an attempt is made to measure the attitudes, behaviour, beliefs, intentions and opinions of the public. Political opinion polls are primarily concerned with voting intentions and opinions relating to current issues and personalities. Their purpose is to enable conclusions to be drawn about the opinions and intentions of the public as a whole by analysing and presenting data drawn from small, though representative, samples. As a result they have emerged as a means by which the incoherent opinions of the public are formulated and then communicated to those active in the political process.

Opinion polls have undoubtedly contributed to Government action or inaction in some cases. For example, they were a significant factor in the debate concerning abortion law reform in the mid-1960s. A series of opinion polls was commissioned by the Abortion Law Reform Association and the findings were used to demonstrate to the Government and to Parliament that public opinion was on the side of reform. Similarly, it is apparent that Government activity in important areas of policy has been influenced by opinion polls. For example, opinion poll findings which demonstrated the great unpopularity of the Poll Tax were influential in persuading the Conservative Government under Margaret Thatcher to modify the impact of the tax in ways designed to reduce its adverse impact.[24]

Overall it can be said that although politicians pay close attention to opinion polls, the action which they take is not necessarily based upon them. The clearest case in which public opinion as revealed by opinion polls has been conspicuously and continuously ignored is on the issue of capital punishment. To begin with, in 1965 the death penalty was abolished provisionally for a five-year period by a free vote in the House of Commons – a decision taken in the face of considerable public opposition evidenced by over-whelming opinion poll majorities of 80 per cent or more in favour of its retention.[25] Despite the fact that every poll taken since that time has also revealed a large majority of the population in favour of restoring the death penalty, Parliament has repeatedly and clearly voted against such a step. A different example can be drawn from the sphere of European policy. Parliament voted against the holding of a referendum on the ratifica-tion of the Maastricht Treaty despite public opinion poll evidence that a large majority of the public were in favour of such a step.[26]

Surveys and enquiries

At the turn of the century a number of social enquiries into living conditions which involved extensive house-to-house surveys – such as Charles Booth's *Life and Labour of the People of London* (1897) and Seebohm Rowntree's *Poverty: a study of town life* – had a significant impact upon the climate of political opinion at the time and provid-ed much factual support for the drive towards social reform and public welfare. More recently, Lord Scarman's *Report into the Brixton Disorders of 10-12 April 1981* owed a lot to the oral evidence provided by more than fifty witnesses including police officers, journalists, members of the emergency services and residents of the area who had wit-nessed the course of events, as well as written evidence from 284 organisations and indi-viduals and some 450 letters from members of the public.[27] Described by the *Daily Mirror* as 'one of the great social documents of our time', it influenced the subsequent political debate on the inner cities, the police and the ethnic minorities. The same could be said of the Report of the Archbishop of Canterbury's Commission on Urban Priority Areas (*Faith in the City*, 1985), which drew extensively upon evidence taken by the Commission all over the country.[28]

As the range of Government activity has become greater and the role of Government correspondingly larger, so the requirement for information has grown, both to estimate social needs and to monitor the effects of Government action. Fundamental to this process is the Census carried out every 10 years, the most recent in 1991. In addition, the Office of Population Censuses and Surveys carries out surveys and research on a regular and continuing basis which provides essential factual information for policy makers in Government. The Family Expenditure Survey and the International Passenger Survey are both examples of this work. Individual Government Departments are also involved in gathering data. For example, the Department of Transport's Cross Channel Passenger and Freight Traffic Report of 1992 was an extensive and detailed analysis of people who cross the English Channel.[29] We should also mention in this context the public opinion research done for large-scale planning Inquiries, such as those which examined proposals for a Third London Airport, the Sizewell B nuclear power station, and the Channel Tunnel Rail

Link. All of these investigations were intended to contribute to the quality of policy making.

Direct contacts between MPs and the public

There are a variety of opportunities available to Members of Parliament directly to ascertain the views of the public. *Firstly*, there are the letters which MPs receive both from their constituents and more widely from the general public. A typical MP now receives more than 150 letters a week, receiving in one day the amount of correspondence which would have been received in one week in the 1960s. Sir Robert Rhodes James, MP for Cambridge between 1976 and 1992, calculated that he received and replied to 249,000 letters from his constituents, an average of 300 letters a week, and that answering them sometimes took three hours a day.[30] *Secondly*, Members of Parliament are lobbied with increasing frequency by sometimes very large delegations which turn up at the Palace of Westminster demanding to see their MP (or indeed any MP) and put their case. *Thirdly*, nearly all MPs now hold what are described as 'Surgeries' or 'Advice Bureaux' in their constituencies either once a week or twice a month. These provide yet another source of information on public feelings, although because of their self-selecting characteristics, such aggrieved constituents may not be representative of the broader swathe of public opinion.

Organised groups

Pressure groups have been covered in Chapter 6, so it is sufficient here simply to point out that individuals can join with others of a like mind in an attempt to get a particular opinion or set of opinions across to politicians of all parties and to the Government of the day and by so doing seek to secure political action consistent with those opinions.

Political parties

Political parties were covered in Chapter 5, so we need merely point out here that individuals can join the political party whose broad ideological approach most closely matches their own and then work within its structures in an attempt to influence party policy as it emerges.

The media

Although the subject of the media has been covered in Chapter 7, it is nonetheless necessary briefly to mention two matters in this chapter. *Firstly*, there is the issue of the extent to which the media truly reflects public opinion. Certainly members of the public have access to the media via, for example, the letters pages of newspapers and magazines, radio phone-in programmes and public participation programmes on television. Yet all of this is only a tiny proportion of total media output and may not reflect much more than the views of those who push themselves forward. *Secondly*, there is the issue of the extent to which the media are simply acting as neutral channels of communication between the Government and the governed, or rather are seeking to lead, form, mould and even distort public opinion. On this last point it is argued by some that the only reality is that created by the media, since it is the media which assess what the people think and want and then relay the results to others. However, others (especially those actively engaged in politics) contend that reality is often very different from what the media choose to convey at any time and that all politicians labour under the burden of media distortions and consequently public misconceptions. The simple conclusion must be that both sides of this argument have valid points and that wisdom consists in eschewing dogmatic or permanent conclusions.

8.3 The effects of opinion

More deferential politicians

Public opinion in Britain has a variety of political effects. It is arguable that one effect has been to make most politicians more deferential to the wishes of the electorate. While this tendency may seem to have reached its zenith in the time of Harold Wilson, who as Leader of the Labour Party (1963-76) paid assiduous attention to opinion polls and other psephological data (such as by-election and local election results), it has remained significant at all times in post-war politics, especially when General Elections are imminent. Certainly it has been true in the negative sense that leading politicians both in and out of office usually take considerable care not to put forward policies or take positions which seem destined to encounter powerful opposition from public opinion. Even the redoubtable Margaret Thatcher, who more than any other leader sought to do what she believed to be right regardless of the political consequences, adjusted Conservative policy on some occasions in order to take account of the public responses which might have been expected if she and her Ministerial colleagues had pressed ahead with certain radical policies in an unaltered form.[31]

This draws our attention to the elusive and controversial concept of '*political impossibility*' which has played such an important part in so many political calculations by leading politicians over the years. In essence it can be defined as the influence upon political decision-makers of anticipated public reaction. Some have argued that this is a harmful influence upon politics, since it can prevent the adoption of radical policies which may be justified as an appropriate response to many of Britain's deep-seated national problems. Others have argued that it is a beneficial influence, since it can be seen as a contribution to British national cohesion, especially during difficult periods of disappointment and relative decline when a less sensitive political approach could prove very damaging. The argument is really between those who regard the conservatism of British public opinion as something of a saving grace, since it constitutes a significant obstacle to the ambitions of the zealots in each main party, and those who see it as a tragedy, since it has often constituted a virtually insuperable barrier to radical action. If the overriding priority is to guard against radical change, then the former view ought to be commended; if it is to make radical change, then the latter view ought to prevail. In any event the outcome is likely to depend upon the personal temperament of the leading politicians who have to carry the responsibility of Government.

Under Margaret Thatcher's leadership in the 1980s the Conservative Government tended to press for what it believed to be right almost regardless of the immediate political consequences. Under John Major's leadership in the 1990s the approach has been much less ideological and more pragmatic in a way strangely reminiscent of Harold

Wilson's period as Prime Minister. John Major's supporters have justified his pragmatism on two principal grounds. Firstly, he was elected leader of his party in 1990 precisely because he was not Margaret Thatcher, and secondly, he has had to give his highest priority to holding his party together – something which was made that much more difficult after the 1992 General Election when the Conservative majority in the Commons was reduced to a small fraction of the majority that Margaret Thatcher had enjoyed.

A counterweight to pressure groups

Another important effect of public opinion has been the way in which it has provided a useful counterweight to the influence of pressure groups in the British political system. As we noted in Chapter 6, there have been times when it has become very difficult for any Government to resist the claims of certain powerful interest groups, such as the National Union of Mineworkers in the 1970s or the British Medical Association in the late 1980s, without appealing over the heads of the group concerned to the general public. This is essentially what Edward Heath sought to do when he called a General Election in February 1974 on the issue of 'who governs?' It is also what the 1979-83 Conservative Government sought to do when it introduced legislation to provide for secret ballots in trade unions affairs. In each case the intention of Ministers was to appeal over the heads of obstructive interest groups to the wider public in an effort to fulfil their political purposes. Of course, the success of this tactic depends upon the power of the opposing interest group and the degree of public sympathy or support which it can generate for its cause. For example, the NUT's campaign against the Conservative Government's attempts to introduce national curriculum assessment in the early 1990s depended upon the credibility of its propaganda, the willingness of its members to remain solidly behind the union line and the sympathy of parents.

Whenever politicians of the Right or Left invoke the views of the wider public in support of their cause, it is usually a sign that they have been obstructed or opposed by a small but powerful group which seeks to set its sectional interest above that of the general community. This has been as true when Labour Ministers have complained about the pernicious influence of the City of London as when Conservative Ministers have criticised the abuse of trade union power. In each case they have sought to defend the principle that general public opinion has more inherent legitimacy than any sectional group. On the whole it is hard to oppose this principle, since general public opinion has a sounder and more altruistic record than sectional groups on most political issues. Yet every political system also needs safeguards against the tyranny of the majority (or even of a minority of the electorate exploiting a Parliamentary majority), since in most societies there have been times when majority opinion has been unfair or unenlightened and temporarily defeated minorities have needed protection against it. Thus a balance has to be struck which allows fair opportunities for both majority and minority opinion, while retaining a democratic presumption in favour of the former.

The influence of opinion polls

Yet another effect of public opinion has been to give political opinion polls an influence out of all proportion to their true value. Such polls have become the most systematic expression of public opinion between General Elections. When sensibly interpreted, they can provide a useful navigational aid for politicians, whether in Government or Opposition. The systematic analysis of opinion poll data has enabled the parties to identify key target groups of voters – for instance, the wives of blue collar workers in the case of the Conservative Party or the public sector salariat in the case of the Labour Party – and then to concentrate and organise their efforts with particular target groups in mind. Opinion polls also guide the Prime Minister of the day in making the decision about when to call a General Election and they can affect the morale of party activists if the findings are either very good or very bad for a particular party or its leader.[32] While opinion polls are not normally used to determine policy or decision making, it is understandable that they should influence both the development and the presentation of policy. On the other hand, there is a widely held view among practising politicians that both local and European elections (but not usually Parliamentary by-elections) are a better guide to the public mood, if not necessarily an infallible indicator of voting behaviour at a future General Election.

Special considerations apply to the role of opinion polls during election campaigns. Some experts have argued that the polls produce a bandwagon effect which assists the party that seems to be on a winning streak. Others have argued for the backlash effect which leads doubting voters to rally to the party that appears to be the underdog. One thing seems certain, however, and that is that opinion polls can have a much more powerful effect upon the actual result at by-elections than at General Elections, since on such occasions they signal to the local electorate which is the best vehicle for effective tactical voting and, as a result, political protest. This was certainly evident during the Bermondsey by-election in 1983, the Greenwich by-election in 1987 and the Glasgow Govan by-election in 1988.[33]

The use of referenda

Still another effect of public opinion is visible in the way in which the growing self-confidence and declining deference of the general public has led to periodic demands for national referenda. These demands have arisen on a variety of political issues, notably those which demonstrate that Parliamentary opinion is out of tune with public opinion, for example on the emotive issue of capital punishment. Of course, national referenda have certainly not been a defining characteristic of the constitutional arrangements in Britain and most MPs in all parties have been determined to see that this remains the position. Yet there is always a temptation for political demagogues or other publicity seekers to break ranks with their colleagues in Parliament by calling for national referenda on certain issues when they believe that the results of a plebiscite would be in their favour, as Margaret Thatcher and others did by campaigning for a referendum on British ratification of the 1992 Maastricht Treaty.

The important and much publicised referenda on Britain's membership of the European Community in 1975 and on devolution to Scotland and Wales in 1979 are still generally considered to have been exceptions which prove the rule. The publicly stated reason for holding referenda in these special cases was that they were conducted on constitutional issues of great importance in which the very future of Parliament itself was involved. However, this would not explain why there was no such referendum on the issue of the ratification of the Maastricht Treaty, an issue which undoubtedly presaged major constitutional change. Rather, the actual reasons for holding referenda in 1975 and 1979 owe more to the intra-party political and Parliamentary circumstances of the times. They were clearly exceptions to the general rule that Britain is a Parliamentary rather than a plebiscitary democracy. On the other hand, it is possible that, as such precedents have been set, it may prove increasingly difficult for Members of Parliament to resist future demands for referenda on a wide range of political issues, especially when a majority in the House of Commons is seen to be out of tune with the overwhelming opinion of the general public, when public feelings are running high, or when powerful cause groups become involved.[34]

The impact of direct action

Finally, we should not neglect the impact of direct action as a powerful form of non-verbal and non-literate political communication. We should note the fact that at various stages in British history public protest, whether spontaneous or induced, has played an important, sometimes decisive, part in the expression of public opinion. We need only instance Wat Tyler and the Peasants' Revolt in 1381, the Peterloo Massacre in 1819, the Chartist Movement in the 1840s, the Suffragette demonstrations in the early 1900s, the Invergordon 'mutiny' in 1931, and the Jarrow and other unemployment marches in the 1930s. More recent examples of the power of direct action would include the inner city riots in the summer of 1981, the miners' dispute of 1984-85, the Greenham Common demonstration against American cruise missiles in the mid-1980s, the campaign of civil disobedience against the Poll Tax in the late 1980s, the demonstrations against the actions of the Child Support Agency in 1993-94, and the activity of Animal Welfare protesters against the live animal export trade in 1994-95.

Nowadays lawful public demonstrations are usually organised for publicity purposes by minorities who feel strongly about an issue, but who also feel excluded from the regular channels of influence and representation in society. The fact that some people have recourse to such methods may cast doubt upon the validity of their arguments, but more often it reflects their assessment of the chances of attaining their objectives by more orthodox institutional means, such as Parliamentary pressure or official contacts in Whitehall. For example, those who believed in the merits of unilateral nuclear disarmament chose to squat outside the Greenham Common air base or to march in large processions through London, since they did not believe that the more conventional means of putting their case would have had any impact upon the decision-makers. Similarly the Muslim demonstrations in London, Bradford and other cities against Salman Rushdie and his 'blasphemous' novel *The Satanic Verses* illustrated the anger and frustration of the minority Muslim community at the apparent inability of Parliament to respond to their deeply felt concern. Public demonstrations of this kind have always been a recognised way of seeking publicity for a grievance or support for a cause, and most are conducted in a peaceful and law-abiding manner. Yet they do not always succeed in influencing political decisions in their chosen direction, since the impact upon the general public is often adverse and occasionally counterproductive.

8.4 Public opinion in context

The question has often been asked about the circumstances in which politicians should follow, lead, educate, cajole or simply ignore public opinion. The issue is certainly not new. Edmund Burke writing to his constituents in 1774 stated what is the classic case for representatives arriving at their own judgements, completely independent of what their constituents' views might be. His view was that: 'Your representative owes to you not his industry only, but his judgement; and he betrays, instead of serving you, if he sacrifices it to your opinion.'[35] It is this approach, this reasoning, which has been cited by MPs over the years when refusing to bow to the demands of public opinion for the restoration of capital punishment, for example.

The traditional position in Britain is simply stated, namely that the public are expected at a General Election to choose the party which they wish to see in Government through until the next General Election, not to assume responsibility themselves for any part of the governmental process once it is in operation. As one quality newspaper put it in 1992, 'it is the job of Members of Parliament to understand and decide on issues after open debate and with due regard for the opinions of the voters'.[36]

The alternative view is one derived from the philosophy of Jean-Jacques Rousseau who declared that: 'the deputies of the people are not and cannot be their representatives, they can only be their commissioners, and as such they are not qualified to conclude anything definitely. No act of theirs can be a law, unless it has been ratified by the people in person; and without their ratification nothing is a law.'[37] This view (often described as 'direct democracy') has never gained much support in Britain, not least because it clearly conflicts with the concept of Parliamentary supremacy. Yet it seems likely to gain ground in the future given that British society is less deferential to its leaders and already appears less prepared to give the benefit of the doubt to the indirect democracy represented by Parliament at Westminster.

Traditional discussion of the part that public opinion ought to play in the formation of public policy tends to assume that members of the public have valid opinions to communicate. Such an assumption, however, is not necessarily borne out by experience. It should also be recognised that the relationship between public opinion and decision-making is two-way with the flow of influence rarely, if ever, running smoothly from the former to the latter. Indeed, no simple causal relationship is apparent. Public opinion never moves in a single direction without setting up contradictory and countervailing forces. Nor does it exist in a vacuum. Rather it is an integral and inseparable part of any political system, even when suppressed in an authoritarian system.

It follows that the correspondence between public opinion and political action tends not to be exact or immediate. Public opinion – in the sense of a viewpoint widely held – is only likely to have an effect, whether positive or negative, if channeled or exploited by politicians, pressure groups or the media. It is more often a factor of constraint, setting limits to what the public accepts in a pluralist society rather than providing new opportunities for action by decision-makers or opinion-formers. Indeed, all Governments have to make calculations when deciding upon their courses of action (or inaction), as to whether or not the public will wear it. In this sense the art of governing in a Parliamentary democracy is the ability to calculate when too many people will say 'no', but before they have an opportunity to do so.

Consensus and controversy

There has been both consensus and controversy in British politics since the war. Generally, Government has relied to a very great extent upon at least the tacit acquiescence, if not the positive consent, of the various groups and interests with which they have to deal, and on the whole they have preferred discussion, compromise and agreement to the imposition of policy on unwilling institutions, groups and interests.

The 1945-51 Labour Government under Clement Attlee established the post-war consensus under which Britain was governed for more than a quarter of a century thereafter. There were six main elements in this consensus: (1) a mixed economy with extensive state intervention, including a large industrial public sector; (2) a commitment to maintain full employment; (3) an extensive welfare state – with provisions 'from the cradle to the grave'; (4) progressive taxation with high marginal rates in order to pay for public expenditure; (5) acceptance of the trade unions as legitimate economic and social partners in the process of government; (6) a belief that Government should pay at least lip service to a fairer and more equal society. In short, there was a belief in activist Government; a belief that it was the function of Government to find solutions to problems, whenever and wherever they arose.

Although this consensus was either modified or extended by successive Governments of both parties, there was no substantial or sustained challenge to it until the mid-1970s.[38] In these circumstances the political argument was largely confined to disputes about the best way to manage the mixed economy and to distribute the fruits of economic growth. Admittedly, there were some deep divisions of opinion about some issues, notably in the sphere of foreign policy. For example, the Suez expedition in 1956, the process of decolonisation in the late 1950s and early 1960s, and Britain's relationship with the European Community all caused serious dissension between and within the main parties. Yet such arguments took place against a background of basic agreement upon many other issues of fundamental importance.

This particular view of the world was challenged during the latter part of the 1960s and finally defeated in the mid-1970s. There were a number of powerful reasons for this. *Firstly*, inflation began to soar in the mid-1970s as a consequence of the quadrupling of the price of oil in the world energy crisis of that time. *Secondly*, as the recession went deeper, the economy began to contract and the public finances plunged into debt. *Thirdly*, in the new climate of monetarism imposed by the IMF in 1976, Keynesian remedies came to seem as part of the problem rather than the solution. *Fourthly*, first the Labour Government and then the Conservative Government after 1979 were faced with the problems of managing, or even lowering, public expectations in the light of the new realities. In such circumstances it was not surprising that the post-war consensus came to an end. The Labour Party moved to the Left and the Conservative Party to the Right, thus producing a degree of political polarisation in the early 1980s which had not been seen in Britain since the 1930s. Margaret Thatcher and her political supporters in the Conservative Party, matched by the so-called 'hard Left' in the Labour Party, were the outward and visible manifestations of this period of political polarisation.

From 1979 to 1990 the three successive Thatcher Administrations effectively demolished much of the post-war economic, social and political order. As Norman Tebbit, one of Margaret Thatcher's political allies, explained at the time: 'our task is to establish the new political consensus within which our opponents, too, must work'.[39] The commitment to full employment was abandoned, the battle against inflation was given priority, the role and responsibilities of the state were deliberately reduced, and the power of the trade unions was curbed. In the process public attitudes and perceptions were changed, leading to a greater sense of economic realism, more respect for market forces and greater acceptance that people should not look to Government for solutions to every problem. By the end of the 1980s the result was the establishment of a new 'common ground', one with which the Government's opponents were obliged to come to terms. Among the political casualties were the Labour Party, which lost a considerable part of its support to the newly formed 'Alliance' of Liberals and Social Democrats, and the so-called 'Wets' within the Conservative Party who had sought, but failed, to uphold the principles of the post-war consensus.

Now in the mid-1990s, the new Labour Party under the leadership of Tony Blair appears prepared to accept at least some of the tenets of the Thatcherite legacy, and seems quite likely to be returned to power in due course in recognition of the 'historic compromise' which it has made with its ideological opponents. However, nothing ever stands still in British politics, so we should not be surprised to notice that the new middle ground seems to be occupied by all three main parties which acknowledge the new, post-Thatcherite consensus. Its guiding principles seem to include a readiness to accept most of the implications of living in a market economy, off-set in Labour's case by an urge to intervene (at any rate at the European level) and to redistribute income and wealth via a 'fairer' tax and social security system; and in the Conservative case by a wish to regulate the liberalised economy no more than strictly necessary and to concentrate social provision principally upon those who really need it.

Informed opinion and mass opinion

Differences between Left and Right are not the only significant cleavages in British public opinion. There is also the important gulf which exists between informed opinion and mass opinion.

Informed opinion may be defined as opinion held by the minority of people who are 'in the know' about political issues and whose views are usually, but not always, the result of a recognisably rational process of thought. Typically it is the opinion of politicians at Westminster, civil servants in Whitehall, political journalists, pressure group spokesmen and those prominent in some other walks of life, such as public corporations, local government, medicine, education, the law, the church and the City. In view of the metropolitan character of British political opinion, it often derives disproportionately from interacting London elites, although it can also be influenced by ephemeral intellectual trends which often originate in the universities and in so-called 'think tanks', such as the Institute for Economic Affairs, the Institute for Public Policy Research, Demos, and the Social Market Foundation. It is therefore essentially the opinion of the current Establishment and its licensed critics.[40]

Mass opinion, on the other hand, is often little more than ignorant sentiment, although it is usually based upon significant attitudes, beliefs and ideas which are rooted in popular experience. This means that it has often to be conjured up before it can be said to exist. As V. O. Key observed, 'public opinion does not emerge like a cyclone and push obstacles before it; rather it develops under leadership'.[41] The extent of public ignorance about the basic facts of politics obviously contributes to this situation and has been a matter of record for some time. For example, in 1964 almost a quarter of a representative sample did not know that the coal industry had been nationalised for nearly 20 years. In 1971 another opinion poll showed that only 13 per cent of those questioned could name the six member states of the European Community at a time when the British

Government was engaged in widely publicised negotiations for British entry. In 1978 only 46 per cent of those questioned in a national poll could give the name of their MP and a poll in 1979 showed that 77 per cent of those questioned did not know what was meant by the acronym NATO – 30 years after the foundation of the North Atlantic Treaty Organisation.

The high level of public ignorance of the facts of politics has persisted ever since. For example, in June 1986 when presented in a Mori Poll with photographs of all the leading Conservative politicians, a representative sample of the public were 100 per cent correct only in their recognition of Margaret Thatcher, 66 per cent correct with Norman (later Lord) Tebbit, and 51 per cent correct with Sir Keith (later Lord) Joseph. Yet in all other cases less than half of the public correctly identified such senior figures as the Foreign Secretary, the Chancellor of the Exchequer, and the Home Secretary. Recognition of politicians was no better at local level, since a Gallup Poll in April 1988 showed that 44 per cent of a representative sample could could give neither the name nor the party affiliation of their local Councillor. As for the major issues of policy, a Gallup Poll in June 1988 showed that only 29 per cent of a representative sample knew what was meant by the much publicised date of '1992', while 15 per cent associated it incorrectly with the Poll Tax and 42 per cent confessed to having no idea at all. In an NOP survey in 1995 almost a third of under 35s questioned put their apathy about politics down to 'not knowing enough about it'.

Bearing in mind all the political communication which takes place, it is perhaps a little difficult to understand why such a degree of public ignorance and apathy has persisted. The explanation could be that those politicians and others who have something to say are not saying it with sufficient clarity or repetition. It could be that the channels of communication in the mass media are defective for this purpose. It could even be that the public is perfectly able to hear, but not really prepared to listen because of a widespread mood of cynicism and even alienation from the whole process of party politics. Simple observation would suggest that politicians and other opinion formers try hard to impart a great deal of fact and opinion to the general public, perhaps even too much for easy assimilation. It would also suggest that the media, and especially television, are more pervasive and influential than ever before. Yet it is equally clear that these factors do not necessarily produce a well-informed or enlightened public.

It is possible to identify several plausible reasons for this unsatisfactory state of affairs. It may be because the conduct of political argument on aggressive party lines is not the best way of explaining to the public many of the complicated issues raised in contemporary politics. It may also be because the imperatives of modern journalism and the fierce commercial competition in the media have discouraged editors and producers from giving sufficient coverage or adequate explanation of many difficult political issues. After all, the popular national newspapers are more noted for their coverage of sport, scandal and sex than for intelligent or subtle discussion of important political issues. Equally, the radio and television programme makers are more concerned to compete for a mass audience and to win the battle of the ratings than to provide much serious coverage of political news and views. As for the attitudes of the general public, anecdotal evidence suggests that most British people are largely uninterested in party politics, are suspicious of the apparent untrustworthiness of politicians, and feel cynical, even perhaps alienated, from the whole process whenever they do pay attention. If these understandable public reactions to the volume of information made available and the intractability of most of the problems are taken into account, it would seem to be more a case of a public which is not very keen to listen than of politicians and other opinion formers who are not trying to communicate.

In short, mass opinion on most political issues consists of a large component of ignorance, a considerable lack of interest, a high degree of cynicism, a certain amount of prejudice, an assortment of received ideas, a smattering of popular mythology, a dose of wishful thinking, and considerable rationalisation of personal experience. If this appears to be something of a caricature, then it must be said that there is not much evidence from opinion polls or other systematic sources to disprove it. It seems to be the political reality in Britain, and it will probably continue to be the case until such time as a more positive and less cynical political culture develops.

8.5 Conclusion

Governments are undoubtedly influenced by public opinion. However, the extent to which they choose to pay attention to public opinion depends upon how important a part they consider public opinion plays in the resolution of a particular issue.

The extent to which a Government follows public opinion will depend upon how it interprets the views of informed opinion. The opinions expressed from these quarters certainly carry considerably more weight than mass opinion. Besides which, it must always be remembered that public opinion is only one of the pressures and constraints operating upon Government in the highly complex world of policy and decision making. It is the task of the Government of the day to determine the relative importance of each factor. It is likely, for example, that the constraints imposed by the markets or by the international environment will have considerable influence upon national decisions in the modern world. Nonetheless, it is evident that all those involved in political decision making have to take full account of public opinion. Where they differ is over their definitions of public opinion, how it should be measured and assessed and the significance to be attached to what they find out. The fact that in many cases Governments have felt constrained to make decisions which are consistent with perceived public opinion at the time, is an indication of the importance of public opinion in the British political system.

The conclusion must be that public opinion in Britain influences, but is not necessarily a determinant of, what happens in British politics. The degree of its importance in any case depends mainly upon three factors: its *intensity*, its *durability* and its *specificity*. The more intense, durable, and specifically focused it is, the greater the degree of influence it is likely to have. Whatever shape it takes or force it demonstrates, public opinion in Britain can be regarded as a source of political legitimacy, a counterweight to the influence of pressure groups, a form of political intelligence and occasionally even a 'Court of Appeal' in matters of strong public concern or great importance. Yet its true value is limited by the fact that, in complex issues of national policy, it is usually not based upon sufficient knowledge or experience and is often more of a reflection than an inspiration for the positions taken by leading politicians and other opinion formers. It is undoubtedly a dynamic factor in the working of the British political system, since it involves a constant and continuous process of two-way communication between the politicians and the people.

Political leadership will always have a major part to play in the formation of public opinion. Yet, if such leadership is to be really effective, it will have to make itself felt beyond the limited confines of Whitehall and Westminster. Metropolitan elites will need to leave the corridors of power and make more frequent contact with the general public in all parts of the country. In any event all opinion-formers will need to have a clearer idea of what they want to say and how best to say it. The key people in the media will need to offer more political news and views and to present such material in balanced and responsible ways. Schools and other institutions of learning will need to put more emphasis upon political literacy in all its forms. Yet, even assuming a reasonable degree of success with all these endeavours, the politicians will still have to keep their fingers crossed and hope that the British people really want to play an active part in the nation's pluralist political process.

Suggested questions

1 How is public opinion formed and influenced in Britain?
2 What are the ways in which public opinion is brought to the attention of politicians in Britain?
3 What are the effects of public opinion upon British Government and politics?

Notes

1. B. Parekh (ed.), B*entham's Political Thought* (London: Croom Helm, 1973), p. 212
2. Quoted in A. H. Birch, *Representative and Responsible Government* (London: Allen and Unwin, 1964), p. 172.
3. Cited in A. Andrews: 'Quotations for Speakers and Writers' (London: Newnes Books, 1969), p. 376.
4. *Ibid*
5. *Ibid*.
6. *Ibid*
7. See A. V. Dicey, *Introduction to the study of the Law of the Constitution* (10th edn) (London: Macmillan, 1967), pp. 59. 60, 71-85.
8. See A. V. Dicey, *Law and Opinion in England in The Nineteenth Century* (London: Macmillan, 1905), p. 10.
9. V. O. Key, *Public Opinion and American Democracy* (New York: Knopf, 1961), p. 14.
10. R. Rose in R. Rose (ed.), *Studies in British Politics*, 3rd edn (London: Macmillan, 1976), p. 254.
11. See D. E. Butler and D. Stokes, *Political Change in Britain*, 2nd edn (London: Macmillan, 1974), pp. 19-151.
12. In H.R. Penniman (ed.), *Britain at the Polls*, 1979 (Washington, DC: American Enterprise Institute, 1981), p. 282.
13. See N. D. J. Baldwin, *The Conservative Party: an instinct to survive* (Barnstaple: Philip Charles Media, 1990).
14. See R. Jenkins, *Mr Balfour's Poodle* (London: Heinemann, 1954).
15. See K. Middlemass and J. Barnes, *Baldwin: a biography* (London: Weidenfeld & Nicolson, 1969).
16. Ibid
17. See J. Campbell, *Edward Heath: a biography* (London: Capes, 1993).
18. See I. Bulmer-Thomas, *The Growth of the British Party System* (Vol. II) (London: John Baker, 1965), pp. 103-104.

19. See A. H. Home, *Macmillan* (Vol. II) (London: Macmillan, 1984), pp. 331-351.
20. See J. Bruce-Gardyne, *Mrs Thatcher's First Administration* (London: Macmillan, 1984), pp. 113-114.
21. See D. Butler and U. Kitzinger, *The 1975 Referendum* (London: Macmillan, 1976).
22. See W. Whitelaw, *The Whitelaw Memories* (London: Aurum Press, 1989), pp. 108-109.
23. See V. Bogdanor, *The People and the Party System* (London: Cambridge University Press, 1981).
24. See M. Thatcher, *The Downing Street Years* (London: Harper Collins, 1993) pp. 642-667.
25. See F. Teer and J. D. Spence, *Political Opinion Polls* (London: Hutchinson, 1973), p. 138.
26. For example, a MORI poll of June 1993 showed 73 per cent of respondents in favour of a referendum as opposed to 18 per cent against and 9 per cent 'don't knows.
27. See *The Scarman Report* (London: HMSO, 1981).
28. See *Faith in the City: a call for action by Church and State* (London: Church House, 1985).
29. *Cross-Channel Passenger and Freight Traffic Report* (London: HMSO, 1992).
30. R. Rhodes-Jones, 'Politics in the postbag', in *The Times*, 22 October 1992.
31. For example, Mrs Thatcher and her ministerial colleagues deliberately postponed an all-out confrontation with Arthur Scargill and he National Union of Mineworkers until 1984 when all the relevant preparations for a long industrial dispute had been made by the Government and the electricity utilities.
32. It was the fact that the Conservatives trailed a long way behind Labour in the opinion polls during the final 16 months of Mrs Thatcher's leadership which, more than anything else, was responsible for the Cabinet-led back-bench revolt which brought about her downfall in November 1990.
33. See P. Norris, *The Volatile Electorate: British by-elections since 1900* (London: Oxford University Press, 1990).
34. See D. E. Butler and A. Ranney (eds), *Referendums: a comparative study of practice and theory* (Washington, DC: American Enterprise Institute, 2978), for a fuller discussion.
35. F. O. Goman, *Edmund Burke: his political philosophy* (London: Allen and Unwin, 1973), pp. 55-56.
36. *The Independent*, 17 June 1992.
37. J. J. Rousseau, *The Social Contract* (New York: Harper, 1949), p. 85.
38. See D. Kavanagh and P. Morris, *Consensus politics from Attlee to Thatcher* (Oxford: Basil Blackwell, 1989).
39. Norman Tebbit, *The Times*, 7 October 1987.
40. See A. Sampson, *The Changing Anatomy of Britain* (London: Hodder & Stoughton, 1982), for a vivid description of the Establishment in Britain.
41. V. O. Key, *Public Opinion and American Democracy* p. 285.

Further reading

Clemens, J., Polls, *Politics and Populism* (London: Gower, 1983).
Johnson, N., *In search of the Constitution* (London: Methuen, 1980).
Jowell, R., et al., *British Social Attitudes* (London: Gower, 1990).
Ranney, A. (ed.), *The Referendum Device* (Washington, DC: American Enterprise Institute, 1981).
Teer, F., and Spence, J. D., *Political Opinion Polls* (London: Hutchinson, 1973).
Worcester, R. M., and Harrop, M. (ed), *Political Communications* (London: Allen & Unwin, 1982).
Wybrow, R.J., *Britain Speaks Out, 1937-87* (London: Macmillan, 1989).

PART 3

Parliament

9　The Monarchy

The object of this chapter is to place the Monarchy in its contemporary context. Before doing so, however, some knowledge of the past is necessary, because in order to be able to understand and appreciate the position of the Monarchy within today's constitutional framework, some knowledge of its history and consequent development is essential. In Britain continuity and change have gone hand-in-hand. Continuity has been the dominant feature of British constitutional development, yet this has not meant the absence of change as age-old institutions have evolved and adapted to fulfil purposes often very different from those for which they were originally created. As a result there is often a striking contrast between the theory and practice of the British constitution. Nowhere is this more true than in the case of the Monarchy.

In formal terms the Monarchy is one of the institutions of Parliament. With a Queen on the throne every Government is 'Her Majesty's Government', the Opposition is 'Her Majesty's Loyal Opposition' and the Monarch still has an important, if largely formal, part to play in Britain's constitutional arrangements. It is the Queen who opens each new session of Parliament, who reads 'the Queen's Speech' from the throne on such occasions, and who gives her Royal assent to Bills, without which they could not become Acts of Parliament and hence the law of the land.

9.1 Origins and historical development

In Saxon times kings were guided by the 'Witan' or 'Witenagemot', an assembly of the most important men – lay and ecclesiastical – in the kingdom. The membership was not static and consisted of those individuals whom the King chose to summon to the three or four meetings held annually. As Ronald Butt put it, 'his natural advisers were the elders; the men of strength, standing, influence, experience and knowledge'.[1] Those present included the chief officers of the Royal household and others who held high state office, the 'Earldormen' who represented central Government in the shires, Bishops and other senior churchmen, and the principal men who held land directly from the King. The functions of the Witan were ill-defined, but included 'discovering and declaring' the law, in other words being a consultative and law-consenting assembly. In addition, the

Witan sat as the King's supreme Court of Justice. Its actual power was inversely proportional to that of the King at any given time. Together the King and the Witan were the highest authority in the nation.

A new stage in the development of the nation's political institutions was ushered in when Duke William of Normandy defeated Harold, the Saxon claimant to the throne, at the battle of Hastings in 1066. William the Conqueror (as he came to be known) launched a series of campaigns which, in the fullness of time, left him in undisputed control of the country. It was William's claim that he had succeeded to the throne through inheritance. As a result he laid claim to an element of continuity and sought to maintain many of the laws of his Saxon predecessors. At the same time, however, he brought with him from Normandy a new approach to government, namely the feudal system, whereby the greater part of the country was governed by tenants-in-chief, or barons, who held their land directly from the King on condition that they defended the conquered territory for the King. By the time of the Domesday survey of 1085-86, only about eight per cent of the land remained in English hands; indeed, of the tenants-in-chief only two appear to have been English.

The Norman barons assembled in the Court of their sovereign to regulate the affairs of their tenancies, settle disputes between each other and organise the military subjection of the conquered lands. The tenants-in-chief thus assembled – both lay and ecclesiastical – became known as the 'Magnum Concilium' or Great Council. This gathering assisted the King in determining state policy, supervised the work of public administration, acted as the highest Court of Justice, and made or modified the laws of the land. It met only three or four times a year, and then only for a matter of days at a time. For this reason there grew up the 'Curia Regis' or 'Court of the King' – an inner circle of the Great Council – whose function it was to assist the sovereign on a day-to-day basis during the long periods when the Great Council was not assembled.

This system of government worked well for a while, but towards the end of the twelfth century tensions between the King and his 'great men' began to increase. Matters were brought to a head by the abuse of autocratic power by King John. Consequently the barons seized an opportunity in 1215, when the King's position was weakened by war and misrule, to force him to sign a *Magna Carta* or Great Charter, setting out some clear principles and safeguards against further abuse of power by the Monarch. The intention of the barons was not to create a new system of government, but rather to ensure better government under the existing system. The agreement foreshadowed three of the main principles upon which the development of Parliament was later to be based: (1) that the King himself was subject to the law; (2) that the King could only make law and levy taxation with the consent of the governed; and (3) that the King's subjects did not owe the King absolute or unconditional obedience.[2] In short, it asserted the limited nature of kingship – the principle of conditional or 'constitutional' Monarchy – which was to be the mainspring of Parliamentary action against the Crown in the seventeenth century.

Within three months of the King's seal being affixed to Magna Carta, however, the concordat which it was supposed to symbolise broke down. John died in October 1216 to be succeeded by Henry III, then a boy of nine. Henry occupied the throne for the next 56 years during which time politics were dominated by the struggle between the Crown and the barons. The relationship between the King and the barons deteriorated eventually to the point of armed conflict in which the barons under Simon de Montfort were victorious. In 1265 de Montfort convened a Parliament (literally a 'talking gathering') which was attended not only by the barons, clergy and knights of the shires, but also by two burgesses from each of the Boroughs known to be supportive of the baronial cause. This occasion has since been widely recognised as the real beginning of Parliament at Westminster, and it is the recognition of this date which allows the British Parliament to claim that it is one of the oldest Parliaments in the world.

During the decades and centuries which followed, the holding of 'Parliaments' containing representatives of the counties and towns became the accepted custom and practice and 'Parliament' itself became a feature of the governmental system. At no time was Parliament definitively established, it merely evolved as a consultative forum for the King and the politically important sections of his realm. By about 1485 – the beginning of the Tudor period – it may be said that the institutional foundations of Britain's constitutional Monarchy had been laid. See Figure 9.1 for a chronological table of Monarchs.

The Tudor Monarchs found that there was political advantage for them in having their national policies – such as Henry VIII's break with the Catholic Church or Elizabeth I's determination to oppose the Spanish kings – supported and endorsed by the people's representatives in Acts of Parliament. For this reason no Tudor Monarch sought to dispense with Parliament and each member of the dynasty in turn put its support to good use. However, sessions of Parliament were infrequent and brief. Even during the 45-year reign of Elizabeth I, when Parliament counted for more than had previously been the case, the two Houses (Lords and Commons) were in session on average for little more than three weeks a year. During this period, the House of Lords became predominantly a secular body, while the House of Commons was increased in size by more than a third to about 300 members. By the end of the sixteenth century Parliament had become second only to the Monarch as a power in the land.

Constitutional tensions came to the fore under the Stuarts, especially James I and Charles I, who laid claim to the 'divine right of kings' and sought to reduce or deny the privileges acquired by Parliament under the Tudors. The mounting disagreements between Crown and Parliament eventually led to the Civil War (1642-1649), the triumph of the Parliamentary forces, the execution of Charles I and the abolition of the Monarchy itself. For the next few years the country was ruled by Oliver Cromwell in what was called a Protectorate. It was not until after Cromwell's death in 1658 that the Monarchy was restored, Charles II assuming the throne for the Stuarts in 1660. However, the relationship between the Monarch and Parliament was not a great deal better than before the Civil War and matters worsened under James II as he sought to reassert the divine right of kings. The eventual result was that Parliament and people combined against the King who fled the country in 1688 and was replaced by William of Orange (from Holland) and his English wife Mary – daughter of Charles I – in 1689. This peaceful transfer of constitutional power from one Monarch to another – but actually from the Monarchy to Parliament – has been described by Whig historians as 'the Glorious Revolution'. The new constitutional settlement was given statutory recognition in the 1689 Bill of Rights. The 'pretended power' of the Crown to suspend or dispense laws, or to govern without the consent of Parliament was declared illegal, as was the levying of taxation by Royal prerogative without the authority of Parliament. The 1689 Bill of Rights and the 1700 Act of Settlement confirmed the victory of Parliament in the struggle against the Crown. Constitutional Monarchy was developed in place of the unfettered rights of Kings and Queens, and Parliamentary supremacy in the government of the country was well and truly established.

Figure 9.1 British Monarchs since the Norman conquest

William I (the Conqueror)	1066-1087	**The Stuarts**	
William II	1087-1100	James I	1603-1625
Henry I	1100-1135	Charles I	1625-1649
Stephen	1135-1154	*The Interregnum*	
		(Oliver Cromwell)	1649-1660
		Charles II	1660-1685
The Plantagenets		James II	1685-1688
Henry II	1154-1189	William III & Mary II	1689-1702
Richard I (the Lionheart)	1189-1199	Anne	1702-1714
John	1199-1216		
Henry III	1216-1272	**The Hanoverians**	
Edward I	1272-1307	George I	1714-1727
Edward II	1307-1327	George II	1727-1760
Edward III	1327-1377	George III	1760-1820
Richard II	1377-1399	George IV	1820-1830
Henry IV	1399-1413	William IV	1830-1837
Henry V	1413-1422	Victoria	1837-1901
Henry VI	1422-1461		
Edward IV	1461-1483	**Saxe-Coburg / 1917: Windsor**	
Edward V	1483	Edward VII	1901-1910
Richard III	1483-1485	George V	1910-1936
		Edward VIII	1936
The Tudors		George VI	1936-1952
Henry VII	1485-1509	Elizabeth II	1952-
Henry VIII	1509-1547		
Edward VI	1547-1553		
Mary I	1553-1558		
Elizabeth I	1558-1603		

From the beginning of the Hanoverian dynasty in 1714, the role of the Monarch was reduced still further. George I (1714-1727) was a German, speaking no English and knowing nothing of English ideas and ways. George II (1726-1760), although more interested in his adopted land, lacked the ability to make himself felt in government affairs. In these circumstances the powers which their predecessors had so jealously sought to preserve fell into disuse or into the hands of the English aristocracy who effectively ran the country throughout the eighteenth century. George III (1760-1820), perhaps more English than Hanoverian, tried to recapture the Royal position that had been lost. His influence upon Government and politics was far greater than that of his two predecessors to the extent that in 1780 the House of Commons felt driven to declare that the 'influence of the Crown has increased, is increasing, and ought to be diminished'.[3] After the resignation of Lord North as Prime Minister in 1782, the tide turned back in favour of Parliament, and during the last decades of his reign, the King was discredited by madness. By then a satisfactory way of running the Government without the active participation of the Monarch had been developed. This fact, soon to be buttressed by successive extensions of the franchise in the nineteenth century, meant that no Monarch could turn back the clock. Admittedly, Queen Victoria (1837-1901) occasionally sought to play a partisan political role, but her attempts were increasingly marginalised by a long chain of Prime Ministers who countered her ambitions by variously ignoring, opposing or flattering her.

The result is that since Victorian times no British Monarch has been seriously tempted to step outside the bounds of constitutional Monarchy.

9.2 Powers and functions

The Monarchy has long been regarded as one of the 'dignified' rather than 'efficient' parts of the constitution, to use Walter Bagehot's nineteenth-century terminology. As a result the powers which the Monarchy possesses today are more theoretical than real. They are based upon convention and residual Royal prerogatives, namely the residue of discretionary or arbitrary authority legally left in the hands of the Monarch. This means that they can only be used within the confines of well-established custom and practice. If such conventions were ever broken by the Monarch, it would discredit and possibly do fatal damage to the institution of the Monarchy itself. If the Monarch were to exercise constitutional power without reference to acknowledged advisers – including notably the Prime Minister of the day – it could provoke a constitutional crisis.

Today the powers and functions of the Monarchy essentially fall under two broad headings which can be termed the *political* and the *symbolic*. The constraints placed upon independent action by the Monarch in the political sphere have traditionally bolstered the strength of the Monarchy in the symbolic sphere. We shall now address the *political sphere* and deal with each power or function under that heading.

The choice of Prime Minister

Whereas George III chose and dismissed Prime Ministers almost at will, the last Monarch to choose a Prime Minister without advice was Queen Victoria in 1894, and today Elizabeth II is 'free' to choose as Prime Minister only the elected leader of the party which commands majority support in the House of Commons. It would only be in the exceptional circumstances of a so-called 'hung Parliament' – that is one in which no single party has an overall majority in the Commons – that the Monarch could be faced with alternatives, either calling upon the leader of the largest single party to form a minority Government or possibly looking for a senior political figure with a better chance of forming a Government which could command the support of a majority in the Commons.

During the first 20 years after the war, however, the position was more shaded, at any rate in relation to the choice of Conservative Prime Ministers. In January 1957, when Anthony Eden became too ill to continue as Prime Minister after the debacle of the Suez expedition, the Queen took advice from Sir Winston Churchill and the Marquess of Salisbury before inviting Harold Macmillan to form a new Government. In October 1963, when Harold Macmillan became seriously ill and a successor had to be found for the position of Prime Minister, the Queen again took advice – this time from Harold Macmillan himself in hospital – before inviting Lord Home to form a new Government. In both cases a new leader of the Conservative Party was said to have 'emerged' from the process of informal soundings which characterised the decision making of the party in those days. On the last occasion, the behaviour of the so-called 'magic circle' was strongly criticised by Iain Macleod and Enoch Powell, who subsequently both refused to serve in the Administration of Sir Alec Douglas-Home (the style to which Lord Home reverted after renouncing his peerage in order to sit in the Commons as Prime Minister).

Since 1965 in the case of the Conservative Party and 1922 in the case of the Labour Party, there have been systematic arrangements to ensure that a new leader is rapidly elected to succeed one who retires or dies. The result is that the role of the Queen is now confined to choosing as Prime Minister whoever has already been elected as leader of the governing party. Of course, when there is a clear change of Government following a decisive result in a General Election, the Queen sends for the leader of the victorious party and invites that individual to form a new Government.

There has always been the possibility of a more significant role for the Monarch at a time of national crisis or when a General Election has produced a 'hung Parliament'. An example of the first eventuality occurred in 1931 when George V was instrumental in encouraging the formation of the National Government under Ramsay MacDonald in order to get through the Commons the deflationary economic measures which had not been acceptable to a significant part of the Parliamentary Labour Party when it had been in power on its own.[4] Another example occurred in 1940, when George VI had some influence upon the choice of Winston Churchill to succeed Neville Chamberlain as Prime Minister after the latter had been discredited by the significant number of abstentions within the Conservative Parliamentary Party at the end of a crucial debate of confidence on the conduct of the war.[5]

An example of the second eventuality occurred in February 1974 when it seemed possible for a while that the Queen could have been drawn into party political controversy by Edward Heath's attempt to retain power for the Conservatives by offering a pact (and seats in his Cabinet) to the Liberals after his party had been defeated at the General Election. As things turned out, it proved impossible for the then Liberal leader, Jeremy Thorpe, to persuade his party to do such a deal with the Conservatives. Thus a few days later Harold Wilson was duly invited by the Queen to form a minority Labour Government.

Certainly the scenario of a hung Parliament is one which could give rise to the Monarch being involved in some very awkward decisions which could have very far-reaching political consequences. In such a situation the Monarch would be expected to send initially for the leader of the largest single party in the Commons who would then have to see whether a minority Government could be formed or whether some sort of understanding with one or more of the other parties was possible. Either course would be quite plausible and it would only be in the unlikely event of complete Parliamentary deadlock that the Monarch might be advised to send for another party leader or political figure to form a viable Government – rather than agree to a dissolution very soon after the previous General Election. Whatever happened, the Monarch might be obliged to play a significant, even decisive, role in the process of Government formation. This is not something which either a Monarch or a Monarch's advisers would relish, since it might well cast doubt upon the traditional impartiality of the Monarchy in party political matters. Nonetheless, the possibility remains that the Monarch might have to exercise the discretion which constitutionally rests in the Monarch's hands if there seemed to be no alternative.

Dissolution of Parliament

It is now a well-established convention that the Monarch can only dissolve Parliament at the request of the Prime Minister in office within the five-year maximum life span of a Parliament. It is necessary to go back to the reign of Queen Anne to find the last example of a Monarch exercising this Royal prerogative in an independent way. Even in 1913, when it was argued by some that George V might have been within his constitutional rights to have dissolved Parliament in order to give the electorate a chance to pronounce upon the Liberal Government's Bill for Irish Home Rule, A. V. Dicey, the eminent constitutional expert, was not prepared to recommend such a step to the King for fear that it would compromise the neutral constitutional position of the Monarchy.

Since that time various views have been advanced about the power of dissolution. One view, which was advocated by some after the very close General Election result in 1950, holds that if the Prime Minister in office is not prepared to recommend a dissolution in circumstances where it might be considered in the national interest to have one, then the Monarch is entitled to seek other leading figures in the Commons who might be prepared to recommend such a course. In the event such a view did not prevail in 1950 and it has not prevailed ever since. The Monarch is therefore bound by the established view and obliged to accept only the advice of the Prime Minister in office.

There may be a valid distinction, however, between the Monarch's constitutional right *to refuse* a dissolution on the grounds that it would lead to a premature and unnecessary General Election and the now unsustainable claim by any Monarch *to impose* a dissolution against the wishes of the Prime Minister in office. As far as the right to refuse a dissolution is concerned, no such request has been refused since the middle of the nineteenth century, although dissolutions have been refused more recently by Governors-General acting on behalf of the Monarch in Commonwealth countries. As for the right to impose a dissolution upon the Government of the day – in essence the dismissal of the Government – no British Government has been dismissed by the Monarch since George III dismissed the Fox-North Coalition (under the titular leadership of the Duke of Portland) in 1783.

There is another way in which the Monarch could become involved in controversy surrounding a dissolution. This would be if the Monarch suggested a dissolution – and hence a General Election – before agreeing to a request from the Government to exercise the Royal prerogative. This was the position in 1910 under both Edward VII and George V with regard to Herbert Asquith's request to create enough new Liberal peers to ensure the passage of the Parliament Bill in the House of Lords. On that occasion, successive Monarchs made it clear that they would not feel justified in creating new peers until the electorate had a chance to express its views on the issue in a General Election.[6] In practice, of course, the exercise of any such form of Royal initiative today would run the serious risk of totally discrediting the whole idea of constitutional Monarchy in Britain. It would involve the Monarchy in apparently taking sides in the political battle and that would destroy one of its vital assets, namely political impartiality.

Notwithstanding the conventional wisdom on this matter, there are some conceivable circumstances in which a Monarch might be justified in exercising the Royal prerogative of dissolution in defiance of the wishes of the Prime Minister in office. For example, if it became clear in the course of a 'hung Parliament' that a minority Government had outlived its usefulness and was simply standing in the way of a timely General Election which might produce a clearer Parliamentary result, those who advise the Palace on constitutional issues might be prepared to emphasise the arguments for such a dissolution. Such a course of action might also have to be considered if the Government broke the most basic of electoral rules, namely the five-year maximum life-span of a Parliament, without the necessary all-party support for doing so, as existed, for example, during both World Wars.[7]

Another possibility is that an unpopular Prime Minister might carry out a threat to call a General Election in mid-Parliament rather than agree under pressure from senior Cabinet colleagues either to change policy or even to resign as Prime Minister. In such circumstances established political conventions would support the position of the Prime Minister, even if there appeared to be sufficient support in the governing party for a change of policy or a new Prime Minister or both. Whatever might be the private views of the Monarch and the Monarch's advisers, it seems clear that they would be obliged to grant the wish of the Prime Minister in office, however unpopular that might be with most of the governing party. It would therefore be for the governing party to sort out its own problems of policy and personality rather than for the Monarch to intervene in the dispute. It must be stressed, however, that these are all hypothetical circumstances which would be most unlikely to arise in modern political conditions.

If the Monarch did proceed along these lines, it is likely that no more than a pyrrhic victory would be won, since such steps would almost certainly lead to a 'Monarch versus the people' clash at the ensuing General Election. This would probably be won by the aggrieved party and might put in jeopardy the very continuation of Britain's constitutional Monarchy. Indeed, the exercise of Royal prerogative by the Governor-General in Australia in 1975 – when Sir John Kerr dismissed Gough Whitlam's Labour Government – was undoubtedly an important factor behind the rise of republican sentiment in that country. The practical conclusion is that the Monarch in Britain today has no sensible alternative to accepting the advice of the Prime Minister in office, whatever might appear to be the arguments for doing otherwise.

Assent to legislation

Royal assent to legislation is another aspect of the Monarch's prerogative which has become purely formal over the years. In the seventeenth century Charles II managed to postpone or quash Bills of which he disapproved by the simple expedient of mislaying them. Queen Anne was the last British Monarch to veto legislation outright when in 1707 she withheld assent from the Scottish Militia Bill. George III certainly encouraged the House of Lords to reject the India Bill in 1783, while George IV managed to delay legislation on Catholic emancipation by letting it be known that he was not happy with the idea. Queen Victoria was the last Monarch seriously to consider withholding assent, although there is some evidence that in 1913 George V toyed with the idea of refusing assent to the Government of Ireland Bill which was then being put through Parliament under the Parliament Act of 1911. Today it is a well-established convention that the Monarch accepts and acts upon the advice of Ministers. As such, Royal assent is a mere formality and any attempt to make it otherwise would precipitate a constitutional crisis.

Creation of peers

The Monarch has the power to create new peers and in certain cases it is believed that the Palace still has some influence over the final selection from the various names proposed. Certainly there was a time when the use of this particular Royal prerogative was formidable indeed. For example, in 1711-12 Queen Anne, on the advice of her Ministers, created 12 new peers precisely to ensure ratification by the House of Lords of the Treaty of Utrecht. In 1831 even William IV's threat (at the instigation of his Whig Prime Minister, Lord Grey) to create new peers helped to ensure the passage of the first Reform Bill against fierce Tory opposition. In 1911 the willingness of George V to create as many as 400 new Liberal peers (discreetly made known by the Prime Minister, Herbert Asquith) caused the hereditary majority of Conservatives in the upper House to give way to the Liberal majority in the House of Commons over what was to become the 1911 Parliament Act.[8]

Whereas in the past Monarchs took a keen interest in such matters – Queen Victoria, for example, refused to sanction the creation of individual peers on a number of occasions during her reign – in contemporary circumstances the creation of new peers by the Monarch has become little more than a constitutional formality. Appointments to the peerage are normally made twice a year when the names of the newly created peers appear in the Honours Lists. The appointments are made on the basis of advice given and co-ordinated by the Prime Minister in office, although anyone can make suggestions which are then discreetly sifted and assessed by a small unit of civil servants attached to 10 Downing Street before the Prime Minister of the day makes the formal recommendations.

Since 1964 life peerages have been the usual order of the day, mainly because successive Prime Ministers since that time have not felt generally inclined to recommend the creation of any more hereditary peerages. Yet this is no more than a convention of fairly recent times and as such it has been capable of modification. For example, immediately after the 1983 General Election William Whitelaw and George Thomas were made hereditary peers on the recommendation of Margaret Thatcher. The former was in recognition of William Whitelaw's long and distinguished service to the Conservative Party and the nation, culminating in his period as deputy leader of the party from 1975 to 1983 and to enable him to take over as leader of the Lords. The latter was in recognition of George Thomas's distinguished period as Speaker of the House of Commons from 1975 to 1983. In each case the Queen complied with the Prime Minister's wishes, as is now customary in such matters, although the element of controversy in restoring the principle of hereditary peerages was reduced by the fact that William Whitelaw had no male heir, only daughters who were not eligible to inherit the title, and George Thomas was a bachelor. More recent departures from the modern norm in favour of life peerages were the granting of an hereditary Earldom to Harold Macmillan – who had male heirs – in 1984, and to Prince Andrew on the eve of his wedding to Sarah Ferguson in 1986.

Some argue, however, that difficulties could arise for the Monarch if a future Labour Government were committed to the abolition of the House of Lords and hence the creation of a unicameral Parliament. This would probably entail the creation of up to 1000 new peers whose sole task upon taking their seats in the House of Lords would be to vote for a House of Commons Bill designed to bring about their abolition.[9] In such circumstances much would depend upon whether the Monarch considered that the Government had a clear mandate for such a far reaching constitutional change. If so, the Monarch and the Monarch's advisers would probably conclude that there was no alternative but to go along with the idea. Yet it is not absolutely certain that the Monarch would acquiesce in this procedure, since the Monarch might be convinced that the demise of the House of Lords foreshadowed the demise of the Monarchy itself. What is clear is that any attempt by the Monarch to block such a measure would probably have fatal consequences for the future of the Monarchy itself.

Granting of honours

The Monarch is also formally involved in the granting of honours, both civilian and military, to those whom it is customary for the nation to recognise and reward in this way. As with the creation of peerages, this usually happens twice a year when the Honours Lists are published. However, there can be special investitures to recognise special events: for example, the honours awarded to those whose acts of conspicuous gallantry had been recognised during the 1982 Falklands campaign and more recently the 1990-91 Gulf War. In nearly all cases the system is a popular and effective way of recording public recognition for those who have made notable contributions to the well-being of British society and who have shone in various walks of life. It also adds lustre to the institution of Monarchy and provides regular opportunities for rewarding service to the community in ways which do not involve bribery or corruption.[10]

Nearly all such honours are awarded by the Monarch on the formal recommendation of the Prime Minister who, in turn, is advised by a small civil service unit attached to 10 Downing Street. Once again this unit sifts and assesses a wide range of recommendations made by MPs and others. Even so, a few honours have remained in the personal gift of the Monarch – for example, the Order of the Garter, the Order of the Thistle, the Order of Merit, and the Royal Victorian Order. Usually these awards have no political significance, but are simply a way of signifying the Monarch's personal recognition of an outstanding person, such as Mother Theresa, the Catholic nun working for the hungry and the destitute in Calcutta, who was awarded the Order of Merit by the Queen on her visit to India in 1983, or Nelson Mandela, President of South Africa, who was awarded the Order of Merit by the Queen during her state visit in 1995. Very occasionally such awards do have political significance, albeit marginally, as was the case in 1990 when the Queen awarded Margaret Thatcher the Order of Merit following her resignation as Prime Minister and Denis Thatcher an hereditary Baronetcy in recognition of his role in support of his wife.

Public appointments

The Queen plays a formal role in a vast range of public appointments, since all important posts in the civil service, the police, the judiciary, the BBC and the Church of England are filled in the name of the Monarch, not to mention, of course, the Ministerial appointments in every Government. Once again such appointments are usually made on the basis of advice given or co-ordinated by the Prime Minister, often with the help of the small civil service unit attached to 10 Downing Street which processes the recommendations from all quarters. Senior appointments in the Diplomatic Service are made on the advice of the Foreign Secretary, in the Armed Services on the advice of the Defence Secretary, in the police on the advice of the Home Secretary, and in the judiciary on the advice of the Lord Chancellor. However, many other senior Ministers effectively have considerable power of public patronage which they exercise in the name of the Monarch and every Prime Minister takes a close personal interest in all the main appointments.

In these circumstances it is not surprising perhaps that some concern has been expressed from time to time about the nature and scope of such political patronage, which is Royal in name but Ministerial in fact.[11] A number of politicians – notably Tony Benn and others in the Labour Party – and some journalists have been concerned about the lack of public scrutiny or subsequent democratic accountability of such public appointments, not to mention the implications for public expenditure in the wide range of public bodies to which such people are appointed. The problem is compounded in the eyes of many observers when one party has been in office continually for many years and the tendency grows for public appointments to be made to a considerable extent on party political criteria. Yet this kind of political patronage has not led the critics to attack the Monarchy, since it is well understood that the Monarch is merely acting as a dignified rubber stamp for appointments which are not really within her control.

Mercy and pardon

The prerogatives of mercy and pardon are still vested in the Monarch, who is entitled to exercise them on the advice of the Home Secretary of the day. Yet since the House of Commons voted in 1965 to abolish the death penalty on a provisional basis, and since that decision has subsequently been confirmed in successive free votes over the years, it now seems that this particular aspect of the Royal prerogative has fallen into disuse. Pardons are granted only after conviction and sentence in rare cases when there is some special reason why a sentence should not be carried out or a conviction should be quashed – for example, a discovery that the evidence on which a conviction was based is actually false. Thus the exercise of this aspect of the Royal prerogative has been both formal and rare.

Other formal functions

Several important, formal functions are exercised in the name of the Monarch, but actually by Ministers. These include important matters, such as the concluding of international treaties, declarations of war, the introduction or amendment of colonial constitutions and the establishment of public corporations. In each case the Monarch is acting as a splendid and dignified veil for decisions which are actually taken by Ministers in the Government of the day.

In the conduct of foreign policy *the Royal prerogative to conclude treaties* enables Ministers to reach legally binding agreements with other Governments or international organisations without having to secure the *prior* approval of Parliament. For example, the 1972 Treaty of Accession which took Britain into the European Community was signed by Edward Heath as Prime Minister in Brussels without the Government having had to secure the prior approval of Parliament at Westminster. The same procedure applied to the 1986 Single European Act and the 1992 Treaty of Maastricht, both of which involved initiatives taken by Ministers in the name of the Crown which had the effect of committing the United Kingdom to certain highly controversial courses of action *before* Parliament had an opportunity to give a formal opinion. Unlike the position in the United States, where treaties negotiated by the Administration have to secure the 'advice and consent' of the Senate before they can become American Law, or the position in the European Union where the European Parliament has to give its formal opinion before the Council of Ministers and the Commission can conclude a new European treaty in the name of the European Union, the position in Britain is that only if treaties have legislative consequences in the United Kingdom does the Government have to involve Parliament. Even then, this need only be done after a treaty has been signed by a Minister on behalf of the Crown.

A declaration of war is made officially in the name of the Monarch, although in the nuclear age such formalities would be of little real interest if time were very short. In the event of a war which directly affected Britain, it would be for the Prime Minister and a few senior colleagues and military advisers to take all the key decisions. Such decisions would merely be made known to and later ratified by the Monarch as and when appropriate. In the case of the 1982 Falklands conflict, Britain did not declare war upon Argentina, since there were compelling technical and legal reasons for not doing so in the light of British diplomatic efforts at the United Nations and elsewhere. Although the Queen was not therefore required to sign a declaration of war, she was kept informed by the Prime Minister at every stage of the conflict.

Colonial constitutions are promulgated or changed in the name of the Monarch. For example, the constitution of Zimbabwe, which British Ministers under Lord Carrington had negotiated with the representatives of all the parties at Lancaster House in 1979-80, was eventually promulgated in the name of the Queen and later given statutory authority in the Zimbabwe Independence Act of 1980.

The creation of public corporations is also done in the name of the Monarch through the granting of Royal Charters to the bodies concerned. For example, the BBC became a public corporation by Royal Charter in 1926. The various New Towns, such as Milton Keynes, which were built over the years since the Second World War, were established in a similar way.

The significant growth of so-called QUANGOs (Quasi-Autonomous Non-Governmental Organisations) under all post-war Governments, but especially Conservative Administrations since 1979, has been another aspect of central Government activity facilitated by the use of the Royal prerogative. This has simplified the procedures of public appointments by Ministers and assisted the 'unelected state' to grow without undue hindrance from Parliament or other elected bodies.[12]

Unpublicised functions

Within the political sphere the Monarch also performs some unpublicised functions, the most notable of which are the regular and confidential conversations with the Prime Minister of the day. On such occasions the Monarch enjoys what Walter Bagehot once described as 'the right to be consulted, the right to encourage and the right to warn'.[13] In modern circumstances these rights are exercised during private meetings every week at Buckingham Palace (when the Monarch is in residence) and once a year for a week-end in the late summer when the Monarch is resident at Balmoral in Scotland.

Queen Elizabeth II's experience of the affairs of state is unrivalled in modern times, since in more than 40 years on the throne she has been served by nine different Prime Ministers and 16 different Governments. She came to the throne in 1952 when Winston Churchill was Prime Minister, President Truman occupied the White House and Stalin still ruled in the Kremlin. She has the undisputed right to see all state papers and in consequence she is almost certainly better informed about key political developments than virtually anyone else in Britain. Her private advice to all Prime Ministers must be invaluable in view of the length and variety of her experience of matters of state. Indeed one former Prime Minister apparently accepted the analogy of paying a weekly visit to a psychiatrist and admitted that he could say things to the Queen that he could not say even to his closest political colleagues.[14] The functions of the Monarchy are summarised in Figure 9.2.

Figure 9.2 Functions of the Monarchy

Political functions	*Symbolic functions*
Royal Assent to Bills	State Opening of Parliament
Dissolution of Parliament	Head of the Commonwealth
Choice of Prime Minister	State visits abroad
Creation of peers	Entertaining foreign Heads of State in UK
Granting of Honours	Patronage of good causes
Public appointments	Visits to all parts of UK
	Military ceremonial
Unpublicised functions	Religious ceremonial
Personal contacts with the Prime Minister	
Confidential advice to the Government	*Formal functions*
	Conclusion of treaties
Quasi-judicial functions	Declaration of war
Prerogative of mercy	Introduction or amendment of
Prerogative of pardon	colonial constitutions
	Establishment of public corporations

Symbolic functions

The Monarch and other members of the Royal family play an important symbolic role in many different ways. For example, Queen Elizabeth II and Prince Philip have made frequent State visits to countries in all parts of the world. Queen Elizabeth II has also played an important role at successive Commonwealth Conferences and in entertaining foreign Heads of State or Government when they visit Britain. In all such activities the Monarch and other members of the Royal family are serving the national interest, as defined by the Government of the day. As far as the Monarch's travels are concerned, Royal trips abroad are judged to be good for British foreign policy and for the promotion of British trade. Furthermore, the making or withholding of a Royal visit can be used by the British Government as a way of indicating approval or disapproval of political regimes in other countries. For example, in 1995 the Queen paid official visits to President Yeltsin in Russia and President Mandela in South Africa.

In relation to the Commonwealth, Queen Elizabeth II plays a particularly significant role as titular head of that free association of nations and she is known to attach particular personal importance to it. This has involved her and other members of the Royal Family in travelling tens of thousands of miles to different parts of the world to see and be seen by many thousands of people in the 51 member states of the Commonwealth (in sixteen of which, in addition to the United Kingdom, the Queen is also Head of State). It has also led her to attach considerable personal importance to her annual Christmas broadcasts to the people of Britain and the Commonwealth.

Within Britain the Monarch and other members of the Royal family are involved by custom and tradition, and often at the instigation of the Government of the day, in the promotion of good causes and in various forms of public ceremonial designed to raise the morale or reinforce the unity of the British people. For example, the Queen usually leads the nation in paying respect to the dead of two World Wars, and other conflicts in which the British armed services have been involved, at the Cenotaph in Whitehall on Remembrance Sunday every year. The Queen and other members of the Royal family also pay conspicuous visits to all parts of the United Kingdom, including notably those where the people have suffered from natural disaster (as when hundreds of school children were killed by a coal-tip landslide at Aberfan in 1966) or been involved in serious social unrest (as in the inner city areas of London, Bristol and Liverpool after the 1981 riots). In these and many other ways the Monarchy makes a valuable contribution to the underlying cohesion and morale of the people in the United Kingdom – England, Scotland, Wales and Northern Ireland. See Figure 9.3 for a summary of the Royal Family's working year.

Figure 9.3   The Royal Family's working year

	Official visits, opening ceremonies and other engagements	Receptions, lunches, dinners and banquets	Other engagements, including investitures, meetings attended and audiences given	Total number of engagements in the United Kingdom	Engagements while abroad on official tours
Queen Elizabeth II	147	64	275	486	187
Duke of Edinburgh	158	119	26	303	359
Queen Mother	34	13	16	63	0
Prince of Wales	194	82	99	375	152
Princess of Wales	13	7	14	34	8
Duke of York	50	15	11	76	93
Prince Edward	49	50	23	122	157
The Princess Royal	277	99	72	448	229
Princess Margaret	96	35	5	136	7
Duke of Gloucester	134	35	20	189	64
Duchess of Gloucester	122	30	7	159	23
Duke of Kent	127	39	33	199	96
Duchess of Kent	154	22	10	186	74
Princess Alexandra	85	25	13	123	65

Source: *The Times*, 3 January 1995

9.3 Financing the Monarchy

Although any well-researched attempt at a comprehensive cost-benefit analysis of the British Monarchy would almost certainly show that it generates a financial profit for the nation, for many years the annual publication of the Civil List (the grants from tax-payers for the upkeep of the Royal family) tended to provoke considerable media and public interest – and in many cases criticism – not least because of the Queen's great private wealth and tax-free status at the time. In 1990, in an attempt to defuse these issues an agreement was reached between the Queen and the Government setting an annual sum of £7.9 million on the Civil List to be averaged over the period 1991-2000 for the support of the Queen, with further annual allowances totalling £1.9 million net to be paid to the Duke of Edinburgh, the Duke of York, the Queen Mother, Princess Margaret, the Princess Royal and other active members of the Royal family. The income of the Prince of Wales is derived from the rental income and other revenues of the Duchy of Cornwall. In addition, the costs of maintaining the Royal residences (except for Balmoral and Sandringham), the Royal Flight and the Royal Yacht *Britannia* continued to be met from public funds. See Figure 9.4 for a summary statement of the cost of the Monarchy.

Unfortunately for the Monarchy, the fate of the Royal family seemed to go from bad to worse in the early 1990s. One result of this was that in November 1992 it was announced – on the initiative of the Queen herself – that the Monarch would start paying Income Tax on her private fortune and that she would finance the Civil List payments made to members of her family other than herself, her husband and her mother. This unexpected announcement seemed to meet much of the public criticism head on, as did the announcement in June 1994 – again on the Queen's personal initiative – that the Royal Yacht Britannia would be decommissioned in 1997 and the Royal family would in future pay for their private use of the Queen's Flight. In short, the methods of financing the British Monarchy have changed very significantly in the 1990s as the Royal Family and the whole institution of Monarchy have come under much more widespread media exposure and public criticism.

Figure 9.4   Cost of the Monarchy

	£ million
Civil list (palace staff etc.)	7.9
Duchy of Lancaster (privy purse)	3.1
SPENT BY WHITEHALL	
Palace Maintenance	26.5
Royal Yacht	9.3
Queen's Flight	6.7
Royal Train	2.2
Civil air fares	0.8
Overseas visits	0.6
Publicity	0.4
Honours admin.	0.2
Equerries	0.2
Yeomen of the Guard	0.04
Security	Unknown
TOTAL	£57 million

Source: *The Economist*, 25 January 1992

These costs should be set against the annual revenue of the Crown Estate (£81 million in 1993–94) surrendered to the Exchequer by each Sovereign at the beginning of each reign since 1760.

9.4 The Monarchy, the media and the public

Traditionally, the Monarchy has been one of the most revered of Britain's national institutions. An opinion poll in 1969 demonstrated considerable public support for the Monarchy in that only 13 per cent thought it should be ended, 30 per cent thought it should continue as it was, and 50 per cent thought it should continue but change with the times (7 per cent had no opinion).[15] A similar opinion poll in 1980 showed that the continuing appeal of the Monarchy was derived to a significant extent from the fact that it was usually projected to the people as the 'Royal Family', which 80 per cent of those questioned thought to be 'a marvellous example to everyone of good family life'.[16] The same poll also showed that 90 per cent preferred the idea of Monarchy to a Republic of the French or American type. This was a point emphasised by another poll in 1984 in which 77 per cent of the respondents considered that Britain would be worse off and only 5 per cent thought that Britain would be better off as a Republic.[17]

Since the mid-1980s however, both the respect for and the popularity of the Monarchy have plummeted, with polls showing that those who consider that Britain would be better off without the Monarchy have increased to 13 per cent in 1987, 20 per cent in 1992 and 27 per cent in 1995.[18] The institution and its leading personalities have been subjected to an unprecedented degree of media scrutiny, disclosure and criticism. In March 1992 it was confirmed that the Duke and Duchess of York were to separate. Equally, there was increasing concern about the marriage of the Prince and Princess of Wales. Media speculation and public prurience reached fever pitch with the publication of a book by Andrew Morton entitled *Diana: her true story*, in which it was claimed that the Princess of Wales was 'trapped in a loveless marriage' and was so unhappy that she had attempted to commit suicide on six occasions. In November 1992, during a Royal visit to South Korea, the awful relationship between the Prince and Princess of Wales became painfully apparent to TV audiences, thus increasing speculation about separation and even divorce for the Royal couple. Throughout this time some Members of Parliament were agitating for a reduction in the financial privileges enjoyed by the Monarchy. Such agitation reached a peak after a fire destroyed part of Windsor Castle on 20 November 1992 and the Government announced that it would cover all the costs involved. On 24 November 1992, in a speech at the Guildhall, the Queen spoke of how the year of her fortieth anniversary on the throne had deteriorated from a celebration to what she termed an '*annus horribilis*' (awful year). She admitted that the Monarchy and other institutions were not above reproach, but suggested that less savage and more constructive criticism would be appreciated. The year ended with *The Sun* newspaper's premature publication of the Queen's Christmas broadcast, and 1993 began with the Monarch successfully suing the paper for breach of copyright – an action which was settled out-of-court-in the Queen's favour.

In recent years, therefore, the gap between myth and reality in public perceptions of the Monarchy has widened and people have been painfully reminded that the Royal Family consists of frail human beings rather than public symbols. As a result, the moral authority of the Monarchy has sharply declined. However, as British society has become less deferential, it has become harder, perhaps even impossible, to maintain the magic and the mystery surrounding the British Monarchy. As Jack Straw, a leading Labour front-bench spokesman has written: 'it is increasingly clear that the current Royal system, with its large number of participants and its emphasis on show business, has little serious future [. . .] there is little mystery about a soap opera'.[19] Paddy Ashdown, leader of the Liberal Democrats, has called for much of the pomp and circumstance surrounding the Monarchy to be stripped away, while Dr John Habgood, when Archbishop of York, raised doubts about the Monarch's continuing role as 'Defender of the Faith' and Head of the Church of England.[20] Some opinion formers, such as Ludovic Kennedy, have even argued that the Monarchy has had its day and the time has come for a Republic.[21] Indeed, the results of an opinion poll published in April 1993 revealed that only 37 per cent of those questioned thought Britain would be worse off as a Republic (compared with 77 per cent eight years earlier).[22]

It is apparent from the sad saga of recent years that public attitudes towards the Royal family as public figures and the British Monarchy as an institution have become much less positive, certainly since the media began to give saturation publicity to the breakdown of Royal marriages, notably those of the Prince and Princess of Wales and the Duke and Duchess of York. These developments, along with apparently lurid revelations about the personal lives of other members of the Royal family, have severely tarnished the 'ideal family' image which advisers at Buckingham Palace had earlier sought to present. The result has been a combination of prurience and ridicule which has led some observers to speculate that Prince Charles might not succeed to the throne at all, his place being taken instead by his eldest son, Prince William. Obviously it is enormously difficult, particularly for the younger generation within the Royal family, to live anything resembling a normal married life (whatever that may be these days) when they have to do so in the glare of such unremitting and intrusive media publicity. Furthermore, it has been possible for some members of the Royal family to overcome their personal problems and go on to restore their reputation in the eyes of the public through assiduous good work and public service, as Princess Anne, the Princess Royal, has done. In an age when the traditional 'nuclear family' has become a minority model rather than the social norm and when as many as one in two new marriages are destined to end in divorce, it may be that a more tolerant and indifferent public is simply amused and titillated by what has befallen certain members of the Royal family. Yet older generations are probably less amused by what has happened over recent years and it is in those quarters that support for the Royal family has declined the most.

When in 1969 Queen Elizabeth II first decided to accept the advice that she should allow the television cameras in to show not only her public face but also her more private and family activities, a fateful decision was made from which it has been difficult to retreat, even though at times she must have been sorely tempted to do so. To begin with, all went well in that the Silver Jubilee celebrations in 1977 and the Royal Wedding in 1981 of Prince Charles and Lady Diana Spencer demonstrated a flair for publicity and spectacular ceremonial which worked positively for the Monarchy and indeed the whole Royal family. Such glittering pageantry, as well as the more homely Christmas broadcasts by the Queen to the nation and the Commonwealth, did much to tighten the bonds of sentiment and loyalty between the Royal family and the wider public. Yet, as we can now see with the advantage of hindsight, there was always a risk in this strategy, namely, that the greater sense of familiarity which the Queen and their extended family engendered by allowing the mass media to pry and eavesdrop upon their lives would breed, if not contempt, then a larger degree of public cynicism and hence a loss of public respect not only for members of the Royal family but also the institution of Monarchy. Distance and mystique were previously important – some would say vital – elements in the public appeal of the Monarchy. Now that the media have to a large extent demystified the public image of the Monarchy, it will be much more difficult to restore a sense of public deference and to reinforce the sense of public respect which is still felt for the Queen herself.

Nevertheless on many occasions before in its long history the Monarchy has engendered great controversy and experienced extensive public criticism, and yet has managed to survive such crises. For example, the Prince Regent and William IV were deeply unpopular and heavily ridiculed in the early nineteenth century; Edward VII, as Prince of Wales, was the butt of many jokes and much public ribaldry; and Edward VIII effectively split public opinion down the middle during the Abdication Crisis in 1936 when he chose marriage to an American divorcee, Wallis Simpson, in preference to the throne. It may well be, therefore, that the Monarchy will survive its present troubles as well and that in some years time all the current controversy will be largely forgotten. After all, the present Queen, Elizabeth II, is not only one of the most respected Monarchs in the world, but also likely to remain on the throne as long or longer than her illustrious predecessor Queen Victoria. This very longevity and continuity in the person of the Queen herself is likely to stand the institution of Monarchy in good stead and may be enough in itself to counter and eventually bury the recent wave of strident media criticism and malicious innuendo against the most vulnerable or foolish members of the Royal family. Time alone will tell.

9.5 Conclusion

The Monarchy still holds the supreme position at the apex of British society, yet it does so at the expense of its previous claims (before 1837) to wield real political power. Today it serves as a powerful symbol of continuity and community which is particularly valuable to the nation in difficult or troubled times.

The Monarchy also provides an excellent example of the many paradoxes which abound in the British political system. It is an inherently conservative institution which can facilitate change. Whatever else may be altered, the Monarchy appeals to most people as an unchanging icon, a reassuring symbol. Such seemingly permanent and unchanging institutions can make it easier for people to accept even radical change in other areas of their lives. The Monarchy therefore plays an important part in preserving the cohesion of British society and it contributes significantly to the sense of underlying national unity which helps to hold the British people together. Nonetheless, its reputation in the eyes of a significant number of British people has been damaged by recent revelations about the private lives of some members of the Royal family. Hence it will not be easy, or perhaps even possible, for the Monarch and the Monarch's advisers to restore the position to what it was before.

Suggested questions

1 What are the functions of the British Monarchy?
2 Does the Monarch have any real power in Britain today?
3 'The Queen reigns but does not rule.' What does this mean?

Notes

1. R. Butt, *A History of Parliament: the Middle Ages* (London: Constable, 1989), p. 2.
2. *Ibid.*, p. 60.
3. The Dunning Motion – a resolution by John Dunning in April 1780 and approved by 233 votes to 190. See: J. Brooke, *King George III* (London: Constable, 1992), pp. 201-218.
4. See F. Hardie, *The Political Influence of the British Monarchy 1868-1952* (London: Batsford, 1970), pp. 150-153, and W. I. Jennings, *Cabinet Government* (London: Cambridge University Press, 1951), pp. 40-42.
5. See S. Bradford, *George VI* (London: Weidenfield & Nicolson, 1989), pp. 310-312.
6. See. F. Hardie, *The Political Influence of the British Monarchy* 1868-1952) , p. 67.
7. The Parliaments elected in 1910 and in 1935 were each extended by all-party agreement, in the former case until 1918 and in the latter case until the 1945 election which took place soon after the agreed ending of the 1940 Coalition Government.
8. Some historians have argued that in 1831 the threat of the mob and in 1911 and threat of rebellion in Ireland also played a part in persuading the Conservative peers to give way to the Government of the day in the Commons.
9. This was the proposal advocated in the later 1970s for a future Labour Government by Tony Benn.
10. Although there have been occasions in the past when the honours system was abused for political purposes – for example, by Lloyd George as Prime Minister when Maundy Gregory was active on his behalf in offering peerages in return for financial support.
11. Among those who have expressed concern about this are Tony Benn in *Arguments for Democracy* (London: Jonathan Cape, 1981), and P. Holland and M. Fallon in *Public Bodies and Ministerial Patronage* (London: CPC, 1978).
12. See Chapter 15, pp. 323–7 for a full discussion of QUANGOs.
13. W. Bagehot, *The English Constitution* (London: Fontana/Collins, 1063) p. 111.
14. A point made by Dr David Butler in correspondence with one of the authors.
15. *The Sunday Times*, 23 March 1969.
16. *Now*, 8 February 1980 (a weekly news magazine which later ceased publication).
17. *The Times*, 22 April 1993.
18. ICM Pools, *The Guardian*, 9 January 1995.
19. *The Guardian*, 19 January 1993.
20. *The Guardian*, 25 January 1993.
21. See 'Who should be President of Britain?', *The Times*, 18 January 1992.
22. *The Times*, 22 April 1993.

Further reading

Barnett, A., *Power and the Throne: the Monarchy debate* (London: Vintage, 1994).

Bogdanor, V., *The Monarchy and the Constitution* (London: OUP, 1995).

Borthwick, R., *Long to Reign Over Us? The Future of the Monarchy* (London: John Stuart Mill Institute, 1994).

Borthwick, R., *The Monarchy* (Barnstaple: Philip Charles Media, 1990).

Dimbleby, J., *The Prince of Wales* (London: Little Brown, 1994).

Flamin, R., *Sovereign* (London: Bantam, 1991).

Hall, P., *Royal Fortune: tax, money and the Monarchy* (London: Bloomsbury, 1992).

Hardie, F., *The Political Influence of the British Monarchy 1868-1952* (London: Batsford, 1970).

Holden, A., *The Tarnished Crown* (London: Bantam, 1993).

Keay, D., *Elizabeth II: portrait of a monarch* (London: Ebony Press, 1992).

Ziegler, P., *Crown and People* (London: Collins, 1978).

10 The House of Lords

As we saw in Chapter 9, an important – possibly the most important – feature of the British constitution is its capacity gradually to adapt to changing circumstances. In this respect the House of Lords is a microcosm of the British constitution, since throughout its long history it has been able to do just this. In contrast to other second Chambers elsewhere in the world which have been specifically created with powers and composition clearly defined in basic constitutional documents, the House of Lords is the product of history. It was not created by founding Fathers or under a Basic Law, it has simply developed and changed organically in the soil of British history. This is not to say that its evolution has been linear or continuous; on the contrary, it has been haphazard, spasmodic and uncertain. Yet it has survived for a very long time and its evolutionary adaptability will probably enable it to survive a good while longer.

10.1 Origins and historical development

As the product of evolution rather than deliberate creation, it is not possible to say exactly when the House of Lords originated, for Parliament as a whole had no single genesis. Rather it came into being gradually 'from the medieval Court and Council where Plantagenet kings consulted the great men of the realm to secure support and offer their people justice'.[1] Nonetheless, as we saw in the previous chapter, it is possible to find the deepest roots of the British Parliament in the consultative customs of the Saxon kings who took periodic advice and support from the 'Witan'.

From the late thirteenth century onward there was a gradual and halting alignment of the membership of Parliament into two principal groups: the House of Lords and the House of Commons – the former composed of men who attended in response to individual summons from the Monarch and the latter of people elected in the Counties and Boroughs who attended in a representative capacity. By 1485 – at the outset of the Tudor period – the institutional foundations of Parliament had been laid. As we also noted in the previous chapter, the power of Parliament (especially the Commons) made steady progress throughout the Tudor period, to such an extent that the historic clash in the seventeenth century with the pretensions of the Stuart Monarchy became inevitable. In consequence the nation experienced a Civil War (1642-49), the execution of the King (1649), an interregnum under Oliver Cromwell (1649-58), the restoration of Charles II as King (1660), and the so-called 'Glorious Revolution' (1688-89) before a new constitutional order was firmly established.

As the principle of representative and responsible government developed in the eighteenth century, the power of control over the Executive fell increasingly to the House of Commons rather than the House of Lords. It was to the Commons, not the Lords, that individual Ministers and the Government collectively came to be held responsible. However, the Lords did not meekly accept the constitutional superiority of the Commons, and the leading territorial magnates in the upper House managed to retain effective control over the lower House by controlling the processes of election to many seats in the Commons, especially the so-called pocket or rotten boroughs. The personification of this manipulative power in the second half of the eighteenth century was the Duke of Newcastle who, in co-operation with his noble friends and relatives, managed to control as many as 80 to 100 seats in the House of Commons – enough 'placemen' to ensure that he and his faction either formed or dominated many Administrations.

The Reform Act of 1832, which enlarged the electorate from about three to five per cent of the adult population and which abolished many of the rotten boroughs, deprived the House of Lords of much of the political power which it had enjoyed in the eighteenth century. The Tory peers had strongly opposed it, but in the end were forced to concede to a combination of Liberal reformers in both Houses (led by Earl Grey) and popular pressure from what was called 'the mob' – that is, angry public demonstrations in favour of reform. The Monarch, William IV, also played a significant part on the side of reform by indicating his willingness to create a large number of new peers who, if necessary, could have swamped the die-hard opposition in the Lords. In the event, this threat, along with the other pressures mentioned, was sufficient to get the legislation passed.

The expansion of the suffrage and the development of more modern electoral arrangements between 1832 and 1867 gave the House of Commons a growing claim to genuinely representative credentials. At the same time, the power of the landed interest was in decline in the wake of the growth of the industrial towns and, after the repeal of the Corn Laws in 1845, the enormous impact of free trade upon the economy and society. These and other factors brought about a gradual shift of political power away from the House of Lords to the House of Commons – for example, the proportion of peers in the Cabinet declined from about three-quarters to about a third of the total. During these years the House of Lords was able to head off challenges to its legal powers and to the hereditary basis of its membership as long as the peers were content to play second fiddle to the Commons. Indeed, in many ways the leading figures in the Lords were careful not to alienate or challenge their counterparts in the Commons for fear of provoking further instalments of constitutional reform which would have weakened their institutional position still more. As Walter Bagehot explained the position of the Lords in 1867: 'the House has ceased to be one of the latent directors, and has become one of the temporary rejecters and palpable alterers' (of legislation passed by the Commons).[2] He went on to describe the House of Lords as a Chamber with powers of delay and revision, but little else and concluded that: 'its danger is not in assassination, but atrophy; not abolition but decline'.[3]

It was not long, however, before the validity of Bagehot's observations was challenged, since during the last decades of the nineteenth century and the first decade of the twentieth century there was recurrent conflict between the Tory and Unionist majority in the Lords and the Liberal majority in the House of Commons. This finally came to a head in the constitutional crisis of 1909-11. In 1893 the Conservative and Unionist majority in the Lords had heavily defeated William Gladstone's Liberal attempt at Irish Home Rule. In 1906 the Liberal Education Bill had been very drastically amended by the Lords, and consequently abandoned by the Commons. The Lords had rejected the Land Valuation Bill in 1907 and again in 1908, the Licensing Bill in 1908, and finally (and fatefully) the Liberal Finance Bill of 1909. The quarrel between the two legislative Chambers – a quarrel, in Winston Churchill's words 'often threatened, often averted, long debated, long delayed, always inevitable' – had come to a head at last.[4]

The House of Commons immediately voted to declare the House of Lords' action unconstitutional and a breach of privilege. Parliament was then dissolved. In the ensuing General Election the Liberals were returned to power, although with a much reduced majority. However, when the Parliament Bill to curb the power of the Lords was introduced into the Commons in April 1910, the Liberals were able to count upon Labour and Irish Nationalist support. The first consequence of the new Parliamentary arithmetic was that the 1910 Liberal Budget was passed by the Commons and then accepted by the Lords without a vote. However, owing to the death of King Edward VII on 6 May 1910, the Parliament Bill itself was not proceeded with. Following the failure of attempts to negotiate an agreed settlement at a constitutional Conference, the Liberal Government decided that a second General Election should be held in 1910 before it could legitimately proceed with the Bill. The Prime Minister (Herbert Asquith) also obtained a promise from the new King, George V, that should the Liberals win the election he would agree to create enough new Liberal peers to overcome the die-hard Conservative opposition to the Bill in the Lords. The new House of Commons (elected in November 1910) was almost identical in composition with the old, so the Liberals remained in office, reintroduced the Parliament Bill and promptly secured a Parliamentary majority for it in the Commons. This time the Lords gave it a Second Reading, but watered it down in Committee. On its return to the Commons, the lower House refused to accept most of the amendments proposed by the Lords and promptly returned it to the peers. On 10 August 1911, after considerable behind the scenes activity and argument within the Conservative and Unionist peers, the majority in the upper House were reluctantly prepared to accept the Bill as it then stood as the lesser of two evils. Consequently, the Lords voted not to insist on their amendments by 131 votes to 114, with some 300 Conservatives abstaining.

The 1911 Parliament Act removed the Lords' power to reject Money Bills, while their powers to veto ordinary Public Bills were replaced with a power of delay for a maximum of two years. This meant that if a Bill were approved by the Commons in three successive Sessions, it automatically became law at the end of that time whether or not their Lordships were content. Together with the reduction in the maximum permitted span of a Parliament from seven to five years, this meant that any Bill passed by the Commons in the first two sessions of a five-year Parliament would inevitably become the law of the land if insisted upon by a majority in the Commons. Although the Bill curbed the powers of the Lords, the composition of the upper House was not addressed, any more than the whole issue of the appropriate functions for a curtailed second Chamber.

In 1917 a constitutional Conference of 32 distinguished individuals under the chairmanship of Viscount Bryce was set up with the object of finding solutions to the problems of reforming both the powers and the composition of the House of Lords. In its report the following year it proposed that a reformed upper House should have three quarters of its members indirectly elected by MPs on a regional basis, while the remaining quarter should be chosen by a joint committee of both Houses. As far as powers were concerned, it proposed that legislation which was the subject of dispute between the two Houses should be submitted to a 'free conference', consisting of a small number of Members from each House who should be given very great power in determining whether or not the legislation should pass and in what form. There was, however, a substantial dissenting minority within the Bryce Commission and this disagreement was sufficient to prevent the Government of the day from acting upon its majority recommendations. Even though many other proposals were made between the wars for reforming the House of Lords and the Labour Party Conference became committed to the abolition of the second Chamber, the constitutional position remained unchanged until after the Second World War.

In 1945 the victorious Labour Government did not put forward any proposals for reform or abolition of the House of Lords, since it had many other more pressing legislative priorities – such as the creation of the National Health Service, various nationalisation Bills, and the legislation to bring about independence for India. Furthermore, the Conservative peers under the leadership of Lord Salisbury adopted a deliberate convention of self-restraint under which they did not oppose at Second Reading any legislative measures emanating from the 1945 Labour Manifesto, although they were prepared to press amendments to Labour Bills in the name of 'improving' the legislation. By 1947, however, the mood of the Conservative majority in the upper House had changed and it became clear that, at any rate in relation to the proposed nationalisation of the iron and steel industries, the Conservative peers were prepared to use their inbuilt majority against such legislation. Faced with this threat from their Conservative opponents in the Lords, Labour Ministers secured approval in the Commons for a further Parliament Bill designed to reduce the delaying power of the upper House to one year. In spite of efforts to find a compromise between the respective majorities in the two Houses, agreement proved impossible. The Government went ahead without all-party agreement, using provisions of the 1911 Parliament Act to ensure the passage of what was to become the *1949 Parliament Act*. This effectively reduced the period of delay to less than thirteen months, cut from three to two the number of Sessions in which a disputed Bill had to be passed by the Commons, and from three to two years the period of delay following Second Reading in the Commons. Once again, however, the Act did nothing to change the composition or the functions of the second Chamber. When the Labour Party lost office and the Conservative Party returned to power in 1951, and whole issue of comprehensive reform fell out of the reckoning.

A number of minor reforms did, however, take place during the late 1950s and early 1960s. In 1957 daily allowances were introduced for travel to and from and attendance at the House of Lords. In 1958 the *Life Peerages Act* made possible the creation of Life Peers (that is, peerages which can not be inherited), including peerages for women in their own right. In 1963 the *Peerage Act* enabled female hereditary peers to sit and allowed hereditary peers to renounce their titles – while in no way impinging upon the rights of their heirs and successors – in order to make themselves eligible for membership of the House of Commons.[5] In the wake of these minor changes, the right of hereditary peers to sit in the House of Lords remained, as did the rights of the House as a whole to reject subordinate legislation, Private Bills and Bills to confirm provisional Orders.

In addition, the minimal delaying power which the upper House still possessed not only gave the Peers the ability to dislocate considerably the Government's legislative programme, but also, at the end of a Parliament, to defeat a Government Bill in its entirety.

The 1964 General Election saw the return of a Labour Government, which in the 1966 General Election managed to increase its majority in the Commons to nearly 100. One result of this was the subsequent introduction of the ill-fated *Parliament (No. 2) Bill* in 1968, which involved both a reduction in the total number of peers and an attack upon the hereditary principle. The Bill secured a comfortable majority on Second Reading in the House of Commons. However, when it went into Committee on the floor of the House (as is conventional with constitutional measures), it was effectively defeated by a sustained and devastating filibuster by back-benchers on both sides of the Commons led by Enoch Powell and Michael Foot. Such traditionalists in the Commons opposed further reform of the House of Lords mainly on the grounds that a reformed second Chamber was likely to be a strengthened second Chamber, whereas they were determined to preserve the primacy of the House of Commons. In the face of this time-consuming and highly effective opposition, the Wilson Government abandoned the Bill, leaving the upper House still unreformed in both composition and functions.

10.2 Composition

Today the membership of the House of Lords is still divided between ecclesiastical and lay members, formally described as 'Lords Spiritual' and 'Lords Temporal'. The *Lords Spiritual* are the senior clergy of the Church of England, namely the Archbishops of Canterbury and York, the Bishops of London, Durham and Winchester, and the twenty-one most senior among the other diocesan Bishops. They cease to be members of the House when they retire as Bishops and so are the only Members who are not members for life. They sit on the bishops bench and do not take a party whip. The *Lords Temporal* are the peers of England, Scotland, Great Britain and the United Kingdom. All peers of this type who are aged 21 or over, not bankrupt, of British Commonwealth or Irish nationality, and have not been convicted of treason (until pardon or completion of sentence) are entitled to take their seats in the House of Lords. The various categories of the peerage are shown in Figure 10.1.

Figure 10.1   Composition of the House of Lords

Peerage Category	No	%
Hereditary peers (male)	741	61.6
Hereditary peers (female)	17	1.4
Created Hereditary peers (all male)	15	1.2
Life peers (male)	320	26.6
Life peers (female)	63	5.2
Law Lords (all male)	22	1.8
Bishops (all male)	26	2.2
Total	1204	100.0

Hereditary peers

The vast majority of Members of the House of Lords are hereditary peers, namely those whose title is held by virtue of inheritance. Most hereditary peerages pass through the male line, although certain peerages can pass through the female line in default of a male heir, while special provision has occasionally been made for a title to pass to a female – for example that of Earl Mountbatten of Burma in 1979. Only since the passage of the 1963 Peerage Act have female holders of hereditary peerages been able to sit in the House of Lords.

The peerage is an ancient order –for example the Baronies of de Ros and Mowbray date back to 1264 and 1283 respectively, the Earldom of Shrewsbury to 1442 and the Dukedom of Norfolk to 1483, each of which still have title holders today. However, very few peerages which are still extant date back that far in British history and most of them have been created since the beginning of the nineteenth century; indeed, many such peerages were created during the early years of the twentieth century. Very few hereditary peerages have been created since 1964, because successive Prime Ministers since that time have believed (in line with public opinion) that such creations were 'a thing of the past'. Labour Prime Ministers have been ideologically opposed to the expansion of the hereditary peerage, while most Conservative Prime Ministers have not wanted to appear provocative on the issue. Yet there have been a few notable departures from this custom and practice. For example, in June 1983 William Whitelaw (deputy leader of the Conservative Party 1975-83) and George Thomas (Labour Speaker of the House of Commons 1975-83) were created hereditary peers on the recommendation of Margaret Thatcher, and in February 1984 Harold Macmillan finally accepted the hereditary Earldom of Stockton which he had previously declined on ceasing to be Prime Minister in October 1963. It should not be assumed that all hereditary peers are mere 'backwoodsmen', since some of them have played a distinguished part in British Government. For example, Lord Home was Foreign Secretary in Administrations led by Harold Macmillan and Edward Heath; Lord Shackleton was a senior member of Harold Wilson's Administration (1964-70); and Lord Carrington was Defence Secretary in Edward Heath's Administration (1970-74) and Foreign Secretary under Margaret Thatcher (1979-82). The hereditary peerage has also produced some able and enthusiastic younger peers who have been useful and effective Ministers in successive Governments.

Life peers

Life peers are those whose title is limited to the lifetime of the title-holder. They fall into two categories: those created under the *1876 Appellate Jurisdiction Act* and those created under the *1958 Life Peerages Act*. The former Act provided for a limited number of Lords of Appeal in Ordinary (Law Lords) who are appointed to hear and determine judicial appeals. The general category of Law Lords also includes those other peers who have held or are currently holding high judicial office in a superior Court – for example, present and former Lords Chancellor.

The 1958 Life Peerages Act enabled distinguished men and women from many walks of life to have peerages conferred upon them in recognition of their political or public services to the nation. Such Life Peers may be former civil servants or diplomats; distinguished soldiers, sailors or airmen who rose to the highest military ranks; successful industrialists or prominent trade union leaders; distinguished scientists or other academics; renowned actors or other leading figures from the world of the arts and the media. In November 1994 there were 80 women peers, an increase compared with earlier times, but still rather a small number and only 6.6 per cent of the total membership.

By far the largest single category of life peers is composed of politicians who have previously sat in the House of Commons or been active in local government. In the former case, they tend to have been either retired Ministers or previously eminent backbenchers whom the Prime Minister of the day and the other party leaders wish to reward with a seat in the Lords and whose political skills can be kept in play in the upper House. In the latter case, they tend to have been distinguished figures from the world of elected local government whose experience in that sphere is seen as an attribute for membership of the Lords. In both cases we can agree with Ian Gilmour who observed that: 'the House of Lords does something to reduce the hazards of a political career and embalms without burying a number of useful politicians'.[6]

Political affiliations

The Conservative and Unionist peers are by far the largest grouping in the House of Lords, accounting in 1995 for 39.8 per cent of the total eligible membership. The Conservative ranks in the upper House are disproportionately made up of hereditary peers (69.3 per cent) while the much smaller Labour contingent is mainly composed of life peers (89.5 per cent). The ranks of Liberal Democrat peers have tended to be drawn in approximately equal parts from hereditary and life peers. There is also an increasingly significant and influential group of *cross-benchers*, who represent not only the interests of the law and the church, but also independent-minded laymen.[7] See Figure 10.2 for information on political affiliation in the House of Lords.

Any analysis of political affiliations in the House of Lords has to take account of a number of variables, such as the subject under discussion, the persuasive power of certain individuals, the day of the week and even the hour of the day. When these factors are taken into account, it becomes apparent that the complete Conservative control of the upper House, which was evident in the early and middle part of the century, has since

Figure 10.2 Political affiliation in the House of Lords

Party/Group	No.	Sub %	Total %
Conservative	479	45.9	39.8
Labour	114	10.9	9.4
Liberal Democrat	54	5.2	4.5
Cross-bench	287	27.5	23.8
Other	83	8.0	6.9
Bishops	26	2.5	2.2
Sub-total	1043	100.0	86.6
Lords without writs or summons	84	–	7.0
Peers on leave of absence	77	–	6.4
Total	1204	–	100.0

disappeared. Gone are the days when a Conservative Government need have no fear of defeat in the Lords. Indeed, in the years since 1979 the Lords have been a frequent embarrassment, irritant and even obstruction to successive Conservative Administrations. Thus, although in the past there was an in-built Conservative majority in the Lords, these days there is at best only a *potential* Conservative majority in the upper House. Certainly it is still easier for the Conservatives to win divisions than it is for Labour, but such outcomes are no longer inevitable. In short, one of the little-known secrets of the contemporary House of Lords is that no single party can rely unreservedly on its support.

Whatever the party political implications of recent developments in the House of Lords, it is as well to note that political divisions on party lines in the upper House are not usually as sharp or bitter as they can be in the Commons. This is apparent in the often relaxed and courteous style of debate in the Lords. Furthermore, most of the speech-making and legislative work is done by perhaps 100 to 150 particularly active peers, although a larger number usually take part in divisions. There have been occasions over the last five decades when the latent Conservative majority has sought to amend or delay Labour Government legislation of which it disapproved and a surprising number of occasions on which similar treatment has been meted out to Conservative legislation. Yet, as we shall see later in this chapter, the Conservative peers have usually been rather careful not to use even the limited constitutional power which has been left to them in ways which would provoke a Labour Government or seriously embarrass a Conservative Government. This is essentially because the House as a whole has an instinct for self-preservation and peers of all affiliations have recognised that incautious action on their part could lead to significant constitutional conflict with the Commons and even perhaps the eventual abolition of the second Chamber.

10.3 Powers and functions

The classic statement of the powers and functions of the second Chamber in the British political system was made in the Bryce Commission Report of 1918.[8] The present activities of the House of Lords can be considered in the light of the four powers and functions in that report. These were:

1   *The power of legislative delay* – that is, the ability to delay for about one year the passage of a Bill approved by the Commons.
2   *The power of legislative scrutiny and revision* – that is, the ability to amend and improve a Bill inadequately drafted or considered by the Commons;
3   *The power of well-informed discussion and deliberation* – that is, the ability to debate the issues of the day in a better-informed and less partisan way than is often the case in the Commons;
4   *The power to initiate non-controversial legislation*, thus relieving the Commons of at least some of the legislative burden at the beginning of every session of Parliament.

To this list suggested by the Bryce Commission in 1918 we should add:

5   *The judicial powers and functions of their Lordships*, exercised by the so-called Law Lords sitting in either one or two Appellate Committees.

6 *The scrutiny powers and functions*, exercised by special committees of peers established for the careful consideration of Private Bills, delegated legislation flowing from Whitehall Departments, and draft European Legislation flowing from European institutions in Brussels.

Legislative delay

In theory, the power of legislative delay is used by the Lords when they refuse to approve legislation already passed by the Commons. The 1911 Parliament Act laid the foundation for this by enabling the Lords to delay legislation (with the exception of Money Bills) for up to two years. Subsequently the 1949 Parliament Act reduced the delaying period to one year. In practice, since 1911 this power has been used only sparingly, because the latent Conservative majority in the upper House has been well aware of the danger that excessive use of this power could hasten the day when a Labour Government might decide to reform radically or even to abolish the Lords altogether. The only Bills which passed into law under the terms of the 1911 Parliament Act were the *1914 Welsh Church Act,* the *1914 Government of Ireland Act*, and the *1949 Parliament Act.*

Until the *1991 War Crimes Act*, no Bills passed into law under the terms of the 1949 Parliament Act. However, the Conservative majority in the Lords did seek to use its constitutional delaying power on two occasions in the mid-1970s when the then Labour Government pressed ahead with highly contentious legislation (namely the *1975 Trade Union and Labour Relations Bill* and the *1976 Aircraft and Shipbuilding Industries Bill*) at a time when it had little or no overall majority in the Commons. In both these cases, the Labour Government called the bluff of the Conservative peers by reintroducing the legislation a second time under the terms of the Parliament Acts. This proved sufficient to persuade their Lordships to back down and each of these Bills duly became law at the second time of asking. The moral of the tale is that the majority in the Commons can always get its way in the end if it really wants to do so, although in recent years particularly Conservative Governments have felt obliged to take account of opposition to their legislation in the Lords and to respect the limited delaying power still available to the upper House.

Legislative scrutiny and revision

The power of legislative scrutiny and revision exercised by the House of Lords has often been regarded as its most important function, especially when dealing with particularly complex or controversial Government Bills. This is mainly because MPs very often make inefficient use of the Parliamentary time available in Standing Committees when they are supposed to scrutinise and debate Bills clause by clause and line by line. The result is that there is often a need for additional legislative revision. This falls upon the House of Lords, where many of the necessary amendments and new clauses are introduced by Ministers when the Government has had second thoughts about aspects of its own legislation.

Sometimes this is in response to suggestions made in the House of Commons or to sustained pressure from interest groups which have lobbied for or against aspects of the legislation. Sometimes it is simply a matter of doing in the Lords what should have been done in the Commons, if there had been enough Parliamentary time to do so and if all parties when in Opposition did not spend so much of the time in committee simply filibustering on the early clauses of Government Bills. Although the close scrutiny of Bills involves a great deal of often painstakingly dull work, it is clear that the House of Lords performs an essential and invaluable Parliamentary function in this respect. In doing so, it does invaluable work which would otherwise have to be done by the House of Commons or which would simply be left undone to the detriment of the quality of legislation. It also helps to see that the Courts do not have to spend too much of their time subsequently clarifying the original intentions of Parliament via the medium of case law.

It is argued by some that when acting as a revising chamber, the House of Lords has sometimes been involved in wrecking Government legislation from the lower House of which a majority of their Lordships may strongly disapprove. In 1969, for example, the Conservative peers insisted upon amendments to the *House of Commons (Redistribution of Seats) No. 2 Bill*, the purpose of which legislation was to free the Labour Home Secretary, James Callaghan, from the legal obligation to lay before Parliament the reports of the independent Parliamentary Boundary Commissions. The amendments had the desired effect for the Conservatives in that the Labour Government backed down and the danger of 'gerrymandering' by Labour was averted.

Deliberative function

The deliberative function of well-informed debate upon the great issues of the day is another worthwhile aspect of the activities of the House of Lords. This is because the level of knowledge and the standard of argument in the upper House is often very high and because the issues are usually approached in a serious and relatively dispassionate way. Indeed, the Lords can often find time to debate important and topical issues which might not get an airing in the more partisan and busy conditions of the Commons. In such debates the Lords can also draw upon the great knowledge and experience which is available in their ranks, especially among the life peers who include Fellows of the Royal Society, leading industrialists and others of great intellectual and professional distinction. This is therefore one of the ways in which their Lordships can have considerable influence in Whitehall and Westminster and upon the climate of informed opinion in the country as well.

Initiation of non-controversial legislation

This procedure is particularly appropriate with Government legislation which is both complex and technical, such as Bills on data protection, energy conservation and patent law for example. It is also popular with many of their Lordships – more particularly those less inclined to play an active part in proceedings on a day-to-day basis – because it improves their chances of getting away from London to their country estates or grouse moors well before the 12th of August every year, an aspiration which can be thwarted if the upper House has to deal with too much legislation coming from the Commons during the second half of each annual Parliamentary session.

Judicial powers and functions

Theoretically, there is no distinction between the House of Lords in its judicial role as the final Court of Appeal in Britain and in its other activities. In practice, the judicial proceedings are quite separate from all other proceedings as only the Law Lords participate in hearing appeals, legal sittings are separate from the sittings of the whole House, and the Law Lords may sit in their judicial capacity even after the House has been prorogued or dissolved.

Judgements on appeal to the Law Lords are delivered by members of the Appellate Committee meeting in the Chamber of the Lords, but since 1963 these have taken the form of a written opinion from each individual judge. Usually appeals are heard by a committee of five Law Lords and decisions are reached by a majority. The judgements have great authority and have influenced the development of English Law over centuries. For a long time the Law Lords regarded themselves as bound by legal precedents established in their earlier decisions, but since 1966 they have been prepared occasionally to modify that doctrine by departing from their previous decisions when it has appeared right to do so.

Scrutiny powers and functions

The House of Lords is actually quite effective at scrutinising the activities of the Executive in Britain. There are several ways in which their Lordships do this beyond their normal participation in debates and in the legislative process. For example, peers may ask up to four Questions for oral answer each day that the House is sitting, each of which can lead to Supplementary Questions. Unstarred Questions, Private Notice Questions and Questions for written answer are also available. In addition, the most important statements of Government policy made in the House of Commons are usually made simultaneously in the House of Lords and on such occasions peers have the opportunity to probe or criticise Ministerial decisions. In recent years, the House of Lords has also made very good use of its Select Committees which, in some cases, have built up unrivalled reputations for their expert knowledge and the quality of their reports. Examples in recent years would include Science and Technology (1979-), Unemployment (1979-82), Overseas Trade (1984-85) and Murder and Life Imprisonment (1988-89). In all these ways members of the House of Lords scrutinise the activities of the Executive, sometimes more effectively than their counterparts in the House of Commons.

There are three other forms of scrutiny exercised by the House of Lords most of which are highly technical, but nevertheless rather important in the overall process of Parliamentary control. These are the careful scrutiny of Private Bills, of delegated legislation (Statutory Instruments) flowing from Whitehall Departments under previous primary legislation and of draft European legislation flowing from the European institutions in Brussels.

Private Bills (which are Bills to alter the law relating to a particular locality or to confer rights or relieve liabilities from a particular person or category of persons) may be assigned to a committee of five peers for detailed consideration once the legislation has been through the earlier stages of public notification and Second Reading. Such committees have some of the attributes of quasi-judicial proceedings in that the promoters and opponents of Private Bills are usually represented by legal counsel and may call evidence in support of their arguments. Once this committee stage is successfully concluded, the Bill is reported to the House where its subsequent stages are similar to those of a Public Bill.

In the case of *Statutory Instruments*, the original Act may confine to the House of

Commons the responsibility for scrutiny, as is the case with all fiscal measures. However, in most other instances the Lords have the same scrutiny powers as the Commons. These powers are usually exercised by the Joint Committee on Statutory Instruments (consisting of seven peers and seven MPs) which has the duty to consider whether or not the attention of both Houses should be drawn to a particular Statutory Instrument on any of a number of different grounds. These include, for example, whether it would impose a charge on public funds, whether it would be retrospective in its effects, whether its publication has been unjustifiably delayed, or whether there were doubts about it being *ultra vires* – that is, outside the acknowledged legal competence of the Minister and Department concerned. In short, the Joint Committee may report on a Statutory Instrument on any one of such technical grounds, as long as it does not seek to address the merits or demerits of the policy.

In spite (or perhaps because) of the fact that there is a large and growing number of Statutory Instruments issued by central Government, very few are referred by the Joint Committee for further debate in this way. However, those which are subject to the negative procedure and those subject to the positive procedure which have been reported on unfavourably by the Joint Committee, can be 'prayed against', which means made the subject of a critical motion put down by peers or MPs for debate on the floor of either House. The main effect of these procedures, in which peers play a full part, is to keep Whitehall officials up to the mark by discouraging them from drafting sloppy or unjust secondary legislation.

As for Parliamentary scrutiny of *European secondary legislation* (that is, Directives issued by the European institutions in Brussels), Committees of each of the two Houses of the Westminster Parliament have been in existence since 1974 with scrutiny powers and functions similar to those of the Joint Committee just described which deals with national Statutory instruments. In fact, the House of Lords Select Committee on the European Communities (as it is known) more than matches the House of Commons Select Committee on European Secondary Legislation, and is considered by many knowledgeable observers to be unrivalled in its expertise and depth of scrutiny of European legislation. Both the Lords' and Commons' committees are continuously involved in the scrutiny of draft European legislation, and both may report to their respective Houses with recommendations that particular legislative proposals should be debated in plenary session. Thus the House of Lords plays a leading role in this increasingly important area of Parliamentary activity.

Overall assessment

In many ways, in spite of its anachronistic image, the House of Lords is still in a position to act as an important constitutional check and as a safeguard of judicial independence in Britain. This significant role for the Second Chamber derives at least partly from the fact that the consent of the Lords is required before the lower House can extend the life of an elected Parliament beyond five years (as happened in both World Wars); and the fact that High Court judges can only be dismissed on an address to the Monarch from *both* Houses of Parliament, thus giving the Lords an effective veto against any serious attempt at political interference with the independence of the judiciary.

However, the position of the House of Lords in Britain's constitutional arrangements does not depend only, or even mainly, on these two aspects of its powers and functions.

It derives at least as much from the weight of British history and the fact that custom and practice in Britain have ensured a bi-cameral legislature capped by a constitutional Monarchy. The three elements of this institutional structure need to be considered as a whole. Yet within this framework, the House of Lords is now the weaker partner *vis-à-vis* the House of Commons and, as Janet Morgan warned their Lordships some years ago: 'it is only by monitoring their own behaviour and remaining sensitive to their image in the world outside [Westminster] that they can avoid infringing a web of sanctions explicitly formulated or implicitly understood'.[9]

10.4 The work and impact of the Lords

As far as the work of the House of Lords is concerned, the first thing to be aware of is the fact that a substantial proportion of the membership chooses either not to attend or to attend only occasionally. For example, during the 1993-94 Session 29.5 per cent of their Lordships did not attend at all, while a further 4.5 per cent attended only a single sitting. In all 48.8 per cent of those who did attend did so on fewer than a third of the 142 possible sitting days. It is apparent, therefore, that there is a marked difference between the total potential participation and the actual participation which takes place.

Nevertheless, the introduction of life peers gradually caused the style and working methods of the House to alter. This reflects the fact that a large proportion of the Life Peers are former MPs, former leading lights in local government or people with other kinds of party political experience. More and more of the peers drawn from these categories have tended to approach their role as members of the House of Lords with a degree of political professionalism not shared by all their hereditary counterparts. Indeed, in most cases they are now appointed to the upper House on the recommendation of the respective party leaders in the Commons to be what are openly called 'working peers' – to differentiate them from others who are appointed more in recognition of their previous distinguished contributions to British national life in spheres which are not necessarily related to party politics. In this respect, the character of the House of Lords is gradually changing and its membership and behaviour are moving closer to the character of the House of Commons – with the obvious differences that none of their Lordships is currently elected to the second Chamber and in the Lords there are a significant number of independents (the cross-benchers). The changing nature and scope of work in the House of Lords is shown in Figures 10.3 and 10.4.

It is clear from these tables that the number of peers attending sittings has greatly increased and that their Lordships are spending more time in Parliament and are involved in more Parliamentary business than before. Whereas peers could at one time count on working only Tuesday to Thursday with each working day often confined to the hours between 4.00pm and 7pm; currently the House sits more often, the working week has expanded, and the sittings go on much longer to accommodate the greater volume of legislation and other Parliamentary business. Logically, therefore, the procedures of the House of Lords have gradually been changed to meet the new requirements. Their Lordships have seemed keen to do this and, since the House is a self-regulating institution with relatively few Standing Orders, it has been able to respond more flexibly to changing needs and requirements.

Figure 10.3 Sessional statistics, 1950–51 to 1993–94

Statistical item	1950-51	1960-61	1970-71	1980-81	1990-91	1993-94
Average daily attendance	86	142	265	296	324	378
Number of sitting days	100	125	153	143	137	142
Number of sitting hours	294.45	599.00	966.53	919.53	885.52	971.45
Average length of sitting	2.57	4.47	6.18	6.25	6.28	6.51
Sittings after 10 pm	1	5	38	53	42	64
Monday sittings	0	21	22	28	29	34
Friday sittings	-	-	-	11	9	4

Figure 10.4 The work of the House of Lords, 1950–51 to 1993–94

Type of Work	1950-51	1960-61	1970-71	1980-81	1990-91	1993-94
Starred questions (a)	119	290	511	537	531	540
Questions for written answer	38	73	283	857	1304	1974
Unstarred questions	12	12	39	31	42	56
Motions leading to debate	(b)	(b)	46	47	71	61
Public Bills Introduced:						
Government Bills (c)	6	7	11	12	10	6
Private Members Bills	2	2	14	23	8	15

	1951-52	1962-63	1970-71	1980-81	1990-91	1993-94
Amendments made:						
Government Bills Commons	30	456	558	418	544	821
Bills Commons	27	29	15	49	24	31
Government Bills Lords	75	283	207	940	1012	467
Bills Lords	0	8	75	53	5	84
Totals	132	776	855	1460	1595	1403

The 1970-71 Session was longer than usual because it began after 1 June election.

(a) In 1954 the limit was put up to three per day on any Sitting Day; previously it had been three only on Tuesday and Wednesdays. In 1959 the limit was raised to four per day on any Sitting Day.

(b) Figures not available.

(c) Excluding Consolidation Bills.

Throughout the 1980s, when a determined and sometimes highly ideological Conservative Government had a commanding position in the House of Commons, the House of Lords often asserted its constitutional independence. During that time the peers sought to provide some of the effective scrutiny and opposition which they felt that the House of Commons was unable to provide. For example, in March 1980 the *Education (No.2) Bill*, which was later to become the 1981 Education Act, ran into trouble with their Lordships on a clause which sought to allow Local Education Authorities to impose transport charges for children in rural areas. The proposal offended both rural and religious interests in the Upper House and in any case had been strongly attacked in the Commons when 13 Conservative MPs had voted against it and 16 more had abstained. The campaign was led in the Lords by the Duke of Norfolk, supported by two former

Conservative Secretaries of State for Education, and in the end the Government was heavily defeated by 216 votes to 112 with no fewer than 38 Conservative peers voting against the Government. The sheer scale of the defeat and the prospect of having to face further back-bench dissent in the Commons and a second defeat in the Lords, encouraged Ministers to climb down. No further attempt was made to resurrect the clause and the Treasury was obliged to forgo an estimated public expenditure saving of up to £30 million. In all, 50 defeats, ten of them significant, were inflicted upon the Conservative Government by the Lords in the 1979-83 Parliament. Most were on specific points of particular concern to their Lordships – for example, the treatment of pensioners and the disabled, rural issues, respect for existing minority rights, and matters of constitutional etiquette.

During the 1983-87 Parliament further Government defeats in the Lords ensued – a total of 62. Perhaps the most significant was when the Government's plan to cancel the May 1985 elections to the Greater London Council and six other Metropolitan County Councils was defeated by 191 votes to 143 on a Labour amendment which came before the House in its deliberations on the *1984 Local Government (Interim Provisions) Bill.* The Government then offered a compromise in the light of the defeat which allowed the existing Councils to continue for an extra year, but which still cancelled the election due in 1985. Such an example clearly indicated that the Lords have been both willing and able to administer salutary and timely rebuffs to Conservative and Labour Governments alike.

During the 1987-92 Parliament the Lords inflicted a further 72 defeats upon the Government and since then an additional 35 defeats during the *1992-93 and 1993-94 sessions.* For example, in April 1991 during consideration of *The Criminal Justice Bill* the peers defeated the Government by passing an amendment to do away with the mandatory life sentence for murder, an amendment which the Government later overturned in the Commons. In 1993, during passage of *The Railways Bill,* the peers voted to give British Rail an equal chance to bid for rail franchises alongside the private sector, twice defeating the Government on the issue and thus ensuring that the Government later came forward with a compromise solution. More recently, the *Police and Magistrates' Courts Bill* and the *Criminal Justice and Public Order Bill* both suffered defeats or forced concessions at the hands of their Lordships – for example, on the proposed power for the Home Secretary to appoint Police Authority chairmen; to end local government majorities on Police Authorities; to introduce a new offence of male rape; to challenge in the Courts the film censor's criteria on video violence, and to allow judges to draw the attention of juries to a defendant's exercise of the traditional right to silence when charged with a criminal offence. In all these cases their Lordships demonstrated considerable self-confidence in playing one of their legitimate roles as a constitutional critic and check upon the power of the Government of the day. Yet it must equally be pointed out that Governments have usually been able to overcome such objections in the upper House by using Parliamentary power in the lower House when they have really needed to do so.

10.5 Proposals for change

There is a lively and continuing debate about the future of the House of Lords which has taken place within and between all parties. Proposals for change have tended to fall into one of four broad categories:

1 Abolish the House of Lords altogether, creating a unicameral Parliamentary system, as was the case for a few years following the execution of Charles I in 1649;
2 Abolish the House of Lords, but create in its place a wholly new body with different composition, powers and functions;
3 Change the composition of the House of Lords, but keep its powers and functions as they are;
4 Reform both the composition and the powers and functions of the House of Lords.

Set against all these various forms of possible change, of course, is the conservative view (with a small 'c') that the House of Lords should be left as it is now ('if it ain't broke, don't fix it'). On the whole those Conservatives (with a capital 'C') who are interested in this matter have tended to press for reform of the upper House in order to strengthen and entrench its position in relation to the Commons. The Labour Party has wavered over the years between a wish to reform it, a wish to replace it, and a wish to abolish it altogether. The Liberal Democrats have tended to see reform of the House of Lords as part of a new constitutional settlement in a much wider context.

Conservative proposals

Traditionally the Conservative Party has been quite interested in reforming the House of Lords, since it has seen such ideas as a way of putting the upper House on a more secure constitutional basis. Winston Churchill and L. S. Amery were among those who flirted in the 1920s with the idea of turning the Lords into a more functional body capable of directly representing both sides of industry as well as the hereditary peerage.[10] In the late 1940s and early 1950s the Marquess of Salisbury, as Conservative leader in the Lords, concentrated upon encouraging his noble colleagues to exercise political self-restraint, especially when they faced the radical post-war Labour Government. For example, agreement was reached not long after the 1945 General Election that the upper House, with its overwhelming Conservative majority, would not divide on the Second Reading of any Government Bill which had been foreshadowed in the 1945 Labour Party Manifesto.

It was not until the 1970s that serious reform proposals were forthcoming once again from the Conservative side. In 1977 Lord Carrington, then Conservative leader in the Lords, proposed the creation of a reformed second Chamber whose members would have been elected by proportional representation from large regional constituencies. His argument was that such a Chamber would reflect public opinion rather differently from the Commons, since the type of constituencies, the method of election and the timing of the elections would all have been different from those of the lower House. His main objective was to produce a reformed second Chamber with sufficient democratic legitimacy to survive and prosper as a constitutional check or counterweight to the House of Commons. In 1978 a Conservative committee chaired by Lord Home produced another set of reform proposals which recommended that the membership of the Lords should be reduced to about 400, of which one-third would have been nominated by the political parties and two-thirds elected on a basis of proportional representation from about 250 large territorial constituencies. Neither of these proposals – or anything resembling them – was implemented then or since. This is mainly because the Conservatives in the Commons have never given a high priority to Lords reform and because the vast majority of the Conservative Party in the Commons is opposed to the introduction of proportional representation.

Labour proposals

The Labour Party has traditionally been less interested in reform than in abolition of the House of Lords. Indeed, it has been nominally committed to the abolition of the Lords in their present form since 1934. However, no Labour Government has ever come forward with proposals to abolish the Lords. The closest Labour ever came in office to fulfilling this stated objective was when in the late 1960s the second Wilson Administration came forward with the Parliament (No.2) Bill which was eventually abandoned in the face of sustained opposition from both sides of the House of Commons. Since that experience the Labour position has oscillated from abolition (approved overwhelmingly at Party Conference in 1977) to reform based upon the idea of substituting for the present hereditary element representatives drawn from new regional Assemblies in England and new 'national' Assemblies in Scotland and Wales (as proposed in the 1989 Labour Policy Review).

In its 1992 Manifesto the party promised to replace the House of Lords with an elected second Chamber which would have the power to delay, for the lifetime of a single Parliament, legislation that threatened to reduce individual or constitutional rights. More recently, Tony Blair, the Labour leader, has indicated a greater degree of caution towards the idea of wholesale Lords' reform by suggesting that a future Labour Government would introduce legislation to confine rights of active participation and voting in the Upper House to Life Peers and so-called first holders of hereditary peerages, thus effectively submitting the House of Lords to the power of party political appointments, but seemingly postponing any other changes in its powers or functions.

Liberal Democrat proposals

Liberal Democrats have sought to place the 'modernisation' of what they describe as 'Britain's antiquated and ineffective constitution' at the head of their policy priorities. They have therefore advocated reform of the House of Lords as part of a new constitutional settlement incorporating a codified constitution, an entrenched Bill of Rights, home rule for Scotland and Wales, regional Assemblies throughout England, and proportional representation for all elections. As far as the second Chamber is concerned, they advocate transforming the House of Lords into a directly elected Senate with the task of representing the various nations and regions of the UK. Members of such an Upper House would be elected by Single Transferable Vote for fixed terms of six years, with one third retiring every two years. They would be empowered to delay legislation, with the exception of Money Bills, for up to two years and would have a power of veto over proposed constitutional changes emanating from the lower House.[11]

10.6 Conclusion

A study of the House of Lords in recent years provides clear evidence that it is not in danger of atrophy or decline; indeed, quite the reverse. The House of Lords has demonstrated a remarkable ability to evolve and adapt to changing circumstances. This stems very largely from its extraordinary character, a character derived from the fact that it has never been the brainchild of constitutional draftsmen, but has been shaped by a small number of Parliamentary Statutes and influenced by tradition, custom and practice dating back at least to medieval times.

The House of Lords, as it exists today, is thus the product of a long evolutionary process. It may appear to be an illogical institution in that it is hard to believe that anyone would set out to establish a second Chamber quite like it. Yet its unusual character can be regarded as a strength in that it encompasses a delicately balanced combination of real effectiveness and limited competence which makes a significant contribution to the work of Parliament and the British political system. If it did not exist, it would almost certainly need to be replaced with a new Parliamentary institution of comparable purpose and utility.

Suggested questions

1. Analyse the composition of the House of Lords in Britain today.
2. What are the functions of the House of Lords and how well is it able to perform them?
3. What are the implications of reforming or abolishing the House of Lords?

Notes

1. R. Butt, *A History of Parliament the Middle Ages* (London: Constable, 1989), p. 1.
2. W. Bagehot, *The English Constitution* (Glasgow: Fontana/Collins, 1963), p. 128.
3. *Ibid.*, p. 149
4. Quoted in R. Rhodes James (ed.), *Churchill Speaks* (Leicester: Windword, 1981), p. 178.
5. The 1963 Peerage Act was the direct result of the efforts of Tony Benn, who had inherited the title of Viscount Stansgate, to get the law changed so that he and other hereditary peers could disclaim their titles and consequently no longer be disqualified from standing for election or re-election to the House of Commons.
6. I. Gilmour, *The Body Politic* (London: Hutchinson, 1969), p. 302.
7. The term cross-bencher is used to describe those peers who are not formally aligned with any political party, but who belong to an unofficial group which meets each week, with a convenor in the chair to discuss forthcoming business. These members receive written notice of future business, the difference between this and a party whip being that it is issued without the additional matters on divisions and so on which are included in a party whip.
8. See Report on the Reform of the Second Chamber, Cmnd 9038 (London: HMSO, 1918).
9. J. P. Morgan, *The House of Lords and the Labour Government, 1964-70* (Oxford: Clarendon Press, 1975), p. 8.
10. See L. P. Carpenter, 'Corporations in Britain, 1930-45' in the *Journal of Contemporary History* 11 (1976), pp. 9-14; and references to 'Industry and the State' published in 1927 by Harold Macmillan and others.
11. See 'Here We Stand: proposals for modernising Britain's democracy', Liberal Democrat Federal White Paper, No. 6, September 1993.

Further reading

Bagehot, W., *The English Constitution* (London: Fontana, 1978).

Baldwin N. D. J., *The House of Lords* (Barnstaple: Philip Charles Media, 1990).

Bromhead, P. A., *The House of Lords and Contemporary Politics* (London: Routledge & Kegan Paul, 1958).

Morgan, J. P., *The House of Lords and the Labour Government, 1964-70* (Oxford: Clarendon Press, 1975).

Norton, P. (ed.), *Parliament in the 1980s* (Oxford: Basil Blackwell, 1985).

Shell, D., *The House of Lords* (Oxford: Philip Allan, 1988).

Shell, D. and Beamish, D. (eds.), *The House of Lords at Work* (Oxford: Clarendon Press, 1993).

11 The House of Commons

Unlike the Monarchy or the House of Lords, the House of Commons still has real power in the British political system, at any rate on those occasions when it is willing and able to use it. Yet the nature of its power is different from what it was in the nineteenth century when most of the traditional notions about the House of Commons were established. The modern House of Commons is neither the Government of the country nor even the principal place where official decisions or legislative proposals are conceived. It is essentially the sounding board for popular representation and redress, one of the stages on which the party battle is fought, the principal forum within which legislation and other decisions of Government are scrutinised, and the framework for Parliamentary control of the Executive – one of the tasks which it shares with the House of Lords.

The essential purposes of the House of Commons have not changed significantly since the last quarter of the nineteenth century. W. I. Jennings described them as being 'to question and debate the policy of the Government and in doing so to bring home . . . the unpopularity (or popularity) of a particular line of policy'.[1] L. S. Amery described them as being 'to secure full discussion and ventilation of all matters . . . as the condition of giving its assent to Bills . . . or its support to Ministers'.[2] Such descriptions are still broadly valid today.

11.1 Composition

The present House of Commons is composed of 651 members elected on a uniform national franchise from single member constituencies of about 66,500 electors on average. The Speaker and the three deputies, who are all elected MPs, take no partisan part in the proceedings (unless a vote is tied, in which case they are expected to vote for the *status quo*), since they are responsible in the chair for seeing that the rules of order are maintained. At the time of writing (January 1996), and with two by-elections pending – one Conservative seat, one Labour seat – of the remaining 645 MPs, 325 were Conservative, 270 were Labour, 25 Liberal Democrats, 13 Ulster Unionists of various kinds, 4 Scottish Nationalists, 4 Plaid Cymru (Welsh Nationalists) and 4 Social Democratic and Labour (moderate Irish Republican). Therefore, following the fact of the defection of two Conservative MPs –

Alan Howarth to Labour and Emma Nicholson to the Liberal Democrats – the Conservative Government of John Major had a Commons majority of 5 over all other parties.

MPs as representatives

Members of Parliament can be seen as more or less representative in two quite different senses. *Firstly*, we can consider the educational and occupational backgrounds of individual MPs. This reveals that all sorts and conditions of men and a small, but growing, number of women can be found in the House of Commons. We can illustrate the point by using figures derived from the 1992 General Election results. These show that 39 per cent of Conservative and 42 per cent of Labour MPs came from middle class or professional occupations, while only one per cent of Conservative and 22 per cent of Labour MPs came from traditional working class occupations. These figures demonstrate the growing *embourgeoisement* of the political class which is turning the House of Commons steadily into a meritocracy. This process has been further stimulated by the fact that 86 per cent of Conservative MPs and 84 per cent of Labour MPs had experienced further or higher education – one of the most significant predictors of upward social and occupational mobility. Of the Conservative MPs 45 per cent had been to university at Oxford or Cambridge, whereas the comparable figure for Labour MPs was only 16 per cent. Equally, there was a significant divergence in the proportions of those who had been to public schools (private education) with 62 per cent of Conservative but only 14 per cent of Labour MPs having had this dubious privilege.

Thus British MPs as a whole are still something of an elite in educational and occupational terms, although notably less so than they were some years ago. Of course, much depends upon whether one refers to the individuals concerned or to their family backgrounds. If the latter criterion is adopted, the social and class differences between the parties remain greater – a fact which is best explained in this context by the rapid upward social mobility experienced by many people in Britain in recent years. In general, however, it is evident that as the middle class as a whole has become larger, so, predictably, its contingent of MPs has become larger as a direct reflection of changes in society as a whole. Equally, the influence of the prestigious public schools and the universities of Oxford and Cambridge has continued to decline – even in the Conservative Party – with the result that there is growing educational and social convergence between the Parliamentary representatives of the two main parties. This has greatly diminished the presence of MPs from each end of the conventional social spectrum, although it is worth a wry note that old Etonians have been prominently represented in the ranks of the Conservative Government, especially at the Foreign Office and the Treasury.

Secondly, we can consider the extent to which the composition of the House of Commons reflects the composition of the electorate as a whole and especially those sections of the population which traditionally have been under-represented in nearly all the leading British institutions.[3] The most obvious example of a disproportion between representation at Westminster and in the population as a whole is that of *women*, who account for 52 per cent of the electorate but only about 9 per cent of all MPs. In the past this has been largely due to the prejudices of Conservative women on constituency selection committees who have seemed opposed to choosing those of their own sex as candidates for winnable seats, and the male chauvinism of many traditional Labour activists when choosing candidates for winnable Labour seats. However, in recent years things have begun to change in this respect – at any rate in the Labour and Liberal Democrat parties where there is now a degree of positive discrimination in favour of women candidates. Such developments have been less noticeable in the Conservative Party where the proportion of women MPs is now significantly smaller than in the Labour Party, in spite of the experience and example of Margaret Thatcher!

Another marked disparity (as we have already noted in Chapter 3) is that those who vote for the Liberal Democrats are penalised by the 'unfair' working of the British electoral system which discriminates against all third parties unless their votes are geographically concentrated (and sometimes even then). Consequently at the 1992 General Election the Liberal Democrats got 18 per cent of the votes cast across the nation, but only 3 per cent of the seats in the House of Commons. Moreover, some groups in the electorate are not directly represented in the House of Commons at all – for example, those under 30 or over 80 years old. On the other hand, there are other groups which seem to be over-represented; notably lawyers, consultants, and company directors in the Conservative Party; and lecturers, journalists and public sector white-collar workers in the Labour Party. Nevertheless many MPs develop a wide range of interests (both paid and unpaid) during their time in the House and this can turn them into quite prominent 'virtual representatives' of various categories and interests in the electorate.[4]

Front-benchers

Paid office-holders in the present Government (those who are entitled to sit on the Government front bench) make up about 90 of the 326 Conservative MPs. This figure includes 14 Government Whips who facilitate the business in the Commons, but who do not speak in debates or share in the running of Government Departments in the way that other Ministers do. The so-called payroll vote (that is, those who are expected to support the Government on all occasions) is now supplemented by about 40 Parliamentary Private Secretaries (PPSs) who sit on the second bench just behind their Ministers and who are expected to be completely loyal to the Government in the same way as the Ministers whom they serve. At the heart of the Government front bench is the Cabinet which (in August 1995) had 23 members, of whom 21 sat in the Commons, since only the Lord Chancellor and the Leader of the Lords sat in the upper House.

On the Opposition side, the Labour front bench is made up of the Shadow Cabinet and the other Opposition front bench spokesmen who support their more senior colleagues. The Labour Shadow Cabinet consists of 20 senior members of the Parliamentary Party of whom 15 are elected each year by their colleagues in the Parliamentary Party. The other five who sit *ex officio* are the Leader, the Deputy Leader, the Opposition Chief Whip, the Chairman of the Parliamentary Party and the Leader of the Opposition in the Lords (who is formally co-opted by the Party Leader). When the Conservative Party is in Opposition, the members of the Shadow Cabinet are all appointed by the Leader of the Party. Beneath the Shadow Cabinet there are about 40 to 50 junior Opposition spokesmen who are appointed by the Leader usually after consultation with senior colleagues to share the front bench duties of shadowing the various Ministers. In addition, there are about 10 Opposition Whips led by the Opposition Chief Whip who, together with the Leader of the Opposition and the Opposition Pairing Whip, are the only members of the Opposition to receive additional salaries from public funds in recognition of their additional Parliamentary responsibilities.

Back-benchers

The 430 or so MPs who have no direct involvement in Government or in the tasks of front-bench Opposition make up the generality of back-benchers.[5] Some are senior, have been in the House a long time, may well have been Ministers at an earlier stage in their careers, and wield a good deal of influence within their parties. A few carry considerable weight in the House as a whole and still attract a larger than normal audience of their colleagues when they speak in debate. However, by far the greater number of back-benchers are relatively junior, have been in the House for less than three Parliaments and try to make their way in politics as well as they can. This means that they are likely to spend a great deal of their time trying to attract the attention and approval of their party Whips by playing an active and helpful part both in proceedings in the Chamber and in Committee 'upstairs'.

The principal duty of back-benchers when their party is in Government is to support it with their votes in the division lobbies and, to a lesser extent, with their voices during Parliamentary proceedings. When their party is in Opposition, their principal task is to harry the Government on every suitable occasion both in the Chamber and in Committee 'upstairs'. Some back-benchers may choose a more notorious and difficult path by becoming rebels within their own party, as the so-called Euro-sceptics did within the Conservative Party in the 1990s. Others come to be seen by the party hierarchy (and are often dismissed) simply as mavericks or eccentrics. Such deviant behaviour is not normally recommended for those who are ambitious for Ministerial office, but there are some formidable exceptions who usually get taken into Government before long in order to turn them into team players.

The life of a back-bencher in the modern House of Common is usually more fun in Opposition than in Government. This is because, in the former case, there are more opportunities to play a prominent part in the party battle (since by definition there are always fewer MPs on the Opposition benches than on the Government side) and to make a favourable impression on the party leadership. It is also because nothing which is said or done by Opposition back-benchers matters very much and such politicians can therefore enjoy (at least at Westminster, if not in their constituencies where their role is different) the luxury of considerable irresponsibility. When their party is in Government, back-benchers have to tread the much more difficult, narrow path between sycophancy and rebellion. In such conditions they can be forgiven for thinking that all their Whips really want is their presence in the division lobbies at the appointed times to support the Government.

Certainly back-benchers in both main parties have cause to complain about the privileges granted to Privy Councillors (that is, very senior back-benchers nearly all of whom have held Ministerial office at an earlier stage in their careers) and to the spokesmen of minor parties, since both categories are almost certain to be called to speak in debates at favourable times and to catch the Speaker's eye if they wish to intervene at Question Time or following Ministerial Statements. This is mainly a reflection of the seniority principle which influences the pecking order at Westminster and indeed in virtually every other Parliament around the world. It is also a reflection of the well established Westminster convention that the Speaker should try to ensure a hearing for minority points of view and indeed for dissidents within the main parties as well. For example, the so-called Maastricht rebels were able to speak frequently and sometimes at length during the course of the legislation to implement Britain's adherence to the Maastricht Treaty in the early 1990s, and back-benchers who intend to abstain or vote against their party (especially if it is in Government) will normally be given a chance to explain their reasons during the course of the relevant debate.

Pay and conditions of work

All MPs receive a Parliamentary salary from public funds (£31,687 in 1994) which is linked to a percentage of the pay awarded to civil servants in Grades 5 to 7, together with a Parliamentary allowance for office costs of up to £41,308 (in 1994)). They are also entitled to free, first class travel within the United Kingdom as long as they are on Parliamentary or constituency business, and to one free trip a year to the institutions of the European Union on the Continent. At Westminster they do not have to pay for telephone calls within the United Kingdom and have the benefit of free, first class post for written communication with their constituents and others (for example, public bodies) in connection with their constituency duties. For those with motor cars there are generous mileage allowances for travel to and from (and within) their constituencies. Inner London MPs qualify for a London allowance (£1223 in 1994), while all other MPs are entitled to claim a so-called Additional Costs Allowance (£10,958 in 1994) which is supposed to take account of the extra costs of having to have two homes as a function of Parliamentary life.

Ministers, who have the same constituency duties as their back-bench colleagues (excluding peers), receive various levels of salary from public funds according to their positions in the Government, together with a proportion of their Parliamentary salaries (£23,854 in 1994). In 1995 Ministerial salaries ranged from £120,179 for the Lord Chancellor (the senior legal officer in the land who is more highly paid than the Prime Minister) to £21,961 for the lowliest Parliamentary Under-Secretary and £18,620 for an Assistant Government Whip. However, when the proportion of their Parliamentary salary to which they are entitled is included, the latter two figures rise to £45,815 and £42,474 respectively.

Compared with their counterparts in comparable democracies, British Ministers and Members of Parliament do not enjoy very lavish salaries. However, their overall package of pay and allowances is probably as good as the average in many other countries. Ever since MPs began to award themselves significant pay and allowances in 1964, the issue has been controversial and ostensibly unpopular with the media and the general public. In spite of the automatic link between the pay of MPs and a percentage of civil service pay at a determined level and in spite of the work of the Top Salaries Review Board which makes recommendations on Ministerial pay, it seems that there is never a right moment for Members of Parliament, Ministers (and indeed peers who get modest daily allowances for their attendance at the House of Lords) to increase their remuneration even if only in line with the cost of living. Furthermore, the situation has been exacerbated in recent years by a succession of sensational revelations in the media of MPs allegedly being prepared to take money from outside interests in return for asking Parliamentary Questions, and this has opened up a much wider debate about the propriety or otherwise of MPs having paid outside interests in addition to their public duties. All outside interests (both paid and unpaid) are supposed to be declared in the Register of Members' Interests which is kept up-to-date by a senior Parliamentary clerk and hitherto the principle of full, voluntary disclosure was thought to be sufficient. However, public interest in these matters became much more acute in the 1990s and it seems likely that recommendations from the Nolan Committee – established by the Prime Minister in 1994 – will lead to a number of new guidelines for higher standards in public life which may pave the way, eventually, for a complete ban on paid outside interests for MPs.

Apart from the Speaker and the three Deputies, the only MPs not in the Government who have additional salaries paid from public funds are the Leader of the Opposition (£37,495 in 1994), the Opposition Chief Whip (£28,936 in 1994) and the Opposition Pairing Whip (£18,620 in 1994). Once again their total remuneration is increased in each case by £23,854 which (in 1994) was the proportion of their Parliamentary salary to which they were entitled in respect of their duties as constituency MPs. These financial arrangements symbolise the longstanding commitment in Britain to the idea of constitutional Opposition and give financial expression to the traditional term 'Her Majesty's Loyal Opposition'. Indeed, Britain was the first Parliamentary democracy to make such financial arrangements for leading members of the Opposition in recognition of their constitutional duty to oppose the Government of the day.

The conditions of work for MPs have improved dramatically over the last two or three decades, although some of the arrangements reflect the lingering amateurism which still characterises some of the more traditional habits and assumptions at Westminster. For example, when the Chamber of the House of Commons was rebuilt after the Second World War, it was decided to leave the size and shape as it had been before the German attack which had destroyed it, namely rows of opposed benches and a total seating capacity of no more than two thirds of those entitled to take a seat. This was consciously done to reflect both the combative nature of British Parliamentary politics and the conversational, occasionally intimate, atmosphere of many debates and other proceedings.

Although some nearby buildings at 1 Parliament Street and 7 Millbank were refurbished for MPs and their personal staff in the late 1980s and early 1990s and although a completely new Parliamentary office building is planned for completion in the late 1990s, there is currently a shortage of suitably equipped office premises for individual MPs at Westminster and a number of them still have to make do with a desk, telephone and filing cabinet in rooms shared with their colleagues. The traditional approach to these matters has reflected a certain caution on the part of successive generations of MPs at the prospect of having to defend the spending of large amounts of taxpayers' money on facilities for themselves, and this has been reinforced by the reluctance of every British Government to encourage MPs not in the Administration to become professional, full-time politicians capable of monitoring the Executive on anything like equal terms.

Furthermore, most MPs now have such a burden of constituency work and committee work at Westminster that they spend relatively little time in the Chamber, except when present for Questions to Ministers or particular debates in which they hope to take part. Of course, this trend has been somewhat modified by the televising of the Commons, which has lured many more MPs into the Chamber at any rate during prime time (that is, when the media are paying attention) since they hope to be seen in glorious political action by their constituents and the general public. Nevertheless it remains broadly true that until quite recently MPs have had to perform an increasingly varied and time-consuming range of political tasks in physical conditions which were largely unchanged since the mid-nineteenth century when the present Palace of Westminster was built.

11.2 The power of the Commons

The tasks of the House of Commons are diffuse, variable and rather difficult to define in a permanent and authoritative way. They are not set out in any single document or defined in any Court ruling. In cases of dispute the most reliable guide is *Erskine May*, the reference book which covers the whole of Parliamentary procedure in the lower House according to the precedents established over centuries by successive Speakers and codified by successive Clerks of the Commons.[6]

Theory and practice

In theory, the House of Commons has very great power in the British constitution. This could be said to include the power to make and unmake Governments, to topple Prime Ministers, to safeguard the liberties of British subjects, to bring to light and remedy injustices, and even to legislate itself out of existence or the country into a dictatorship.

In practice, the power of the Commons is usually subsumed in the power of the Government of the day, which governs through Parliament as long as it retains the voting support of an overall majority in the House of Commons. It is usually misleading to refer to the powers of the Commons in any way which implies that such powers can be divorced from those of modern single-party Government which has been the norm in recent times. In normal Parliamentary conditions, when one of the main parties on its own has an overall majority in the Commons, the power of the House as a representative institution seeking to monitor and control the Government of the day is wielded principally by the Opposition parties in their constant efforts to draw attention to the shortcomings of Government policy and to criticise, delay and occasionally obstruct the progress of Government legislation. There is, however, an important, if delicate role for Government back-benchers as representatives of those in the electorate who voted for the party in office and as critics of Government policy when they believe it is reneging on party commitments or falling short of public expectations.

Only on rare occasions this century has the power of the House of Commons really made itself felt. One of the most famous examples was in May 1940, when the poor result of a vital confidence debate on the conduct of the war (when the Chamberlain Government won the vote with a reduced majority, but entirely lost the argument and the mood of the House) led Neville Chamberlain to resign as Prime Minister and so make way for Winston Churchill to succeed him as the country's war-time leader. Another memorable example was in March 1979 when, at the end of a confidence debate following the so-called Winter of Discontent, all the Opposition parties united to defeat what was by then a minority Labour Government and so precipitated the May 1979 General Election which brought the Conservatives under Margaret Thatcher to power.

A more recent example of Parliamentary power was the ability of the small band of Euro-sceptics on the Conservative back-benches to threaten and almost to defeat the Government legislation to give legal effect to the Treaty of Maastricht in Britain. In this case a disparate group of between 10 and 20 back-benchers, often in tactical alliance with the Labour Opposition, were able to alarm and annoy Ministers for months on end while the Bill concerned was slowly grinding its way through the legislative process. The practical effect of this sustained Parliamentary campaign – which had some powerful support in parts of the media and in many Conservative-held constituencies – was to debilitate and discredit John Major's Administration and, in so doing, to sow the seeds of its subsequent loss of authority in the country at large. On the whole, however, all such examples of raw Parliamentary power have been rare in modern times, since on most occasions Governments have been able to count upon the voting support and loyalty of their own back-benchers.

The power of influence

In most normal circumstances the House of Commons has to rely upon the power of influence – that is, influence upon Ministers in the Government, influence upon the policies of the Government, and influence upon the media and public opinion. Effective influence in the Commons is frequently exercised in a discreet manner *before* the event, whether in party committees, formal delegations or informal conversations. On the other hand, the exercise of overt Parliamentary power (as in the examples already given earlier in this chapter) is usually confined to the comparatively rare occasions when the authority of a Minister or sometimes of the Government as a whole is in jeopardy or may even have broken down. For example, when it became clear at the beginning of April 1982 that Ministers in the Foreign Office and the Ministry of Defence had lost the confidence of the bulk of the Conservative Parliamentary Party following the Argentinian invasion of the Falklands Islands, Lord Carrington and most of his Ministerial team at the Foreign Office resigned and John Nott at the Ministry of Defence offered his resignation, but had it refused at the time by Margaret Thatcher because the nation was by then effectively at war with Argentina. In crude and capricious Parliamentary conditions this was a vivid example of the power of the Commons or, more precisely, the power of Government back-benchers when they are no longer prepared to support Ministers because of grievous failures of policy – perceived or actual.

Another example is provided by the case of Nicholas Ridley, Secretary of State for the Environment from 1986 to 1989, who became increasingly accident prone and unpopular with the electorate because of his obvious disdain for the usual shibboleths of 'green' politics. His incorrigible attitudes made life very difficult for Conservative back-benchers who conveyed their anxiety to the Conservative Whips with increasing frequency and intensity. The result was that by 1989 Margaret Thatcher was left with no alternative but to move him from the Department of the Environment in her Cabinet reshuffle of July that year, even though he remained one of her personal favourites. More recent examples of Ministerial vulnerability to Parliamentary displeasure – notably on the Government back-benches – were provided by the cases of Norman Lamont and Nicholas Scott. The former, when Chancellor, came to seem increasingly inept and accident prone, especially during the long economic recession of the early 1990s. Conservative MPs were bombarded with demands from their constituents and from the wolf-like media for a human (political) sacrifice. The situation became even more embarrassing following Black Wednesday on 16th September 1992 when Britain was effectively ejected by the financial markets from the European Exchange Rate Mechanism to which the Government's entire anti-inflation policy had been anchored – at least rhetorically. Although Norman Lamont clung onto office as Chancellor of the Exchequer for a few more months, his case became hopeless and his eventual fate was sealed. Accordingly, John Major unceremoniously sacked him in May 1993. The latter case of Nicholas Scott was equally painful in that he had been a long-serving and personally popular Minister for the Disabled. Yet his Ministerial position became fundamentally untenable in the summer of 1994 when his Department was involved in some Parliamentary 'dirty tricks' designed to spike the chances of a far-reaching Private Member's Bill on behalf of the disabled ever reaching the statute book. In this case the Parliamentary operation was a 'success', but the Minister 'died' in that he was sacked by John Major in the mid-term reshuffle soon after. Both cases exemplified the political truth that when a Minister becomes a significant liability or embarrassment to the party in office and especially to Government back-benchers, sooner or later the unfortunate individual gets the sack.

Over the long period since the Second World War such examples of raw Parliamentary power have been relatively rare, although more recently in the febrile atmosphere of mass media politics the vulnerability of errant or fallible Ministers appears to have increased. Certainly such things seem to happen faster and with grater sensationalism these days than was the case even twenty years ago and in this respect, as in many others, the nature of British politics has changed significantly over the years. Nowadays Parliamentary reputations are built up and then demolished sometimes with alarming rapidity. The more that certain Ministers are thrown into the limelight, the more rapidly they seem to become vulnerable to destruction at the hands of the media and their own back-bench 'colleagues'. In all such cases the most decisive criteria for Ministerial survival are the degree of political embarrassment caused to the rest of the Government, the extent to which Government back-benchers are prepared to weather it, and whether the Prime Minister eventually wishes to sacrifice or stand by the Minister in question. In each and every case the chain of events and the eventual outcome is subtly different, although it may not seem that way to the victims of such political 'assassination'.

The background reality which lies behind all this is that at nearly every General Election since the war the electorate has voted and the electoral system has worked in such a way as to ensure that one of the main parties has had an overall majority in the Commons large enough to withstand most back-bench rebellions and the political erosion which takes place due to death and retirement during the normal span of a Parliament. In such circumstances the power of the Commons has not normally been manifested in successful attempts to censure Ministers, still less to defeat Governments. Instead it has been exercised through constant back-bench influence upon Ministers and the constant interplay between Governments striving to get their policy approved and their legislation onto the Statute book and Oppositions striving to criticise their actions and delay or frustrate their progress.

Parliamentary culture

The House of Commons has sometimes been described as 'the best club in London', although doubtless there would be many members of clubs, such as Whites or the Garrick, to challenge this claim. However, it does say something about the Parliamentary culture in Britain. It is an atmosphere in which the cut and thrust of the party battle is balanced by a political camaraderie which often makes it easier to form friendships across the floor of the House than with other members on the same side. It is an institution which relies upon the assumption that all its members are 'honourable' (although this may have become harder to sustain in the context of alleged Parliamentary 'sleaze' in recent years) and all are equal in terms of democratic legitimacy.

Yet in an institution in which there are supposed to be no second-class members, it is remarkable how some are more equal than others, and how front-benchers and Privy Councillors seem to get all the best parts. The main explanation, of course, is that traditional Parliamentary procedure, much of which dates from the 1880s, assumes that debate and discussion will be conducted largely by the political giants of the day and that the rest will be content with minor roles as spear-carriers or cheer leaders. This established tendency is reinforced by the simple fact that the Chamber itself is rather small (deliberately so) and that no more than about two thirds of those entitled can possibly find a seat on the green benches when the House is full – for example, on Budget Day or on Tuesdays and Thursdays during Prime Minister's Question Time. In short, there are only limited opportunities for MPs to shine during prime Parliamentary time at Westminster and most of these are taken by senior Ministers and their 'shadows' on the Opposition front bench.

Another interesting aspect of Parliamentary culture in the House of Commons is the extent to which the institutionalised, almost ritual, party conflict is organised by the party Whips working through what are known as 'the usual channels'. This phrase is a euphemism for the sometimes heated and vigorous discussions which take place behind the scenes and off the record between the two front benches. Without the benefit of such discussions, which can include the Prime Minister and the Leader of the Opposition on occasions, the whole place would probably grind to a halt.[7] As it is, the essential deal between the two sides is based upon two key assumptions: (1) that the Government must 'get its business' (that is, get its legislation passed more or less intact); and (2) that the Opposition must have full opportunities to oppose and, within limits, to decide what is newsworthy and urgent or what is uncontentious and acceptable and hence suitable for full cooperation between the parties. In support of this generally pragmatic approach to the conduct of Parliamentary business is the basic British idea that it is the duty of Her Majesty's Loyal Opposition to oppose the Government of the day, coupled with the understanding that there are few problems which cannot be solved in Parliament by the so-called 'business managers' on each side acting in tacit cooperation.

Indeed, the cooperative principle is reflected in the attitude and behaviour of individual MPs who strive very hard as soon as they get to Westminster to secure 'a pair' – that is, a member on the other side of the House who will agree on specific occasions (normally 2-line whips) to stay away from the division lobbies when the votes are called, so that the overall result of the vote is not affected. Such 'pairing' is an invaluable practice for those with long Parliamentary careers and can serve to mitigate what would otherwise be the tedium and exhaustion of staying up half the night to vote on matters about which most members may know little and care even less. However, such personal arrangements (which have to be registered with the Whips on each side) are only allowed to operate on the less contentious items of Parliamentary business which usually attract no more than a 2-line whip – signifying that in the eyes of the parties the issue is not at the heart of the party political battle. See Figure 11.1 for typical 'whips' giving guidance to Conservative and Labour MPs.

A final aspect of Parliamentary culture which is worth mentioning is the fondness of MPs in all parties, but especially on the Conservative side, for dining clubs and informal political gatherings of all kinds. It is sometimes said that the morning and afternoon hours at Westminster resemble those of a coffee shop or works canteen, while the evening hours are often whiled away in the Smoking Room (where fewer people now actually

Figure 11.1 Typical party 'whips'

(a) Conservative

<u>SECRET</u> The House will meet:

<u>MONDAY, 24th April, 1995</u> at 2.30 p.m. for Welsh, Attorney General's and Foreign and Commonwealth (Overseas Development) Questions.

Pensions Bill (Lords): 2nd Reading, Money and Ways and Means Resolutions.

Important divisions will take place, and your attendance

===

at 9.30 p.m. for 10.00 p.m.. and until the Money and Ways

===

and Means Resolutions which are not debatable are

===

obtained, is essential.

===

Motion on Team and Group Ministries which is a Church of England (General Synod) Measure. (EXEMPTED BUSINESS for 90 minutes)
<u>Your attendance is requested.</u>

<u>TUESDAY, 25th April</u>, at 2.30 p.m. for Education Questions and Prime Minister's Questions.
Tabling for Employment Questions and Prime Minister's Questions.

10 Minute Rule Bill: Road Traffic Reduction. (Mr Cynog Dafis)

Medical (Professional Performance) Bill: 2nd Reading and Money Resolution.

Divisions will take place, and your attendance at 9.30

===

p.m. for 10.00 p.m., and until the Money Resolution

===

which is not debatable is obtained, is essential unless

===

you have registered a firm pair.

===

Figure 11.1 continued

WEDNESEDAY, 26th April at 10.00 a.m.

PRIVATE MEMBERS' DEBATES

1. Mr Andrew Row - Responsibility to children.
2. Mr David Hinchcliffe - The future of Rugby League.
3. Mr Archy Kirkwood - Non-domestic rates in Scotland.
5. Mr Nigel Spearing - The National Health Service in East London.

At 2.30 p.m.. PROMPT.
Scottish Questions.

Tabling for Trade and Industry Questions.

10 Minute Rule Bill: Professional Football Compliance. (Kate Hoey)

Criminal Appeal Bill: Remaining stages.

Important divisions will take place, and your attendance

at 3.30 p.m. and until the business is concluded is

essential

NOTE: A Motion to suspend the ten o'clock
rule will be moved at 10.00 p.m.

THURSDAY, 27th April, at 2.30 p.m. for Northern Ireland Questions and Prime Minister's Questions.
Tabling for Treasury Questions and Prime Minister's Questions.

Debate on China and Hong Kong on a Motion for the Adjournment.

Your attendance is requested.

FRIDAY, 28th April, at 9.30 a.m.

PRIVATE MEMBERS' BILLS
Road Traffice (New Drivers): Remaining Stages. (Dr. Michael Clark

Referendum Bill: 2nd Reading. (Mrs Teresa Gorman)

Tampons (Safety) Bill: 2nd Reading. (Dawn Primarolo)

Your attendance is requested.

Figure 11.1 *continued*

(b) Labour

MONDAY 24th April 1995,

PARLIAMENTARY LABOUR PARTY
The House will meet at
2.30 p.m.

1. Wales, Attorney General, & O'seas Devpt questions.

2. PENSIONS BILL (LORDS): SECOND READING.
   (Donald Dewar and Adam Ingram).

YOUR ATTENDANCE BY 9 P.M. IS ESSENTIAL.

3. Motion on the Team and Group Ministries Measure which
   is a Church of England (General Synod) Measure.
   (Frank Field).

YOUR CONTINUED ATTENDANCE IS REQUESTED.

TUESDAY 25th April,

the House will meet at
2.30 p.m.

1. Education questions, tabling for Employment.

2. Ten Minute Rule Bill: Road Traffice Reduction. –
   C Dafis.

3. MEDICAL (PROFESSIONAL PERFORMANCE) BILL: SECOND
   READING. (Nick Brown).

YOUR ATTENDANCE IS REQUESTED.

WEDNESDAY 26th April,

the House will meet at
10 a.m.

1. PRIVATE MEMBERS' BUSINESS.
   10 – 11.30 am   Responsibility To Children. –
                    A Rowe.
                    (Llin Golding)..

   11.30 am – 1 pm   The Future of Regby League. –
                      D Hinchliffe, (Tom Pendry).

2. Scotland quetions, Tabling for Trade &
   Industry.

3. Ten Minute Rull Bill: Professional Football
   Compliance. - K Hoey.

4. CRIMINAL APPEAL BILL: REMAINING STAGES.
   (Jack Straw and Alun Michael).

YOUR ATTENDANCE FROM 4.30 P.M. IS ESSENTIAL.

Figure 11.1 continued

THURSDAY 27th April,   the House will meet at
                                     2.30 p.m.

1.Northern Ireland questions,   tabling for Treasury.

2. Debate on China and Hong Kong on a Motion for the
   Adjournment of the House. (Robin Cook).

YOUR ATTENDANCE IS REQUESTED.

FRIDAY 28th April,   the House will meet at
                                     9.30 a.m.

1. PRIVATE MEMBERS' BILLS.
   Road Traffic
   (New Drivers) Bill: Remaining Stages.
   (Joan Walley)   Michael Clark.

   Referendum Bill: Second Reading.
   (Joyce Quin)   Teresa Gorman.

MONDAY 1st May,   the House will meet at
                                     2.30 p.m.

1. Social Security, &   tabling for National
   Chancellor of the Duchy of Heritage, Church
   Lancaster questions,   Commissioners, & Lord
                                     Chancellor's Dept.

2. CHILDREN (SCOTLAND) BILL: REMAINING STAGES.

2. Members should be ready to
   respond to a THREE LINE WHIP.

                                    DEREK FOSTER.

EUROPEAN STANDING COMMITTEES

European Standing Committee B will meet on Wednesday 26th
April at 19.30 am to consider the unnumbered explanatory
memorandum submitted by the Foreign and Commonwealth
Office on 13th December 1994, relating to the accession of
new member states to the European Union.

smoke), on the Terrace overlooking the Thames in summer, or around various dining tables among self consciously exclusive groups of like-minded MPs. In the Labour Party the various groups usually like to meet and talk in the Tea Room – a rather scruffy canteen and sitting area confined to MPs and officers of the House. In the Conservative Party they prefer the Member's Dining Room or private rooms on the Terrace level or even their London homes. The common denominator on all these occasions is the self indulgent exchange of political gossip and ideas, something which is the very stuff of politics in all Parliamentary assemblies around the world.

The views of these internal party groups, as and when they are clarified, are propounded and taken forward by the MPs concerned who usually lose little time in passing on the essence of their discussions to their party whips and sometimes, in suitably veiled form, to lobby journalists. It is in these ways and at these *symposia* (in the Greek sense of the word) that much political opinion at Westminster is moulded and developed. If a full account is to be given of life in the House of Commons, attention should be paid to these political groupings within at least the two main parties. In the Labour Party, the Tribune Group and the Campaign Group each organise their own slates of candidates for the annual elections to the Shadow Cabinet. In the Conservative Party, the 92 Group, the Macleod Group, One Nation, The Progress Trust and the No Turning Back Group are among the much more numerous informal groupings which compete for influence over party policy and Ministerial appointments.

11.3 Main functions

In 1867 Walter Bagehot suggested that the House of Commons needed to perform the following functions if it was to do its duty: 'elect a Ministry, legislate, teach the nation, express the nation's will and bring matters to the nation's attention'.[8] If we were to translate his words into modern terms, we would say that the House of Commons has to provide most of the Ministers in any Government, to scrutinise and pass legislation, to give a lead to public opinion on the great issues of the day, and to seek redress for the grievances and concerns of the general public. There are, of course, other vital functions performed by the modern House of Commons, notably Parliamentary control of the Executive and party political conflict on the Parliamentary stage. Yet the essential functions of the House have not changed very much since the time when Walter Bagehot made his authoritative observation. The functions of the Commons are summarised in tabular form in Figure 11.2.

Representation and redress

The oldest function of Members of Parliament is to represent the interests of their constituents and to seek redress for their grievances by the Government of the day. This function, which has been performed ever since the establishment of Parliament in the thirteenth century, is still a vital task for MPs in modern conditions. There are a number of different ways in which it is carried out. These range from having a quiet word with a Minister in the division lobby to signing an Early Day Motion with other MPs in order to signal the breadth and depth of support for a particular cause or concern.

Figure 11.2 Functions of the House of Commons

Representation and redress	*The party battle*
On behalf of constituents	In the Chamber
On behalf of interest	In Committees
On behalf of causes	In the media
The legislative process	*Parliamentary control*
First Reading	Debates in the Chamber
Second Reading	Oral and written Questions
Committee Stage	Select Committee work
Report Stage	Representations to Ministers
Third Reading	Representations to Agencies

They include such techniques as writing a letter to a Minister enclosing documentary evidence of a constituent's complaint, leading a delegation to lobby a Minister in Whitehall, putting down a Parliamentary Question for written answer in order to get a Ministerial response on the record in *Hansard*, putting down a Question for oral answer in order to be able to make a point in a supplementary question on the record in the Chamber, and applying to the Speaker for an Adjournment Debate at the end of the day's Parliamentary proceedings or an Emergency Debate immediately after Oral Questions and any Ministerial Statements. As must be evident from this brief description, there are many channels of representation available to MPs when performing this aspect of their duties. It is normal for them to begin with one of the lower key methods and to resort to the more dramatic ones only if the former do not have the desired effect. This wide range of possible techniques for publicising the concerns or grievances of their constituents gives back-bench MPs a real degree of influence in their representations to Ministers and civil servants.

If MPs did not speak up and intervene on behalf of their constituents when the latter feel frustrated by the bureaucracy of central Government or other public agencies, many people might conclude that Parliamentary democracy was a bit of a sham and withdraw their support for it. Even as things stand, the general public has a pretty cynical attitude towards the role and utility of MPs and it is not usually until people experience a positive response from their MP that they are prepared to reconsider their habitually low opinion of the political process. On the other hand, when a conscientious MP is able to provide effective help for a constituent, it can make the beneficiary of such political action more likely to appreciate the value of having an MP in the first place. To the extent that MPs exert themselves in this way – and nearly all of them do – it provides at least one recognisable justification for the British Parliamentary system.

The party battle

Another function of Members of Parliament is to act as combatants for their party when it is in Government and critics or opponents of the Government when their party is in Opposition. The party battle, which was particularly polarised in the 1970s and 1980s, has been deplored in many quarters, especially by the minor parties whose interests are not very well catered for in the procedural arrangements at Westminster. However, there are some points to be made in its favour. It encourages the voters to take an interest in national politics between General Elections, to consider at least two sides to every political argument and to pay some attention to topical policy issues. Without the drama of the party battle at Westminster and, of course, in the columns and studios of the media, the political process would lose much of its vitality and the influence of the bureaucracy would increase. While there are those who would welcome such an alternative way of conducting British political life, even they would have to concede that it would probably produce a less accountable and less democratic form of government.

Although in Britain many people pay little or no attention to the processes of politics, there would probably be even less public interest and even more public apathy without the stimulus and often annoyance of the party battle. Evidence over a long period suggests that the degree of success or failure of the Opposition parties in criticising the Government of the day and putting forward their own proposals does have a cumulative effect upon public opinion and subsequently upon the voting behaviour of at least the more attentive voters. Opposition parties very often fail to get all the publicity which they would like (especially for their own policy proposals), by they are often successful in sowing the seeds of doubt and resentment about the performance of the party in office in the minds of the voters. In this way, more than any other, there tends to be a negative bias in the British party battle which breeds zero sum attitudes in the minds of many voters. Yet it is hard to see how things could be otherwise as long as Britain retains its present 'winner takes all' electoral system.

The legislative process

Another well recognised, but not always well understood, function of Members of Parliament is the scrutiny and passage of legislation. It is the function most often mentioned by members of the public when asked to describe the activities of Parliament. Over the years it has absorbed an increasing proportion of Parliamentary time as the scope and complexity of legislation have increased and as the public – notably pressure groups – have made greater demands upon Governments of all political persuasions. Only in the last few years have there been some signs that public expectations may have moderated under the long-standing influence of the protracted economic recession of the early 1990s. Nevertheless there does not seem to have been any fundamental change in public attitudes and expectations which have been culturally conditioned by a much longer period (during most of the twentieth century) of rising living standards and growing political willingness to countenance an expanding role for the state.

The legislative process in the Commons begins with *First Reading*. This is the name of the formal stage at which printed copies of a Bill are made available in the Vote Office for all MPs and others who are interested to read and consider it. After an appropriate interval, this is followed by *Second Reading* (usually about two weeks later) when a wide ranging debate takes place for about six hours during which the broad purposes of a bill are discussed and at the end of which a vote is usually taken which shows whether or not the House approves of a Bill in principle. This is the stage of the debate when the senior Minister in charge of a Bill sets out the broad arguments for it, the chief Opposition spokesman sets out the broad arguments against it (unless a Bill is wholly uncontentious, in which case detailed criticism and constructive suggestions are more likely to be offered), interested back-benchers on both sides of the House make national or constituency points, and junior Ministers and Opposition spokesmen wind up the debate during the final hour by answering (or sometimes ignoring) the various points made by others during the course of the debate. At the end of such debates on all Government Bills the votes are whipped, which means that MPs are expected to support the position of their own party, unless they have overwhelming reasons for doing otherwise – for example, conscientious objections to a Bill or overriding constituency reasons for opposing it.

Assuming that a Bill is approved by the House at Second Reading, it is then referred to a committee, usually a *Standing Committee* 'upstairs' where it is debated in detail and at length by a committee of between 16 and 50 MPs chosen to reflect the party balance in the House as a whole.[9] This means that a typical Standing Committee may be made up of two or more Ministers in charge of the Bill, a Government Whip and perhaps a dozen or more back-benchers on the Government side, ranged against a variety of Opposition MPs who will invariably include two or more Opposition spokesmen and an Opposition Whip as well as a number of interested Opposition back-benchers who between them usually share the burdens of scrutinising and opposing the Bill.

The task of a Standing Committee is to debate and scrutinise a Bill clause by clause and line by line. This usually involves the members of the Opposition side putting down a considerable number of critical or even wrecking amendments, some merely probing but some seeking to alter fundamentally or even destroy the effect of a Bill. The Ministers in charge of a Bill have to answer each separate debate and, if necessary, to persuade their own back-benchers to vote against any amendments unacceptable to the Government if the Opposition is not prepared to withdraw them at the end of each debate. Once all the debates on amendments and on each clause 'stand part' have been concluded, new clauses can be proposed and debated, provided they fall within the scope of the long title of a Bill.

In the case of unusually complex and controversial Bills, the latter stages in committee often have to be timetabled as long as the Government can persuade the House as a whole to vote for a so-called 'guillotine' motion at the end of a three-hour debate in the Chamber, thus ensuring that the proceedings are timetabled for the remainder of the committee stage. This procedural device is supposed to ensure that all parts of a Bill are discussed, however briefly, and that the passage of a Bill through committee is not unreasonably delayed by Opposition filibustering. Yet even with the benefit of this timetabling procedure, some Bills may involve a committee stage of 100 hours or more and large parts of some Bills may still not be adequately discussed in important respects.

After an appropriate interval (usually several weeks to give time to officials and legislative draftsmen to take account of amendments put forward in committee), the Bill is then returned to the floor of the House for the final Commons stages of *Report and Third Reading*. These are usually taken on the same day and may last for six hours or more– in other words, at least one full day's debate in the Chamber. The Report stage is the time when the House as a whole (especially those who did not serve on the Standing Committee) have a chance to speak and vote upon any new amendments or new clauses which have been accepted by the Speaker for debate on the floor of the House. It is out of order for opponents of a Bill to go over ground already traversed during earlier stages of the legislative process. Third Reading, which follows immediately, is usually no more than a fairly brief debate on the general merits or demerits of a Bill as it then stands, and provides what is usually a final opportunity for the House as a whole to record its views. The debate is concluded by yet another vote on the main principles of the Bill in which MPs tend once again to vote on party lines.

By this stage of the legislative process the House of Commons has usually concluded its scrutiny of a Bill, unless subsequently the House of Lords insists upon making some substantial amendments which Ministers decide to resist. If this happens (and it is a fairly rare occurrence), the Commons have later to give further consideration to the Bill as amended by their Lordships. If all the Lords amendments are acceptable to the Commons (which really means to the Government of the day), the lower House simply sends a message to the upper House signifying its agreement. If, however, some of the Lords amendments are not acceptable to the governing party in the Commons (even if they have been passed by a majority in the Lords containing peers who normally support the Government), the lower House sends a message containing its reasons for disagreement and possibly some counter amendments of its own. It is then for the Lords to decide whether to persist with their opposition to the Commons or to give way gracefully in the light of the fact that under the constitutional provisions of the 1911 and 1949 Parliament Acts, the House of Commons can ultimately get its way. On nearly all occasions since 1949 their Lordships have considered discretion to be the better part of valour and accordingly have given way to the will of the majority in the Commons.

Since nearly all Lords amendments are inspired by the need for technical or drafting improvements in Government Bills (nearly all of which are made at the instigation of Ministers in the light of criticisms voiced during earlier stages of the legislative process), such amendments usually cause no difficulties in the lower House. They merely underline the usefulness of having a bi-cameral legislature. Once a Bill is out of the Lords, it is virtually complete and awaits only the formality of Royal Assent by the Queen. The whole process from First Reading to Royal Assent normally takes between six months and one year. However, it can be speeded up dramatically in cases of emergency legislation – for example, Bills to deal with terrorism or civil disorder which (with the benefit of agreement between the parties) can be put through all stages of the legislative process in 24 hours if necessary.

Parliamentary scrutiny and control

Yet another vital function of Members of Parliament is to scrutinise and seek to control the activities of the Executive. This is probably the most necessary, but also the most difficult function to be performed by the House in modern conditions, essentially because there is no formal separation of powers in Britain between the Executive and the Legislature as there is in so many other comparable countries. This means that in Britain the Government of the day – provided it has a secure overall majority in the House of Commons – is more often able to dominate Parliament than the other way around.

Traditionally, it was assumed that Ministers' responsibility to answer the questions and debating points of Members of Parliament constituted adequate and respectable Parliamentary control of the Executive. Yet with the remorseless extension of the perceived responsibilities of Government over the last 50 years and more, it has become painfully clear that this traditional and complacent assumption does not meet public expectations and needs to be reinforced if central Government and its agencies are to be properly scrutinised, let along controlled by the elected representatives of the people.

The fundamental problem here is that with typical British ambiguity there is a clash between two different versions of democratic legitimacy – that of the party elected into office at the previous General Election to govern the country for a period of years according to the principles and policies which it put before the electorate, and that of the House of Commons as a whole as the overall, democratic manifestation of the will of the people at a particular time.

In modern times Parliamentarians (that is, members of both Houses) have sought to square this circle by making increasingly full and effective use of *Select Committees*. In the House of Commons these are committees reflecting broadly the political balance in the House at any time which are charged by the House as a whole with scrutinising and controlling the activities of the Executive in given policy areas. Originally, in the nineteenth century, they were set up by the House *ad hoc* to look closely into particular issues of public concern – for example, Britain's military shortcomings in the Crimean War. They can also be traced back to the attitudes of William Gladstone and other Parliamentarians in the 1850s who, in their determination to guarantee the probity and efficiency of public expenditure, established the *Public Accounts Committee* as a permanent committee of the House of Commons designed to enable the House as a whole to be satisfied that public money was being correctly and properly spent.

From these nineteenth-century beginnings through to modern times, the fortunes of Select Committees have waxed and waned. They have tended to be more powerful when the Government of the day has had only a very small majority in the Commons or no majority at all (as in the late 1970s), but considerably less powerful when the Government of the day has had a commanding majority which it could use, if necessary, to steamroller any flickering challenge from largely impotent Select Committees. Indeed, there has been a whole school of thought at Westminster for many years – well represented by people like Enoch Powell and Tony Benn – that holds that the correct way to scrutinise and control the Executive is on the floor of the House and that Select Committees are little more than a self-important and time consuming distraction from what should be the cockpit of Parliamentary control in the Chamber.

Against this background it was fortuitous and somewhat surprising that the incoming Conservative Government in 1979 decided to propose a comprehensive reform of the Select Committee structure which was willingly accepted by most Government backbenchers and certainly by the Opposition parties.[10] Following this fundamental reform, there is now one of these all-party and largely non-partisan committees for each area of central Government activity, as well as a number of non-Departmental committees which have deeper roots in Parliamentary soil as has already been explained. These Select Committees, each of which is usually composed of about 11 MPs broadly reflecting the party political balance in the House as a whole, meet regularly (perhaps two days a week when the House is sitting and on other occasions as well) to oversee and investigate their particular area of Government activity. In the course of their investigations, which can include foreign travel, they can call for persons and papers, and their findings are normally written up in substantial reports drafted by their clerks and expert advisers and usually redrafted and amended by members of the committee. Once published in the form of reports to the House as a whole, such documents are intended to inform both Parliamentary and public debate. Occasionally, they can have real influence upon the course of Government policy.[11]

In normal circumstances Select Committees have no legislative role, so they are not really analogous to the Congressional committees in the United States. However, on a few occasions they have been used as Parliamentary mechanisms for the exploration of policy options at a pre-legislative stage.[12] Whatever their shortcomings and inhibitions, they do represent a systematic attempt to improve Parliamentary scrutiny and control of the Executive and its agencies in Britain, which has come to seem all the more necessary as it has been increasingly recognised that the traditional forms of Ministerial accountability to the House as a whole do not guarantee the achievement of this important Parliamentary objective.

In recent years the influence (if not the power) of Select Committees has increased in that their public hearings are quite often televised and hence attract a degree of extra media and public interest. This makes them more formidable interlocutors for Ministers and senior civil servants and a more central part of the whole Parliamentary publicity machine. The Chairmen of such committees can become (or may already be) influential and newsworthy MPs who are often called to speak early in debates on the floor of the House and can be much in demand for media interviews. Yet it would be a mistake to believe that this extra visibility for Select Committees has altered to any real extent the fundamental imbalance of power in the House of Commons between a self-confident Government with a secure Parliamentary majority and the rest of the House, no matter how effective the Opposition may be or how keen certain MPs may have become to use Select Committees and other Parliamentary procedures more effectively to hold Ministers and the Executive to account.

The experience of the Westland Crisis in 1986 and other clashes between Members of Parliament and the Executive before and since underlines the fact that Parliamentary control of the Executive in Britain is not, and may never be, as effective as its proponents or some members of the general public would like.[13] In the final analysis Select Committees, and indeed Parliament as a whole, are likely to remain relatively weak when faced with a strong and determined Government which is confident of its ability to use its voting support on the floor of the House to overcome any challenge. The only circumstances in which this situation might be changed in future would be if a Government were committed to, or had imposed upon it by dint of its minority status in the Commons, a new constitutional settlement including extensive Parliamentary reform, a new Bill of Rights, an independent Supreme Court, legislation to guarantee freedom of information, and the introduction of proportional representation for elections to Westminster. Hitherto such comprehensive reforms have seemed most unlikely to come about, although it must be said that some such reforms now appear to be a real possibility in view of the stated policies of both the Labour and Liberal Democrat parties.[14]

As Professor Bernard Crick wrote about thirty years ago, we should not read too much into the idea of Parliamentary control in Britain because it means 'influence not direct power, advice not command, criticism not obstruction, scrutiny not initiative, and publicity not secrecy'.[15] Yet even these attenuated forms of Parliamentary control should not be underestimated in a political system which has never been characterised by clearcut and unambiguous power relationships. Furthermore, a degree of Parliamentary control to match that exercised by Congress in the United States would only be possible in Britain if it were decided to move to an explicit separation of powers set out in a newly codified constitution and guaranteed by an independent Supreme Court. Such revolutionary change is unlikely to be brought about in a political system in which it is the Government of the day and the official Opposition front bench (the putative alternative

Government) which effectively control the nature and scope of Parliamentary power. The irony is that it is in the name of 'Parliamentary supremacy' that Governments still dominate the political sphere in Britain, although this observation has increasingly to be qualified in the light of constitutional developments in the European Union.

11.4 The progress of reform

The progress of Parliamentary reform has been limited by the fact that the power of Parliament in Britain has usually been a euphemism for the power of Government ruling through Parliament. It has also been limited by the inherent tension between the interests of the Executive and those of the Legislature which is supposed to control it – in other words, between actual and potential Ministers on the one hand and all back-benchers on the other. In most normal circumstances, when the governing party has an overall majority in the House of Commons, any reform (that is, strengthening) of the power of the Commons is likely to mean a relative weakening of the power of Government. The only developments which are really likely to alter this state of affairs would be the introduction of electoral reform, together with a number of institutional and constitutional reforms. Since those who believe that they benefit from the present arrangements (the two front benches and a few self-styled 'great Parliamentarians') have been sceptical of the advantages of making such radical changes, it is easy to see why the cause of Parliamentary reform has only made modest headway.

Although the progress of Parliamentary reform has been slow and the reforms made have been rather marginal, recent experience in the 1990s has shown that it is possible if agreement can be reached between the two front benches. The new, generally warmer disposition towards the cause of Parliamentary reform has stemmed largely from the changing composition and outlook of all parties, but especially among Labour and Liberal Democrat MPs who, at least in their more 'modern' elements, have become increasingly impatient with those of their colleagues who cling to the traditional ways of doing things at Westminster. Reformist pressures have come strongly from the growing contingent of women MPs in the Opposition parties who have generally been very critical of the unsocial hours and archaic procedures of Parliament which militate against anything like a normal family life. Reform has also been spurred by the gathering institutional and legislative implications of Britain's membership of the European Union, notably the need for national Parliaments to equip themselves better to deal in a timely fashion with the spate of European legislative proposals emanating from the European institutions and with those European competences which are now being 'repatriated' to the member states under the doctrine of subsidiarity.[16]

In February 1992 the so-called Jopling Report of an all-party Committee chaired by a former Conservative Chief Whip recommended a number of far-reaching procedural reforms, including the time-tabling of all Government Bills and a variety of other proposals designed to enable the House to rise no later than 10.30 p.m., while allowing for the standard half hour for adjournment debates.[17] On this occasion the response from the Conservative side, both front-bench and back-bench, was generally favourable, while the die-hard tendency on the Opposition side seemed to be overcome by the party leadership. The result, after some prevarication and delay, was that the House eventually debated and approved a package of procedural reforms in the spirit of the Jopling Report on 19th December 1994.[18]

The reforms, which were introduced initially for a trial period of a single session (1994-95), seem likely to endure and, possibly, to be built upon in future, because they are in keeping with the new reformist mood in all parts of the House. The key points in the package were: (1) the curtailing of debate upon the Ways and Means Resolutions of Money Bills to a maximum of 45 minutes; (2) reference of most Statutory Instruments and European legislative proposals to a Standing Committee on Statutory Instruments with any debates on the floor of the House normally being limited to one and a half hours; (3) the House would no longer sit on eight Fridays during the annual session which MPs could then be sure of reserving for their constituency commitments; (4) the House would meet in plenary session every Wednesday between 10.00 a.m. and 2.30 p.m. to debate matters on an adjournment motion (in other words, unwhipped business); and (5) the subjects for debate on Wednesdays would be chosen by ballot and the rest of the time on Wednesdays would be concerned with Questions to Ministers and other normal Parliamentary business in the Chamber.

The spirit and purpose of this package of Parliamentary reform was to reduce somewhat the time-consuming demands of debates and votes in the Chamber, to provide more clear time for MPs to be in their constituencies during Parliamentary sessions, and to limit proceedings late in the evening so that all MPs could normally leave Westminster after voting at 10:00 p.m. – if not earlier when the business of the House permits. Belatedly, therefore, it was an attempt to modernise and humanise some of the House's antiquated procedures and to limit its secular tendency to sit for longer hours to less and less good effect.

The other area of procedural reform in which the House of Commons has made significant strides in recent years is in the sphere of financial procedure. As long ago as 1980 the so-called Armstrong Report produced by a Committee chaired by a former Cabinet Secretary recommended that the Commons consider both sides of the public accounts together and that such a unified Budget should be heralded a few months before by a 'green Budget' setting out the Chancellor's provisional ideas for revenue raising and public expenditure in the following year.[19] The essential ideas behind this proposal were that a unified Budget would be a more coherent way of presenting the public accounts than the traditional practice of dealing with revenue and expenditure in different Whitehall cycles, and that opportunities should be created for Parliament and other interested bodies to influence the fiscal policy of any Government at an earlier and more formative stage of policy making.

Subsequently, the first Thatcher Administration (1979-83) went some way towards accepting these ideas by increasing the range and quality of financial information made available to the House of Commons in the annual economic forecasts published by the Treasury. This reformed procedure was brought into effort for the first time in 1982 and subsequent Autumn Statements published by the Treasury became enlarged and more informative documents as a result. However, it was not until the first Major Administration (1990-92) that the Government accepted the idea of having a unified annual Budget, although it rejected the idea that this great Parliamentary occasion should be preceded a few months before by a provisional 'green Budget'. The result was that in 1993 there were two Budgets in the year (one on the old basis in the spring and one on the new basis in the autumn) and from 1994 a unified Budget has been presented by the Chancellor in November soon after the opening of each annual session of Parliament.

One effect of this procedural change has been to focus the Parliamentary debate on the Budget more on the Chancellor's public expenditure decisions than was the case before, although understandably any controversial tax changes still get the lion's share of immediate Parliamentary and media attention. Needless to say, not everyone at Westminster is content with the new arrangements. MPs in all parties have called for an extra debate on the economy each July to replace the debate on the Autumn Statement which used to take place in November or December, and for the annual Finance Bill to be split into two parts – a relatively brief 'political' Bill containing the really controversial measures and a much longer and more technical Taxes Management Bill designed to keep the Inland Revenue administration cost-effective and up-to-date. At the time of writing, the present Government has accepted the former suggestion, but rejected the latter on the grounds that it is based upon an artificial and untenable distinction in tax law.

The impact of radio and television

Since November 1989 the proceedings in the Chamber of the House of Commons and sometimes 'upstairs' in Select Committees have been broadcast on radio and television. The idea had been under discussion in Britain at least since the 1960s and had been promoted by both media and academic interests with growing support from MPs in all parties. For a long time there was nothing more adventurous than a limited experiment which began in the late 1970s with live radio transmission of a few particularly newsworthy exchanges or debates in the Commons. This tended to concentrate upon Prime Minister's Questions every Tuesday and Thursday and a few significant debates or Parliamentary occasions of particular media interest, such as the Chancellor's annual Budget Statement, the May 1978 debate on nuclear fuel reprocessing, the April 1982 debate on the outbreak of conflict over the Falkland Islands, and the January 1986 debate on the Westland crisis.

The present position (in 1995) on radio is that producers use edited extracts from the tape recordings of proceedings in the Chamber and in committee 'upstairs' as the raw material for programmes which are usually broadcast after the event, such as the BBC programmes *Today in Parliament* or *The Week in Westminster*. On television it has been possible since November 1989 for the general public both in Britain and abroad (courtesy of the C Span channel on satellite television) to watch coverage of proceedings both in the Chamber and 'upstairs' in committee. Although originally accepted only as an experiment, the House voted on a free vote in July 1990 to make the arrangements permanent and it now seems inconceivable that the television cameras will ever be withdrawn.

No one can be absolutely sure what will be the long term effects of allowing television cameras into the House of Commons and it is probably still too soon to suggest a definitive conclusion. On the one hand, the proponents of televising the Commons have argued that it brings the proceedings closer to the public – indeed, right into the sitting rooms of people in Britain and abroad – and thus can enhance public understanding and support for the working of British Parliamentary democracy. They have also argued that, if the House had continued to resist the televising of its proceedings, it would have condemned itself to increasing quaintness and irrelevance in the eyes of people everywhere who have become used to being able to watch all the leading political figures perform in front of the cameras.

The opponents of televising the Commons, on the other hand, have argued that it can have the effect of trivialising and sensationalising the proceedings, partly because the media are always more interested in the trivial and the sensational than the dull but worthy aspects of what happens and partly because many MPs are not able to resist the temptation of playing to the gallery of perhaps millions of viewers on big occasions. The opponents have also argued that, notwithstanding the special arrangements which were made to limit what may be shown by the cameras (for example, no reaction shots of any-one unless an MP is specifically referred to by the MP who has the floor at the time); eventually the imperatives of 'good television' (from the producer's point of view) are likely to predominate over a more restrained approach to portraying Parliamentary prac-tice. They have had to admit, however, that many of their worst fears have not actually been borne out in practice and that both Parliament and people have emerged relatively unscathed from the experience so far. Indeed, it could be said that life at Westminster continues very much as before.

11.5 Conclusion

The House of Commons has a range of powers and functions which can be formidable or merely nominal, depending upon the Parliamentary arithmetic at any time and the mood or inclinations of the 651 MPs. In what might be described as normal circum-stances, when the governing party has an effective overall majority, the Government of the day is able to get its way on the things which really matter, provided only that it retains the confidence and voting support of its own back-benchers. In the rarer circumstances when the result of a General Election has produced a very small majority for the governing party or even a so-called 'hung Parliament' (in which the Government has no overall majority), there can be a serious risk of defeat at the hands of combined Opposition parties. Indeed, even when a Government has a modest, but sufficient overall majority, it can still encounter great danger in Parliament if a signifi-cant and cohesive group of its own back-benchers are in revolt on a political issue where they have a good slice of public opinion on their side – as John Major and his Ministerial colleagues discovered in the early 1990s when the so-called 'Euro-sceptics' on the Conservative back-benches harried and nearly brought down the Government during the passage of the legislation designed to bring British law into line with the 1992 Maastricht Treaty.

There are many paradoxical aspects of the House of Commons which ought to discourage sweeping generalisations. All that can really be said is that the House carries out its various tasks with varying degrees of efficiency and success. It is reasonably effective as a forum for popular representation and redress. It is best known as a dramatic stage for party political conflict, especially now that it is broadcast to a potentially large audience by radio and television. It is quite good at the detailed scrutiny of legislation (although it still does not make the most efficient use of this time), but almost incapable of modifying legislation against the wishes of the Government of the day unless a group of party rebels are prepared to stick to their guns to the point of defying the party Whips. It is gradually becoming more effective as a mechanism for the scruti-ny and control of the Executive, although in this respect it cannot emulate the power and independence of the American Congress as long as there is no formal separation of powers in Britain.

In short, while the House of Commons is theoretically supreme in the British political system, in practice it is usually controlled by the Government of the day in tacit collusion with the official Opposition. In order words, the power of all MPs – and especially the preponderance of back-benchers – is severely limited by the rules and conventions of Britain's 'front-bench constitution'. This position is unlikely to change significantly unless and until there is all-party agreement to far-reaching reforms of Britain's electoral and constitutional arrangements. Such changes are unlikely to be made unless a new Parliamentary consensus emerges to support them, even though an incoming Government might believe that it had a mandate for such radical action. The scope for delay and obstruction is simply too great, especially since there are probably still enough entrenched traditionalists in all parties to thwart the most ambitious plans of the Parliamentary and constitutional reformers. In these circumstances it is unwise to make dogmatic statements about the House of Commons, not least because the mood and priorities of every Parliament are different and in politics no one can really know the future.

Suggested questions

1   To what extent do Members of Parliament reflect the views and interests of their constituents?
2   How well does the House of Commons perform its main functions?
3   What changes need to be made to improve Parliamentary control of the Executive?

Notes

1. W.I. Jennings, *Parliament*; 2nd edn, (Cambridge: CUP, 1969), pp. 7-8.
2. L.S. Amery, *Thoughts on the constitution* (Cambridge: CUP, 1947), p. 12.
3. Until recently ethnic minorities were significantly under-represented in all parties in Parliament. However, the Labour Party has made some successful efforts to recruit more MPs from Asian and Afro-Caribbean backgrounds - for example, Keith Vaz from Leicester and Diane Abbott from Hackney.
4. 'Virtual representation' was best defined a long time ago by Edmund Burke in 1797 when he wrote in a letter to Sir Hector Langrishe that it was 'representation in which there is a communion of interests and a sympathy in feelings and desires between those who act in the name of any description of people (that is, MPs) and the people in whose name they act (that is, particular sections or interests in the community), though the trustees (the MPs) are not chosen by them (but by the voters)'. Today 'virtual representation' raises topical and controversial issues about the outside interests of MPs.
5. It is significant that in 1995 less than one third of all MPs had had direct experience of Government as Minister or a Whip at any stage in their Parliamentary careers.
6. The latest (21st) edition of *Erskine May* was published in 1990 and was edited by the then Clerk of the Commons, Sir Clifford Boulton. It is particularly useful as a work of reference on current procedure and practice in the Commons.
7. Indeed, following the Conservative Government's decision to guillotine the Statutory Sick Pay Bill in December 1993, the then Leader of the Opposition, John Smith, retaliated by withdrawing all official pairing for divisions in the House and becoming unco-operative in dealings through 'the usual channels'. This gesture of Opposition displeasure with the Government only lasted until the following spring, but it did serve as a reminder of the extent to which the

House of Commons can only operate satisfactorily by consent and tacit cooperation between the two front benches.

8. W. Bagehot, *The English Constitution* (London: Fontana, 1978), p. 170.

9. Constitutional measures – such as the Maastricht Bill – have to be taken in a committee of the whole House in the chamber.

10. Since 1979 there have been the following Select Committees: Agriculture; Defence; Education; Employment; Energy (now absorbed by Trade and Industry); Environment; Foreign Affairs; Health and Social Security (since split into two committees); Home Affairs; Scottish Affairs; Trade and Industry; Transport; Treasury and Civil Service; and Welsh Affairs. Following the 1992 General Election additional Select Committee were established to cover National Heritage; and Science and Technology. In 1994 Northern Ireland was added to the list of Select Committees as part of the price exacted by the Ulster Unionists for their support of the Conservative Government at that time. The seven non-departmental Select Committees, which in many cases have been long established, are; Parliamentary Commissioner for Administration; Public Accounts; Statutory Instruments; European Legislation; Consolidation Bills; Procedure; and Broadcasting of the House. The arrangements for all Select Committees are co-ordinated by a small liaison committee composed of the chairman of all the various committees. There are also four 'domestic' committees dealing with the internal arrangements of the House of Commons; Information; Accommodation; Administration; and Catering.

11. For example, the Foreign Affairs Select Committee published a very influential report on the misuse of ODA support for the Pergau Dam project in July 1994, the Social Services Select Committee had a good deal of influence upon the reform of the Child Support Agency, and the Treasury and Civil Service Select Committee helped to shape the new Code for the Civil Service.

12. Examples of this sort of work are now rather dated, but in the 1970s Select Committees were occasionally used to investigate ideas for further fiscal legislation – for instances, Corporation Tax in 1970-71, Tax Credit in 1972-73 and Wealth Tax in 1974-75.

13. The different, but overlapping aspects of the Westland crisis were examined by no fewer than three Select Committees - Defence; Trade and Industry; and Treasury and Civil Service. See especially the Defence Select Committee Report entitled 'Westland plc, the Government's decision making', HC 519 (1985-86), for further details.

14. The Labour Party under Tony Blair seems committed to the establishment of 'national' Parliaments in Scotland and Wales and, for those who want them, regional Assemblies in England. The Liberal Democrats are committed to wide-ranging constitutional and electoral reform, including the introduction of proportional representation for elections to Parliament at Westminster.

15. B. Crick, *The Reform of Parliament* rev. edn (London: Weidenfeld and Nicolson, 1968), p. 80.

16. See Chapter 18, for further discussion of the doctrine of 'subsidiarity'.

17. See Select Committee Report on the Sittings of the House (1991-92), HC 20, (London: HMSO, 1992).

18. See *Hansard* 13 July 1992, Cols 833-907.

19. See W. Armstrong *et al., Budgetary Reform in the United Kingdom* (Oxford: OUP, 1980) for a fuller exposition of these ideas.

Further reading

Biffen, J., *Inside the House of Commons* (London: Grafton Books, 1989).

Drewry, G. (ed.), *The new Select Committees*; rev. edn (Oxford: OUP, 1989).

Garrett, J., *Westminster: does Parliament work?* (London: Gollancz, 1992).

Griffith, J.A.G. and Ryle, M., *Parliament, functions, practice and procedures* (London: Sweet and Maxwell, 1989).

Heatherington, A. *et al., Cameras in the Commons* (London: Hansard Society, 1990).

Norton, P., *Does Parliament matter?* (London: Harvester Wheatsheaf, 1993).

Norton, P., *The Commons in Perspective* (Oxford: Martin Robertson, 1981).

Radice, L., *Member of Parliament* (London: Macmillan, 1987).

Ryle, M. and Richards, P.G. (eds), *The Commons under Scrutiny* (London: Routledge and Kegan Paul, 1988).

Walker, R. and Criddle, B., *Almanack of British Politics,* 5th edn (London: Routledge, 1996).

Walkland, S.A. (ed.), *The House of Commons in the Twentieth Century* (Oxford: Clarendon Press, 1979).

PART 4

Central Government

12 Prime Minister and Cabinet

12.1 Historical development

The use of the term *Prime Minister* was no more than a tenuous convention from the time of Robert Walpole (1721-1742) to the time when Lord North insisted that his Administration resign *en bloc* in 1782 when he lost favour with King George III. Indeed, on a number of occasions during the eighteenth century, the most powerful politician of the time, Lord Chatham, was actually the leading Secretary of State in various Administrations headed by others, such as Lord Pelham or Lord Newcastle. Until the beginning of William Pitt's Administration in 1784, all Prime Ministers were chosen because of their good relationships with the Monarch and they survived in office because of their ability to manage the House of Commons.

The term *Cabinet* is older in origin and was first used during the reign of Charles II. At that time the King used to summon a few favoured members of his Privy Council for consultations in his private apartments and such courtiers became known as members of his 'Cabinet' after the French word for 'private quarters'. For a time they were also known as the 'Cabal', which happened to be an acronym for the names of those involved – Clifford, Arlington, Buckingham, Ashley and Lauderdale.

The office of Prime Minister and the institution of the Cabinet evolved together throughout the nineteenth century. Until the 1832 Reform Act the Prime Minister and Cabinet were answerable to the Monarch almost as much as they were to Parliament. The extension of the franchise in 1832 meant that the Prime Minister and Cabinet became more answerable to and dependent upon shifting majorities in the House of Commons. Further changes occurred after the 1867 Reform Act as the growing power of nationally organised political parties began to limit the independence of individual MPs. One of the consequences was to accord increased political stature to the main party leaders, such as William Gladstone and Benjamin Disraeli, who alternated as Prime Minister for nearly 20 years. In 1878 the title of 'Prime Minister' was officially recorded in a public document for the first time when Benjamin Disraeli signed the Treaty of Berlin on behalf of the British Government. Another equally important development during this period was the growth of the power of the Cabinet in relation to the House of Commons. Thus by the time of Lord Salisbury's second Administration (1886-92) Britain had moved essentially from Parliamentary government of the classic type to Cabinet government of the modern type – that is, government through Parliament rather than government by Parliament.

Statutory recognition of the office of Prime Minister was not formally complete until 1937 when the Ministers of the Crown Act provided the Prime Minister of the day with a salary and a pension from public funds. Yet to this day the powers and responsibilities of the Prime Minister have not been defined in statute. Like the institution of the Cabinet, the office of Prime Minister provides a classic example of the importance of conventions in British constitutional arrangements.

In theory, the Cabinet now constitutes the supreme decision-making body in the British political system. Yet in practice, as we shall see, the Prime Minister can be more than first among equals in any modern British Government. In political terms the most effective sanctions against Cabinet decisions of which people may disapprove are a decisive back-bench revolt in the governing party or the verdict of the electorate at the subsequent General Election. The Prime Minister and the Cabinet are also influenced in an imprecise but real way by the shifting views and feelings of their back-bench supporters in the House of Commons; the need to take account of the Opposition's demands which can affect the progress of Government legislative business in Parliament; their relations with party activists, pressure groups and the media; and their assessment of public opinion on any given issue at any given time. All these factors can qualify and refine the power and authority of the Prime Minister and Cabinet in modern conditions. Figure 12.1 lists all British Prime Ministers since Sir Robert Walpole.

Figure 12.1   Prime Ministers since Robert Walpole

Sir Robert Walpole	1721–42	Henry Temple, 3rd Viscount Palmerston	1855–58
Spencer Compton, Earl of Wilmington	1742–43	Edward Stanley, 14th Earl of Derby	1858–59
Henry Pelham	1743–54	Henry Temple, 3rd Viscount Palmerston	1859–65
Thomas Pelham-Holles, Duke of		Earl Russell	1865–66
Newcastle	1754–56	Edward Stanley, 14th Earl of Derby	1866–68
William Cavendish, 4th Duke of		Benjamin Disraeli	1868
Devonshire	1756–57	William Ewart Gladstone	1868–74
Thomas Pelham-Holles, Duke of		Benjamin Disraeli, Earl of Beaconsfield	1874–80
Newcastle	1757–62	William Ewart Gladstone	1880–85
John Stuart, 3rd Earl of Bute	1762–63	Robert Gascoyne-Cecil, 3rd Marquis of	
George Grenvill	1763–65	Salisbury	1885
Charles Wentworth, 2nd Marquis of		William Ewart Gladstone	1886
Rockingham	1765–66	Robert Gascoyne-Cecil, 3rd Marquis of	
William Pitt, Earl of Chatham	1766–68	Salisbury	1886–92
Augustus Fitzroy, 3rd Duke of Grafton	1768–70	William Ewart Gladstone	1892–94
Frederick, Lord North	1770–82	Archibald Primrose, 5th Earl of	
Charles Wentworth, 2nd Marquis of		Rosebery	1894–95
Rockingham	1782	Robert Gascoyne-Cecil, 3rd Marquis	
William Fitzmaurice, 2nd Earl of		of Salisbury	1895–1902
Shelburne	1782–83	Arthur James Balfour	1902–05
William Cavendish-Bentinck, 3rd Duke		Sir Henry Campbell-Bannerman	1905–08
of Portland	1783	Herbert Henry Asquith	1908–16
William Pitt, the younger	1783–1801	David Lloyd George	1916–22
Henry Addington	1801–04	Andrew Bonar Law	1922–23
William Pitt, the younger	1804–06	Stanley Baldwin	1923–24
William Wyndham, Lord Grenville	1806–07	James Ramsay MacDonald	1924
William Cavendish-Bentinck, 3rd Duke		Stanley Baldwin	1924–29
of Portland	1807–09	James Ramsay MacDonald	1929–35
Spencer Perceval	1809–12	Stanley Baldwin	1935–37

Figure 12.1 continued

Robert Jenkinson, 2rd Earl of Liverpool	1812–27	Arthur Neville Chamberlain	1937–40
George Canning	1827	Winston Churchill	1940–45
Frederick Robinson, Viscount Goderich	1827–28	Clement Attlee	1945–51
Arthur Wellesley, Duke of Wellington	1828–30	Sir Winston Churchill	1951–55
Charles, 2nd Earl Grey	1830–34	Sir Anthony Eden	1955–57
William Lamb, 2nd Viscount Melbourne	1834	Maurice Harold Macmillan	1957–63
Sir Robert Peel, 2nd Baronet	1834–35	Sir Alec Douglas-Home	1963–64
William Lamb, 2nd Viscount Melbourne	1835–39	James Harold Wilson	1964–70
William Lamb, 2nd Viscount Melbourne	1839–41	Edward Heath	1970–74
Sir Robert Peel, 2nd Baronet	1841–46	James Harold Wilson	1974–76
Lord John Russell	1846–52	Leonard James Callaghan	1976–79
Edward Stanley, 14th Earl of Derby	1852	Margaret Thatcher	1979–90
George Gordon, 4th Earl of Aberdeen	1852–55	John Major	1990–

12.2 The Cabinet and its support

The Cabinet in modern Britain has been composed of between 19 and 24 senior Ministers (including the Prime Minister) who meet every Thursday morning (but not usually throughout August) around the large coffin-shaped table in the Cabinet room at 10 Downing Street. It subsumes a large network of committees, both Ministerial and official, and it depends for its efficient operation upon the work of the Cabinet Secretary and 56 other civil servants in the Cabinet Office. The latter is the administrative nerve-centre of central Government and responsible for recording all Cabinet and Cabinet committee decisions, and then communicating them to those who need to know in the various Departments in Whitehall. The Cabinet Secretariat also has an important role in progress chasing, scheduling meetings, setting agendas, checking that papers are circulated in good time and cover the subject properly (for example, financial and European aspects), and briefing the chairmen of the committees concerned.

Certain very senior Ministers have a place in every Cabinet – for example, the Chancellor of the Exchequer, the Home Secretary and the Foreign Secretary. Some other Ministers have a place by dint of the area of the country which their Department represents – for example, the Secretaries of State for Wales, Scotland, and Northern Ireland. Occasionally some important Ministers, such as the Secretary of State for Transport, have been included in the Cabinet at one time and excluded from it at another, depending upon the competing claims of other Departments and the personal preferences of the Prime Minister of the day. In a few rare cases a senior Minister may belong to the Cabinet, but draw no public salary for it. This may be because the Prime Minister of the day has decided to breach the upper limit on the permitted number of such positions (currently 23), but more usually it reflects the convention that party political appointments to the Cabinet (such as the Chairman of the Conservative Party) should be paid from party rather than public funds. Nowadays the Government Chief Whip is not formally a member of the Cabinet, but invariably attends all Cabinet meetings – as the Prime Minister's Parliamentary Private Secretary (the channel of communication with Government back-benchers) has done since Margaret Thatcher introduced the practice in 1983.

The Cabinet meets formally once a week about 11 months a year (seldom in August) and for up to one and a half hours at a time, although extra meetings are arranged as and when the need arises. Owing to the size of the Cabinet, there is no question of all its members taking a full part in all the items under discussion, although John Major is relatively unusual in encouraging complete discussion around the table if everyone wishes to speak on a certain issue. In what might be described as normal circumstances, however, some members of the Cabinet remain silent because their Department is not involved in the issue under discussion and some may be unavoidably absent on the day in question (which is quite often the case with the Foreign Secretary). In such circumstances the Minister concerned may submit views in writing to the Prime Minister, so that these can be taken into account in the discussion. It is just as well that the Cabinet proceeds in this way, since if every Cabinet Minister spoke on every item of Cabinet business, the agenda would never be covered in the time available. At the invitation of the Prime Minister other non-Cabinet Ministers (for example, the Law Officers) may attend and speak at Cabinet meetings when their views are needed.

Cabinet Committees are an essential and integral part of Cabinet government. They are usually composed of the relevant Ministers according to the subject under discussion and chaired by the Prime Minister or another senior Cabinet Minister, such as the First Secretary of State and Deputy Prime Minister, the Leader of the House or the Chancellor of the Duchy of Lancaster. They are normally empowered to take decisions on behalf of the entire Cabinet. Only in cases of serious disagreement are matters referred back to the full Cabinet for final resolution. Few substantial issues are considered by full Cabinet which have not already been dealt with in some way in bilateral meetings between the Prime Minister and the relevant Departmental Minister or by the relevant Cabinet committee. Thus one of the main purposes of such meetings is to reach decisions which can then be put to full Cabinet simply for formal ratification. When Cabinet committees cannot reach agreement or when the issues under discussion are too important to be settled at a smaller meeting, the whole Cabinet has to argue things out in order to reach conclusions which then bind the entire Government.

Cabinet committees can conveniently be divided between *Standing Committees* – such as the Economic Committee, the Home and Social Affairs Committee, the Overseas and Defence Committee and the Legislation Committee – and the *Ad Hoc Committees* which are usually classified under 'Miscellaneous' or 'General' headings and which remain in being only as long as is necessary to resolve a particular issue of policy. Many of the Standing Committees and the sub-committees spawned by them are chaired by the Prime Minister, since they deal with the most important issues of policy. Decisions reached in such committees do not necessarily require subsequent ratification by the Cabinet as a whole, but are usually reported to the full Cabinet.

Miscellaneous or General Committees are normally chaired by either the Prime Minister or another senior Cabinet Minister (for example, The First Secretary of State and Deputy Prime Minister, the Foreign Secretary, the Home Secretary or the Chancellor of the Exchequer) and they meet for as many discussions as necessary in order to resolve the matters at issue. For example, in the 1980s such committees dealt with the Royal Navy's replacement of the Polaris weapons system with Trident, the abolition of the Greater London Council and the other Metropolitan Councils, the imposition of public spending cuts, the de-indexing from average earnings of social security benefits, the annual rate support settlement for local authorities, and the reform of the National Health Service. In the 1990s such committees have dealt for example, with the treatment of refugees arriving in Britain from the former Yugoslavia and the replacement of the Poll Tax with the Council Tax. It is normal for the decisions of such committees to require subsequent approval by the full Cabinet or at least one of its Standing Committees. Yet in all cases the key to the successful working of such committees is that they are empowered to take decisions on behalf of the whole Cabinet and in most cases they do so without any political or constitutional difficulty.

Senior civil servants and the military Chiefs of Staff are not formally members of the Cabinet or its committees, at any rate in peace-time. Yet the Chief of the Defence Staff regularly attends the main Overseas and Defence Policy Committee of the Cabinet, although he is not formally a member of it. In the broader framework of Cabinet government, junior Ministers play a frequent and useful part in Cabinet committees where junior Ministers can relieve senior Ministers of many of the burdens of collective decision making. Indeed, junior Ministers are the workhorses of the Cabinet committee system and they can make or mar their reputations when performing this aspect of their Ministerial duties. For an illustration of the range and scope of the Cabinet committee system see Figure 12.2.

Figure 12.2   Cabinet Committees: October 1995

Ministerial Committee on Economic and Domestic Policy (EDP)
Terms of reference
'To consider strategic issues relating to the Government's economic and domestic policies.'

Ministerial Committee on Science and Technology (EDS)
Terms of reference
'To review science and technology policy.'

Ministerial Committee on Defence and Overseas Policy (OPD)
Terms of reference
'To keep under review the Government's Defence and Overseas policy.'

Ministerial Committee on Hong Kong and Other Dependent Territories (OPDR)
Terms of Reference
'To keep under review the implementation of the agreement with the Chinese on the future of Hong Kong and the implications of that agreement for the Government of Hong Kong and the well-being of its people; and to keep under review as necessary the Government's policy towards other Dependent Territories.'

Ministerial Committee on Nuclear Defence Policy (OPDN)
Terms of Reference
'To keep under review the Government's policy on nuclear defence.'

Ministerial Committee on Northern Ireland (NI)
Terms of Reference
'To oversee the Government's policy on Northern Ireland issues and relations with the Republic of Ireland on these matters.'

Ministerial Committee on the Intelligence Services (IS)
Terms of Reference
'To keep under review policy on the security and intelligence services.'

Ministerial Committee on the Environment (EDE)
Terms of reference
'To consider questions of environmental policy.'

Ministerial Committee on Home and Social Affairs (EDH)
Terms of Reference
'To consider home and social policy issues.'

Figure 12.2 continued

*Ministerial Committee on Industrial,
Commercial and Consumer Affairs (EDI)*
Terms of Reference
'To consider industrial, commercial, and
consumer issues including questions of
competition and deregulation.'

*Ministerial Committee on Local Government
(EDL)*
Terms of Reference
'To consider issues affecting local
government, including the annual allocation
of resources.'

*Ministerial Committee on Regeneration
(EDR)*
Terms of reference
'To consider regeneration policies and their
coordination.'

*Ministerial Committee on Public Expenditure
(EDX)*
Terms of Reference
'To consider the allocation of the public
expenditure control totals and make
recommendations to the Cabinet.'

*Ministerial Committee on the Queen's
Speeches and Future Legislation (FLG)*
Terms of Reference
'To prepare and submit to the Cabinet drafts
of the Queen's Speeches to Parliament, and
proposals for the Government's legislative
programme for each Session of Parliament.'

Ministerial Committee on Legislation (LG)
Terms of Reference
'To examine all draft Bills; to consider the
Parliamentary handling of Government Bills,
European Community documents and Private
Members' business, and such other related
matters as may be necessary; and to keep
under review the Government's policy in
relation to issues of Parliamentary
procedures.'

*Ministerial Sub-committee on Health Strategy
(EDH(H))*
Terms of reference
'To oversee the development, implementation
and monitoring of the Government's health
strategy, to coordinate the Government's
policies on United Kingdom-wide issues
affecting health, and report as necessary to the
Ministerial Committee on Home and Social
Affairs.'

*Ministerial Sub-committee on Public Sector
Pay (EDI (P))*
Terms of Reference
'To coordinate the handling of pay issues in
the public sector, and report as necessary to
the Ministerial Committee on Industrial,
Commercial and Consumer Affairs.'

*Ministerial Sub-committee on European
Questions (OPD(E)*
Terms of Reference
'To consider questions relating to the United
Kingdom's membership of the European
Union and to report as necessary to the
Ministerial Committee on Defence and
Overseas Policy.'

*Ministerial Sub-committee on Terrorism
(OPD(T))*
Terms of Reference
'To keep under review the arrangements for
countering terrorism and for dealing with
terrorist incidents and their consequences and
to report as necessary to the Ministerial
Committee of Defence and Overseas Policy.'

*Ministerial Sub-committee on Drug Misuse
(EDH(D))*
Terms of Reference
'To coordinate the Government's national and
international policies for tackling drugs
misuse, and report as necessary to the
Ministerial Committee on Home and Social
Affairs.'

Figure 12.2 continued

Ministerial Sub-committee on Women's Issues (EDH (W))
Terms of Reference
'To review and develop the Government's policy and strategy on issues of special concern to women: to oversee their implementation; and to report as necessary to the Ministerial Committee on Home and Social Affairs.'

Ministerial sub-committee on London (EDL(L))
Terms of Reference
'To coordinate the Government's polices on London.'

Ministerial Group on Sanctions Against the Federal Republic of Yugoslavia (Gen 27)
Terms of Reference
'To keep under review the implementation of the sanctions against the Federal Republic of Yugoslavia imposed under United Nations Security Council Resolutions 757, 787 and 820, and to report to the Ministerial Committee on Overseas and Defence Policy as necessary.'

Ministerial Group on Competitiveness (GEN 29)
Terms of Reference
'To keep issues affecting the United Kingdom's competitiveness under review; and to update, in whole or part, as appropriate, from time to time the White Paper on Competitiveness for consideration by the Ministerial Committee on Economic and Domestic Policy.'

Ministerial Group on Card Technology (GEN 34)
Terms of Reference
'To consider the developing technology of card systems, and the potential demand for such systems from Government Departments, to ensure a co-ordinated approach across the Government taking account of the impact on the individual citizen.'

Support in Whitehall

Meetings of the Cabinet and its committees would not proceed as smoothly as they usually do if it were not for the fact that the Ministerial meetings are prepared and supported by official meetings of senior civil servants from the various Departments concerned. It is this parallel structure of official committees which keeps Government business moving along and makes it possible for the Cabinet and its committees to dispatch a great deal of Government business in a rather expeditious way. Cabinet Office officials usually chair these official committees which are intended to maximise the areas of potential inter-Departmental agreement and to define, if not minimise, the areas of potential disagreement. Since each Department tends to respect the interests and responsibilities of every other Department and since there is an established pecking order in Whitehall with 10 Downing Street and the Treasury at the top and the smaller or newer Departments at the bottom (for example, the Department of Transport or the Department of National Heritage); the outcome of inter-Departmental discussions at official level often reflects the balance of bureaucratic power in Whitehall. This may facilitate the collective decision-making process, but it can also make for minimalist, inter-Departmental compromises which may lower the quality or reduce the effectiveness of the decisions actually taken. In other words, a significant political price can be paid for the collegiate conventions of Whitehall.

The outcome of Cabinet discussions and of inter-Departmental discussions at official level is also affected by the relative standing and authority of the various Ministers whose Departments are involved in a political issue at a given time. Thus if the Chancellor of the Exchequer and the Chief Secretary have won battles with their Cabinet colleagues over the control of public spending, the Treasury is likely to be even more formidable than usual in its dealings with other Departments. Equally, if Foreign Office Ministers have been proved wrong, or even had to resign, over sensitive issues – for example, the Argentinian invasion of the Falkland Islands in April 1982 – then that Department will find its authority and standing in Whitehall at least temporarily diminished. About the only sure rule in British central Government is that it is usually wise to enlist the support of 10 Downing Street in any important inter-Departmental battle.

In the process of central Government the Cabinet Office has a vital role to play in ensuring fast and efficient communication of inter-Departmental decisions to all who need to know of them throughout Whitehall. This central secretariat, which consists mainly of civil service high-flyers seconded from other Departments, communicates Government decisions in the form of extracts from Cabinet or Cabinet committee minutes to those parts of the central Government machine which have to act upon them. This means that in the first instance such decisions are communicated to the Private Offices of the Ministers involved in the implementation of the policy and then further relayed from there within the respective Departments. Such minutes are drawn up by officials of the Cabinet Office under the overall supervision and direction of the Cabinet Secretary. It is open to the Prime Minister, or indeed any other Cabinet Minister, to see the minutes in draft, to point out errors and then ask for suitable amendments. Yet if this is to be done, it has to be done quickly. Consequently, requests are not frequently made and even less frequently granted. In short, Cabinet Office officials keep a tight and effective grip upon this aspect of Cabinet government.

From 1971 to 1983 the Cabinet was assisted in its deliberations by the *Central Policy Review Staff* (CPRS).[1] This was set up by Sir Edward Heath when Prime Minister (1970-74), as a small advisory body within the Cabinet Office designed to give intelligent and dispassionate advice to the Cabinet as a whole on matters of policy affecting the entire Government. Under the initial direction of Lord Rothschild it seemed to achieve its objective and proved itself to be a useful source of independent and sometimes heretic advice to Ministers. Yet subsequently it seemed to lose its way and suffer diminished effectiveness. This was partly because it encountered formidable opposition from senior officials in the Treasury and Cabinet Office who disapproved of some of its work – notably on public expenditure and political priorities in the early 1970s – and partly because the Labour Government in the late 1970s drew it away from its original purpose into short-term, inter-Departmental trouble-shooting which put it too much in the political limelight for its own good. The final straw, which probably precipitated its demise, was the fact that it was not able to preserve the confidentiality of its sensitive reports to Ministers during the 1979-83 Conservative Government. One notorious example in the autumn of 1982 involved a report which questioned the future ability of the public purse to finance much of the Welfare State and notably growing demands upon the National Health Service. This caused considerable embarrassment to Margaret Thatcher and her Ministerial colleagues and no one was really surprised when the CPRS was abolished soon after the Conservative victory at the 1983 General Election.

10 Downing Street

In addition to the formal structure of Cabinet government just described, successive Prime Ministers since Lloyd George (1916-22) have taken steps to have other sources of advice and support available to them at 10 Downing Street. Lloyd George had the services of a so-called 'Kitchen Cabinet' of advisers and cronies during the First World War and immediately after. During the Second World War Winston Churchill had the help of Lord Cherwell (known as 'the Prof'); after the war Clement Attlee had assistance from Francis Williams (a political journalist); Harold Macmillan derived support and comfort from John Wyndham (an aristocratic personal friend); Harold Wilson during his three terms as Prime Minister (1964-66, 1966-70, and 1974-76) had personal support from Marcia Williams (his political secretary); and Margaret Thatcher had several personal advisers including Sir Anthony Parsons (a retired diplomat) and Sir Alan Walters (an academic economist).

Since 1974 there has also been a *Policy Unit* in 10 Downing Street consisting normally of fewer than a dozen advisers brought in to serve the Prime Minister of the day and to assist with political tasks. The personnel of this Unit have varied from Government to Government, depending upon the outlook and preferences of the Prime Minister of the day. For example, Harold Wilson and James Callaghan depended quite heavily upon Dr Bernard Donoghue, an academic from the London School of Economics; Margaret Thatcher had advice and support from Sir John Hoskyns, a businessman, Ferdinand Mount, a journalist, John Redwood, a banker and later a politician, and Brian Griffiths, an academic and lay preacher. John Major has depended upon the advice and support of Sarah Hogg, a journalist, and Norman Blackwell, a management consultant. Whether such advisers are installed as head of the Policy Unit or work more informally for the Prime Minister of the day in a 'kitchen cabinet', their contributions to the policy making process can be very significant. They often act as speech-writers and help the Prime Minister of the day to develop a distinctive personal agenda, and they can act as political trouble-shooters, when necessary, between conflicting interests in the Government.

12.3 Prime Ministerial power

The Prime Minister of the day could be described as the most powerful person in Britain. Certainly the reality of Prime Ministerial power has been recognised for some time by practising politicians and academic observers alike. Yet the nature and extent of such power is a matter of controversy and there are some significant constraints upon its exercise, no matter who occupies the premises at 10 Downing Street.

Conflicting interpretations

There have been at least two strongly conflicting interpretations of Prime Ministerial power in Britain. On the one hand, Harold Wilson concluded that 'the predominantly academic verdict of overriding Prime Ministerial power is wrong'.[2] In making this forthright comment, Lord Wilson was probably reflecting upon his own experience of having to preside over several Labour Cabinets which contained powerful and determined personalities who did not take kindly to excessive Prime Ministerial leadership. On the other hand, Lord Morley (in the nineteenth century) in his biography of Sir Robert Walpole (Prime Minister from 1721-42 – the first and still longest serving) wrote as long ago as 1889 that 'the flexibility of the Cabinet system allows the Prime Minister [in this case he was thinking rather of his Liberal friend and colleague William Gladstone] to take upon himself a power not inferior to that of a dictator, provided always that the House of Commons will stand by him'.[3] This view has had its strong adherents ever since, including Sir Anthony Eden (Prime Minister 1955-57) who wrote in his Memoirs that 'a Prime Minister is still nominally *primus inter pares* [first among equals], but in fact his authority is stronger than that'.[4]

The best way of assessing these conflicting interpretations is to examine the various aspects of Prime Ministerial power in order to see which of the two schools of thought is best supported by the evidence of history. Yet even at this early stage in our investigation it is tempting to agree with the common sense view expressed by Herbert Asquith (Prime Minister 1908-16) in his Memoirs which he wrote about 70 years ago that 'the office of Prime Minister is what its holder chooses and is able to make of it'.[5] In the light of the long history of the office, it is difficult to dissent from this concise view expressed by one of its most distinguished occupants.

The power of patronage

The Prime Minister of the day has the power of political patronage. This is manifested principally in the power of appointment to and dismissal from Ministerial posts in Government. Having accepted the Royal commission to form a new Government, the party leader concerned can fill the 100 or so Ministerial posts in the Commons and the Lords in the most appropriate ways. Yet for reasons of practical politics there are always a number of senior figures in any party who virtually select themselves for Ministerial office and some others whom it would be imprudent for any Prime Minister to exclude. Other considerations which come into play in the course of Government formation are regional balance, ideological balance and simply age, as well as political debt and personal loyalty. Thus, although Prime Ministers have done almost as they liked when making Ministerial appointments, their freedom of manoeuvre has always been limited in practice by common prudence and sensible calculation of their own strength or weakness at any time.

Equally, the Prime Minister can ask for the resignation of any member of the Government at any time on the grounds that the Minister concerned is not up to the job or is too old to continue or the office is needed for someone else. Although the most usual motives for Prime Ministerial dismissal of a senior Minister are to improve the general effectiveness and political balance of the Cabinet, there have been occasions when the Prime Minister of the day has deliberately sought to create a more politically congenial array of senior Ministers. For example, in September 1981 Margaret Thatcher sacked three Cabinet Ministers (Lord Soames, Sir Ian Gilmour, and Mark Carlisle) at least two of whom she found ideologically uncongenial, and appointed three new ones (Nigel Lawson, Norman Tebbit, and Lady Young) at least two of whom were very close to her own brand of Conservatism. John Major, by contrast, has been more loath to use his power of dismissal and has tended to use it only when the passage of events has forced it upon him. For example, when he sacked Norman Lamont as Chancellor of the Exchequer in May 1993, it was a belated attempt to placate public hostility to the pain caused by the economic recession of the early 1990s, and his extensive reshuffle of July 1995 was a clear attempt to put a new face upon the Government following his own re-election as Leader of the Conservative Party in the same month.

The Prime Minister of the day also has a wider and more general power of political patronage which stems from the right to advise the Monarch on public appointments made in the name of the Crown. This means that a large number of important and influential positions in the higher ranks of the British Establishment – and nowadays at the top of the large and growing number of QUANGOs (Quasi-autonomous non-governmental organisations) – are effectively in the gift of the Prime Minister of the day and senior Ministerial colleagues when they fall due for appointment or replacement. For example, the Permanent Secretaries of Whitehall Departments, Bishops in the Church of England (albeit on the advice of the Ecclesiastical Appointments Committee), the Governor of the Bank of England, the chairmen of public corporations such as the BBC or the ITC, and key appointments to a host of other public bodies all depend to a considerable extent on finding favour with the Prime Minister of the day, although other senior Ministers obviously have a good deal of influence in their own Departmental spheres. In view of the influential nature of many of these positions and the steady emasculation of local government under the Conservatives since 1979, these political appointments can have great significance. Thus Prime Ministerial patronage, whether exercised positively in favour of some or negatively to blackball others, is a formidable and growing aspect of Prime Ministerial power in Britain.

Power within Government

It probably does not need saying that the Prime Minister of the day normally has considerable power within the Government. Indeed, many would argue that a strong Prime Minister has the ability to dominate the Government by personally setting its strategic agenda and political priorities. This is done in a number of different ways, all of which are facets of Prime Ministerial power. It is achieved through the Prime Minister's control of the Cabinet agenda, the right to establish Cabinet committees and to pick their membership, the right to chair the most important committees and discussions, the right to summarise the conclusions of Cabinet meetings, the right to have the best available advice from the civil service and outside, the ability to take an overall and non-Departmental view of political issues, the power of Ministerial appointment and dismissal, the pre-eminent position in the eyes of the media and the public, and, most of all, the leadership of the governing party in the House of Commons.

During the 1980s when Margaret Thatcher was at 10 Downing Street, the power of the Prime Minister within the Government increased very largely at the expense of the Cabinet as a whole. This happened for a number of reasons. It was partly an obvious consequence of Margaret Thatcher having led her party to three consecutive General Election victories. More insidiously, however, it was a consequence of her ability gradually to transform the membership of the Cabinet over a period of years from one which she largely inherited from Edward Heath to one which she could call her own, because all but one of its members (Sir Geoffrey Howe as Lord Howe of Aberavon was then) owed their positions in Cabinet directly to her. It was also a consequence of her marked preference for bilateral meetings with key Ministers as an effective and disciplined way of resolving policy problems rather than having recourse to the more traditional but less controllable methods of Cabinet committees or full Cabinet meetings. No one should really have been surprised by these developments, since Margaret Thatcher gave due warning of her intentions and her preferred method of working in Government when she told Kenneth Harris in a famous newspaper interview given before the Conservatives came to power in 1979 that 'it [her Administration] must be a conviction Government – as Prime Minister I could not waste time having any internal arguments'.[6]

During John Major's period at 10 Downing Street in the 1990s, the power of the Prime Minister within the Government has not been so obvious – indeed, he has sometimes seemed to be almost a prisoner of some of his senior colleagues or of rebel back-benchers in his own party. This should not come entirely as a surprise, partly because from the beginning of his time as Prime Minister he set out to be more collegiate in his approach to leadership than his combative predecessor, but mainly because during his time as party leader and Prime Minister the Parliamentary arithmetic has been much less comfortable for the Conservatives than at any time when Margaret Thatcher was Prime Minister. These plain facts have not prevented the media and some of his Parliamentary colleagues from contrasting him unfavourably and unfairly with his predecessor and have almost certainly contributed to his remarkably low rating in the public opinion polls. For our purposes here the moral of the tale is that in the space of even a few months – let alone a few years – the perception of a given Prime Minister can change dramatically, as even the careers of Winston Churchill, Harold Macmillan and Margaret Thatcher showed so clearly.

The extent and nature of Prime Ministerial power within Government can therefore change frequently and sometimes almost without warning – as was the case with John Major's loss of authority following 'Black Wednesday' on 16 September 1992. Such power has been a matter of continuing controversy under all Prime Ministers. Furthermore, the available evidence is often relayed by observers or participants in the process of British politics who are strongly committed for or against a particular Prime Minister (or indeed by former Prime Ministers themselves), while most academic accounts are largely speculative in view of the unreliable quality of their sources. The honest investigator is left with not much more than a series of impressions of one Prime Minister as compared with another or of the same Prime Minister at different phases of electoral and political fortune. The dilemma is that those who might be reliable and fairly objective witnesses of the drama do not normally gain real first-hand access to the political theatre, whereas those who were privileged to be on stage at the relevant time have not usually been the most reliable witnesses – especially when writing their memoirs some time afterwards. Since no final or definitive conclusions can therefore be drawn, it would be wise to rest upon the observation that Prime Ministerial power in Government has varied greatly from one Administration to another and indeed from one time to another during a particular Prime Minister's tenure of the office.

Power in Parliament

Most Prime Ministers have usually had formidable power and authority in Parliament.

This is partly because the power of appointment to and dismissal from posts in the Government can do so much to determine the political fortunes of MPs in the governing party, and partly a reflection of their leading role in the gladiatorial battles between the parties both in the House and on the media. Clearly the extent and nature of such power has varied from time to time, depending upon the personal fortunes of each Prime Minister and the political standing of the governing party at any time. Much also depends upon the extent to which the Prime Minister can rely upon the loyalty and support of Parliamentary colleagues, the efficiency and subtlety of the Government Whips, and the personal standing of the Prime Minister in the eyes of the media and the general public.

On the whole Conservative Prime Ministers seem to have been more powerful in relation to their Parliamentary followers than Labour Prime Ministers in relation to theirs, although there have been exceptions to the rule from time to time. The general position reflects the contrasting origins, organisation and instincts of each main party. Whereas the Conservative Party has been traditionally both hierarchical and deferential towards its leader, the Labour Party has tended to be more democratic in its aspirations and egalitarian in its attitude towards the leader. In most cases this has made it easier for Conservative Prime Ministers to preserve their Parliamentary authority than for Labour Prime Ministers to preserve theirs, although the contrast should not be exaggerated. Not only is it true that there have been relatively strong and decisive Labour Prime Ministers - for example, Clement Attlee from 1945 to 1950 or Harold Wilson from 1964 to 1967 – it is also true that there have been relatively weak and indecisive Conservative Prime Ministers – for example, Sir Anthony Eden from 1955 to 1957, or Sir Alec Douglas-Home from 1963 to 1964. We should also bear in mind that all political relationships in Britain have become much less deferential over the years and that the media have become more powerfully destructive, so it is not surprising that the authority of all modern Prime Ministers is probably not as great as their illustrious, but less widely criticised predecessors.

In general, all peace-time Prime Ministers in Britain during this century have been able to exercise predominant power in Parliament as long as they have retained high standing in the eyes of the media and the public, and have been able to count upon the loyal support of the vast majority of their own back-benchers.[7] In many ways the exceptions have been more interesting than the rule. For example, there were several times after the devaluation of the Pound in 1967 when Harold Wilson had to head off the threat of serious revolts against his damaged political authority – which came from those of his Cabinet colleagues who were particularly close to the trade unions (such as James Callaghan) and from those who more or less openly resented his leadership or coveted his job (such as Roy Jenkins). Equally, there have been times during John Major's tenure at 10 Downing Street when he has been openly defied by some of his Cabinet colleagues (notably by the so-called 'bastards' – Michael Portillo, Peter Lilley, and John Redwood: the latter resigning from the Cabinet in June 1995 in order to challenge for the leadership) and by troublesome back-benchers on issues of policy, such as Norman Lamont in relation to the preservation of the UK against threats alleged to emanate from Britain's deeper involvement in European integration and from the so-called 'peace process' in Northern Ireland. Indeed, the sniping at John Major became so damaging in 1994 and 1995 that he felt obliged to resign the leadership of the Conservative Party in June 1995 in order to challenge his adversaries in the party 'to put up or shut up'. In the event his gamble paid off and he was re-elected Leader of his party by a convincing margin against his sole challenger, John Redwood.

Party political power

It must also be obvious that the Prime Minister of the day can have great power over the fortunes and destiny of the governing party. In the Conservative Party, this stems from the degree of deference traditionally accorded to the party leader, especially when that person is also Prime Minister. In the Labour Party, the party political dominance of the leader has not usually been so clear-cut, since within the Labour movement even Prime Ministerial power has had to be shared with the rest of the Parliamentary Party, the affiliated trade unions and the constituency parties, all of whom have acknowledged roles even under the newly reformed Labour party constitution. Furthermore, Labour Prime Ministers have quite often had problems with the National Executive Committee of the party, since nearly all the members of this committee have their own independent power bases within the Labour movement. Whereas the authority of any Conservative Prime Minister is usually recognised, if sometimes resented, within the party, the paramount position of Labour Prime Ministers has not always been recognised and, indeed, has often been challenged by party colleagues both in private and in public. Nevertheless, we should not over-simplify this distinction between the two main parties, since in this fickle age of mass media politics no Prime Minister is ever all-powerful or completely secure for long – as even the career of Margaret Thatcher so clearly demonstrated.

In terms of the party political context, the power of any British Prime Minister is probably at its greatest (and certainly most lonely) in the exclusive right of the occupant of the office to recommend to the Monarch the time of dissolution within the five-year maximum span of a Parliament. The exercise of this aspect of Prime Ministerial power can have lasting effects for good or ill upon the political fortunes of the party and the destiny of the country. It is a formidable power, as Margaret Thatcher demonstrated in 1983 and 1987, when on each occasion she called an election a year before she had to and so ensured the continuation in office of the Government which she led. Neverthe-less it is a power with a double edge, as can be well illustrated by a few historical examples.

In 1951 Clement Attlee decided to call a General Election, even though the Labour Government which he led had an overall majority of five in the Commons and more than three years of its full Parliamentary term still to run.[8] The result of the election was a narrow victory for the Conservatives and the beginning of 13 years of Conservative rule. In February 1974 Edward Heath decided to appeal to the country by holding a General Election on the issue of 'who governs?' He was persuaded to do this by Conservative Central Office even though the Government which he led had a comfortable majority in the Commons and nearly 18 months of its Parliamentary term still to run. The result was a narrow victory for the Labour Party (largely on the issues of industrial peace and the rising cost of living) and the beginning of more than five years of Labour rule. His unwise and premature decision also had lethal consequences for his own position in the party and within little more than one year he had lost the leadership.

On the other hand, James Callaghan appeared to err in the other direction when he decided *not* to call a General Election in October 1978 against the advice and instincts of nearly all his senior colleagues and contrary to the confident expectations of many of his most powerful trade union allies. The main political consequence was that the Labour Party missed what was probably its best opportunity to win another term of office at a time when there was relative industrial peace and some evidence of economic recovery. When the postponed General Election did eventually take place in May 1979, it was against a background of the so-called 'winter of discontent' with the trade unions and the Parliamentary defeat of the Labour Government in the Commons on a vote of confidence in March 1979. The result of these events was the election of a Conservative Government under Margaret Thatcher on the basis of the largest swing at a General Election since 1945. In all these cases we have mentioned it can be argued that this particular aspect of Prime Ministerial power had very significant political consequences.

Power on the national and international stage

In contemporary political conditions Prime Ministers in Britain – as in other democracies – have considerable power and prestige on the national and international stage, even allowing for demystified public attitudes and widespread public cynicism. Of course, the symbols and trappings of Prime Ministerial power should not be confused with the substance. Yet they are significant nevertheless as part of the aura of power which tends to surround all heads of Government in the modern media age. Certainly this particular aspect of power can be strongly reinforced by the excessive attention which the media sometimes devote to nearly every aspect of a Prime Minister's life. It is also dramatised by the need for the Prime Minister of the day to attend frequent summit meetings with counterparts in other countries, all of which serve to elevate the leading figures to a political level well above other Ministers.

On the other hand, we have seen in the cases of Harold Wilson after the 1967 devaluation of the Pound and John Major after the 1992 departure of Britain from the European Exchange Rate Mechanism that the media (and hence public opinion) have a marked tendency to turn swiftly against such leaders whom they may have admired only a little while before. As far as the media are concerned, this may happen because they believe they have genuine cause to reassess the competence or integrity of the Prime Minister in question, or, more cynically, it may be because it suits their commercial purposes (that is, boosting circulations or editorial egos in apparently equal parts) to build up even the most senior politicians only to have the pleasure of knocking them down some time later. Either way, these characteristics underline the strong trend towards presidentialism in Britain and many other Parliamentary democracies.

Needless to say, these aspects of Prime Ministerial power are enhanced every time there is a real international crisis or a requirement for particularly swift or decisive national leadership. This is especially true in time of war, but it is also true in relation to matters of national security in time of peace. For example, it is normally the Prime Minister of the day who has to act decisively in the event of a spy scandal or a major industrial crisis which threatens essential services. Equally in foreign affairs, it is for the Prime Minister to give a clear lead when British national interests are threatened – as Sir Anthony Eden did at the time of the Suez crisis in 1956 or Margaret Thatcher did at the time of the conflict over the Falkland Islands in 1982. Similar requirements for Prime Ministerial leadership apply to the so-called 'peace process' in Northern Ireland as we have seen since the Downing Street Declaration in December 1993, and to the recurrent rows which have taken place between Britain and her partners in the European Union. They would also apply in the now unlikely event of Britain being involved in a possible nuclear confrontation or having to respond to the threat of nuclear blackmail from a maverick dictator or terrorist group. Although these dangers have mercifully diminished since the end of the Cold War, they still cannot be completely discounted in an uncertain or delicate phase of international relations.

12.4 Cabinet government

It is difficult to consider the idea of Cabinet government in Britain in a way which separates it from the role of the Prime Minister. Yet there are some important points about the ideas of Cabinet government and collective responsibility which serve to illustrate some of the limitations upon the exercise of Prime Ministerial power. Many years ago John Mackintosh provided a useful framework of analysis for such questions when he argued that the main tasks of the British Cabinet were 'to take or review the major decisions (of central Government), to consider (though not necessarily at the formative stage) any proposals which might affect the future of the Government, and to ensure that no Departmental interests are overlooked thus giving the work of Government a measure of unity (and coherence)'.[9] It may, therefore, be helpful if we consider each of these aspects in turn.

Important decision making

In theory, the Cabinet is the most important decision-making body in British central Government. It is supposed to play this vital role because there is no other institution so well placed or qualified to meet the need for decisive arbitration at the apex of central Government. After all there is formally no chief executive in British central Government and all executive power is vested by statute in the various Secretaries of State and other Ministerial heads of the Whitehall Departments. Thus whatever the impact of real Prime Ministerial power, the Cabinet is supposed to be the most important decision-making body and to give institutional expression to the principle of collective responsibility.

On the other hand, some have argued that in modern times it has invariably been the Prime Minister of the day who has taken all the really important political decisions, albeit usually after appropriate discussion with senior Ministerial colleagues. There is historical evidence to support this view in the 1947 decision to develop a British nuclear weapons capability, the 1956 decision to invade the Suez Canal Zone, the 1982 decision to send a Task Force to recapture the Falkland Islands, and the 1993 Downing Street Declaration on the future of Northern Ireland. The argument is also borne out when speed of response is an essential factor in Government decision making, as was the case, for example, with the decision in September 1992 to leave the European Exchange Rate Mechanism. Yet all these essentially Prime Ministerial decisions had to be cleared with a few very senior Ministers and advisers and were subsequently endorsed by the whole Cabinet.

There are several reasons why the Prime Minister of the day usually comes out on top in the decision-making process of British central Government. The main reason is that in every modern Cabinet the Prime Minister has usually been more than first among equals. This is partly for the reasons already given in the earlier section on Prime Ministerial power, but also because the civil service is accustomed to dealing with Ministers in an hierarchical way. Indeed, it is usually convenient to have a Prime Minister who is regarded as being head and shoulders above the rest of the Cabinet, since this provides opportunities for competing Ministers to outflank or trump the efforts of their colleagues by securing the support of 10 Downing Street at a decisive stage in any important inter-Departmental argument.

Nearly every Cabinet in modern times has divided quite conveniently into two layers: a 'first eleven' of very senior Ministers who carry real weight and authority in the Government and a 'second eleven' who, although in charge of Departments and holding Cabinet rank, count for less in any Government. At one time in the early 1950s Winston Churchill sought to formalise this division by nominating a few 'Overlords' from among his most senior Cabinet colleagues to supervise and co-ordinate the work of clusters of other Cabinet Ministers. The experiment did not really work and was soon abandoned because of Ministerial resentment and jealousy. In the late 1960s Harold Wilson also experimented with the idea of creating an 'inner Cabinet' composed of fewer than half a dozen of Labour's real political heavyweights at that time. Once again the idea did not really work in practice for similar reasons and was soon abandoned. More recently, Michael Heseltine's appointment as 'First Secretary of State' and Deputy Prime Minister in John Major's July 1995 reshuffle provided yet another example of a move in this direction. However, in this case it is too soon to tell what, if any, will be the effects on the conduct of Cabinet government.

In every Cabinet it is the Prime Minister who usually holds most of the high cards in dealings with Cabinet colleagues. The Prime Minister can determine the membership of Cabinet committees at any rate at the margin by including additional members who can be relied upon for their support, although the bulk of the membership of such committees is really determined by the nature and scope of the issues under discussion. The Prime Minister can exploit the use of bilateral meetings with individual Ministers in order to divide and rule any collective opposition within the Cabinet to preferred policies. Indeed, as long as a political axis is preserved between the Prime Minister and the Chancellor of the Exchequer, there are few, if any, occasions on which the two of them are likely to be defeated by the rest of the Cabinet.

All of these realities are underpinned by the doctrine of *collective responsibility*. This means that the invidious choice facing any member of the Cabinet (or indeed any other Minister or PPS) who is really unhappy about an aspect of Government policy is either to threaten resignation, with the high risk that such a threat might be called, or to keep quiet and so risk losing political credibility if it is widely known in Westminster and Whitehall that the Minister concerned is at odds with Government policy. Clearly this can never be an attractive choice, yet on most occasions in modern times Ministers faced with this dilemma have chosen the latter course and remained within the Government. All of which really underlines that it is not sensible for even a very powerful Cabinet Minister to threaten resignation unless the Minister concerned is fully prepared to carry out the threat, especially since all the actors in the drama of modern British politics are aware that few resignations even from the Cabinet have enhanced the prospects of the individual taking such a momentous step. In most cases in modern times it has proved to be a ticket to political obscurity.

In the *Conservative Party*, it is necessary to go back to *Anthony Eden* who resigned in opposition to the policy of appeasement in 1938 or *Peter Thorneycroft* who resigned because of his inability to carry the Prime Minister and other Cabinet colleagues with him on his policy of public expenditure cuts in 1958 to find examples of senior Cabinet Ministers who chose to resign on significant issues of policy. Yet notwithstanding this, Ministers in successive Governments have been notably accident-prone and media calls for resignation have been all too frequent.

The resignation of *Lord Carrington* and Ministerial colleagues at the Foreign Office in April 1982 was relatively unusual in that it was a direct and immediate atonement for the policy failure of their Department to foresee or prevent the Argentinean invasion of the Falkland Islands, even though it was widely agreed that the Ministry of Defence was equally culpable. The dramatic resignation of *Michael Heseltine* in January 1986 was also partly on policy grounds when he concluded that he was losing his argument in favour of a European future for Westland Helicopters, but it was mainly an act of exasperation at the way in which Margaret Thatcher had conducted Cabinet government over many years. The resignations of *Nigel Lawson* in 1989 and *Norman Lamont* in 1993 exemplify somewhat different phenomena. The former had become increasingly exasperated during his later years as Chancellor with the baleful influence of Sir Alan Walters over Margaret Thatcher, but – more importantly – he and his powerful neighbour in Downing Street had eventually drifted apart on one of the key issues of economic policy, namely the weight to be given to stability of the exchange rate in the conduct of monetary policy. The latter, who had offered to resign on the ignominious 'Black Wednesday' in September 1992, became understandably resentful about having to take subsequent sole blame for the unpopular effects of Britain's membership of the European Exchange Rate Mechanism – a policy which he claimed he had not really believed in even when he was having staunchly to defend it.[10] Most dramatic – and consequential – of all recent examples was the resignation of *Sir Geoffrey Howe* as Leader of the House and 'Deputy Prime Minister' in November 1990, an act which gave him the opportunity to make an uncharacteristically electrifying personal statement to the House of Commons indicting Margaret Thatcher and her whole approach to political leadership especially on European policy, and thus precipitating her downfall.

These various examples of Conservative Cabinet resignations, at any rate since 1979, demonstrate two different general phenomena. The cases of Lord Carrington and Norman Lamont were in their different ways clear examples of the need for ritual sacrifice to atone for previous policy failures by the Government as a whole. The cases of Michael Heseltine, Nigel Lawson, and Geoffrey Howe, however, were in their different ways all expressions of exasperation at having to deal with Margaret Thatcher as she became increasingly obdurate and unreasonable on matters of policy. Thus issues of policy and personality were inextricably connected, as is so often the case in politics.

In the *Labour Party*, it is customary to refer to the cases of *Aneurin Bevan, Harold Wilson*, and *John Freeman* in 1951 who resigned against the Treasury's insistence upon introducing charges for false teeth and spectacles within the National Health Service, and *George Brown* in 1968 who resigned in a fit of pique against Harold Wilson's continued prevarications on European policy. In both these celebrated cases clashes of personality and the influence of personal ambitions were bound up with differences of fundamental importance. It was no coincidence that Aneurin Bevan and Hugh Gaitskell (the Labour Chancellor in 1951) were obvious rivals for the succession to Clement Attlee, and that George Brown had been defeated by Harold Wilson in the 1963 Labour leadership contest following Hugh Gaitskell's untimely death.

As interesting and revealing, however, were the counter-examples of *Michael Foot* and *Tony Benn*, two of the leading Left-wingers in the 1974-79 Labour Governments of Harold Wilson and James Callaghan, neither of whom resigned from the Cabinet at any stage – even when faced with the appalling need (from a Socialist point of view) to make deep and immediate cuts in public expenditure at the behest of the International Monetary Fund in the autumn of 1976.[11] These cases demonstrate not only the addiction to high office of even previously rebellious individuals, but also the cunning and good sense of successive Labour Prime Ministers in keeping some of their most potent, potential adversaries inside rather than outside the tent in the words of the traditional Arab aphorism.

Given all the effective constraints and inhibitions of collective responsibility, there has been a tendency in all British Governments for disaffected or unhappy members of the Cabinet to convey their disapproval of certain aspects of Government policy either via private and unattributable conversations with Lobby journalists (see Chapter 7, pp. 133-4) or in carefully coded public speeches designed to be just within the bounds of collective responsibility, while marking out important differences designed to distance them from the prevailing Government orthodoxy. The use of such techniques can be regarded as a tribute to the durability and elasticity of collective responsibility in British central Government.

The latitude provided by these techniques was used with impunity by Tony Benn during the period in the 1970s when he was the self-styled Socialist *enfant terrible* of the Wilson and Callaghan Administrations. It was equally exploited by the leading Tory 'Wets', such as Peter Walker and James Prior, during their surprisingly long Ministerial careers under Margaret Thatcher. More recently, in the 1990s, similar techniques were exploited by the so-called 'bastards' in the Major Cabinet (Michael Portillo, Peter Lilley, and John Redwood) who occasionally made coded speeches undermining John Major's policy on Europe, but who were not sacked for their impertinence. In all such cases behaviour of this kind is only possible as long as the Prime Minister of the day feels unable or disinclined to punish it. Yet it is also worth noting that John Redwood eliminated himself from the Cabinet in June 1995 by resigning to fight John Major in the leadership election at that time.

Notwithstanding such drama and difficulty, the Cabinet is still the forum within which the most important decisions of Government in Britain are ratified, if not actually taken. It is the body in whose name the Government acts and its ostensible unity is vital to the continuation in office of any Administration. At times it can be a formidable brake upon Prime Ministerial power and individual Ministerial initiative alike. Yet in modern British politics it has had a notably varied role as illustrated by the contrast in its fortunes and behaviour under Margaret Thatcher and John Major respectively.

Review of key problems

Another vital role of the Cabinet is the review of key problems which can affect the future of the Government and the country. To the outside observer this would appear to be an activity upon which any Cabinet worth its salt ought to be engaged. After all, where else but around the Cabinet table should there be serious and timely discussion of such vital subjects as the concept of sustainable development, the continuing task of defeating infla- tion, or the difficulties of meeting public expectations in the modern Welfare State? Yet sadly the truth seems to be that this aspect of the work of the Cabinet has often been neglected in favour of dealing with more urgent political issues.

In recent years the agenda of every regular Cabinet meeting has included an item on the following week's Parliamentary business (when Parliament is sitting), an item which permits the Prime Minister or Foreign Secretary to give a brief report on current international developments or recent international conferences with implications for Britain, and often an item which allows the Chancellor of the Exchequer to report upon the state of the economy as indicated by the latest official statistics. Of course, any mem- ber of the Cabinet may apply to the Cabinet Secretary to have a particular item includ- ed on the agenda of a future meeting, but it is not uncommon for such requests to be turned down or for the matter to be referred to the appropriate Cabinet committee at the behest of the Prime Minister who is in effective control of the Cabinet agenda. On most occasions when Prime Ministers do this, they are merely acting as good chairmen by seeking to get decisions taken at the appropriate level consistent with the political impor- tance of the issue. However, in the case of a real emergency or if a Cabinet Minister is not prepared to accept the decision of a Cabinet committee, the Prime Minister will nor- mally ensure that the matter is put immediately on the agenda of the full Cabinet. Any other response would lead to a deterioration in the general atmosphere of mutual trust in the Cabinet and this would not be in the interest of any Prime Minister, however pow- erful. In general, therefore, the preparation and timing of Cabinet decisions is very much in the hands of the Prime Minister, which gives the holder of that office a real advantage over the rest of the Cabinet.

The fact that successive Prime Ministers and senior officials in the Cabinet Office have not always encouraged the Cabinet as a whole to discharge its responsibility for strategic policy review of this kind can be explained in a number of ways. Firstly, it is doubtful whether regular Cabinet meetings are the appropriate occasions on which to attempt this task, since senior Ministers are always very busy and short of time – they have their own Departmental business to manage, the demands of Parliament to which to respond, and a variety of public engagements in Britain and abroad to fulfil. Secondly, the Cabinet exists mainly to settle or endorse the big decisions which have already been carefully prepared in Whitehall and which may even have been taken (in effect at any rate) by the Prime Minister and a few senior Ministerial colleagues in advance of regu- lar Cabinet meetings. In these circumstances it is not surprising that the Cabinet has an unimpressive record in this respect.

Just occasionally, of course, the Cabinet does engage in intensive and extensive dis- cussions of this kind. This happened, for example, with the discussions in the Churchill Cabinet about British withdrawal from Egypt in 1954, in the Macmillan Cabinet about Britain's relationship with the rest of Western Europe in the late 1950s, in the Heath Cabinet about policy towards Northern Ireland in 1972-73, and in the Callaghan Cabinet in 1976 when it was necessary to agree upon a package of public expenditure cuts to satisfy the conditions of the IMF loan to Britain. Reflective discussions also take place from time to time in the more informal setting of Chequers (the Prime Minister's official country res- idence), but these are usually focused on a single theme (for example, the protection of the global environment under Margaret Thatcher in the late 1980s) and do not necessarily involve the entire Cabinet. In general, most regular Cabinet discussions are largely pre-ordained and even a little ritualistic. The Cabinet remains the supreme decision-making body in the British political system, but it has often been a disappointment to those who have looked to it for deep or original discussion of the key political issues of the time.

Under John Major's leadership Cabinet government in Britain seems to have staged something of a revival, at any rate as compared with his immediate predecessor. He appears to believe in genuine discussion before important decisions are taken and he is not in the habit of stating his desired conclusion at the outset of every important agenda item, as was all too often the practice of his predecessor. However, at the same time there have been some issues which he has felt the need to control more closely – such as the future of Northern Ireland or Britain's relations with the rest of the European Union – because of political sensitivities and internal party disagreements of a potentially acute kind. All of which serves to remind us of the provisional and tentative nature of any general observations about Cabinet government in Britain.

Inter-Departmental coordination

The third important role of the Cabinet is to ensure inter-Departmental coordination in the development of Government policy. In the opinion of many well informed observers this has long been the most notable role of the Cabinet in Britain. It is obviously a vital aspect of Cabinet activity, since it helps to impart a degree of coherence and unity to Government policy and so reinforces the doctrine of *collective responsibility*. Indeed, it could not really be otherwise, since senior Ministers cannot be expected to be bound by Cabinet decisions affecting their spheres of responsibility if their Departmental interests and political points of view have not been adequately taken into account. Such inter-Departmental coordination helps to guard against the taking of political decisions by one Department which may have unintended or adverse consequences for other Departments. It is also meant to contribute to the administrative efficiency of any Government, in that it can help to avoid both unnecessary duplication in Whitehall and the creation of awkward or damaging gaps in the scope of official action.

Since individual Cabinet Ministers are not always good 'team players' by temperament or calculation, it is necessary to bolster the unity and collegiality of the Cabinet with a number of institutional devices. For example, the Permanent Secretaries of all the various Whitehall Departments speak to each other from time to time and have regular weekly meetings under the chairmanship of the Cabinet Secretary. The Press Officers in all the various Departments are also in frequent contact and work collectively under the overall guidance of the Press Secretary at 10 Downing Street. The Private Offices of all Cabinet Ministers keep in touch and include an increasingly significant sub-network of Political Advisers, each of whom works directly for a Cabinet Minister and is paid from party rather than public funds. The Policy Unit at 10 Downing Street works exclusively for the Prime Minister of the day and occupies itself principally with political trouble-shooting, speech-writing and party political initiatives. It has sometimes tried to provide long-term or synoptic ideas on policy for the Government as a whole, but more often it works as a sort of policy clearing-house and political 'thought police' at the heart of central Government. All these various Whitehall networks are there to reinforce the coherence of Government policy and the unity of the Government as a whole.

It is clear that single party Government in Britain needs to be united Government if the political system is to work satisfactorily. The Cabinet is the main institutional expression of this unity and it is therefore vital that its decision-making procedures should contribute to rather than detract from the essentially collegiate nature of central Government in Britain. Whenever a Cabinet is seriously split on policy – as the Callaghan Cabinet was in 1976 over the IMF demand for public expenditure cuts or the Thatcher Cabinet was in 1979-81 over the general thrust of economic policy or the Major Cabinet has been on Britain's approach to further development of the European Union – the morale and effectiveness of the whole Government suffers. It can also lead to reduced levels of public support when the media and the general public perceive that the Cabinet is divided on important issues of policy or personality. It is therefore not surprising that all Prime Ministers strive mightily to avoid such splits and try to deal promptly with them when they occur.

12.5 Conclusion

Considerable controversy continues to surround the issues raised by the respective roles of the Prime Minister and Cabinet in modern British politics. There is no consensus of opinion among academic observers or practising politicians, although in Margaret Thatcher's time at 10 Downing Street most people were persuaded that British central Government was becoming increasingly presidential. Equally, during John Major's time as Prime Minister very different conclusions have been drawn.

In view of this contradictory evidence, some observers agree with John Mackintosh who wrote a considerable time ago that 'the weight of evidence does suggest that British Prime Ministers are in a position of great strength as against their colleagues and within the whole framework of British Government'.[12] Others agree with George Jones who wrote more recently that 'the Prime Minister is the leading figure in the Cabinet whose voice carries most weight, but he is not the all-powerful individual which many have claimed him to be'.[13] In the light of John Major's time at 10 Downing Street, these would seem to be well judged cautionary words. However, Robert Blake probably came to the most timeless conclusion when he wrote that 'the powers of the Prime Minister have varied with the personality of the Prime Minister or with the particular political circumstances of his tenure'.[14] On the whole this judgement seems to accord most closely with the evidence over the centuries. It allows for the fact that there have been times when Prime Ministers have carried all before them – for example, in the immediate aftermath of General Election victories or other personal political triumphs – and times when powerful Ministers or the Cabinet collectively have asserted their authority over weak, lazy, sick, politically damaged or discredited Prime Ministers. Indeed, Prime Ministerial power is like a fortress built on sand: it can look impregnable, yet can be washed away by a turn in the tide.

Although we have been looking in this chapter at two distinct components of the British political system, the fortunes of the Prime Minister and Cabinet are always inextricably linked. Whatever their respective roles and capabilities, neither can function satisfactorily without the consent and cooperation of the other. In so far as each is limited in the exercise of political power, the constraints are essentially political rather than constitutional, practical rather than theoretical. It is the other actors in the political process – the political parties, pressure groups, the civil service, the media, the markets, Britain's European partners and public opinion – which keep both Prime Minister and Cabinet in check. Moreover in the modern world it is the passage of events, very often in other countries, and the verdict of the British electorate which usually determine their fate.

Suggested questions

1   Describe the structure and problems of Cabinet government in Britain.
2   How powerful is the Prime Minister in modern Britain?
3   Does collective responsibility raise or lower the quality of decision making in British central Government?

Notes

1. See T. Blackstone and W. Plowden, *Inside the Think Tank* (London: Heinemann, 1988), for a fuller account of the Central Policy Review Staff.
2. H. Wilson, *The Governance of Britain* (London: Weidenfeld & Nicolson, 1976), p. 8.
3. Quoted in R. Blake, *The Office of Prime Minister* (Oxford: Oxford University Press, 1975), p. 50.
4. A. Eden, *Full Circle* (London: Cassell, 1960), p. 269.
5. H.H. Asquith, *Fifty Years of Parliament, Vol. II* (London: Cassell, 1926), p., 185.
6. *The Observer*, 25 February 1979.
7. This last condition of Prime Ministerial power is critical, as was made clear by the circumstances which led to Michael Heseltine's challenge to Margaret Thatcher for the leadership of the Conservative Party in November 1990 and hence the office of Prime Minister. This challenge to a very powerful Prime Minister and her subsequent downfall was the culmination of consistently low opinion poll ratings since July 1989 and a growing belief in both the Cabinet and the rest of the Conservative Parliamentary party that it would be impossible to win another General Election under her leadership.
8. On the other hand, it has been argued that Clement Attlee did not really have an effective choice, since his most senior Cabinet colleagues had either died (for example, Ernest Bevin and Stafford Cripps) or were exhausted after 11 years continuously in office both in war and in peace (for example, Herbert Morrison and Hugh Dalton), and since he was under pressure for some of his other Cabinet colleagues to hold a General Election at that time in any case.
9. J.P. Mackintosh, *The British Cabinet,* 3rd edn (London: Stevens, 1977), p. 414.
10. These two prominent examples of high-level Ministerial resignation underlined how important it is for all Prime Ministers to stay on good working terms with their Chancellors of the Exchequer and how dangerous it can be if an occupant of 11 Downing Street, or a former occupant, becomes completely disaffected.
11. See Tony Benn's *Diaries*, 1973-76, Vol. , pp. 661-690; and Denis Healey's *Memoirs*, 'The Time of My Life', pp. 426-435, for more detailed accounts of this critical period in the life of the 1974-79 Labour Government.
12. In A. King (ed.), *The British Prime Minister* (London: Macmillan, 1969), p. 198.
13. In A. King (ed.), *The British Prime Minister,* 2nd edn (London: Macmillan, 1985), p. 216.
14. R. Blake, *The Office of Prime Minister*, p. 51.

Further reading

Benn, A., *Diaries, Vols. I-IV* (London: Hutchinson, 1987-90).

Blake, R., *The Office of Prime Minister* (Oxford: Oxford University Press, 1975).

Callaghan, L.J., *Time and Chance* (London: Collins, 1987).

Hennessy, P., *Cabinet* (Oxford: Blackwell, 1986).

Hogg, S. and Hill, J., *Too Close to Call: Power and Politics – John Major in No. 10* (London: Little, Brown, 1995).

Howe, G., *Conflict of Loyalty* (London: Macmillan, 1994).

James, S., *British Cabinet Government* (London: Routledge, 1992).

Kavanagh, D., *Thatcherism and British Politics* (Oxford: Oxford University Press, 1987).

Lawson, N., *The View from Number 11* (London: Bantam Press, 1992).

Shell, D. and Hodder-Williams, R. (eds), *Churchill to Major: The British Prime Ministership since 1945* (London: Hurst and Company, 1995).

Thatcher, M., *The Downing Street Years* (London: Harper Collins, 1993).

Young, H., *One of Us*, rev. edn (London: Pan Books, 1990).

13 Ministers and Departments

Britain is a country with a long tradition of centralised Government. Some of the public offices of central Government have been in existence for centuries. For example, the first Lord Chancellor pre-dates the Norman Conquest of 1066 having been appointed by Edward the Confessor, the Exchequer developed in the twelfth century, and the office of Lord President of the Council dates from 1497. Some of the Departments of central Government are now over 200 years old, with two of the most prestigious Departments having been established in 1782 under George III when both a Department for Foreign Affairs and a Department for Home and Colonial Affairs (now the Home Office) were created.

Since the mid-nineteenth century Departments of central Government have been created, reorganised and dissolved. For example, the Board (Department) of Education was established in 1870 with a Minister directly responsible to Parliament for the whole area of public education. The Board of Agriculture and Fisheries was converted into a Ministry in 1919 after the struggle to feed the nation during the First World War. The Air Ministry was created in 1937 to organise what at the time was a revolutionary new arm of warfare. More recent examples include the Department of the Environment, which was established in 1970 as one of a number of super-Departments designed to secure better co-ordination in Whitehall; the Department of Energy, which was established in 1974 as a partial response to the energy crisis at that time (and re-absorbed into the Department of Trade and Industry in 1992); and the Department of National Heritage, which was created in 1992 to bring together in one Department the Government's responsibilities for the arts, sport and the media.

The organisation of Departments has often been changed in response to changes in Government functions and in political priorities. The 1974-79 Labour Government split the super-Departments into several smaller Departments – for example, the Department of Transport was re-established as a separate Department outside the Department of the Environment and the Department of Trade and Industry was split into a Department of Industry, a Department of Trade, and a new Department of Prices and Consumer Affairs. Equally, the 1979-83 Conservative Government abolished the Civil Service Department and redistributed its functions between the Treasury and the Cabinet Office; the 1983-87 Conservative Government recreated the Department of Trade and Industry, but transferred some of its functions to an enlarged Department of Transport; the 1987-92

Conservative Government split the Department of Health and Social Security into separate Departments of Health and Social Security respectively; while the Conservative Government elected in 1992 did away with the Department of Energy, redistributing its functions to the Department of Trade and Industry, and in 1995 merged the Department of Employment with the Department for Education. Thus it is apparent that there has been both change and continuity in the organisation of British central Government.

13.1 The structure and work of Departments

Throughout the entire period of Departmental government in Britain there has been only one fundamental examination of the overall structure of central Government. This was carried out by a committee chaired by Lord Haldane which reported to Lloyd George's Government in 1918.[1] The two main recommendations of the report were that Departmental boundaries should be based upon functional criteria (such as health, agriculture or defence), and that the Cabinet should be kept as a compact policy-making body at the apex of central Government. Neither recommendation has been fully implemented over subsequent years. Thus it has been quite common for Departments based on function (such as the Department of Health) to coexist with some based on responsibility for a mixture of subjects and functions (such as the Home Office) and others based on geography (such as the Scottish Office, the Welsh Office and the Northern Ireland Office). Furthermore, Cabinets have had as few as five members (Winston Churchill's War Cabinet in 1940) or as many as 24 members (Harold Wilson's Cabinet in 1975 and James Callaghan's Cabinet in 1977).

A limited attempt at Departmental reorganisation was made by the Heath Government in 1970. This stemmed from careful preparation in Opposition and was set out in a White Paper published soon after the Conservative election victory.[2] It marked the culmination of a trend in the 1960s towards the creation of super-Departments, the adoption of a managerial style of government, and deliberate attempts to strengthen the central co-ordinating Departments in relation to the rest of Whitehall. Yet only the emphasis upon the strengthening of the central Departments (such as the Treasury and the Cabinet Office) really substantiated the rhetoric about a new style of government. See Figure 13.1 for a diagram of the structure of central Government.

Department structure

The Departmental structure in Whitehall today consists of 22 Departments, including the Cabinet office and the three legal Departments. In political terms the most important are the Treasury, the Foreign Office and the Home Office. Yet in terms of the public spending for which they are responsible, the Department of Social Security, the Department of Health, and the Department for Education and Employment are the most significant. In formal terms there is no Prime Minister's Department, although the staff at 10 Downing Street and in the Cabinet Office provide effective civil service support for the Prime Minister of the day. Having said this, however, it should be noted that the Cabinet Office, and indeed the Cabinet Secretary, advise the Cabinet as a whole, not just the Prime Minister. See Figure 13.2 for a diagram of the Cabinet Office and Office of Public Service.

Figure 13.1 The structure of central Government (July 1995)

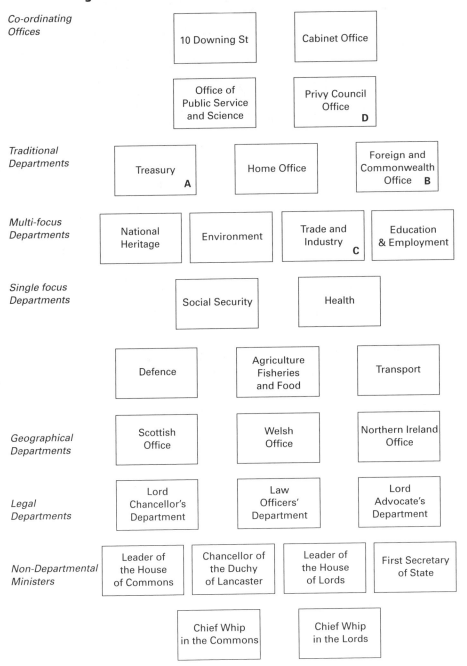

Co-ordinating Offices

10 Downing St

Cabinet Office

Office of Public Service and Science

Privy Council Office **D**

Traditional Departments

Treasury **A**

Home Office

Foreign and Commonwealth Office **B**

Multi-focus Departments

National Heritage

Environment

Trade and Industry **C**

Education & Employment

Single focus Departments

Social Security

Health

Defence

Agriculture Fisheries and Food

Transport

Geographical Departments

Scottish Office

Welsh Office

Northern Ireland Office

Legal Departments

Lord Chancellor's Department

Law Officers' Department

Lord Advocate's Department

Non-Departmental Ministers

Leader of the House of Commons

Chancellor of the Duchy of Lancaster

Leader of the House of Lords

First Secretary of State

Chief Whip in the Commons

Chief Whip in the Lords

A. Includes the Board of Customs and Excise, the Board of Inland Revenue and the Paymaster General
B. Includes the Overseas Development Administration
C. Includes Energy and the Export Credits Guarantee Department
D. Includes the Lord President of the Council and the Lord Privy Seal

Figure 13.2 Cabinet Office and Office of Public Service

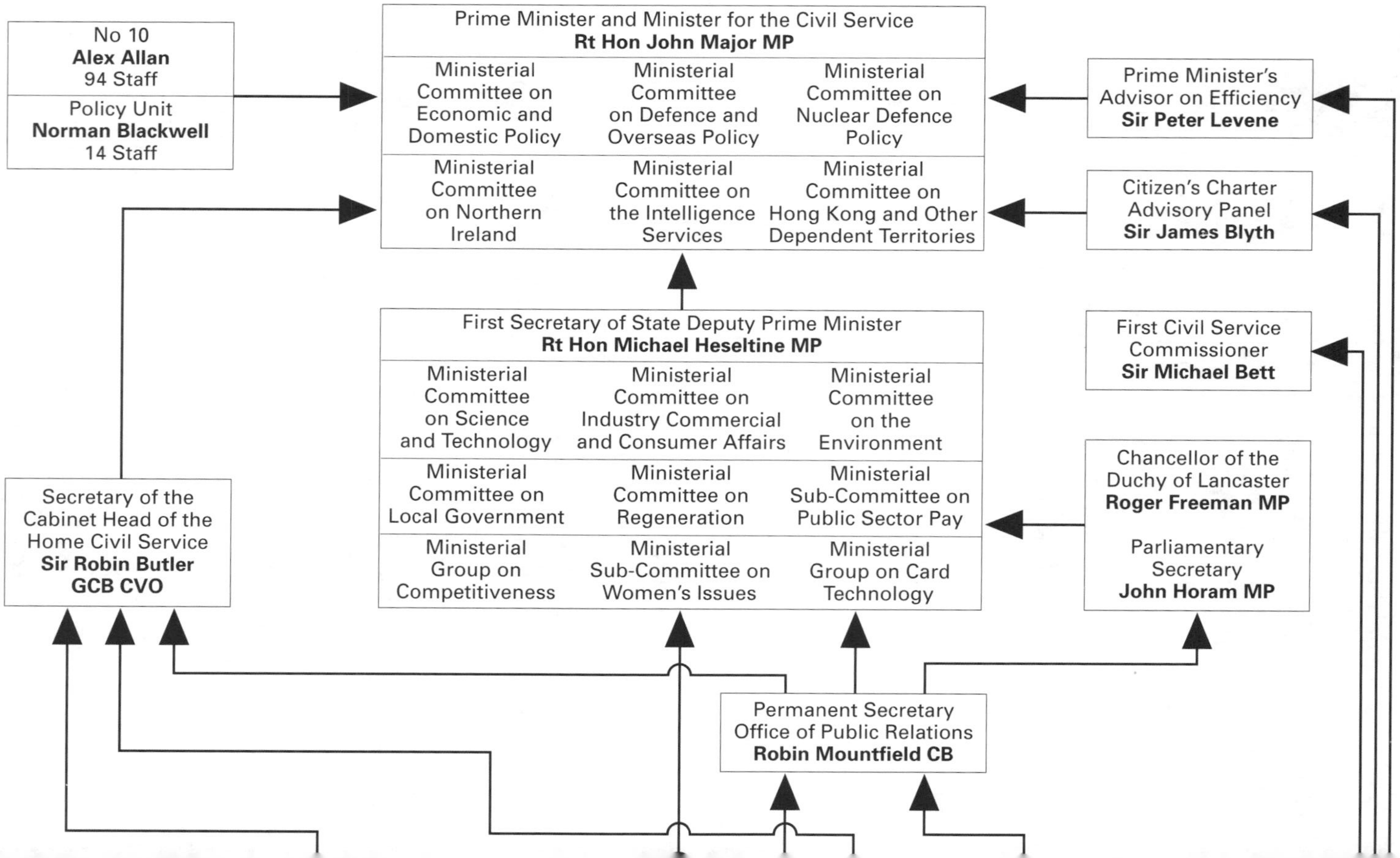

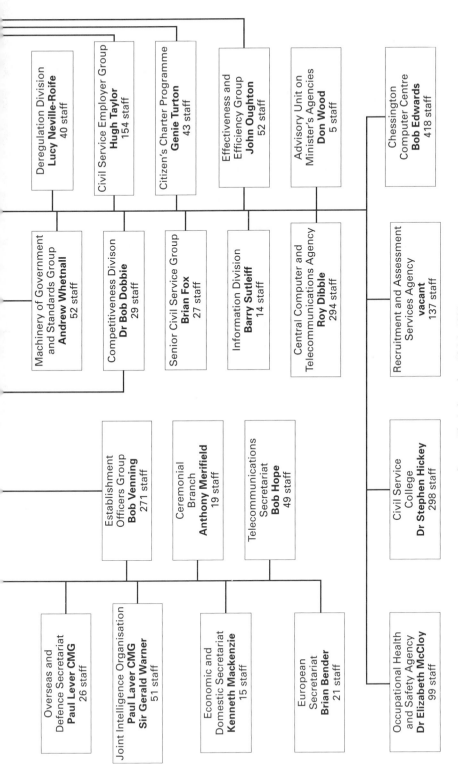

| Deregulation Division **Lucy Neville-Rolfe** 40 staff | Civil Service Employer Group **Hugh Taylor** 154 staff | Citizen's Charter Programme **Genie Turton** 43 staff | Effectiveness and Efficiency Group **John Oughton** 52 staff | Advisory Unit on Minister's Agencies **Don Wood** 5 staff | Chessington Computer Centre **Bob Edwards** 418 staff |

| Machinery of Government and Standards Group **Andrew Whetnall** 52 staff | Competitiveness Division **Dr Bob Dobbie** 29 staff | Senior Civil Service Group **Brian Fox** 27 staff | Information Division **Barry Sutleiff** 14 staff | Central Computer and Telecommunications Agency **Roy Dibble** 294 staff | Recruitment and Assessment Services Agency **vacant** 137 staff |

| Establishment Officers Group **Bob Venning** 271 staff | Ceremonial Branch **Anthony Merifield** 19 staff | Telecommunications Secretariat **Bob Hope** 49 staff | Civil Service College **Dr Stephen Hickey** 298 staff |

| Overseas and Defence Secretariat **Paul Lever CMG** 26 staff | Joint Intelligence Organisation **Paul Laver CMG Sir Gerald Warner** 51 staff | Economic and Domestic Secretariat **Kenneth Mackenzie** 15 staff | European Secretariat **Brian Bender** 21 staff | Occupational Health and Safety Agency **Dr Elizabeth McCloy** 99 staff |

Source: *The Independent*, 10 July 1995

Apart from the Prime Minister, there are a few other non-Departmental Ministers, such as the Lord President of the Council and the Lord Privy Seal and now, of course, the First Secretary of State and Deputy Prime Minister. It is also possible to appoint a Minister 'without portfolio'.[3] Such offices can be a convenient way for the Prime Minister of the day to include close political colleagues in the Cabinet without burdening them with Departmental responsibilities, as was the case with John Major's appointment of the Chairman of the Conservative Party, Dr Brian Mawhinney, as Minister without portfolio in July 1995.

Within each significant Department the normal pattern is for there to be a Secretary of State or Minister of equivalent Cabinet rank as Departmental head, supported by at least one Minister of State at the second level and perhaps two or more Under-Secretaries at the third level. There are, however, variations in this pattern which flow mainly from the nature and scope of each Department's responsibilities. For example, following an extensive reshuffle in July 1994 the Department of the Environment had one Cabinet Minister, three Ministers of State and two Under-Secretaries, whereas the Welsh Office had only a Cabinet Minister and two Under-Secretaries. The Treasury is distinctive in many ways, not least in having two Cabinet Ministers – the Chancellor of the Exchequer and the Chief Secretary – and normally the backing of the Prime Minister as well (who is known formally as the First Lord of the Treasury).

Just as the number and importance of Ministers varies from one Department to another, so the number of civil servants working in each Department also varies considerably. For example, in the middle 1990s the Ministry of Defence and the Department of Social Security each employed more than 80,000 non-industrial civil servants, whereas the Treasury only employed about 1400 (although this figure did not include those employed by the Inland Revenue or Customs and Excise), the Department for Education employed 2407 and the Department of National Heritage 1030. The explanation for these wide differences is that in the former category are to be found Departments whose functions cover a wide range of policy functions and the provision of extensive public services, whereas in the latter category are to be found Departments whose functions are limited to policy advice and supervisory responsibilities. Despite varying considerably in size and function, there is nevertheless a recognisably standard structure for each Department in Whitehall.

Government functions

It is difficult to generalise about the way in which central Government works in Britain. So much depends upon the personality, outlook and experience of the senior Ministers concerned and also upon the calibre and performance of the senior civil servants involved, as well as upon the various Departmental habits and traditions. According to the traditional view propounded by Sir Ivor Jennings, the essential features of British central Government are 'the clear division between politicians and public servants and the close relationship between policy and administration'.[4] This emphasises one of the key paradoxes of British central Government. On the one hand, there is a clear theoretical distinction between the role of Ministers, who are supposed to determine the policy and take all the decisions, and that of civil servants, who are supposed to advise Ministers and see that the business of Government is conducted in conformity with the policy laid down by Ministers. On the other hand, there is the *practical* impossibility in modern British Government of sustaining such a clear distinction. In short, it has become increasingly apparent that the theory that Ministers take the political decisions and civil servants carry them out has long since been overtaken by reality. Hence we find yet another example of the inherent contradictions in the British political system.

Most Ministers have to work very hard, often for between 12 and 18 hours a day. There are policy discussions to conduct, official papers to be considered and, where possible, approved, Ministerial correspondence to be dealt with, frequent meetings both within their own Departments and bilaterally with other Departments or 10 Downing Street, meetings of the Cabinet or Cabinet Committees to attend, meetings to be held with outside bodies and the representatives of various pressure or interest groups, Parliamentary committees to attend, Parliamentary Questions to be answered, Parliamentary debates in which to take part, official visits to be made to various parts of the country and abroad, foreign visitors to be welcomed and entertained, journalists and others in the media to be briefed, interviews to be given, meetings of the European Union and other international organisations to attend, constituents and party activists to be kept content as well as constituency work to attend to.

A graphic illustration of the demands of Ministerial life was given by Tony Benn, when describing how he allocated his time in 1977 when he was Secretary of State for Energy.[5]

(1) Fulfilled fifty public engagements in the constituency, made twelve general speeches in Bristol, held sixteen constituency surgeries, and handled more than 1000 personal cases.

(2) Attended four General Management Committee meetings of the Bristol South East Labour Party; attended twenty ward meetings, and five Labour Group meetings to discuss policy.

(3) Attended twelve meetings of the Parliamentary Labour Party, and made fourteen speeches to various sub-group meetings of MPs.

(4) Dealt in Parliament with three Energy Bills, produced fifty-four Statutory Instruments; presented thirty-three explanatory memoranda to the House on European Community energy matters; answered fifty-one oral questions and 171 written questions; had 154 meetings with non-Governmental groups; produced 1821 Ministerial minutes on papers taken home in the official red box; made 133 public appointments to various bodies.

(5) Attended forty-two Cabinet meetings and 106 Cabinet Committee meetings; submitted four Cabinet papers and forty-five Cabinet Committee papers; received 1750 Cabinet papers covering the whole range of Government policies.

(6) Made nineteen visits abroad, and received thirty-two Ministers and Ambassadors from foreign countries.

(7) In the first half of 1977, presided over the Energy Council of the European Community, which involved taking the chair at six Council meetings and having sundry other official meetings on European energy questions.

(8) Attended fifteen meetings of the Labour Party National Executive Committee and sixty-two other Labour meetings.

(9) Made eighty speeches up and down the country, gave eighty-three radio interviews, fifty-seven television interviews and thirty-four press

conferences, wrote sixteen articles, had thirty interviews with individual journalists, and received or answered 1000 letters which did not involve constituency casework or Ministerial responsibilities.

This is a considerable amount of work by any standards, but it is by no means untypical of Ministerial life today. However, any inventory can only provide a superficial and incomplete sketch of the full range of Ministerial activities, since it is impossible to give a definitive description of a working life which is inherently so varied and unpredictable.

In addition to the problems which can be caused by what can be termed 'Ministerial musical chairs' whenever the Prime Minister has a reshuffle, incoming Ministers usually get no time to prepare for their jobs and little or no advice from their predecessors. New Ministers seldom have anything more than superficial knowledge or understanding of their new responsibilities unless they have been promoted from within or are returning to a Department which they already know. The normal assumption is that they will learn on the job with the assistance of their Ministerial colleagues and civil service advisers. Indeed, the ability to get to grips with a complex brief in a short period of time is considered to be one of the main qualifications for Ministerial office in British central Government.

Civil servants for their part, and notably those in the senior administrative grades who advise Ministers, do their best to ensure that Ministers are adequately briefed on all matters with which they have to deal. Yet at the same time they try to see that Ministers are not over-burdened with unnecessary paperwork or matters which can be handled by officials. This means that one of the key roles of senior civil servants, and especially those who work in Ministerial Private Offices, is that of 'gate-keeper' in the information-gathering and decision-making process of central Government. Every day such civil servants have to decide whether to refer matters to Ministers for information or decision or whether to deal with issues themselves within the confines of established Government policy. Although there is a natural tendency for civil servants to err on the side of caution by referring all politically sensitive matters to Ministers, their 'gate-keeper' role gives them considerable influence within central Government and the veil of official secrecy behind which they work makes it hard for the outside observer – and sometimes even Ministers – to evaluate just how satisfactorily they perform their tasks.

Perhaps the most characteristic aspect of activity in Whitehall is the work which is done in the extensive network of *inter-Departmental committees* both at political level in Cabinet Committees and bilateral Ministerial meetings and at official level in the inter-Departmental Committees made up of officials from the Departments concerned. Since many of the issues with which central Government has to deal are too broad and complex to be handled within the sphere of a single Department, the process of inter-Departmental co-ordination by officials, prior to collective Ministerial decisions, is vital to much of the policy- and decision-making process. It puts a considerable burden upon officials in the Cabinet Office, who have to see that the various strands of policy are pulled together. The process of government would not work so smoothly without such inter-Departmental co-ordination by officials.

Another important aspect of the work of British central Government is the frequent and extensive consultation which takes place between officials and various client or pressure groups. Nowadays nearly every Department finds it useful to consult widely with such groups, not so much about which policy to adopt as about the detailed effects and implications of policy already determined by Ministers. For example, the Ministry of Agriculture has worked very closely (some would say too closely) with the National Farmers' Union in accordance with the statutory duties of consultation laid down in the 1947 and 1957 Agriculture Acts. Equally, the Department of Trade and Industry has kept in contact with the Confederation of British Industry and the wide range of Chambers of Commerce and Trade Associations, although less so during the 1980s and early 1990s than before because of the non-corporatist instincts of the Thatcher and Major Governments. In short, nearly all Departments make it their business to keep in touch with the various interest and cause groups which have a stake in their spheres of Departmental responsibility, although the extent and intensity of these contacts, at any rate at Ministerial level, has diminished under the post-1979 Conservative Governments. Certainly any Government which totally spurned or neglected such contacts would not only find its tasks made more difficult, but also lay itself open to serious criticism in Parliament and in the media. As a consequence, political prudence dictates that Ministers and officials at least go through the motions of consultation, and usually much more than that.

13.2 The role of Ministers

The role of Ministers in British central Government can be simply defined as taking the lead in, and making decisions on, matters of policy, and the defence and promotion of that policy in Whitehall, Westminster, Brussels and the world at large. Within their Departments Ministers act essentially as political jurymen who take decisions on the basis of advice supplied to them by their civil servants and others. Of course, Ministers are always free to question, ignore or discard such advice, but this can be unwise. Civil servants do not usually recommend courses of action or inaction which they know would be politically unacceptable to Ministers at the time. Ministers for their part sometimes may not have the time or the inclination to question or reject the policy advice which is put to them. Usually only strong, self-confident and experienced Ministers, or those who are engaged upon implementing clearly established party policy, manage to dominate all policy work in their Departments.

Every Government since the war has contained a few senior Ministers who have been able, more often than not, to get their way with officials, with their Ministerial colleagues and with Parliament. Of course this has applied particularly to strong and determined Prime Ministers, such as Clement Attlee and Margaret Thatcher. Yet it has also applied very clearly to some other leading figures who have not been Prime Minister. One obvious example of such a Ministerial heavyweight would be Ernest Bevin, who was Minister of Labour in the wartime Coalition Government and Foreign Secretary in the post-war Labour Government. Another example would be Duncan Sandys, who was successively Commonwealth Secretary and Defence Secretary in Conservative Governments in the 1950s. Yet another would be Denis Healey, who was Labour Defence Secretary, 1964-70, and Labour Chancellor of the Exchequer, 1974-79. More recently one could cite Viscount Whitelaw, who was successively Leader of the House of Commons and Northern Ireland Secretary in the 1970-74 Heath Government, and Home Secretary and then Leader of the House of Lords in Margaret Thatcher's first two Administrations; and Nigel Lawson, who was Chancellor of the Exchequer in Margaret Thatcher's

Government from 1983 to 1989. During the 1990s examples can be cited of Kenneth Clarke, who served as a Cabinet Minister at the Departments of Trade and Industry, Health, and Education under Margaret Thatcher, and as Home Secretary and then Chancellor of the Exchequer under John Major; Michael Heseltine, who first entered the Cabinet in 1979, serving as Environment Secretary and Defence Secretary under Margaret Thatcher before resigning in 1986 over the Westland Affair and subsequently rejoining John Major's Cabinet in 1990 again as Environment Secretary and later as President of the Board of Trade and then First Secretary of State and Deputy Prime Minister; and Douglas Hurd who was successively Northern Ireland Secretary, Home Secretary and then Foreign Secretary under the leadership of Margaret Thatcher and John Major. It is not easy to define what qualities such Ministers have had which have earned them the accolade of 'political heavyweights'. Yet politicians and pundits alike know one when they see one. Force of character and political judgement undoubtedly play an important part, but so do Ministerial competence and Prime Ministerial backing.

It is evident that the balance of experience and ability can often determine the balance of power between Ministers and senior civil servants. In the final analysis it is apparent that a variety of factors are involved. These include the degree of popular support for a policy (especially as manifested by the media), whether or not it appeared in the party Manifesto, the degree of Prime Ministerial and Cabinet support, the availability of sufficient time in which to carry it through to fruition, the absence of other overriding policy priorities or distracting emergencies and crises, the extent of support among senior civil servants and Parliamentary colleagues, the feelings among party activists and members, and the leadership given by a competent and determined Minister.

Ministerial responsibility

Ministerial responsibility is both individual and collective. It is still one of the key concepts in British central Government. It has endured since the nineteenth century because it has advantages for Ministers and civil servants alike. Ministers have benefited from the fact that it puts them in a privileged position in which they are the main recipients of official information and advice. Traditionally, civil servants have also benefited from the fact that it has give them considerable influence over Government policy and decision making without the formal need to accept public responsibility for the outcome.[6] However, these traditional characteristics have been changed significantly in recent years by the growth of so-called 'Next Steps Executive Agencies' which have had the effect of putting responsibility for the *administration* of public policy fairly and squarely on the shoulders of the much more visible Chief Executives who lead them and who can, occasionally, be sacked if their performance does not come up to expectations.[7]

With regard to *individual responsibility*, the senior Minister in a Department is theoretically responsible for everything which happens or fails to happen within the Department and can be held to account by Parliament and the media for acts of omission as well as commission. The classic view holds that Ministers are responsible for every act of their civil servants, regardless of whether or not they are properly aware of what is happening in their Departments. The most often cited example of this doctrine was the resignation of the Minister of Agriculture, Sir Thomas Dugdale, in the 1954 Crichel Down Affair. More recent examples cited usually include the resignation of Lord Carrington and most of his

Ministerial colleagues at the Foreign Office in April 1982 in recognition of his Department's failure to foresee and prevent the Argentinean invasion of the Falkland Islands. On the other hand, there are a large number of examples of senior Ministers *not* resigning, even when their policies and personal reputations were in tatters. For example, John Davies did not resign as Secretary of State for Trade and Industry in 1971 in the wake of the Court Line collapse or in 1972 after the failure of Vehicle and General. Equally, Norman Lamont did not resign as Chancellor of the Exchequer in September 1992 following the collapse of the fixed exchange rate policy and the forced withdrawal of Sterling from the Exchange Rate Mechanism of the European Monetary System. Similarly Michael Howard did not resign as Home Secretary in April 1995 when the Courts threw out his cost-cutting Crime Injuries Scheme, even though they accused him of abusing power and flouting the will of Parliament. Indeed, Prime Ministers have often challenged the whole concept of Ministerial responsibility. For example, Margaret Thatcher refused to accept the resignation of William Whitelaw as Home Secretary following a widely publicised breach of security at Buckingham Palace in 1982 or James Prior as Secretary of State for Northern Ireland following a mass escape from the Maze prison in September 1983.[8]

It is apparent, therefore, that there are no hard and fast rules which determine the nature of Ministerial responsibility in all cases and the outcome depends upon an unpredictable mixture of precedents and political circumstances. In contemporary conditions the factors which determine whether or not Ministers resign from office seem to depend more upon the extent to which they still command the confidence of the Prime Minister, the Chief Whip and their own backbenchers than upon any objective assessment of the incompetence or impropriety of the action or inaction for which they may be criticised. In other words, holding on to Ministerial office seems to have taken precedence over principled resignation in modern British Government.

The chain of responsibility in a Department is hierarchical, which means that civil servants and junior Ministers alike report to senior Ministers at the head of their Departments and it is the latter who have to take the ultimate responsibility for their action or inaction. Of course, there have been times when junior Ministers have been so out of sympathy with a particular policy of their Department or the Government as a whole that they have felt bound to resign. This was the case, for example, with Ian Gow who resigned as Minister of State at the Treasury in 1985 in protest against the Anglo-Irish Agreement.[9] Others have resigned in order to be free to criticise Government policy more generally. Yet on the whole junior Ministers stay at their posts and only tender their resignations if they are obliged to do so in the course of a Ministerial 'reshuffle' organised by the Prime Minister of the day or as a result of political pressure arising from some scandal publicised by the media.

Indeed, it seems that *individual Ministerial responsibility* has been blurred and eroded in modern times by the size and complexity of modern Government. This means that it has been effectively impossible for senior Ministers to be aware of, let alone control, everything which happens or fails to happen in their Departments. For example, thousands of planning appeals have to be decided every year by the Secretary of State for the Environment, many of them important and nearly all of them complicated and contentious. Yet no Minister in that position can possibly hope to consider all of them personally, so junior Ministers and civil servants effectively take the decisions in the senior Minister's name in all but a few outstanding cases. Thus in most cases individual Ministerial responsibility has become little more than a constitutional 'cloak', a convenient fiction for Parliamentary and civil service purposes, but a convention which is put strictly into practice on very few occasions.

On the other hand, *collective Ministerial responsibility* is more of a reality in modern political conditions, because it reflects the collegiate and usually cohesive nature of single party Government in Britain. It is really a way of expressing the fact that all Ministers and Whips – and, indeed, Parliamentary Private Secretaries – are bound by Government policy and are expected to stand by it and to speak and vote for it. While politicians cannot really be expected to believe totally in everything which they have to support in public for reasons of party loyalty, those whose activities are covered by collective Ministerial responsibility are expected nevertheless to support the Government on all occasions. If they feel unable or unwilling to do so, they are supposed to resign or can expect to be dismissed – as was the case in 1981, for example, when Keith Speed, the junior Navy Minister, was sacked for speaking out publicly against planned cuts in the Royal Navy budget, or in 1989 when Nicholas Ridley, then Environment Secretary, was sacked for speaking out against the Germans.

It should come as no surprise, however, that the convention of collective responsibility has not always been observed. Indeed, on those, admittedly rare, occasions when Governments have been so split that enforcement has been effectively impossible, temporary suspension has become the only effective course. For example, in 1931 there was an open 'agreement to differ' in the National Government on the issue of tariff reform, and in 1975 during the European Referendum campaign Labour Cabinet Ministers were allowed to argue against each other on public platforms. It is unwise, however, for those covered by collective responsibility to test the boundaries of the permissible too obviously or too often, since in doing so they are quite likely to invite dismissal by the Prime Minister of the day. On the whole, therefore, collective Ministerial responsibility is a reality in modern British government, but it is no longer the effective mechanism of Parliamentary accountability which it was originally meant to be.

Parliamentary accountability

In theory, the proper constitutional check upon the power of the Executive in Britain is to be found in Ministerial accountability to Parliament. This is supposed to be achieved in three ways. None of these is adequate on its own, but taken together there are some safeguards for the public interest.

Firstly, there are the opportunities for MPs to hold Ministers to account during proceedings in the Chamber of the House of Commons (and, to a lesser extent, for peers to do so in the House of Lords) – that is, at Question Time, following Ministerial statements and during debates. Yet the scope for effective Parliamentary influence in such proceedings – through challenge, criticism and attack – is limited by the ability of most competent Ministers to answer points in the House without revealing any new or substantial information if they do not want to do so. Experience also shows that such proceedings are often rather an empty ritual, since any attempt at a strong Parliamentary challenge usually gives way to mere party-political point-scoring. Also, invariably the media have discovered (or been briefed about) the points at issue long before Parliament gets its chance, in effect reducing the impact of Parliament.

Secondly, there are the opportunities for MPs and peers to probe Ministerial thinking and Government policy during Select Committee investigations and during the committee stage of Government Bills. These have proved to be somewhat more effective mechanisms for Parliamentary influence. Yet, in the former case, the usefulness of such investigations is limited by an unwillingness often shown by Governments to act upon the findings of Select Committees and occasionally even to allow key Ministerial or official witnesses to appear before the committee at all.[10] In the latter case, legislative scrutiny by the Opposition in Standing Committees has to be set against the normal voting power of the Government majority, both in the Committees and subsequently on the floor of the house at Report and Third Reading. Such proceedings provide a form of Parliamentary accountability and influence, but not effective Parliamentary control, unless, of course, the Government of the day has a relatively small or no majority in the Commons or a large enough number of its own back-benchers feel inclined to rebel.

Thirdly, there are the various opportunities for MPs and peers to use their power of publicity to dramatise the errors of Ministers or the shortcomings of Government policy. The principal effect of this form of Parliamentary accountability has been to encourage an attitude of defensiveness on the part of civil servants and to reinforce the tendency for Whitehall Departments to play safe in the conduct of Government business. Indeed, it is the capricious and unpredictable quality of such Parliamentary accountability which has led both Ministers and officials to treat it with wary respect. This has had a marked influence upon attitudes and working practices in Whitehall and has sometimes discouraged bold or imaginative decision making by Ministers. It may, therefore, have lowered the quality of decision making in British central Government.

Thus, if we examine the various forms of Parliamentary accountability, we discover that none of them has proved to be a guarantee of representative and responsible Government. The lack of proper accountability has been most marked in the detailed areas of policy covered by *Statutory Instruments*, the secondary legislation which is drafted by civil servants in the name of Ministers and lawfully implemented under the authority of existing statutes. In effect, legislation of this type is no longer within the realm of effective Parliamentary control. Although there is a Joint Committee of the Lords and Commons which has the task of overseeing the spate of secondary legislation which pours out of Whitehall, the problem has really become unmanageable now that there are more than 2000 Statutory Instruments issued each year. The volume of such secondary legislation and the shortcomings of existing Parliamentary procedures for dealing with it are such that genuine Parliamentary accountability is really unattainable.

The other notable area in which Parliamentary accountability is clearly defective is that of *European legislation*. Under the 1972 European Communities Act the British Government is obliged to implement automatically the *Regulations* issued by the European Commission, notably in the spheres of agriculture, trade and competition policy, and to find appropriate national means of carrying out the *Directives* which flow from decisions taken by the Council of Ministers. In 1974 both the House of Commons and the House of Lords established special Select Committees to sift draft European legislation and to make recommendations as to whether or not the various items contained therein were sufficiently important to merit a debate on the floor of their respective Chambers. As things have turned out, such debates (in the House of Commons at any rate) are normally brief and late at night, if and when the 'usual channels' find time for them at all. In some cases it has not even proved possible to find time to debate a particular draft European proposal before it is considered by the Council of Ministers or before it is promulgated by the Commission as directly applicable European legislation. This means that it may well become law in Britain before there has been any consideration of its merits or otherwise by MPs on the floor of the House of Commons or by peers on the floor of the House of Lords.

One answer to the problem of insufficient Parliamentary accountability in this area of Executive action is for the tasks of scrutiny to be performed by the directly elected European Parliament which does have some enlarged rights of 'co-decision' with the other European institutions in specific areas of European Union activity. Yet this is not a complete answer, and in any case many of the national Parliaments remain jealous of their historic rights to legislate and to hold Ministers to account. The result is that there is what has been called a 'democratic deficit' in the European Union which could be closed either by a great leap forward towards fuller political integration in Europe with much greater powers for the European Parliament, or by a dramatic reassertion of democratic control by national Parliaments which seems both unlikely and possibly unattainable.[11] Other possible solutions would be to make at least some British Members of the European Parliament also members of the House of Lords; or for the member states to create a second Chamber of the European Parliament, made up of members drawn proportionately from the national Parliaments.

In reflecting generally upon the history of Parliamentary accountability in Britain since the Second World War, we must conclude that it has been notable more for the tendency of Ministers to escape the shackles of real accountability than for the ability of Parliament to impose its will and control upon Ministers.[12] While there were the celebrated cases of the Crichel Down affair in 1954 and the Argentinean invasion of the Falkland Islands in 1982, each of which led to the resignation of the Cabinet Minister considered most culpable, in modern times such cases have seemed to be exceptions to the general rule that Ministers and civil servants can make grievous mistakes without ever really being subjected to full and effective Parliamentary accountability. They may get sacked later on when the heat has died down and the public attention has turned elsewhere, yet at the relevant time when they ought to be held strictly to account in Parliament, Ministers are often able to get away with suffering no more than Parliamentary and media censure because their own party colleagues rally to their support.

13.3 The problems of Government

The problems of Government vary from Department to Department and from time to time. The key question which has to be faced by all Governments is whether or not Ministers are really in full control of their Departments and therefore able to give the necessary political impetus to the Government as a whole. In this section we shall examine some of the problems which make it hard to give a convincing, affirmative answer to this basic question.

Ministerial workload

As touched upon previously, one major problem of British central Government is the heavy workload which Ministers have to bear, especially Cabinet Ministers in charge of large Departments such as Defence, Social Security or the Environment. The very size, scope and complexity of such Departments militate against the idea that senior Ministers can readily dominate or control every aspect of their Department's activities. Yet this is what they are expected to do, notwithstanding the extra requirements imposed by the insatiable demands of the modern media and the growing obligations of European Union membership. Indeed, in view of the collegiate nature of Cabinet government in Britain, it is a problem with which all senior Ministers have to cope.

One way of lightening the burden upon Ministers has been to reduce the size of the public sector. This has happened since 1979 as a result of the Conservative Government's policy of privatisation, which by the mid-1990s had reduced the state industrial sector by about two-thirds compared with its size when the Conservatives came to office. Thus the areas of activity for which Ministers are held directly responsible has diminished, even if the extent to which the general public seems to blame Ministers for things which go wrong has increased with the growing politicisation of daily life in Britain and other advanced countries largely as a result of the relentless activity of the media.

Another possibility would be to reduce the range of tasks which Ministers are expected to perform – for example, by relieving them of their constituency duties as in France, or their responsibilities for the administration of policy as in Sweden. While the former idea may seem unthinkable in Britain, because back-benchers like to ensure that Ministers have to encounter and deal with the same constituency problems as themselves, considerable progress has been made towards implementation of the latter idea with the establishment of so many Departmental Agencies to do the run-of-the-mill administrative tasks previously done by Departments.

Of course, the problems of Ministerial workload are exacerbated by some of the conventions of central Government in Britain, notably the assumption that Ministers will consult widely and systematically before taking major decisions or introducing important new legislation. Admittedly, many of these consultations with interest groups and relevant experts are conducted by civil servants on behalf of Ministers. Yet Ministers still have to lay down the political guidelines for such discussions and in the most important cases often have to take a leading part in them as well. A balanced solution to the problem would take account of all these factors. Yet no matter which solutions are adopted, Ministers will always require great personal energy and strong political will in order to perform all their tasks successfully.

Departmental policy

Another major problem of central Government is the continuously powerful influence of established Departmental policy. This may not make itself felt very much during the first year or two of a Government's term of office, but it can assume considerable importance as time goes by if the political momentum of the party in office begins to falter. This phenomenon was particularly noticeable during the period of the post-war consensus from 1945 to 1973 and especially in the well-established Departments with long traditions and considerable self-confidence, such as the Foreign Office or the Home Office. Yet the outcome of disputes between Ministers and civil servants has never been a foregone conclusion. Much depends upon whether Ministers individually – and notably the Prime Minister – are determined to carry out their policies and to impose their authority upon the Government. If they are so determined, both the realities of political power and the conventions of Whitehall enable them to get their own way whatever the personal preferences or reservations of senior civil servants. If they are not so determined, then the underlying strength of Departmental policy may triumph in the end.

The strength of Departmental policy, or at least the influence of senior civil servants, is enhanced by the habits of Ministerial life. This is because it has been customary for Prime Ministers to shift Ministers and move them from post to post quite frequently, sometimes simply to assert Prime Ministerial authority, but usually to broaden the experience of their most promising Ministerial colleagues. Typically, a Cabinet Minister holds office for about two and a half years on average and most Secretaries of State last only two years in a particular post.[13] However, these figures mask the fact that there are considerable differences between Departments. For example, between 1964 and 1995 there were only six Lords Chancellor, but 23 Secretaries of State at the Department of Trade and Industry. Hence many Ministers are precluded from making anything more than a temporary or marginal impact upon the political issues with which their Departments have to deal.

The strength of Departmental policy is also enhanced by the habits of civil service life. This is because it has been customary to move civil servants in the higher administrative grades frequently from one job to another both within a single Department and sometimes between Departments. In many instances this means that key administrative staff may stay in post for only a year or two, with the result that they do not really have time to develop their own expertise in the policy area concerned. This happens mainly for reasons of career development and is largely for the benefit of those who have been identified as 'high flyers' early in their civil service careers. Although an able civil servant is very good at breaking into new policy areas – after all this is one of the professional skills which mark them out as 'high flyers' – nevertheless, the inevitable consequence is that even the best civil servants rely heavily upon their Departmental 'experts' and especially upon what is already in the Departmental filing cabinets – in other words the accumulated wisdom of established Departmental policy. Such tendencies can only be overcome by sustained political will on the part of Ministers and significant changes in civil service career development policy, changes which are already beginning to come about.

The quality of advice

Another problem of central Government is the quality of official information and advice available to Ministers. While such material is a source of strength for Ministers in relation to the Opposition and all back-benchers, it does not necessarily strengthen their position within their own Departments. This is because it is not unusual for politicians who become Ministers to be posted to a Department about which they know little or nothing in advance and which deals with areas of policy of which they have had little or no previous experience.[14] Even when Ministers appoint expert personal advisers from outside the civil service, such outsiders are likely to be 'domesticated' by their Department and are unlikely, on their own, to be able to provide their Minister with sufficiently weighty countervailing advice to match or defeat the established Departmental view. The result is that, unless Ministers are engaged in the implementation of clear Manifesto commitments or are pushing through other forms of unambiguous party policy, they are seldom provided with a sufficiently compelling view of the available alternatives to existing policy and are therefore often obliged to rely upon the advice from their Departmental civil servants, and will tend to do so provided they are convinced that it will persuade the Cabinet and Parliament.

This is an unfortunate state of affairs for two reasons. Firstly, the best answers to many of the most difficult problems of central Government are not necessarily to be found either in the liturgy of party Manifestos or in the drawers of Departmental filing cabinets. Secondly, and often for partisan political reasons, the policy- and decision-making process can be deprived of a good deal of high-quality information and advice from 'outsiders' who are both expert in their field and independent of Government. Some of this has changed with the tendency for Prime Ministers to hold all-day seminars and other 'brainstorming' sessions at Chequers or 10 Downing Street. It has also been modified by the growth in the number, although not necessarily the quality, of so-called 'special advisers' working directly for senior Ministers. Yet there is undoubtedly still room for the quality and breadth of advice available to Ministers to be improved.

13.4 Conclusion

Well-qualified observers of British politics and some distinguished practitioners have argued for years about whether Ministers are really in control of their Departments. As long ago as the 1850s Lord Palmerston wrote to Queen Victoria that 'Your Majesty will see how greatly such a system [of government] must place in the hands of the subordinate members of public Departments [civil servants] the power of directing the policy and the measures of the Government, because the value, tendency and consequence of a measure frequently depends as much upon the manner in which it was worked out [that is, administered] as the intention and spirit with which it was planned.'[15] This was one of the earliest and most perceptive statements of the now familiar argument that in the process of government the power to administer can be as important as the power to decide. In other words, civil servants can have nearly as much effective power as Ministers, even though the constitutional conventions do not admit it.

On the other hand, Herbert Morrison wrote in the 1950s that 'if the Minister in charge [of a Department] knows what he wants and is intelligent in going about it, he can command the understanding, co-operation and support of his civil servants.'[16] This statement from a senior Labour Minister with Departmental experience dating back to before the Second World War could be interpreted as an affirmation of Ministerial dominance in Whitehall. Yet it could also be interpreted as a back-handed compliment to the power of the civil service and a warning that Whitehall officials tend to fill any vacuum which may be left by Ministers. Clearly it is necessary to refine the conventional statement that Ministers decide the policy and civil servants simply carry it out. The contemporary realities are more subtle, and the traditional model takes insufficient account of the complexities of modern Government.

What we see is an *interdependent working relationship*. Civil servants look to Ministers to be clear about the policy objectives they wish to pursue, to heed advice on their likely consequences and methods of implementation, to be able to carry their Ministerial colleagues with them (including notably the Chief Secretary and the Chancellor of the Exchequer), and to present a convincing case for the policy to Parliament, the media and the general public. Ministers look to senior civil servants to be responsive to their political directions, to provide prompt, accurate, candid, clear and constructive advice on policy, and to manage the administration of policy and the Department itself under overall Ministerial guidance.

A case can, of course, be made for radical changes in the positions of both Ministers and civil servants – and indeed the Major Government's reforms of the civil service are having a significant impact upon the traditional assumptions of central Government in Britain. However, the administrative continuity and the political impartiality which still characterise the British civil service provide a healthy antidote to the Ministerial system of party government which can involve at different times both partisan dogma and political indecision.

In modern political conditions it is, of course, possible for Ministers to exercise clear leadership, but this has usually become less likely as each General Election has receded further into the past. In this respect Margaret Thatcher and her senior Ministerial colleagues were distinctly unusual and might be regarded as one of the exceptions which prove the rule. Senior Ministers may believe that they are in complete charge of their Departments. Yet civil service control of official advice to Ministers, the long time-scale and great complexity of decision making in Government, and the limited scope for truly autonomous political action – especially if attempted purely at national level – all tend to reduce the impact and effect of Ministerial leadership. The broad conclusion must be that Ministers may be in charge of their Departments and of the Government as a whole, but only within the limits set by established administrative procedures and the uncompromising political and economic realities in Britain and abroad.

Suggested questions

1 Describe the structure and work of British central Government.
2 "The tradition that Ministers take the political decisions and civil servants carry them out has long been overtaken by reality." What factors give rise to such a view and how valid are they?
3 What are the problems of British central Government? Are they capable of solution within existing institutions and conventions?

Notes

1. See R*eport of the Committee on the Machinery of Government,* Cd 9230 (London: HMSO, 1918).
2. See *Report on the Reorganisation of Central Government,* Cmnd 4506 (London: HMSO, 1970).
3. The *Lord President of the Council* is formally responsible for the Privy Council Office and he takes charge at the infrequent formal meetings of the Privy Council, while the only remaining formal task of the *Lord Privy Seal* is to arrange Royal Proclamations. The formal responsibility of the *Chancellor of the Duchy of Lancaster* is for the general administration of the Duchy of Lancaster estates and revenues, but the real work is done by the professional staff concerned.
4. W. I. Jennings, *Cabinet Government,* 3rd edn (London Cambridge University Press, 1959), p. 133.
5. Cited in P. Kellner and Lord Crowther-Hunt, *The Civil Servants* (London: Macdonald, 1980), pp. 215-216.
6. The conventional wisdom on this matter has been significantly eroded in modern times by the fact that all recent Governments have, to some extent, abandoned the pure theory of Ministerial

responsibility. The point was very well made by the late David Watt at the time of the 1986 Westland crisis when he wrote: 'if Ministers allow blame to rest with individual, identifiable civil servants, they must expect two consequences: critics of Government actions will hold officials publicly responsible; and the civil servant will claim, and deserve, the right to defend himself in public, if necessary by shifting blame back on the Ministers' (*The Times*, 7 February 1986).

7. See pages 297-303 in Chapter 14.
8. See J. Prior, *A Balance of Power* (London: Hamish Hamilton, 1986), pp. 232-33, and W. Whitelaw, *The Whitelaw Memoirs* (London: Anrum Press, 1989), pp. 211-13.
9. See M. Thatcher, *The Downing Street Years* (London: Harper Collins, 1993), p. 403.
10. For example, when the Expenditure Select Committee sought to cross-examine Labour Ministers on public financial support for Chrysler UK in the 1970s, the then Prime Minister, James Callaghan, prevented any of his Cabinet colleagues from appearing before the Committee. Equally not all the key official witnesses were permitted by Margaret Thatcher, when Prime Minister, to testify before Select Committees in the wake of the 1986 Westland crisis.
11. In 1989 the House of Commons began belatedly to address this problems when the Select Committee on Procedure considered the matter and issued a cautious report entitled *Scrutiny of European legislation*, H.C. 622, 1988-89, Vols. I and II. See also the Government's response: *Scrutiny of European legislation*, Cmnd 1081 (London: HMSO, 1990).
12. See A.H. Birch, *Representative and Responsible Government* (London: Allen & Unwin, 1964), pp. 141-48; J. Bruce-Gardyne and N. Lawson, *The Power Game* (London: Macmillan, 1976), pp. 10-37; and S. James, *British Cabinet Government*, (London: Routledge, 1992), pp. 5-10.
13. See R. Rose, 'Too Much Reshuffling of the Cabinet Pack?', *IEA Inquiry No. 27* (London: IEA, 1991).
14. As Harold Macmillan laconically observed in 1955 when moving – after only eight months – from the Foreign Office to the Treasury, 'After a few months learning geography I've got to learn arithmetic.' See N. Fisher, *Harold Macmillan* (London: Weidenfeld & Nicolson, 1982), p. 154.
15. Quoted in H. Parris, *Constitutional Bureaucracy* (London: Allen & Unwin, 1969), p. 114.
16. H. Morrison, *Government and Parliament* (London: Oxford University Press, 1959), p. 311.

Further reading

Birch, A. H., *Representative and Responsible Government* (London: Allen & Unwin, 1964).
Bruce-Gardyne, J., *Ministers and Mandarins* (London: Sidgwick & Jackson, 1986).
Drewry, G., and Butcher, T., *The Civil Service Today*, 2nd edn (Oxford: Basil Blackwell, 1991).
Hennessy, P., *Cabinet* (Oxford: Basil Blackwell, 1986).
Hennessy, P., *Whitehall* (London: Secker & Warburg, 1989).
James, S., *British Cabinet Government* (London: Routledge, 1992).
Kaufman, G., *How to be a Minister* (London: Sedgwick & Jackson, 1980).
Kellner, P., and Crowther-Hunt, Lord, *The Civil Servants* (London: Macdonald, 1980).
Nairne, P., *The Civil Service: Ministers and Madarins* (Barnstaple: Philip Charles Media, 1990).
Young, H., and Sloman, A., *No Minister* (London: BBC, 1982).
Young, H., and Sloman, A., *But, Chancellor* (London: BBC, 1984).

⬡14 The Civil Service

In Britain the standard definition of a civil servant is still based upon the one which was formulated by the Tomlin Commission in 1931, namely 'a servant of the Crown employed in a civil capacity who is paid wholly and directly from money voted by Parliament'.[1] In April 1994 this definition covered about 533,000 permanent staff. Of this total about 487,000 were non-industrial civil servants and 46,000 were industrial civil servants employed mainly by the Ministry of Defence. In addition, there were some 21,000 casual staff. Twenty per cent of all civil servants work in London, a further 16 per cent in the rest of South East England and 64 per cent in other parts of the country.

In this chapter we are concerned mainly with the civil servants who work directly for Ministers (popularly known as 'Whitehall' after the street in the centre of London in which a number of Government Departments have their headquarters) and more especially with those in the higher grades (Grades 7 and above) who are closely involved in policy work. We are therefore considering the administrative elite at the heart of British central Government.

14.1 Composition and functions

The 22 Departments in Whitehall vary greatly in size, mission and character. For example, the Treasury with about 1400 civil servants (whose number is currently being reduced still further) is the most powerful and prestigious Department in British central Government and has the endlessly difficult tasks of controlling public spending and advising the Chancellor of the Exchequer on economic policy; whereas the Ministry of Defence with more than 80,000 non-industrial civil servants has the tasks of ensuring civilian control of the nation's military effort and providing civilian support for the armed forces. Indeed, the three largest Departments in terms of personnel (but not necessarily budgets) are Defence, Social Security and the Inland Revenue, which together employ just over half the total number of civil servants. In terms of public expenditure the most significant Departments are Social Security, Health, Education and Employment, and Defence – with the last one now lower down the spending league following the end of the Cold War.

In a typical Department (if we can assume such a thing), perhaps half of the civil servants are involved in the administrative tasks of central Government, while the remainder perform a range of technical, scientific and support tasks. In central Government as a whole around 25,000 civil servants are involved in the policy and decision-making process at the centre of the various Departments, although of these only perhaps 3000 at the most senior levels have close and frequent contacts with Ministers. It is this small elite which has set the conventions of Whitehall and determined much of the character of the civil service in Britain.

The personnel

In the higher administrative grades of the British civil service the traditional dominance of experienced 'generalists' still holds sway – that is, civil servants recruited largely in their twenties on the basis of their personal qualities and general academic attainments rather than any specialist skills (for example, as scientists, economists, or lawyers). This influences both the character and the quality of the service at every level and there are three principal reasons for it.

Firstly, the civil service has not completely escaped from the long-lasting influence of the 1854 Northcote-Trevelyan Report which defined the role of civil servants as being 'to advise, assist, and to some extent influence those who are set over them from time to time' (that is, Ministers).[2] The legacy of this seminal view of the civil service is that in the higher administrative grades at any rate no particular value has been placed upon the possession of specialist skills, except the skills of public administration and of working effectively with Ministers, which are considered to be best acquired mainly by experience in the job.

Secondly, there has traditionally been a disdain for technical expertise which was well expressed by Lord Bridges (Secretary to the Cabinet between 1938 and 1947) when he defined a good civil servant as someone 'who knows how and where to find reliable knowledge, can assess the expertise of others at its true worth, can spot the strong and weak points in any situation at short notice, and can advise on how to handle a complex situation'.[3] As the saying goes, the experts are supposed to be on tap but not on top. However, specialists now have considerable influence in a number of Departments and many generalist policy makers spend much of their career in a single Department, thus developing substantial expertise in its work.

Thirdly, there has been a traditional tendency for the young recruits into the administrative grades to come disproportionately from middle-class family backgrounds and to have arts degrees from Oxford or Cambridge. Certainly this was true when the composition of the civil service was analysed for the Fulton Committee in 1967.[4] It appeared still to be true in the 1970s and 1980s when similar analyses were done.[5] However, in more recent times the Civil Service Commission has been making great efforts to recruit into the administrative grades people from universities other than Oxford and Cambridge, more women, and more people from ethnic minorities.[6] Nevertheless it is still true that those who qualify for the career path which leads to the most influential positions in the civil service are very much the product of the values and outlook of their predecessors who have such influence over their selection. On this basis the service still attracts some of the best and brightest in every generation. Yet as long as there is such continuity of recruitment, the character of the top civil service is likely to change only slowly. See Figure 14.1 for a table of civil service and staffing levels.

Figure 14.1 Civil Service staffing levels

a Civil Service staff in post at 1 October 1994 by full/part-time etc

| | Permanent staff | | | Casual staff | | |
| | | of which, | | | of which, | |
	Total	Agencies	All on Next Steps lines	**Total**	Agencies	All on Next Steps lines
Head count						
Non-industrial full-time	454,215	222,017	296,757	–	–	–
Non-industiral part-time	51,026	29,460	39,662	–	–	–
Non-industrial total	505,241	251,477	336,419	–	–	–
Industrial full-time	43,466	14,963	14,963	–	–	–
Industrial part-time	1,575	352	352	–	–	–
Industrial total	45,041	15,315	15,315	–	–	–
All full-time	497,681	236,980	311,720	–	–	–
All part-time	52,601	29,812	40,014	–	–	–
Full-time equivalent						
Non-industrial	479,728	236,747	316,588	17,402	11,258	12,464
Industrial	44,254	15,139	15,139	1,739	578	578
Total	**523,982**	**251,886**	**331,727**	**19,140**	**11,836**	**13,042**

b Civil Service permanent staff in post at 1 October 1994 by sex

	Men	Women	Total
Head count			
Non-industrial full-time	248,628	213,598	462,226
Non-industrial part-time	2,374	48,044	50,418
Non-industrial total	251,002	261,642	512,644
Industrial full-time	38,850	6,223	45,073
Industriial part-time	176	1,508	1,684
Industrial total	39,026	7,731	46,757
All full-time	287,478	219,821	507,299
All part-time	2,550	49,552	52,102
Total	**290,028**	**269,373**	**559,401**
Full-time equivalent			
Non-industrial	249,815	237,620	487,435
Industrial	38,938	6,977	45,915
Total	**288,753**	**244,597**	**533,350**

Sources: Civil Service Statistics 1994 Table 4 and Quarterly Staff in Post Return 1 October 1994

Main functions

The main functions of the higher administrative grades of the civil service can be summarised as follows: informing and advising Ministers; helping them to formulate policy
and, if it involves legislation, to get it through Parliament; carrying out the ensuing administrative tasks; representing Ministers in meetings with and dealing with Ministers'

correspondence from, other Departments, interest groups and members of the public; and managing the bureaucratic machine of central Government. We shall now look briefly at each of these functions in turn.

Civil servants are the main source of information and advice for Ministers. When Ministers need to know something or have to prepare for a meeting, make a speech, answer questions in Parliament or on the media, it is the civil servants in their own Departments (and sometimes in other Departments as well) who provide the necessary information and advice. Usually this is provided in writing in the form of background briefs or other internal memoranda. It is often supplemented (or even replaced) by oral information and advice given at internal Departmental meetings, since this can be quicker in an emergency and some Ministers prefer to be briefed in this way. On the whole civil servants do not produce original work for these purposes, since they have neither the time nor the aptitude for the research upon which such work would have to be based. They therefore act essentially as filters and interpreters of existing information and advice which they derive mainly from Departmental sources and accessible outside experts whose discretion can be trusted.

Civil servants help Ministers to formulate policy and to make decisions by presenting them with option papers which usually encompass a range of possibilities and policy recommendations. They also provide most of the information and advice against which Ministers can test the soundness or otherwise of their own ideas and their party political commitments. The complex role of civil servants in the policy and decision making process is described more fully in Chapter 19.

Civil servants carry out the administrative tasks of central Government in accordance with the political guidelines laid down in Ministerial decisions. If this is not possible in certain cases when new situations arise, reference is usually made to the appropriate Minister or Ministers for further policy instructions. Although the administration of policy can be as important as the actual decisions made by Ministers, civil servants (and now the staff of Executive Agencies as well) are supposed to avoid action or inaction which embarrasses Ministers or prejudices Ministerial decisions. On the whole they seek faithfully to carry out the policies and decisions which they have helped Ministers to produce.

Civil servants have an important role as representatives of Ministers at meetings in Whitehall and elsewhere. These may be meetings with officials from other Departments, with the spokesmen of various pressure groups or with members of the general public. On occasions civil servants may speak on behalf of Ministers within the carefully defined limits of established policy – for example, when giving evidence to a Select Committee or taking part in an inter-Departmental committee – and they write numerous letters, memoranda and circulars on behalf of the Ministers for whom they work. On some occasions civil servants may state their Department's position in somewhat speculative terms if they are involved in exercises of 'kite-flying' or devil's advocacy in order to test some aspect of the conventional wisdom or the likely media response to a particular policy idea. Normally there is a clear distinction between the latitude allowed to them in the privacy of internal Whitehall meetings with Ministers and other civil servants, and the orthodox and cautious way in which they are supposed to reflect Government policy in meetings or written communications with outsiders.

Finally, there is the very important function of senior civil servants, namely that of seeing that the machinery of central Government is managed in an efficient and cost-effective way. This has long been one of the principal functions of those in the top two grades of the civil service (at Permanent Secretary and Deputy Secretary levels), but it has assumed greater prominence during the years of Conservative Government since 1979 because Ministers have attached greater importance to it. Indeed, the spread of Executive Agencies since 1988 (see pp. 300–1 for more details) has been one of the most significant manifestations of the drive for greater efficiency and cost-effectiveness in the delivery of public services. By the autumn of 1994 there were about 100 such bodies charged with the delivery of services to the public and already they had proved to be a more businesslike, if sometimes controversial, way of meeting the objectives of Government policy.

Ever since the implementation of the Northcote-Trevelyan reforms in the second half of the nineteenth century, the Permanent Secretary of each Department has had to take personal responsibility as the senior official for the management of the Department and to act as its Accounting Officer. Each Accounting Officer is responsible for the complete activity and expenditure of the Department concerned within financial limits agreed each year by the Cabinet and central guidance provided by the Treasury and the Office of Public Service and Science on financial management and personnel matters. Indeed, the efficient management of the civil service was regarded by the Thatcher Administration as being of such importance that at one time all senior Ministers were urged by the Prime Minister (often without much success, it must be said) to play a direct and continuous part in the management of their Departments alongside their Permanent Secretaries. On the whole this rather revolutionary idea did not appeal to busy Ministers preoccupied with their political responsibilities or to the most senior officials who felt that it was an invasion of their territory. It was, therefore, not very surprising that by 1990 the emphasis of Government policy was switched towards implementing the Agency principle which has devolved both management and public accountability to a much greater extent than before onto the shoulders of Permanent Secretaries and Agency Chief Executives.

To summarise: the civil service in Britain today has at least five distinct but interconnected functions to perform. These are the analysis of policy issues, the formulation of policy under Ministerial direction, the implementation of decisions once taken by Ministers, the delivery of services to the general public, and the management of public resources.[7] Whereas traditionally the higher administrative grades were involved almost exclusively in the first three functions, they have been drawn more deeply into the last two by successive Conservative Administrations since 1979.

14.2 Key issues

There are several key issues in the continuing debate about the civil service in Britain today. In this section we shall concentrate upon those which have had a significant effect upon the development of the British political system. Accordingly, we shall begin by considering some of the most influential Whitehall conventions and ways of working, and then go on to review the strengths and weaknesses of the service, including the issues raised by the nature and limits of civil servants' loyalty to Ministers. In nearly all cases we shall discover that it is not sensible to generalise about the role of civil servants, since they perform very different functions in relation to Ministers and the general public respectively.

Whitehall conventions

The civil service in Britain works within established conventions which have shaped its practices for many years. Foremost among these are: support of Ministers both individually and collectively; accountability through Ministers to Parliament; integrity and objectivity in advice and service delivery; political impartiality at all times; equitable treatment of citizens under the law; and selection and promotion on merit without political patronage or interference.[8]

Higher grade civil servants tend to see their main role and duty as the support of Ministers in those areas of Departmental business to which Ministers attach importance. This means that in the past they have tended to give a higher priority to servicing the needs of their Ministers on matters of policy and assisting them in their dealings with Parliament, the media and the public than to meeting the managerial requirements of running their Departments.[9] The tasks of bureaucratic management and control have tended to be seen as rather tedious and unattractive chores by the most of the talented officials who have reached the top of the civil service over the years. Both the Thatcher and the Major Administrations set out to change this rather grand attitude with the result that senior civil servants have been obliged to adopt more of the so-called 'new managerialism' both within their Departments and in dealings with the general public under the rubric of the Citizen's Charter originally set out by John Major in July 1991.[10] However, notwithstanding the significance of these developments, policy advice for Ministers still has to come first when it is really needed, especially if Ministers are faced with urgent demands from Parliament or the media.

Another well established convention is that civil servants should take their instructions only from their superiors in their own Departments or sometimes directly from Ministers, but not from anyone else. This means that the lines of authority and reporting are strictly vertical and that to get anything new done in a Department of central Government it is usually necessary for Ministers, either directly or through officials, to give the initial policy instructions, or at least to indicate to civil servants that a possible alternative policy can be examined. This tends to put considerable burdens upon the Ministers themselves and upon the officials working most closely with them in their Private Offices. It means that if the Minister concerned is not an innovator or is very cautious, quite senior officials elsewhere in the Department may be quite lightly employed for considerable periods. It also underlines the fact that without a clear and decisive lead from Ministers, Departments are not usually very good at shaping a new agenda or responding to events speedily or with imagination.

Another well established convention is that the administration of policy should be carried out according to the highest standards of probity and equity, while at the same time avoiding any form of political embarrassment for Ministers. This last consideration has often put a premium upon a rather defensive and cautious approach to policy and decision making with particular emphasis being laid upon avoiding risk and trying to see that neither Parliament nor the media get too many opportunities to identify shortcomings or failures in Government policy which could turn the public against the party in office.

Another fundamental convention in Whitehall, which might better be defined as an aspiration, is that the Government of the day should at all times have a coherent and defensible position on every policy issue with which it has to deal. This is regarded as a minimum requirement for satisfactory Cabinet government, which has to be based upon the principle of collective responsibility. It means that a great deal of civil service time and effort is spent upon producing agreed positions with which all Departments can concur, even if such positions may represent little more than a lowest common denominator within Whitehall. Notwithstanding the sometimes Herculean efforts of the most influential civil servants to formulate agreed policy positions to which all Ministers can adhere, there are times when the pressure of events becomes too great for coherence and unity to be maintained – as has been evident, for example, in some aspects of Conservative European policy in the 1990s.

Another insight into the problems which can arise when Departments struggle to agree policy between them and seek to keep these problems from the public gaze was provided by the controversy over arms-related exports to Iraq. Media revelations of the Matrix-Churchill affair in 1992 led the Prime Minister, John Major, to establish a public inquiry under Lord Justice Scott. Right from the beginning, the evidence given to the inquiry highlighted the way in which the highest standards in public life can be compromised when Ministers and senior civil servants assume that their definition of 'the public interest' should override all other considerations, including in this case the legal right of certain British businessmen involved in international trade with Iraq to conduct a full and effective defence against the arms-trading offences with which they were charged.

Essentially, all these Whitehall conventions flow from traditional adherence to the twin principles of Ministerial responsibility and Parliamentary accountability. The former has always meant that senior civil servants regard the support of Ministers as their principal and overriding duty. The latter means that civil servants can be cautious, even unimaginative, in the way they perform their tasks. In both cases these conventions derive from assumptions long held by politicians and officials alike, and from the political imperatives of Parliamentary government.

Strengths and weaknesses

The British civil service has both strengths and weaknesses which stem mainly from the nature of British Parliamentary government and the people involved in it. In many cases the weaknesses are merely the counterparts of the strengths which have been widely recognised for many years. Since the position can be regarded from at least two contrasting angles, it is unwise to be dogmatic when making an assessment. In any case, the situation has been changing quite fast and significantly under the Thatcher and Major Administrations, so judgements should be tentative and provisional rather than dogmatic and definitive.

One obvious strength is the intellectual and administrative ability of those in the higher grades of the civil service. This reflects the high entry and selection standards for this group, and the continuing attractions of the administrative grades for many of the ablest students from the universities. It also reflects the fact that the elite group of 'fast stream' graduate entrants (now known as Trainees in Policy Management) have quickly benefit from accelerated promotion to positions of responsibility in the service, although 58 per cent of the Senior Open Structure in October 1993 (Grade 3 and above) had *not* entered the service through the administrative fast stream. In general, the result of this recruitment policy has been the formation and continuing renewal of a small cadre of clever and competent people who become skilled practitioners in the art of public administration and whose main strengths are the ability to advise Ministers on policy and to carry out Ministerial decisions effectively.

On the other hand, it has been argued that this elite group has smooth and generalist qualities which are not necessarily the most appropriate for tackling the challenges of Government in the modern world. Unfavourable contrasts have been drawn with their opposite numbers in the higher grades of the French civil service, for example, who are seen by some to have the dual advantage of intellectual distinction and a more specialised technical training in the arts of public administration before they enter the public service.[11] Other criticisms have been levelled at Britain's bureaucratic elite by those on the Left of British politics who have complained about the socially and educationally unrepresentative composition of the group and have argued that the situation will not be satisfactory until such cadres are recruited from a much wider background.[12] However, the situation is changing and recent figures show a steady move towards a less exclusive profile among those who enter the administrative grades.[13]

Another strength of the British civil service has been the tradition of political impartiality and the ability to work satisfactorily for Ministers of very different political persuasions. Although individual civil servants retain their own private political views, in their professional lives they have to carry out the policies of the Government of the day without complaint or obstruction (as long as Ministers act lawfully). Resignations from the civil service on policy or political grounds are therefore very rare, although a number of civil servants do leave the public service every year for the different challenges and often higher financial rewards of the private sector – for example, the Inland Revenue Inspectors who leave to join private accountancy firms.

On the other hand, there have been critics of the British civil service who have interpreted this acknowledged political impartiality as tantamount to patient and practised obstruction of the more radical purposes of democratically elected Governments. Complaints of this kind have been expressed on both the Left and the Right of British politics. On the Left, Tony Benn and others have made the point in speeches, articles and memoirs reflecting upon the experience of the 1974-79 Labour Government.[14] On the Right, Sir John Hoskyns (a businessman who was for a time head of the Policy Unit under Margaret Thatcher) criticised civil servants for withholding the last five per cent of commitment to the policies of any Government in order to preserve their credentials for serving a future Government of a different political persuasion.[15] It would seem from such matching complaints that the civil service is at least even-handed in its instinct for political impartiality and against excessive enthusiasm. Yet we should also note that by the mid-1990s after more than 16 years of continuous Conservative Government, very different concerns have been expressed to the effect that some civil servants might have allowed their impartiality to be compromised by becoming too accustomed to doing the bidding of one political party.[16]

As for the almost complete absence of corruption in the British civil service (at any rate in the financial sense), this must obviously be regarded as a virtue by any measurement. With very few exceptions British civil servants have demonstrated over the years that they are people of the highest personal integrity who do not succumb to the temptations of bribery and corruption which damage the reputation of Governments in many other countries. It is local government in Britain which has been more vulnerable to such venality, mainly because it offers more opportunities for officials to do favours in return for personal financial gain.

Obviously no one would claim that the almost total absence of corruption in the British civil service is anything other than a great strength of the system. However, during the 1990s doubts have been raised about whether more insidious forms of political corruption might have afflicted at least some senior civil servants and heads of Executive Agencies because of the unusually long period of government by one political party. Critics on the Opposition benches in Parliament, as well as in academia and the media, have been disturbed by what they have seen as inappropriately zealous commitment to some of the more controversial Conservative policies, such as market testing or occasional privatisation of public services traditionally delivered only by public servants. Evidently such people would have been happier if civil servants had withheld at least the last few ounces of commitment to the policies of a Government which such critics have strongly opposed – although we can only speculate whether they would retain this view if their own party were in power.

Loyalty issues

The British civil service has long been admired for its sense of dedication and commitment to public duty. This is based upon the traditional civil service ethic which holds that civil servants must be scrupulously correct in their dealings with Parliament and public alike. It reflects what has sometimes been described as the 'mandarin culture' of Whitehall which has been transmitted from the centre and the top to all parts and layers of the service with varying degrees of success. In its most theoretical form it is based upon the belief that there is something which can be called 'the public interest' which is supposed to be defined by Ministers in the Government of the day, but which occasionally has to be defined and defended by senior civil servants (notably the Cabinet Secretary) when it seems to come under unreasonable political threat or when there is a tricky constitutional point on which it may be impossible for Ministers to take an objective view. In this respect very senior civil servants can find themselves obliged to perform delicate acts of constitutional arbitration – such as ruling on questions of proper conduct and procedure for Ministers – in a way which could be considered analogous to the duty of the Monarch and her advisers to define and defend the public interest against the possibility of reckless action by Ministers – for example, if the Prime Minister of the day were ever unreasonably to ask for a premature dissolution of Parliament at a time when there was no constitutional justification for it (see Chapter 9, pp.176–8).

There are at least two views of this aspect of the civil service ethos in Britain. One view is held by those who really do not trust any politicians in office – seemingly an increasingly widespread view in Britain – and who therefore welcome the existence of what might be described as bureaucratic stabilisers in the political system. In the eyes of such people, who include notably the managers of large companies and other modern technocrats, it is always preferable to have a high degree of continuity and predictability in Government policy and regulatory arrangements laid down by law. In so far as British politics is thought by such people and their sympathisers to have suffered from a surfeit of political ideology and polarisation in the 1970s and 1980s, they have often looked to the civil service to provide the stability and moderation which was thought to have been missing. It is the argument for what might be described as the gyroscopic role of the civil service – that is, its presumed ability to draw most policy and nearly all Governments back to the middle ground of British politics before too much damage can be done by radical extremists.[17]

Another view, which is held with equal vehemence by so-called 'conviction politicians' of the Left and the Right, is that the British political system must be based upon the principle of 'winner takes all' and that this means that whatever the shortcomings and foolishness of Ministers, they have an absolute democratic right to define the public interest at any time. Consequently, according to this view, it is the duty of civil servants simply to carry out their Ministers' wishes in the most effective way unless and until the latter are dismissed by the Prime Minister or the whole crew is sent packing by the voters at a General Election.

For most of the time this controversy does not arise in acute form, since civil servants are usually very adept at steering an appropriate middle course between these two points of view. However, there have been some notable occasions when civil service power within powerful Whitehall Departments has been very much in evidence. Possibly the most vivid and recurrent examples have been associated with the power and influence of the Home Office bureaucratic Establishment. In the 1950s at least two Conservative Home Secretaries were persuaded by their civil servants of the need to retain capital punishment for murder, notwithstanding the publicly declared abolitionist views of the Ministers concerned when they first took charge of the Department. Equally, in the late 1980s and early 1990s Home Office Ministers were persuaded by their civil servants of the case against custodial sentences for young offenders, notwithstanding the perennial commitment of nearly all Conservatives to greater emphasis upon retributive forms of justice. These two examples are made all the more telling by the fact that during the intervening period the 'penal policy Establishment' completely changed its bias from a retributive to a permissive position, and yet was able apparently to get its way on each occasion.

The idea of civil servants seeking to set their own definitions of the public interest above that of Ministers was best illustrated perhaps by the case of Clive Ponting, a senior civil servant in the Ministry of Defence, who in 1984 deliberately passed two classified documents concerning the sinking of the Argentinian cruiser *Belgrano* during the Falklands conflict to Tam Dalyell, a Labour back-bencher who had been hounding Ministers on the issue since 1982.[18] When this was discovered after a rigorous internal investigation in Whitehall, Clive Ponting was charged with a criminal offence under Section 2(1) of the 1911 Official Secrets Act and taken to Court where he pleaded not guilty. The principal grounds of his defence were that it had been his duty 'in the interests of the state' to inform Parliament (in the person of Tam Dalyell), since Ministers had misled the House of Commons and the Select Committee investigating the matter was in danger of being misled as well. Although the trial judge said in his guidance to the jury that 'the interests of the state' were synonymous with the policies of the Government of the day, the jury evidently thought otherwise, as it found Clive Ponting not guilty.

For our purposes two main issues were highlighted by this interesting case. Firstly, it had to be established whether civil servants have a legal right to communicate classified information against the wishes of Ministers on the grounds that they have a higher duty to see that Parliament and the public are not misled. Secondly, there was the question of whether civil servants have a professional duty to their own conceptions of 'the public interest' and if so, whether this can ever be regarded as superior to their duty to serve Ministers. In his summing up in the Ponting case, the judge argued against both these propositions, but the jury – and much of the media and public opinion – were more inclined to sympathise with the defendant's point of view. The outcome was a technical victory for Clive Ponting and a moral victory for all those who believe that the Government of the day has no monopoly right to define the public interest. Yet Ministers and the Government's supporters in the country were entitled to argue in reply that if a civil servant really feels unable on grounds of principle or conscience to accept a Ministerial decision, then the correct course of action is for the civil servant to resign rather than break the terms and conditions of employment.

The public interest

It has always been difficult to define 'the public interest' in an objective and enduring way. As has already been pointed out, the traditional view in Britain is that it is for Ministers, who are accountable to Parliament, to define. It is rare for civil servants, such as Clive Ponting, who have been in direct and frequent contact with Ministers, to press their objections to the extent of knowingly breaking the law, because they recognise that their prime and overriding duty is to Ministers, provided the latter do not actually break the law.

In modern political conditions more frequent dilemmas arise in those cases in which the arguments for confidentiality and transparency clash. This was illustrated most vividly during the course of the Scott Inquiry into the so-called Matrix-Churchill affair.[19] In this case a few Ministers and civil servants were involved in secret efforts to circumvent the Government's own ban on arms sales to Iraq. This involved providing information both to Parliament and to the public which was misleading and the use of so-called Public Interest Immunity Certificates, the effect of which was to prevent certain British businessmen accused of breaking the law from using vital documents in their own defence when the case came to Court. In other words, it was alleged that Ministers and civil servants, after guidance from the Attorney-General, were ultimately prepared to see innocent British citizens convicted and sent to jail simply to safeguard what they had defined as 'the public interest' – which in this case involved *not* telling the media and the public the truth about the Matrix-Churchill affair.

Other current concerns

There are several other current concerns about the British civil service which need to be mentioned at this stage. *Firstly*, it is often alleged that civil servants are disinclined to approach the problems of Government in the round and in a sufficiently long-term perspective. According to this view, there is too much focus in Whitehall upon immediate political issues within the sphere of each Department. In so far as this can be true, it stems from a natural bureaucratic instinct to play safe and working habits in Whitehall which have long attached importance to the orderly division of labour between the various Departments. Furthermore, in a system of government which is so heavily influenced by the political requirements of Ministers, it is naive to expect civil servants to pursue a broader or more long term strategy than that of the Ministers whom they serve. Indeed, bearing in mind the sensitive issues discussed in the previous section, it would not be well received by Ministers if civil servants deliberately set out to do this.

Secondly, there is the familiar refrain in some political quarters that civil servants seem unwilling or unable fully to embrace radical policies (when set out by Ministers) or even radical departures from existing policy. It is argued that civil servants demonstrate this tendency by filtering or diluting many of the new and challenging ideas which do not fit the conventional wisdom in Whitehall. Yet nearly everything depends upon the derivation of radical new ideas. If these come from the Prime Minister and other senior Ministers, there is a very good chance that they will be accepted and implemented, albeit sometimes with private misgivings. On the other hand, if new ideas come from other less impeccable sources (such as back-benchers or unfashionable intellectuals), civil servants are rather unlikely to take them on board and will tend to regard them as political heresy until given the green light by senior Ministers.

Thirdly, in the mid-1990s perhaps the most notable element of informed concern about the civil service stemmed from the fact that one party (the Conservatives) had been in office for more than 16 years and had allegedly changed or destroyed the traditional ethos of public service in Britain. Such concerns have been based upon trade union dislike of market-testing (that is, putting civil service activities out to tender to see if the private sector can perform them more cost-effectively) and, in some cases, outright privatisation of certain traditional state functions – such as low security prisons. Initially, this concern also included misgivings about the spread of Executive Agencies, but gradually, these are coming to be accepted as a valid and cost-effective way of delivering services directly to the public – for example, social security benefits or advice and help for job-seekers.

Finally, the critics of the recent Conservative policy of civil service reform have expressed a general anxiety about the growth of 'the unelected state' and the infiltration of the civil service with undesirable standards and practices more usually associated with activity in the private sector.[20] Certainly the traditional homogeneity of the public service has been reduced by the creation of a large number of 'extra-governmental organisations' which are beholden to Ministers and within the orbit of central Government, but no longer an integral part of it or influenced to the same extent as Whitehall Departments by the traditional civil service codes of behaviour. Such developments have been criticised by the House of Commons Public Accounts Committee when it drew attention to certain tendencies for some Health Authorities and Development Agencies to cut corners in relation to the usual civil service standards of probity and financial accountability.[21] They have also been fiercely attacked by Opposition politicians who resent the fact that the power and financial responsibilities of local authorities have been steadily eroded by Conservative legislation since 1979, leading to what they see as usurpation by the 'unelected state'.

According to the Conservative point of view, however, much of this criticism has come predictably from Opposition politicians who do not like Government policy and public sector trade unions which see their members' job security threatened by Conservative reforms. Under various charters since the Citizen's Charter of 1991, Conservatives have argued that traditional notions of public accountability need to be changed and up-dated, so that accountability to the *users* of public services is set alongside the traditional forms of accountability to Members of Parliament and local Councillors, who are the democratically elected guardians of the public interest. Until quite recently, the sphere of central Government was one of the few areas of institutional activity which had not felt the full effects of Conservative determination to diminish the role of the state. Now that civil servants are among those who are being affected by the process of reform, it is not surprising that they and their allies have become more concerned and less complacent.

14.3 Methods of control

Over the years in Britain politicians in office have developed a number of different methods for controlling the civil service and seeing that it does what elected Ministers want it to do. Each of the methods has been used to a certain extent, but none has proved sufficient. It has therefore proved necessary to use all of them in combination in a continuing effort to achieve real and lasting political control.

Ministerial responsibility

The classic method of controlling the civil service in Britain is based upon the traditional doctrine of Ministerial responsibility. This may have been effective during the second half of the nineteenth century when the scope and complexity of central Government was very much smaller than it is today. In modern conditions, however, its efficacity is much more dubious, as recent experience has shown and a number of well placed witnesses have pointed out.[22]

In theory, Ministerial responsibility is supposed to mean that Ministers are held to account and take responsibility for everything which happens or fails to happen within the allotted spheres of their Departmental responsibility. It is also supposed to mean that Ministers will offer their resignation or be sacked when things go seriously wrong in areas of policy and administration over which they are supposed to be in charge.

In practice, modern central Government and its agencies have become so large and complex that Ministers, however dutiful and energetic, cannot possibly be aware of, let alone determine, everything which happens or fails to happen within their allotted spheres of 'responsibility'. Consequently, the best that sensible Ministers can do is to insist that their civil servants draw to their attention in a timely way (that is, at a stage when Ministerial intervention could make a difference) all the important or politically sensitive issues which arise within their allotted spheres of responsibility. This means that civil servants who work closely with Ministers should be able to distinguish between sensitive political issues and run-of-the-mill administration. If such assumptions cannot safely be made (as seems to have been the case with Ministerial 'responsibility' for the prison service), then the whole idea of Ministerial responsibility is revealed to be fatally flawed and out of date.

One attempt to make more of a reality of the doctrine, at any rate in relation to the costs of central Government, was launched by Margaret Thatcher in the early 1980s under the heading of a new Management Information System for Ministers (MINIS). This was supposed to make it possible throughout Whitehall for senior Ministers to know the costs and benefits of every aspect of their Departments' activities, so that waste and duplication could be rooted out and efficiency and effectiveness could be enhanced.[23] In the event this systematic approach did not appeal to all senior Ministers, many of whom did not believe that such managerial activity constituted the best use of their own limited time and energy. Furthermore, it still did not address the fundamental problem that there are only 24 hours in a day and most senior Ministers have neither the time nor the inclination nor, realistically, the possibility of supervising everything which happens or fails to happen within their Departmental spheres – especially now that there are more than 100 Executive Agencies in which the chief executives are supposed to take 'operational responsibility'. The net result of all this is that senior Ministers rarely resign on grounds of policy failure and virtually never on grounds of defective public administration.

Bureaucratic hierarchy

Partly because of the shortcomings of Ministerial responsibility, bureaucratic hierarchy has become the orthodox method of trying to control the machinery of central Government in Britain. Once again in origin it dates from the nineteenth century and the reforms of Whitehall which flowed from the 1854 Northcote-Trevelyan Report. It has always presupposed a simple and clear division between the responsibility of Ministers for policy and the responsibility of senior civil servants for the public administration which carries out the policy.

In theory, such a simple division of labour appears to be well established in Whitehall. After all, as mentioned earlier, every Permanent Secretary and every head of an Executive Agency is responsible for the money spent by the Department or Agency as the case may be. Procedurally, the executive heads of the Agencies report to the Permanent Secretaries of their parent Departments and thence to the Public Accounts Committee of the House of Commons for the public money which they spend. Yet in an era of greater functional accountability at lower levels of the civil service than before, this procedure will need to be modified to take account of the new 'managerial ethos' at nearly every level of the bureaucracy.

In practice, the very senior civil servants at the top of the various Departments (and increasingly some of the Agency chief executives) can be so preoccupied with their role as leading policy advisers to senior Ministers that they have little time to spend on the rather detailed tasks of managing their Departments (or Agencies). Thus much of the load of day-to-day management has to be delegated to more junior officials in the hierarchy. In fact, far from being a problem, this natural response to the realities of the situation may be part of a more effective solution in that it obliges more civil servants at many levels to take charge of (and responsibility for) their own activities. Notwithstanding this necessary devolution and delegation of responsibility down the bureaucratic hierarchies of central Government, Permanent Secretaries have striven to respond positively to the present Government's 'managerial' initiatives, and effective staff leadership and management are now seen as key parts of their jobs.

Administrative efficiency

Another method of controlling the civil service is based upon the principle of administrative efficiency. This assumes that it is possible to apply to the civil service some of the business and management techniques used in the private sector. As long ago as 1968 this idea was one of the main thrusts of the Fulton Report and it has been promoted intermittently by Governments in Britain ever since. For example, this approach attaches special importance to the achievement of a given level of output with less financial and other inputs, to the comparison of different methods to achieve a given objective, and to the use of cost-benefit analysis in the process of decision making.

It is fair to say that such techniques imported from the private sector have not always proved to be easily transferable to the public service where the goals, constraints and criteria of success or failure have tended to be rather different. In the private sector, the main goal is usually profit, the constraints are largely imposed by the market, and the criteria of success or failure include assessments made by investors and the rate of return on capital. In the public service, on the other hand, the goals tend to be more open-ended and changeable, the constraints include considerations of equity and 'the public interest' – not to mention the problems of Parliamentary and public accountability – and the criteria of success or failure depend very much upon the changing priorities and prejudices of senior Ministers.

In spite of the inherent problems of applying this approach to public administration in the civil service, the Thatcher Government demonstrated that it was possible to make progress in this direction. The so-called 'Rayner scrutinies' (named after Lord Rayner who was a managing director of Marks & Spencer before becoming Margaret Thatcher's first adviser on the efficiency of Government) identified potential financial savings in some of the routine support services in Whitehall – for example, typing pools, messenger services and Ministerial transport. Subsequently his scrutiny of Government research and development establishments revealed potential financial savings of at least 15 per cent, while a review of the non-office activities of central Government – such as H.M. Coastguards or the Property Services Agency – indicated further areas of possible savings.[24]

On the other hand, not all the Rayner scrutinies were a success, especially when the proposals seemed politically unacceptable to Government back-benchers. For example, in 1981 it was suggested in one such scrutiny that certain payments made to pensioners through Sub-Post Offices should be made every other week rather than weekly or, in some cases, no longer made at all. This was anathema to millions of elderly people living on fixed incomes who raised such a storm of protest with MPs that Ministers soon decided to drop the idea. Notwithstanding such early setbacks, the general idea of seeking the maximum administrative efficiency within the public service has now become commonplace in Britain and would probably be accepted by any Government.

Judicial scrutiny

A final method of controlling the civil service in Britain is that of judicial scrutiny by the Courts and quasi-judicial bodies, such as Administrative Tribunals. The attraction of this method is that it can provide a framework of standards for good administrative practice without usually becoming too legalistic.[25] Yet so far it is doubtful whether the system of administrative law in Britain is sufficiently well developed really to achieve its purposes in this respect. This is because the Courts have remained fairly cautious in the face of the continuing doctrine of Ministerial responsibility, and have tended to confine their interventions to cases based upon the *ultra vires* doctrine when Government Departments or local authorities are alleged to have gone beyond the proper limits of their competence.[26] Although this principle of judicial review is applied only sparingly to the work of central Government, its very existence normally has a considerable impact upon Departmental legal advisers and hence indirectly upon Ministers and civil servants.

However, in the more legalistic atmosphere engendered by the incursion of European law into more and more areas of British national life, the Courts in Britain may become bolder in their political interventions if they choose to follow the European example.[27] In any case litigants in Britain now appeal more often to the European Court of Justice in Luxembourg on issues within the legal competence of the European Union and to the European Court of Human Rights in Strasbourg. Consequently it seems clear that the civil service in Britain (and of course in all the other member states) is likely to be more rather than less affected by the processes of judicial review in future.

Before concluding this section, mention should also be made of the decision taken by Parliament as long ago as 1967 to establish a *Parliamentary Commissioner for Administration* (popularly known as the Ombudsman) with statutory authority to investigate public complaints of maladministration in central Government Departments and, later, in the National Health Service as well.[28] Although the Ombudsman has so far been limited by the fact that the office has no powers of initiative or legal enforcement and can only respond to complaints referred (usually by MPs), the office has been successful over the years in rectifying faulty procedures in the civil service and occasionally in persuading Whitehall Departments to make *ex gratia* payments by way of compensation to people with clear and justifiable grievances. The powers of publicity and persuasion, backed by the House of Commons Select Committee which monitors its work, have proved to be valuable and significant additions to the range of methods available for imposing some control upon the civil service in Britain.

14.4 Executive Agencies and beyond

There have been a number of further developments in the nature and tasks of the civil service in Britain in recent years, especially in relation to Executive Agencies since 1988, which are clearly of considerable significance. Some have been logical extensions of reforms initiated by the Thatcher Administration. Others have been carried forward more purposefully during John Major's time at 10 Downing Street with potentially far-reaching implications. All are worth considering, because of their likely effects upon the British political system. See Figure 14.2 for a list of all the Executive Agencies in December 1994.

Tighter financial management

The initial thrust of civil service reform under the Conservatives was in favour of tighter financial management and this tendency has been evident throughout the period since 1979. It all began with the so-called Rayner Scrutinies mentioned above. These are estimated to have saved £1,500,000 from 1979 to 1991 and currently to be generating savings of about £100-200 million a year. Lord Rayner originally suggested that each Department should conduct an annual scrutiny of some aspect of its activities. His successor, Sir Peter Levene, placed greater emphasis upon trans-Departmental scrutinies and no longer expected each Department to undertake a scrutiny every year. The result of this shift of emphasis was that the 1993 programme, for example, included 10 scrutinies from 8 Departments, since most of the obvious candidates for scrutiny had already been scrutinised.

The Financial Management Initiative launched in 1982 was the next attempt by the Conservative Government to get better value for money in the civil service. It sought to do this partly by giving Ministers greater personal responsibility for the management of

Figure 14.2 Executive agencies (in December 1994)

Accounts Services Agency
ADAS
Army Base Repair Organisation
Benefits Agency
Building Research Establishment
Buying Agency
CADW Welsh Historic Monuments
Central Office of Information
Central Science Laboratory
Central Statistical Office
Central Veterinary Laboratory
Chemical and Biological Defence Establishment
Chessington Computer Centre
Child Support Agency
Civil Service College
Coastguard
Companies House
Compensation Agency
Contributions Agency
Defence Accounts Agency
Defence Analytical Services Agency
Defence Animal Centre
Defence Clothing and Textiles Agency
Defence Operational Analysis Centre
Defence Postal and Courier Services
Defence Research Agency
Disposal Sales Agency
Driver and Vehicle Licensing Agency
Driver and Vehicle Licensing (Northern Ireland)
Driver and Vehicle Testing Agency
Driving Standards Agency
Duke of York's Royal Military School
Employment Service
Fire Service College
Forensic Science Service
Government Property Lawyers
Highways Agency
Historic Royal Palaces
Historic Scotland
HM Customs and Excise (29 Executive Units)
HM Land Registry
HM Prison Service
HMSO
Hydrographic Office
Information Technology Services Agency
Inland Revenue (29 Executive Units)
Insolvency Service
Intervention Board
Laboratory of the Government Chemist
Logistic Information Systems Agency
Maintenance Group Defence Agency
Marine Safety Agency

Medical Devices Agency
Medicines Control Agency
Meteorological Office
Military Survey
National Physical Laboratory
National Weights and Measures Laboratory
Natural Resources Institute
Naval Aircraft Repair Organisation
NEL
NHS Estates
NHS Pensions Agency
Northern Ireland Child Support Agency
Occupational Health Service
Ordnance Survey
Ordnance Survey of Northern Ireland
Patent Office
Paymaster, Office of HM Paymaster General
Pesticides Safety Directorate
Planning Inspectorate
Public Record Office
Public Trust Office
Queen Elizabeth II Conference Centre
Queen Victoria School
Radio communications Agency
RAF Signals Engineering Establishment
RAF Training Group Defence Agency
Rate Collection Agency
Recruitment and Assessment Services Agency
Registers of Scotland
Resettlement Agency
Royal Mint
Royal Parks
Scottish Agricultural Science Agency
Scottish Fisheries Protection Agency
Scottish Office Pensions Agency
Scottish Prison Service
Scottish Record Office
Security Facilities Executive
Service Children's Schools (North West Europe)
Social Security Agency (Northern Ireland)
Student Awards Agency for Scotland
Teachers' Pensions Agency
Training & Employment Agency
Transport Research Laboratory
UK Passport Agency
Valuation and Lands Agency
Valuation Office
Vehicle Certification Agency
Vehicle Inspectorate
Veterinary Medicines Directorate
War Pensions Agency
Wilton Park Conference Centre

their Departments, but mainly by introducing a more managerial and cost-conscious attitude into the procedures and practices of civil servants in the administrative grades. This has involved increasing the responsibilities of line managers, securing better management information, ensuring that Departments pay the real price of common services, putting greater emphasis upon managerial skills in civil service training, and looking for increased efficiency at all levels of the bureaucracy. For a number of reasons it proved difficult to get this new managerial ethos established and accepted in the civil service, not least because most of the senior civil servants have tended to find policy work more interesting than financial management. In an attempt to counteract this, posts in charge of executive operations have been openly advertised and people with managerial skills brought into the civil service. Following the 1994 Civil Service White Paper, this process of open competition for senior posts is likely to be further extended.

The most recent thrust towards tighter financial management has come from the *Competing for Quality* programme launched in November 1991 as part of the Citizens Charter policy. At the beginning the market-testing and contracting-out which this involved was expected to produce 25 per cent savings which could then be ploughed back into Departmental programmes. It has involved requiring in-house civil service teams to bid for specific tasks against competition from the private sector and in this competitive tendering process civil servants have won the contracts in more than half the cases (measured by the value of the work to be performed). The Government estimated that by December 1993 (about 2 years after the launch of the new approach) total savings of £135 million had been achieved representing an average saving of 22 per cent. However, the 1991 White Paper also made it clear that there would be circumstances in which the Government might make strategic decisions *not* to continue as a direct provider of certain public services and that there should be a general presumption that all *new* public services would be contracted out to the private sector without going through the procedures of competitive tendering at all.[29]

Information subsequently provided by the Government in 1994 made it clear that 113 activities previously valued at £768 million had been contracted out with no opportunity for an in-house civil service bid over the period from November 1991 to the end of December 1993.[30] The rationale given by Ministers for this more radical approach involving the private provision of public services was that so-called 'strategic contracting-out' was justifiable when in-house provision might detract from a Department's ability to concentrate upon its core functions or when the private sector was better equipped to provide a particular public service.

Clearer distinction between policy and administration

Another objective has been the achievement of a clearer distinction between policy and administration in central Government. In Britain some of the earliest steps in this direction were taken by the Heath Government in the early 1970s when it experimented with the idea of 'hiving off' sections of Whitehall Departments in quasi-autonomous Agencies, such as the Civil Aviation Authority in 1971 or the Manpower Services Commission in 1973. The principle was taken a good deal further by the Thatcher Government following an influential report in 1988 by Sir Robin Ibbs, head of the so-called Efficiency Unit.[31] This recommended that to the greatest possible extent the executive (that is, administrative) functions of central Government should be carried out not by traditional Departments but by specially designed Agencies within the orbit of Whitehall's influence – the so-called Next Steps Agencies. The idea immediately appealed to Conservative Ministers and since then it has spread rapidly to nearly every sphere of central Government administration, so much so that by the autumn of 1994 there were more than 100 such Agencies in existence with two thirds of the total number of civil servants working in them or the executive structures of the Revenue Departments.

Each Agency works within the terms of a Framework Agreement laid down by Ministers in the relevant Department and on the basis of an annual business plan seeks to meet a range of targets set by Ministers. The staff continue to be civil servants under the direction in each case of a Chief Executive who is in turn accountable to the relevant Minister for the Agency's performance in relation to its objectives and targets. Increasingly, the Chief Executives of Agencies respond directly to Parliamentary representations and complaints on behalf of constituents, although Ministers have argued that the traditional channels of political accountability also remain, since if an MP is dissatisfied with a direct response from an Agency Chief Executive, the matter can still be taken up directly with the Minister concerned.

Among the first Executive Agencies to be established were the Stationery Office, the Meteorological Office, and the Employment Services within the then Department of Employment. Since then the model has been applied throughout Whitehall to include such large bureaucracies as the Inland Revenue, the Customs and Excise, and the Benefits Agency. In every case the main goals have been to clarify and increase accountability, while enhancing through greater delegation the freedom to manage resources in the most effective ways. In pursuit of these objectives, at least one third of all Agencies are operating as trading funds or under the discipline of net running cost controls. These mechanisms are designed to enable them to have the flexibility to meet the changing needs of their customers or users, while remaining under constant pressure to increase efficiency. With the further backing of Citizen's Charter principles, serious and successful attempts have also been made to improve the quality and reliability of all public services.

Hitherto these aspects of civil service reform under the Conservatives have attracted all-party political support at Westminister.[32] However, the progress of reform has thrown into sharper focus the various definitions of public accountability put forward by the different parties. While Ministers in the Major Government have spoken and acted increasingly in terms of *direct* accountability to the users or customers of public service (whether taxpayers, social security claimants or NHS patients, for example), the spokesmen for the Opposition parties still tend to think of public accountability in terms of the duty of everyone in the public service to respond to the inquiries and complaints of elected politicians – in other words, *indirect* accountability via the people's elected representatives, whether in local authorities or the national Parliament. Furthermore, strong opposition to the development of these Agency principles has come from the civil service and public service trade unions which are naturally worried about the apparent fragmentation of what used to be a unified civil service, and about the perceived threat to the job security, pay and conditions of their members.

Given the obvious success of the Agency principle in the recent Conservative reforms, Ministers evidently believe that it can be extended beyond the sphere of routine public administration to the core civil service functions of policy advice and public sector regulation. This argument was powerfully put in the so-called Trosa Report written by a senior French civil servant who was invited to review progress in 1993. Ministers then drew upon this independent advice to extend the Agency principle still further when they published a long-awaited White Paper on the Civil Service in July 1994.[33]

The 1994 White Paper proposed that the core Departments in Whitehall should benefit from the Agency principle in at least three important ways. Firstly, greater freedom to manage is to be delegated to other Whitehall Departments by the Treasury and the Office of Public Service and Science, albeit within overall financial limits set by controls on Departmental running costs. Secondly, the quality of management information within Departments is to be further improved by switching from current cost accounting to resource-based or accruals accounting similar to that normally used in the private sector. Thirdly and more generally, Ministers are continuing to change the overall culture of the civil service by reducing the layers of senior management wherever possible and by consciously moving all Departments towards a more limited policy role which leaves virtually all the routine work of public administration to the newly formed Executive Agencies.

The erosion of the state

When Margaret Thatcher launched the idea of Next Steps Agencies in February 1988, she assured the House of Commons that the new institutions would be 'generally' within the civil service and their staff would therefore continue to be civil servants. Yet since that time it has become ever more apparent that Executive Agency status can be something of a half-way house on the way to full-scale privatisation of activities which traditionally have been regarded in Britain as part of the apparatus of the state. We can already see that the effect of this process has been gradually to shift the boundaries of central Government and to erode the sphere of the nation state.

This process started from modest beginnings with the privatisation of *Forward*, the civil service catering organisation, and the Driver, Vehicles and Operators Information Technology Agency. It has since spread to encompass the Crown Agents, the Transport Research Laboratory, the National Engineering Laboratory and a number of other technical Agencies within the civil service. In all cases the thinking behind the policy is based upon the Conservative belief that many, if not most, of the support functions for central Government Departments would benefit from the greater managerial and financial freedom of the private sector. It is quite possible that the principle will be further extended in future (at any rate under a Conservative Government), since the future of each Executive Agency is to be reviewed at five-year intervals and on each occasion the reviews will include careful consideration of the case for privatisation and the case for abolition.

The pursuit of this policy, however, has already proved to be something of a mixed blessing in that while the threat (or promise) of privatisation may be said to keep the staff of the Executive Agencies on their toes, it has also served to demoralise at least some of the more traditionally minded staff who did not join the civil service in the first place in order to work in insecure conditions analogous to those in the private sector. The policy has therefore given rise to strong opposition from the civil service trade unions and has raised serious doubts about the chances of maintaining a unified civil service which upholds a common ethos of public service values and traditions.

Underlying many of the concerns which have been expressed about the erosion of the state is the belief held by some academics and other observers unsympathetic to the Conservative cause that the higher reaches of the civil service have been undesirably politicised by the unusually long period of one-party rule in Whitehall and at Westminster. It was these concerns which led some distinguished witnesses who gave evidence to the Treasury and Civil Service Select Committee of the House of Commons in 1993-94 to suggest that there was a need for a new consolidated Civil Service Code, a new independent appeals procedure for civil servants, and a Civil Service Act to put the new arrangements on a firm statutory basis.[34] These ideas were broadly accepted by the all-party Select Committee in its 1994 report, and by the Major Government in most significant respects, save the idea of a new Civil Service Act upon which Ministers said they wished to reflect further.

The net numerical effect of all the changes and reforms covered in this section has been to reduce the overall size of the civil service in Britain by previously improbable proportions. In May 1979 when the Conservatives came to office there were 732,000 civil servants, since when this number has been steadily reduced to a total of 524,000 in November 1994, with the prospect that it will fall still further to 477,000 by the end of the present Parliament .[35]

From trust to contract

When considering the future of the civil service in Britain, it is instructive to reflect upon the extent to which relationships within the civil service and between civil servants and Ministers have moved gradually from trust to contract. Put simply, this means that civil servants have increasingly been obliged to master the new language and assumptions of contractual relations with their superiors and with Ministers instead of the more traditional relations based upon the principles of trust and hierarchy. The 1994 White Paper on the future of the civil service proposed the establishment of a new Senior Civil Service at Grade 5 and above – roughly the top 3000 or so policy advising civil servants.[36] It also embraced the idea, previously suggested by the Efficiency Unit, of explicit written employment contracts for civil servants designed to promote a new culture in the Senior Civil Service. This did not go as far as the reforms in New Zealand, where a network of fixed term contracts was introduced for all senior officials within a legislative framework provided by the 1988 State Sector Act. However, it seemed to have been informed by New Zealand experience.

This radical approach appears to have worked rather well when applied to the Chief Executives of the Next Steps Agencies which, in most cases, are charged with delivering specific services to the general public of a largely uniform and routine character. It is less certain how useful it will be when applied to the more unpredictable activity of policy advice and the close, sometimes capricious, relationship between Ministers and civil servants.

There is also the strong possibility that the civil service, like some other national institutions in Britain, will be increasingly affected by the influence of administrative practices on the Continent as the development of the European Union becomes more significant for many aspects of the British polity. If this turns out to be the case, the British will have to get used to living under a more highly developed system of administrative law, some of it derived directly from new European law binding upon Britain and some of it derived from British law increasingly influenced by Continental experience. Such developments would probably entail a more explicit separation of powers between the Executive, the Legislature and the Judiciary in Britain which, in its turn, would only be realistic if Parliament at Westminster legislated for a new codified constitution and a new structure of administrative Courts capped by a constitutional supreme Court on the lines of the *Conseil d'Etat* (Council of State) in France or the *Bundesverfassungsgericht* (Federal Constitutional Court) in Germany.

Needless to say, such far-reaching legal and constitutional changes in Britain would transform the context within which the civil service and all other institutions of Government operate, and it would require all-party agreement to have a chance of implementation. At present such an outcome seems rather unlikely and remote, but it cannot completely be discounted in the uncertain political conditions of the mid-1990s. After all, the realities of Britain's membership of the European Union and the dynamic aspects of the continuing process of European integration have already affected much of the context and many of the assumptions of civil service work in Britain and may do so to an even greater extent in future.

14.5 Conclusion

On the basis of the evidence highlighted in this chapter, it is reasonable to conclude that civil servants wield considerable power and influence within British central Government, especially in the new Executive Agencies. They can have considerable influence over policy, but this tends to be greater when the party in office has lost some of its ideological momentum after many years in office or towards the end of a Parliament. Nevertheless the realities of British politics mean that Ministers remain in charge and their political rights are seldom questioned even by the most independent-minded or awkward civil servants. Officials are there to guide, assist and advise Ministers, not to control them. If the relationship between Ministers and officials works as it is supposed to, there need be no problems caused by over-mighty or manipulative officials.

On the other hand, the traditional ethos and conventions of Whitehall have been known to frustrate the intentions of Ministers (especially junior Ministers) and these factors may sometimes have lowered the quality or reduced the vitality of policy and decision making in British central Government. In this chapter we have also noted the extent to which it is civil servants more than Ministers who tend to feel that some of their basic assumptions are under threat from the process of radical change. Yet at the same time we should not forget that well established institutions – such as the most powerful Whitehall Departments – have traditions of their own which outlast even the most determined and long-serving Ministers.

At the outset of this chapter we made it clear that we would focus mainly upon the higher administrative grades of the civil service, since these are the people who are most closely involved with Ministers in the process of policy and decision making. However, under the cumulative influence of Conservative reforms since 1979, we should also note that the executive and regulatory functions of the civil service have become relatively more important, the significance of which is underlined by the fact that the vast majority of civil servants are involved either in routine administrative tasks or in delivering largely standardised public services to the general public. It is, therefore, the great mass of officials who have felt most threatened by the process of change since 1979 and who tend to lament the much more insecure role projected for them in future if the present policy is sustained. Even the core civil service will probably get smaller as long as Ministers maintain the present thrust of reform. Yet the position could change significantly if the Conservative Government loses its reforming zeal or if a different party (or parties) are elected into office at the next General Election.

Suggested questions

1 Describe the structure of the civil service in Britain both in general and within a 'typical' Department.
2 What are the functions of the civil service, and to what extent do they reveal strengths and/or weaknesses?
3 What is the traditional role of the civil service in Britain and how has this been affected by the Conservative reforms since 1979?

Notes

1. Report of the Tomlin Commission Cmnd 3909 (London: HMSO, 1931).
2. Quoted in the Fifth Report of the Treasury and Civil Service Select Committee, 'The role of the civil service', Vol. I, HC 27-I, 1993-94 (London: HMSO, November 1994), para 65.
3. E. Bridges, *Portrait of a Profession* (London: Cambridge University Press, 1950), p. 25.
4. See the Report of the Fulton Committee, Cmnd 3628 (London: HMSO, 1968).
5. See B. Sedgemore, *The Secret Constitution* (London: Hodder & Stroughton, 1980), pp. 148-53; also P. Kellner and N. Crowther-Hunt, *The Civil Servants* (London: Macdonald, 1980), pp. 121-3.
6. See Civil Service Commissioners' Report, 1993-94; especially Tables 5-7.
7. See the Interim Report of the Treasury and Civil Service Select Committee on 'The role of the civil service', HC 390-I, 1992-93, para 6 (London: HMSO, July 1993) from which this definition of functions is drawn.
8. The authors are grateful to Richard Mottram, Permanent Secretary at the Office of Public Service and Science in 1994, for his expert guidance on the established conventions of the civil service.
9. See D. Howells, 'Marks and Spencer and the Civil Service, a comparison of culture and methods', *Public Administration*, Autumn 1981.
10. See the *Citizen's Charters*, Cmnd 1599 (London: HMSO, July 1991).
11. For example, in a Report on the Civil Service by the House of Commons Select Committee on Expenditure, HC 535, 1977.
12. See B. Sedgemore, *The Secret Constitution*, pp. 11-48.
13. See Civil Service Commissioners' Report, 1993-94, for evidence of this trend.
14. See T. Benn, 'Manifestos and Mandarins', in W. Rodgers *et al*, *Policy and Practice, the Experience of Government* (London: RIPA, 1980), pp. 57-78.
15. See J. Hoskyns, 'Whitehall and Westminster, an outsider's view', *Fiscal Studies*, November 1982.
16. See in particular the evidence given to the Treasury and Civil Service Select Committee in May 1993 by Lord Callaghan, Interim Report on 'The role of the civil service', HC 390II, pp. 138-9.

17. Of course, the so-called 'middle ground' of British politics is an elusive and changing concept, as can be illustrated by the apparent policy convergence between John Major's Conservative Party and Tony Blair's 'new Labour' Party.

18. For a fuller analysis of 'the public interest' defence used in the Courts, see R. Thomas, 'The British Official Secrets Acts, 1911-39 and the Ponting Case', in R.A. Chapman and M. Hunt (eds), *Open Government* (London: Routledge, 1989), pp. 95-122.

19. Lord Justice Scott is expected to submit a report to the Prime Minister on completion of his judicial inquiry into illegal arms sales to Iraq.

20. See especially the evidence given to the Treasury and Civil Service Select Committee in 1993-94 by the civil service unions in 'The role of the civil service', HC 27-II, pp. 132-52.

21. See the Eighth Report of the House of Commons Public Accounts Committee, 1993-94, on 'The proper conduct of public business' (London: HMSO, 1994) for further elaboration of this argument.

22. A good example was the non-resignation of Norman Lamont as Chancellor of the Exchequer in September 1992 immediately after 'Black Wednesday' when the British Government suffered the humiliation of having Sterling forced out of the European Exchange Rate Mechanism by huge financial movements in the markets.

23. MINIS was well described in para 23-26 of the Third Report of the Treasury and Civil Service Select Committee, HC 236-I, 1981-82.

24. By early 1991 the total cumulative savings from the Efficiency Scrutinies came to £1,500,000, *Hansard*, 7 February 1991, Col. 215.

25. See G. Drewry, *Law, Justice and Politics* (London: Longman, 1975), pp. 75-6.

26. For example, in the 1981 case of *Bromley Council* v. *Greater London Council*, in which the Law Lords ruled that the GLC had acted *ultra vires* by subsidising London Transport fares to an excessive extent via precepts upon the rates of the London Boroughs.

27. See Chapter 18, section 18.2 below for discussion of the legal and constitutional implications of Britain's membership of the European Union.

28. See Chapter 17, section 17.6 below for a fuller description of the role and statutory limits upon the activities of the Ombudsman.

29. See the White Paper 'Competing for Quality', Cmnd 1930 (London: HMSO, November 1991).

30. See the White Paper on 'The Civil Service, continuity and change', Cmnd 2627, July 1994, p. 93.

31. See 'The financing and accountability of Next Steps Agencies', Cmnd 914 (London: HMSO, 1989) for a fuller explanation of Conservative Government thinking on the Executive Agencies.

32. This point is best illustrated by successive reports of the all-party Treasury and Civil Service Select Committee in the late 1980s and early 1990s, culminating in the November 1994 Report on 'The role of the civil service'.

33. See Sylvie Trosa, *Next Steps – moving on*: a progress report to Government (London: Office of Public Service and Science, February 1994).

34. See the White Paper 'The Civil Service, taking forward continuity and change', Cmnd 2748 (London: HMSO, 1995).

35. See Treasury Press Release 141/94, 30 November 1994.

36. See the White Paper 'The Civil Service, continuity and change', Cmnd 2627, paras 4.13 - 4.22.

Further reading

Bruce-Gardyne, J., *Ministers and Mandarins* (London: Sidgwick & Jackson, 1986).

Drewry, G. and Butcher, T., *The Civil Service Today* (Oxford: Blackwell, 1988).

Dyness M. and Walker, D., *The Times Guide to the New British State: The Government Machine in the 1990s* (London: Times Books, 1995).

Giddings, P., *Parliamentary Accountability: a study of Parliament and Executive Agencies* (London: Macmillan, 1995).

Hennessy, P., *Whitehall* (London: Secker & Warburg, 1989).

Metcalfe, L. and Richards, S., *Improving Public Management* (London: Sage, 1989).

Pyper, R., *The British Civil Service* (Hemel Hempstead: Prentice Hall/Harvester Wheatsheaf, 1995).

Treasury and Civil Service Select Committee Report on *'The role of the Civil Service'*, HC 27 I-III (London: November 1994).

White Paper on *'The Civil Service, continuity and change'*, Cmnd 2627 (London: HMSO, July 1994).

White Paper on *'The Civil Service, taking forward continuity and change'*, Cmnd 2748 (London: HMSO, January 1995).

Williams, W., *Washington, Westminster and Whitehall* (London: Cambridge University Press, 1988).

PART 5

Other Public Institutions

⬡15 **The Public Sector**

In this chapter the term 'public sector' is taken to include public corporations, non-Departmental public bodies and other extra-Governmental organisations. It does not include the Departments of central Government which we dealt with in Chapters 13 and 14 or the institutions of local government which we shall deal with in Chapter 16. In this chapter we shall begin by looking at the problems which have been posed by the public corporations over the years, and then go on to examine the issues raised by privatisation which have assumed particular importance in the political debate since the early 1980s. The various types of institution to be found in the British public sector are shown diagrammatically in Figure 15.1.

Figure 15.1 *The composition of the public sector*

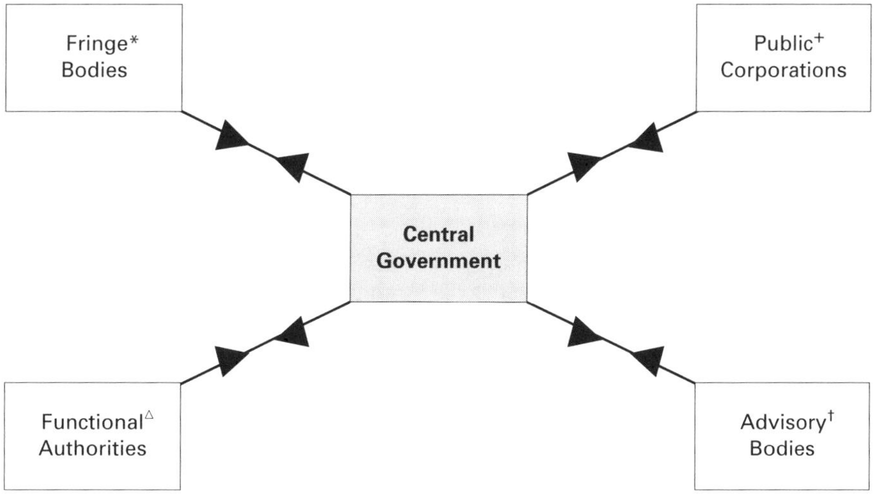

* Notably several hundred QUANGOs
+ Nationalised industries
△ Notably the Health Authorities
† Notably Advisory and Departmental Committees

15.1 Public corporations

In Britain public ownership and control have traditionally been associated with the model of the public corporation. Yet there have been many different forms of public ownership and control which have been tried over the years. In the second half of the nineteenth century, the early Socialists advocated *municipal ownership* and control of key industries. Those who pressed for this 'gas and water Socialism' considered local authorities to be the best institutional mechanism for providing these essential public services. Before the Second World War more than two thirds of electricity supply and about one third of gas supply were under municipal ownership and control, as is still the case in some Continental countries today (for example, Denmark). Over the years a number of municipal authorities also provided passenger transport services, civic amenities and other local services through their direct labour departments. After 1945 the focus of public ownership and control shifted to *nationalisation*, since the post-war Labour Government gave priority to considerations of national planning, economies of scale, and distributional equity. This model of centrally administered nationalised industries remained the archetypal public sector institution until 1979 when the alternative policy of privatisation began to be brought to the fore in Britain.

Notwithstanding the dominance of nationalisation as the model for the public sector in Britain from 1945 to 1979, other forms of public ownership and control were attempted with varying degrees of enthusiasm for shorter or longer periods during that time. These alternatives included *administrative control by Whitehall Departments* with Ministers directly accountable to Parliament for the running of nationalised industries, as with the Post Office until 1969; *financial control by state holding companies*, such as the Industrial Reorganisation Corporation in the late 1960s or the National Enterprise Board in the late 1970s; and the establishment of *state-owned financial institutions*, such as the Post Office Giro Bank in 1969.

In spite of these variations, the dominant model continued to be *public corporations*, more usually known as nationalised industries. At their peak in 1982 such institutions employed about 1,759,000 people (about 7 per cent of those in work at the time), they created about 11 per cent of Gross Domestic Product (GDP), and accounted for about 17 per cent of total fixed investment in the British economy.[1] They had come to dominate four vital sectors of the economy: energy, transport, steel, and communications. They included long established institutions, such as British Rail and British Coal, as well as some relatively new institutions, such as British Telecom and the British National Oil Corporation. In their heyday they were important customers and suppliers of the private sector, and they had a profound and pervasive effect upon the health of the British economy and the course of British politics.[2]

Common characteristics

Public corporations have a number of common characteristics which have set them apart from other industrial and commercial undertakings in Britain.[3] (1) They have been established by Acts of Parliament as statutory bodies responsible for the production of goods or the provision of services specified in the legislation. (2) They have been publicly owned in the sense that any securities which they issue carry no private risk and usually pay fixed rates of interest, although in some successful cases they have paid public dividends to the Exchequer. (3) They have been subject to Government control via the indirect mechanisms of required rates of return on capital, external financial limits on investment and borrowing, and periodic Ministerial appointments of their Chairmen and Board members. (4) In return for meeting these politically determined obligations, they have enjoyed varying degrees of day-to-day managerial autonomy, their employees have not been civil servants (unlike in France or Germany, for example), and they have enjoyed some limited financial freedoms from Treasury control, but increasingly less as the years went by.

Essential problems

There are a number of essential problems which have beset public corporations in Britain over the years. To a considerable extent these problems stemmed from the conflicting pressures which gave rise to the establishment of public corporations in the first place. For example, there was the Socialist impulse of the 1918 Labour Party constitution, followed by the more pragmatic felt need for national economic planning and industrial reorganisation under successive Governments between the two World Wars. During the Second World War, there was growing acceptance within the Coalition Government of final state responsibility for the level of employment and the management of the economy, and by 1945 there was a political consensus in favour of adequate national welfare and social security as well.

It was against this background that the post-war Labour Government led by Clement Attlee felt able to take some giant strides towards the public ownership and control of a considerable part of the national economy, especially those sectors of industrial production which were considered to be 'the commanding heights', such as coal and steel. This was done principally in the name of Socialist economic planning in a sincere attempt to improve the prospects of national economic recovery after the war. It was also done for the sake of employment in an attempt to relieve some of the chronic insecurity which so many workers had experienced during the period between the wars. Moreover, the policy was pursued with a high degree of political commitment to Clause IV of the Labour Party constitution which had called for 'the common ownership of the means of production, distribution and exchange'. This was, therefore, the heroic period of nationalisation in Britain.

Since that time, however, it has become clear to nearly everyone in Britain that the policy of nationalisation and the model of the public corporations were seriously flawed in practice. *Firstly*, the theory of public ownership assumed that the major issues of macroeconomic policy could be kept separate from the day-to-day matters faced by the management of public corporations, and that Ministers and nationalised industry Boards could play distinct and complementary roles which would not clash. In practice, these were soon shown to be heroic or naive assumptions, since in a modern mixed economy Ministers are inevitably involved in the biggest decisions of public corporations. This was partly because of their economic weight and political importance in the British economy, which meant that their corporate decisions were bound to have a significant effect upon the success or failure of Government policy. It was also because, whereas the Socialist ideal had been that the state should own the most vital industrial sectors on behalf of the people, all too often the reality was characterised by trade union demands for the state to rescue backward or uncompetitive undertakings (for example, the railways or ship-building) largely for the sake of keeping the employees in work.

Secondly, the problems of dealing with the public corporations were not made any easier by their great diversity which was reflected in their widely differing economic fortunes. For example, at various stages over the last four decades, British Airways, British Gas, British Telecom and the Post Office have each generated impressive profits which have been returned in large part to the Exchequer in the form of public dividends, whereas British Rail, British Coal, British Shipbuilders and London Transport have each had economic difficulties and have seldom been able to generate an overall profit for the nation. The former group provided examples of successful industries (often with monopoly benefits) which were capable of generating good returns on their capital and labour employed, whereas the latter group provided examples of strife-torn industries with economically debilitating social and regional obligations. It is therefore sensible only to make observations about particular public corporations at particular times.

Thirdly, the public corporations have suffered over the years from the fact that their very existence has been the subject of bitter and long-lasting political conflict both between and, occasionally, within the two main parties. In many respects they have been treated as a political football to be kicked back and forth between two entrenched ideological positions on the Left and the Right of British politics. The hard Left of the Labour Party has invariably pressed for an enlarged public sector and the nationalisation (or renationalisation) of key economic sectors. The free market wing of the Conservative Party has consistently sought to reduce the size of the public sector and, since the early 1980s in particular, to privatise as many public corporations as possible. Indeed, the extent of this determined drive to privatise is demonstrated by the fact that since 1979 there have been at least 50 significant acts of privatisation in Britain which by 1994 had reduced the remaining nationalised industries to a mere 4 per cent of GDP employing only 1.7 per cent of the total workforce.[4]

In the face of this massive and sustained onslaught upon the public sector in Britain by the Conservatives in office, the Labour Party has felt obliged in the 1990s to revise its traditional policy favouring nationalisation and renationalisation. At the 1994 Labour Party Conference Tony Blair declared his intention to re-write the 1918 Labour constitution and especially the party's long-standing commitment to public ownership of the means of production, distribution and exchange enshrined in Clause IV – something which the party did in 1995. Thus at the time of writing there are convincing signs that the twentieth-century struggle over nationalisation and de-nationalisation may have come to an end, or at any rate it may have been transformed into a more subtle debate about regulation and control in the public interest.

Finally and most crucially, the central problem of the public corporations in Britain has been the difficulty of establishing a satisfactory arm's-length relationship between the Boards of the nationalised industries and Ministers in the Government of the day. In so far as this was ever achieved, it involved reconciling managerial freedom for the Boards with the constant political temptation for Ministers to interfere with the managerial ground-rules of the public sector. Traditionally the public corporations were charged in their founding Statutes with twin duties: to break even financially taking one year with another, and to operate in the public interest. Needless to say, these duties were often incompatible and when they were, it was usually the latter (as defined by Ministers) which prevailed. This might have been all right if there had been a clear and lasting consensus between the two main political parties about what constituted 'the public interest' at any given time. Yet such a consensus never really existed, since there was an inherent conflict of interest between the interests of the employees of public corporations who wished to maintain their jobs and improve their rewards (backed by Labour) and the interests of taxpayers and others in the wider community who wished to contain the levels of financial support for the public corporations and who were invariably backed by the Conservatives.

In short, experience over at least five decades in Britain has demonstrated the great difficulties in maintaining a satisfactory arm's-length relationship between public corporations and the Government of the day. All too often the former were required by the Treasury to reduce or defer their investment programmes for the sake of wider objectives of national policy, notably Government determination to limit or reduce the level of public sector borrowing. On other occasions they were obliged to subordinate their commercial judgement to the political priorities of Ministers. For example, there were occasions when British Coal wanted to close uneconomic pits, but the Government of the day insisted that these be kept open for social or political reasons. There were other occasions when British Steel was required to invest heavily in new plant and equipment at the behest of Ministers (notably by the Conservatives in 1972-73) only to find, when the new plant came on stream, that the forecast expansion of the market to justify it did not materialise. Even the rhetorically non-interventionist Conservative Government in the early 1980s instructed the nationalised gas and electricity industries to raise their prices by more than their commercial judgement suggested was wise simply to increase the flow of revenue from these public corporations to the Exchequer. In all such cases it could be argued that the nation as a whole suffered the effects of policies which combined the worst of both worlds.

15.2 Regulation and control

Since 1976 there have been some significant developments in the ways in which successive Governments in Britain have sought to regulate and control the public sector. We take 1976 as our starting point, since it was then that the Labour Government was obliged by the International Monetary Fund (IMF) to introduce a system of rigorous cash limits upon all forms of public spending, which included tighter financial controls upon the public corporations. This system was refined and extended by the Conservative Government in the 1980s with the result that most public corporations were adversely affected both by the tight financial limits set by Ministers and (in the early 1980s at any rate) by the financial consequences of the economic recession at that time. Two of the most unfortunate consequences of these developments for the public corporations were that they had to put up their prices by more than the rate of inflation (which they did not then wish to do) and that their capital investment programmes had to be cut back. Although in theory the Boards had the freedom to operate at arm's length from the Government of the day, in practice the political constraints upon them severely reduced their capacity to do so. In such conditions the methods of external control fell into at least one of three main categories: Ministerial oversight, Parliamentary control, and other regulatory mechanisms. We shall now examine each of these in turn.

Ministerial oversight

Ministerial oversight has been the most common method of controlling the public sector. It is really a short-hand for supervision of the public corporations by Ministers and senior civil servants. It has usually taken the form of frequent conversations between Ministers and the Boards of public corporations on significant issues of policy, such as plans for large-scale corporate investment, key pricing decisions, important pay negotiations, and significant matters to do with the impact of corporate activity upon the wider environment – for example, an airport runway extension or the siting of a new power station. In these relationships Ministers have sought to preserve the fundamental distinction between day-to-day management decisions (usually matters for the Boards) and long-term strategic decisions with a high political content in which they have felt obliged to take a close interest. In such contacts Ministers have sometimes been tempted to blur or ignore this vital distinction – indeed it has not always been apparent that there has been such a distinction – although in the event they have usually shied away from directly usurping the role of senior management.

On those occasions when Ministers have decided to intervene, they have usually exercised their statutory right to do so by issuing a directive to the Board concerned. They have also been tempted to influence Board decisions in more informal ways known as 'lunch-time directives' of which no written record is kept. This technique may well have been used to put pressure upon British Rail to keep open certain uneconomic branch lines, on the Post Office to buy British rather than foreign equipment, and on British Coal in connection with the pace and scale of pit closures. However, under the Conservatives since 1979 the sustained policy of privatisation has left fewer and fewer public sector issues to be resolved in these ways.

When there has been serious conflict between Ministers and the Boards of public corporations, it has often been because the latter have chosen to interpret their statutory duties more narrowly (and commercially) than the sponsoring Departments would have wished. This has then faced the Minister concerned with an invidious choice between doing nothing about an unpopular Board decision and so risking public and political criticism for apparent inactivity, and intervening in a particular Board decision and so perhaps jeopardising the commercial prospects of the public corporation. On the whole Ministers have chosen the latter course more often than the former, which is a reflection of the fact that the general public and Parliament have more clout than the Board of any public corporation.

Parliamentary control

Another method of control, which is really the counterpart of Ministerial oversight, has been achieved by making public corporations directly or indirectly accountable to Parliament at Westminster. When this has been exercised indirectly via a Minister, it has not been very satisfactory, since Ministers have tended simply to tell MPs that they will draw the issues of concern to the attention of the relevant Chairman and Board. A greater degree of Parliamentary accountability has been achieved via the mechanism of Select Committees – notably the Select Committee on Nationalised Industries in the 1950s and 1960s – in which the decisions and practices of public corporations have been scrutinised and criticised.

However, perhaps the most powerful and effective way of exercising political control and Parliamentary accountability has been the straightforward practice of MPs writing to senior management of public corporations whenever and wherever they have cause to do so on behalf of their constituents. Such written representations can be supplemented by the use of meetings and delegations, as well as backed up by the implied threat that the MPs concerned will raise the issue on the floor of the House if suitable steps are not taken to meet the point. Since ultimately all public corporations depend for their continued existence upon the support and approval of Parliament, and since most of them have needed substantial support from public funds at any rate at times, MPs have had both the ability and the right to be quite demanding of public corporations when they need to be.

Other regulatory mechanisms

From time to time other regulatory mechanisms have been used in attempts to exercise some additional political control over institutions in the public sector. For example, the *Monopolies and Mergers Commission* has conducted efficiency audits of many of the public corporations under the powers provided for it in the 1980 Competition Act.[5] This has served to sharpen up the performance of a number of public corporations, such as the Post Office or British Rail.

Occasionally, Ministers have decided to establish a *Royal Commission* or *Committee of Inquiry* to conduct a full-scale review of a public corporation when its current activities or future prospects have caused an unusual degree of public interest or concern. For example, in 1985 the Thatcher Government established the Peacock Committee to look into the future financing of the BBC.[6] Its controversial report, which was nevertheless a disappointment to the more radical elements in the Thatcher Government, subsequently triggered the far-reaching 1990 Broadcasting Act which set the legislative framework for British broadcasting in the 1990s, but was soon overtaken by the dynamism of financial markets and media technology. In general, however, successive Conservative Administrations have seemed rather allergic to the use of Royal Commissions, largely because of their traditional reputation as civil-service-inspired devices for gathering the opinion of 'the great and the good' and then recycling this back to Ministers in elegant prose.

Finally, some of the public corporations have been provided from the outset with statutory *Consumer Councils* to monitor their activities from a consumer point of view. The Electricity Consumers Council and the Post Office Users National Council were two examples of this institutional device which invariably turned out to be a disappointment to campaigning bodies such as the Consumers Association. Moreover, as is sometimes the case in arrangements of this kind, the practice of regular monitoring was often vulnerable to 'agency-capture' – in other words, a situation in which the watch-dog is tamed and rendered ineffective by the very institution which it is supposed to watch.

15.3 Privatisation and its consequences

We have seen in the previous sections of this chapter some of the intractable problems which were caused for all British Governments after 1945 by the constant attempts to maintain a satisfactory arms's-length relationship between Ministers and public corpo-rations. By 1979 the lesson of experience was that the public corporations were bound to pose serious problems for any Government, at any rate in so far as their commercial performance was so frequently disappointing and their impact upon taxpayers and the rest of the economy invariably unwelcome.

Against this background it was not surprising that some senior figures in the new Conservative Government which came to power in 1979 wanted to embark upon a pol-icy of radical and extensive privatisation. However, at that time many of their colleagues were still inhibited by the long-lasting influence of the post-war settlement which had led the nationalised industries to be regarded by both main parties as an inevitable, if not necessarily desirable, part of the British national economy. Although the Heath Government had come to office in 1970 pledged to begin a process of de-nationalisation, it soon felt compelled to do some nationalisation of its own – notably of Rolls-Royce and Upper Clyde Shipbuilders – in order to stave off the prospects of bankruptcy and large-scale unemployment in the aerospace and shipbuilding industries. This experience had left its mark upon some of Margaret Thatcher's senior colleagues who felt disinclined to attempt too much too soon by way of privatisation after 1979.

As things turned out, the 1979-83 Conservative Government returned six large pub-lic corporations to the private sector, although only two (British Aerospace and Amersham International) were sold to investors in one go. We should also notice, however, that this period of Conservative Government was marked by the 1980 Housing Act, the most sig-nificant feature of which was the introduction of a statutory right for all Council tenants to buy (at generous discounts in most cases) the properties in which they lived as Council tenants. This triggered an enormous shift of wealth and power from the public to the pri-vate sectors and did a good deal to popularise the wider cause of privatisation. By the end of the 1980s it had resulted in the creation of more than 1 million extra people in owner-occupation and the raising of about £10,000 million in asset sales.

Following their victory at the 1983 General Election, Margaret Thatcher and her senior colleagues felt more confident about applying the principle of privatisation to more parts of the public sector. Accordingly, the Conservatives legislated in the 1983-87 Parliament for the return to the private sector of a larger number of state-owned industries, including two giant public utilities – British Telecom and British Gas. The gross proceeds of these two sales in 1984 and 1986 amounted to nearly £9,000 million and in each case the shares were bought extensively (at a discount to the real market price) by first-time shareholders and employees of the industries concerned. By the mid-1980s the policy of privatisation had gathered real political momentum and it has been carried forward by the Conservatives in office ever since, although not perhaps with the same degree of verve and conviction under John Major's leadership after 1990. Nevertheless, the cumulative result at the time of writ-ing is that more than 50 significant privatisations have taken place under the Conservatives since 1979 which have yielded accumulated proceeds for the Exchequer of at least £66,000 million. See Figure 15.2 for a list of these privatisations and the money raised in each case.

Meaning and extent

It should already be apparent that the full meaning and significance of privatisation is really to be found in the withdrawal of the state from the production of goods and the provision of services into the more limited, but necessary roles of purchaser and regula-

Figure 15.2 Privatisations since 1979

		Written Answers			27 APRIL 1995					Written Answers			
		gross proceeds of sale			Privatisation Costs (£ million)								
Privatisation	Year of sale	equity	debt	total	'Sale Costs	Cash injection	'Debt written off	Employee incentives	Loyalty incentives	Interest on application monies	Total costs	As per cent of total gross proceeds	Net proceeds
British Aerospace[3]	1981	149	–	149	6	100	60	–	–	–	166	111.4	–17
Cable and Wireless[2]	1981	224	–	224	9	35	–	–	–	–	44	19.6	180
Amersham International	1982	63	–	63	3	–	–	–	–	3	0	0	63
NFC	1982	54	–	54	0	49	100	–	–	–	149	278.5	–96
Britoil	1982	549	–	549	13	–	–	–	–	–	13	2.3	536
Associated British Ports[2]	1983	48	25	73	3	–	81	1	–	1	85	116.1	–12
Enterprise Oil	1984	392	–	392	11	–	–	–	–	1	10	2.5	382
BT[3]	1984	3,916	3,500	7,416	185	–	2,790	56	82	4	3,109	41.9	4,307
British Gas[2]	1986	5,434	2,500	7,934	187	–	–	37	185	7	402	5.1	7,532
British Airways	1987	892	–	892	35	–	160	15	8	4	213	23.9	679
Royal Ordnance	1987	190	–	190	4	–	–	1	–	–	5	2.7	185
Rolls Royce	1987	1,348	–	1,348	34	283	–	14	–	5	326	24.2	1,022
BAA	1987	1,225	–	1,225	46	–	44	3	17	2	108	8.8	1,117
National Seed Development Organisation	1987	66	–	66	1	37	–	–	–	–	38	58.3	28
Professional and Executive Recruitment	1988	6	–	6	1	–	–	–	–	–	1	15.0	5
British Steel	1988	2,500	–	2,500	58	–	4,489	18	–	2	4,564	182.5	–2,064
General Practice Finance Corporation	1989	145	–	145	1	–	–	–	–	–	1	0.4	145

Source: *Hansard* 27 April 1995, Cols 647–8

Figure 15.2 continued

		Written Answers						27 APRIL 1995			Written Answers		
		gross proceeds of sale										As per cent of total gross proceeds	
Privatisation	Year of sale	equity	debt	total	Sale Costs	Cash injection	Debt written off	Employee incentives	Loyalty incentives	Interest on application monies	Total costs		Net proceeds
Harland and Wolff	1989	8	–	8	1	205	422	–	–	–	629	8,275	–621
Short Brothers	1989	30	–	30	2	366	390	–	–	759	2,529	2,529	–729
Regional Electricity Companies	1990	5,182	2,815	7,997	[5]202	–	–	51	64	34	–[6]	–[6]	–[6]
Generating Companies[2]	1991	2,228	768	2,996	[5]85	–	–	24	41	6	–[6]	–[6]	–[6]
Scottish Electricity Companies	1991	2,918	626	3,544	114	–	1,044	11	53	1	1,219	34.4	2,325
NTL	1991	48	22	70	2	–	–	–	–	–	2	3.1	68
Insurance Services Group	1991	[4]70	–	[4]70	7	50	–	–	–	–	57	81.0	13
BTG	1992	28	–	28	3	–	–	–	–	–	3	10.5	25
Northern Ireland Electricity	1992–93	704	70	774	29	–	–	2	15	–	47	6.0	727
DVOIT	1993	5	–	5	2	–	–	–	–	–	2	50.0	2
Forward	1994	5	–	5	1	–	–	–	–	–	1	10.9	4
DTELS	1994	7	–	7	2	–	–	–	–	–	2	27.3	5
Belfast International Airport	1994	33	15	48	4	–	–	–	–	–	4	7.4	44
British Coal	1994	963	–	963	35	–	1,633	–	–	–	1,669	173.3	–706

Privatisation Costs (£ million)

Notes:
[1] Costs to Government often some costs will fall to the company).
[2] Excludes costs and proceeds of secondary sale(s).
[3] Since 1979
[4] Includes up to £5 million to be paid in 1996.
[5] Costs to 31 December 1991 excluding VAT and stamp duty.
[6] Lack of information on VAT and stamp duty costs means this is not available on a consistent basis.

tor of goods and services now provided mostly by the private sector. [7] Seen in this light and bearing in mind the sustained Conservative commitment to the policy, it is not an exaggeration to say that privatisation has had the effect of redefining the national consensus about the appropriate role and extent of the state and its agencies in contemporary Britain. This assertion is corroborated by the fact that the Labour Party no longer argues a case for extensive renationalisation of the undertakings which have been privatised by the Conservatives – rather its new policy under Tony Blair concentrates upon the ideas of better regulation and accountability.

In these circumstances the broad definition of privatisation includes everything from the sale of state-owned enterprises to private investors (previously known in Britain as de-nationalisation), to the sale of public assets (such as public land or Council housing), to the contracting out of public services (such as cleaning or rubbish collection), to radical ideas for providing education or health services via individual vouchers cashable at public or private institutions. It can also be said to include aggressive liberalisation of many sectors of the economy, such as bus and coach services, cable television and telecommunications. Nor should we fail to note in this broad context the sustained Conservative policy of reducing the size of the civil service, and the policy of eliminating some of the tiers of local government - such as the Greater London Council and the other Metropolitan County Councils. In all these various ways successive Conservative Administrations since 1979 have sought to curtail and redefine the role of the state and its agencies, while simultaneously encouraging market forces in the areas of the economy from which public sector institutions have been withdrawn.

By the mid-1990s it is hard to be sure about how much further the policy of privatisation can or will be taken in Britain. It is perhaps significant that it has never been foisted upon Northern Ireland or Scotland to the same extent as England and Wales – in the former case because all Governments in London have been careful not to exacerbate 'the troubles' with insensitive 'English' policies and in the latter case because Scots of all political persuasions have always been very good at persuading the English that they are different. For example, the idea of privatising the Forestry Commission was eventually shelved because of strong Scottish resistance and the privatisation of the Scottish water industry left it as a hybrid under the control of Scottish local authorities. In England and Wales, the policy of privatisation has been carried forward under John Major's leadership, but seemingly with less conviction than under his more ideological predecessor. This is partly because there is not much left to be privatised and partly because (in the case of Royal Mail, for example) a number of Conservative back-benchers successfully rebelled against the policy. On the other hand, the Conservative Government proceeded with the privatisation of what remained of British Coal in 1994 and it is currently proceeding with its privatisation plans for British Rail and Rail Track.

On the Labour side, opposition to every new privatisation remains strong. However, once an industry or activity has been privatised, the new Labour Party under Tony Blair seems rather loath to commit itself to expensive re-nationalisation which could have unattractive implications for its allegedly cautious attitude towards any policy which might involve the need for higher taxation. The current dominance of the so-called 'modernisers' in the party leadership means that there seems little likelihood of 'New Labour' committing itself to extensive re-nationalisation. In general, it seems that Labour in office would proceed cautiously on a case-by-case basis and would probably not go beyond taking an increased public stake in some of the privatised utilities.

Arguments for and against privatisation

The arguments for privatisation were originally based upon the view that the public sector in Britain had become too large and burdensome on the rest of the economy and that, in the absence of effective reforms within the public sector itself, there was no sensible alternative to de-nationalisation. In the minds of radical Thatcherite Conservatives there was also the strongly held belief that the spread of free enterprise was an unqualified plus for any economy with other beneficial consequences for the spread of political freedom, whereas a state-owned enterprise was seen by them as virtually a contradiction in terms.

By the mid-1980s the policy of privatisation had been refined in the light of experience and a fuller and more convincing range of arguments were adduced in its support.[8] These were essentially as follows. (1) It was argued that privatisation serves to reduce Ministerial involvement in industrial decision making and is therefore conducive to a more commercial approach. (2) It enabled the industries concerned to raise funds for investment from the capital markets without suffering from the limitations imposed by the Public Sector Borrowing Requirement. (3) Once such industries became profitable, it meant that they paid Corporation Tax to the Exchequer which could then be used by the Chancellor either to cut other taxes or to increase public spending or to repay public debt or any combination of these. (4) It could help to promote wider share ownership both by attracting new private shareholders and by encouraging the growth of employee share ownership. (5) It is held to increase economic efficiency and corporate performance in the sectors concerned, as was demonstrated by the greatly improved performance in the private sector of, for example, Cable & Wireless and the National Freight Corporation. (6) It replaces a political system of regulation and control via state ownership with a more legalistic system involving independent regulatory agencies, such as the Office of Telecommunications or the Office of Gas Supplies. (7) Finally and more generally, it helped to create more of an enterprise culture in Britain by replacing state-owned industries which could not go bankrupt with privately owned industries which could, thus forcing the undertakings concerned to make themselves more competitive in order to survive in the market.

Apart from old-style Socialists who still prefer state ownership on long-standing ideological grounds, *the arguments against privatisation* have come mainly from those who believe that the costs of the policy tend to outweigh the benefits for employees, consumers and taxpayers. Such people have adduced the following arguments. (1) They have argued that when public corporations have been privatised, the sales have been either under-subscribed or under-priced. In the former case, exemplified by Cable & Wireless in 1983 or Enterprise Oil in 1984, the sales were by tender and hence the market was able to set the price. This led to situations in which not all the shares were initially taken up and the underwriters had to purchase the balance of unsold shares. In the latter case, exemplified by British Telecom in 1984 or British Airways in 1987, the sales were made at a fixed price directly to the financial institutions and the general public. This led to situations in which the shares were initially under-priced and therefore traded at a premium at the end of the first day on the market. The critics pointed out that such premia, which by 1987 were estimated to have amounted to more than £4,000 million in total, represented a loss to taxpayers and the nation as a whole of considerable proportions. (2) The critics have argued that Conservative Ministers have simply been 'selling the family silver', as the Earl of Stockton (the former Prime Minister, Harold Macmillan) put it in a memorable phrase, in order more easily to finance either tax cuts or extra public expenditure or a mixture of the two. The gravamen of this charge has been the argument that the policy of privatisation has amounted to little more than the stripping of public assets for private gain. There has been evidence to support this argument in cases such as the sale of the Royal Ordnance factories to British Aerospace in 1987 or the sale of the Water Authorities in 1989 to a variety of British and foreign buyers who then proceeded to strip the assets of valuable land and property. (3) They have argued that there is no real benefit to consumers or the public at large if privatisation involves simply the transformation of a public monopoly into a private monopoly which can subsequently exploit its privileged market position to the disadvantage of its customers and competitors. It is easy to see how the Conservative Government has laid itself open to this charge, because some of the leading candidates for privatisation were natural monopolies - for example, British Gas or the Water Authorities. It has also been easier to privatise public corporations with the active support of senior management and this has tended to be less forthcoming if a privatisation entailed the break-up of the public undertaking concerned. Moreover, it is impossible to ignore the fact that the sale of a monopoly is always likely to provide greater proceeds for the Exchequer than the sale of a public corporation which has been broken up (before the sale) for reasons of competition policy. (4) In recent times the newly privatised industries have frequently been criticised for the greed of their top management in voting themselves enormous increases in pay and share options at a time when they have been laying off large numbers of their employees and confining those who remain to very modest or no salary increases at all. This line of criticism from the mass circulation media and the Opposition parties has been compounded by the related criticism of some company Boards for their appointment of recently retired Conservative Ministers – in some cases the very people who had taken key Ministerial decisions when the industries were privatised. (5) Finally, some critics of the policy on the ideological Right have argued that Conservative Ministers seemed to stumble into the policy of privatisation without a coherent strategy or a set of sensible priorities to guide them. Such people have asked whether the prime purpose of the policy has been simply to sell all the assets which can be sold at the best available price, or whether there are some more intellectually respectable reasons for privatisation - for example, on grounds of improved economic performance – which should therefore have been underlined in explanation of the policy.

Problems and consequences of privatisation

We have seen how privatisation in Britain was regarded in the 1980s both as a blessing and as a curse, depending upon the political point of view of the observer. Even in the eyes of its most enthusiastic proponents, however, real problems have been posed which have made privatisation as controversial as the various forms of public ownership which preceded it.

Perhaps the key problem posed by privatisation is the paradox that the transfer of activities from the public to the private sectors has actually necessitated more elaborate forms of regulation than was the case before. In other words, the liberalisation implicit in the policy of privatisation has required *re-regulation*, not de-regulation, in a more explicit and legalistic form. Whereas in dealing with public corporations it was often necessary for Ministers to intervene in order to protect the interests of taxpayers against the commercial inefficiencies of nationalised industries; in dealing with privatised under-takings, it has been necessary for the independent regulators –such as OfTel, OfGas or OfWat (see Figure 15.3) – to protect the interests of consumers against any exploitation of disproportionate market power by the privatised utilities. For example, without such regulatory intervention, (and many have argued that the initial approach by the regula-tors was too lenient with the newly privatised undertakings), it would have been possi-ble for British Telecom to charge very high prices for services of which it was the dominant supplier during the early years after privatisation (such as domestic phone calls) and thus cross-subsidise its attractively low charges for long distance and commercial phone calls where it faced more direct competition from Mercury and others. It is for this reason that the independent regulators have set complicated formulae to control the prices which the utilities may charge in an attempt to ensure that regulation acts as a proxy for competi-tion in areas of activity where there is not a fully liberalised market. Although the utilities have complained and the stock market has reacted against the degree of regula-tory uncertainty, spokesmen for consumer groups and the general public have often com-plained of exploitation at the hands of monopoly or near-monopoly corporations.

A more general problem caused by the regulatory consequences of privatisation has been the difficulty in achieving forms of regulation which are both fair to the privatised undertakings and acceptable to the general public. This has been a difficult balance to achieve, not least because the action of the regulators has often seemed to be both arbitrary and capri-cious. However, one principle is already clear: the more genuine competition there is in a particular sector, the less need there ought to be for elaborate regulation. This is because real competition should ensure that most customer requirements are met at the lowest cost con-sistent with the need to make sufficient profit to pay the employees, reward the sharehold-ers and finance future investment. However, as long as explicit regulatory arrangements are necessary, it seems likely that we shall find the four following characteristics in such regu-lation. (1) It should be cost-effective and not too burdensome for the privatised undertak-ings concerned. (2) It should involve the least and simplest restrictions upon the commercial freedom of the industries consistent with adequate protection of the consumer and public interest. (3) It should bring benefits to consumers which outweigh the compliance costs upon the industries, since these costs will tend to be passed on in prices especially in monopolis-

Figure 15.3 The new regulatory framework

Establishment Date	Body	Statutory Basis
1984	Office of Telecommunications	Telecomunications Act 1984
1985	Secuirities & Investment Board	Financial Services Act 1986
1986	Office of Gas Supply	Gas Act 1986
1989	Office of Electricity Regulations	Electricity Act 1989
1989	Office of Electricity Regulation Scotland	Electricity Act 1989
1991	Radio Authority	Broadcasting Act 1990
1992	Independent Television Commission	Broadcasting Act 1990
1992	Office of Electricity Regulation N. Ireland	Electricity (N. Ireland) Order 1992
1992	Office for Standards in Education	Education (School) Act 1992.
1993	Office of the Rail Regulation	Railways Act 1993

tic markets. (4) As far as possible, it should be imposed in ways which do not make it vulnerable to 'agency capture' – that is, the situation which exists when the regulator becomes the servant rather than the master of the undertakings which are regulated.

A final and politically significant consequence of the drive to privatisation in Britain in the 1980s and 1990s has been the development of more legalistic and contractual relationships between the private sector and the state. This has been brought about by a combination of market-led developments (notably in the financial services sector) and political necessity, which has meant that a liberalising Government has sometimes been damaged by the behaviour of its friends and supporters who have appeared to benefit disproportionately from privatisation at the expense of employees, consumers and the wider public. Conservative Ministers have responded by strengthening the established regulatory bodies, such as the Office of Fair Trading and the Monopolies and Mergers Commission; and by creating new regulatory bodies, such as the Office of Telecommunications and the Securities and Investment Board. What this has amounted to over the past decade or more is that the state and its agencies have largely withdrawn from their previous combined roles as producers, purchasers and regulators to a more limited position of informed purchasing and independent regulation. In short, there has been a purchaser-provider split and a shift from trust to contract as the basis for ensuring continued provision of essential public goods and services.

15.4 Non-Departmental public bodies

In a chapter on the public sector in Britain we have to examine many more forms of institution than simply the public corporations. This is because there has been a significant growth of other public sector bodies which are neither an integral part of central Government nor an integral part of local government, but which nevertheless are clearly located within the public sector. These bodies have been variously described at different times as 'non-departmental public bodies' (NDPBs), 'quasi-autonomous non-governmental organisations' (QUANGOs), or simply 'extra-governmental organisations' (EGOs). No matter what the subtle differences in nomenclature, it is possible to recognise these institutions when one sees them. Furthermore, they require investigation and analysis, because they have become a matter of considerable media interest and political controversy under both Labour and Conservative Governments in Britain.

In one of the earliest official surveys of this part of the public sector, Geoffrey Bowen identified 252 non-Departmental public bodies which he defined as 'organisations which have been set up or adopted by Departments and provided with public funds to perform some function which the Government wishes to have performed, but which it does not wish to be the direct responsibility of a Minister or a Department'.[9] They were generally divided into three categories: executive bodies, advisory bodies, and administrative Tribunals. They therefore included a wide range of very different institutions exemplified by the British Library, the Equal Opportunities Commission, the Gaming Board, Trinity House, the Wales Tourist Board, the White Fish Authority, and the Supplementary Benefits Appeals Tribunals.

When this varied part of the public sector was reviewed again in the 1980 Pliatzky Report, it appeared that the number of such institutions had grown to 2167, they employed about 217,000 people and were responsible for a range of activities costing about £6150 million in all.[10] By April 1988, following a deliberate cull of such institutions by Conservative Ministers, the total number had apparently fallen to 1648, of which 1066 were advisory bodies, 390 were executive bodies and 65 were administrative Tribunals. This lower figure represented the net position after taking account of the 417 new bodies which had been created and the 937 old bodies which had been abolished since 1979. Most of the net reduction took place between 1979 and 1983 when the QUANGO hunt was at its peak. Since that time the enthusiasm of Conservative Ministers for this particular sport seems to have waned with the result that, according to a study published in 1994 by Democratic Audit and Charter 88 Trust, there were 5521 'extra-governmental organisations' responsible for £47,000 million of public spending in 1992-93 and providing at least 65,000 jobs directly or indirectly in the gift of Ministers.[11] As Figure 15.4 shows, this provides extensive Ministerial patronage.

Common characteristics

On closer inspection it becomes clear that these various public bodies have a number of common characteristics. (1) They derive their existence from Ministerial decisions and can be answerable to Ministers for what they do or fail to do. (2) Their creation normally requires legislative approval by Parliament and most of them produce annual reports which have to be laid before Parliament and can be debated there. (3) They are usually financed by Exchequer grants, but may sometimes be given the power to raise their own statutory levies. (4) Each Chairman and Board are appointed by a Minister for a fixed term of office and can be dismissed or reappointed by a Minister at the end of such a term. (5) Such bodies recruit their own staff (who do not usually have the status of civil servants), although their pay and conditions are often comparable with those of the civil service. (6) The annual accounts of such bodies are audited either commercially or by the National Audit Commission which means that high standards of financial accountability ought to be achieved. In short, they represent an identifiable and growing sub-species of public administration in Britain.

Advantages and disadvantages

Those who have investigated this opaque area of the public sector have identified a number of advantages and disadvantages in the existence of such bodies. At the outset it must be said that the advantages usually seem more obvious to the supporters of the Government of the day, whilst the disadvantages usually seem more obvious to its opponents. This is mainly because the public appointments concerned are made by the party in office for what are usually considered by its supporters to be good reasons.

On the positive side, the following points can be made for non-departmental public bodies. (1) They permit certain activities of importance to the state to be conducted outside the confines of Government Departments, yet within the Whitehall sphere of influence. (2) They permit such activities to be conducted free from direct or frequent oversight by Parliament and therefore to some extent insulated from the party battle at Westminster. (3) They enable Parliament to pass what is essentially framework legislation in some areas of public administration with the confidence that any problems which may arise can be solved in a practical manner. (4) They make it easier to achieve a broad continu-

Figure 15.4 The network of ministerial patronage

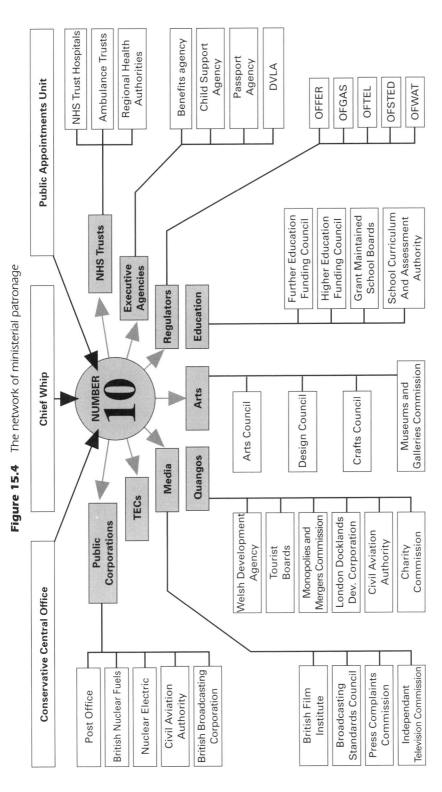

ity of policy in a largely apolitical way. (5) They relieve civil servants of many tiresome administrative chores and so enable the Departments of central Government to concentrate more on policy advice and financial control. (6) They provide useful opportunities for the dispensing of political patronage by the party in office.

On the negative side, the following points can be made against non-departmental public bodies. (1) There has been a lack of clarity or agreement about just how many such bodies there really are at any time and whether all those which have been identified by some as being in this category have been correctly categorised. (2) The growth of such bodies has produced an institutional proliferation which has proved expensive to administer and difficult to supervise and control. (3) The large number of appointments to such bodies has provided too much scope for political patronage on a scale which has been politically and ethically undesirable. (4) There has been a lack of effective democratic control over these bodies and a parallel lack of financial control over the public funds which are spent by them. In short, they have been seen by their critics as a 'new magistracy' which has involved the steady replacement of elected local government with appointed local administration in a country which used to be able to pride itself upon its institutional and political pluralism.

In January 1988 Margaret Thatcher announced to Parliament the results of a comprehensive review of NDPBs and made it clear that such bodies would be subjected to further review at least every five years.[12] She told the House of Commons that such reviews would consider whether or not there was a need for each and every body, how well or badly it was fulfilling its objectives, and whether or not its financial and other management systems were adequate. Since that time this category of public administration has grown considerably. Grant Maintained Schools, NHS Trusts, Further Education Colleges, Training and Enterprise Councils, Urban Development Corporations – all these and many more institutions could be said to have joined the category as Conservative Ministers have taken a range of powers and responsibilities away from elected local government.

The main criticism of these developments in the academic and political worlds has been that such bodies are not subject to the control of locally elected politicians (or indeed Members of Parliament) and that what they spend is not adequately audited at national level (only one third of all NDPBs have their financial affairs scrutinised by the Audit Commission or the National Audit Office). On the other hand, Ministers in the Major Government have argued the merits of direct accountability to those whom they describe as 'the customers' of NDPBs. As William Waldegrave put it when he was the Minister responsible for the public service, the issue is 'not whether those who run our public services are elected, but whether they are . . . consumer responsive'.[13] This definition of 'public accountability' stems from two strong feelings held by the Conservatives under both Margaret Thatcher and John Major: the desire to by-pass what they have seen as the unreasonably obstructive attitudes of many Labour and Liberal Democrat controlled local authorities, and the wish to improve the performance of the public sector by setting higher standards for the public services under the rubric of the Citizens Charter. This means that the political parties in Britain now espouse contrasting definitions of public accountability. The Opposition parties put the accent upon the traditional definition in Britain which stresses *upward* accountability to the elected representatives of the people at national and local level, whereas the Conservatives put the accent upon their new definition which stresses the *downward* accountability directly to the people themselves in their various roles as consumers, users, customers or beneficiaries of the goods and services delivered at the behest of the state.

15.5 Other public bodies

In considering the remainder of the public sector in Britain, we shall refer briefly to Royal Commissions and Committees of Inquiry, as well as the myriad of advisory committees to be found within the orbit of British central Government. We shall also describe the special purpose authorities, such as the Health Authorities and the Water Authorities, which have been either abolished or privatised by the Conservatives but which could be recreated by a future Labour Government.

Royal Commissions and Committees of Inquiry

The appointment of a Royal Commission or Committee of Inquiry is an act of the Executive which requires no prior Parliamentary approval, although it is often a Ministerial response to political pressures. As Lord Benson and Lord Rothschild put it in an article some time ago, the purposes of such bodies are 'first to ascertain all the relevant facts, next to assemble them fairly and impartially, and finally to form balanced conclusions'.[14] Once established, bodies of this kind usually invite written and oral evidence from all interested parties both inside and outside the web of central Government. They may also undertake or sponsor research of their own in order to get a clearer understanding of the issues which they have to investigate. When their work is complete, they normally publish both their reports and records of the evidence submitted to them as a contribution to subsequent debate in Parliament and in public. Only when dealing with matters of national security or commercial confidentiality are such reports published with certain omissions and, very occasionally, a decision may be taken by Ministers not to publish at all.

Over the period 1954-69 which was reviewed by Lord Benson and Lord Rothschild, 24 Royal Commissions and more than 600 Committees of Inquiry were established. Most of them were disbanded when their tasks were complete, although a few were allowed to continue as Standing Commissions or Committees on a permanent basis – for example, the Royal Commission on Environmental Pollution or the Law Commission. Among the most significant Royal Commissions or Committees of Inquiry in more recent times have been the Kilbrandon Commission on the Constitution (1969-73), the Bullock Committee on Industrial Democracy (1975-77), the Wilson Committee on Financial Institutions (1977-80), the Scarman Committee on the Brixton Disorders (1981), and the Banham Commission on Local Government Boundaries (1991-94). When such bodies have reported, it has been for Ministers to decide what to do about their recommendations. Sometimes this has led to administrative action, sometimes to new legislation. In many cases, however, it has been used as little more than a convenient device for deflecting criticism, defusing controversy or simply putting off difficult decisions on issues about which there may be little or no political agreement. Sometimes it has been used as a way of burying issues altogether, which is why Margaret Thatcher and other self-styled 'conviction politicians' have usually eschewed this institutional device. However, the more pragmatic John Major has been better disposed than his predecessor to the use of such bodies and at the time of writing although only one Royal Commission had been set up[15] (as Figure 15.5 shows) a total of 61 Committees of Inquiry had been established during his time at 10 Downing Street, including the Scott Inquiry into the Matrix-Churchill Affair in 1992 and the Nolan Committee on Standards in Public Life in 1994.

Figure 15.5 Departmental Committees of Inquiry November 1990–May 1995

Dept	Committee	Established	Chairman
MAFF	Advisory Committee on Flood and Coastal Defence Research and Development	December 1990	Mr P Ackers
MAFF	Expert Group on Animal Feeding-stuffs	February 1991	Prof. G E Lamming
MAFF	Committee on Sea Level and Wave Recording	February 1991	Mr M J Tucker
MAFF	Committee on the Ethics of Genetic Modification and Food Use	September 1992	Reverend Dr J C Polkinghorne FRS
MAFF	Review of the Hygiene and Structural Requirements in a Sample of Slaughterhouse which have applied for temporary derogations under the Fresh Meat (Hygiene and Inspection) Regulations 1992	October 1992	Dr A M Johnston Mr B J Spurr
MAFF	Committee to Review Fertility Aspects of Sewage Sludge Application to Agricultural Land.	January 1993	Prof. A D Bradshaw
MAFF	Ad Hoc Committee to consider the Ethical Implications of Emerging Technologies in the Breeding of Farm Animals.	May 1993	Prof. Michael Banner
Attorney General	Possible merger of SFO with CPS	July 1994	Rex Davie
MOD	MOD Policy Study	December 1993	Sir John Blelloch
MOD	Independent Review of Armed Forces' Manpower, Career and Remuneration Structures	April 1994	Michael Bett
MOD	Review of Representational Entertainment in the Armed Forces	October 1994	Sir Peter Cazalet
DFE	Review of the Further Education Unit and Further Education Staff College	January 1993	Ken Young CBE
DFE	Review of the National Curriculum and Assessment Framework	April 1993	Sir Ron Dearing

Figure 15.5 continued

Dept	Committee	Established	Chairman
DFE	A short study to investigate the potential of emerging technologies to improve the effectiveness of the learning process for pupils of statutory school age.	January 1995	Peter Seaborne
DFE	Review of the 16–19 Qualifications Framework	April 1995	Sir Ron Dearing
DOE	Inquiry into the Rating of Plant and Machinery	June 1991	Derek Wood QC
DOE	Enquiry into the Planning System in North Cornwall District	August 1992	Miss Audrey M Lees
DOE	Task Force on Government Departments' Empty Houses	December 1992	John Baker
DOE	Inquiry into the Investment arrangements of the National Rivers Authority	March 1993	Sir Michael Kerry
DOE	Review of the Procurement and Contracting in the Construction Industry	July 1993	Sir Michael Latham
DoH	Committee of Enquiry into Complaints about Ashworth Hospital	April 1991	Sir Louis Blom-Cooper
DoH	Fundamental Review of the Existing System of Remuneration of General Dental Practitioners	July 1992	Sir Kenneth Bloomfield KCB
DoH	Panel of persons appointed under the Medicines Act 1968 to hear company representations on the proposed revocations of the product licences for Halcion/Triazolam.	January 1993	Miss Diana Cotton QC
DoH	The Allitt Enquiry	May 1993	Sir Cecil Clothier
DoH	Review of NHS Complaints Procedures	June 1993	Prof. Alan Wilson
DoH	Advisory Group on Osteoporosis	November 1993	Prof. P J Barlow
DoH	Task Force to Review Services for Drug Misusers	May 1994	Reverend Dr John Polkinghorne FRS
DoH	Expert Group to Investigate Cot Death Theories	November 1994	Lay Sylvia Limerick
HO	Enquiry into Police Rewards and Responsibilities	July 1992	Sir Patrick Sheehy

Figure 15.5 continued

Dept	Committee	Established	Chairman
HO	Enquiry into the Escape of IRA Prisoners from Whitemoor Jail	September 1994	Sir John Woodcock
HO	Enquiry into Prison Security	December 1994	Sir John Learmont
LCD	An Inquiry into t Access to Civil Justice	March 1994	Conducted by Lord
DNH	Review of press Self-Regulation	July 1992	Conducted by Sir David Calcutt QC
DNH	Fire protection measures for the Royal Palaces	January 1993	Sir Alan Bailey
NI	Taxi Industry	November 1991	Mr R Stirling
NI	Operational Policy in Belfast Prison from Management of Paramilitary Prisoners	December 1991	Viscount Colville of Culrose QC
NI	Overtime Inquiry	January 1993	Sir John Blelloch
NI	Northern Ireland Energy Efficiency Action Group	March 1993	Dr William J McCourt
NI	Stormont Fire and Safety in Crown Buildings	January 1995	Sir Reginald Doyle
OPSS	Expert Working Group on Human Genome Research	February 1993	Prof. Kay E Davies
OPSS	Review of UK Microbial Culture Collections	January 1994	Prof. Roger Whittenbury CBE
OPSS	Committee to Review the Contribution of Scientists and Engineers to the Public Understanding of Science, Engineering and Technology	January 1995	Sir Arnold Wolfendale FRS
PM	Committee on Standards in Public Life	October 1994	Lord Nolan
SO	Committee to review Curriculum and Examination in the Fifth and Sixth years in Secondary Education in Scotland	March 1990	Prof. John M Howie CBE
SO	The Cairngorms Working Party	March 1991	Magnus Magnusson KBE
SO	The Loch Lomond and Trossachs Working Party	November 1991	Sir Peter Hutchinson Bt CBE
SO	Committee to review Initial Training of Further Education College Lecturers	May 1992	Prof. Janette Anderson

Figure 15.5 continued

Dept	Committee	Established	Chairman
SO	Inquiry into Cervical Cytopathology at Inverclyde Royal Hospital, Greenock	April 1993	Dr Euphemia McGoogan
DSS	The Pension Law Review Committee	June 1992	Prof. Roy Goode
DTI	Coal Task Force	November 1990	Dr Eoin Lees
DTI	Renewable Energy Advisory Group	September 1991	Dr Martin Holdgate
DTI	Radio Spectrum Review Committee Stage 3: 28–4760 Mhz	July 1992	Sir Colin Fielding CB
DTI	Inquiry into the Export of Defence Equipment and Dual-Use Goods to Iraq 1984–90	November 1992	Sir Richard Scott
DTp	Review of London Underground Limited's response to fires and other emergencies	September 1991	Dr Brian Appleton
DTp	Inquiry into river safety	December 1991	John W Hayes
DTp	Inquiry into the prevention of pollution from merchant shipping	January 1993	Lord Donaldson
DTp	Assessment of what further work should be undertaken to identify the cause of the sinking of the MV Derbyshire	March 1995	Lord Donaldson
DTp	Review of Coastguard actions during and after the Lyme Bay canoe tragedy	May 1995	John Reeder QC
DTp	Study into aircraft noise mitigation measures at Redhill Aerodrome and Wycombe Air Park.	November 1990	A J O'Connor
HMT	Inquiry into the Supervision of the Bank of Credit and Commerce International	July 1991	Rt Hon Lord Justice Bingham
HMT	Report on the role and functions of the Securities and Investments Board	July 1992	Andrew Large

Source: *Hansard*, Written Answer, 25 May 1995

Departmental Advisory Committees

As for the many advisory committees which assist Whitehall Department in the course of day-to-day public administration, these provide a clear illustration of the extent to which regular consultations with acknowledged experts and interested groups, whether formal or informal, have become a notable characteristic of British central Government.

As we saw in Chapter 6, such advisory committees can meet the needs of Whitehall Departments for expert information and advice, while satisfying the claims of sectional interest groups for access to central Government and influence upon policy making. They also provide one more means by which any Government can seek to gain and retain the consent of the governed – at any rate those who may be most directly affected by the consequences of a given Government policy.

Such advisory committees are particularly useful to Whitehall Department in the detailed preparation of secondary legislation and technical Statutory Instruments. The need for this advice arises because many Acts of Parliament put statutory responsibilities upon Ministers to consult certain specified advisory bodies when drawing up subsequent secondary legislation. For example, under the 1964 Police Act the Home Secretary was obliged to consult the Police Council which had been set up specifically to advise on regulations concerning the administration and conditions of service in police forces throughout the country. Equally, under the 1975 Social Security Act the Secretary of State for Social Security was obliged to consult the National Insurance Advisory Committee on all regulations issued in relation to National Insurance.

There have also been examples of such detailed consultations which have taken place on a non-statutory basis over the years – for example, within the framework of the National Economic Development Council (NEDC) from its inception in 1962 to its abolition in 1992. During its heyday this provided a useful forum for regular meetings between the Government of the day (represented mainly by Ministers) and what were known at the time as 'the two sides of industry', namely employers and trade unions. However, with the considerable change in the political climate on industrial policy during the Thatcherite years, Ministers saw less and less need for the NEDC and associated it increasingly in their minds with the corporatist politics of the 1960s and 1970s. Of course, Ministerial attitudes to such consultations may well change under a future Labour Government, since the Labour Party is strongly committed to 'industrial partnership' and favourably impressed by the more collectivist models of government still in fashion on the Continent of Europe.

Special Purpose Authorities

Until the privatisation of the water industry in the late 1980s, there were 10 *Water Authorities* in England and Wales (and separate ones in Scotland and Northern Ireland) responsible in the public sector for about three quarters of the water supply, water treatment and sewerage services. The remaining water services were provided by smaller private water companies which had been in existence for a long time in some parts of the country. The Water Authorities provided a good example of special purpose authorities in the public sector, since they had been established in 1974 by Act of Parliament with clear statutory duties to provide comprehensive water services within hydrologically determined geographical areas.

For many years *Health Authorities* provided another good example of special purpose Authorities. Their institutional structure was originally determined by the post-war Labour Government under the terms of the 1948 National Health Service Act. They were essentially unchanged for a quarter of a century, but then reorganised in 1974, 1982 and again in 1993 following the Conservative Government's far-reaching health service reforms in the early 1990s. The current outcome of this period of institutional upheaval is that in England the structure of the National Health Service is capped by the National Management Board led by a Chief Executive responsible to the Secretary of State for Health. Below the National Board there are currently 8 Regional Health Authorities, although these are being abolished under current legislation going through Parliament. This will leave 206 District Health Authorities as the main bodies responsible for managing and purchasing health care at the local level. Unlike the situation before the 1990 health service reform, health care is now provided (largely under contracts) by GPs working in primary practice, hospitals organised as NHS Trusts, and some other specialist facilities (including a few private ones). Together with the so-called NHS Outposts of the Department of Health in the various parts of the country and the few remaining special purpose Authorities (such as the Health Education Authority), these institutions make up the managerial, purchasing and regulatory structure of the National Health Service in England. Separate, but similar arrangements have been made in Wales and Scotland, while Northern Ireland remains an exception with Health Boards answerable directly to a Minister in the Northern Ireland Office.

Under the aegis of the 1990 Health Service Reform Act the organisation of the NHS has therefore been radically transformed for the first time since its creation in the late 1940s. A clear distinction has been drawn between those responsible for *purchasing* health services on behalf of their local communities – that is, the District Health Authorities and Family Health Service Authorities (which oversee the primary health care provided by GPs) – and those responsible for *providing* the services – for example, the NHS Trusts, private hospitals and other specialist facilities. In primary care, a controversial distinction has been drawn between the growing proportion of GPs who have become so-called 'fund holders' with the freedom to use their practice budgets to purchase specialist, acute or primary health care for their patients from wherever they deem most appropriate, and all the others (currently about 50 per cent of all GPs) who remain tied to the services provided within their areas according to the priorities set by their District Health Authorities and Family Health Service Authorities. It remains to be seen whether or not this internal market in the NHS will be better for patients and their families than the traditional command model which it replaced. The critics of this reform claim that it has produced an excessively bureaucratic and more inequitable health service. The proponents of the reform argue that the new system is delivering better value for money and hence a lower burden upon taxpayers than would otherwise have been the case. If Labour is returned to office at the next General Election, it seems clear that local Councillors will be given a greater role on health Authorities (as they had before 1982) and that the development of the internal market may be halted or even put into reverse.[16]

15.6 Prospects for the public sector

None of the familiar problems of the public sector in Britain has been made any easier to understand or solve by the various myths which have permeated the political debate over the years. There has been the myth that in dealing with public corporations it is possible to draw a clear and convincing distinction between political and commercial issues. There has been the myth that these hybrid institutions can act both in the public interest and as profit-maximising commercial undertakings. There has been the myth that there can be either full Ministerial control or complete managerial autonomy for these institutions.

All of these mythical ideas, and many more, have damaged both the image and the performance of the public corporations, and have contributed to the demise of many of them.

The reality, of course, has been rather different. It is that all British Governments since the war have been doomed to relations of inherent ambiguity with public corporations and, to a lesser extent, with all the other institutions in the public sector as well. This was certainly true during the period before 1979 when Ministers in all Governments felt inhibited from moving either decisively towards tighter political control or decisively towards extensive privatisation of the public sector institutions. In so far as many of the problems of dealing with the public sector have diminished since the mid-1980s, this is because since then Conservative Ministers have taken the policy of privatisation about as far as it can go in a modern mixed economy. Yet this very radicalism has produced other problems of regulation, equity and accountability which are proving almost as difficult to deal with now that so many public corporations have been privatised.

Signposts to the future

Against this background of extensive privatisation, it is difficult to be sure and unwise to be dogmatic about the future of the public sector in Britain. Although the Conservatives have been strongly committed to privatisation for a decade or more, they now seem to have doubts about taking the policy much further. On the other hand, Labour politicians seem very wary of committing themselves to renationalise industries which have been privatised, partly because they are worried about the image which such a stance would project to the electorate and partly because the implementation of such a policy in Government could be both expensive and unpopular at a time when there would probably be other more urgent priorities for public expenditure. With the outlook of the two main parties perhaps tending to converge towards a new middle ground, it is possible only to suggest a few signposts to the future.

Firstly, it would seem that in the mixed economy of modern Britain there are certain goods and services which may be more suitably provided by public sector institutions if they are to be provided at all, such as loss-making postal services for outlying areas of the country or uneconomic commuter and rural rail services. Yet recent developments in Conservative policy suggest that Ministers believe that even in these cases it ought to be possible for private providers to compete on the basis of the lowest possible rate of subsidy from the public purse. According to this radical view, as long as the safety and quality of such services can by guaranteed by strict and effective regulation, then there is no reason why almost any public service should not be provided by the private sector in this way.

Secondly, there will usually be compelling considerations of national policy and national interest which make it virtually essential that the public sector should take charge of certain large and risky high technology projects, such as civil nuclear power, since it is difficult or impossible for the private sector to raise the necessary capital or secure the necessary insurance cover for its public liabilities. Nevertheless, even assumptions of this kind have been challenged in the 1990s not only by the so-called private finance initiative within the public sector whereby both the profits and the risks of certain capital projects are shouldered by the private sector, but also by the impending privatisation of civil nuclear power.

Thirdly, there will continue to be a good deal of political argument about how far it may be possible to apply private sector managerial techniques and accounting conventions to the core state activities which seem almost certain to remain within the public sector. Such issues have already been addressed via the processes of compulsory competitive tendering, market testing and resource accounting – all of which have been substantially piloted in the civil service. Yet the debate will continue about whether public goods and services really ought to be provided by the residual public sector as a point of political principle, or whether even this shibboleth can be safely discarded as long as public goods and services can be more cost-effectively and satisfactorily provided by the private sector within a framework of rigorous public sector regulation. When public services are inherently more of a gift relationship than a commercial transaction – for example, in the case of state education or the National Health Service – then they will almost certainly have to remain within the public sector as public goods. In such cases the services concerned are likely to remain largely free at the point of use, although there will be continuing political and public debate about how much of these 'free goods' can be afforded at any time. Core public services and the drive for a more commercial approach within the public sector have been difficult or impossible to reconcile in the past, but there is some reason to suppose that this dilemma may be easier to deal with in future.

15.7 Conclusion

In this chapter we have seen that the most notable characteristics of the public sector in Britain have been its remarkable size and diversity, as well as the fierce political argument which has raged over its scope and obligations. Such problems have been seen in sharpest relief in the chequered history of public corporations, but the rest of the public sector has not proved much easier to manage or control.

In political and constitutional terms, the public sector has posed problems for Governments of the Left and the Right alike. For example, the original Morrisonian model of the public corporation did not in the long run prove to be a satisfactory means of delivering public goods and services in both a cost-effective and a democratically accountable way. In the end few people derived much real benefit from such hybrid institutions, except perhaps the unionised employees of the nationalised industries in their heyday and the civil servants in the sponsoring Departments. Everyone else seems to have been frustrated or thwarted by public corporations, including notably their private sector competitors and the Ministers who were supposedly held to account for their actions. There was seldom sufficient trust between Ministers and the managers of public corporations; continuity of policy was prejudiced by the incessant party political conflict over the scope and the ground-rules of the public sector; and the holy grail of real public accountability seems to have eluded every attempt to achieve it.

It is not surprising, therefore, that since 1979 the Conservatives have been determined to reduce the size and burdens of the public sector through their policy of privatisation, and that the modern Labour party under Tony Blair has wanted at least to redefine, if not to abandon, its previous commitment to nationalisation and public ownership. In such fluid political conditions it is not possible to forecast the eventual outcome of these developments. Yet in the mid-1990s it seems distinctly possible that the main political parties may converge upon a new zone of political consensus which supports the idea of a public sector much smaller but more effective than the traditional model in Britain.

Suggested questions

1 Assess the contribution of public corporations in Britain since 1945.
2 Has privatisation changed everything?
3 To what extent should we be concerned by the 'new magistracy' of unelected government in Britain?

Notes

1. See *National Income and Expenditure* 1983, Tables 1.10 and 10.3; and *Economic Trends*, February 1983, Appendix 1, Table 1.
2. For example, in 1982 public sector purchases from the private sector amounted to about £9000 million, while public sector sales to the private sector amounted to about £11,000 million.
3. These generalisations refer essentially to the nationalised industries and not to all public corporations, some of which – such as the BBC created by Royal Charter in 1926 – were established for very different purposes.
4. See *Privatisation 1979-94* (London: CPC, 1994).
5. Examples have included efficiency audits of the London letter post, the Severn–Trent Water Authority, the Central Electricity Generating Board, and British Rail commuter services in London and the South East.
6. See the Report of the Committee on the financing of the BBC, Cmnd 9824 (London: HMSO, 1986).
7. See C. Veljanovsky, *Selling the State* (London: Weidenfeld & Nicolson, 1987), for further elaboration of this argument.
8. For example, in J. Moore, *Privatisation in the UK* (London: Aims of Industry, 1986).
9. G. Bowen, *Survey of Fringe Bodies* (London: Civil Service Department, 1978).
10. See L. Pliatzky, *Report on Non-Departmental Public Bodies*, Cmnd 7797 (London: HMSO, 1980).
11. See S. Weir and W. Hall (eds), *Extra-Governmental Organisations in the United Kingdom* (London: Charter 88 Trust, 1994); also *Independent on Sunday*, 30 January 1994, on the subject of QUANGOs.
12. *Hansard*, 28 January 1988, Cols 313-314.
13. Quoted in *Independent on Sunday*, 22 May 1994.
14. Lord Benson and Lord Rothschild, 'Royal Commissions, a memorial', *Public Administration*, Autumn 1982.
15. The single Royal Commission was on Criminal Justice and was chaired by Lord Runciman.
16. Over the period 1990–93 the Conservative reforms of the NHS produced a 10 per cent increase in the number of clerical and administrative staff, but more than a doubling in the number of general and senior managers, from 9700 to 20,000.

Further reading

Asher, K., *The Politics of Privatisation* (London: Macmillan Education, 1987).
Glynn, J., *Public Sector Financial Control and Accounting* (Oxford: Blackwell, 1987).

Pirie, M., *Privatisation – theory, practice and choice* (London: Wildwood, 1988).

Plummer, J., *The Governance Gap – QUANGOs and accountability* (London: Demos, 1994).

Prosser, T., *Nationalised Industries and Public Control* (Oxford: Blackwell, 1986).

Pryke, R., *The Nationalised Industries – policies and performance since 1968* (Oxford: Martin Robertson, 1981).

Redwood, J., *Popular Capitalism* (London: Routledge, 1988).

Ridley, F. F. and Wilson, D. (eds), *The Quango Debate* (London: Oxford University Press, 1995).

Veljanovsky, C., *Selling the State* (London: Weidenfeld & Nicolson, 1987).

Weir, S. and Hallfield, W., *Ego Trip – extra governmental organisations in the UK* (London: Charter 88, 1994).

White paper on 'The Citizen's Charter', Cmnd 1599 (London: HMSO, July 1991).

16 Local Government

The United Kingdom is a unitary, multi-national state. Consequently, all political authority is ultimately centralised. Constituencies in all the component parts of the United Kingdom – England, Scotland, Wales, and Northern Ireland – send representatives to the national Parliament at Westminster. Even within the nations and regions of the country, the words 'local government' are a somewhat misleading term used to describe what has become largely the implementation and delivery of national policies under the guidance of locally elected Councillors. Local authorities (another term for the units of local government in the United Kingdom) do not have any real autonomy and are constitutionally subordinate to Parliament at Westminster. What they can and cannot do is specified in Acts of Parliament (as interpreted by the Courts), which means that Parliament at Westminster can both create and abolish local authority powers and, indeed, local authorities themselves.

It is, therefore, important to distinguish at the outset between *local government*, which can be defined simply as directly elected local authorities, and *local administration*, which includes the regional and local offices of central Government and its Agencies (see Chapter 14) and the local administration of justice (see Chapter 17). The focus in this chapter is upon directly elected local authorities – in other words, primary local government.

16.1 Structure and personnel

The structure of local government is different in the different parts of the United Kingdom. It is represented diagrammatically in Figure 16.1

England and Wales

The structure of local government in England and Wales was reformed by the 1972 Local Government Act which came into effect in 1974. It reduced the previous mosaic of about 1400 local authorities to six large Metropolitan Councils (outside Greater London, which had been created as a single Authority by the 1963 Greater London Act), 47 County

Figure 16.1 *The structure of local government*

England (outside London)
35 County Councils
14 Non-Metropolitan Unitary Councils
36 Metropolitan District Councils
274 Non-Metropolitan District Councils

London
32 London Boroughs
The City of London

Scotland
29 Single-tier Authorities
3 Unitary Island Councils

Wales
22 Single-tier Authorities

Northern Ireland
26 District Councils

Councils (for example, Devon, Kent, Norfolk, Dyfed), 36 Metropolitan District Councils (of which the largest was Birmingham with a population of more than one million), and 333 County District Councils (representing areas with local populations ranging from 60,000 to 100,000 in most cases). Thus a total of about 420 local authorities replaced the previous 1400 or so, and the interdependence of town and country became the guiding principle of the structure of local government.

At the most local level, the former *Parish Councils* were retained and their powers were increased, although to a limited extent. About 300 former Urban Districts and small Boroughs became Parish Councils. Parishes of more than 200 inhabitants were required to elect a Council, whereas those with fewer inhabitants than this were encouraged to practise the direct democracy of parish meetings.

The Greater London Council and the six other Metropolitan Counties were abolished by Acts of Parliament in 1984 and 1985 which came into effect on 1 April 1986. This meant that the large conurbations – namely Greater Manchester, Merseyside, South Yorkshire, Tyne and Wear, West Midlands, and West Yorkshire – no longer had any democratic representation at that level of local government. The functions of the Metropolitan Counties were reallocated to the Borough and District Councils, statutory joint boards and other unelected public bodies. The abolition of these upper-tier authorities was intended to remove a source of bitter conflict with central Government, save money after incurring some transitional costs, and provide a simpler and more accountable structure of local government in the large Metropolitan areas.

The Local Government Act of 1992 created a new Local Government Commission, under the chairmanship of Sir John Banham, to review local government structures and boundaries in England. Its task was to tour the country examining the structures of local government in the different localities. The intention was that its resulting recommendations would lead to Parliamentary legislation designed to make a wide variety of structural changes (or no changes at all) according to the strength and direction of local representations. In this process there was to be no single model of local government reform for England, although Ministerial guidance in Circulars from the Department of the Environment indicated a general preference for the abolition of the Counties and the introduction of sizeable unitary authorities based upon enlarged Districts. Early in March, 1995 Sir John Banham resigned after the Environment Secretary, John Gummer, announced that he would not accept many of the Commission's recommendations. None the less, a number – 14 – of Unitary Authorities were introduced in time for the May 1995 Local Government Elections – for example in Bristol, the Isle of Wight, Middlesborough and Hull – taking over their responsibilities in April 1996.

In Wales, the Secretary of State took direct responsibility for reorganisation, and in March 1993 a White Paper was issued which proposed 21 unitary authorities. In fact 22 single-tier Authorities were created in time for elections in May 1995, with the resulting Councils taking over their responsibilities in April 1996.

Scotland

Until 1995 the structure of local government in Scotland was determined by the 1973 Local Government (Scotland) Act which came into effect in 1975. This involved the creation of nine Regional Councils (with populations ranging from about 2,500,000 in Strathclyde to fewer than 100,000 in The Borders) and 53 District Councils within the regions. The division of functions between the two levels of local government was in many ways similar to that in England and Wales. The structure was also similar, except that the three island areas (Orkney, Shetland, and Western Isles) each became single, all-purpose local authorities.

As in Wales, the Secretary of State for Scotland has direct responsibility for the reorganisation of local government. In July 1993 a White Paper proposed reorganisation into single-tier Councils. These proposals - which were heavily criticised at the time because of what was said to be their arbitrary and politically inspired nature - were given statutory effect in the 1994 Local Government (Scotland) Act which created 29 single-tier Councils to go along with the three unitary Island Councils.

Northern Ireland

The present structure of local government in Northern Ireland was largely determined by the 1972 Local Government (Northern Ireland) Act which came into force in 1973. It created a single level of local government by establishing 26 District Councils based upon the main population centres in the Province. The Districts vary considerably in area and resources, with populations ranging from about 13,000 to about 350,000. Under a subsequent reorganisation of local government in 1977, which was precipitated by the way in which the Protestant majority had abused its position of local power, the District Councils were stripped of all but some minimal functions, such as street cleaning and sanitation, markets and abattoirs, and recreational facilities.

All the more important functions of local government in the Province are carried out either by central Boards under the Northern Ireland Office (dealing, for example, with housing, police, fire services and electricity supply) or by area Boards (dealing, for example, with health, personal social services, education and libraries) or directly by the Northern Ireland Office (town and country planning, water and sewerage services, roads and car parks, vehicle registration and licensing, for example). Although the local Councillors in Northern Ireland have severely circumscribed direct functions, they have some indirect influence when they sit as nominees on the various area Boards and some consultative influence when they hold formal discussions with Ministers and officials in the Northern Ireland Office.

There is currently no mechanism for revising the structure of local government in Northern Ireland, although given the nature of the situation in Northern Ireland it would be within the general ambit of the Secretary of State. As a result there is no reason to expect early changes. However, if the so-called 'peace process', involving London, Dublin and all political parties in Northern Ireland which have forsworn the use of violence, were to create the conditions for significant change in the government or status of the six Counties; then the structure of local government in Northern Ireland (and indeed, conceivably, in the whole of Ireland) could change.

Councillors and officials

The composition of local authorities in England and Wales can be summarised by saying that each Unitary Council has between 40 and 70 elected Councillors, each County Council has between 60 and 100 elected Councillors and each District Council has between 30 and 80 elected Councillors. In each case, Councillors are elected for fixed terms. At present those elected to the London Borough Councils, the Unitary Councils, the County Councils and the non-Metropolitan District Councils are elected every four years, whereas in 107 of the Non-Metropolitan District Councils and in the Metropolitan District Councils outside London one-third of the Councillors are elected every third year. For electoral purposes some of the Unitary Councils and all of the Counties are divided into single-member constituencies, whereas the District and London Boroughs and some Unitary Councils are divided into wards, each represented by between one and three Councillors, depending upon geographical area and population.

At every level of local government the Chairman of the Council is elected annually by fellow Councillors. In those Councils which are predominantly urban, the Chairman takes the honourary title of Mayor and presides in that capacity over the Council proceedings. However, the real power in all Councils is wielded by the leader of the majority party and, to a lesser extent, by the political chairmen of the key committees – for example, education, finance, environment and social services. Most Councils have a Policy and Resources Committee (or its equivalent) which normally includes the chairmen of all the main committees and acts as a sort of 'Cabinet' for the local authority. Councillors of all political persuasion usually serve on more than one committee and the membership of committees reflects the relative strengths of the political parties in the local authority concerned. Since many local authorities are politically dominated by one particular party, this usually means that the key committees are controlled by the majority party in the locality and are run in conformity with that party's political ideas and interests. However, in so-called 'hung Councils' in which no single party has an overall majority, political power – for example, the key committee chairmanships – is usually shared between two, or indeed more, parties.

Councillors are not much more representative of the general public than are Members of Parliament. To be eligible for election, however, they must live or work in the local authority area concerned. There is not a great deal of statistical evidence about their make-up and socio-economic characteristics. A survey conducted in 1964 revealed that only 12 per cent of Councillors were women, only 19 per cent were blue-collar workers, and the average age was 55 years.[1] In 1977 the Robinson Report confirmed that the general characteristics of Councillors had not changed very much, since at that time they were still predominantly male, middle-aged and middle-class, although the proportion of women had risen slightly to 17 per cent.[2]

Research into the characteristics and attitudes of Councillors carried out for the Widdicombe Committee in 1985 showed that fewer than one in five Councillors were women and that the majority of Councillors were still aged 55 or more.[3] However, with the exception of the English shires and the Welsh local authorities, all local authorities showed an increase in the number of Councillors aged 45 or less, with the most marked increases in London and Scotland. In general, Metropolitan Councillors have been getting younger on average, while Shire Councillors have retained their older age profile. Councillors had higher educational qualifications than the public as a whole and were more likely to have stayed on at school beyond the age of sixteen. Almost a quarter of the Councillors who took part in the survey had obtained a degree or higher qualification, compared with only 5 per cent of the general population and 12 per cent of the population aged 25-69 by 1995.

The Widdicombe Report also showed that in the period since the Robinson Report there had been an appreciable fall in the proportion of Councillors in paid employment – 60 per cent in 1985 compared with 72% in 1976. This fall was matched not by an increase in the number declaring themselves to be unemployed, but rather by an increase in the number defined as retired. Councillors were drawn from a much narrower range of occupational backgrounds than would be found in the population as a whole, with 41 per cent coming from professional or managerial backgrounds and only 5 per cent from semi-skilled or unskilled manual occupations. Of those Councillors in paid employment at the time of the survey, 36 per cent were employed in the public sector (exactly the same as the population as a whole at the time) and of those almost half were employed in local government, notably as teachers, lecturers, social workers or administrators. The practice of people being Councillors in one local authority while being employed as officials in another local authority caused some controversy and even hostility, especially among Conservatives in their attitude towards Labour-controlled local government. It was one of the things which the Widdicombe Committee was asked to examine and it led to the inclusion of a measure in the 1989 Local Government and Housing Act which enabled the Government to prohibit Council officials on salaries of more than £19,500 a year from standing for election in local government.

In 1994 a new study showed that there had been a steady increase in the proportion of women Councillors since Widdicombe, with women making up 25 per cent of Councillors. The study also showed that there had been a marked improvement in women Councillors' representation in leadership positions, with the proportion being virtually identical with those of men. Changes had also occurred in the educational background of Councillors, with a growth in graduates (to 28%) and a decline in the proportion of Councillors with no educational qualifications (to 18%). With regard to employment the study found that 58% of Councillors were in paid employment (32% in full-time work, 7% in part-time work and 19% self-employed), while 4% were unemployed, 31% were retired and 8% were not working for other reasons. In common with the Widdicombe findings, the 1994 study found that the majority of Councillors were employed in the private sector (63%) with only 37% in public sector employment. With regard to Councillor turnover, little had changed: 38% of the Councillors who took part in the survey had served for more than 10 years, compared with 35% reported by Widdicombe, while it found that Councillors spent on average 74 hours a month on Council business, exactly the same figure recorded by the Widdicombe survey.[4] (See Figure 16.2.)

Figure 16.2 *Average hours per month Councillors spent on Council duties*

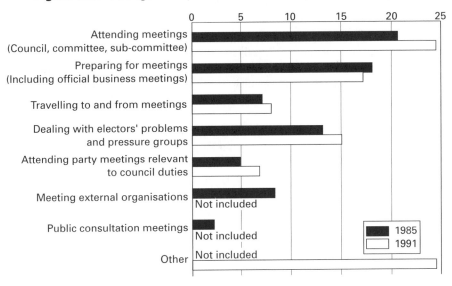

Source: *The Guardian,* 3 May 1994

Local authority officials are the other vital element in local government. In general, they assist Councillors in much the same way as civil servants assist Ministers, but there are some significant contrasts with the civil service, especially the fact that the key officials in local government are normally well-qualified professionals in the particular sphere of local government activity in which they are engaged. Thus Chief Education Officers and their senior colleagues are often former teachers, Directors of Social Services and their senior staff are often former social workers, and Chief Planning Officers and others within the planning department are often qualified planners, surveyors or architects. The key point is that Departments of local government are staffed by professionals and, as such, have a considerable influence upon the policy of their local authorities.

The main similarity between local government officials and civil servants in central Government is that both are expected to remain politically neutral and faithfully to carry out the policies of their political masters. In local government the principal effect of such political neutrality is that most policy decisions are heavily influenced by the technical and expert advice of the officials concerned. Of course, the decisions are always taken by the Councillors, but there can be occasions when they appear to be acting as little more than political spokesmen for the officials. On the other hand, there has also been some concern – especially in the Conservative Party – that some local government officials appear to be uncomfortably 'political' in their motivation and their actions, notably in Labour-controlled local authorities in inner city areas. Doubtless similar perceptions are held in the other direction by some of those strongly committed to the Labour Party when they look at the behaviour of local government officials in Conservative-controlled local areas. A balanced conclusion would seem to suggest that these things are largely in the eye of the beholder, although it should be added that both local and central Government seem to have gone through a particularly 'political' phase in the 1980s.

16.2 Powers and functions

The powers and functions of local government in England and Wales are set out in the relevant statutes, notably the 1972 Local Government Act. Such legislation specified the powers which are to be exercised by the various levels of local government, and there is a clear understanding that all powers which are not statutorily designated for local authorities remain the preserve of central Government – assuming that Parliament has provided the necessary statutory powers in the first place. Indeed Parliament is able to modify or even abolish aspects of local government in the United Kingdom, as was witnessed in 1972 when the Northern Ireland Stormont Parliament was suspended and its powers transferred to Parliament at Westminster, and when legislation was put through Parliament in 1984 and 1985 to abolish the GLC and the other Metropolitan County Councils.

Statutory duties

Local authorities are given statutory duties in Acts of Parliament. The Westminster legislation sets out what the statutory duties shall be in each case. This means that local authorities have to perform certain functions which Parliament has assigned to them and they carry out their duties in accordance with the terms of the legislation. For example, the 1944 Education Act stipulated that local authorities should be responsible for providing public education for all children in their areas who are within the statutory age range for school education. (This duty was diminished in importance by subsequent Conservative legislation which provided for the establishment of Grant Maintained Schools accountable solely to their own governing bodies and financed by the Funding Agency for Schools.) Equally, the 1972 Chronically Sick and Disabled Persons Act laid statutory duties upon local authorities to provide care for all such people within their areas in the various ways prescribed in the legislation. Or again the 1977 Homeless Persons Act imposed a statutory duty upon local authorities to house the homeless, provided the latter satisfy certain prescribed conditions and have not made themselves deliberately homeless. Similarly, the 1992 Community Care Act obliged all local authorities to take the lead in organising suitable care and support for all those who need care in the community, including the chronically sick and those with physical or mental handicaps. However, such statutes are sometimes vague, while circulars from central Government are not binding. This can lead to considerable variation in standards. Consequently the professions concerned have become an important source of standardisation.

Discretionary powers

Local authorities are also given discretionary powers in Acts of Parliament. Once again the Westminster legislation sets out in each case the areas and the extent to which such powers may be exercised. This means that local authorities are endowed with discretionary powers to provide certain services, if they wish to do so and assuming they can raise the necessary finance. For example, the 1969 Children and Young Persons Act gave local authorities the discretionary powers to do all sorts of caring and compassionate things for young people in trouble, but failed to make available the extra money without which it proved difficult to implement large sections of the Act. During the period of public expenditure restraint imposed by the Conservative Government since 1979, many local authorities pressed for discretionary rather than mandatory powers whenever they were affected by new legislation, so that they might have a better chance of living within the tight financial limits set by central Government. Thus the discretionary powers, which used to be seen as a way of extending local provision of national services, are now regarded by many local authorities as a way of saving money, since this allows them to reduce or withdraw such services without incurring legislative or judicial penalties.

Division of functions

The division of functions between the various levels of local government is fiendishly complicated and has been subject to a number of changes over the years. At present, *the County Councils* have statutory responsibilities for transport, highways, police, fire service, Court administration, overspill housing, strategic planning, consumer protection, refuse disposal, education, public libraries and personal social services. *The non-Metropolitan District Councils* have statutory responsibilities for housing, local planning, environmental health, minor roads, licensing of public houses and places of entertainment, and the registration of births, marriages and deaths. *The Metropolitan District Councils* have the same statutory responsibilities as the non-Metropolitan District Councils, with the addition of education, public libraries and personal social services. The upper and lower levels of Metropolitan local government used to share statutory responsibility for museums and art galleries, parks and open spaces, municipal swimming baths, regional airports and land acquired for development. However, since the abolition of the Metropolitan Counties in 1986, these tasks have been taken on by the Metropolitan Districts. Only police, fire services, and public transport were transferred to statutory joint boards, while a few residual functions (such as land drainage, flood protection and some arts sponsorship) were transferred to other public bodies.[5] The single-tier Unitary Authorities introduced in England, Wales and Scotland in 1995/96 took over all aspects of local government within their geographical area. The distribution of responsibilities between the various different kinds of local authority and the vesting of functions in special purpose bodies bypassing local government is shown in tabular form in Figure 16.3.

Figure 16.3   The distribution of local government responsibilities

Non-Metropolitan areas

District Councils
Archives[1]
Arts[1]
Building Regulations
Concessionary Fares[1]
Economic Development[1]
Environmental Health
  and Public Protection
Housing
Land Use Planning (Local Plans and
  Development Control except Minerals and
  Waste Disposal)
Local Museums and Galleries[1]

Off-street Parking[1]
Parks and Open Spaces
Playing Fields and Sports Facilities
Refuse Collection and Street Cleaning
Tourism[1]
(Grants to Voluntary Bodies)[1]
Local Tax Collection
Register of Electors

County Councils
Archaeology
Archives[1]
Arts[1]
Careers Service
Civil Defence

Figure 16.3 *continued*

Coast Protection
Concessionary Fares[1]
Coroners
Economic Development[1]
Education
Land Use Planning (Structure Plans and
 Development Control for Minerals and Waste
 Disposal)[2]
Fire
Libraries
Local Highways and Traffic Management
Local Museums and Galleries and County-wide
 Museum Services
Magistrates' Courts
Off-Street Parking[1]
Personal Social Services
Police[3]
Probation Service
Public Transport
Tourism[1]
Trading Standards
Waste Disposal and Regulation
(Grants to Voluntary Bodies)[1]

Coroners
Economic Development
Education
Environmental Health and Public Protection
Housing
Land Use Planning (Unitary Development Plans
 and Development Control)[6]
Libraries
Local Highways and Traffic Management
Local Museums and Galleries
Magistrates' Courts[7] (except Inner London)
Off-Street Parking
Parks and Open Spaces
Personal Social Services
Playing Fields and Sports Facilities
Refuse Collection and Street Cleaning
Tourism
Trading standards
Waste Disposal and Regulation (most
 Metropolitan County areas)

(Grants to Voluntary Bodies)
Local Tax Collection
Registration of Electors

**Greater London and Metropolitan County
 areas**

Unitary Authorities
Archaeology[4] (Metropolitan County Areas)
Archives
Arts
Building Regulations
Careers Service
Coast Protection
Concessionary Fares[5]

Statutory joint arrangements
Civil Defence
Concessionary Fares[5] (Metropolitan County
 areas)
Fire
Police[7] (Metropolitan County areas)
Probation Service[7] (except Inner London)
Public Transport[8] (Metropolitan County areas)
Waste Disposal and Regulation (London and
 some Metropolitan County areas)

1. Concurrent functions of county and district councils.
2. Development control in most National Parks is handled by National Parks Committees which
   include representatives of the constituent county and district councils. Separate arrangements
   operate in the Lake District and the Peak Park.
3. This service is administered by Police Authorities which can cover two or more counties.
4. This function is the responsibility of English Heritage in the Greater London area.
5. Concurrent function of Passenger Transport Authorities and Metropolitan District Councils in
   Metropolitan County areas.
6. The London Planning Advisory Committee advises the Secretary of State on planning for London
   as a whole.
7. The Home Secretary has special responsibilities for the Metropolitan Police, the Inner London
   Magistrates' Courts Service and the Inner London Probation Service.
8. This function is performed by London Regional Transport in the Greater London area.

Under the pressure of successive phases of Westminster legislation passed at the behest of the Conservative Government in the 1980s and 1990s, elected local government has been required to 'market test' many of its own services, to introduce compulsory competitive tendering (CCT), and to cede to the growing category of 'special purpose bodies' or QUANGOs (quasi-autonomous non-governmental organisations) many of the duties, powers and functions which it previously performed within the legislative framework set by Parliament.[6] This gradual erosion of the role of local government as a *provider* (as distinct from a purchaser or regulator) of local services has been commended by its Conservative proponents as a drive towards the creation of 'enabling' local authorities.

16.3 Financial arrangements

The financing of local government has long been both complicated and controversial in Britain. From the early 1950s local authority spending grew steadily and usually at a faster rate than the economy as a whole. This growth was bearable in the 1950s and 1960s when the British economy was growing at about 3 per cent a year and there was general public and political support for a constantly expanding public sector. However, since the 1976 financial crisis, when the then Labour Government had to call in the IMF, successive Governments of both main parties have felt it necessary to control all forms of public spending. Local authority spending, which has accounted for about one quarter of the total, has been no exception to this rule. In such circumstances relations between local and central Government became strained and in the 1980s struggles over local government finance and local government spending were exacerbated by sharp differences of party politics between Conservative central Government and Labour and Liberal Democrat-controlled local authorities.

The financial problems of local government have not been made any easier by the fact that so much new legislation proposed by central Government and passed by Parliament has had financial implications for local authorities for which they have not always been sufficiently compensated by the Exchequer. Many new statutory duties were placed upon local authorities over the years in fields such as housing, education, social services and community care. Yet under Conservative Governments since 1979, local authorities have not received all the financial support from the centre which they felt they needed, while at the same time they were prevented by law from raising the extra finance which they needed from local sources – traditionally domestic and business rates.

The methods of local government finance

The methods of financing local government have varied over the years in Britain. In general, however, local authorities relied upon revenue from local rates (property taxes) levied according to a complicated formula on domestic, commercial and industrial (but not agricultural) buildings within their designated areas; together with financial support in various forms from central Government and income from rents, fees and charges. A breakdown of local Government expenditure and income is provided in Figure 16.4.

Rates, which traditionally raised nearly half of the revenue needed to finance local

Figure 16.4 Local government expenditure and income

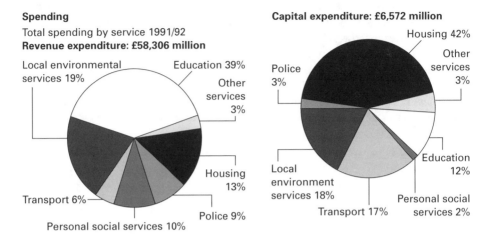

Spending

Total spending by service 1991/92
Revenue expenditure: £58,306 million

Local environmental services 19%
Education 39%
Other services 3%
Housing 13%
Transport 6%
Personal social services 10%
Police 9%

Capital expenditure: £6,572 million

Housing 42%
Other services 3%
Police 3%
Education 12%
Personal social services 2%
Transport 17%
Local environment services 18%

Income

Income by source 1991/92
Total £64,977 million

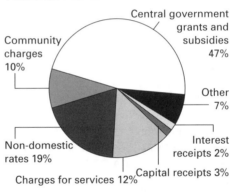

Community charges 10%
Central government grants and subsidies 47%
Other 7%
Non-domestic rates 19%
Interest receipts 2%
Charges for services 12%
Capital receipts 3%

Source: *The Guardian*, 3 May 1994

services, were assessed on the rateable value of the land or buildings concerned. In theory they represented the rent at which the property could be let (if there were a market for such lettings), minus the notional cost of repairs, insurance and other maintenance expenses. They were paid every year (normally in two or more instalments) and the abstruse calculations upon which they were based were reviewed about every 10 years by the Inland Revenue in periodic revaluations which took account of inflation and any improvements to the property over the intervening period. Although rates were an unpopular form of taxation, it was never easy to identify a simpler or more cost-effective way of raising large sums of revenue from local sources.[7]

The rest of the money needed for local government revenue support came traditionally from a system of central Government grants to local authorities. These took two main forms. Firstly, there were specific grants in aid of particular local purposes – for example, 50 per cent of local police expenditure or 90 per cent of mandatory student grants, or specific housing subsidies for poorer tenants. Secondly, there were general grants to the rate funds of individual local authorities in order to increase their overall income, notably in those parts of the country with a poor rateable base.

The total amount of *Rate Support Grant* (RSG) was fixed every year by the Department of the Environment in co-operation with the Treasury and after consultation with the local authority Associations and the Consultative Council on Local Government Finance. The RSG was composed of a *needs element* assessed for each local authority mainly on the basis of demographic factors, a *resources element* paid to those authorities where the rateable base was below the national average, and a *domestic element* designed to bring some relief to all domestic ratepayers. The most notable characteristics of the system were a bias in favour of income redistribution from the richer to the poorer parts of the country, and considerable power for central Government in its ability to switch or withhold grants from individual local authorities.

By the middle 1970s, however, the whole system of local government finance was seen by many as inherently flawed – indeed, even in a state of crisis. In 1975 the then Labour Secretary of State for the Environment, Anthony Crosland, declared that 'the party is over', meaning that it was no longer realistic or acceptable for local government spending to continue rising at a rate above inflation and faster than the growth of the economy as a whole.

When the Conservatives returned to power in 1979, they were determined to give a high priority to controlling local government spending, encouraging local authorities to deliver services more efficiently, and reducing the number of detailed controls over local government. Under the *1980 Local Government Planning and Land Act* the Government sought to introduce a better framework for the distribution and control of public funds for local government. To do this it decided that the Department of the Environment would determine the appropriate spending level for each Council and introduced block grants paid to every local authority. This system was designed to ensure that all local authorities of the same kind (for instance, all Shire Counties or all London Boroughs) could provide a similar standard of local services if they levied a similar rate in the pound. It also sought to escape from reliance upon past expenditure as a measure of local need and to base such measurements upon an objective view of the costs of typical standards of local service. While the new system was supposed to discourage local authorities from overspending, it was also supposed not to reduce the freedom of local authorities to determine their own local priorities within financial limits.

Under the *1982 Local Government Finance Act* the first Thatcher Government went one stage further in its policy of tightening the financial controls upon local authorities. The Act prevented local authorities from raising supplementary rates and precepts during the course of the financial year and subjected their activities to further financial scrutiny by the newly established Audit Commission. Under the *1984 Rates Act* a further legislative attempt was made to curb excessive rate increases by individual local authorities and to provide a general reserve power for the limitation of rate increases by all local authorities. This policy of '*rate-capping*' had some limited success in controlling the overspending by what Ministers saw as spendthrift local authorities and hence shielded ratepayers from some of the worst financial consequences. However, it also led some local authorities into the greater complexities of so-called 'creative accounting'. In essence it succeeded in reducing the rate of increase in local authority spending from about 3 per cent per year in real terms at the beginning of the 1980s to about 1 per cent per year in real terms by the end of the decade.

In spite of all these efforts by central Government, the system of local government finance with all its controls and anomalies became increasingly discredited, with the result that Ministers felt obliged to look for even more radical solutions. As Nicholas Ridley, then Secretary of State for the Environment, made clear at the 1986 Conservative Party Conference, the Government had a clear choice: 'either we go on legislating until we have a framework of law within which the abuses can be contained with more central control; or we make local authorities fully accountable to their electors and ensure that those who vote for local extravagance and depravity [sic] pay for it'.[8] It was not long thereafter that the Government clearly chose 'local democratic accountability' and came forward with a new set of proposals which figured prominently in the 1987 Conservative Party Manifesto. These proposals involved the abolition of domestic rates, their replacement with a *Community Charge* – the so-called *Poll Tax* (levied on nearly everyone aged 18 or over within each local authority area), the introduction of a *Uniform Business Rate* in place of non-domestic rates, and a simplified system of block grants to local authorities according to their population numbers and their needs in place of the previously complicated RSG formula.

On being returned to power at the 1987 General Election, the Conservative Government set about implementing its Manifesto pledge to reform the system of local government finance at the earliest possible date. Even though there was considerable opposition and misgiving in Conservative ranks, a Bill was introduced early in the Parliament which later passed onto the Statute Book as the *1988 Local Government Finance Act*. Ministers argued that the Community Charge would improve democratic accountability for local authority spending, since about twice as many people would have to pay as had paid domestic rates before (36 million as opposed to 18 million in the former system in England). They also argued that it would be fairer than domestic rates, since the cost of local government services would be spread more evenly over all those who used them. In short, it was seen by the Government as an extension of the charging principle (hence the name Community Charge) and a useful way of promoting financial discipline in local government by creating a larger constituency of support for the restraint of local spending. As for the Uniform Business Rate, Ministers argued that it would prevent profligate local authorities from putting up their business rates to pay for their ambitious political and social spending programmes and that it would protect business ratepayers (once the initial revaluation had been made) from future rate increases above the rate of inflation.

The Government's original idea was to phase in both the Community Charge and the Uniform Business Rate over a period of years. However, that idea was largely abandoned as far as the Community Charge was concerned following grass-roots pressure at the 1988 Conservative Party Conference, mainly from Scottish Tories who had pioneered the shift to the new form of local government financing a year before their fellow citizens in the rest of the United Kingdom. The consequence was a decision to introduce the Community Charge in England and Wales in April 1990 at levels which were mitigated for some local authorities and exacerbated for others by the effects of the so-called 'safety net' arrangements. These were to last for one year only and ensure that local authorities with low spending patterns and those with high rateable values would have to subsidise to some extent others with high spending patterns and low rateable values. A further complexity was introduced at the 1989 Conservative Party Conference when the then Local Government Minister, David Hunt, announced that additional steps would be taken to see that no individual Community Charge payer would be more than £3 a week worse off as a result of the change in the first year of the new system, provided that the local authority in which they lived did not spend at a level higher than its so-called Standard Spending Assessment. On the other hand, the Uniform Business Rate, which was introduced on the basis of the first rating revaluation in England and Wales since 1973, was phased in over a five-year period from April 1990 with safety net arrangements to limit the size of both the gains and the losses from the new system in any one year. Thereafter there are to be regular statutory revaluations of business property every five years.

In the event the Community Charge as amended and the Uniform Business Rate proved highly unpopular with very many in the electorate. There were a minority of clear gainers, such as single-person households in low-spending local authority areas, those who lived in houses larger than they needed (unless they had two or more grown-up children living at home) and businesses in previously high-rated or high-spending local authority areas. Yet, as is so often the case in politics, the gainers said very little in favour of the changes, while the losers said a very great deal against them.

The Community Charge made the then Conservative Government deeply unpopular, divided the Cabinet, and contributed to the downfall of Margaret Thatcher as Prime Minister in November 1990.[9] The new Prime Minister, John Major, made it one of his first tasks to get rid of it and with the help of Michael Heseltine, once again Secretary of State for the Environment. The Community Charge was therefore replaced by the *Council Tax*, which came into effect on 1 April 1993.[10] This tax, which is levied on each and every residential household, is calculated largely on the basis of property values as reflected in broad valuation bands based upon prices in April 1991. However, it does take some account of the number of people living in each dwelling by allowing a 25 per cent discount for people living alone. It was also introduced at relatively low levels thanks to a considerable Exchequer subsidy paid for by increasing the standard rate of VAT (Value Added Tax) from 15 to 17.5 per cent, while its early impact was also mitigated by transitional relief phased over a number of years. The Uniform Business Rate was retained, although efforts were made to ameliorate its adverse impact – especially upon new business premises in the South-East of England – by adjusting the transitional reliefs. Agricultural land remained unrated. As for the system of Exchequer support to local authorities, this was also retained in its new simplified form, although here again the Major Government was more prepared than its predecessor to respond sympathetically to complaints from the local authority Associations.

16.4 Central-local relations

The relations between local and central Government have seldom been easy or unambiguously defined. In the nineteenth century there was a lengthy search for a system of local government which would be both efficient and democratic, although not necessarily for a relationship with central Government that was designed to be mutually beneficial. Throughout the twentieth century there have been notable occasions when the usual habits of co-operation between local and central Government have broken down and thus given rise to serious misunderstanding and conflict. In general, however, local authorities have sought faithfully to perform their statutory duties and have acted within the statutory constraints laid upon them by Parliament.[11]

Constitutional relations

The constitutional relations between local and central Government have varied greatly over the centuries in Britain. Between 1688 and 1835 the effective independence of local government could hardly have been greater, since there was virtually no interference from central Government and only minimal control. However, since the 1835 Municipal Corporations Act, the powers and influence of central Government have grown steadily and there has been an apparently remorseless tendency towards the centralisation of political power. This should not be thought particularly surprising in a unitary state, such as Britain, in which all the legal power and authority of local government has always derived from Acts of Parliament and in which local government has been able to rely only on local elections and local pride to buttress its sense of legitimacy in dealings with central Government.

Today the constitutional relationship between local and central Government is invariably described by Ministers as a partnership, but by Councillors in much less flattering terms and, occasionally, as a central dictatorship. In Whitehall and Westminster not much more than lip-service is paid to the idea of partnership with local government, partly because many local authorities tend to be controlled by local politicians from the Opposition parties, but mainly because local government is now on average dependent upon the decisions of central Government for about 85 per cent of its income and, ultimately, for its very existence.

There is, therefore, a paradoxical aspect to the relationship between local and central Government which is explained partly by the historical fact that until modern times virtually all civil government in Britain was local government (for example, through Justices of the Peace), partly by the important tradition that national services should wherever possible be provided locally, and partly by the traditional tendency for central Government to act via the agency of local authorities rather than directly via its own regional and local organisation. It might have been more logical to have clear-cut statements and constitutional rules about the division of powers and responsibilities between local and central Government, and then to have entrenched such arrangements in a new constitutional settlement. Yet the principle of Parliamentary supremacy did not permit such an outcome and it seems rather unlikely that it ever will, unless such a move is brought about by Britain's membership of the European Union. Consequently the compromise which has been reached gives local government a clearly subordinate constitutional position, while allowing it a more co-ordinate relationship with central Government when dealing with a wide variety of practical issues which arise on a day-to-day basis.

Political relations

Political relations between local and central Government have not been easy in modern times, since they are often characterised by inherent conflict of interest and incompatible political objectives. This was especially true in the 1980s when an ideological Conservative Government in Whitehall had a long-running battle with several local authorities led by left-wing Labour politicians of a campaigning disposition. Of course, there is bound to be tension or worse in a relationship which depends upon mutual understanding and co-operation between inherently unequal partners. Furthermore, the relationship is bound to become rather bitter when central Government seeks to impose tighter financial constraints upon local authorities and when many local authorities are run by politically motivated men and women with principles and objectives which are entirely at odds with those of Ministers. Since 1979 the Labour Party has been particularly strong in urban local government, especially in the inner city areas and the great conurbations of the Midlands and the North. Equally, the Liberal Democrats have steadily gained political control of more local authorities, notably in the West Country and the suburbs of London, where disgruntled voters who previously supported one or other of the main parties have responded positively to the appeal of Liberal Democrat community politics. Consequently, mutual suspicion and resentment came to characterise the relationship between local and central Government, much to the detriment of the traditional conventions which previously facilitated comparatively civilised relations between the two levels of elected government in Britain.

Even in difficult economic circumstances, and with fraught political relations, the partnership between local and central Government is supposed to involve some sharing of decision-making powers. Yet most people in local government would probably agree with N. P. Hepworth when he wrote that 'local government does not share in the decision making of central Government; it makes representations, but that is not the same thing'.[12] On the other hand, from the point of view of central Government, the partnership can seem quite real, in that many aspects of Government policy depend for their success upon the active and willing co-operation of local government. For example, overall public expenditure restraint is dependent upon local government co-operation - at a time when local authorities account for one quarter of total public spending, even if the planning total was at one time redefined to exclude those categories of local spending which are financed exclusively from local revenue. Similarly many of the statutory obligations placed upon local government by Parliament are couched in broad terms of principle which leave the precise methods of implementation very much in the hands of local authorities, not to mention the discretionary powers whose use or non-use depends entirely upon local government decisions. Furthermore the local authorities have learned to combine in order to maximise their influence upon central Government. They do this through their representative bodies – the Association of Metropolitan Authorities, the Association of County Councils and the Association of District Councils, and in strictly financial matters through the Consultative Council on Local Government Finance.

While the relationship between local and central Government is reasonably clearcut in constitutional terms, it has often been ambiguous and even hostile in political terms. Neither level of government can really afford to alienate the other and neither can achieve all its objectives without the co-operation of the other. Local government now depends more heavily than before upon central Government grants and the Uniform Business Rate whose level in any year is determined by central Government. On the other hand, central Government depends heavily upon local government for the local administration of national services, although increasingly from 1979 the Conservative Government has insisted upon the purchaser-provider split in local government –

driven forward by privatisation and the contracting-out of services – and sought to outflank elected local government by making more extensive use of Urban Development Corporations and other special purpose bodies, as well as the enhanced regional offices of central Government.[13]

16.5 Methods of central control

There are four principal methods by which central Government seeks to control local government: namely, legislative control, policy control, administrative control and financial control. Of these financial control is the most important, but we shall consider each of them in turn.

Legislative control

It is the legislative control in Acts of Parliament which establishes the nature and extent of the subordinate powers conferred upon local government. As J. A. G. Griffith has explained, 'within the terms on which these powers are bestowed, local authorities are autonomous bodies and a Department [of central Government] which proposes to control the way in which or the extent to which local authorities exercise their powers must be able to point to statutory provisions authorising this intervention'.[14] Thus legislative control provides legal safeguards for local government as well as a means of control for central Government.

One of the most widespread criticisms of central control of local authorities, however, has stemmed from the excessive frequency of new Westminster legislation designed to limit, if not remove, what little is left of local government's legal discretion. It has been calculated that at least 150 Acts of Parliament have been put on the Statute Book since 1979 which were designed in one way or another to diminish the powers of local authorities, and its has been forcefully argued that this has done more than anything else to disable and demoralise both Councillors and officials in local government.

Such legislative control can take various forms. In many cases the original legislation confers upon Ministers the power to make detailed regulations which are binding upon local government. For example, it is customary for Whitehall to issue Statutory Instruments which set out the building regulations to be observed in the construction of buildings and the planning regulations to be observed in carrying out local property or transport developments. In some cases local authorities are given power to make by-laws about public footpaths and other very local matters. Yet it is always made clear in the original Westminster legislation that these by-laws must be confirmed by the relevant Minister. Of course, this legislative control involves two-way influence and communication, since the representative bodies of local government are often consulted in the preparation and always consulted on the implementation of Westminster legislation which affects local authorities.

Policy control

Another form of central control is provided by the power and influence of Government policy. This can take various forms, depending upon the priorities of the party in office and the legal basis of the relationship between local authorities and the different Departments of central Government. For example, the 1948 Children Act and the 1969 Children and Young Persons Act each stipulated that local authorities should exercise statutory functions in this area of policy under the guidance of the relevant Ministers, which has meant in effect the policy pursued by the Government of the day. Similarly the Secretary of State for Education has a supervisory and promotional role in relation to the organisation of schools and the supply of teachers in all the local education authorities in England and Wales. This power derives from the 1944 Education Act, as amended by the 1988 Education Reform Act, and it has been exercised by successive Governments in accordance with their own particular education policies and with increasing force and frequency in relation to the implementation of the national curriculum in all state-funded schools since its introduction in 1988.

Other examples of policy control by Ministers and their civil servants in Whitehall can be found in the sphere of housing and other local services. Successive Conservative Governments have promoted policies of home ownership and home improvement, while Labour politicians have promoted policies of public sector house building and rent control. In these ways the policy of the Government of the day has had a considerable influence upon the behaviour of local authorities. Sometimes it has led to bitter conflict between the two levels of government, with local authorities vainly seeking to resist the policy favoured by central Government – for example, resistance to the right-to-buy provisions of the 1980 Housing Act by Labour-controlled Norwich or general resistance from both Labour and Liberal Democrat-controlled local authorities to the Conservative policy of compulsory contracting out and competitive tendering for local services. Yet in the end central Government has the whip hand, since, if the existing statutory position is not sufficiently compelling, the party in office can always use its Parliamentary majority to put through further Westminster legislation to curb or eliminate what it may see as intolerable resistance by local government.

Administrative control

Administrative control is another form of central control which derives from central Government's responsibility for setting national standards and promoting the efficiency of local government. Ever since the nineteenth century it has been accepted that many functions of government in Britain should be national services locally administered. This has always implied the need for administrative control via national standards drawn up by Whitehall civil servants and enforced in many cases by powerful, independent Inspectorates. For example, in the case of education Her Majesty's Chief Inspector of Schools monitors – through the Office of Standards in Education (OFSTED) – levels of quality in schools and regulates the work of the independent registered inspectors. In the case of the police, the payment of central Government grants to police authorities is conditional upon there being satisfactory reports from Her Majesty's Inspectorate of Constabulary about policing in the different areas of the country covered by different police forces.

Although the range and power of administrative controls exercised by central Government over local authorities has become increasingly formidable over the years, there have been instances when a countervailing tendency has been evident. For example, the 1979-83 Conservative Government sought to reduce the number and scope of certain controls upon local government in the hope of thereby reducing the burden of compliance costs upon the private sector. It is also believed that, by freeing local authorities from many forms of detailed supervision and administrative control, it would be possible for them to perform their statutory duties in a more cost-effective way. Some provisions in the 1980 Local Government and Planning Act were designed for precisely this purpose. Equally, the 1994 Deregulation Act sought to reduce the scope and quantity of detailed regulations which bear so heavily upon local authorities, private firms and other public bodies alike, and which in consequence add to costs and create unnecessary delays. Indeed, there is a constant need to deregulate in modern government simply to prevent the inexorable tendency towards more and more regulation, whether driven from London or Brussels, from getting out of hand. Nonetheless, the general tendency has been rather the other way, with central Government seeking to control the activities of local government ever more closely.

Financial control

Certainly, one of the most powerful forms of central control has always been the financial control exercised by central Government. This can be traced back at least to the 1929 Local Government Act in which the earlier system of assigned revenues was abolished and replaced with a system of specific grants, together with a block grant from central Government to each local authority. In 1948 this system of financial control was supplemented by a system of deficiency payments to those local authorities with rateable values below the average, and in 1958 the whole system was rationalised to enable a new block grant (the Rate Support Grant) to replace the wide variety of specific grants which had grown up over the years. At every stage from then until the present day financial support from central Government has been synonymous with financial control by central Government, especially as the proportion of total local government spending financed by central Government grants or locally raised taxation entirely under the control of central Government has now risen to about 85 per cent. Little more than lip-service has been paid by central Government to the idea of encouraging real financial independence for local authorities, because the Treasury has always been determined not to relax its control over any significant category of public spending nor to relinquish the right to tax to subnational (or supranational) levels of government.

Today the financial control of central Government over local government takes essentially four forms. *Firstly*, central Government in essence sets a spending limit for each Council via the Standard Spending Assessment. *Secondly*, local government revenue-expenditure is supported – that is, controlled – to the tune of about 57 per cent on a national average basis by the Aggregate Exchequer Grant paid to each local authority according to its needs and its population. *Thirdly*, about 24 per cent of all local authority spending is financed by the proceeds of the Uniform Business Rate which is set by central Government at a level which should not rise by more than the rate of inflation and which might be held below that. This was intended to eliminate the excessive rises in business rates which were previously imposed by high-spending local authorities, but it also eliminated any incentive to local authorities to set their Business Rates at a relatively low level in order to attract mobile business investment. *Fourthly*, local authority capital expenditure is tightly controlled by the Treasury, since local authorities are not encouraged to borrow directly (and more expensively) from the markets and not allowed by the Treasury to spend more than 25 per cent of their receipts from the sale of housing and 50 per cent of receipts from other sources in any one year. From its election in 1979 the Conservative Government was as keen to control local government capital expenditure as it was to control local government current expenditure. Initially this was part of its campaign to reduce and then eliminate public borrowing. By the early 1990s, however, when the length and depth of the recession produced an unparalleled public sector deficit, it was motivated principally by a desire to curb the current expenditure implications of all capital projects.

A final point which relates to central Government financial controls over local government is that between 1979 and 1994 a total of £24 billion of annual expenditure was transferred from local authorities to Government appointed special purpose bodies. This transfer greatly reduced the amount of public spending over which elected Councillors had some influence and enhanced the degree of central financial control from Whitehall.

16.6 Whither local government?

With common sense and goodwill on both sides it should be possible to achieve fruitful co-operation between local and central Government. There appear to be three basic conditions for this. *Firstly*, it must be generally accepted that there are certain minimum nationwide standards for national services which are provided locally. *Secondly*, it must be accepted that local authorities are best placed to co-ordinate, if not necessarily provide, many of the public services which people expect. *Thirdly*, it must be accepted that the relationship between local and central Government can only work satisfactorily on the basis of trust and mutual respect. Unfortunately, the second and third of these conditions have proved difficult, if not impossible, to fulfil, because in the period since 1979 the Conservatives at Westminster have conducted something close to warfare against Labour and Liberal Democrat controlled local government, and politicians in all parties in local government have been opposed to many aspects of Conservative national policy towards local government.

The politicisation of local government

Local government in Britain is in a parlous state. The Conservative Government re-elected in 1992 was determined to carry through another restructuring of local government and continued the pressure towards centralisation and the marginalisation of elected local government with greater emphasis upon special purpose bodies and the regional outposts of central Government. On the other hand, Labour and the Liberal Democrats, as well as the Nationalist parties in both Scotland and Wales, have been committed to varying degrees of decentralisation and devolution of power to the localities. In considering the future of local government in the United Kingdom, a great deal will therefore depend upon the outcome of the next General Election, indeed of subsequent General Elections as well.

If the Conservatives are returned to power at Westminster, it seems likely that a tight rein upon more than 80 per cent of local authority spending will be maintained via the mechanism of central Government grants, the Uniform Business Rate and capping. Conservatives were doubtless relieved that the replacement of the Community Charge with the Council Tax went comparatively smoothly in the early 1990s. However, this probably reflected the generosity of the transitional arrangements. The public may not be so sanguine once the period of effective subsidy expires and many householders find that they have to pay substantial sums in local taxation because their homes were effec-tively over-valued in 1991 when each was allocated to a particular band of Council Tax.

The other main consequence of the Government's decision to scrap the Community Charge was the wide-ranging review of local government boundaries announced in November 1990. This rolling review of local government in England – originally under the chairmanship of Sir John Banham – and similar reviews carried out in both Scotland and Wales by the respective Secretaries of State – encountered considerable opposition to its proposals which were put forward piecemeal in the various parts of the country. While people may have accepted, indeed welcomed, the abolition of artificial entities like Avon, Cleveland and Humberside and the return of Rutland, there did not seem to be much support for yet another costly and far-reaching reform of local government, even one based upon the original principle of trying to create a single tier of enlarged unitary authorities. For many the whole process appeared too much like change for change's sake. As previously noted, 14 Unitary Authorities were introduced for the May 1995 Local Elections, taking over their responsibilities in April 1996. Further changes are due in April 1997 and beyond. (See Figure 16.5 for a map of local authority boundaries and possible future changes.)

If the Labour Party is returned to power at the next General Election, it is possible that it will take legislative steps to introduce a measure of regional government with the creation of perhaps 10 regional assemblies in England (if these are wanted in the regions), including a new Greater London Authority, to which would be allocated some of the strategic planning responsibilities of the Counties as well as the regional responsibilities of central Government Departments. This means that a new Labour Government would perhaps abolish the existing County Councils and pass their most significant responsi-bilities – for example, education and social services – down to enlarged and strength-ened District Councils.[15] As far as finance is concerned, it is possible that the Council Tax would be scrapped and replaced with a reformed system of domestic rates based on capital values and household income and that the Uniform Business Rate would be scrapped and replaced with the old system of business rates; although – presumably – the system of financial support from central Government would continue much as before. Above all, Labour has felt offended – as indeed have some others – by the enormous growth of extra-governmental organisations under the Conservatives – in other words, unelected local government by QUANGOs and other public bodies based upon Ministerial appointments and political patronage. It is therefore likely to return many of these func-tions – for example, Urban Development Corporations, the Funding Agency for Schools and the NHS Trusts – to the democratic control of Regional Assemblies and strength-ened local authorities.

In addition, under a future Labour Government it is probable that Scotland would be given a directly elected Scottish Parliament with substantial legislative and tax-rais-ing powers, so that most decisions affecting Scotland would be taken in Scotland. The Parliament would have a substantial budget of its own comparable in size to all the money now allocated to Scotland under the auspices of the Scottish Office.

Figure 16.5 Actual and proposed local authority boundaries

● Possible 'unitary'
councils – further review
1. Blackpool
2. Blackburn
3. Warrington
4. Halton
5. The Wrekin
6. Norwich
7. Peterborough
8. Huntingdonshire
9. Northampton
10. Gloucester
11. Basildon and Thurrock
12. Medway Towns
13. Exeter

Areas where there will be just one tier of local government, with a 'unitary' council covering the full range of functions.

No change. There will continue to be two tiers with county and district councils.

Metropolitan areas not covered by the review. They already have unitary councils.

Figure 16.5 *continued*

1. City of Aberdeen
2. City of Dundee
3. Argyll and Bute
4. Dumbarton and Clydebank
5. East Dumbartonshire
6. North Lanarkshire
7. City of Glasgow
8. East Renfrewshire
9. Renfrewshire
10. Inverclyde
11. Clackmannan
12. Falkirk
13. West Lothian
14. City of Edinburgh
15. Midlothian
16. East Lothian
17. South Ayrshire
18. East Ayrshire
19. South Lanarkshire

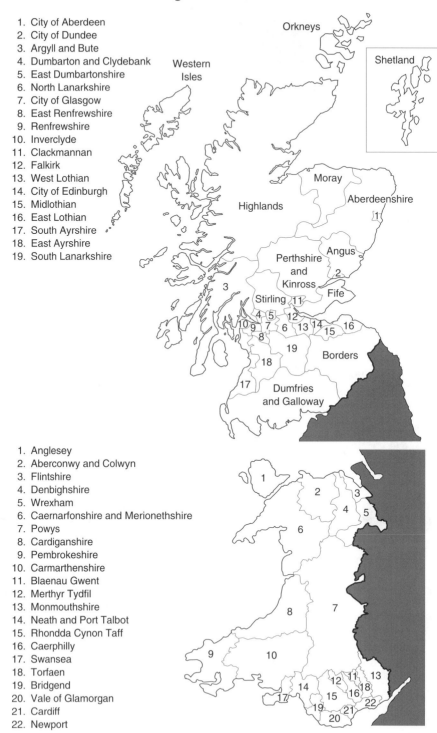

1. Anglesey
2. Aberconwy and Colwyn
3. Flintshire
4. Denbighshire
5. Wrexham
6. Caernarfonshire and Merionethshire
7. Powys
8. Cardiganshire
9. Pembrokeshire
10. Carmarthenshire
11. Blaenau Gwent
12. Merthyr Tydfil
13. Monmouthshire
14. Neath and Port Talbot
15. Rhondda Cynon Taff
16. Caerphilly
17. Swansea
18. Torfaen
19. Bridgend
20. Vale of Glamorgan
21. Cardiff
22. Newport

In Wales, it seems likely that an incoming Labour Government would introduce an elected body for Wales responsible for Welsh Office functions and the work of nominated bodies in the Principality.

In Northern Ireland, the Labour Party has been more cautious about advocating structural change, saying simply that it will work with the political parties there to establish a devolved, power-sharing administration in Belfast. It is not clear what fate the party has in store for the 26 District Councils, but presumably it would leave them in place as the basis of local government in the Province.

As for the various positions of the other parties on local government reform, because it is unlikely that any of them will win even a share of power at Westminster after the next General Election, there is not much point in spending too much time examining their proposals in detail. Suffice it to say that the *Liberal Democrats* advocate the introduction of a Local Income Tax, related to the ability to pay and collected by the Inland Revenue, to replace the Council Tax; and the replacement of the Uniform Business Rate with Site Value Rating, locally administered and based on the taxation of land values (with exemption for agricultural land and domestic properties). With regard to local government itself, the Liberal Democrat approach is to take power away from Westminster and Whitehall, and give it to stronger, more independent and more democratic local Councils. The party therefore advocates not only the reform of local Councils into a unitary system based on 'natural communities' and 'local wishes'; but also home rule for Scotland, with the creation of an elected Scottish Parliament; home rule for Wales, with the creation of an elected Welsh Synod; and the creation of fully democratic regional governments in England.

The *Scottish National Party* is committed to an independent Scotland within the European Union, while *Plaid Cymru* advocates a 'self-governing Wales within a democratic European confederation'. Thus *all* the Opposition parties are, to a greater or lesser extent, well disposed towards greater power and autonomy for sub-national government, and only the Conservatives seem to favour the continuation of the United Kingdom as the most unitary state in the European Union.

Local autonomy or further centralisation?

The relationship between local and central Government in Britain also has to be considered in the light of broader arguments for greater local autonomy on the one hand or further centralisation on the other. We shall deal with each side of this important debate in turn.

The arguments in favour of greater local autonomy include: (1) the need to diminish the remoteness of government from its citizens; (2) the desirability of enhancing democratic accountability at local level; (3) the opportunities which could be created for greater public participation; (4) the improved efficiency of smaller units in public administration; and (5) the reduced financial burden upon the Exchequer.

The arguments in favour of further centralisation include: (1) the need for common national standards of public provision; (2) the uniformity of public expectations as to what Government should provide; and (3) the attractions for Ministers and civil servants of a more direct and reliable form of control over local authorities.

With many tendencies in British society moving in favour of greater homogeneity and even uniformity (see Chapter 1, pp 6-10) there is obviously a strong countervailing case for more local autonomy. As Professors Jones and Stewart have argued, greater autonomy should be encouraged 'not to let loose rampant and uncontrolled localism and the sharpening of geographical inequalities, but to maintain a more balanced array of pressures in public policy making'.[16] In other words, there is strength in diversity and value in variety, not least as a way of minimising the risk of replicating mistakes on a large scale.

With the increasing politicisation of local government, central Government has been drawn to interfere more and more with the activities of local authorities. Since 1979 successive Conservative Governments have taken this tendency almost to its limit by imposing the unpopular Community Charge to finance one quarter of all local government spending (although this was later replaced by the Council Tax), reducing still further the Aggregate Exchequer Grant to local authorities as a proportion of their total resources, and introducing the Uniform Business Rate which had the effect of removing local incentives to attract new business investment to a given local authority area with business rates at an attractively low level. Beyond that the ultimate Conservative objective for local authorities would seem to be the transformation of this layer of government into 'enabling authorities' which would have duties of service specification, purchase and regulation, but which would only rarely be involved in the actual provision or delivery of public services at local level.[17]

In short, Conservative politicians at national level have tried to increase central Government control over local government and to by-pass elected local government altogether whenever it was seen as an obstacle to the attainment of their national objectives. On the other hand, Labour and Liberal Democrat politicians at least appear to have remained faithful to the cause of devolution, whether to a national Parliament in Scotland and an assembly in Wales or to regional assemblies and strengthened unitary authorities in England. Only a new constitutional settlement, guaranteed by a new Bill of Rights and interpreted by an independent Supreme Court, would be able to safeguard local government against the fashions and prejudices of the politicians in power at Westminster.

16.7 Conclusion

It should be clear from this chapter that the position of local government in Britain is neither immutable nor easy to describe. However it can be assessed in terms of its *efficiency, vitality, adaptability* and *capacity for genuine partnership with central Government*. Let us conclude by considering each of these aspects in turn.

With regard to the *efficiency* of local government, it seems clear that the present division of functions is a fairly defensible one and does not put such a high premium upon the interests of local democracy that the interests of efficiency are unduly compromised. For example, the emphasis upon techniques of corporate management within local authorities and the discipline of tough financial limits set by central Government appear to have had a positive effect upon the efficiency of local government – certainly that is what their advocates argue. On the other hand, the morale of those in local government has undoubtedly suffered in this relentless drive for greater efficiency, not least because many of the traditional functions and the traditional financial resources of local government have been steadily taken away from them by central Government.

With regard to the *vitality* of local government, the available evidence is somewhat contradictory. On the one hand, the normal turnout at local elections is seldom more than about 40 to 50 per cent of those entitled to vote, and at local by-elections it sometimes falls below 30 per cent. This suggests rather scant public interest in the democratic process of local government. On the other hand, even a cursory glance at the columns of the local press in any part of the country reveals considerable public interest in the actual decisions of local government. For example, Council Tax payers are very interested in seeing that value for money is secured in local authority spending, while beneficiary groups usually favour the expansion of existing services or the creation of new ones. Public interest is also reflected in the volume of correspondence sent to Members of Parliament and Councillors about local authority matters.

With regard to the *adaptability* of local government, the record over the years has been quite good. However, throughout the 1980s, when many social needs increased, the financial resources made available by central Government to local government were consistently squeezed, so that the Aggregate Exchequer Grant now covers less than half of total local authority spending compared with nearly two-thirds more than 10 years ago. The response of local authorities has been one of angry criticism, especially from Labour-controlled local authorities in inner city areas where the social problems are often greatest. It is clear that local Councillors of all parties resent the financial restrictions which have been imposed by central Government and would like to have a system of local authority finance which enabled them to perform all their statutory duties in a more satisfactory way.

As for the capacity of local government to maintain a *genuine partnership* with central Government, this has been determined partly by the diminishing extent to which it has retained sole responsibility for providing local services. Successive Conservative Governments in the 1980s and 1990s made determined attempts to encourage the privatisation of local services and to separate the idea of local government *provision* from local government *responsibility* – for example, in the field of Community Care. However, the main explanation for the rather lopsided partnership between local and central Government in recent years has been the failure of the former to secure any significant degree of real financial autonomy. Indeed, with the switch from local business rates to the Uniform Business Rate and the use of central Government financial capping, the extent of local government financial autonomy has decreased still further. It is, therefore, hard to demonstrate that local government has anything like a genuine or equal partnership with central Government, and it seems very unlikely to achieve this unless it is granted greater revenue raising powers by a future Parliament.

Even allowing for all these problems and shortcomings, local government in Britain still has several *points in its favour*. Its diversity contributes to political pluralism in Britain. Its institutions offer an important sphere of political activity to a considerable number of elected Councillors. It stimulates public interest in the local provision of national services. Apart from Parliament at Westminster and the European Parliament, it provides the only level of elected representation in British democracy. Such positive attributes should not be underestimated or ignored, notwithstanding the fact that they have been significantly limited by central Government over the past 15 to 20 years.

Suggested questions

1 How and why has the structure of local government changed in the United Kingdom in the 1990s?
2 'Local government can do only what central Government wants it to do, so local autonomy is a farce.' Is such a view justified?
3 'The United Kingdom is a unitary state with all political authority ultimately centralised.' Discuss.

Notes

1. Report of the Maud Committee on local government management (London: HMSO, 1967).
2. Report of the Committee of Inquiry into the system of remuneration of members of local authorities, vol. 2 Cmnd 7010 (London: HMSO, 1977).
3. See 'The conduct of local authority business', Cmnd 9797 (London: HMSO, 1986), paras 2.23-2.31 for more information on the socioeconomic profile of modern councillors.
4. See K. Young and N. Rao, *Coming to Terms with Change? The Local Government Councillor in 1993* (London: Joseph Rowntree Foundation, 1994).
5. The functions transferred to the Borough and District Councils included: planning, highways and traffic management; waste regulation and disposal; housing; trading standards and related functions; support for the arts, sport and historic buildings; civil defence and emergencies; funding for Magistrates' Courts and the probation service; Coroners; school crossing patrols; building control; tourism and the licensing of places of entertainment; archives and libraries; recreation, parks and Green Belt land; safety of sports grounds; registration of common land and town or village greens; public rights of way and the registration of gipsy sites.
6. See S. Weir and W. Hall, *Ego Trip: Extra-governmental Organisation in the UK* (London: Charter 88 Trust, 1990).
7. See 'Local government finance' (the Layfield Report), Cmnd 6453 (London: HMSO, 1976); the Labour Government's response to the Longfield Report, Cmnd 6813 (London: HMSO, 1977); and 'Alternatives to domestic rates', Cmnd 8449 (London: HMSO, 1981), for a fuller discussion of these issued.
8. Quoted in the 1987 Conservative Campaign Guide, p. 331.
9. See N. D. J. Baldwin, *The Conservative Party: an instinct to survive* (Barnstaple: Phillip Charles Media, 1990).
10. See 'A new tax for local government', Department of the Environment Consultation Paper, April 1991.
11. See K. B. Smellie, *History of Local Government* (London: Allen & Unwin, 1968), for a more detailed account.
12. N. P. Hepworth, *The Finance of Local Government,* 4th edn (London: Allen & Unwin, 1978), p. 255.
13. See M. Dynes and D. Walker, *The Times Guide to the New British State: The Government Machine in the 1990s* (London: Times Books, 1995).
14. J. A. G. Griffith, *Central Departments and Local Authorities* (London: Allen & Unwin, 1966), p. 49.
15. See 1992 Labour Party Manifesto 'Time to get Britain working again' for a succinct and authoritative statement of Labour's approach to local government reform.
16. *The Times*, 14 August 1981.
17. See M. Forsyth, *Re-servicing Britain* (London: Adam Smith Institute, 1980), N. Ridley, *The Local Right: enabling not providing* (London: Centre for Policy Studies, 1988), and A. Seldon, *The State is Rolling Back* (London: E & L Brooks/Institute for Economic Affairs, 1994), for a fuller discussion of this approach.

Further reading

Alexander, A., *Local Government in the 1990s* (Barnstaple: Phillip Charles Media, 1990).

Butcher, H., *et al., Local Government and Thatcherism* (London: Routledge, 1990).

Butler, D., Adonis, A., and Travers, T., *Failure in British Government: the politics of the Poll Tax* (Oxford: OUP, 1994).

Gray, C., *Government Beyond the Centre* (London: Macmillan, 1993).

Hampton, W., *Local Government and Urban Politics*, 2nd edn (London: Longman, 1991).

Leach, S., *et al., The Changing Organisation and Management of Local Government* (London: Macmillan, 1994).

Rhodes, R.A.W., *Beyond Westminster and Whitehall* (London: Routledge, 1992).

Stoker, G., *The Politics of Local Government,* 2nd edn (London: Macmillan, 1991).

Wilson, D., Game, C., et al., *Local Government in the UK* (London: Macmillan, 1994).

Young, K. and Rao, N., *Coming to Terms with Change? The Local Government Councillor in 1993* (London: Joseph Rowntree Foundation).

17 The Legal System

There are five main aspects of the legal system in the United Kingdom.[1] All of them are significantly affected by the peculiar nature of the British constitution, which is uncodified and which vests supreme legal power and authority in Parliament rather than in any Court. *Firstly*, there is the sphere of *criminal justice* which involves the application of the criminal law to cases brought to Court by the prosecuting authorities and others. *Secondly*, there is the sphere of *civil justice* which involves the application of the civil law to cases brought by various plaintiffs, including individuals, corporate bodies and the Law Officers of the Crown. *Thirdly*, there is the process of *judicial appeal* which allows those who are dissatisfied with the verdicts of lower Courts or Tribunals to seek redress or reversal of judgement in the higher Courts of Appeal. *Fourthly*, there is the important sphere of *rights and duties* which determines the complex legal relationship between citizens and the state. *Finally*, there is the sphere of *administrative law* which enables the courts to review the actions of Ministers, local authorities and other public bodies. This chapter reviews each of these aspects in turn. It does so against a contemporary backdrop which reveals declining public confidence in the police and the judicial system, an increasingly relevant European context, and mounting pressure for significant reform.

For our purposes in this chapter, the most important single feature of the British constitution is Parliamentary supremacy which in most circumstances permits the Executive to dominate the political sphere through Parliament. There is no formal separation of powers; rather, the Executive and the Legislature are intertwined and together are able to override the Judiciary. This position is derived from the traditional idea (dating from the seventeenth century) that Parliament can do anything it wishes: it can make, amend or repeal any law, with the consequence that primary legislation passed by Parliament can override any decisions made by the Courts and not even the Law Lords (the highest Court in the land) can rule that an Act of Parliament is unlawful or unconstitutional.[2] As a result Britain has traditionally been a country with a comparatively weak judiciary - certainly when compared with the United States or other constitutional systems based upon codified constitutions. This has shaped and influenced much of the legal system in Britain, and made even very senior judges cautious about explicitly challenging the authority of Parliament.

From the start it should also be noted that Common Law and Statute Law are two distinct sources of law, and the power given to judges through the doctrine of precedent and the use of Common Law as a basis for judgement is of some constitutional significance. Similarly, it should be noted that judges are appointed from the ranks of legal professionals with experience in advocacy, that there is an independent body of barristers or advocates and that Court procedures are based for the most part on a preference for adversarial rather than inquisitorial types of proceeding.

17.1 Criminal justice

Machinery and procedure

The majority of criminal cases are disposed of in *Magistrates' Courts* and only a minority are tried in the higher Courts. Trial in a Magistrates' Court is summary (that is, without a jury) and takes place before a bench of two or more Justices of the Peace or one legally qualified Stipendiary Magistrate. Most cases are brought by the Crown Prosecution Service which prefers charges against the defendants on the basis of police evidence and legal advice.

In the minority of cases which go to *Crown Courts* the procedure is one of trial by jury before a High Court Judge, a Circuit Judge or a Recorder (that is, a practising barrister or solicitor sitting in a judicial capacity). Most of the more serious cases are transferred automatically to the Crown Courts, although even in less serious cases the defendant can opt for trial by jury in a Crown Court rather than summary trial in a Magistrates' Court – and many do in the hope and expectation that they will stand a better chance of acquittal in front of a jury.

The most serious cases (for example, murder, rape, or armed robbery) must be tried in the *High Court*. Other serious cases (for example, manslaughter or serious assault) are usually tried by a High Court Judge, but sometimes released to a Circuit Judge or a Recorder. Cases which involve lesser indictable offences or those in which the defendant has opted for trial by jury are usually tried by Circuit Judges or Recorders. In all these cases the most important role of the judge is directing the jury on matters of law. Yet the passing of sentence on convicted defendants has become increasingly significant, at any rate in very serious cases, since judges have tended increasingly to make specific recommendations about the length of prison sentence which should be served, largely to pacify public opinion which has become increasingly vexed not only over what is widely regarded as insufficient or too lenient sentencing, but also by the practice of granting parole or remission of sentence sometimes when as little as a third or a half of a sentence has been served. It was for this reason that in the 1988 Criminal Justice Act the Attorney General was given the power to refer certain cases to the Court of Appeal if he thought the sentence imposed by a Crown Court Judge was unduly lenient. See Figure 17.1 for a diagram of the system of criminal courts.

Controversial issues

There are many controversial issues in the criminal law. Most of them were considered by the *Royal Commission on Criminal Justice*, set up under the chairmanship of Lord Runciman in March 1991 and which published its report in July 1993.[3] Previous to this

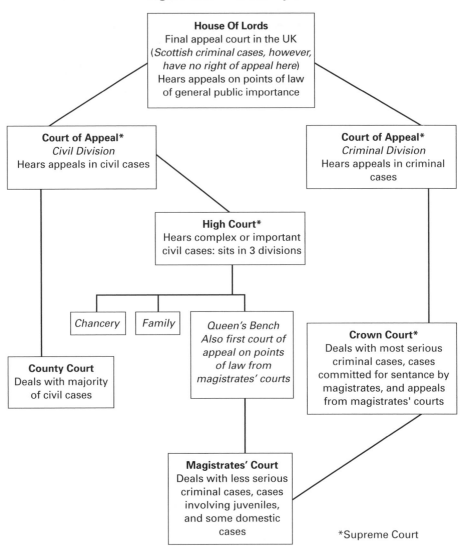

Figure 17.1 The Court system

House Of Lords
Final appeal court in the UK
(*Scottish criminal cases, however,
have no right of appeal here*)
Hears appeals on points of law
of general public importance

Court of Appeal*
Civil Division
Hears appeals in civil cases

Court of Appeal*
Criminal Division
Hears appeals in criminal
cases

High Court*
Hears complex or important
civil cases: sits in 3 divisions

Chancery *Family*

*Queen's Bench
Also first court of
appeal on points
of law from
magistrates' courts*

Crown Court*
Deals with most serious
criminal cases, cases
committed for sentence by
magistrates, and appeals
from magistrates' courts

County Court
Deals with majority
of civil cases

Magistrates' Court
Deals with less serious
criminal cases, cases
involving juveniles,
and some domestic
cases

*Supreme Court

there had been a similar investigation by the *Royal Commission on Criminal Procedure* which had been set up in 1977 and which reported in 1981.[4] Under the chairmanship of Sir Cyril Philips it had touched on the right of silence for criminal suspects, the exclusion of evidence which had been improperly obtained, the definition of arrestable offences, the extent of police powers to stop and search, the limits on detention in police custody, and the use of tape-recordings in interviews of criminal suspects. The result was the 1984 *Police and Criminal Evidence Act*. Nonetheless, there has continued to be considerable controversy, not least because there are always considerable tensions between the rather reactionary views and prejudices of the general public – often eagerly nurtured by the tabloid press which does little to dispel public ignorance of the principles and procedures involved – and the more enlightened, often pragmatic, views of judges, magistrates, police and prison service.

The Runciman Commission was established in the wake of a number of prominent miscarriages of justice, not least the case of the 'Birmingham Six' who had served more than 16 years in prison for a terrorist crime they did not commit. The 1993 Report included a total of 352 recommendations on virtually every aspect of the criminal justice system, including a defendant's right to silence, the use of DNA profiles, the issue of confessions, continuous tape-recording in custody suites in police stations, police disciplinary action, greater supervision of police investigations, the training of police, lawyers and judges, the ending of a defendant's right in certain cases to opt for trial by jury, discounts on sentences to encourage defendants to plead guilty, the abolition (where possible) of pre-trial committal hearings, time limits on the preparation of cases, and the establishment of an independent body to carry out investigations into alleged miscarriages of justice. By way of response the Government brought forward two pieces of legislation, both of which attracted considerable criticism from the judiciary, lawyers, the police, pressure groups and Opposition parties. Nevertheless the Conservative Government's legislative proposals became law in the shape of the 1994 *Criminal Justice and Public Order Act* and the 1994 *Police and Magistrates' Courts Act*.

One of the difficulties in reaching balanced and lasting conclusions in this sphere of the law is that many of the issues raise important questions to do with the relationship between the police and the public, especially in some inner city areas where the relationship can be very strained between police officers and individuals from the ethnic minority communities.[5] Problems have arisen particularly in the area of police powers to stop and search people for offensive weapons, such as knives and other sharp instruments. There have also been intermittent complaints from suspects that they have not been able to consult a solicitor before being charged or that they have been 'fitted up' by the police with fabricated evidence and induced to make false confessions. Such problems are likely to persist as long as there are shortcomings in police practice, great media and public pressures upon the police to catch and charge someone for offences of a particularly heinous character, and a deep and lasting mistrust of all law-enforcement agencies among some disaffected individuals and groups.

A more general problem is caused by the constant need to strike a fair and effective balance between the interests of the law-abiding majority, which wants the police and the Courts to maintain law and order in a strong, even draconian way, and those of certain vociferous minorities who are often more concerned with the protection of civil liberties and the maintenance of civil rights. Since it is always difficult to strike an appropriate balance between such strongly conflicting interests, the solution has typically involved attempts to balance increased powers for the police and the Courts with more effective legal safeguards for the law-abiding community. This was the intended approach behind both the 1984 Police and Criminal Evidence Act and the 1994 Criminal Justice and Public Order Act, although there was far from universal agreement that this was in fact the result.

Those who are strongly committed to the maintenance of law and order have invariably argued for changes in the criminal law – for example, the return of capital punishment - which they believe would enable the police and the Courts to deal more effectively with the current levels of crime and lawlessness. Indeed, very few people have argued for a more permissive attitude towards crime – except those who wish to decriminalise the purchase and use of soft drugs or legalise and regulate prostitution – or more lenient procedures for dealing with convicted criminals. However, growing concern has been expressed, not only by liberal-minded opinion-formers, about the large and growing number of people sent to prison in Britain compared with other advanced countries and about the smaller (but highly publicised) number of incidents of wrongful conviction, such as the Guildford Four, the Birmingham Six, the Maguire family, the Tottenham Three, and Stefan Kiszko. Others have argued the need for improved procedures to deal with complaints against the police, since a growing number of people believe that there should be a genuinely independent element in any body established to investigate claims of police malpractice. Finally, there is a section of largely intellectual, left-wing opinion which is disturbed by what it sees as alarming tendencies for British society to develop in an authoritarian direction wholly at variance with British liberal-democratic traditions. Such people usually cite as evidence for their concern the occasional tendency for the police, the security services and the para-military units of the modern state to overstep the traditional bounds in a few highly publicised instances of brutality, excessive surveillance and democratically unacceptable uses of force – citing examples such as the actions of the South Yorkshire Police against miners at the Orgreave Coke Plant during the 1984-85 strike (for which they were obliged to pay £500,000 compensation), the death in 1993 of Joyce Gardner, a Jamaican woman living in London, who collapsed during a struggle with police officers from the deportation squad, and some of the actions of the police during the protests by Animal Rights campaigners outside the Essex port of Brightlingsea in 1995.

17.2 Civil justice

Machinery and procedure

Most civil cases are heard initially either in County Courts by Circuit Judges or in one of the three civil Divisions of the High Court by High Court Judges. Magistrates' Courts have original jurisdiction in some cases involving the summary recovery of certain kinds of debt and some domestic proceedings, such as separation and maintenance, guardianship or adoption.

In the *County Courts* the jurisdiction is both local and limited. Such Courts deal with actions founded on the law of contract and tort where the claim of the plaintiff does not exceed the sum of £20,000; equity cases up to a value of £30,000 which affect trusts, mortgages and the dissolution of partnerships – both figures set in 1995 – and actions concerning the recovery of land. They also deal with matters arising from social legislation, such as the adoption of children, the validity of hire purchase agreements, and disputes arising from the various Rent Acts. Since 1977 undefended divorce cases have been dealt with under a 'special procedure' at a Divorce County Court. The procedure is administrative – there are no formal hearings, while complaints of racial discrimination are heard in Tribunals specially designated for the purpose in which procedures are intended to be less formal than in Court. While both barristers and solicitors may appear on behalf of those who come before these Courts and Tribunals, the judge often has to hear the case on the basis of submissions made without the benefit of lawyers.[6] In none of these cases is there call for a jury.

In the High Court, *the Queen's Bench Division* deals principally with actions founded upon the law of contract and tort.[7] It also deals with actions on bills of exchange, insurance claims, shipping actions and some landlord and tenant actions. Only a small proportion of the actions actually come to Court and few are fought to a conclusion, since those involved are usually keen to avoid the high legal costs associated with fighting such cases. Either party may request a trial by jury in cases involving defamation of character, malicious prosecution, false imprisonment, fraud or seduction. The final decision as to whether or not a jury shall try such a case rests with the judge concerned. Another important function performed by this Division is the supervision of the lower Courts and Tribunals. This is done on an application for Judicial Review by issuing prerogative orders, such as a *prohibition, mandamus* or *certiorari*, as well as an order of *habeas corpus*.[8] Whereas in former times these rights were available only to the Monarch, they can now be issued by the High Court upon application from an ordinary plaintiff.

The Chancery Division of the High Court, which was established in London in 1873, has effective jurisdiction over the estates of deceased persons, the execution of trusts, the dissolution of partnerships, disputes in private companies and the redemption or foreclosure of mortgages. In 1921 bankruptcy jurisdiction was added to its various responsibilities, and breach of contract can be investigated here or in the Queen's Bench Division.

The Family Division of the High Court dates from 1971, when cases to do with wills and divorce were separated from those to do with shipwrecks, with which they had been incongruously lumped since 1873 when the Probate, Divorce, and Admiralty Division was established.[9] Today the Division deals with all domestic and matrimonial cases, guardianship and probate. Most of its work is concerned with divorce proceedings in an age when one in three of all marriages end this way.

Controversial issues

The main controversial issues in the civil law today are connected with the public image of the law and lawyers, and with the costs and delays in the processes of the law. We shall, therefore, look briefly at each of these issues in turn.

It is a widely held belief among the general public that the attitudes of lawyers and judges – indeed, the whole paraphernalia of the law – are distinctly old-fashioned and middle class. Indeed, ever since the notorious Taff Vale case in 1901, many have believed that the judiciary has been biased against trade unions, and the development of judge-made case law over the years has not done much to dispel that belief. As Gavin Drewry has pointed out, 'most of the really telling criticism of lawyers centres upon their failure to win the confidence of working-class people and their inability to achieve an image of independence from the Establishment'.[10]

When hearing cases, judges are supposed to be strictly impartial. This means not only that they must not show any personal bias or prejudice, but also that they must exclude from their judgements any political or moral views which they may hold as individuals. Naturally, this is difficult if not impossible for anyone to achieve, so there have been times when judges have appeared to be far from impartial in the eyes of those who come before them. There is at least circumstantial evidence for these misgivings.

Firstly, judges have tended to be drawn disproportionately from the ranks of the upper and middle classes, they are usually white, male and inevitably tend to be quite elderly by the time that they reach the bench. As J. A. G. Griffith has argued, 'they have by their education and training and the pursuit of their profession as barristers acquired a strikingly homogenous collection of attitudes, beliefs and principles which to them represents the public interest.'[11] In the 1990s the Lord Chancellor, Lord Mackay of Clashfern, sought to open up the system of judicial appointments, at least at the lower level, with posts being advertised and the process being subjected to a slightly higher degree of public scrutiny.

Secondly, Griffith and others have argued that the judicial conception of the public interest has invariably been based upon the interest of the state, notably the preservation of law and order, the protection of property and the promotion of certain other political views normally associated with the Conservative Party. In so far as this may be so (and in some ways it would be surprising if it were not), it is almost inevitable that there are some people, especially among ethnic minority groups and embattled sections of the community, who believe that judges are inherently biased against them and their interests. Nonetheless, any investigation into recent cases of Judicial Review would fail to show a judiciary wholly supportive of the actions of Conservative Ministers.

Thirdly, there is a widely held view that access to the law, for those who want to have it, is not equally available to people from all classes and walks of life. Indeed, it is commonly said that only the very rich (who can afford it) and the very poor (who qualify for legal aid from the state) can now afford to go to law. In the latter category, the extent of legal aid available to any litigant has been limited by two tests: whether a solicitor, apart from the consideration of costs, would advise going to Court in the particular case; and whether the applicant falls within the prescribed means-tested limits for legal aid.[12] Over the years the effect of these two provisions has been to exclude quite a large number of fairly poor people from qualifying for legal aid, to penalise those who might otherwise want legal representation when appearing before administrative Tribunals, and to put at a disadvantage litigants with a strong case who are not legally aided when their opposing parties are. Of course, there are other forms of free legal advice available to people, for example, from Citizens' Advice Bureaux, Neighbourhood Law Centres and even Members of Parliament. Yet there still remains a large potential demand for legally aided litigation which probably goes unsatisfied, largely because of Treasury opposition to the mounting public expenditure cost.[13]

Fourthly, there is the deterrent effect of delays in the legal system. It is not just in Dickens' novels that characters sometimes die before their legal case is over. In Britain the problems of delay can be ascribed to the rising demand for litigation, the relative shortage of judges to hear cases, the time taken in amassing all the relevant evidence for use in Court in a convincing way, and the traditional commitment to an adversary procedure which involves the very time-consuming business of hearing and cross-examining witnesses testifying on oath. Some of the problems have been mitigated by improvements in the procedure of small claims Courts, which have served to speed up that particular kind of justice. Yet further progress could undoubtedly be made if more judges could be appointed and if more use could be made of written evidence, at any rate in all those cases where the facts of the matter are not seriously contested by the various parties.

Finally, some have argued that the very nature of the legal system and the middle-class image of the law and lawyers deter many poor or inarticulate people from seeking the benefit of legal advice or legal services. To many people traditional legal procedures seem very off-putting, not to say alarming, with all the wigs and processions and general mumbo-jumbo. Indeed, this is exactly why some of the procedures have been simplified and made more 'user-friendly' in recent years, notably in cases involving families and children.

17.3 Judicial appeal

Machinery and procedure

The process of judicial appeal in Britain can be applied equally to cases of criminal and civil law. Most of the *criminal appeals* are heard by the criminal Division of the Court of Appeal. This is presided over by the Lord Chief Justice or a Lord Justice of Appeal. Queen's Bench judges sit with Appeal Court judges and there are usually three judges on the bench for any hearing. When a case raises an issue of general public importance, a further appeal may be made to the House of Lords, but in criminal cases such appeals are rare.

Most of the *civil appeals* are heard by the Master of the Rolls and the Lord Justices of Appeal, although the Lord Chancellor, the Lord Chief Justice and a few other very senior legal figures may sit *ex officio* (by virtue of their offices) in exceptional circumstances. An odd number of judges (usually three) hears such appeals and decisions of the Court are taken by majority.

On important points of law with wider legal application there is the possibility of further appeal to the House of Lords. Such appeals are made to the *Appellate Committee*, which is the final Court of Appeal and which can only be overruled by Parliament as a whole passing new legislation. The work of the Appellate Committee is done by the Law Lords – the Lord Chancellor, 10 Lords of Appeal and a few other very senior legal figures who may sit by virtue of having previously held high judicial office.[14] The Committee is usually made up of five Law Lords and their judgements take the form of motions, with each judge expressing a judicial opinion on the matter in question. Prior to 1966 the House of Lords had always been bound by its own previous decisions; since 1966 it has been able to overrule them.

Mention should also be made of the *Judicial Committee of the Privy Council* which was established by statute in 1833. This hears appeals on cases authorised by the Courts in the Isle of Man and the Channel Islands, in Britain's remaining colonial Dependencies (for example, the Falkland Islands and, until 1997, Hong Kong) and in those member states of the Commonwealth which have chosen to retain the right of legal appeal to it.[15] It also hears appeals from Admiralty Courts, ecclesiastical Courts, and the disciplinary committees of the General Medical Council and General Dental Council. The Lord Chancellor is nominally its president, but in practice nearly all the work is done by Lords of Appeal. It hears about 20 appeals each year and is the final arbiter of constitutional issues in the various territories and jurisdictions concerned.[16]

Since Britain's accession in 1973 to the European Community – now known officially as the European Union – Britain has been subject to the jurisdiction of the *European Court of Justice* in all those areas of national life covered by European law. This has meant that in an increasingly significant area of legal competence the European Court has provided a final level of judicial appeal higher even than the House of Lords, indeed even Parliament itself. Under Section 2 of the 1972 European Communities Act and subsequent legislation the Westminster Parliament is under a self-imposed legal duty at all times not to pass legislation which would conflict with any European legislation. Thus it can be said that in the areas of European competence, as defined by European treaty obligations, European law takes precedence over national law and an appeal to the European Court of Justice trumps any appeal to a national Court. Following on from this, and as a direct consequence of the *Factortame Ltd* judgement, 1990, it is quite clear that if an Act of Parliament is inconsistent with European Law, a domestic Court in Britain would have to refuse to give it effect. In this context it is worth reiterating the fact that the *European Court of Human Rights* also has compulsory jurisdiction in Britain.

Controversial issues

The process of judicial appeal does not normally give rise to great political controversy, except on those rare occasions when issues of wider political importance are raised in particularly contentious cases. When this happens, judgements in the House of Lords are final, except when they trigger the Government of the day to introduce fresh legislation to overturn or confirm the previous legal position or when the British legal system is overruled by the European Court of Justice.

Early examples of the first of these alternatives were provided by the 1906 Trade Disputes Act, which overturned the House of Lords judgement in the 1901 Taff Vale case, and the 1913 Trade Union Act, which overturned the House of Lords judgement in the 1910 Osborne case. A later well known example was the 1965 War Damage Act, which overturned the 1965 House of Lords judgement in the case of Burmah Oil. A notable example in more recent times was the 1983 Transport Act, which took account of the 1982 House of Lords judgement in the case of *Bromley Borough Council* v. *the Greater London Council* on the politically contentious issue of passenger transport subsidies in Greater London on the bus and underground services. In all such cases, when matters of political importance have been involved, the Government of the day has felt obliged to introduce legislation either to overturn or to take account of the legal position as defined by the House of Lords.

Over the years there have been periods of judicial activism and creativity, and periods when the behaviour of the judiciary has been characterised by conservatism and a determination to defend the established legal order. On the whole judicial conservatism has been the more prevalent. This is partly a reflection of the inherently conservative background and outlook of the judiciary in Britain, to which reference has already been made. Yet is also reflects the well-established constitutional attitude held by the judiciary over many years and most succinctly expressed by Lord Reid on several occasions. In 1961, in *Shaw* v. *the Director of Public Prosecutions*, he observed that 'where Parliament fears to tread, it is not for the Courts to rush in', and in 1972 he maintained that cases which raised political issues should be decided 'on the preponderance of existing authority'.[17] A challenge to Parliament's constitutional right to ratify the 1992 Maastricht Treaty was rejected by the High Court on 30 July 1993, a decision which was undoubtedly influenced by the Speaker of the House of Commons who reminded the Courts in no uncertain terms of the supremacy of Parliament as established in the Bill of Rights in 1689. In rejecting the challenge, the Court declared that ratification involved an exercise of the Royal Prerogative, not a transfer of that Prerogative without Parliamentary approval.[18]

In these matters much has depended upon whether the judiciary construes the law passed by Parliament literally and narrowly or contextually and broadly. For example, Lord Denning in his many years as Master of the Rolls and Chairman of the Court of Appeal (1962-82) was usually inclined to interpret the law in a way which was well disposed towards whichever litigant he considered to be the underdog. Naturally, this did not endear him to those organisations which he deemed oppressive (for example, Trade Unions) or indeed to the Law Lords, who often had to review his judgements on further appeal. Much has also depended upon the extent to which the judiciary has thought it proper or prudent to flex its muscles in defiance of the Government of the day. It has been said that on the whole Labour Governments have found themselves in conflict with the judiciary more often than their Conservative counterparts. However in the 1980s the judiciary was something of a brake upon the radical intentions of the Thatcher Government and in the early-to-mid 1990s, the judges were not only some of the sharpest critics of the Major Government's proposals to reform the criminal justice system, but also not infrequently ruled against Government Ministers in the Courts. Indeed, it could be argued that such facts demonstrate not so much judicial hostility to any particular Government, Left or Right, as the simple reality that there is always likely to be a conflict between the judiciary, with its invariable commitment to the preservation of the existing legal order, and any Government which wishes to make radical change.

Since the bitter debates in Parliament and elsewhere over the application of the 1992 Maastricht Treaty to Britain, perhaps the most controversial legal issues have arisen from the clash of jurisdictions between British legal institutions and those of the European Union. In essence this has meant a *political* struggle between, on the one hand, those politicians and others who wish to preserve the legal sovereignty of Britain's national Courts and, ultimately, of Parliament itself; and, on the other hand, those politicians, officials, interest groups and others who see sectional and national advantage in Britain being prepared to subordinate its legal arrangements to those of the European Union, certainly in those policy areas where, by freely concluded treaty commitments between the Governments of all the member states, it has been agreed that the matters concerned shall be justiciable not only in the national Courts but also, ultimately, in the European Court which has the supreme authority in all legal disputes involving European law. This fundamental clash of competences and jurisdictions – which some see as an inevitable but acceptable aspect of Britain's membership of the European Union, and others see increasingly as a reason to transform the terms and conditions of the entire project into an international rather than a supranational adventure – seems likely to become more acute and difficult to resolve as time goes by.

17.4 Citizens and the state

In the modern world the complex relationship between citizens and the state raises political and legal issues of great importance. Citizens expect to enjoy certain inalienable rights, including freedoms of both a positive and negative kind. There are the freedoms *to* do certain things, and the freedoms *from* having certain things done to you. Each category of freedom is equally valuable. Yet in every case the rights concerned have to be qualified or counterbalanced by certain rights of the state or its agencies to act on behalf of the community as a whole. It is in holding this balance between the rights of citizens and the interests of the state that the legal system in Britain has had to try to resolve some of the most difficult problems of modern society. Furthermore, the basis of civil rights in Britain is to some extent precarious, since there is neither a codified constitution nor an effective Bill of Rights with which to constrain the possibility of Parliamentary tyranny, by which is meant the tyranny of any transient Parliamentary majority in the House of Commons. It is therefore as well to be circumspect when pronouncing upon the important issues which are raised in this section.

International Conventions

There are issues which arise from the wide range of civil rights declared in international Conventions and in many cases subsequently embodied in British law by Parliament at Westminster. For example, the principle that all citizens should be equal before the law is a worthy aspiration in Britain as in other countries, but in Britain's constitutional arrangements it is not enshrined in a codified constitution. From the mid-1960s Parliament has legislated against racial discrimination (in 1965, 1968 and 1976) and against sexual discrimination (in 1975), although its stance on discrimination against the disabled or the aged or gay people has not be so clear-cut. Attempts have been made to counter and eventually eradicate both racial and sexual discrimination from all public behaviour, with public sector institutions (such as the civil service) often required to set an example to the private sector. Many of the initiatives in these spheres have been taken by the Commission for Racial Equality and the Equal Opportunities Commission, both of which were established by Labour Governments to act as watch-dogs and agenda-setters in these areas of policy. Thus, if individual citizens feel aggrieved on racial or sexual grounds, they can use the law, often with the help of these bodies, to take cases to Court in order to seek redress or reinstatement.

The protection of civil rights is a matter of wide international concern. Indeed pressure groups, such as Amnesty International, have been established, often with bases in Britain, to draw attention to human rights abuses and to campaign world-wide against such practices. National Governments have been prepared to make purposeful moves in this direction at least since the 1948 UN Declaration of Human Rights and the 1950 European Convention on Human Rights. The latter, which was ratified by the British Parliament in 1951, provides judicial procedures by which alleged infringements of civil rights in Britain may be examined at international level. The European Convention provides an overt constraint upon the legislative supremacy of Parliament in that successive British Government have not wished to be found in breach of its provisions. However, the Convention has not been incorporated within British national law on the somewhat complacent grounds that civil rights in Britain are adequately protected by British law and that such incorporation would be inconsistent with the traditional British claim to legal supremacy for Parliament at Westminster. It was not until 1966 that the United Kingdom formally recognised the right of individual petition to the European Commission on Human Rights or the compulsory jurisdiction in Britain of the European Court of Human Rights. Since then various proceedings under the Convention have helped to bring about changes in British law and legal practice, for example the introduction of immigration appeal Tribunals, revised rules on access to lawyers for prisoners and restrictions on the use of corporal punishment. It is also necessary to stress once again the European Union aspect of the matter. For example, the 1992 Maastricht Treaty outlined a range of citizens' rights and created a European 'Ombudsman' to which all citizens of the Union have the right to appeal if they feel in need of redress.[19]

Citizenship and free movement

There are issues which arise from rights of citizenship and free movement. Under the 1981 British Nationality Act all British citizens have the same legal rights and status, although this applies only to those with full British citizenship. The position of others resident in Britain is limited by the various legal provisions governing the control of immigration. The position is qualified to some extent by the free movement provisions in European law by which British citizens are also bound, since once individuals have gained the right of abode in one of the other member states of the European Union, they then have the right to come to Britain in search of work.

Under the 1981 British Nationality Act those who are legally British citizens have the right of abode in Britain, and hence the right to enter the United Kingdom and to remain in the United Kingdom as long as they like. Such people cannot legally be deported. On the other hand, the right to leave Britain can be vitiated if people are without British passports (or at any rate temporary British visitor's passports) if they wish to take up legal residence outside the United Kingdom. Of course, under the provisions of European law, all citizens of the member states have the right to take up residence in any part of the European Union under the free movement provisions of the European Treaties. In practice, this 'right' is not yet used by many people and there are considerable linguistic, cultural and administrative obstacles to its extensive realisation. Indeed, official figures have suggested that only a small number of people from the other member states of the European Union have settled in Britain, and an even smaller number of British have moved to settle in other parts of the European Union.[20]

The 1992 Maastricht Treaty altered the character of the European Community, turning it into a European Union and making every citizen of each member state into a citizen of the European Union with rights to live, work and vote (but not in U.K. Parliamentary elections) anywhere in the Union. In addition, citizens of the Union have been given a 'European Charter of Citizens Rights' and have the right to take national Governments to the European Court, to petition the European Parliament, and to appeal directly to a European Ombudsman.

Emergency powers and state security

There are issues which arise from the use of emergency powers by the Government and its agencies, together with the related problems of state security. In most serious emergencies the police, fire and ambulance services can cope with any problems which arise. Yet there are some occasions when the military has to be called in to assist the civilian power or to deal with particularly serious threats to the life and well-being of the community. In recent times the most notable example has been the need to keep thousands of British troops in Northern Ireland in order to help the civil authorities preserve peace and public order. Other examples have included the need to counter the action of terrorists by calling in the Special Air Service (SAS) and other special military units to assist the police and security services. The legal position on all such occasions is that military personnel have a duty to support the civil power when requested by the latter to do so.

Since such emergencies usually involve sensitive and difficult issues of public safety, they require Ministerial supervision and control at the highest level.

During peace-time a state of emergency may be declared under the authority of the 1920 and 1964 Emergency Powers Acts. These statutes permit the Government of the day to make use of wide-ranging temporary powers designed to ensure the maintenance of essential services, subject to Parliamentary approval at least every seven days. During wartime even more far-reaching powers were available to the Government of the day in the shape of the 1914 and 1915 Defence of the Realm Acts and the 1939 and 1940 Emergency Powers Acts. These statutes, which were later repealed, gave the Government of the day almost unlimited powers, including detention without trial for indefinite periods and the seizure of private property without compensation. Again the legislation was subject to Parliamentary approval at least every 28 days.

In the case of special measures to deal with terrorism, Parliament passed some draconian statutes in 1973 and 1975 to deal with the threat in Northern Ireland from the IRA and other terrorist organisations, and in 1974 and 1976 to deal with terrorist offences anywhere in the United Kingdom. This legislation conferred very extensive powers upon the Government of the day, which enabled it to take almost any measures deemed necessary to counter such dire threats to national security, including detention without charge for up to seven days (subsequently reduced to three days with the endorsement of a Court in more recent legislation) and the power to exclude undesirable people from the country. In view of the political sensitivity of the terrorist threat from Northern Ireland over the years, the Prevention of Terrorism (Temporary Provisions) Act and the Northern Ireland (Emergency Provisions) Act have been re-enacted on many occasions and been put to Parliament for renewal on an annual basis.

The interests of state security have also been invoked to justify the passage of the 1989 Official Secrets Act, the retention of the D Notice system and the interception of private communications by telephone-tapping and other techniques of electronic surveillance. These practices have continued on the basis of rather tenuous legal authority, subject to no more than indirect control by Ministers (notably by a Cabinet Committee on the Intelligence Services chaired by the Prime Minister) and virtually no control by Parliament. Traditionally security matters of this kind have been kept under review by the Security Commission, a small supervisory body of Privy Councillors chaired by a Law Lord, which reports regularly to the Prime Minister and occasionally to Parliament. Although the whole process has been shrouded in mystery, since the early 1990s a little more information has been made available about MI5 and MI6: the Security Service has been put on a statutory footing and a special committee of senior Privy Councillors has been established to oversee this area of state activity.[21]

In these circumstances it is not surprising that there has been continuing pressure for reform and the replacement of the existing law with new legislation which would put more emphasis upon the rights of ordinary citizens and less on the needs of national security (which are sometimes a cover for Ministerial convenience). There has been an active, all-party campaign for freedom of information throughout the sphere of Government and the public sector, which has had some success at least in relation to local government and the release of environmental information. The problems of striking an appropriate balance between the needs of official secrecy (and commercial confidentiality) on the one hand and the rights of the citizen on the other have been very great and, some would say, insoluble. The difficulties have been exacerbated by the growing use of computers throughout the public sector and by the development of what is known as the Government Data Network. Public concern about the possible misuse of personal information kept on official files led to the 1984 Data Protection Act, which provided some safeguards against malpractice in relation to nearly all official information which is mechanically processed and stored – but not simple card-index systems.

In 1994 a new Code of Practice came into effect obliging Government Departments to respond to 'reasonable' requests for information. The code stipulated that information would be provided 'as soon as practicable', with a target of twenty working days for 'simple requests for information'. Where information cannot be provided, then Departments are obliged to provide an explanation. Breaches of the code were to be monitored by the Parliamentary Ombudsman. There were, however, a wide range of exemptions, including all 'policy advice' to Ministers unless the Government considered it 'relevant and important'; 'original documents', with Ministers being obliged to disclose only information in digest form; and information harmful to national security, defence or international relations.

In addition, the Major Government has been pledged to the concept of the 'Citizen's Charter' which it described as ' the most far-reaching programme ever devised to improve quality in public services'. This was an attempt to improve standards of public service by treating citizens more as customers or clients. The main themes were quality, choice, standards and value for money. These formed the basis for a number of key principles including the setting, monitoring and publication of explicit standards for public services; the provision of full, accurate and easily understandable information on public services; an emphasis on greater responsiveness to the public and greater accessibility for the public; and the creation of effective procedures for complaints and redress of grievances.[22] These initiatives have not, however, defused the pressures for freedom of information, not least from groups such as the 'Campaign for Freedom of Information' and 'Liberty'. Indeed, both the Labour Party and the Liberal Democrats are pledged to introduce legislation providing for freedom of information, so at the very least the issue is not going to go away.

Personal liberty and property

There are issues which arise from rights of personal liberty and property. Magna Carta in 1215 stipulated that 'no free man shall be taken or imprisoned or dispossessed or outlawed or in any way destroyed [. . .] unless by the lawful judgement of his peers or the law of the land'. This was an early expression of what became known as the 'rule of law' – in essence a belief that all are equal before the law and that no one can be punished without due process of law. Although British citizens are free people, in certain circumstances they can lawfully be detained – for example, after arrest and pending trial on a criminal charge (assuming bail is refused by a Magistrates' Court) or when a local authority decides within its statutory rights to take a child into care. Any such departure from the principle of personal liberty can raise issues of considerable controversy and has sometimes led to investigations by a Royal Commission or the passage of new legislation. Powers of arrest, which are normally exercised by the police (but are legally available to any citizen) are regulated principally by the 1984 Police and Criminal Evidence Act. However, a number of other Acts, such as the latest version of the 1981 Prevention of Terrorism (Temporary Provisions) Act, have an important bearing upon these matters as well.

As for property rights in Britain, these have never been regarded as absolute or sacrosanct. Parliament has legislated on many occasions to limit such rights when they have conflicted with what is deemed by Ministers to be the public interest – for example in the spheres of public health, nationalisation or compulsory purchase. As a general rule in modern times there has not been as much determination to use the law to defend economic or property rights as there has been to defend rights of personal liberty. This is in accordance with the European Convention on Human Rights which has a similar bias. Having said this, however, it should be noted that some have certainly regarded recent employment legislation as giving more weight to economic or property rights than rights of personal liberty.

Wrongful interference with the rights of personal liberty and property can be countered by the use of various legal remedies. These include civil action for damages, prosecution for assault, exercise of the right of self-defence, use of the police complaints procedure, and even the invocation of *habeas corpus*.[23] Yet there are no final or definitive solutions to these problems, since the law governing these aspects of civil rights can be changed from time to time by Act of Parliament – for example, the 1994 Criminal Justice and Public Order Act or the 1991 Child Support Act which created the Child Support Agency – and in any case it has to be seen increasingly within a European context.

Freedom of expression

There are issues which arise from rights of free expression and their necessary limitation. In this sphere British law has usually relied upon the principle that anything which is not prohibited is permitted. Yet the extent to which restrictions have been imposed in civil or criminal law has varied from time to time. For example, the law of defamation protects individuals from slander and libel, or rather it provides a form of legal redress if the person concerned can afford to fight a case. Substantial damages may be awarded for injury to a person's reputation, and in some cases even the threat of such legal action can be sufficient to secure a retraction or to get a newspaper to publish a (usually inadequate) note of correction. In some cases those accused of defamation can plead absolute privilege (typically in fair and accurate reports of such proceedings). The defence of 'fair comment' can also protect expressions of opinion on matters of public interest, even if someone thinks what has been said is defamatory.

In the criminal law there are the offences of sedition, blasphemy, obscenity and criminal libel which theoretically protect society from some of the excesses of free expression. Yet in practice actions are rare and of dubious utility, since it is difficult to get juries to convict on the basis of such ancient laws. Furthermore, as was seen in the much publicised instance of Salman Rushdie's *Satanic Verses*, the law (in this case the law of blasphemy) does not always apply. In this instance an alleged blasphemy against the prophet Mohammed fell outside the terms of the statute, which concerns itself only with blasphemy in a Christian context. However, it certainly focused public attention on the utility of such a law in a modern, multi-cultural society.

Freedom of expression in the media has traditionally been controlled to some extent by a combination of self-discipline on the part of the more responsible media and the intervention of certain statutory bodies whose task it has been to maintain what are regarded as 'proper' standards. In the case of newspapers, the Press Complaints Commission has had an unimpressive record in preventing and an even less impressive record in punishing severe lapses of taste or decency, or unacceptable invasions of privacy. The same can be said in the case of broadcasting with regard to the Broadcasting Complaints Commission. However, in this area the BBC Board of Governors, the Independent Television Commission (ITC) and the Radio Authority have great powers over the broadcasters in radio and television, although they have taken few opportunities to use their powers, especially if urged to do so by the Government of the day. In the sensitive areas of sex and violence on television the Broadcasting Standards Council has wielded its statutory powers with apparent enthusiasm, causing some observers to comment upon what they regard as the creation of a general climate in which legitimate artistic expression may be inhibited. In the world of cinema and video the British Board of Film Classification has the task of certifying films for public release and can prohibit exhibition on the grounds that it 'would offend against good taste or decency or would be likely to encourage or incite to crime or to lead to disorder or to be offensive to public feeling'. As far as advertising is concerned, standards of public taste and decency are monitored by the Advertising Standards Authority, although again with rather little obvious effect. In certain respects the media have become much more unrestrained with the liberalisation of the airwaves in the 1990s and increasingly intense competiton between tabloid newspapers. It will also be difficult to regulate the electronic media as the new technologies become cheaper, more competitive and potentially global in their reach.[24]

Finally, it should be noted that it is not unknown for Governments to attempt to exert pressure on broadcasters in relation to particular programmes. For example, in 1985 the Conservative Government leaned heavily on the BBC to withdraw the *Real Lives* programme which focused on a prominent member of the IRA (the programme was withdrawn, although shown at a later date following minor changes); while in December 1987 the Government took out an injunction to prevent the broadcast of a Radio 4 series *My Country Right or Wrong*. Nonetheless, those who work in the media jealously guard their freedom and seek vigorously to resist such Government interference. This was evident in the strength of the media reaction to the *Real Lives* controversy and to similar Government attempts in 1988 to ensure that a *This Week* programme, 'Death on the Rock', was not broadcast, because of its portrayal of an SAS killing of three IRA terrorists in Gibraltar. Government can, however, use the law to curtail freedom of expression, as happened between 1984 and 1994 when the media were not allowed to broadcast the actual voices of members of the IRA and Sinn Fein, even though their pictures could be shown and their words could be spoken by an actor.

Meetings, procession and protest

There are issues which arise from rights to meet, process and protest freely, subject only to various necessary restraints in the interest of public order. In modern times, however, this has been a particularly difficult balance to strike, since it is bound to involve constant adjustment and compromise between conflicting interests. In principle, such freedom is not extended to senior civil servants, the armed services, the police, or registered charities. However, the civil service is heavily unionised at all levels (with the exception of GCHQ, the Government's communications headquarters, where membership of trade unions was prohibited in 1984), and the police of lower ranks have powerful representation from the Police Federation. There is also undoubtedly a grey area covering registered charities and their ability apparently to circumvent some of the legal limitations of their charitable status. The provisions of the 1986 Public Order Act and the 1994 Criminal Justice and Public Order Act curtailed what may lawfully be done on the streets and in public places by providing the police with stronger powers to avert public disorder. For example, the 1986 Act introduced a new offence of disorderly conduct to deal with some forms of modern hooliganism and the 1994 Act created new offences concerning various forms of trespass and causing intentional harassment, alarm or distress, which was designed to deal with racial violence and other forms of harassment.

Public and private meetings for any purpose are constrained not so much by the law as by the need to secure prior permission from the owners of suitable halls or open spaces. However, the 1994 Criminal Justice and Public Order Act contained powers to ban certain 'trespassory assemblies' altogether, while public meetings may not lawfully be held on the public highway and any such obstruction is an offence under the 1959 Highways Act. This has special relevance to the right to picket, which is supposed to be confined under the 1980 Employment Act to peaceful persuasion in contemplation or furtherance of a trade dispute by people attending either at their own place of work or that of so-called 'first customers' and 'first suppliers'.[25] Legal protection against disorderly conduct at a public meeting is still provided by the 1908 Public Meetings Act, as amended by the 1936 Public Order Act; although in modern conditions this has little practical bearing upon such matters.

In general, the preservation of public order in processions and public meetings depends upon the police, who can exercise considerable discretion. Among the powers available to Chief Officers of Police under the 1986 Public Order Act are the power to specify routes for marches and demonstrations and to impose conditions on public meetings. The 1994 Criminal Justice and Public Order Act gave Chief Officers additional powers to apply to the relevant District Council for a ban on public meetings for up to four days within a specified area, and for a ban lasting not more than three months on any category of public procession and occasionally on all public processions.

17.5 The role of the police

For much of their contemporary history the police in Britain have been held in high regard, placed on a pedestal by public opinion as exemplifying an ideal model of behaviour and character. In short, the 'British Bobby' came to be seen as representing all that was 'right and proper' in British society. One survey in the early 1960s showed that no less than 83 per cent of those interviewed professed great respect for the police.[26] This level of public support had been the result principally of four particular features of policing in Britain. *Firstly*, with certain exceptions such as the Diplomatic Protection Group and the police in Northern Ireland, the police do not normally carry firearms. Indeed, only about 10 per cent of the police are trained in the use of firearms and no untrained personnel would ever be issued with a firearm. *Secondly*, individual police forces are locally based and locally controlled. There is no 'national' police force, but rather 52 local police forces in the United Kingdom – 43 in England and Wales, 8 in Scotland and one in Northern Ireland. Outside London each force is under the direction of a Chief Constable who, in turn, is responsible to a local Police Authority. In London – with the exception of the City of London – the Metropolitan Police force is under the command of the Commissioner who, in turn, is responsible to the Home Secretary. *Thirdly*, there is the belief, indeed the knowledge, that there is only one category of police officer whether uniformed or plain-clothed, rather than a range of special police forces answerable to different parts of Government as is the case in many other countries. *Finally*, there is the perception that the police are non-political, non-partisan and impartial. Indeed, it is to preserve this position that the police are kept at arms length from direct Government control and there are a number of local forces rather than a single national force. These features have combined to produce an image of the police as local, disciplined, unarmed, and free from political direction. Thus, traditionally, the police in Britain enjoyed an enviable reputation - at any rate by international standards.

However, from the latter half of the 1960s not only has violence become a more apparent feature of British society, but also the reputation of the police has increasingly been tarnished in the eyes of the media and the public - at any rate those elements in society which come more frequently into contact with the police. For example, although a survey in 1990 showed that 77 per cent of those questioned felt that the police did either a 'very good' or a 'fairly good' job as against 21 per cent who felt that they did a 'poor' or 'very poor' job; the same survey showed that 31 per cent of respondents under the age of 25 said that the police did a poor job.[27] A survey published at the end of 1992 showed that while 76 per cent of white respondents said that the police did a 'very good' or 'fairly good' job; this figure was 62 per cent among Asian respondents and 52 per cent among Afro-Caribbean respondents.[28] Another survey carried out in 1994 showed that only 36 per cent of the public were satisfied with the way their own area was policed - down from 51 per cent in 1992, 67 per cent in 1985 and 75 per cent in 1981 – while only 41 per cent thought the police 'wonderful' – down from 62 per cent in 1983.[29] This movement of public opinion has been the cumulative consequence of five developments, namely: police corruption and other scandals, changes in policing methods, police malpractice in certain areas, problems of police powers and accountability, and rising levels of crime. We shall comment upon each of these points in turn.

With regard to *police corruption and other scandals*, public confidence in the police received a severe jolt in 1969 when *The Sunday Times* revealed the existence of institutionalised corruption in the Metropolitan Police, a situation made worse when it became apparent that members of the police were covering up for each other. More revelations concerning corruption came to the fore, resulting in a massive internal police investigation known as 'Operation Countryman'. This reported in 1978 and although it failed to substantiate most of the allegations, the damage had clearly been done. The public perception was that there had been a police cover-up, whether or not there had been any substance to the allegations. Since then a number of cases have come to light in which innocent people were convicted on the basis of falsified or distorted testimony in which police officers were implicated. There were the notorious cases of the Guildford Four, the Birmingham Six, the Maguire family, and the Tottenham Three. If these had been the only examples, they could perhaps have been explained away as special cases involving terrorism in the first three instances and the brutal murder of a police Constable in the fourth. Yet there have been other cases involving serious police malpractice, for example in the West Midlands Serious Crime Squad in the 1980s and in the case of Stefan

Kiszko who spent 16 years in prison because irrefutable evidence, which showed that he could not possibly have committed the crime for which he had been sentenced, was withheld from the Court by the police. The cumulative result of all such cases has been to damage the image and standing of the police in the eyes of large sections of the British public.

Turning to *changes in police methods*, the main factors have been the reorganisation of the foot patrol system into a motorised unit system in the late 1960s and the growing use of new police equipment. The unintended consequence of the first development was to make the police seem more remote and less reassuring to the law abiding public. The consequence of the second development – the escalating use of new police equipment, such as helmets with vizors, riot shields, long truncheons, CS gas, and the increasing use of firearms – was to disturb and alienate many members of the general public. Such high pressure policing may have become inevitable in certain violent circumstances – for example, the direct action by the miners in 1984-5 or the Poll Tax Riots in the late 1980s – but it has done nothing to enhance the traditional British doctrine of policing by consent.

With regard to *police malpractice in certain areas*, the police have increasingly been accused of bias in their dealings with certain minority groups, not least ethnic minorities. Allegations of police racism have grown, with the police being accused of taking a heavy-handed approach especially towards members of the Afro-Caribbean community. One survey showed that Afro-Caribbeans were 50 per cent more likely to be stopped in their vehicles than white people and nearly four times more likely to be stopped on foot.[30] Indeed, one of the reasons given for the riots which took place in a number of inner city areas in the early 1980s and the early 1990s was the aggressive attitude of the police towards the black community. Similarly, the police have been accused of taking a provocative stance when dealing with public demonstrations and have been blamed – at any rate by extremist elements - for outbreaks of violence on occasions such as the Trafalgar Square Poll Tax riot of 1990 or the Hyde Park riot against what is now the 1994 Criminal Justice and Public Order Act in October 1994. In short, some have come to see police misconduct as widespread – evidenced by the £1.7 million paid in out-of-court settlements to victims of misconduct by the Metropolitan Police in 1993-94.

Turning to *problems of police powers and accountability*, these have also become more salient since the 1980s. As previously pointed out, traditional policing in Britain was usually kept distinct from the party political fray. However, with the breakdown of the post-war consensus in the late 1960s and early 1970s, and with rising levels of public concern about crime and lawlessness, issues of law and order and especially the role of the police inevitably became more controversial. At the same time a number of senior police officers – for example John Alderson in Devon and Cornwall and James Anderton in Greater Manchester – became prominent public figures in their own right. The adequacy of the powers of the police and the effectiveness of legal safeguards against police abuse became highly controversial topics, with civil liberties groups demanding additional safeguards and the 'law and order' lobby demanding greater police powers. Those on the Left of the political spectrum were associated with the former view and those on the Right with the latter. In all this the need to address the apparent lack of police accountability became ever more evident and an increasing cause for public concern.[31]

Finally, there has been *the rising level of crime and lawlessness*. In the early years of the twentieth century the British police recorded fewer than 100,000 offences each year. This figure rose gradually to reach 500,000 by 1950. Since then - and even taking account of the fact that there are today more offences on the statute book - recorded crime rates have risen dramatically – reaching a figure of 5.4 million offences recorded by the police in the 12 months to the end of June 1994.[32] At the same time the proportion of crimes cleared up declined from 41 per cent in 1979 and 26 per cent in 1993. Despite the obvious difficulties associated with such statistics, they have provided the focus for much of the debate in the 1990s, because little public benefit appears to have been gained from the 65 items of law and order legislation passed by Parliament in the period 1979-95, or from the more than 15 per cent increase in police numbers and the 70 per cent real increase in spending on the police during the same period. These trends have undoubtedly eroded public confidence in the police, created a climate of cynicism and even paranoia in some sections of the public, and fostered a sense of anxiety bordering almost on despair among politicians and public alike.

In March 1993 the Government published a White Paper on *Police Reform*.[33] Shortly thereafter the *Report of the Inquiry into Police Responsibilities and Rewards* – the Sheehy Report – was published.[34] At the end of 1993 the Government brought forward its legislative proposals - already considerably modified – in the shape of the *Police and Magistrates' Courts Bill*. This, along with the *Criminal Justice and Public Order Bill*, dominated much of the 1993-94 Parliamentary session, not least because both Bills were a target for some of the most substantial and sustained Parliamentary criticism of recent years. Originally the Police and Magistrates' Courts Bill had contained proposals to enable the Home Secretary to set objectives for and even to merge police forces, to reduce the size of Police Authorities, to appoint five members and the chairman of each Police Authority, to grant new powers to Chief Constables, to establish new disciplinary procedures, and to introduce fixed-term contracts and performance-related pay for Magistrates' clerks. In the event, the Conservative Government compromised with its critics and came forward with amended proposals which were passed into law as the 1994 Police and Magistrates Courts Act.

It is too soon to tell what will be the longer term effects of these developments. Suffice it to say that profound social factors underlie the issues which have generated controversy about the police. Since the late 1960s the social conditions which must underpin what can be termed 'policing by consent' have been eroded; economic and social inequality has increased; British society has become less homogeneous and less deferential than before. Consequently, as was pointed out by Lord Scarman in his Report into the 1981 Brixton disorders, it is no good blaming the police for rising crime and declining respect for the law. Indeed, it is difficult to escape the conclusion that all sections of society must take responsibility for what has happened and act constructively together to deal with both the causes and the consequences of crime and public disorder.

17.6 Administrative law

From a political point of view it is administrative law which is probably the most important aspect of the legal system in Britain. H. W. R. Wade defined this area of the law as 'the body of general principles which govern the exercise of powers and duties by public authorities'.[35] Since the end of the nineteenth century there has been a great expansion of Parliamentary legislation and hence a notable multiplication of administrative bodies created by statute. This has led to growing judicial and quasi-judicial intervention in the field of public administration. Members of the general public have felt the need to appeal to Tribunals and ultimately to the Courts on many points of administrative law. For its part the judiciary has attempted to compensate for the failure of Parliament adequately to protect citizens from the shortcomings or injustices which can be perpetrated by the public administration.

Administrative Tribunals

In the modern British political system there is a bewildering array of administrative Tribunals which have been created by Acts of Parliament. Some, such as the National Insurance Tribunals which decide disputed claims to benefits, were established as a function of the Welfare State. Some, such as the Industrial Tribunals which adjudicate on claims of industrial injury, unfair dismissal, and other employment disputes, are related to the problems of industrial relations. Some deal with housing disputes, some with pensions or unemployment, some with immigration, some with the National Health Service, and some with education disputes. All exist in order to provide simpler, cheaper, quicker and more accessible forms of justice than are available in the Courts; certainly these are the intentions underpinning this approach.

The main characteristics of Administrative Tribunals are as follows. They are normally established by Act of Parliament. Their decisions are quasi-judicial in the sense that they investigate the facts of the case and then apply certain legal principles in an impartial manner. They are independent in the sense that their decisions are in no way subject to political or administrative interference. Their membership varies, but they usually consist of a legally qualified chairman and two lay members representing relevant interests. They are assisted by clerks who are usually civil servants from the relevant Department. Appeals against their decisions can be made in various ways, since Parliament has laid down no consistent procedures. Appeals may lie to a Minister, a superior Tribunal, a superior Court, or there may be no provision for appeal, as is the case with the National Insurance Commissioners or the National Health Service Tribunal.

The main advantages of Administrative Tribunals are as follows. They offer relatively quick, cheap and accessible procedures which are essential, for example, in the administration of welfare schemes involving large numbers of small claims. Another advantage is that they are well suited to deal expertly with highly technical matters, such as those referred to the Income Tax Commissioners or the Medical Appeal Tribunals. On the other hand, *the main disadvantage* of Administrative Tribunals is their institutional proliferation and jurisdictional complexity. Over the years the growth of these bodies has produced over 50 different types of Tribunal, all of which fall within the definition laid down in the 1971 Tribunals and Inquiries Act. They range from those which are very active, for example Supplementary Benefit or Rent Tribunals, to those which have heard no cases at all, such as the Mines and Quarries Tribunals.

In such a complex structure there are inevitable problems of overlapping and competing jurisdictions, and little has been done so far to amalgamate or group Tribunals according to their various functions. Considerable attention has also been paid to the search for effective ways of controlling and supervising this part of the legal system. None of the existing methods has proved wholly satisfactory, which is why some have looked to practice on the Continent and others to overall constitutional reform for appropriate answers. Consequently, it is necessary to consider each of the various solutions in turn.

Ministerial control

The traditional view of the problems of administrative law is that the public interest can best be safeguarded by Ministers responsible to Parliament. Yet this idea has been something of a constitutional fiction ever since its mythical properties were first revealed by Lord Hewart and Professor Robson more than 60 years ago.[36] The criticism then, and even more so today, is that Ministers cannot possibly be well informed about, still less truly accountable for everything which happens (or fails to happen) within all the various administrative Tribunals and other quasi-judicial bodies for which they may be nominally responsible.

Even before the Second World War, it was recognised that Parliamentary control of Ministers was vitiated by the growth of delegated legislation, just as the purity of judge-made laws was threatened by the growth of quasi-judicial powers exercised by civil servants in the name of Ministers and by Administrative Tribunals. Yet for many years little was done to tackle these problems, since the pressing challenges of war and reconstruction had to be given a higher priority. It was not until after the notorious Crichel Down affair in the early 1950s that some effective action began to be taken.[37] A committee chaired by Sir Oliver Franks was established to look at all these matters and in 1957 it produced a report which was broadly acceptable to the Conservative Government of the day. This led to the 1957 Tribunals and Inquiries Act which provided for the creation of the Council on Tribunals to oversee the whole sphere of administrative law. Subsequently the legislation was consolidated and has most recently been brought up-to-date in the 1992 Tribunals and Inquiries Act.

In general, Ministerial control has not been an adequate response to the problems of overseeing and reviewing this type of law. In effect, it has sought to deny the significance of the problems by assuming that public administration is bound to reflect the public interest as long as in each Departmental area it is headed by a Minister responsible to Parliament. Such an idea is obviously defective in contemporary conditions, now that the whole process of Government has become so large and complex. In circumstances in which few Ministers achieve complete control over their Departments and Parliament has even less effective control over Ministers, it is naive to pretend that the Ministerial principle provides a satisfactory answer.

The Ombudsman

Another approach to solving the problem has been the creation of an independent institution specifically designed to limit serious abuses of administrative power and to deal firmly with any which arise. In Britain, as in other countries – for example, New Zealand and Scandinavia – this has been achieved by the Parliamentary Commissioner for Administration, commonly known as the Ombudsman.[38] The institution was created by Act of Parliament in 1967 in a further attempt to ensure that the administrative procedures of central Government and its agencies are correctly followed and that any allegations of maladministration are investigated and, if possible, rectified.

The Ombudsman, who is usually a former lawyer or civil servant, is appointed by the Crown on the advice of the Lord Chancellor. The constitutional status of the position is similar to that of a High Court judge, namely completely independent of Government. As is the case for a judge, the salary is fixed by statute and charged automatically to the Consolidated Fund. The Ombudsman can only be removed from office by the Crown after addresses by both Houses of Parliament; in other words the incumbent is effectively unsackable during a five-year term of office. The staff of the Ombudsman are usually drawn from the ranks of the civil service. The jurisdiction of the Ombudsman is confined to the Departments of central Government and certain non-Departmental public bodies. However, in addition to the Parliamentary Ombudsman, there are Health Service Ombudsmen in England, Scotland and Wales whose job it is to investigate complaints about NHS authorities including NHS Trusts; Local Government Ombudsmen in England (where there are in fact three), Scotland and Wales whose job it is to investigate complaints made against local government bodies; and an Ombudsman for Northern Ireland whose job it is to investigate complaints made against Government Departments and other public bodies in the Province. Nonetheless, the jurisdiction of the Ombudsman does not cover either the police or public corporations. Similarly, although the Ombudsman can investigate complaints about the way in which Departments have discharged their functions, the jurisdiction does not extend to international relations, Court proceedings, employment issues, or the commercial transactions of central Government. Furthermore, there is no right to investigate cases where the complainant has a right of recourse to an Administrative Tribunal or a remedy in the Courts. Nor can complaints be investigated if made more than one year after the date when the complainant first had notice of the matter. In short, Parliament did not exactly give the institution *carte blanche*, largely because at the outset it was seen by many MPs as an interloper in their territory.

It is essentially for this reason that to this day most complaints are made to the Ombudsman via a Member of Parliament. Once the complaint has been officially received, it is first for the Ombudsman to decide whether or not it properly falls within their jurisdiction. In fact, fewer than half the complaints received fall within the Ombudsman's jurisdiction and can therefore be investigated. All official documents, except Cabinet papers, have to be produced for inspection at the request of the Ombudsman who has the same powers as a High Court judge to compel any witness to give evidence. When an investigation is complete, a report is normally sent to the MP concerned, who then sends it on to the complainant.

The Ombudsman has no executive powers, but the reports concerned often suggest appropriate remedies upon which the Department involved normally takes action. The remedies may include financial compensation from public funds, remission of taxation, administrative review of earlier decisions, or revised administrative procedures. For example, in the 1989 Barlow Clowes report the Ombudsman recommended that the private investors who had lost all their money to two investment funds which were not properly supervised by the Department of Trade and Industry should receive substantial financial compensation for their losses on a diminishing scale as the amounts increased. This reflected implied culpability on the part of the supervisory Department and, following a lengthy Parliamentary campaign by back-benchers for recompense for their constituents, led Ministers to offer taxpayers' money for the purpose. MPs work quite happily in partnership with the Ombudsman in joint efforts to secure redress for their constituents. In formal terms this relationship has been cemented by the work of a Select

Committee of the House of Commons which supervises the work of the Ombudsman and takes evidence, where appropriate, from Departments which are the subject of such investigations. This all helps to ensure that the recommendations are carried out.

Judicial review

Another way of dealing with injustices or abuses which are perpetrated by the public administration is judicial review. The basic leverage for the judiciary is provided by the doctrine of *ultra vires*, which holds that acts of public administration can be unlawful if they offend against the rules of natural justice or otherwise go beyond interpretations of the statutes which reasonable people could reasonably accept. It is this doctrine which enables the High Court to set aside administrative decisions which, although perhaps within the literal scope of the statutes, are plainly unreasonable. The issues involved are inevitably controversial, since the nub of the argument is usually the degree of discretionary power which can properly be exercised by a public body. The judiciary has the difficult responsibility of interpreting the meaning of statutes on the basis of what reasonable people would reasonably decide. This can be approached in a narrow and literal sense or a broad and contextual sense, and the outcome of such cases will often depend upon which of the two approaches is adopted.

When a complaint against the public administration is brought before the High Court, several legal remedies are available to the plaintiffs. There are the traditional prerogative remedies which were originally vested in the Monarch, but which are now available to ordinary citizens. These are *certiorari* to quash an administrative decision already made; *prohibition* to prevent a public authority from considering a matter which it has no statutory right to consider; and *mandamus* to compel a public body to perform a public duty. Then there are the two non-prerogative remedies which are often more useful nowadays. These are an *injunction* to prohibit a public body from doing something and a *declaration* which is simply a statement by the Court clarifying the legal position, so that the powers and duties of a public body can be defined more precisely.[39]

Judicial review is impartial in the sense that it is in no way influenced by the position of the complainant or the power of the public body about which the complaint has been made. Yet there are weaknesses in such procedures. For example, the Courts can only intervene if a plaintiff starts legal proceedings; it can only deal with the case before it; it usually lacks the detailed expertise of the public administration which it seeks to control; it cannot oversee the way in which its remedial orders are carried out; and it proceeds so slowly and expensively that many would-be plaintiffs are deterred from going to law in the first place.

In conducting the process of judicial review, the judges tend to be guided essentially by the principles of natural justice. These are the right of the complainant to be heard before the relevant decision is taken and the absence of prejudice on the part of the Court or other public body charged with the duty of adjudication. Clearly, there is a difficult balance which has to be struck by the Courts between the interests of the plaintiff and those of the general public as represented by the decisions of public bodies. The balance has shifted back and forth over the years. Yet as Hartley and Griffith have pointed out, the Courts have tended to be guided 'more by policy than by precedent, more by what they think is fair and reasonable than by rigid rules.[40] Judicial review is therefore a more than usually political form of justice.

Since about the mid-1960s the judiciary in Britain has taken more account of the principles of natural justice and has been prepared to play a more active part in arguments of political principle.[41] This has been evident especially in cases which bear upon the definition of individual rights, such as personal property, liberty, freedom of movement, retention of office and access to employment. It could also be argued that over these years the tide of judicial opinion turned against some unpopular groups of which others in society tended to disapprove, such as trade unionists or students. Notwithstanding the fluctuations in both judicial and public opinion on these and other questions, the judiciary has shown a growing willingness to use the process of judicial review to deal definitively with disputes which can arise in the sphere of public administration.

The number of applications for judicial review has risen sharply over recent years, from 160 in 1974 to 1500 in 1987 to 2800 in 1993 and successive Governments have had the Courts find against them. For example, in 1976 the Courts struck down a direction by the then Secretary of State for Education, Shirley Williams, to Tameside Council to implement a scheme to convert a number of grammar schools to comprehensive schools. In 1981 the High Court ruled that the then Secretary of State for the Environment, Michael Heseltine, had acted improperly in refusing to listen to representations from various London Boroughs concerning his decision to reduce their rate support grant. In 1990 the High Court overruled Government guidelines on the administration of the Social Fund introduced in 1988. In 1993 the Law Lords ruled that the then Home Secretary, Kenneth Baker, had been in contempt of Court when deporting a Zairean refugee in May 1991. In 1994 the High Court found that the Foreign Secretary, Douglas Hurd, had acted illegally in authorising aid worth £234m for the Pergau Dam in Malaysia. Finally, in 1995 the Law Lords ruled that the Home Secretary, Michael Howard, had abused his powers and flouted the will of Parliament when he introduced a cheaper, fixed rate Criminal Injuries Compensation Scheme. Although not all cases involve the action of Ministers, and notwithstanding the fact that in those that do, not all result in the action of the Minster being struck out, the apparently greater willingness of the Courts to play an active role in this respect has undoubtedly modified the balance of power somewhat in favour of the ordinary citizen.

Continental solutions

There are some who argue that Britain should look further afield to find the most effective ways of supervising and controlling the public administration. Specifically, they maintain that the best solution would be to establish in Britain a new Administrative Division of the High Court (similar to that which exists in France) or a new Administrative Appeals Tribunal (along the lines of that which exists in Sweden). Such approaches have been advocated by those members of the judiciary who would like to see the process of judicial review extended into all corners of the public administration.

Such solutions would almost certainly be opposed by those who already harbour a deep suspicion of the judiciary and hence a strong unwillingness to allow them a more influential political role. Certainly many of those on the Left of British politics would oppose any extension of the powers and competence of the judiciary unless and until they could feel satisfied that the judiciary had ceased to be drawn from such a deeply conservative section of the population. At the same time many of those on the Right would resist it on the grounds that it is undesirable to import foreign judicial practices into Britain. Yet, as Britain becomes more deeply drawn into the process of European integration, it seems almost certain that the impact of European law and especially the influence of the European Court will be increasingly felt in both the public and private sectors.[42] Indeed, much of the acrimonious debate between the so-called 'Euro-sceptics' – those opposed to further European integration – and the so-called 'Europhiles' – those supportive of further European integration – has centred upon the growing concern of the former about the intrusion of the European Court into more and more areas of British national life.

Constitutional reform

Finally, some eminent legal figures, such as Lord Scarman and Lord Hailsham, have argued the case for comprehensive constitutional reform entailing a new Bill of Rights and the introduction of an entrenched and codified constitution which would be interpreted and protected by a newly established and completely independent Supreme Court.[43] Those who favour this way of dealing with the problems of administrative law have to contend with the traditional British response that civil rights and political liberties are most secure if founded upon the established custom and practice of common law. Of course, they would probably reply in their turn that the traditional approach has become obsolete in view of the scope and complexity of public administration in contemporary political circumstances. This would then lead them to the conclusion that a new Bill of Rights should include a formal statement of civil rights and public duties.

Whatever the attractions of this idea, there would be several considerable difficulties with such an approach in Britain. There would need to be a codified constitution which anyone could invoke in the event of a dispute with the public authorities. There would need to be a wholly new Supreme Court quite independent of the political considerations which are sometimes seen as influencing the judgements of the Law Lords. There would need to be public acceptance of a very different and more distinctive role for the senior members of the judiciary. Above all, Members of Parliament would have to be willing to acknowledge that Parliament itself could no longer claim its traditional political and constitutional supremacy. Of course, the irony here is that the idea of Parliamentary supremacy is already rather dated, being challenged by Britain's membership of the European Union, and is likely to be further eroded if more national sovereignty is pooled in the process of shared decision making in the Council of Ministers and democratic power sharing between Westminster and the European Parliament.

Among those who favour such all-embracing changes, Nevil Johnson has argued that 'the challenge is to construct a different relationship between law and politics and in so doing to give law [. . .] a new and wider part in the regulation of the affairs of society'.[44] We have seen in Chapter 15 how this has already been happening in response to the new regulatory needs highlighted by the policy of privatisation. It may yet be taken further if politicians in all parties can get used to the idea of playing second fiddle to judges in the determination of some of the really big legal and constitutional issues in British society.

17.7 Conclusion

It remains to be seen whether the legal system in Britain will develop in a more creative and independent direction, or whether it will remain fundamentally conservative and obedient to the idea – however mythical – of Parliamentary supremacy. There are clearly major implications for the traditional doctrines of Ministerial responsibility and Parliamentary accountability if the judiciary does develop more independent and creative powers. Yet it must be said that such a development is likely to depend essentially upon the Government of the day voluntarily agreeing to be limited by the Courts rather than upon any inclination of the judges to strike more heroic postures. Such a condition seems unlikely to be met in the future irrespective of the political complexion of the Government of the day.

The Labour Party has put forward proposals for a 'Charter of Rights', backed up by a complementary and democratically enforced Bill of Rights, in order to establish in law the specific rights of every citizen. It also advocates additional anti-discrimination legislation, Freedom of Information legislation, a Right to Privacy Act and a Security Services Act; proposes to create a Department of Legal Administration, to improve access to legal aid and to extend its availability to Tribunal hearings; and proposes to diminish Ministerial patronage in the sphere of QUANGOs and to create elected Police Authorities. If implemented, all of this – together with proposals for reform of the House of Lords and the establishment of new Assemblies in Scotland and Wales as well as the option of regional assemblies in England – would undoubtedly add up to the greatest package of legal and constitutional reform in this century.

However, competition for legislative time in Parliament is invariably fierce and of all Labour's constitutional proposals, only the plan to establish a Scottish Parliament has been promised for the first session under a new Labour Government. Thus it would be wise to suspend judgement not only on the practicality but also possibly on the sincerity of such proposals, since students of these matters can recall their disappointment on previous occasions when politicians in office appeared to lose sight of their impressive commitments in Opposition, or failed to deliver the end product because of an insufficient appreciation of the complexity of what was involved and the strength and persistence of the opposition to such reform proposals.

One of the reasons why Labour's proposals may well fall some way short of delivering a constitutionally guaranteed Bill of Rights or even the simple enactment into British law of the European Convention on Human Rights is that the Labour Party (and indeed many politicians in other parties as well) have not overcome their traditional antipathy towards the judiciary. Obviously, there is not a great deal which the judges can do about this in the short term at least – even if they were minded to do so – because of their chastening experience of traditional subordination to the governing majority in the House of Commons at all times. As H. W. R. Wade rightly pointed out, 'if they [the judges] fly too high, Parliament may clip their wings'.[45] In other words, constitutional reform of this kind is unlikely to come about unless the Judiciary *and* the Legislature make common cause against the Executive, and that is highly improbable in the British political system.

It is well to remember that there never has been a truly effective separation of powers in Britain. Such a triangular balance nearly came about in the eighteenth century, when central Government was at its weakest. Yet in more modern times the politicians in Government have definitively asserted their position and the judiciary has been careful not to step too far out of line with the Government of the day. This is because in the last resort the politicians in office can always use their whipped majority in the House of Commons to trump any judicial challenge. For example, when in 1985 the High Court quashed a decision by the then Secretary of State for Transport, Nicholas Ridley, to require the Greater London Council to pay £50 million to support the London Transport Authority, the decision was reversed by subsequent legislation.

Of course, relations between the Judiciary, the Executive and the Legislature may change in future in response to more demanding public attitudes or different constitutional arrangements. For example, the public may come to expect more from the Courts by way of judicial protection and redress against over-mighty or unrepresentative Government. The influential all-party lobby, Charter 88, has pressed for the incorporation into British law of certain, fundamental constitutional principles long since enshrined in the European Convention on Human Rights. Its pressure may prove successful in the longer term if it can become more of a popular movement. Equally, the supremacy of European law over British law, at least in the areas of expanding European competence, may hasten the day when the traditional doctrine of Parliamentary supremacy (which really means the temporary supremacy of the political majority in the House of Commons) can no longer be sustained as the cornerstone of the British constitution. Yet the strong suspicion remains that it will be only in the event of there being a significant measure of electoral reform that the door may really be unlocked to comprehensive constitutional reform in Britain.

Suggested questions

1   What is the nature of the legal relationship between the state and its citizens in Britain today?
2   Describe the structure and problems of either the criminal justice or the civil justice system in contemporary Britain.
3   How appropriate and effective are the arrangements for applying and reviewing administrative law in Britain?

Notes

1. There is no single legal system – either in terms of judicial organisation or body of law – which is applicable throughout the United Kingdom. Rather, there is one set of arrangements in England and Wales, one in Scotland, and one in Northern Ireland. In the detailed descriptions of civil and criminal courts and proceedings which follow, the focus is on the system as applicable to England and Wales. Nevertheless, these five points are essentially applicable throughout.
2. This concept has, however, been modified in significant respects by Britain's membership of the European Union. See Chapter 18 for more on this.
3. See Report of the Royal Commission on Criminal Justice, Cmnd 2263 (London: HMSO, 1993).
4. See Report of the Royal Commission on Criminal Procedure, Cmnd 8092 (London: HMSO, 1981).
5. For a fuller discussion of these issues see the Scarman Report on the Brixton disorders, Cmnd 8487 (London: HMSO, 1981).

6. Solicitors are the branch of the legal profession chiefly concerned with advising clients and preparing their cases, while Barristers who have been 'called to the Bar' (qualified) are entitled to practise as advocates in superior Courts.

7. These are breaches of duty leading to liability for damages, but non-contractual in the case of tort.

8. *Prohibition* prevents a public authority from considering a matter which it has no statutory right to consider. *Mandamus* enables the High Court to compel a public body to perform a public duty which it is statutorily obliged to perform. *Certiorari* enables the High Court to quash an administrative decision already made by a public body. A writ of habeas corpus is supposed to prevent the police from detaining without charge for more than 24 hours those suspected of non-serious offences, although in the case of suspected terrorists there is statutory provision for this time limit to be extended to 3 days inland and 7 days at a port of entry.

9. The reason for this incongruous grouping was simply that all jurisdictions had a common basis in Roman law.

10. G. Drewry, *Law, Justice and Politics* (London: Longman, 1975), p. 128.

11. J. A. G. Griffith, *The Politics of the Judiciary* (London: Fontana, 1977), p. 193.

12. In 1992-93 eligibility for legal aid was reduced to those with disposable incomes of less than £2213 per annum. Consequently whereas it was estimated that 79 per cent of households were eligible for legal aid in 1979, by 1992-93 this had declined to 48 per cent.

13. Legal aid has however grown dramatically over the years. For the first 20 years of the scheme the total cost of aid did not exceed £10m a year. By 1980 the cost had risen to £100m, by 1990 to £1bn, and it was still rising. In 1989 2.3 million people obtained legal aid. By 1993 this figure had risen to 3.5 million. At the same time the average cost of each individual action has also risen: in 1989 the average cost was £204; in 1994 it stood at £350. See R. Rice, 'Trapped in a time warp', *The Financial Times*, 4 October 1994.

Net expenditure on legal aid in 1993-94 was:

	£ million
Criminal legal aid	
Criminal Higher	236
Criminal Magistrates'	192
Duty Solicitor Schemes	78
Criminal Green Form (advice and assistance)	14
Total criminal Legal Aid	520
Civil legal aid	
Civil Legal Aid	544
Assistance by way of representation	19
Green form (advice and assistance)	127
Total Civil Legal Aid	690
	1380
Total net expenditure	1900

14. Formerly there was no restriction upon the participation of lay peers in the judicial proceedings of the House of Lords. However, after the O'Connell case in 1844, in which their intervention would have had the effect of overturning the decision of the Law Lords (that is, the Lord Chancellor, the Lords of Appeal and such peers as held or had held high judicial office in a superior Court), it became an established convention that they should not take part in the judicial work of the House. Because of the ensuing shortage of peers who had held highly judicial office, the 1876 Appellate Jurisdiction Act provided for the appointment of two Lords of Appeal and declared that appeals to the Lords should not be heard unless at least three Law Lords were present. In 1948 the Lords authorised (on a temporary basis at first) the hearing

of appeals by an Appellate Committee drawn from the 11 appointed Lords of Appeal (including the Lord Chancellor) and the other senior legal figures already mentioned. After a time this innovation became permanent, so that nearly all appeals to the House of Lords are now heard by the Law Lords sitting as either one or two Appellate Committees, depending upon the number of cases to be heard.

15. These are Trinidad and Tobago, Singapore, Dominica, Kiribata, and The Gambia.

16. The Judicial Committee has been available as a source of advisory opinion for the Crown on matters of public concern or legal difficulty which cannot otherwise be brought conveniently before the Courts, for example cases relating to disqualification from the House of Commons or those to do with Parliamentary privilege. It had a role under Section 5 of the 1920 Government of Ireland Act in that, until Stormont was dissolved in 1972, the Government in London was empowered to refer to it questions relating to the interpretation of the Act, notably issues of legislative competence. As things turned out, this provision was used only once, in 1936. It would also have had a similar role of constitutional arbitration if the devolution legislation of the 1974-79 Labour Government had been brought into effect. However the 1979 Scottish and Welsh Devolution Acts remain inoperative, because the referenda held in those parts of the United Kingdom did not achieve the required levels of public support to trigger the legislation.

17. Both quoted in J. A. G. Griffith, *The Politics of the Judiciary*, p. 179 and p. 183. See also *Journal of the Society of Public Teachers of Law* (1972), vol. 12, p. 22.

18. Queen's Bench Divisional Court, *Regina v. Secretary of State for Foreign and Commonwealth Affairs, ex parte Rees-Mogg*, 30 July 1993, see Law Report, *The Times*, 31 July 1993.

19. See: Part 2, Articles 8-8d, Treaty on European Union (Luxembourg: EUR OP, 1992).

20. In 1992 800,500 EU citizens had settled in Britain; in the five years to 1992 an average of 58,300 British citizens per year had left Britain to settle in other parts of the EU. See Eurostat, University of London (*The Guardian*, 16 February 1995) and *The Times*, 26 January 1995.

21. For example, see 'Central Intelligence Machinery' (London: HMSO, 1993).

22. See 'The Citizen's Charter', Cmnd 1599 (London: HMSO, 1991).

23. This is the name given to a Writ addressed to an individual who holds another in custody, directing them to produce the individual held and show cause for their detention. Where a Writ is granted the individual held must be released at once. Failure to do so amounts to contempt of Court. See Note 8 for more information.

24. This problem has been addressed in attempts to reach agreement between the nations in the Council of Europe. However, no international broadcasting agreement is likely to be completely effective in an increasingly de-regulated, global media market.

25. This restricted legal immunity from civil action in the Courts to the employees of the firm in dispute or the employees of a direct supplier or customer of the firm in dispute, thus theoretically limiting the scope for 'blacking' or sympathy strikes.

26. See Report of the Royal Commission on the Police, Cmnd 1728 (London: HMSO, 1962).

27. See 'Operational Policy Review' (Police Federation, 1990).

28. See 'Public Satisfaction with Police Services', Home Office Research and Planning Unit, Paper 73, December 1992.

29. See MORI survey carried out 20-24 January 1994 on behalf of *Readers Digest* magazine, and published in the April 1994 issue.

30. See 'Public Satisfaction with Police Services', Home Office Research and Planning Unit, Paper 73, December 1992.

31. See T. Jones, T. Newbury, and D. Smith, *Democracy and Policing* (London: Policies Studies Institute, 1994).

32. Many offences are never reported to the police, and some of those that are do not get recorded. The British Crime Survey published in November 1993 showed that only about one in three offences was recorded in official statistics. As a result the British Crime Survey

estimated that there were over 15 million crimes in England and Wales in 1991. See British Crime Survey.

33. See 'Police Reform', Cmnd 2281 (London: HMSO, 1993).

34. See the *Report of the Inquiry into Police Responsibilities and Rewards*, Vols I and II, CM 2280-T/CM 2280-II, 30 June 1993.

35. H. W. R. Wade, *Administrative Law*, 4th edn (Oxford: Clarendon Press, 1979), pp. 5-6.

36. See Lord Hewart, *The New Despotism*, 2nd edn (West Point: Greenwood, 1945), and W. Robson, *Justice and Administrative Law*, 3rd end (London: Stevens, 1951).

37. The Crichel Down affair involved an area of farm land in Dorset about which misleading replies and false assurances were given by a junior civil servant in the Ministry of Agriculture. Subsequent inquiries established that there had been muddle, bias, inefficiency and bad faith on the part of a few officials, as well as weak organisation in the Department. This led eventually to the resignation of the Minister, Sir Thomas Dugdale.

38. See C. M. Clothier, *Ombudsman: jurisdiction, powers and practice* (Manchester: Manchester Statistical Society, 1981), for a fuller description of the role of the Ombudsman in Britain.

39. An *injunction* and a *declaration* are two of the legal remedies generally available to litigants and they are not confined to cases in which citizens seek to challenge public authorities.

40. T. C. Harley and J. A. G. Griffith, *Government and Law* (London: Weidenfeld & Nicolson, 1975), p. 230.

41. Notably in the Court of Appeal where Lord Denning had a long and active period as Master of the Rolls from 1962 to 1982.

42. See Chapter 18, pp. 402–8 for more on the European Court of Justice and its role in European integration.

43. See Lord Scarman, *English Law, the New Dimension* (London: Stevens, 1974), and Lord Hailsham, *The Dilemma of Democracy* (London: Collins, 1978).

44. N. Johnson, *In Search of the Constitution* (London: Methuen, 1980), p. 149.

45. H. W. R. Wade, *Administrative Law*, p. 30.

Further reading

Clothier, C. M., *Ombudsman: jurisdiction, powers and practice* (Manchester: Manchester Statistical Society, 1981).

de Smith, S. and Brazier, R., *Constitutional and Administrative Law*, 6th edn (London: Penguin, 1990).

Dickson, B., *The Legal System of Northern Ireland,* 2nd edn (1989).

Griffith, J. A. G., *The Politics of the Judiciary*, 4th edn (London: Fontana, 1991).

Jackson, R. M., *et al., The Machinery of Justice in England*, 8th edn (London: CUP, 1989).

Morris, T., *Crime and Criminal Justice since 1945* (Oxford: Blackwell, 1989).

Reiner, R., *The Politics of the Police*, 2nd edn (London: Harvester Wheatsheaf, 1992).

Robertson, G., *Street's Freedom: the individual and the law*, 6th edn (London: Penguin, 1989).

Stainsby, P., *Tribunal Practice and Procedure* (London: Law Society, 1988).

Wade, H. W. R., *Administrative Law*, 6th edn (Oxford: Clarendon Press, 1988).

Walker D.M., *The Scottish Legal System*, 6th edn (1992).

Wright, A., *Citizens and Subjects* (London: Routledge, 1993).

PART 6

Democracy in Britain

18 Britain in Europe

No modern textbook on the British political system can afford to ignore Britain's membership of the European Union and still be an accurate and complete reflection of contemporary political realities. The vast network of economic and political relationships which this involves and especially the legal and constitutional issues which it raises, are essential to a proper understanding of contemporary British politics. Things have not been the same for Britain ever since it joined the European Community (as the European Union was then called) in January 1973. Even more significant changes are taking place under the aegis of the 1986 Single European Act (which made possible the European Single Market) and the 1992 Treaty of Maastricht (which foreshadows European Monetary Union by the end of the century). It is therefore essential to include in this book a substantial chapter on Britain in Europe and to take full account of the European dimension of British politics in every other chapter where it is relevant.

18.1 Historical background

The origin of post-war European integration can be found in the decision of six states – France, West Germany (as it was then), Italy, Holland, Belgium and Luxembourg – to establish the European Coal and Steel Community in 1950. This experiment in supranationalism, from which Britain decided to stand aside, involved the pooling of national economic sovereignty in the two vital sectors of coal mining and steel making which were then regarded as 'the sinews of war'. The founding fathers – Jean Monnet and Robert Schuman (both Frenchmen), Konrad Adenauer (a German), Alcide de Gasperi (an Italian), and Paul-Henri Spaak (a Belgian) – chose these two sectors quite deliberately because they had been at the heart of national war-making capacities for the previous century or so. By pooling these national resources irrevocably and then allowing them to be managed and controlled by a new supranational 'High Authority', it was confidently expected that war in Europe between European nations would thus be rendered impossible once and for all.

Although Britain had participated in all the *international* organisations which had been established after the Second World War – such as the Brussels Treaty Organisation in 1948 (which in 1955 became the Western European Union), the Council of Europe and the North Atlantic Treaty Organisation in 1949 – the political leaders in Britain at that time could not bring themselves to participate in *supranational* organisations of which the European Coal and Steel Community was the prominent example. There were various reasons for this, but the principal explanation was that the realities of Britain's weakened position in the post-war world had been masked by her war-time achievements and post-war preoccupations with her Empire and embryonic Commonwealth. After all, Britain had stood alone against the might of Hitler's Germany in 1940, she had been acknowledged as one of the three victorious Powers in 1945 (along with the United States and the Soviet Union), and British politicians and people alike tended to look to Britain's relations with the United States and with the British Empire and emerging Commonwealth before they considered relations with the nations on the shattered Continent of Europe. Of the famous 'three circles' of British influence in the world – the special relationship with the Americans, the imperial responsibilities in the Empire and Commonwealth, and the various aspects of European entanglements – of which Winston Churchill spoke so eloquently at the time, there was little doubt in British minds about the order of priorities. Relations with the other European nations generally came third in the British world-view. In Churchill's words, Britain was 'with them, but not of them'.

However, during the 1950s Britain was drawn into closer involvement with Continental Europe as her so-called 'special relationship' with the United States suffered a series of blows and disappointments, notably at the time of the ill-fated British and French invasion of the Suez Canal Zone in 1956 and as the process of British de-colonisation produced a Commonwealth which came to be seen by some in Britain as much as a liability as an asset. With the collapse of the attempt to form a European Defence Community in 1954, Britain moved swiftly to sign the 1955 Paris Accords which established the Western European Union, brought West Germany into conventional (but not nuclear) defence arrangements with her European partners, and committed Britain to keep more than 50,000 troops on the mainland of Europe for 50 years. However, when the Six took the process of European integration one stage further by signing in 1957 the Rome Treaties, which established the European Economic Community (EEC) and Euratom in the following year, Britain once again stood aside after having sent only observers to the seminal conference at Messina in 1956. The British Conservative Government then made a futile attempt to negotiate a wider European Free Trade arrangement with the Six in 1957-58. When this was understandably rebuffed by the Six, Britain and the other excluded European nations (Austria, Denmark, Norway, Portugal, Sweden and Switzerland) decided to establish the European Free Trade Area (EFTA) as a partial counterweight to their exclusion from the mainstream of European economic and political integration.

It was not long before the Conservative Government, then led by Harold Macmillan, realised the error of its ways in having stood aside from the mainstream of European integration. Accordingly, in July 1961 the Government initiated negotiations with the European Communities (as they were then called) to see whether a basis existed for future British membership which would be consistent with the interests of Britain, the Commonwealth and EFTA. The subsequent formal statement introducing the application declared that the Government's decision had been reached 'not on any narrow or short-term grounds, but as a result of a thorough assessment over a considerable period of the needs of our own country, Europe and the free world as a whole'.[1] It is interesting to note in passing the clear implication in this statement that 'Europe' was somewhere other than Britain or conversely that Britain was not in Europe. By this stage Britain seemed at last to be set on a course to bring her into full membership of the European Community. Yet in spite of the considerable progress which was later made in resolving many of the technical problems, the negotiations between Britain and the Six had to be broken off following President De Gaulle's veto delivered at a famous press conference in Paris on 29 January 1963.[2]

Throughout the 1960s successive British Governments, both Conservative and Labour, sought to keep alive the possibility of Britain's membership of the European Community. In May 1967 the Wilson Administration made another formal application for Britain to join the European Community, but once again this was baulked by French opposition. However, two years later in April 1969 President De Gaulle staked his political fortune upon the result of a constitutional referendum in France and lost, thus leaving himself with no choice but to resign. This had the effect of opening the way for Britain to renew its application to join the European Community, which was duly done by the Heath Administration immediately after the Conservatives came to power in June 1970.

The detailed negotiations with the Six took little more than one year and were brought to a satisfactory conclusion. Both Houses of Parliament debated and voted upon the principle of British entry in October 1971. The House of Commons voted in favour by 356 to 244, a majority of 112, in which 69 Labour MPs defied a three line whip in order to vote for the Government motion; and on the same day the House of Lords approved the same motion by a larger majority of 393. On 22 January 1972 Edward Heath, as Prime Minister, signed the Treaty of Accession in Brussels on behalf of Britain. Parliament was then required to legislate to bring British law into line with European law and the resulting Westminster statute was the all-important 1972 European Communities Act. The passage of this legislation was fraught with difficulties. It was opposed by a determined minority of Conservative 'anti-Marketeers' (as they were then called) and on occasions the Government only survived because some Labour MPs were prepared to abstain in key votes. Eventually, however, the way was cleared for full British membership of the European Community from 1 January 1973, when Denmark and Ireland also joined (although Norway had earlier decided not to join in a public referendum decision which rejected the view of the Norwegian Government).

Because the Labour Party had been split on the European issue at least since the vote of principle in October 1971, Labour fought the two General Elections in 1974 pledged to a policy of renegotiating what it described as the unacceptable terms of entry. The process of renegotiation which followed was backed by the implicit threat that the renegotiated terms would be put to the British people in a consultative referendum and, if continued membership on such terms were rejected, then the Government would take the necessary steps for British withdrawal. When the referendum was held in 1975, the British people voted by a two-to-one majority in favour of Britain remaining in the European Community and this verdict was accepted (however reluctantly in some cases) by the Government and by Parliament.

Since that time Britain's membership of the European Union has not been seriously in doubt in the sense that British withdrawal is not considered to be a serious option any longer, even by those who have remained or become hostile to the current arrangements. However, there have been long-lasting battles by the British Government – especially during Margaret Thatcher's first Administration from 1979 to 1983 – further to improve the terms of membership, notably in relation to the working of the Common Agricultural Policy (CAP) and the size of Britain's net contribution to the European Budget. By the mid-1980s the 'British Question' seemed to have been more or less resolved, although Margaret Thatcher and other British Ministers were always prepared to fight Britain's corner in the process of European decision making. Nevertheless it was Margaret Thatcher who agreed to an extensive revision of the European Treaties which resulted in the 1986 Single European Act and the Major Administration has been prominent in pressing for the fullest possible progress towards the achievement of a genuine single European market.

At the time of writing things appear to have changed yet again in a number of significant ways. *Firstly*, the development and destiny of the European Union has been greatly influenced by the end of the Cold War and the reunification of Germany. These great events helped to trigger the further enlargement of the European Union to the north and the east to include Austria, Finland and Sweden (but not Norway which once again rejected entry in a referendum in 1994). It also opened the way for the European Union to be enlarged by the year 2000 or thereabouts to include the more developed of the former communist states in Eastern Europe, such as Poland, Hungary, the Czech Republic, Slovakia and Slovenia (see Figure 18.1 on the next page).

Secondly, the existing member states of the European Union (with the notable exception of Britain and possibly Denmark) accept the need to 'deepen' the process of economic and political integration before, or at any rate in parallel with, the next phase in the process of enlargement. This European vocation was enshrined in the 1992 Treaty of Maastricht, especially those sections of it which provided for the creation of European Monetary Union by 1999 at the latest.

Thirdly, the peoples of the various member states (and indeed some of the applicant states) have clearly become more cynical and disenchanted with the whole 'European project'. This has meant that the political elite on the Continent (but not necessarily in Britain) has become dangerously detached from the views and feelings of the various peoples whom they presume to lead. However, the younger generation of political leaders in Europe are not so sentimental about the unalloyed value of closer and deeper European unity and strong campaigns have been fought in France (a key country in the whole issue) against the conventional wisdom. In Britain the Conservative Party has become markedly more 'Euro-sceptic', the Labour Party remains in its newly acquired pro-European posture (but is also still divided on the issue), and only the Liberal Democrats remain consistently federalist and pro-European. All these dynamic political factors seem likely to have a significant impact upon the future of Britain in Europe.

18.2 Legal and constitutional implications

Britain's membership of the European Union has profound legal and constitutional implications which have become increasingly apparent as the member states have continued to enhance the degree of integration with one another. Yet it is fair to say that the problems posed by the incursion of European law into Britain should have been clear from the very beginning when Parliament debated Britain's entry into the European Community in 1971-72. The fact that many MPs and others may not have fully realised what they

Figure 18.1 Greater Europe: the European Union widens

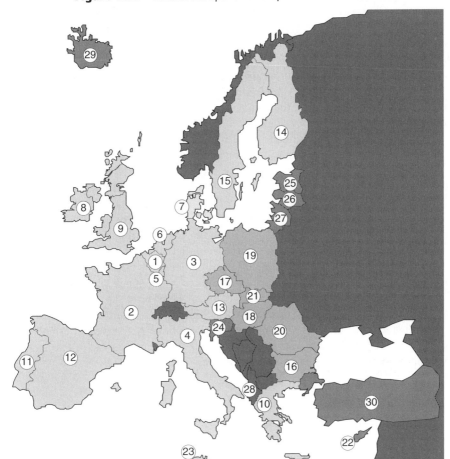

Membership past & present

First there were the Six (1958)

1 Belgium
2 France
3 Germany (west)
4 Italy
5 Luxembourg
6 Netherlands

. . . then the Nine (1973)

7 Denmark
8 Ireland
9 UK

. . . the Ten (1981)

10 Greece

. . . the Twelve (1986)

11 Portugal
12 Spain

. . . and now the Fifteen (1995)

13 Austria
14 Finland
15 Sweden

Towards the next century

c2000

16 Bulgaria*
17 Czech Republic*
18 Hungary*†
19 Poland*†
20 Romania*
21 Slovakia*

EU drawing up proposals for integration into its single market in preparation for full membership

22 Cyprus†
23 Malta†
24 Slovenia

Other potential members

25 Estonia**
26 Lativia**
27 Lithuania**

**EU planning negotiations for association agreements*

28 Albania
29 Iceland
30 Turkey†

†Have formally applied to join*

were letting themselves and subsequent generations in for owed a good deal to the fact that the then Conservative Government, in its understandable wish to secure the approval of Parliament for Britain's entry, was less than completely honest (or significantly under-estimated) the longer term legal and constitutional implications of this great European adventure.[3]

Section 2 (1) of the 1972 European Communities Act made provision for European law to take direct effect in the United Kingdom.[4] It provided for the European Treaties and European legislation under the Treaties to take direct effect in Britain. It also included *future* European law and it made clear that European, rather than British, law would determine whether or not a particular provision was directly effective in Britain. Section 2 (2) of the Act made provision for the implementation of European law by means of subordinate British legislation at Westminster. However, in section 2 (1) it had been made clear that such Statutory Instruments could *not* be used in four specific areas which would require primary legislation: the imposition of new or increased taxation, the creation of new serious criminal offences, retrospective legislation, and sub- delegated legislation. Section 2 (4) determined that both past and future Acts of Parliament should be subordinate to European law in those areas where a conflict might arise. This was reinforced by Section 3 (1) which declared that any question about the effect of European law in Britain should be decided in accordance with the principles of any relevant ruling of the European Court of Justice (ECJ), the most notable of which is the supremacy of European law over national law in all the member states. Thus all these interlocking and mutually reinforcing sections of the 1972 European Communities Act served to establish the supremacy of European law over national law, although it was an Act of Parliament at Westminster which made this possible in Britain.

Important features

The most important features of the relationship between European law and national law in Britain are the direct effect of European law in the British Courts, the supremacy of European law over national law if and when the two conflict, and the procedures by which European law is enforced in Britain and the other member states. It is important to be clear about the meaning and implications of these features and we shall deal with each one in turn.

The concept of direct effect means that a provision of European law grants individual rights to citizens in Britain and the other member states which must be upheld by the national Courts. This principle was clarified for the first time in the *1962 Van Gend en Loos case*, when it was established that the European Court may legitimately determine that a given provision of European law is directly effective.[5] This principle may sound relatively simple, but, as enunciated by the European Court ever since 1962, it has not accorded very easily with the traditional view of such matters in Britain. In the leading case just mentioned the European Court held that the European institutions are 'endowed with sovereign rights, the exercise of which affects member states and their citizens'. It also declared that member states had 'limited their sovereign rights, albeit within limited fields' and that European law can confer rights on individuals 'which become part of their legal heritage'. These were bold assertions on the part of the European Court which the passage of time has since done nothing to dispel. Yet they are some way removed from the theoretical principle of British law which holds that European legislation is applicable in Britain only because the 1972 European Communities Act delegated powers to the European Union to legislate for the United Kingdom in certain designated areas covered by the European Treaties.

The supremacy of European law means that a directly effective provision of European law always prevails over a provision of national law, irrespective of whether the former was agreed before or after the latter. The *1977 Simmenthal case* provided a good example of this.[6] In this leading case the Italian authorities had argued that Italian national law should prevail, because it had been passed *after* the two relevant European regulations, and that Italian law should stand until such time as its conflict with European law had been declared unconstitutional by the Italian Constitutional Court. When the matter was referred to the European Court, the latter held that the national Court had a duty to give full effect to European law and not to apply any conflicting national provisions, even if these were adopted subsequently. It also held that there should be no question of waiting for national law to be set aside by a national constitutional Court or a national Legislature before accepting the supremacy of European law. However, the European Court ruling was limited to Treaty provisions and the directly applicable measures of the European institutions. It did not state that conflicting national provisions were void, merely that they were inapplicable. Moreover, its ruling was concerned not only with conflicting national law, but also with all national laws which 'encroach upon the field within which the Community exercises its legislative power'.

It can be seen from this and other judgements of the European Court that European law prevails over national law in all cases where the former has direct effect, as long as the legal right contained in a given European instrument is invoked against the recalcitrant member state. Indeed, the *1973 French Merchant Seamen case* demonstrated that there is a positive obligation upon member states to repeal national legislation which conflicts with European law, even if the latter is considered inapplicable by the national authorities.[7] Experience in the European Union has also shown that the powers of the member states can be limited or removed even where the conflict with European law is only indirect or potential. For example, under Articles 113 and 238 of the 1957 Rome Treaty the member states have lost the power to enter into commercial or association agreements with third countries, since these powers are explicitly reserved to the European Commission acting on behalf of the European Union as a whole. Equally, the *1978 Pigs Marketing Board case* demonstrated that in the field of the Common Agricultural Policy, if the European Commission has introduced a common market regime for a given farm product, the member states are precluded from adopting any national measures which might undermine or create exceptions to it.[8] The most significant recent confirmation of this principle was the *1991 Factortame case* when the European Court ruled that the 1988 Merchant Shipping Act was in breach of European law by preventing Spanish owned trawler companies from registering in Britain to take advantage of the British fishing quota under the terms of the Common Fisheries Policy. As a result of this decision, the British Government repealed the offending portions of the Act.

The enforcement procedures for European law are the third important feature of the relationship between European law and national law. There are two ways in which European law can be enforced against national Governments in the member states. The first is through legal action taken by private individuals or firms in the national Courts which seeks to apply the doctrine of direct effect. For example, when the Irish Government imposed restrictions upon fishing in Irish waters which were contrary to European law under the Common Fisheries Policy, a Dutch fisherman was able to invoke European law as a defence to a charge of illegal fishing.[9] Equally, when in 1977 the Ministry of Agriculture in Britain imposed a ban upon the import of main crop potatoes, this was challenged by a Dutch potato exporter as contrary to European law.[10] In both cases the European Court upheld the position of the Dutchmen who had challenged national restrictions which were found to be contrary to European law.

The other way in which European law can be enforced against national Governments is by direct legal proceedings against the member state concerned. This can be done under Article 88 of the Paris Treaty (ECSC Treaty), Articles 169-171 of the Rome Treaty (EEC Treaty), and Articles 141-143 of the Euratom Treaty. The procedure is divided into two stages. In the first stage, the European Commission either delivers a 'Decision' under the ECSC Treaty which is binding and conclusive (unless the member state concerned wishes to challenge it in proceedings before the European Court) or it merely delivers a 'reasoned opinion' under the EEC and Euratom Treaties which is not binding. This means that if the member state concerned fails to comply, the European Commission can bring the matter before the European Court for definitive determination.

In the second stage, the European Court proceedings are not a review of the European Commission decision or reasoned opinion, but rather a fresh consideration of the case to establish whether or not a violation of the Treaties has occurred. If the European Court finds that the allegations are proved, it will give judgement against the offending member state. Under the ECSC Treaty this has the effect of confirming the European Commission decision which is binding and it opens the way for the imposition of sanctions against the offender if that proves to be necessary. Under the EEC and Euratom Treaties this takes the form of a declaration setting out how and why the offending member state has failed to fulfil its obligations under the relevant European Treaty. Although the European Court has no power to order a member state either to take or not to take a particular course of action and it cannot declare invalid any national legislation, the member state is obliged to terminate the violation found by the European Court.

Such enforcement procedures have been effective in most cases, even when member states have indulged in deliberate delaying tactics. This is largely because in the leading *Pig Producers case in 1978*, the European Court upheld the European Commission's application for an interim injunction to terminate a British subsidy scheme which had been designed by the British Government to help British pig producers compete against imports which were subsidised at European level. Together with a similar case at about the same time which was brought by the European Commission against Ireland for introducing fisheries conservation measures which were regarded as being contrary to European Treaty obligations, this meant that the principle of using interim measures against offending member states became established.[11] Such developments are evidence of the *political* nature of European jurisdiction. When deciding whether to grant an interim injunction to the European Commission, the European Court takes into account: firstly, the chances of the proceedings being successful; secondly, the extent to which the matter is urgent; and thirdly, such evidence as there may be of irreparable damage being done to the European Union if no judicial action is taken. In those rare cases when a member state has deliberately sought to break European law and to defy the European Court, the issues have only been capable of resolution on a political basis, because it is upon *the continuing will to co-operate* that the satisfactory functioning of the European Union finally depends.

Principal problems

When Britain joined the European Community in 1973, it laid itself open to three principal legal and constitutional problems. However, the essential dilemma was vividly described by Lord Denning in 1979 when he referred to the threat from 'the flowing tide of Community law' and warned that 'we have to learn to become amphibious if we wish to keep our heads above water'.[12] In other words, as long as successive British Governments and Parliaments take the view that Britain's membership of the European Union is *on balance* beneficial to the interests of the country, the British will find themselves increasingly woven into the fabric of evolving European law. As this body of law is extended by agreement in the Council of Ministers into more areas of European activity, the real scope for autonomous action by Britain (or any other member state) will gradually diminish. Only a determined attempt to halt (and then perhaps to reverse) this secular trend in Europe will be able to make any real difference.

The first problem is that legal provision for Britain's membership of the European Community (now called the European Union) could not be made by means of a constitutional amendment – as happened in the case of Ireland for example – but had to be made by passing an Act of Parliament, in this case the 1972 European Communities Act. The reason for this was, of course, the well rehearsed fact that Britain did not have, and still does not have, a codified constitution. We should therefore note the paradox that in Britain's case the legal means of providing for permanent membership of the European Community was the decidedly impermanent mechanism of an Act of Parliament which, by its very nature, can be amended or repealed at any time.

The second problem is that the British attitude towards international law is essentially dualist, which means that in Britain national and international law are regarded as being quite distinct. There never has been a general rule of law in Britain which allows treaties to take effect within the British legal system without the essential enabling mechanism of an Act of Parliament. By contrast, in other European countries which have codified constitutions, such as France or Germany, international treaties signed by their Governments take precedence over national law and have direct effect in their national jurisdictions without any requirement for enabling legislation as in Britain.

The third and most fundamental problem (which really underpins the first two) is the hallowed British constitutional principle of Parliamentary supremacy. This means that there is no legal authority superior to Parliament in the United Kingdom and that any Parliament can overturn the laws of its predecessors – in other words, no Parliament can bind it successors. *In theory*, this peculiarity of the British constitution means that Parliamentary supremacy and the primacy of European law in the areas covered by the European Treaties are fundamentally incompatible. *In practice*, the circle has been squared by the doctrine contained in the 1972 European Communities Act which holds – in Section 2 (1) in particular – that Parliament evidently *intended* that all Acts of Parliament, whether before or after that Act, *should* be subordinate to European law in those areas of jurisdiction covered by the European Treaties and subsequently interpreted by the European Court.

On the face of things, this resolution of the problem seems to be inconsistent with the rule that no British Parliament can bind its successors and the possibility that a future British Parliament might pass an Act which defied European law. Yet in reality such an acute constitutional difficulty is unlikely to arise for two important reasons. Firstly, if a future Parliament at Westminster were determined to pass a new law which flouted established European law, it would probably do so only in circumstances in which a British Government was actively considering British withdrawal from part or all of Britain's legal obligations to the European Union – a situation which does not seem very likely to materialise unless a very different view is taken of fundamental British national interests in future. Secondly, as long as the Government of the day with the support of a majority in the House of Commons values continued British membership more than partial or complete withdrawal, then the situation will not arise in the first place and Britain will continue to comply with its obligations under European law. Indeed, Section 2 (4) of the 1972 European Communities Act makes it clear that Parliament at Westminster is presumed *not* to intend any future statute to conflict with, still less override, any provisions of European law. In other words, as long as successive British Governments, backed by the British Parliament, *choose* to remain in the European Union, European law will be recognised as superior to national law in Britain in the areas covered by the European Treaties.

Since the 1992 Treaty of Maastricht and the debates in Parliament and elsewhere about its legal and constitutional implications, there has been deep and continuing disagreement in Britain and, to a lesser extent, in the other member states of the European Union about the pace and direction of the next phase of European integration. On the one hand, majority political opinion on the Continent appears to be comfortable with Article A of the Common Provisions of the Treaty which stated that 'this Treaty marks a new stage in the process of creating an ever closer union among the peoples of Europe in which decisions are taken as closely as possible to the citizen'. The clear implication of this majority point of view is that the doctrine of *subsidiarity*, which is spelt out in Article 3 (b) of the Treaty, should prevail. This made it clear that new competences should be allocated to the supranational level in the European Union 'only if and in so far as the objectives of the proposed action cannot be sufficiently achieved by the member states and can therefore, by reason of the scale or effects of the proposed action, be better achieved by the Community'. In practice, the application of this doctrine has already led to the repatriation to the member states of a number of competences previously claimed or exercised by the European institutions and has proved attractive to Germany and other member states where national constitutions are explicitly federal in character.

On the other hand, the so-called 'Euro-sceptics' in Britain and, to a lesser extent, in some other member states such as France and Denmark, regard these words in the Treaty as little more than window-dressing designed to reassure the growing number of people throughout the European Union who feel increasingly uncomfortable with the integrationist methods and federalist destiny of the European project. Such people have pointed out that, in the event of constitutional dispute on these matters, it is ultimately the European Court which will arbitrate, and they argue that its record over many years shows a clear institutional and philosophical bias in favour of defending the *acquis communautaire* (the body of European law already established) and advancing the interests of the other supranational institutions of the European Union – notably the European Commission and the European Parliament. For these reasons they argue that cumulative European case law is likely to favour the cause of even closer European integration and all who put their faith in the doctrine of subsidiarity as the best way of limiting the ambitions of the Euro-fanatics are likely to be bitterly disappointed. It must be said that on the basis of the historical evidence it is hard to dismiss such warnings and it would probably be unwise to do so.

18.3 Political and institutional impact

The political and institutional impact of Britain's membership of the European Union has already been significant and seems likely to become more significant in future. Ever since Britain's entry into the European Community (as it was then called) in 1973, the country has been involved to an increasing extent in the process of European integration. This process has been well described by Sir Michael Butler, a former UK Permanent Representative at the European institutions in Brussels, as 'primarily about solving detailed, complicated and usually technical problems by consensus in a political framework which makes it extremely difficult for the national Governments to do other than agree in the end'.[13] It is this apparent irreversibility of European integration which has been both the secret of its success so far and the main cause for concern among those in Britain and some other member states who wish to limit, or even reverse, the process in future. Certainly the drive towards 'an ever closer union of the European peoples' (in the words of the Treaty of Rome) seems to have posed greater political and institutional problems for Britain than for the other member states.

Impact upon Ministers

The impact of Britain's membership of the European Union has been felt first and foremost in the sphere of central Government. This is because Ministers in all British Governments have had to play an active part in the process of European decision making. From the beginning this has involved Departmental Ministers representing Britain and defending British national interests in the Council of Ministers, whether the General Affairs Council composed of Foreign Ministers or the specific 'subject' Councils, such as Agriculture, Finance, Transport or the Environment, depending upon the particular policy area under discussion. Since 1974 it has also involved the Prime Minister of the day participating in what has come to be known as 'the European Council' with the other heads of Government and the President of the European Commission. Such 'summit meetings' are now held twice a year under the chairmanship of whichever member state holds the Presidency of the European Union for the relevant six-month period. The purpose of these meetings has been to provide renewed impetus for the development of the European Union and on a number of occasions this is what has been achieved.

The most obvious consequence for Ministers of all these meetings has been the growing amount of time which they have had to devote to them as the sphere of European competence has been extended by agreement into more areas of policy. For example, there was no mention of environmental policy in the 1957 Treaty of Rome, since at that time there was no general recognition of the importance of acting at European level to deal with environmental problems, whereas nowadays these matters are considered to be significant European concerns. Equally, the 1992 Treaty of Maastricht enshrined an agreement by all the member states (except Britain and Denmark which reserved their national positions) to proceed in stages towards European Monetary Union based upon a single European currency administered and safeguarded by a European Central Bank by 1999 at the latest.

The traditional method of decision making in the Council of Ministers has been to continue the discussion of difficult issues, such as the reform of the Common Agricultural

Policy or the level of Britain's net contributions to the European Budget, until the combined effects of physical exhaustion and the spirit of compromise emerge and combine to make a European decision possible. This so-called 'Community method' has imposed great strains upon Ministers and in recent years since the 1992 Maastricht Treaty it has shown some signs of diminishing returns. However, agreement was by no means easy in much earlier times – especially when President De Gaulle practised an 'empty chair' policy in the mid-1960s. For a schematic representation of the European decision making process see Figure 18.2 on the next page.

It is also important to note that there have been significant changes in the rules of the game since 1986 when the Single European Act became law in all the member states. This important advance in European decision-making procedures involved the introduction of qualified majority voting in the Council of Ministers on all issues to do with realising the Single European Market – with the exception of taxation, immigration, and workers' employment rights, which were reserved for decision making by unanimity. This means that British Ministers – like Ministers from other member states – can find themselves outvoted when the Council of Ministers takes decisions by qualified majority, unless a blocking minority can be assembled which in the late 1980s required at least 23 votes out of a total of 76 and which assumed that two of the larger member states would have to combine with at least one of the smaller ones (apart from tiny Luxembourg) in order to prevent measures from going through.[14] Since that time, of course, the European Union has been enlarged in 1995 to include three new member states (Austria, Finland, and Sweden) with the result that the blocking minority on issues of qualified majority voting has been raised to 26 votes out of an enlarged total of 87 votes.

On the other hand, it is well to remember that qualified majority voting can, and often has, worked in Britain's favour, so the rules of the game cut both ways. For example, it would have been much more difficult to make speedy progress with implementing the Single European Act if the policy had remained subject to decision making by consensus or unanimity. Although there is nearly always considerable pressure to find a compromise even in the most intractable disputes in the Council of Ministers, national Governments sometimes find it quite convenient to be outvoted if they have significant problems with public opinion in their own countries, but nevertheless recognise privately that the decision taken is the right one in the interests of Europe as a whole.

Impact upon civil servants

The impact upon civil servants has probably been even greater than the impact upon Ministers. This is because Britain's membership of the European Union has spawned a vast network of bureaucratic relationships between Whitehall and the European institutions in Brussels, Luxembourg, and Strasbourg – as well as complicated bilateral relations between the various national capitals. Within Whitehall itself it has been necessary for the Foreign Office and the Cabinet Office to co-ordinate the work of all the various Departments involved in the European decision-making process. Those civil servants, who are involved in actual or potential issues of European policy, spend a good deal of their time commuting to and from Brussels for meetings with their counterparts from the other national capitals. Some of them are also stationed at the UK Permanent Delegation in Brussels (UKREP for short) where they have an essential role to play in liaising with the European institutions and the other national delegations. They are also involved in

Figure 18.2 The European decision making process

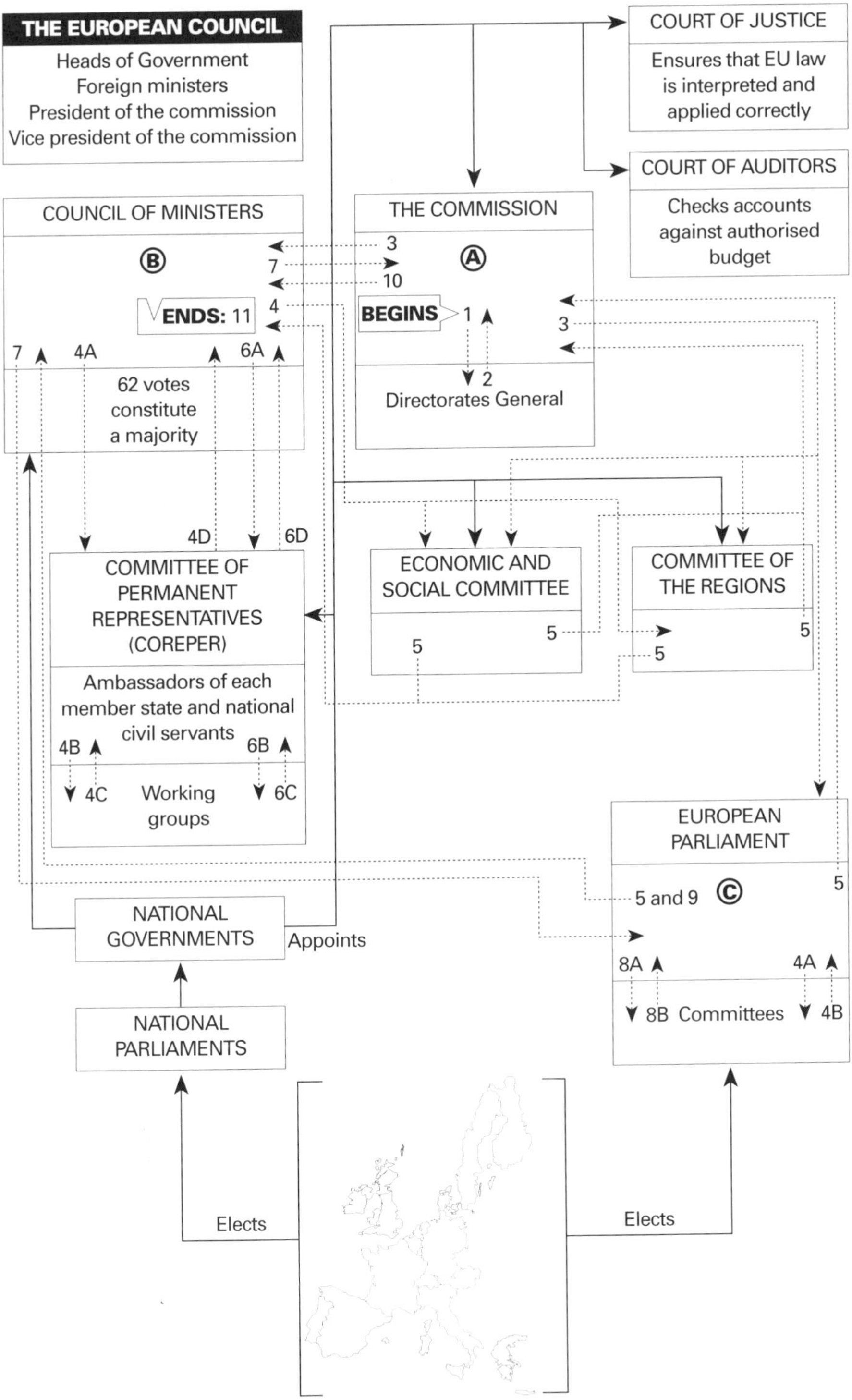

THE EUROPEAN COUNCIL
Heads of Government
Foreign ministers
President of the commission
Vice president of the commission

COURT OF JUSTICE

Ensures that EU law is interpreted and applied correctly

COURT OF AUDITORS

Checks accounts against authorised budget

COUNCIL OF MINISTERS

Ⓑ

3
7
10
4 **ENDS: 11**

THE COMMISSION

Ⓐ

BEGINS 1
3
2
Directorates General

62 votes constitute a majority

7   4A   6A

4D   6D

COMMITTEE OF PERMANENT REPRESENTATIVES (COREPER)

Ambassadors of each member state and national civil servants

4B   6B

4C   Working groups   6C

ECONOMIC AND SOCIAL COMMITTEE

5   5

COMMITTEE OF THE REGIONS

5

5

EUROPEAN PARLIAMENT

5 and 9   Ⓒ   5

8A   4A

8B Committees 4B

NATIONAL GOVERNMENTS   Appoints

NATIONAL PARLIAMENTS

Elects   Elects

Figure 18.2 *continued*

A

Jacques Santer	**Luxembourg**	President
Martin Bangemann	**Germany**	Industrial policy
Ritt Bjerregaard	**Denmark**	Environment
Emma Bonino	**Italy**	Fish, consumers
Sir Leon Brittan	**UK**	Trade, Asia, US
Hans van der Broek	**Netherlands**	Foreign policy, Eastern Europe
Edith Cresson	**France**	Research, training
Joao de Deus Pinherio	**Portugal**	Africa, Caribbean, Pacific
Franz Fischler	**Austria**	Agriculture
Padraig Flynn	**Ireland**	Social policy
Antita Gradin	**Sweden**	Immigration, interior policy
Neil Kinnock	**UK**	Transport
Erkki Liikanen	**Finland**	Budget
Manuel Marin	**Spain**	Mediterranean, Latin America
Mario Monti	**Italy**	Internal market
Marcelino Oreja	**Spain**	Institutional affairs
Christos Papoutsis	**Greece**	Energy
Yves-Thibault de Silguy	**France**	Economic and Monetary affairs
Karel van Miert	**Belgium**	Competition policy
Monika Wulf-Mathies	**Germany**	Regional policy

B

Germany/France/Italy/United Kingdom	Each have 10 votes
Spain	Has 8 votes
Belgium/Greece/Netherlands/Portugal	Each have 5 votes
Austria/Sweden	Each have 4 votes
Denmark/Finland/Ireland	Each have 3 votes
Luxembourg	Has 2 votes
Total	87 votes

C

Germany	99
France/Italy/United Kingdom	87 each
Spain	65
Netherlands	31
Belgium/Greece/Portugal	25 each
Sweden	21
Austria	20
Denmark/Finland	16 each
Ireland	15
Luxembourg	6
Total MEPs	624

preparing the British Government's position at meetings of the Council of Ministers and in assisting their sponsoring Departments in Whitehall. In this way they carry forward the process of permanent dialogue between the European institutions and the British and other Governments of the member states.

In view of the growing volume of European legislation emanating from the institutions in Brussels, civil servants in those Departments particularly involved in European policy have had to spend an increasing amount of their time upon the negotiation and subsequent implementation of European law. For example, the Ministry of Agriculture spends probably three quarters of its official time on the negotiation and enforcement of the Common Agricultural Policy in Britain, while the Departments of Trade and Industry, Transport, and Education and Employment are also among those busiest with European regulations and directives. Even such proud and traditionally independent Departments as the Treasury and the Home Office have been increasingly drawn into the process of European policy making and law enforcement.

In addition, a growing proportion of the issues considered by the Cabinet and its committees has a European dimension of one kind or another, while Whitehall preparation for the meetings of the European Council every six months often involves strenuous work in 10 Downing Street, the Cabinet Office, the Foreign Office and many other Departments. Indeed, it can be argued that the administrative process of the European Union has affected the civil service more than any other component of the British political system. This characteristic is one of the principal reasons for the continuing 'democratic deficit' in what is still a rather bureaucratic European Union.

Impact upon Parliament

The impact upon Parliament of Britain's membership of the European Union has been emphasised by the anti- Europeans and the 'Euro-sceptics' as perhaps the most serious and adverse of all the negative consequences flowing from the original decision to enter the European Community taken by Parliament in October 1971. This argument was put with great conviction at Westminster in 1992-93 when the legislation designed to give legal effect to the Maastricht Treaty in Britain was fought by the Euro-sceptics every inch of the way. Yet the suspicion remains that the doom-laden forecast that Parliament at Westminster (and the other national Parliaments) will be reduced to the status of County Councils has been exaggerated for propaganda effect. Indeed, some recent political developments in the European Union have foreshadowed a revived role for national Parliaments.

Nevertheless both the proponents and the opponents of further political integration within the European Union have recognised that there are a number of real problems, both procedural and substantial, which face the national Parliaments as they endeavour to come to terms with institutional developments at European level. The fundamental difficulties were well expressed in a 1989 Procedure Committee Report which reminded the House of Commons that 'European legislation is initiated almost exclusively by an executive organisation (the European Commission) with which the UK Parliament has no formal relationship and over which it has no direct control'.[15] This means, as the Report went on to explain, that 'while the House may, by changes in its own internal procedures, find ways of bringing to bear more efficiently such authority as it retains over European legislation, it cannot by such means increase its authority or seek to claw back powers which have been ceded by Treaty'. The report concluded that 'the House has never realistically expected to exercise total accountability in relation to Ministers' prospective actions in the Council of Ministers, although it has always demanded explanations and justifications after the event'. In other words, members of the House of Commons realise that they can no longer exercise much democratic control over political developments in the European Union *before* the event, although they can retain some influence upon British Ministers and insist upon Parliamentary accountability *after* the event. This means that in circumstances of qualified majority voting, in particular, it is the European Parliament, rather than any national Parliament, which is better equipped under European law to exercise at least some effective democratic control.

When considering these rather bleak prospects for Parliament at Westminster and the other national Parliaments in the European Union, it is as well to remember that

Ministers in Britain have long been able to conclude Treaties without prior Parliamentary approval by exercising the powers of the Royal prerogative on behalf of the Crown – hence the formal appellation 'Her Majesty's Government'. Thus the largely retrospective nature of Parliamentary control in Britain in relation to developments in the European Union is no different to the limited and retrospective power which MPs are able to exert over Ministers acting within national jurisdiction. However, whereas Parliament at Westminster has long claimed to have supreme jurisdiction over British national laws, it has already had to share jurisdiction with the European Parliament (and to some extent with the other national Parliaments) in the sphere of European legislation introduced under the European Treaties. Indeed, in many respects Parliament at Westminster has to accept what amounts to a subordinate role not only in those areas of legislation where European law takes direct effect (for example, the Common Agricultural Policy), but also in those areas where the European Parliament has acquired powers of co-decision with other European institutions (notably the Council of Ministers) at certain stages of the European legislative process.[16]

In these circumstances there are a number of procedural and other problems for Parliament at Westminster which have been identified by observers and practitioners alike. *Firstly*, there is the volume of European legislation which is hard for the House of Commons to deal with properly within the constraints of an already congested legislative timetable. Attempts have been made to address this problem via the European Scrutiny Committee which sifts draft European proposals for legislation and recommends some for debate by the House as a whole, and more recently via two European Standing Committees to which many European proposals are now referred in order to relieve pressure upon the chamber itself. In many ways the House of Commons seems to have taken some procedural lessons from the House of Lords where these matters have been handled better via a powerful European Communities Committee and its various sub-committees. The size of the problem has been growing with the growing scope of European legislation, especially that which is related to the full implementation of the Single European Market. However, with the new determination since the 1992 Maastricht Treaty to repatriate some European competences to the member states, it may be that this problem of European legislative overload upon national Parliaments will ease in the late 1990s.

Secondly, there has been the problem of the *attitude* of most British MPs towards the seeming spate of European legislation from Brussels. Many MPs, especially in the Conservative Party, bemoan the fact that Westminster is not equipped to deal with this extra legislation, but are equally not prepared to countenance further increases in the powers of the European Parliament which would be the most logical way to close the so-called 'democratic deficit'. The result is that when Westminster does get a chance to debate European legislation, the discussion takes place in clouds of resentment and recrimination often during ill-attended debates after 10.00 p.m. This attitudinal problem will not really be alleviated until more constructive relationships evolve between the two main levels of democratic representation in Europe, although the two European Standing Committees which meet to discuss European proposals on Wednesday mornings at Westminster may assist in resolving some of the problems.

The third and most serious problem for Parliament, which has arisen since the 1986 Single European Act, is that the use of qualified majority voting in the Council of Ministers has reduced the areas in which any member state can veto decisions at European level.

This development has been particularly disturbing for the 'Euro-sceptics', but it has not exactly delighted the great ballast of Parliamentary opinion at Westminster either. There is now widespread concern among MPs in all parties at Westminster that European developments will continue to erode the power and position of national Parliaments, unless the latter exert themselves in a concerted campaign to regain some of the ground which has been lost. At the time of writing there are only limited signs that this view held by British MPs is shared by their counterparts in the other member states.

Whereas the power of Parliament at Westminster in relation to European legislation has been relatively weak and in decline, the European Parliament has come to wield more power than before in the European legislative process via the so-called 'co-operation procedure' which was introduced as part of the 1986 Single European Act and extended under the 1992 Treaty of Maastricht. Once the Council of Ministers has reached a common position by qualified majority, the European Parliament has the power to reject this common position or propose amendments to it which, if then adopted by the European Commission (which made the original proposal for legislation), can only be amended subsequently by the Council of Ministers on a basis of unanimity. The general effect of this procedure so far has been to cause the European Commission to modify its original proposals in perhaps one third of all cases when the European Parliament has used this power.

Impact upon the political system

It is clear that Britain's membership of the European Union has had a significant impact upon the British political system in a number of other ways. This has been manifest in nearly all areas of political activity to a greater or lesser extent, although it has obviously been concentrated in the areas of European legal competence – such as agriculture and external trade. In these circumstances it is fair to say that the evolving European Union provides the economic, political and institutional context within which many of the decisions of British national life are taken. Unless a future British Government backed by a future British Parliament (and probably with the backing of another referendum) were to take Britain out of the European Union, Britain's membership of it (even on a modified basis) is likely to play an increasingly influential part in the lives and well-being of the British people.

In the first place, British political parties are now considerably affected by the need to conduct politics not just at a local and national level, but also at a European level in the European Parliament and the various transnational political groupings in which they play a part. For example, the Labour Party is now the largest national component in its transnational grouping (the Socialist International), whereas the Conservative Party is only loosely associated with the Christian Democratic Group in the European Parliament and plays only a limited role in its transnational political grouping (the European Peoples' Party). For these and other reasons the Labour Party now seems more 'European' than the Conservative Party, although the Liberal Democrats can justifiably claim to represent the most consistently pro-European tendency in British politics.

Secondly, the development of the European Union is having a powerful influence upon pressure groups in Britain and other member states and increasingly upon the private sector in general. As more key decisions of interest to the private sector are taken by European institutions rather than national Governments and national Parliaments, more power has levitated to the European level. For example, British farmers are now at least as keen to lobby the European Commission and the European Parliament via their transnational European organisation COPA (Comité d'Organisations de Producteurs Agricoles) as they are to lobby the Ministry of Agriculture and Parliament at Westminster via the National Farmers' Union and other national pressure groups. This is because they know that most of the key decisions which affect their livelihood – for example, on guaranteed farm prices, agricultural levies, or the rate for the green Pound – are taken at European level rather than national level. Similar conclusions have also been drawn in the industrial and financial sectors as further substantial progress has been made towards the completion of the Single European Market with its common rules and obligations for the entire European Union.

Thirdly, the working of the European Union is having a growing impact upon local and sub-national government in Britain and all the other member states. Increasingly, local authorities in Britain are looking to the European institutions for financial assistance and political support. For example, the large conurbations and outlying regions of the United Kingdom are now very interested in the fruits of the European Social and Regional Funds within the European Budget. They have therefore lobbied persistently and effectively to get their share of European transfer payments under these headings. Equally, the nationalist parties in Wales, Scotland and Northern Ireland see action at European level as one of their best chances of developing political counterweights to the influence of English central Government and Parliamentarians in London whom they regard as mainly unsympathetic to their claims for 'national' independence. It is not surprising, therefore, that the Scottish Nationalists at any rate have adopted the idea of an independent Scotland within Europe as their party's goal.

Fourthly, it is becoming increasingly true that the media, and hence public opinion, in Britain are affected by Britain's membership of the European Union. Of course, the extent of this influence fluctuates depending upon the turn of events. Sometimes there is intense media interest in European issues, as there has been when the British Government has been strongly at odds with its European partners (over fishing for example) or when 'the European issue' has caused deep and bitter divisions within the political parties – as happened with the Conservative Euro-rebels who had the party whip withdrawn from them between December 1994 and April 1995. At other times European issues have taken second place to apparently more pressing national or local preoccupations. Yet as the world has come to seem smaller and as decisions taken in a European framework or by European institutions have seemed to affect people's lives more and more, public awareness of the costs and benefits of being in the European Union seems to have risen and the whole context of British politics seems to have been enlarged.

Obviously, this raised European consciousness in Britain has affected some sections of society more than others. For example, those who travel on behalf of British companies, those with professional contacts on the Continent and most of the internationally mobile younger generation seem to take Britain's membership of the European Union very much for granted and see themselves as much as 'Europeans' as English, Welsh, Scottish, or Northern Irish. On the other hand, it must be admitted that many of the older and more sentimental sections of the British population are still suspicious or resentful of 'Europe' and will take a great deal of persuading that anything good can come out of the European institutions. It will still take a considerable time before many British people can go anywhere in Europe and (in Churchill's words) say with conviction: 'here I feel at home'.

18.4 Possible future developments

It is difficult to foresee how the European Union will develop in the years ahead and almost as difficult to predict how Britain and its political institutions will respond to the challenges involved. Yet there are a few developments already discernible which seem likely to be among the main driving forces of European integration during the rest of this decade and beyond, while there are also some obvious divisive issues which could be factors for disintegration. The outcome will depend upon the balance between the two.

Main driving forces

The first and most obvious driving force in the European Union both now and in the future is the determination of firms and individuals in the private sector to take advantage of the economic and commercial opportunities offered by the increasingly unified European Single Market of about 370 million people. In this sense it is the private sector which is likely to lead the member states in further moves towards European integration. National authorities and public sector organisations which depend upon them are more likely to be relatively unenthusiastic and to lag behind, usually seeking to validate but sometimes trying to obstruct further developments in a supranational direction.

The best examples of this process of private sector integration are to be found in the activities of large companies, whether based within the European Union or outside, which exert pressure in their own corporate interests upon the member states and the European institutions to reach agreement upon a growing web of common rules, standards and obligations which will enable them to exploit the full potential of the European Single Market. The real pace-setters will continue to be the likes of IBM and General Motors, Siemens and GEC, Nomura and Nissan, Deutschebank and Rhone Poulenc, Phillips and Fiat – to name but a few of the most prominent examples. However, such large companies are increasingly joined by a myriad of small and medium sized companies which are finding that they too can exploit valuable niches and opportunities in the large single market. By pursuing their own corporate interests, they are driving forward the whole process of European integration.

A second and equally significant driving force is likely to be the power of the transnational trade union confederations once they begin to act effectively to advance the interests of organised labour at European level. Powerful national trade unions, such as I.G.Metal in Germany or Unison in Britain, will try to forge alliances with their counterparts in other member states and to create supranational representative bodies to increase their influence upon the decisions of employers and national Governments. Sometimes they will do this through the mechanisms of collective bargaining with national or multinational employers. At other times they will put pressure upon the European institutions, especially the European Commission and European Parliament, in attempts to encourage the growth of what is described as 'European solidarity'.

The most obvious examples of such trade-union pressure are the campaigns which have been waged throughout the European Union for a shorter working week and a statutory minimum wage. Of course, such campaigns will tend to be resisted by many employers and by some national Governments (such as the British Conservative Government) which are opposed to measures which would add to industrial costs and which may resent such interference by European institutions in the free play of market forces. Yet it is equally clear that at the level of general principles such initiatives will continue to find favour in the European institutions and in most member states – as was well exemplified by the Social Chapter of the 1992 Treaty of Maastricht which was strongly supported by eleven of the then twelve member states with only the British Conservative Government in strong opposition to the whole idea.

A *third* main driving force will continue to be the power of highly mobile finance capital. We have already seen the emergence of London and Frankfurt as centres of financial operations in the European time zone, filling the gap between Tokyo and New York in global financial markets. Such developments are likely to grow and accelerate in future as capital, currencies and other financial instruments circulate and are exchanged with dramatic ease and rapidity around the globe. The enormous weight of these financial flows (which are effectively beyond the control of any national authorities) can be illustrated by the fact that in 1989 the daily turnover of financial transactions on the New York financial markets was the equivalent of three times the then total gold and foreign-exchange reserves of Britain, and the total value of currency flows in the world (that is, the buying and selling of currencies for speculative, hedging or other financial purposes) has been estimated to be at least 20 times the total value of all currency transactions used to finance the business of world trade in goods and services.

Such developments have already had an awesome influence upon the claimed economic 'sovereignty' of each member state in the European Union and they will probably be one of the decisive factors which will lead at least some of the member states to form a single currency area before the end of the century – in other words, a limited monetary union where the Euro will be legal tender for transactions. If this happens (as the Maastricht Treaty provided that it could), it will be because at least a hard core of the member states regard it as both a vital corollary of the European Single Market and the best available way of exercising (albeit in common) at least some real economic sovereignty in the face of global market forces. The fact that the British Conservative Government negotiated the right in 1991 to opt in or opt out of such arrangements when they are brought forward for decision (probably between 1997 and 1999) does not alter the fact that this provides one of the most powerful examples of a supranational imperative in Europe which will drive at least some of the member states of the European Union to pool even more of their claimed national sovereignties in an attempt to regain some real power jointly to control their common economic and political destiny.

A *final* driving force for the future, which we have already discussed earlier in this chapter, is the incremental development of European law. As we have seen in Section 18.2 above, Britain and the other member states have been and will be affected by the incursion of European law into more areas of activity which were previously subject only to national competence and jurisdiction. This happens every time that the member states resolve to make a further move towards closer integration, as they did in the 1986 Single European Act or the 1992 Treaty of Maastricht. In future, the further development of European law is likely to be driven at least as much by the evolving case law of the European Court as by the political decisions of national Governments to break fresh European legal ground. Indeed, the doctrine of subsidiarity which was agreed within the Maastricht Treaty and the stated determination of Britain and some other member states to repatriate to the member states some powers and competences now exercised by the European institutions at European level suggests that the integrationist forces within the

European Union will not have things all their own way over the years ahead. We may see a titanic struggle emerging between those who favour European jurisdiction and those who wish to retain the legal authority of the member states. Yet whatever the outcome, the European Union seems likely to become at least as much a community of law as a community of politics.

Main divisive issues

Since the very beginning of the drive towards European unity in 1950, there have been a number of divisive issues which have caused difficulty and sometimes crisis for the member states of the European Union. Yet whenever the member states have been plunged into crisis, they have usually emerged with their fundamental unity intact and sometimes even strengthened by the experience. It seems likely that this will continue to be the pattern with the Fifteen, now that the European Union has been enlarged once again to include Austria, Finland, and Sweden. The almost theological dispute between all the member states which wish to 'deepen' the process of European integration as a corollary of enlargement (apparently fourteen member states) and Britain, which under a Conservative Government appears to wish to halt or even reverse the process of integration, seems likely to continue, although perhaps with less acrimony under a future Labour Government in Britain. It is therefore worth devoting a few paragraphs to this most fundamental of all divisive issues in the European Union in the 1990s.

The essential problem arises from the debate about 'sovereignty' in Europe and people disagree fundamentally about what the term means. Indeed, the word has different meanings and elicits different reactions in the various member states and national traditions. Virtually everywhere on the Continent, except perhaps in Denmark and in some sections of French opinion, the idea of pooling national sovereignties for the common good of Europe as a whole does not really cause any difficulties for politicians and constitutional lawyers alike. This is partly because in many cases on the Continent the nation state has had a chequered and even discredited history, whereas in Britain it still largely symbolises the pride of the British (more exactly the English) in their own nationality. It is also because the so-called 'Community method' holds few fears for the Continental Governments and peoples, since they have been committed to working pragmatically towards 'an ever closer union of the European peoples' (in the words of the 1957 Treaty of Rome) for several decades and have become quite used to the habits and compromises of integration; whereas successive British Governments and the British people have been much more alarmed by the prospect of an apparently irreversible loss of national sovereignty every time member states commit themselves to a new phase of European integration. For British 'Euro-sceptics' the implied erosion of Parliamentary supremacy and the perceived threat to national identity have been the most potent bogies.

With regard to the supremacy of Parliament at Westminster, we have already noted in earlier sections of this chapter that those who have been consistently hostile to Britain's membership of the European Union, especially its supranational aspects, have deeply resented the way in which all the key UK Statutes dealing with Britain's membership (notably the 1972 European Communities Act, the 1986 European Communities Amendment Act and the legislation implementing the 1992 Treaty of Maastricht) effectively provided for the supremacy of European law over national law in those areas of policy covered by the European Treaties. However, Conservative Ministers in the Major

Government have argued that the Treaty of Maastricht represented the high-water mark of the traditional approach towards European integration, since its 'architecture' included at least two *international* rather than supranational 'pillars' (foreign policy and internal security policy) and since the newly introduced doctrine of 'subsidiarity' provided for the repatriation of at least some European competences to the national level of decision making. If this latter view gains support at the 1996 Inter-Governmental Conference to review the implementation of the Maastricht Treaty, then there is at least a chance that the development of the European Union in the rest of the 1990s and beyond will not simply be a linear progression from what has transpired over the previous four decades.

As for the preservation of British and other national identities, there are those in Britain who worry that as the member states and societies become more closely integrated within the European Union, the British people (and others) will in some way lose their distinctive national identities in a sort of multi-national *minestrone*. Such misgivings and fears cannot be dismissed or disproved, because they are essentially subjective and affective in character. Yet at the same time it is wise to observe that the French do not seem any less French, the Germans any less German or the Italians any less Italian as a result of their longer involvement in the process of European integration. The real problem for the British in this regard seems to be that their sense of identity is unusually bound up with their proud and apparently independent history (symbolised by the folk memory of 1940-41 when Britain stood alone against Hitler's Germany) and with their long-established institutions of Parliamentary government which sit rather uneasily with the habits and assumptions of Continental law.

The substantial aspect of the debate about national sovereignty within the European Union concerns issues of political and institutional *competence*. It raises important questions about whether or not the member states will have a *legal right* to act unilaterally in the spheres covered by the European Treaties (which in Britain's case would appear to have been retained at least in theory under the doctrine of inalienable Parliamentary sovereignty) and further, more subtle questions about whether or not they have *the capacity to act* effectively in certain areas of policy on their own – a proposition which seems much more dubious in the modern global economy. On the former point, no one really denies that each member state retains the right to act in defiance of European law (at the risk of being disciplined by the European Court) and the ultimate right to adopt an 'empty chair' policy or even to leave the European Union altogether.[17] Yet in contemporary circumstances this is a somewhat theoretical definition of national sovereignty, since its implementation would probably leave the member state that tried it less rather than more able to protect its national interests. On the latter point, we come to the heart of the argument for membership of the European Union and all the previous forms of European integration which preceded it – namely that by freely pooling national sovereignties in certain agreed areas of policy, the member states have discovered that collectively they have a capacity to act which is superior to anything which they could have achieved on their own. Indeed, this is the very *raison d'être* of European integration.

Since a considerable part of political and public opinion in Britain has not been prepared to accept this argument, an arcane and rather obscure discussion has developed about Governmental functions and the most appropriate and effective levels at which these should be exercised in particular cases. This is the debate which is proceeding under the heading of *subsidiarity*, a notion widely canvassed by Jacques Delors when President of the European Commission (1985-95) and now apparently supported by the British and

German Governments in particular.[18] The doctrine is based upon the contention that the loss of national power to the European level of government can be limited by the fact that the member states and the European institutions are said to agree (under Article 3(b) of the Maastricht Treaty) that no functions should be exercised at supranational level which could more appropriately and effectively be exercised at national level and, it should be added, (although this does not seem to be accepted by the British Conservative Government), no functions should be exercised at national level which could more appropriately and effectively be exercised at sub-national level – that is, regional or local government. So far this apparently reassuring doctrine has not made much difference to the way in which the European Union functions and it seems likely that in the majority of cases the member states and national political institutions will continue to lose effective power and real autonomy in the face of real world developments (for example, in global capital markets), quite apart from the growing power and influence of European institutions above them and local institutions below them. In any case the role of the European Court will be crucial, since at present it alone has the legal competence to define and interpret what is 'appropriate' and 'effective' whenever there is a constitutional dispute between a national Government and the European Institutions.

Assuming that national powers and functions levitate upwards to the European level and gravitate downwards to the institutions of sub-national government, many political theorists and practitioners believe that the current 'democratic deficit' in the European Union could get worse unless and until the powers of the European Parliament are enhanced and extended and the powers of democratically elected local authorities are restored and even put upon a newly entrenched constitutional footing. If measures of this kind are not taken, there is a real danger that national Parliaments in the European Union will continue to lose power to European judges and civil servants on the one hand and to unaccountable public bodies and local administration on the other. After all, national Parliaments have found themselves increasingly less able to monitor and control national Governments, so it is not surprising that policy making and public administration at European level have almost completely escaped their grasp.

As far as the future of Parliament at Westminster is concerned, we dealt with the issues of democratic accountability in the European Union in earlier sections of this chapter. Suffice it to say at this point that the 'Euro-philes' in British politics are relatively relaxed about the idea of sharing the responsibilities of democratic control with the members of the European Parliament, whereas the 'Euro-sceptics' wish to emasculate what they see as a rival institution and to insist that the Council of Ministers should take all the important decisions preferably by unanimity and preferably only with the prior consent of national Parliaments. In the longer term, however, it seems likely that the European Parliament (often in alliance with the European Commission and the European Court) will continue to press for increased powers of democratic control at the expense of national Parliaments and that, with powerful German backing in particular, it may well be successful.

18.5 Conclusion

We have seen in this chapter how Britain excluded herself from full participation in the early stages of European integration after the Second World War and how the country paid an economic and political price for this self-imposed exclusion. However, since joining the European Community in 1973, Britain has played a full part in nearly all European developments, even if she has invariably been ranged on the side of those trying to slow down the pace and limit the scope of European integration. This was especially the case when Margaret Thatcher saw in the end of the Cold War and the disintegration of the Soviet bloc in Eastern Europe a chance to enlarge the European Union to the north and to the east and in the process to dilute the strength of European integration. It also seems to be the case with John Major who, although trying very hard to hold his party together on the European issue, is probably more of a 'Euro-sceptic' than was immediately apparent when he took over from Margaret Thatcher in 1990 and said that he wanted Britain to be 'at the heart of Europe'.

The reasons for this cautious approach and this scepticism about the European ideal, as we have seen, have been a widely held British suspicion of supranationalism in all its forms (except perhaps in NATO) and a marked preference for an international approach towards co-operation with the rest of Europe based upon the sovereign rights of the nation states. There is also considerable hostility at Westminster to the prospect that European law will increasingly encroach upon, and perhaps eventually dominate, the sphere of British national law, and widespread resentment at the erosion of real national autonomy – even though this is much more the consequence of real world economic and technological developments than any decisions taken by the European Union. In short, many of the misgivings felt in Britain about membership of the European Union stem from a nostalgic yearning for the era when Britain was truly a Great Power strong enough to be able to steer clear of binding or permanent entanglements on the Continent and to throw her weight from time to time into the European balance of power decisively on one side or the other.

No one can tell how the European Union will develop over the years ahead or exactly what part Britain will play in it. The British Conservative Government is strongly committed to the creation of a genuinely single European market, but is increasingly sceptical about any other moves towards deeper European integration, such as the introduction of a single currency or more European decision making by qualified or even simple majority vote. The Labour Party, on the other hand, seems to be somewhat more *Communautaire* than the Conservatives, at any rate in relation to the Social Chapter of the 1992 Maastricht Treaty and the idea of more powers for the European Parliament. In the political spectrum the Liberal Democrats and the nationalist parties (SNP and Plaid Cymru) remain the most 'European' of all the political formations in Britain. Whatever else happens in British politics over the years ahead, Britain is surely in the European Union to stay and her destiny will be heavily influenced by her European partners – whether or not successive British Governments wish to exert influence 'at the heart of Europe'.

Suggested questions

1 Explain why it was that Britain did not join the Six original member states of the European Union, but nevertheless did so subsequently.
2 How profound and far-reaching are the legal and constitutional implications of Britain's membership of the European Union?
3 What seem likely to be the main driving forces and divisive issues in the European Union in the future, and how will these affect the course of British politics?

Notes

1. See White Paper on 'The United Kingdom and the European Community', Cmnd 1565 (London: HMSO, 1961), para 3.

2. President De Gaulle's verdict was that:
   England in effect is insular, she is maritime, she is linked through her exchanges, her markets, her supply lines to the most diverse and often the most distant countries; she pursues essentially industrial and commercial activities and only slight agricultural ones. She has in all her doings very marked and very original habits and traditions. In short, the nature, the structure, the very situation that are England's differ profoundly from those of the Continentals.

3. The key paragraphs in the 1971 White Paper 'The United Kingdom and the European Communities', Cmnd 4715 (London: HMSO, July 1971) baldly stated:
   there is no question of any erosion of essential national sovereignty; what is proposed is a sharing and enlargement of individual national sovereignties in the general interest (para 29) [and] at present the Communities' institutions are purely economic – but if the development of European policies in non-economic fields calls for new institutions, then as a member Britain will play a full and equal part in devising whatever additions to the institutional framework are required (para 30).

4. Section 2 (1) of the 1972 European Communities Act clearly states:
   all such rights, powers, liabilities, obligations and restrictions from time to time created or arising by or under the Treaties, and all such remedies and procedures from time to time provided for by or under the Treaties, as in accordance with the Treaties are without further enactment to be given legal effect or used in the United Kingdom, shall be recognised and available in law, and be enforced, allowed and followed accordingly; and the expression 'enforceable Community rights' and similar expressions shall be read as referring to one to which this sub-section applies.

5. See Case 26/62 (1963) ECR1.

6. See Case 10/77 (1978) ECR 629.

7. See *Commission* v. *France*, Case 167/73 (1974) ECR 359.

8. See *Pigs Marketing Board* v. *Redmond*, Case 83/78 (1978) ECR 2347.

9. See *Minister for Fisheries* v. *Schoenenberg*, Case 88/77 (1978) ECR 473.

10. See *Meijer* v. *Department of Trade*, Case 118/78 (1979) ECR 1387.

11. See *Commission* v. *Ireland*, Case 61/77 (1978) ECR 417.

12. See *Shields* v. *E. Coomes (Holdings) Ltd* (1979), 1 All ER 456, 461-2.

13. See M. Butler, *Europe, more than a Continent* (London: Heinemann, 1986), p. 169.

14. Qualified majority voting was originally defined in Article 148(2) of the 1957 Rome Treaty. Under this procedure today the votes of each of the 15 member states are weighted as follows: Belgium 5, Denmark 3, Germany 10, Greece 5, Spain 8, France 10, Ireland 3, Italy 10, Luxembourg 2, Netherlands 5, Portugal 6, United Kingdom 10, Austria 4, Sweden 4, Finland 3. To attain a qualified majority, it is necessary to secure 62 votes in favour out of a total of 87 on a proposal from the European Commission or 62 in favour cast by a least 10 members states on any other proposal.

15. See Fourth Report from the Select Committee on Procedure, 1988-89, 'The Scrutiny of European legislation', Vol I, 622-I, 8 November 1989.

16. The limited legislative powers of the European Parliament (the so-called co-operation procedure) are laid down in Articles 6 and 7 of the Single European Act 1986. This means that once the Council of Ministers has adopted 'a common position' by qualified majority, the European Parliament has three months in which to approve, reject or amend it. If the Parliament approves or fails to act, the Council simply adopts the decision. If the Parliament rejects the 'common position', then the Council can act only by unanimity. If the Parliament amends the proposal,

the Council can either accept the Commission's revised proposal by qualified majority or it can reject or amend it in the light of the Parliament's opinion, but only by unanimity.

17. Under the terms of a Protocol to the 1992 Treaty of Maastricht it was recognised that 'the United Kingdom shall not be obliged or committed to move to the third stage of Economic and Monetary Union without a separate decision to do so by its Government and Parliament'. The Conservative Government also secured an 'opt-out' from the Social Protocol attached to the Maastricht Treaty under which 11 of the then 12 member states declared their intention to introduce binding measures to implement the provisions of the 1989 Social Charter which the UK did not sign. However, the pre-existing Social Action Programme, based upon earlier Treaty commitments, was not affected by the UK 'opt-out' and the UK has continued to participate in negotiations on Commission proposals in this area of policy.

18. The doctrine of 'subsidiarity' has its intellectual origin in a pronouncement by Pope Pius XI in 1931 in his *Rundschreiben über die gesellschaftliche Ordnung* (Encyclical on Social Order).

Further reading

Barnes, I. and Barnes, P. M., *The Enlarged European Union* (London: Longman, 1995).

Buchan, D., *Europe, the strange Super-Power* (Aldershot: Dartmouth, 1993).

Butler, M., *Europe, more than a Continent* (London: Heinemann, 1986).

George, S., *An awkward partner, Britain in the European Community*, 2nd edn (Oxford: Oxford University Press, 1994).

Hartley, T. C., *The Foundations of European Community Law,* 2nd edn (Oxford: Clarendon Press, 1988).

Holland, M., *European Integration – from Community to Union* (London: Pinter, 1993).

Neville Brown, L. and Jacobs, F. G., *The Court of Justice of the European Communities,* 3rd edn (London: Sweet & Maxwell, 1989).

Pinder, J., *European Community, the building of a Union,* 2nd edn (London: Oxford University Press, 1995).

Story, C., *Europe in Britain* (London: World Reports, 1993).

Treaty on European Union, Maastricht, 7 February 1992, Cmnd 1934 (London: HMSO, 1992).

Wallace, H., *Budgetary Politics, the finances of the European Communities* (London: Allen & Unwin, 1980).

19 Policy and decision making

In this chapter we are concerned with the policy and decision making process of British national politics, but only with the two main parties since none of the other parties has actually been in office since the Second World War. We may define *policy* as a deliberate course of action or inaction worked out by the leading figures of either of the two main parties with the help of others in order to define their political purposes and, to some extent, the methods by which they intend to achieve them. We may define *decision making* as an act by a Minister or Ministers collectively (and sometimes by civil servants in the name of Ministers) to select a particular course of action or inaction on a matter of public policy. Such definitions may seem rather abstract and general, but if they are to reflect the realities of modern British politics, this is bound to be the case.

At the outset it is worth heeding Richard Neustadt's observation that 'in Britain governing is meant to be a mystery'.[1] This can be attributed to a number of different factors. Firstly, there is the tradition of official secrecy in British central Government, which can be traced back at least to the 1911 Official Secrets Act and which is still firmly established as one of the ruling conventions of conduct in Whitehall. Secondly, there is the tendency for all Ministers and civil servants to exploit the fact that their privileged access to official information is a form of real power in Britain as in any other political system. Thirdly, there are the limitations imposed upon all investigations in this area by the fact that those politicians and others who might be able to shed real light upon what happens are usually unreliable or self-serving witnesses trying to improve the sales of their memoirs or re-write history to their own advantage, while those academics and others who might be more reliable and objective analysts are not usually given sufficient access to the evidence, except thirty years after the event as historians.

For these and other reasons it is not wise to be dogmatic about the policy and decision making process in Britain, and not possible to draw all the right conclusions about what actually happens. Yet an attempt will be made in the following pages, necessarily in a rather schematic way. The process is shown diagrammatically in its sequential stages in Figure 19.1 on the next page.

Figure 19.1 The policy and decision making process

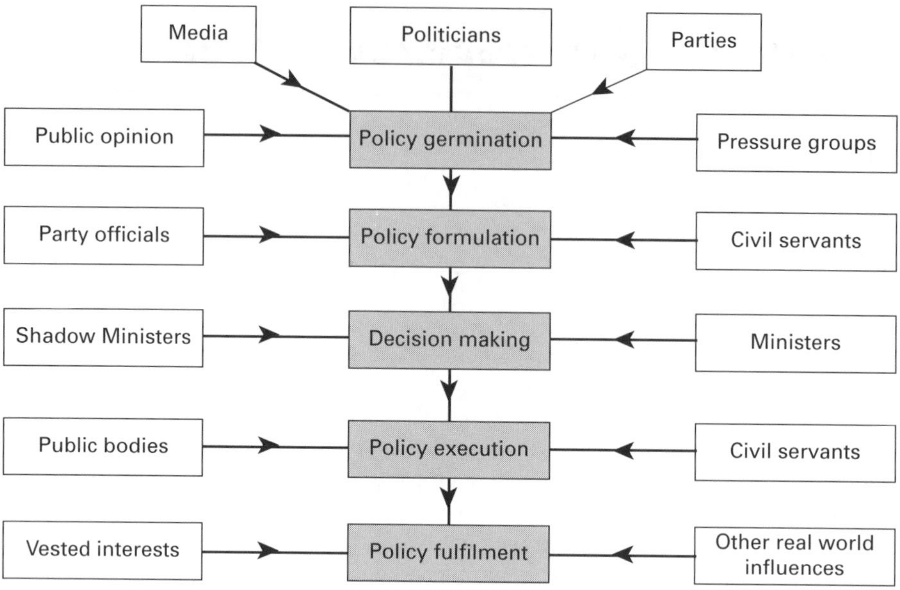

19.1 Stages in the process

In many ways it is somewhat artificial to divide the policy and decision making process into a number of discrete stages, since in reality there is always a good deal more overlap and confusion than such a neat presentation would suggest. However, it is a useful means of clarifying the way the process works and of identifying the key participants and procedures.

Policy germination

The process begins with the stage of policy germination. This usually takes place when a party is in Opposition, although it also has to take place when a party is in Government if the party concerned wishes to win successive General Elections.

In the Conservative Party, what usually happens is that the leadership identifies a problem or a set of problems arising from its previous experience in office or its observation of the current economic and political scene, and then decides upon the need for a new policy or the reconsideration of an existing policy. It has then to see whether there are the necessary sources of information and advice within the party fold to enable it to embark upon the formulation of policy proposals. If it seems that there are, the leadership will probably press ahead by setting up a policy group (or policy groups) to look into it. On the other hand, if it is clear that there are not sufficient sources of information and advice within the party and its orbit, efforts are made to enlist the assistance of sympathetic and expert outsiders who can be trusted to keep a confidence and who have both the time and the inclination to help the party in such policy work.

When Margaret Thatcher was leader of the party (1975-90), the more ideological thrust of Conservative policy was somewhat influenced by self-styled 'think tanks', such as the Institute of Economic Affairs (IEA) and the Centre for Policy Studies (CPS) – the latter having been established by Sir Keith Joseph and Margaret Thatcher in 1975 to help them chart a new course for the Conservatives. The IEA, which had been founded by Ralph Harris and Arthur Seldon in the 1950s, had been an unrelenting campaigner for a free-market approach not only in economic policy but also in social policy and other spheres as well. Throughout the Thatcherite period such bodies had some influence in helping to create an intellectual climate which made Thatcherite policies more acceptable than they might otherwise have been.

Under John Major's leadership since 1990, the influence of such 'think tanks' has diminished, while the influence of the Policy Unit at 10 Downing Street and of senior civil servants has increased as the process of policy and decision making has become more short term and reactive to events. With the Prime Minister usually listening closely to the Chief Whip and fond of a more collegiate style of political leadership, the influence of the Cabinet and indeed of troublesome back-benchers like the so-called 'Euro-rebels' has increased as compared with the position during Margaret Thatcher's time as Prime Minister.

In the Labour Party, policy germinates in a rather different way which reflects the different organisational and ideological traditions of the party. Political power and influence over policy has traditionally been more diffused within the entire Labour movement. Thus ideas and pressure for the germination of policy come from a wider range of sources – such as constituency activists, internal party pressure groups and affiliated trade unions, as well as many friendly academics, intellectuals and experts in mass communications. The role of the Parliamentary leadership has often been to act as something of a brake upon the wilder policy ideas which can emerge, especially at those times in the party's history when the hard Left has been strong in the constituency parties.

The approach to policy making changed following Labour's third electoral defeat in a row in 1987 when Neil Kinnock and his closest colleagues recognised the need for a thorough policy review. In organisational terms, the conclusion that was drawn was the absolute necessity to keep the policy and decision making process firmly within the control of the party leader and a few trusted collaborators. In policy terms, Neil Kinnock came to the conclusion that only a revisionist and modernising approach to Labour policy would suffice if the party were to stand a chance of making a winning appeal to the voters in the 1990s. This new approach was broadly followed by John Smith as leader of the party from 1992 to 1994, although with some caution about the danger of offending key trade union leaders on sensitive policy issues such as public ownership and industrial relations. Since Tony Blair became leader in July 1994, the drive for policy modernisation has been taken further – notably with the reformulation of Clause IV of the party's constitution in modern language, and much else.

In the case of each main party the mechanisms just described may be referred to as the pure models of policy germination. In practice this stage of the process is often more hit-or-miss, since it is influenced by developments in the real world which require a greater or lesser degree of pragmatism depending upon the political correlation of forces at any time. The Labour Policy Review of 1987-89 was a good example of the reactive model of policy germination in that the Labour leadership felt obliged to take full account of the so-called 'new realism' engendered by about ten years of Thatcherism in action. Equally, the almost revolutionary change in Conservative policy from 1975 to 1979 had exemplified another kind of reactive model in that the party leadership was consciously responding to the perceived failures of the second half of Edward Heath's term as Prime Minister from 1970 to 1974.

At this early stage in the policy and decision making process, the key questions are: (1) who defines the problems to be addressed, (2) who sets the priorities of the policy work to be undertaken, and (3) what are the ideological objectives of the various policy groups which are established? When a party is in Opposition, it is invariably the party leadership which takes charge of the agonising reappraisal that is normally thought to be necessary following a decisive defeat at the polls. When a party is in Government, somewhat different motives and considerations usually apply, since the school of experience and the lure of ideas tend to coexist in the process of turning political thought into action.

Policy formulation

The next stage in the process is that of policy formulation. By this we mean the translation into coherent policy proposals of the political ideas which have germinated in the ways already described. This is also a stage which takes place more systematically when a party is in Opposition that when it is in Government, although each situation needs to be examined carefully if we are to get a complete and accurate picture of this stage of the process.

In the Conservative Party, policy formulation is usually the work of party officials and others who draft the papers in which the policy proposals are contained. Of course, such people work under the careful direction and control of the chairmen of the policy groups concerned and indirectly of the party leader and other senior figures in the party. Over many years this drafting work was usually done by officials of the Conservative Research Department (CRD), which had been a relatively small but rather competent back-room organisation staffed mainly by bright young graduates with personal political ambitions. However, the role of the CRD became less prominent after Margaret Thatcher decided to amalgamate it with Conservative Central Office in 1980 and, in any case, it has never seemed so essential when the party has been in Government, since Ministers have been able to rely upon civil servants for factual briefing and support. At the same time it should be noted that civil servants are *not* expected to involve themselves in specifically party political tasks and there is now a whole cadre of 'political advisers' in Whitehall who work for individual Cabinet Ministers on party political matters.

In the Labour Party the work of policy formulation is done by analogous people employed by the party's Research Department. They work under the direction and control of the leading politicians in charge of the various policy groups, which in turn are located within the formal structure of policy committees under the auspices of the National Executive Committee (NEC). Except for the drafting of some of the most important policy documents (for example, some of those produced for the 1987-89 Policy Review), this work is done by party officials who are likely to remain employees of Labour headquarters at Walworth Road if and when the party is returned to Government.

In Government, however, the policy formulation stage tends to be rather different, since the leading politicians concerned are Ministers and can benefit at least from the factual information and advice supplied by civil servants. In these circumstances the real work of drafting and re-drafting policy proposals, which may or may not find their way into the party Manifestos, is done mainly by Ministers and their political advisers, since it would be constitutionally improper for civil servants to be closely involved in such party political tasks.

In the Labour Party the structure of policy groups tends to be as elaborate when the party is in Government as when it is in Opposition, since the NEC provides the framework for the policy-making process at any rate in formal terms. Informally, however, the situation has tended to be rather different in that most recent Labour Party leaders have been able to impose their authority upon the party's policy-making process. Even in the 1970s when this proved to be more difficult for Harold Wilson and James Callaghan, Labour Ministers and Shadow Ministers remained free to decide which of the many policy proposals put forward by the policy groups within the NEC structure they would accept and which they would reject for the purposes of official party policy. When in Government, Labour Ministers also retained considerable flexibility and discretion in deciding upon the methods and the timing of policy implementation, and this is likely to be the case the next time Labour is in office.

In the Conservative Party the structure of policy groups has tended to be less elaborate when the party is in Government than when it is in Opposition. This is because there is no equivalent of Labour's National Executive Committee and because the party leader and other senior figures retain almost complete control of the policy formulation stage of the process. At the appropriate stage in a Parliament policy groups are established at the behest of the leader of the party and these are normally chaired by senior Ministers when the party is in office and by equivalent leading politicians when the party is in Opposition. The actual drafting of policy proposals is usually done by party officials who support the various policy groups. The various policy formulations are considered and reconsidered by the policy groups which will normally be made up of a fairly broad spectrum of interested party opinion from both within and outside Parliament. Once the proposals have been refined and finalised by the policy groups, they are then submitted to the Prime Minister and senior colleagues before any crucial decisions are taken about inclusion or exclusion from the party Manifesto.

It must be added, however, that in both main parties there is some cynicism and even resentment at the way in which the germination and formulation stages of the process seem to have been captured by the party leaders and a few close colleagues. There is evidence for this view which can be drawn particularly from the Thatcher period for the Conservatives and now from the Blair period for Labour. In Labour's case the problem has been mitigated somewhat by the work of the Social Justice Commission under the chairmanship of Sir Gordon Borrie, since this useful body included people drawn from outside the mainstream of Labour politics and even, in a few cases, from other parties. Nevertheless the *cognoscenti* know that it is largely a device to enable the current Labour leadership to put off the time when it has to make firm policy commitments – for example on taxation and transfer payments. In general, it is back-bench MPs in both main parties who have the least opportunities for real influence upon the deliberations of policy groups and the eventual policy decisions which they help to prepare. Even when invited to serve on such groups, there remains the suspicion among back-benchers that they may have been co-opted into what is often largely a placebo exercise with all the big decisions on policy predictably remaining in the hands of the party leaders and their most senior colleagues. In many ways this is no more than an accurate reflection of the realities of power in modern party politics.

Decision making

The next stage in the process is that of decision making. On all important and political-ly sensitive issues this is unavoidably the work of party leaders and their most senior political colleagues.

In Opposition the requirements and procedures are quite simple. Usually all that is necessary is that the Shadow Cabinet should meet to accept or reject the policy propos-als which have been formulated and refined in the ways already described. Of course, there are some issues which require lengthy discussion even at this stage and which can-not be resolved at a single meeting. Yet in most cases, by the time that a policy formu-lation reaches this stage, the actual decisions can be taken quite quickly, not least because the leader of the party and close colleagues will have taken care to prepare the ground for agreement before the meeting.

In Government this stage in the process is both more varied and more complex. Some Government decisions can be taken quite quickly by individual Ministers acting within their allotted spheres of responsibility. Some are taken by groups of Ministers within a particular Department. Yet nearly all important Government decisions affect a variety of Departmental interests and therefore have to be taken at least by a Cabinet committee and often by the Prime Minister and a few very senior colleagues. It is difficult to make any definitive generalisations about decision making at meetings of the Cabinet and its committees. It would appear that in full Cabinet most decisions are taken quite expedi-tiously and it is only when the Cabinet has to deal with the most difficult and contentious political issues – for example, the public expenditure cuts imposed by the IMF upon the 1974-79 Labour Government – that it has had to return to the same issues on several occasions in order to secure agreement. This really underlines the lengths to which Whitehall officials will go to prepare the ground for difficult Cabinet decisions and the efforts which all Prime Ministers make to facilitate smooth Cabinet decision making.

When a Cabinet committee has to make a decision on a particular subject, the terms of reference are usually supplied to the chairman by the Prime Minister or, occasional-ly, by the Cabinet as a whole. It is then for the chairman of the committee to hold as many meetings as necessary in order to reach a decision which can be recommended to the Cabinet, often within an agreed period of time. In the later stages of the 1964-70 Labour Government, it became conventional that any member of the Cabinet who was not on a particular Cabinet committee would not challenge the decisions of the committee in full Cabinet without the prior approval of the Prime Minister or the chairman of the com-mittee concerned. Indeed, the whole rationale of Cabinet committees is that they should be able to take decisions on behalf of the Cabinet without normally having to submit them to a further stage of discussion in full Cabinet. Only if they function in this way can they truly be said to save the time and energy of the Cabinet.

Yet it remains true that the conventions of collective responsibility and the traditions of Cabinet government in Britain entitle all Cabinet Ministers, if they are sufficiently determined, to pursue a particularly sensitive or important political issue in full Cabinet, and they can insist (sometimes backed by a threat of possible resignation) upon having it put on the agenda of a future meeting. To cope with the wide variety of such situations which can arise, some Prime Ministers (such as Harold Wilson) have found it necessary to lay down strict ground-rules for Cabinet decision making, especially if some mem-bers of the Cabinet are not sufficiently amenable to Prime Ministerial leadership. Others (most notably Margaret Thatcher) have not found it necessary to act in this way, because for various reasons they have usually been able to dominate and control their Cabinet colleagues. Others (such as John Major) have developed a more collegiate approach to decision making which encourages the expression of all points of view in Cabinet before collective and binding decisions are reached. In all cases Prime Ministers 'take the voices' around the Cabinet table before important decisions are reached, not least because it is clearly in their own interest to carry their senior colleagues with them and to bind them together on the issues which really matter.

Policy execution

Next comes the stage of policy execution. This is the stage at which civil servants excel, provided decisions have been clearly taken by Ministers and clearly communicated by officials to those who need to know about them. The greatest difficulties tend to occur later in the process, since the law of unintended consequences seems to apply to policy and decision making as much as any other sphere of human activity.

Policy execution normally follows immediately after the previous stages already described. As far as civil servants are concerned, its roots can be traced back to an earlier stage of the process. Once the broad objectives of a party's policy have been set and a General Election campaign has begun, it is normal for civil servants in all Whitehall Departments to prepare position papers designed to assist incoming Ministers to implement their policies, no matter which party wins a mandate from the electorate to form the Government. Thus incoming Labour Ministers may have advice on their desks on how best to implement a policy of economic intervention, while new Conservative Ministers may have comparable advice on how to implement further phases of privatisation. The advice is neither sanguine nor cautious, but merely intended to suggest the most effective ways of executing the policies of the incoming (or returning) Government, while emphasising the practical consequences of implementing the various political commitments.

From then on the initiative is with Ministers and their behaviour varies according to their personal drive and ambition, and the extent to which the party commitments in their own Departmental sphere are given priority by the Government as a whole. If a Minister is charged with the execution of a policy which is given a high political priority and if the commitment is clearly expressed in the party Manifesto or other formal statements by the party leadership, then it will usually be a straightforward matter of taking the appropriate Ministerial decisions for the initiation of administrative action in Whitehall or new legislation at Westminster, whichever is more appropriate. On the other hand, if a Minister has to execute a policy which has been given only a low priority by the party in office, then there will probably be little alternative to preparing the ground with suitable administrative action and Ministerial speeches, while putting in a Departmental bid for a place in the future legislative timetable. In anticipation of such progress, a Minister can try to improve the Department's prospects by stimulating interest in Parliament and the media, and by mobilising the support of the relevant interest groups and among the general public. If all this can be done successfully, it will increase the chances of a Minister making a mark at a later stage of the Parliament.

Assuming that the appropriate Ministerial decision has been taken, the stage of policy execution is initially the responsibility of the Cabinet Office if the decision was taken by the Cabinet or one of its committees. It therefore communicates the decision to all Departments and other agencies which need to know about it. For example, if a decision concerns a nationalised industry, it will be communicated first to the sponsoring Department which will in its turn see that the decision is conveyed to the Chairman of the industry concerned, although this does not necessarily mean that the decision will be faithfully implemented in strict accordance with Ministerial wishes. Thus a decision affecting British Rail would be communicated via the Department of Transport and so on. If the decision involves a matter of local government responsibility (such as local planning, housing or Community Care), it will be communicated to the Department of the Environment for onward transmission to the local authorities in England, and similarly to the Welsh, Scottish, and Northern Ireland Offices for decisions affecting people who live in those parts of the United Kingdom. All such civil service communication is carried out between the Cabinet Office and the appropriate Ministerial Private Offices which are then responsible for onward transmission within the respective Departments. These civil service channels therefore complement and support the direct communications between Ministers which take place in Cabinet committees and on many other more informal occasions in Whitehall, Parliament and elsewhere.

If a decision requires legislation for its implementation, it becomes the responsibility of the Minister or Ministers who will have to pilot the legislation through Parliament. The Department or Departments concerned have to work closely with legal experts from the Office of Parliamentary Counsel who act as the legislative draftsmen for the entire Government. The role of these Parliamentary draftsmen can be of considerable significance, since the precise wording of Bills can sometimes be almost as important as the fundamental principles involved – notably, in the annual Finance Bill which gives legislative expression to every Budget.

If the execution of a Government decision requires new primary legislation, the process begins with an important pre-Parliamentary stage within the confidential confines of Whitehall. This often involves extensive consultations between civil servants in the Departments concerned and relevant experts and other interested groups both within and outside the web of central Government. Such detailed discussions may continue for weeks or even months on the basis of draft legislative proposals and it is not unknown for the results of this work to be rejected by the Legislation Committee of the Cabinet if the timetable is too tight or the legislative programme too full or the likely political outcome too dubious. By the time that a proposed Bill is ready for inclusion in the Queen's Speech at the beginning of a Parliamentary session in November, it can usually be assumed that its content has been fully discussed in this way. On the other hand, there are a few occasions when Ministerial decisions or even draft Bills are introduced at the eleventh hour on the basis of only minimal or perfunctory discussion even within the Government, let alone with relevant outside interests. Examples of this phenomenon would include the decision to abolish the Greater London Council and the Metropolitan County Councils which was taken by Margaret Thatcher and a very small circle of Ministerial colleagues just before the 1983 General Election; or the decision to hold a fundamental review of the National Health Service which seems to have been sprung upon most of the Government by Margaret Thatcher during a television interview on *Panorama* in January 1988.

In other instances the execution of a Government decision may only require the introduction of secondary legislation, in other words a Statutory Instrument issued under the authority of an existing Act of Parliament. Once again there are usually detailed consultations within Whitehall with a wide range of relevant experts and interested groups. Indeed such consultations are particularly important in such cases, since the subsequent procedures for Parliamentary scrutiny of Statutory Instruments are widely regarded as cursory and inadequate.

If the decision falls within the sphere of lawful administrative discretion for Ministers derived from legislation which is already on the Statute Book, the Minister concerned normally acts in an executive capacity and communicates directly with the persons or bodies concerned via Departmental Circular or by ordinary letter or memorandum. In some cases the decision may entail the delegation of executive responsibility to statutory bodies which already have lawful powers in certain specified areas, such as local authorities, public corporations or increasingly the Executive Agencies of central Government. Yet in many cases it is still a matter of Departmental action carried out directly on behalf of the Ministers by the civil servants in the Department.

Policy fulfilment

The final and most problematic stage in the process is policy fulfilment. Recent British history suggests that this is the stage at which the failures of successive Governments have been most marked. Among the reasons for this may be that Governments have tried to do too much, pursued often mutually contradictory objectives, had to share power with formidable interest groups, found themselves constrained by expected or revealed public opinion, and been obliged to work within the limiting framework of established social assumptions and the uncompromising realities of the modern world. Faced with such difficulties, successive Governments have sought to ensure the fulfilment of their policies by using one or more of the following political techniques.

Firstly, there is *the technique of accommodation*. This is a standard political ploy whereby a Government seeks to neutralise any threats to its policies by the simple expedient of accommodating critical points of view and absorbing critical people. It may take the form of co-opting troublesome or obstructive individuals onto official consultative committees or appointing them to positions of responsibility on public bodies or simply holding privileged discussions with powerful groups with a view to incorporating at least some of their ideas or concerns into Government policy. It is certainly one of the most effective and well-tried methods, since it can turn critics or adversaries of Government policy into compliant or at least semi-pacified partners. Yet it is usually not enough to ensure the fulfilment of policy.

A second technique is that of *manipulation*. This is really little more than a sinister term for the well-tried art of political persuasion and it subsumes such often practised skills as news management – that is, attempting to influence public opinion via careful and deliberate guidance of the media. This technique has been used for years with varying degrees of success and it is a normal part of the process of government. Efforts have also been made from time to time to use fiscal policy in an attempt to buy political popularity in the run-up to a General Election by cutting taxes or increasing public expenditure more than would otherwise have been the case. This technique seems to have worked in 1959 for Harold Macmillan and 1992 for John Major. Yet it has become an increasingly uncertain and risky practice inviting swift retribution from the financial markets if badly misjudged in terms of timing or amount. Unexpectedly, John Major led the Conservative Party to victory at the 1992 General Election at the depth of a long recession. This outcome probably owed more to the incredibility of Neil Kinnock as an alternative Prime Minister in the eyes of floating voters than to any of John Major's positive attributes or to the record of his party in office.

A third technique is that of *public opinion mobilisation*. This is really a matter of seeking the support of the 'silent majority' in order to redress the political balance against the excessive influence of vociferous and articulate minorities. As an exercise in political leadership, it is usually no easier than the other techniques already mentioned, and it can often be more difficult in view of the problems involved in trying to hold public opinion constantly to one particular line and then translating it into actual voting behaviour when necessary. Such difficulties are illustrated by the familiar tendency for many people to give strong support in answering public opinion polls to increased expenditure on certain desirable public services, but then to vote in the subsequent General Election for the party which most obviously stands for lower taxation and public borrowing and hence a less indulgent attitude towards public spending. Nevertheless there are various ways in which this technique can be applied. These may involve the use of powerful rhetoric, constant repetition of simple messages, persuasive argument designed to appeal to the general public, symbolic gestures designed to evoke a favourable public response, and specially commissioned political advertising or opinion polls. None of these methods on its own is decisively effective, so sensible politicians usually fall back on the more traditional methods of rational argument and emotional appeal as well.

Finally, there is the technique of *political shock treatment*. This involves confronting the public with the full implications of failing to support Government policy. In a sense this is a technique which was used by the Thatcher Government in its efforts to change public attitudes radically and permanently in the vital areas of economic productivity and industrial performance. It is certainly a technique which has been successful in the past at times of clear and present danger – as in 1940 when Winston Churchill appealed so successfully to the British people as they stood alone against Nazi Germany – and it may also have worked for the Conservative Government during the 1982 Falklands conflict when public opinion rallied strongly behind the British armed forces and the Government. Yet there can be no certainty that it will work in normal circumstances during times of peace and relative prosperity, so Governments are wise not to try it too often or count upon it too much.

19.2 Key aspects

The post-war consensus and its legacy

It should be clear from the foregoing description of the policy and decision making process in Britain that it is essentially a continuous phenomenon which proceeds from week to week, month to month, year to year and even Government to Government. This is mainly because the problems of central Government in Britain have remained broadly the same over the decades since the Second World War, almost regardless of which party has been in office. Every Government has been faced with the need to maintain and improve the competitiveness of the economy, every Government has wrestled with the problems of securing adequate resources for the Welfare State without imposing an intolerable burden upon the wealth creators; every Government – certainly since 1973 – has had to cope with the implications of Britain's relationship with her partners in the European Union. It is also because the civil service has a natural preference for orderly and continuous government, something which is to be expected from a permanent and politically impartial bureaucracy. In view of the institutional inertia in the system, once a policy consensus becomes established, it requires a prolonged period of disappointment with its consequences – even when exploited by radical political leadership fully prepared to embark upon new directions – for the broad thrust of policy to change and a new consensus to emerge. Looking back at the whole period since 1945, we can see that this is how things have happened in Britain.

As we have already noted in Chapter 8, for about 25 years after the Second World War the continuity of Government policy in Britain stemmed from the high degree of policy consensus which had been established within the Coalition Government during the war. This was extended and carried forward with conviction by the post-war Labour Government, widely recognised as one of the great reforming Administrations of the twentieth century in Britain. The consensus continued to apply under both Conservative and Labour Governments in the 1950s and 1960s – hence the term 'Butskellism' which was used to describe the policy approach followed by R. A. Butler (Conservative) and Hugh Gaitskell (Labour) when they were each prominent policy makers within their respective political parties. It was not until the early 1970s – at about the time of the Yom Kippur war between Israel and Egypt and the ensuing oil crisis in 1974-75 – that the post-war consensus in Britain began to crumble, although there had been harbingers of this development in some of the more radical free-market policies attempted by the Heath Government from 1970 to 1972. By 1979, when the Conservatives were returned to office under Margaret Thatcher's leadership, the era of the post-war consensus was effectively over, having been destroyed in the 1970s by the hammer blows of unreliable economic performance and disappointed public expectations. These factors, in turn, created the conditions in which each of the two main parties felt it right to adopt a more ideological approach to politics.

Of course, there were also discontinuities during the period from 1945 to 1979, but these were usually the result of Governments having to respond to great events or other developments over which they had little or no control. This was true, for example, of the decision of the Attlee Government in 1947 to develop an independent nuclear weapons capability for Britain. It was true of the decision of the Eden Government in 1956 to send British forces to invade the Suez Canal Zone. It was true of the decision taken in 1960 by the Macmillan Government to open negotiations with the Six with a view to full British membership of the European Community. It was true of the decision to devalue the Pound taken in 1967 by the Wilson Government, and of the decision taken in 1972 by the Heath Government to impose upon Northern Ireland direct rule from Westminster.

Other more recent examples include the decision taken in 1976 by the Callaghan Government to apply for a massive loan from the International Monetary Fund; the decision taken in 1982 by the Thatcher Government to send a Task Force to the South Atlantic to recapture the Falkland Islands; and the decision taken in 1992 by the Major Government for Britain to leave the Exchange Rate Mechanism of the European Monetary System. These cases provide examples of decisions which entailed notable discontinuities of policy and which could have been said to permit no other response from Government. In all cases they appeared aberrant in the context of the policy consensus prevailing at the time. Yet with the advantage of hindsight we can now see that they were virtually inevitable.

An era of polarised ideologies

After 1979 the British people experienced a new era of polarised ideologies, which had its roots in the bitter industrial disputes of the 1970s but which only came to fruition during Margaret Thatcher's time at 10 Downing Street and particularly in the early 1980s when her brand of radical Conservative ideology was opposed with equal vehemence by Michael Foot's Labour Party and the so-called 'Wets' in her own party who represented the older 'One Nation' tradition of Conservatism. The foundations for the mould-breaking Conservative policies of the 1980s were laid when the party was in Opposition in the late 1970s at a time when it very largely succeeded in winning the intellectual argument against Socialism. For its part the Labour Party had also become more ideological in the 1970s partly as a result of the disappointment felt by its activists with the minimal Socialist achievements of the 1964-70 and 1974-79 Labour Governments and partly as a response to the Thatcherite onslaught of the 1980s. The result of these parallel developments in the two main parties was ideological polarisation and the virtual destruction of the common ground which had been established in the post-war consensus. This shifted the centre of gravity of British politics and laid the foundations for a new neo-Thatcherite consensus which has been largely accepted by the Labour Party under Tony Blair and which has reduced the relative appeal of the Liberal Democrats.

This era of ideological polarisation stemmed from the tendency of each main party, when in Opposition, to return to ideological first principles in an attempt to bring forward purer and more radical policies in preparation for its return to Government. The overall effect of this kind of political response was to lead each of the main parties, when returned to office as a function of the failure of its opponent, to claim that it had a mandate for everything in its Manifesto, no matter how unrealistic or harmful such policy might prove to be in practice. This was one of the main causes of the sharp discontinuities of policy in the 1970s and it left a heavy mark upon the more ideological attitudes of both main parties in the 1980s.

Those who relished the resurgence of ideological politics in Britain in the 1980s and who feel somewhat disappointed with the pragmatic tendencies of all the leading parties in the 1990s are once again finding their voices, especially in the Conservative Party where the ultra-free market and xenophobic hard Right have found new Thatcherite standard bearers in John Redwood and Michael Portillo. So far the 'new' Labour Party has not shown a matching tendency on the Left, largely because all parts of the party in Parliament and in the affiliated trade unions are temporarily united in wishing to do everything possible (including stifling their misgivings) in order to ensure victory for Labour at the next General Election. None of this, however, should obscure one of the most remarkable features of British politics in the 1980s – namely, the extent to which the party in office became *more* rather than less ideological under the singular leadership of Margaret Thatcher.

At the same time it should be made clear that an ideological approach to politics – although not really in the mainstream of the post-war tradition of mutual accommodation in Britain – can bring some real benefits to the country and can be justified as necessary and legitimate on certain important conditions. Firstly, when a party is in Opposition, its leadership should try to mobilise the maximum possible public understanding and support for its fundamental ideas and values. Secondly, during the political campaign running up to and during the General Election, it should make its policy intentions and commitments as clear as possible, so that it will be difficult or impossible for its defeated opponents subsequently to argue that it does not have a mandate for what it does in office. Thirdly, once in Government, the party in office must constantly explain and justify its actions through the media at least for the benefit of the politically attentive public. If it manages to fulfil all these conditions, its policies will have a reasonable chance of commanding public acquiescence, even perhaps positive support.

Towards a new consensus?

In the 1990s, however, it has seemed that the two main parties are converging towards a new policy consensus build upon the post-Thatcherite central ground of British politics. This is partly because Tony Blair and his two predecessors as Labour leader all concluded that it would not be possible for the Labour party to return to power without first establishing credible credentials in the eyes of the English middle class. It is equally because 'the real John Major' seems to be much more cautious and pragmatic than his predecessor and seems to travel with relatively little ideological baggage. Of course, it is possible that this observable policy convergence is more apparent than real and more temporary than permanent, in that it very largely reflects the fact that both main parties have become rather risk-averse. The Conservatives have experienced such deep unpopularity since September 1992 and have suffered such an erosion of their Parliamentary support through by-election defeats and the split with the 'Euro-rebels' that John Major and his senior colleagues seem (temporarily at least) to have lost the inclination for radical initiatives. Labour, for its part, has scarcely been able to believe its luck in being so far ahead in the opinion polls and has followed a deliberate policy of keeping its policy commitments to an absolute bare minimum for fear of dissipating its huge lead in the opinions polls and its chances of returning to power. Yet behind this frozen moderation in both main parties lurk other more radical and ideological figures who would seek to seize either the leadership (in the case of a Conservative defeat at the next General Election) or the policy initiative (in the case of the Labour Party once it is safely returned to office).

During this period of uncertainty and flux, it seems clear that most of the British people are looking for moderation and a sense of security from their leading politicians after quite a period of ideological exhilaration in the 1970s and 1980s. To that extent it seems likely that John Major and Tony Blair are both more in tune with the spirit of the times than any of the more radical figures in their respective parties who might wish to succeed them. There seems to be quite a resonance in British public opinion in the 1990s for a new form of politics based upon such warm and friendly concepts as 'community', 'responsibility' and 'partnership'. Indeed, the leaders of all three national parties seem to have recognised and tried to respond to this public mood. Yet it is also worth remembering that in all parties future policy will have to be developed in conditions of considerable, and possibly growing, uncertainty in view of the volatile developments in the global economy and in technological innovation which are likely to have unpredictable social and political consequences in Britain and many other countries.

19.3 Strengths and weaknesses

There are both strengths and weaknesses in the policy and decision making process in Britain. It is neither one of the best nor one of the worst of its kind in the liberal democracies of the world. It has some characteristics which are universal and some which are peculiar to Britain. In any event it ought to be assessed on its merits and within its own terms.

Strengths

(1) The most obvious strength is the ability of the process to translate party political commitments into Government action or legislation. This derives principally from the way in which the electoral system is capable of turning a plurality of the votes cast in the nation as a whole into a majority of the seats won in the House of Commons. Thus it enables a particular interpretation of the popular will to be transformed into executive or legislative action by the Government of the day, usually without encountering any insuperable obstacles at any rate in Whitehall and Westminster. However, any Government can be vulnerable to a back-bench revolt on its own side – as was evident, for example, in the 1986 defeat of the Thatcher Government on its proposals to liberalise the Sunday trading laws or in the enormous difficulties posed for the Major Government in 1992-93 by the 'Euro-sceptics' on its own back-benches in their determined and sustained opposition to the legislation necessary to align British law with the requirements of the Maastricht Treaty.

(2) Another strength of the process is its efficiency in turning Ministerial decisions into administrative or legislative action. This is a tribute largely to the efficiency of the civil service in Whitehall Departments and Executive Agencies. It means that the writ of Ministers usually runs quite effectively throughout Whitehall and its satellite Agencies, but much less certainly in public corporations and local authorities, and only in the private sector when reinforced by the full power of the law and statutory regulation. For example, the Conservative Administrations since 1979 have had continuing difficulties in imposing public expenditure restraint upon local authorities, even some of those under the control of Conservative Councillors. This is attested by the fact that at least 15 Bills have been introduced by central Government since 1979 in repeated (but not wholly successful) attempts to curb local authority spending by legislative means.

(3) Yet another strength of the process is its ability to cope with abrupt and radical changes of policy. Any institutions of Government which have this ability to accommodate changes of political direction so quickly and completely must be very robust. What is more, such changes are made without any significant change in the administrative personnel involved – something which contrasts sharply with what happens in other democracies such as the United States. Yet even this has changed somewhat in recent years and is reflected in growing concerns about the alleged politicisation of the highest grades of the civil service and the tendency for Conservative and Labour Governments alike over the years to employ more special advisers and other politically motivated people whose involvement in policy making has sometimes been quite influential.[2]

Weaknesses

There are equally some notable weaknesses in the process which might be considered to outweigh the strengths just enumerated. The conclusion to be drawn must depend upon the uses to which the process is put.

(1) It can be argued, for example, that the robust flexibility of the process has permitted too many abrupt and often damaging discontinuities of policy. As has already been pointed out, these have usually stemmed from the determination of politicians in office to implement their Manifesto commitments and, in the 1970s and 1980s, from the polarisation of ideologies.

(2) Paradoxically, another weakness in the process is that there has been too much unimaginative continuity of thinking in Whitehall which has often stymied the prospect of radical policy initiatives. It used to be the case that this had the effect of bringing virtually all Governments back to the safe middle ground of British politics within about two or three years of every General Election. This reflected the gyroscopic influence of the senior policy advisers at the top of the civil service which Shirley Williams (after her time as a Cabinet Minister in the 1974-79 Labour Government) described as 'a beautifully designed and effective braking mechanism'.[3] However, this impression of the influence of the civil service was called into question during the heyday of the Thatcher Administration when allegations were made that the higher grades of the civil service took on too many of the prejudices and assumptions of their political masters.

(3) Another weakness of the process (which is apparent in most democracies around the world) is that it encourages both Ministers and civil servants to pay too much attention to short-term political considerations at the expense of the quest for fundamental long-term solutions to the nation's most serious and intractable problems. While this is partly a function of the relatively short political timescale imposed by the five-year maximum span of a Parliament, it is mainly due to the congenital tendency of nearly all politicians in office to give priority to what appears to be urgent over what they know to be important (when the two categories conflict), largely because the media leave them with little alternative and because they know that most members of the public have impatient expectations.

(4) Another weakness of the process is that both Ministers and civil servants tend to rely too heavily upon a rather narrow range of official information and advice. This is perhaps inevitable, since civil servants control the flow of people and ideas to Minsters and because their advice often reflects essentially the 'Departmental view' supplemented by advice from a rather limited compass of expert opinion. In other words, because of the weight of Whitehall custom and practice and the habits of official secrecy, the policy making process in Britain tends to be much less open than in other Western countries where the governing elites are more receptive to ideas and information from a wide range of sources.

(5) Another weakness of the process has been described as 'Government overload'.[4] Essentially, this means that most Ministers and some senior civil servants working directly for them invariably have far too much to do in too little time. This can be attributed to a number of different causes, among which are the increase over the years in the scope and complexity of modern Government, the growth of the sub-national and supra-national dimensions of policy and decision making, and the impact of modern mass communications which has created a need for Ministers to be informed about and often to

comment at short notice upon a huge variety of developments, allegations and rumours revealed or sometimes created by the media. This is particularly true at the highest levels of Government where the Prime Minister and members of the Cabinet bear disproportionate burdens of paperwork, meetings and media performance.

(6) A final weakness of the process could be said to be the rather limited scope for Parliamentary or public participation. This is mainly because central Government in Britain is regarded as the exclusive and confidential preserve of a chosen few in the relevant 'policy communities'. Policy ideas, especially in their formative stages, are not very widely shared other than among those with a direct need to know or who can be relied upon to give compatible and confidential advice. Perhaps the most notable group among the company of the excluded are back-benchers in the governing party who invariably learn of new policy developments not from their Ministerial colleagues but from the media. Although Parliament is supposed to be the first to be informed (when it is sitting), it is usually quite a long way behind the game as compared with privileged interest groups (who are consulted early on by Whitehall) and the media. This is yet another reflection of the habits of confidentiality which influence so much of the behaviour of British central Government.

19.4 Possible improvements

This is not the place to rehearse in any detail the wide range of possible changes which have been proposed from time to time in order to improve the policy and decision making process in Britain. It is sufficient here to mention only a few of the more familiar suggestions in order to give a flavour of the reformist discussion which has taken place over the years.

Increased support for the Opposition

Some people have argued that there should be increased support for the Opposition parties, so that they can be better informed on the great issues of the day. To this end it has been suggested that there should be created a small but capable Department of the Opposition to enable Opposition politicians to scrutinise and argue with Ministers on a more equal basis. The covert purpose of such an innovation might be to keep the policy making of Opposition parties more closely in touch with the realities and constraints of Government and so reduce the risk that the policy of an incoming Government might reflect little more than the views and prejudices of unrepresentative political minorities. It is also argued that this would raise the quality and sophistication of policy making in Opposition and make it less likely that Parliament as a whole would be dominated by the resources of Government.

Another way of achieving the objective of 'educating' the Opposition would be to give all politicians not in Government much fuller and more frequent access to official information and advice. This happens to some extent in the case of Privy Councillors (former Ministers of senior rank and a few others) who are allowed to see restricted official information and advice on privileged terms. It also happens in a more routine way during the Standing Committee stage of some complicated Government Bills when the

MPs concerned are supplied with Notes on Clauses (civil service explanatory briefing). It is thought that this principle could be extended more widely if Ministers felt sufficiently self-confident and indulgent towards the Opposition to do it.

Yet another way of achieving the objective would be to provide all political parties with substantially greater financial support from public funds – as happens in many other European countries – perhaps in proportion to the votes which each party received at the previous General Election. This would enable parties in Opposition to employ more of their own advisers and so enable at least their front bench spokesmen to be better informed and possibly more effective critics of the Government. However, it could not guarantee a higher overall standard of Opposition, since that is bound to depend most of all on the motivation and capabilities of the politicians concerned.

Wider advice for Ministers

Another proposal which has been put forward is that there should be a wider range of advice available to Ministers from a wider range of people.[5] This could be achieved by bringing into Whitehall a larger number of 'special advisers'. Yet it could as well be achieved by opening up the higher grades of the civil service to recruitment from a wider range of backgrounds in other parts of the public sector and from the private sector as well.[6] To some extent this is now happening under the aegis of the Major Government's policy for open advertising of some senior posts and it could be taken further with the idea of specific short-term contracts. As this more eclectic approach to civil service recruitment gathers momentum, it may well make quite a difference to the traditionally rather narrow and cautious attitudes of the senior mandarins in Whitehall.

Some of the businessmen who have had direct experience of working within British central Government, such as Sir John Hoskyns who headed Margaret Thatcher's Policy Unit at 10 Downing Street during her early years as Prime Minister, have argued that this idea should be taken a good deal further by opening up civil service procedures to permit the recruitment in each Department of perhaps 10 or 20 senior policy officials drawn from the private and voluntary sectors to serve in central Government on fixed term contracts with market-related rates of pay.[7] The argument is that such temporary officials would be likely to offer Ministers support and advice which would be more completely in tune with the political purposes of the Government of the day than anything offered by career civil servants who are always likely to have an eye upon the different views and interests of the official Opposition as the potential future Government.

Such ideas would be all very well in practice if the purposes of the Government of the day were simply to force through Whitehall and Westminster a particular political programme of an unusually radical and determined nature. Yet in view of the fact that much of the work of Government is necessarily reactive as well as proactive, there is a serious risk that other civil servants working for Ministers in such a climate would drastically trim the advice which they gave to Ministers in order to bring it fully into line with the known prejudices of their political masters. This would not be good for the quality of decision making in central Government, since it would deprive Ministers of the cautionary and wise advice normally given by senior civil servants performing their traditional role. It might be a more exhilarating way of proceeding in Government, but there would be no guarantee that it would produce better results for the benefit of the general public.

Structural change in Whitehall

Another proposal which has been made by some is that there should be structural change in Whitehall in order to make the centre more powerful in relation to the various Departments. This has led people, such as Lord Hunt (a former Cabinet Secretary), to propose the creation of a new central Department – either a fully fledged Prime Minister's Department or an enlarged and strengthened Cabinet Office.[8] Such changes have usually been suggested by those who feel a need to strengthen the hand of the Prime Minister in the policy and decision making process and to encourage greater policy coherence throughout Whitehall.

However, in the light of Margaret Thatcher's period at 10 Downing Street, it is by no means self-evident that the shortcomings in the British policy and decision making process derive from insufficient Prime Ministerial power and influence. Indeed, it might seem unwise gratuitously to increase the power of 10 Downing Street when there is already a long-run tendency towards 'presidentialism' in British central Government which can become particularly marked when there is a strong personality at 10 Downing Street who enjoys a comfortable majority in the House of Commons. In any case, the system seems to have a way of correcting itself, as we have seen with the marked personality contrast between Margaret Thatcher and John Major. In so far as there can be a problem of excessive 'Departmentalism' in Whitehall, the most appropriate solution is really the more effective and timely use of the Cabinet and its committees rather than any attempt to bolster the institutional power of the Prime Minister.

Greater role for Parliament

Finally, some people have been attracted by the idea that Parliament should be given a greater role during the formative stages of the policy and decision making process. Such a change would add a creative role to the main functions of Parliamentary activity which are those of scrutiny of the acts of Government and the mobilisation of public consent. To be successful, it would almost certainly require the further development of Select Committees in ways which would enable them to be more deeply involved in the formative stages of policy making. For example, it might mean giving Select Committees the power to consider legislative proposals at a pre-legislative stage or to influence the composition and balance of the public accounts *before* any final decisions are taken by the Chancellor of the Exchequer on the unified Budget.

Such an enhanced role for at least some back-benchers would probably require the strengthening of the sources of expert and independent advice available to Members of Parliament – perhaps through new institutions along the lines of the General Accounting Office or the Office of Technology Assessment which serve the US Congress. In fact, there is already a modest analogue of the latter which serves the House of Commons, although without the visibility and prestige of its larger American counterpart. Yet even with the benefit of such institutional strengthening of the resources available to Parliament, there would still be considerable obstacles to taking such ideas very far forward in a political system in which the essential role of Parliament is to scrutinize and criticise policy rather than to make it.

19.5 Conclusion

A balanced conclusion to the issues raised in this chapter would seem to be that the policy and decision making process works rather well in Britain, but only if its performance is measured in terms of its relatively smooth operation in Whitehall and Westminster. Beyond the walls of these twin citadels the process is not so satisfactory or effective, especially since it is not very good at mobilising the understanding and consent of the general public. Even those interest groups and other privileged bodies which are consulted fairly fully by Ministers and civil servants cannot feel confident that they have much more than marginal influence upon either the process or the outcome of policy making. While they may occasionally pull off a policy *coup*, it is invariably the most senior politicians and their closest political advisers who dominate the policy making discussions and monopolise the decisions. British politics is still very much party politics and this fact of life in Britain leaves little scope for uncommitted or altruistic outsiders. In contemporary circumstances only the increasingly influential media seem to be an exception to this rule.

In the future, the process may well change quite significantly as the world in which national policy making operates becomes more intrusive and more complicated and global events impinge to a greater extent than before on what national politicians can achieve. If Britain is to be 'at the heart of Europe', the process of policy and decision making will also be curtailed and complicated by the requirements of the evolving European Union. Moreover, as and when the general public becomes more aware of the realities of modern politics and wishes to participate directly in a growing variety of ways, politicians and civil servants could find it even more difficult than before to keep up with rising public expectations. In such demanding circumstances all the key participants would be wise to try to explain more fully the inherent limitations of a policy making process based upon sometimes puerile party competition and the clash of artificially polarised policy positions. They would also be wise to emphasise more often the severe limitations imposed by European and global influences which constrain the room for manoeuvre of any national Government. Britain is fortunate in having a robust and mature system of policy and decision making, but there are no grounds for complacency as long as the problems of Government remain so hard to solve.

Suggested questions

1   Describe the policy and decision making process in British central Government.
2   Where does real power lie in the policy and decision making process?
3   How could the process be improved in modern conditions which are so heavily influenced by external factors, such as the media and the markets?

Notes

1.   Quoted in R. Rose (ed.), *Policy making in Britain* (London: Macmillan, 1969), p. 292.
2.   For example, Sir Alan Walters, Margaret Thatcher's personal adviser on economic policy, was a factor in the resignation of Nigel Lawson as Chancellor of the Exchequer in October 1989. This was because his public utterances (in themselves an unusual breach of normal civil service conventions) were an outward and visible sign of the growing differences of view on

policy between Margaret Thatcher and her longest-serving Chancellor. However, it was the growing breach between the two neighbours in Downing Street on the conduct of monetary policy which was the real cause of Nigel Lawson's eventual resignation.

3. In W. Rodgers et al., *Policy and Practice: the experience of Government* (London: RIPA, 1980), p. 81.

4. Lord Hunt of Tanworth, a former Cabinet Secretary who had served four different Administrations, elaborated this point in a lecture given to the Chartered Institute of Public Finance and Accountancy on 9 June 1983.

5. One of the foremost proponents of the idea of wider advice for Ministers from a more open and flexibly recruited civil service is Peter Hennessy in his magisterial book *Whitehall* (London: Secker & Warburg, 1989).

6. See the White Paper 'The Civil Service, continuity and change', Cmnd 2627 (London: HMSO, July 1994), paras 4.13-4.22, for more information on this subject.

7. See J. Hoskyns, 'Whitehall and Westminster, an outsider's view', *Fiscal Studies*, November 1982.

8. Lord Hunt outlined four possible options, but expressed no clear preference: a fully developed Prime Minister's Department, a strengthened Cabinet Office, a recreated and strong Central Policy Review Staff, and an enlarged Prime Minister's Office.

Further reading

Ashford, D.E., *Policy and Politics in Britain* (Oxford: Blackwell, 1981).

Butler, D. et al., *Failure in British Government* (London: Oxford University Press, 1994).

Dynes, M. and Walker, D., *The Times Guide to the New British State: The Government Machine in the 1990s* (London, Times Books, 1995).

Healey, D., *The Time of my Life* (London: Michael Joseph, 1989).

Hennessy, P., *Whitehall* (London: Secker & Warburg, 1989).

Hogwood, B.L., *Trends in British Public Policy* (Milton Keynes: Open University Press, 1992).

James, S., *Policy Making in British Government* (London: Routledge, 1995).

Lawson, N., *The View from Number 11* (London: Bantam Press, 1992).

Rose, R., *Ordinary People in Public Policy* (London: Sage, 1989).

Sanders, D., *Losing an Empire, finding a role – British foreign policy since 1945* (London: Macmillan, 1990).

Savage, S.P. et al., *Public Policy in Britain* (London: Macmillan, 1994).

20 British Parliamentary democracy

British Parliamentary democracy has evolved over the centuries. From Simon de Montfort's Parliament in 1265 to the outbreak of the Civil War in 1642, it was based upon the changing relations between the Monarch and the various estates of the realm. By the time of the Bill of Rights in 1689 a more explicit constitutional contract had evolved between the Monarch's Government and the two Houses of Parliament. From then until the 1832 Reform Act Britain was essentially governed by the landed aristocracy. With successive extensions of the franchise from the 1867 Representation of the People Act to the 1969 Representation of the People Act, a recognisably modern democracy gradually emerged. The contemporary result of this long evolutionary process is that since the entry of the United Kingdom into the European Community in 1973, British politicians and people alike have lived in a Parliamentary democracy which is a constitutional monarchy within the European Union.

20.1 The conditions of democracy

There are a number of conditions which have to be met if the system of Parliamentary democracy in Britain is to function satisfactorily. These are conditions which can be applied to any modern democracy and which Joseph Schumpeter described as 'conditions for the success of the democratic method'.[1]

The first condition is that the politicians active in the political system should be of a high calibre. It would obviously be invidious for the authors to comment in any detail upon this point, save to observe that quality is influenced by attitude in that politicians who adopt a positive and constructive approach to the problems which confront them are often more attractive and persuasive than those whose approach is negative and destructive. Clearly high quality in the political class is a necessary but not a sufficient condition for success in a democracy, while cynical or negative politicians are usually unattractive to the voters.

The second condition is that the range of political activity should be limited. This is obviously a salutary point to make in relation to contemporary politics, since the persistence of unrealistic public expectations – often encouraged by unscrupulous politicians at election time – leads people to suppose that Governments can find a solution to every problem. Unless leading politicians show themselves capable of preaching and practising the virtues of limited government, public disappointment is likely to increase with potentially dangerous consequences for democracy.

The third condition is that there should be a strong and impartial bureaucracy to advise the politicians in office and to administer the decisions of Government. The importance of this condition is perhaps best demonstrated by its absence – for example, in certain countries where the lack of a competent and incorrupt public administration can be a real barrier to political, economic and social development. It is therefore ironic that in Britain the nature and quality of the civil service has sometimes been portrayed as an obstacle rather than an aid to national success, because of the perceived tendency for traditional British bureaucrats to prefer established ideas and procedures to anything new or untried – except when insisted upon by Ministers.

The fourth condition is that vanquished political minorities (notably the losing political parties at a General Election) should acquiesce in their electoral defeat and accept the consequences of the voters' verdict. This condition is fundamental to the satisfactory functioning of a democracy and in Britain the rule of the (Parliamentary) majority has invariably been accepted by all parties. Of course, a healthy democracy ought also to have safeguards for the defeated minorities against possible abuse of power by the majority. Yet in Britain this is difficult to achieve as long as the electoral system enables the victorious party (which normally gains no more than a plurality of the votes cast) to impose its political will upon Parliament and the country simply by dint of its overall majority in the House of Commons.

The final condition is that everyone involved in politics, especially those in the victorious party at a given time, should show tolerance and magnanimity towards the interests and concerns of all those on the losing side at the previous General Election. This is a condition which was broadly fulfilled in Britain during the first 25 years or so after the Second World War. It ought also to appeal to any party in Government which realises that its period in office cannot be indefinite and that sooner or later it will find itself licking its wounds in Opposition. There were signs, however, that a certain Conservative triumphalism in the 1980s infected politicians on the Government side, marking a clear contrast with the more modest behaviour of earlier generations in British politics and, incidentally, with the normal conventions of coalition politics on the Continent of Europe.

20.2 Essential characteristics

It can be said that there are a number of essential characteristics in British Parliamentary democracy which have been widely recognised over the years. We shall take a closer look at each of them in turn.

The first essential characteristic of British Parliamentary democracy is that it is a representative system which is supposed to function in a democratically accountable way. This has some positive consequences for the political system. It endows the Government of the day with democratic legitimacy, although a wise Government will not push its wishes too far or take its own authority for granted. It allows the electorate every four or five years to deliver a verdict on the party in office and on the competing attractions of the other parties. It provides institutional channels of communication between the Government and the governed, although by no means the only channels in a pluralist political system in which pressure groups and the media play such an important part. It can have the effect of magnifying or filtering the force of public opinion according to the nature of the various issues which emerge and the different imperatives for each political party.

Notwithstanding these positive characteristics, the British form of Parliamentary democracy has not always been held in high repute. This is partly because the main actors – the two leading political parties – have been in the habit of raising their party political conflict above all other considerations on almost every occasion. It is partly because public assumptions and expectations of Britain's much vaunted political system have been seriously disappointed on many occasions. It is also because the nature of the political debate as conveyed via the media so often seems to be related scarcely, if at all, to the concerns and aspirations of the general public. For example, the almost theological debate within and between the two main parties about the nature and extent of Britain's participation in the future evolution of the European Union can seem very remote from the more prosaic concerns and aspirations of most people. In these circumstances it is not surprising that some intellectuals and reformers in all parties and in none have been more attracted to the sort of political arrangements which pertain in other countries, notably on the Continent of Europe where coalition Governments based upon broad economic and social consensus tend to be the order of the day and all political relations take place within the framework of a codified constitution.

Needless to say, there are some significant points to be made on each side of this argument. On one side, it is argued that the legitimacy of Government in Britain is largely based upon the fact that the party in office is usually the sole victor of the previous General Election and can therefore command the support of an overall majority in the House of Commons on virtually all occasions. Of course, this is necessarily a qualified legitimacy, since it is normally based upon no more than a plurality of the votes cast at the previous General Election – in other words, the largest single minority of the total national vote – and it is valid for no more than the duration of a single Parliament, which since 1911 cannot exceed a maximum of five years (unless exceptionally extended by all-party agreement, as happened in both World Wars). This means that British representative democracy is really based upon an implicit contract between the Government and the people. Ministers accept that there are limits to the action which they can properly take if they are to remain within the bounds of constitutional convention and public tolerance. The general public accepts (sometimes with deep reservations) that the party in office should be allowed considerable latitude in its attempts to fulfil its election mandate and even more so in the day-to-day government of the country.

The limits of public tolerance and acceptability vary from time to time and from Government to Government. Much depends upon the extent to which policy runs counter to powerful opinion in the political parties and in pressure groups. Much depends upon the generally perceived gravity or urgency of the situation with which Government has to deal. Much depends upon the possibilities of making progress by stealth without attracting media or public attention – something which is now virtually impossible in view of the determination of the media to look under every stone. Some issues will turn on the likelihood of policy reversal in the event of the Opposition winning power at the ensuing General Election. In general, such limits are quite flexible and cannot really be determined in advance.

On the other side, the power of the electorate is largely based upon the fact that, whatever the governing party may do or fail to do during its term of office, it is the voters (especially the floaters) who have the final say at every General Election and can therefore forgive or punish those who have been in power. Yet even this final power of the electorate needs to be qualified in a number of significant ways. Firstly, the voters are able to exercise no more than intermittent democratic control in view of the relative infrequency of General Elections in Britain. At other times, in order to put pressure upon their elected representatives, they have to rely upon stressing the vulnerability of all politicians to rejection in the ballot box if by the end of the Parliament the public's reasonable wishes are not met. Secondly, while the voters are able to exercise a democratic choice, they are only able to do so within the range of electable alternatives offered by the serious political parties. Thus Conservative voters who live in safe Labour seats and who support root and branch reform of the Welfare State are unlikely to be able to return an MP who shares and expresses their views. Equally, Labour voters who live in safe Conservative seats and who support expanded welfare provision are unlikely to be able to return an MP who shares and expresses their views. As for the supporters of minor parties, they seem doomed to cast wasted votes (unless their voting strength is locally concentrated) given the nature and characteristics of the British electoral system. Thirdly, the ignorance and apathy of many voters is another limiting factor in British democracy, since people who vote with little or no real knowledge of the issues or who are too apathetic to vote at all cannot really be said to have a good claim to democratic authority.

The second essential characteristic of British Parliamentary democracy is the vital role played by the political parties as the traditional channels of communication between the Government and the people and as the principal pool of talent from which members of the Government and the Opposition front bench are recruited. Of course, the political parties are by no means the only mechanism of contact, nor indeed the most significant, between Government and people and the figures show that active participation in them has been in secular decline for many years. However, they still manage to channel the energies of political activists in lawful and constitutional directions by representing real class and other interests in British society. As long as the parties are performing their traditional tasks satisfactorily, those who have political causes to advance should feel able to do so within one of the recognised political parties. Once this ceases to be the case on any significant scale – as many people would now argue that it has – there is real cause for concern about the future of Parliamentary democracy.

One of the main reasons for this concern in recent years has been the marked trend in British society away from this traditional form of political participation towards growing public support for and membership of a large number of very active and often influential pressure groups. These groups are very often focused upon a single overriding issue – such as animal welfare or single parents – and they have become all the more formidable because of the degree of personal commitment which they inspire in their members. The reasons for these developments are complicated, but they seem to have a great deal to do with the increased importance and influence of the media in virtually every sphere of modern politics. Indeed, as we saw in Chapter 6, the almost symbiotic relationship between many established pressure groups and the media is one of the main explanations for the growth of their power at the expense of Parliament and the political parties. In these circumstances the main forum for public debate has moved to a considerable extent away from the Palace of Westminster to the columns of the press and the studios of the electronic media.

The third essential characteristic of British Parliamentary democracy is the way in which all Governments feel obliged to try to hold the ring between the various organised and competing interests in the country. This is, of course, a function of the legislative and regulatory role of Government and Parliament. Yet it is also evidence of the relative weakness of every Government in the face of competing power centres in the private sector both in Britain and increasingly abroad. In these increasingly difficult circumstances every Government strives to see that the general interest gets at least an equal hearing above the cacophony of special pleading from sectional interests. This task seems to have become more difficult over the years, not least because too many Ministers can themselves be portrayed as representing narrow sectional interests of an ideological or political variety. Indeed, one of the obvious disadvantages of one party being continuously in office for as long as the Conservatives have been since 1979 is that Ministers can plausibly be accused of equating their party political interests with those of the nation as a whole and so be seen as moving away from the Solomon-like role expected from all Governments. Clearly senior civil servants from the Cabinet Secretary downwards have been mindful of this danger and have sought from time to time to lean against it. Yet their 'constitutional' task is not made any easier by judges and others who have been in the habit of opining that the national interest is, by definition, what Her Majesty's Government says it is at any time.

In forming an objective assessment of this aspect of the political system, the real questions to ask are how far any Government seeks genuinely to represent and hold the ring for the general interest, and how far it demonstrates an ability to do so without simply equating the general interest with its own party political view of the world. Too great an influence for party political objectives lays any Government open to the charge that it is ignoring its wider responsibilities. Too great a willingness to endorse the demands of sectional interests can suggest a feebleness of purpose which can undermine the authority of Government. An unusually altruistic emphasis upon the longer term can earn plaudits perhaps in the history books, but guarantee defeat at a General Election. In short, governing has always been difficult, but it has probably become even more so in a modern democracy.

20.3 Other significant features

British Parliamentary democracy has some other significant features which need to be taken into consideration if we are to get a complete picture of it in modern conditions. Each of the following features has assumed particular importance at different times, but all have shaped the British political system over the years.

Political polarisation

The tendency towards political polarisation in Britain has deep historical roots in the eighteenth-century struggle between the Whigs and the Tories and the nineteenth-century struggle between the Liberals and the Conservatives. During most of the twentieth century it has been the Conservative and Labour parties which have slugged it out with each other, sometimes in a spirit of considerable bitterness and recrimination. For example, in the 1970s and 1980s the two main parties became particularly polarised, partly as a function of internal dissatisfaction within each of the parties with the way in which both Harold Wilson and Edward Heath had followed what were perceived by some fundamentalists in their own ranks to have been weak and vacillating policies, but mainly because it was clear by then that the policies of the post-war consensus had run their course. The result of these matching political developments in each of the main parties was that by the mid-1980s politics in Britain had become less consensual and more polarised than at any time since the 1930s.

This state of affairs was in marked contrast to the much more limited party political differences during the 1950s and 1960s when each of the main parties broadly accepted the political consensus which had emerged in Britain during and immediately after the Second World War. It can also be differentiated from the apparent political convergence in the 1990s between the pragmatic Conservatism of John Major and the 'modernised' Socialism of Neil Kinnock, John Smith and Tony Blair. It would seem that both main parties are now camped upon the post-Thatcherite central ground of British politics which accepts the role of market mechanisms and the need to regulate them, but which is also characterised by an acute awareness of what the media and the general public will tolerate at any time. The irony facing Conservative radicals, who have remained true to the pure faith of Thatcherism, is that their party has held office for so long that it has created the political conditions in which it has been possible for successive leaders of the Labour Party to make the policy and organisational changes required to make the official Opposition electable.

Institutional inertia

Institutional inertia is another significant feature of the British political system which is quite capable of coexisting with the political polarisation just described. Although a number of important institutional changes have been made in Britain over the past 30 years or so – for example, the reform and emasculation of local government, the transformation of the civil service, and the almost complete transfer of the nationalised industries to the private sector – few of these changes have proved to be an unqualified success and all have entailed considerable (often unforeseen) problems. This has led the opponents of institutional change to insist that such initiatives can do more harm than good and are not necessarily a complete remedy for political problems which may be attitudinal or psychological in origin. They have also argued very forcefully that the political upheaval which such institutional changes usually entail brings in its wake a level of cost and disruption which is inimical to the interests of good government.

On the other hand, all those who believe in the value or need for institutional change have tended to argue that it is impossible to entrench really significant policy changes without buttressing them with new, or at least radically reformed institutions. For many such people (especially those who signed up to Charter 88), the most vital institutional and procedural change which has *not* been made in Britain, but which in their eyes ought to be made to facilitate the rest of their agenda, is the introduction of proportional representation for elections to Parliament at Westminster. Unlike the defenders of the *status quo* in each of the two main parties, they argue that Britain's first-past-the-post electoral system is still the most significant obstacle to all the other institutional changes which they tend to favour – such as the introduction of a codified constitution, a new Bill of Rights, and a completely new way of working in Parliament. Naturally, the defenders of the institutional *status quo* cling to the principle of Parliamentary supremacy at Westminster and the uniquely powerful position which it gives to the party which happens to have been victorious at the previous General Election. Of course, there are strong arguments for retaining the existing electoral system in Britain (as we pointed out in Chapter 3), since it does at least give the voters a clear choice at General Elections and provides other opportunities (notably at local elections and Parliamentary by-elections) for the voters to register dramatic protest votes against the Government of the day. Moreover, it needs to be borne in mind that the present electoral system is capable of producing single party Governments which pursue not only consistent and sometimes radical policies, but also cautious and pragmatic policies such as those pursued by the Major Administration in the mid-1990s. In practice, nearly everything depends upon the needs of the times, the policies favoured by the politicians temporarily in office and the nature of the Parliamentary arithmetic at any time. In such provisional circumstances it is probably wise to place the onus of establishing the need for institutional change in Britain upon those who propose it.

Elective dictatorship

Lord Hailsham and others have argued that in certain circumstances British Parliamentary democracy can be virtually an 'elective dictatorship'.[2] This is undoubtedly true in the sense that any British Government with an effective majority in the House of Commons can usually get its way in Parliament, at any rate on the issues which really matter. This fact of British political life has been reflected over the last four decades or so in the ability of successive Labour Governments to impose relatively high rates of direct taxation, to nationalise parts of British industry and to increase the level of welfare benefits; and the ability of successive Conservative Governments to switch the burden of taxation relatively from direct to indirect taxation, to return to private ownership many of the nationalised industries, and to concentrate upon means-tested rather than universal welfare. In each case a principled political agenda has been followed, often almost regardless of the criticism of the Opposition or the hostility from elements of the British public. Such action has been possible because of the relatively high level of political security enjoyed by most majority Governments since the Second World War, at any rate as long as they enjoyed a comfortable working majority in the Commons. Of course, at those times when this essential precondition was not met, talk of 'elective dictatorship' has seemed rather fanciful.

From another point of view it has been argued that an 'elective dictatorship' is an exaggerated description of one aspect of British Parliamentary democracy which tends to be voiced mainly by those who have lost a General Election and are predictably bemoaning the uses to which the governing party puts its power. The reality is that beyond the twin citadels of central Government – Whitehall and Westminster – powerful private-sector interests and mighty external events have demonstrated the ability to frustrate or defeat even the best-laid plans of the most powerful democratic Governments. Two examples drawn from the past two decades in Britain may serve to illustrate the point. In 1983 the Stock Exchange was able to persuade Ministers in the second Thatcher Administration not to submit it to statutory regulation, even though the liberalisation of financial services which was then beginning in Britain seemed already to require a degree of regulation by the state and the Conservatives had a commanding majority in the Commons which they could have used if they had felt so inclined to steamroller through such a reform. Equally, the teacher trade unions were able in the early 1990s to persuade Ministers in the Major Government extensively to modify the regime of standard tests in schools, even though this was a key component of Conservative education policy which was built upon the introduction of the national curriculum. Even more dramatic was the example of 'Black Wednesday' in September 1992 when the centre-piece of the Government's counter-inflation policy – Britain's membership of the European Exchange Rate Mechanism – became impossible to sustain in the face of overwhelming pressures in the financial markets. In all these cases (and in many other examples which could be given) it was made clear that even the most powerful national Governments enjoy only limited and conditional power and that talk of 'elective dictatorship' can often be wide of the mark. In a pluralist, and increasingly global society, national Governments have to share power with the media, the markets and many other powerful actors in both the public and private sectors.

Diminished scope for national Governments

It may seem strange to argue in a book on the British political system that the diminished scope for national Governments and indeed all national authorities is now one of the most significant features of the modern world. Yet this has been borne out in Britain (and indeed in all other nation states) by the mounting evidence which emphasises that the writ of even the most powerful and determined Ministers does not always run unchallenged and can sometimes be defeated. There are several reasons for this diminished power and status of national institutions.

One reason is that in a modern pluralist society the successful implementation of policy often depends to a greater extent than members of the political class are prepared to admit upon at least the tacit acquiescence, if not the active support, of those most directly affected by the policy. It is only necessary to reflect upon the successful Parliamentary and public campaign against the Poll Tax in the late 1980s and early 1990s, or the veto power of the Ulster Unionists in talks within the framework of the so-called 'peace process' in Northern Ireland to see the force of this argument.

Another reason for the limited power of Governments is that so many problems in the world today are not really susceptible to solutions imposed by politicians and civil servants through legislative or administrative action, because they require action by individuals, families and private organisations beyond the effective sphere of any Government. The cautionary tale of Conservative attempts to formulate and implement a 'family policy' under the slogan of 'Back to Basics' serves to illustrate the point. In another sphere, some forms of market activity in the financial services sector (such as derivatives) are so sophisticated and obscure to laymen that it is very difficult for national authorities fully to understand, let alone effectively to regulate and tax these activities. When they do succeed, the most notable effect may be to drive such activities 'off-shore' to more relaxed and welcoming jurisdictions.

The most significant reason, however, why all national Governments seem increasingly by-passed or even left behind by the march of events is that they no longer operate on the levels required to match the most significant developments in the global economy and in the noticeably dynamic interaction between local and global communities – as exemplified by the rapidly growing world of Internet and cyberspace. In these new circumstances the policies and aspirations of even the most powerful national authorities are vulnerable to developments and decisions elsewhere over which they may have little influence and even less control. For example, the free movement of capital around the world, the growing interaction between computer and television technologies, and the looming tendency for millions to migrate across national borders in search of a better life all pose threats to the ambitions and jurisdictions of national Governments. So far their response has usually been to seek ways of combining their power and influence through international organisations. Yet because of the fundamental diversity of national interests which has been revealed, the most successful responses have tended to include supranational elements – as we have seen in the leading post-war examples of NATO and the European Union.

The dilemma for any British Government, and indeed for all national Governments, is that if they stubbornly persist in making claims to exclusive competence and control within their national jurisdictions, they are likely to discredit themselves in the eyes of their electorates because of their almost inevitable inability to deliver all that they have promised. On the other hand, if they give up most of their traditional pretensions, more and more people in their electorates may begin to look elsewhere for satisfaction of their material needs and aspirations. In these circumstances both supra-national and sub-national levels of political authority could begin to come more into their own, while the appeal of self-help in the private sector is already growing fastest of all.

This growing gap between the ambitious objectives of nearly all modern Governments and their rather modest and often disappointing achievements at the end of their period in office has certainly harmed the reputation of Parliamentary democracy in the eyes of many people. In Britain, as in many other countries, it has undermined public faith in national political institutions from the Monarchy to the political parties to the judicial system. The inevitable corollary has been the growth of public cynicism and the emergence in recent years of what can only be described as a culture of mutual contempt. Appropriate remedies are likely to be difficult to find and even more difficult to put into practice. It seems that institutional reform will play a significant part in any remedies proposed and that broadly based campaigns for electoral reform and the more frequent use of referenda will figure prominently in the future.

20.4 Signposts to the future

As we approach the millennium, it seems clear that there are a number of unresolved issues which will influence the shape and nature of British politics in the future. Among the key questions are whether there is scope for significant change in a national political system which is characterised by such ingrained conservatism; and whether, against a background of disappointed expectations, it will be possible to gain and retain public consent for the actions of any Government. At this stage the signposts to the future do not suggest particularly sanguine conclusions.

The scope for change

It is a paradox that although successive Governments in Britain since 1945 have sought to make a radical mark upon national performance and public attitudes, there have been relatively few changes of lasting significance which have been brought about by Governments. This may be explained by the fact that Britain is a very conservative (with a small 'c') country and by the fact that any Government has only limited means at its disposal with which to reshape society. Essentially, Governments can seek to act in one or more of the following ways: they can introduce new policies; they can create, reform or abolish institutions; and they can seek to modify or transform public attitudes. As we have observed during the course of this book, successive Governments have used some or all of these instruments in their quest for achievement.

In the 1950s and early 1960s successive Governments relied mostly upon fairly minor policy adjustments within a well defined and broadly accepted political consensus which had been in place since the Second World War. In the later 1960s and the 1970s successive Governments concentrated more upon trying to make institutional changes as the leading remedies for Britain's national problems. In the 1980s successive Thatcher Administrations attempted a radical programme of change which was akin to a cultural revolution of comparable ambition to that of the great radical Administrations of 1906 (Liberal) and 1945 (Labour). Great claims have been made for the positive impact of this Thatcherite crusade and indeed its ideological legacy is still in evidence in attenuated form in each of the main parties. Yet a sober verdict upon the Thatcher years (1979-90) must be that while a sizeable minority of the British population learned to exploit the opportunities of the new economic liberalism unleashed by the Conservatives at that time, the vast majority of the British people seemed unwilling or unable to make the attitudinal step-changes that were expected of them. This conclusion has since been reinforced by the experience of John Major's time at 10 Downing Street when the most striking characteristics of Government policy have been caution, nostalgia, and pragmatism, and the British people seem to have returned to attitudes of diffidence, resentment and insecurity.

There are various plausible explanations for this assessment. Firstly, the accumulated evidence seems to suggest that the radical instinct does not come naturally or remain very long with most British people who invariably prefer an approach to life which is less strenuous and more comforting. Secondly, when a determined political minority – such as the Thatcherite radicals – manages to establish a temporary ascendancy in Britain, it usually sows the seeds of its own destruction either by going unrealistically far in its chosen direction or by failing to recognise that the world has changed around it. When such developments occur, the conditions are created for the gradual acceptance of political alternatives which come to appear more attractive and more relevant to most people. In this way it appears that the traditionally conservative instincts of the British people are usually too powerful for even the most determined and mould-breaking politicians to overcome.

The importance of consent

Any modern British Government has to give a high priority to the gaining and retaining of public consent, if only because its absence or attenuation can fatally undermine the position of even the most powerful and determined Administration. Of course, in many cases the Government of the day can get by with no more than the tacit acquiescence of the general public. Yet for the assured fulfilment of policy, active consent is usually required and this implies satisfying a number of important conditions. Firstly, it requires a well informed and influential Parliament in which all MPs not in the Government can have real opportunities to influence policy and to scrutinise and control the Executive. Secondly, it requires genuine and extensive consultations with a wide range of interest groups representing the full gamut of sectional interests in modern British society. Thirdly, it requires a serious and responsible approach by the media to the discussion and interpretation of the political issues of the day – something which seems almost impossible to achieve on a reliable and sustained basis. Even if all these conditions are met, the achievement of good government can still be vitiated by complicating factors in the private sector and in government at the European or global levels which increasingly constrain the actions of any national Government.

Thus if any British Government is to deal successfully with the leading problems of our time – for example, the endemic threat of inflation, the powerful effects of new technologies, or the far-reaching consequences of environmental pollution – there will always be a need for responsible and far-sighted leadership by politicians both in Government and in Opposition. In a world in which some things change very rapidly while other things seem to change hardly at all, such leadership will require policies which increase, rather than reduce, the chances of securing public consent. The general public, for its part, will need to recognise that many traditional attitudes and assumptions, which may be held very deeply, can obstruct rather than assist the emergence of new syntheses which are likely to be essential if appropriate and timely action is to be taken. Even on the charitable assumption that politicians and people manage to cooperate in such virtuous ways, it is not likely to be possible to avoid periodic bouts of public disappointment and distress in view of the intractable nature of the challenges which have to be faced.

20.5 Conclusion

It should be clear from this book that British Parliamentary democracy is neither easy to describe nor to explain. Although it is changing in certain respects all the time, in many other ways it remains the same. It is imbued with fascinating paradoxes and contradictions. While the political system allows for and even encourages strong Government, it is less good at legitimising the decisions which are actually taken. This is sometimes because the most controversial decisions are not founded upon a sufficiently broad basis of political consent at the time when they are taken. Yet more often it seems to have been a matter of willing the ends of policy, but not necessarily the means required to achieve them. This provides one of the main explanations for Britain's patchy and often disappointing national performance over many years.

We can see that the political mould set during the Second World War was finally broken by Thatcherite radicalism in the 1980s. This in its turn helped to create the spirit of the 1990s which seems to be an interesting amalgam of post-Thatcherite individualism and pre-Thatcherite collectivism which always owed more to Methodism than Marxism. In the future, as in the past, politicians and public alike will need to strive for mutual understanding and accommodation without which political life is likely to be even more disappointing. In such circumstances there can be no guarantee of success, but it should be possible for Parliamentary democracy to survive in Britain within its European and global frameworks.

Suggested questions

1 What is the essence of British Parliamentary democracy?
2 Is the British political system successful in gaining and retaining the consent of the people?
3 Have British politics been permanently altered by Britain's membership of the European Union?

Notes

1. See J.A. Schumpeter, *Capitalism, Socialism and Democracy,* 3rd edn (New York: Harper & Row, 1962), pp. 289-96.
2. See Q. Hailsham, *The Dilemma of Democracy* (London: Collins, 1978), pp. 280-1.

Further reading

Barker, R., *Political Legitimacy and the State* (Oxford: Clarendon Press, 1990).
Beetham, D., *The Legitimation of Power* (London: Macmillan, 1991).
Brittan, S., *The Role and Limits of Government* (London: Temple Smith, 1983).
Dahrendorf, R., *Life Chances* (London: Weidenfeld & Nicolson, 1979).
Hailsham, Q., *The Dilemma of Democracy* (London: Collins, 1978).
Hirsch, F., *Social Limits to Growth* (London: Routledge & Kegan Paul, 1977).
Luard, E., *The Globalisation of Politics* (London: Macmillan, 1990).
Marquand, D., *The Unprincipled Society* (London: Fontana Press, 1988).
Miliband, R., *Capitalist Democracy in Britain* (London: Oxford University Press, 1984).
Schumpeter, J.A., *Capitalism, Socialism and Democracy,* 3rd edn (New York: Harper & Row, 1962).

Conservative
Labour
Liberal Democrats
Others

Greater
London

How Britain voted in 1992: constituency by constituency

Orkneys

Western
Isles

Shetland

	Conservative
	Labour
	Liberal Democrats
	Others

Name index

Subject index

criminal justice 367–70
judicial appeal 373–5
police (role) 382–5
'Justice' Report (1978) 132

K

Keynesian White Paper (1944) 7
Kilbrandon Commission (1973) 35, 327
'Kitchen Cabinet' 247

L

Labour Party
Cabinet resignations 256–7
candidate selection 96–7
Charter of Rights 392
Clause IV 74, 77, 311, 312, 335–6, 427
Conservative Party (comparison) 91–2
constituency activities 94–7
electoral system 33–4
General Management Committees 95–6
House of Lords reform 206
ideological principles 74–7, 77–81, 436–7
image 58–9
Leader 88, 89, 91, 95
national organisation 88–91, 91–2
NEC 75, 85, 88–9, 92, 97, 252, 428, 429
Parliamentary Committee 89
Parliamentary Labour Party 74, 75, 89,
91, 92, 106, 176
Party Chairman 89
Party Conference 75, 85, 88, 89, 96
policy consensus 7–8
policy formulation 428, 429
policy germination 427
Policy Review 75, 139, 206, 427
political function 84
political inheritance 55
Prime Ministers of 251, 252
Research Department 89, 428
social composition 61, 95
socialism and 74–6, 91, 311, 436
support for 39–40, 47–53, 61–2, 65
Land Valuation Bill (1907) 192
Law Commission 327
Law Lords 195, 200, 366, 373, 390, 391
Law Society 104
League Against Cruel Sports 103
legal aid 372, 394 n13
legal implications of EU membership 21–4,
26, 302–3, 402–8
legal system 16, 366–93

administrative law 385–91
citizens and state 375–82
civil justice 370–3
criminal justice 367–70
judicial appeal 373–5
police (role) 382–5
legislation
delay of 197, 198
emergency legislation 227
European 4–5, 17, 24, 200, 275–6
European secondary 201
House of Commons 225–7
House of Lords 197, 198, 199
non-controversial 197, 199
pre-legislative investigation 229
pressure groups and 116
Royal Assent 171, 178, 227
legislature (effectiveness) 38–9
Lib-Lab pact (1977-9) 41
Liberal Democrats 422
constituency activities 94–7
House of Lords reform 206
ideological principles 77–81
local government 361
national organisation 92–4
Liberal Party 83
'Liberty' group 379
Licensing Bill (1908) 192
Life Peerages Act (1958) 193, 195
life peers 179, 193, 195–6, 202
lobby system 133–4
local autonomy 361–2
local elections 45, 154, 363
local government 338–63
adaptibility 363
Audit Commission 324, 326, 349
boundaries 358, 359–60
central control of 354–7
Community Charge 8, 25, 41, 61, 110,
150, 154–6, 161, 165, 350–1, 358, 362,
384, 452
Council Tax 25, 154, 351, 358, 361, 362
financial arrangements 347–51
functions 343–7
future policies 357–62
powers and functions 343–7
rates/RSG 347–50, 356
Robinson Report 341–2
structure and personnel 338–43
Uniform Business Rate 25, 350–1, 353,
356, 357, 361, 362, 363

powers and functions 175–84
Prime Minister and 175–6
public and 186–8
Royal Assent 171, 178, 227
Money Bills 192, 206, 231
Monopolies and Mergers Commission 315,
323
'multiplier effect' 33
Municipal Corporations Act (1835) 352
municipal ownership 309

N

National Association for the Care and
Resettlement of Offenders 116
National Association of Schoolmasters/Union
of Women Teachers 117
National Audit Commission 324, 326
National Democrats (formerly National Front)
82
National Economic Development Council
(Neddy) 111, 332
National Farmers' Union 104, 110, 115,
271, 416
National Government 152, 176
National Health Service 76, 104, 107–8,
117, 193, 246, 256, 332–3, 386
Trusts 333, 358, 388
National Health Service Act (1946) 104, 332
National Insurance 332, 386
National Liberal Federation 71
National Listeners and Viewers Association
105
National Society for Clean Air 114
National Trust 103, 118
National Union of Conservative Associations
71, 85, 86, 92
National Union of Mineworkers 107–8, 109,
151, 152, 159
National Union of Teachers 117, 159
nationalised industries 182, 309–15
Nationalist parties 81
see also Plaid Cymru; Scottish National
Party
NATO 165, 400
Natural Law Party 83
Neddy see National Economic Development
Council
negative voting 57
New Right 72
new technologies 138–40
New Towns 182

News International 121
Next Steps agencies 25, 272, 299–302
NIMBY groups 119
Nolan Commission (1994) 214, 328
nominations 31
non-controversial legislation 197, 199
non-Departmental public bodies 323–7
advantages/disadvantages 324–7
common characteristics 324
non-voters 46–7
NOP survey (1995) 165
Northcote-Trevelyan Report (1854) 283,
286, 294–5
Northern Ireland 377, 435
Act of Union 4, 16
Anglo-Irish Agreement 82, 273
Downing Street Declaration 26, 78, 254
Home Rule 177, 192
IRA 7, 26, 78, 137, 378, 381
local government 340–1, 361
peace process 251, 254, 341, 452
political parties 81–2
reunification 7
Northern Ireland (Emergency Provisions) Act
378
nuclear disarmament groups 103, 105,
111–12
NUM 107–8, 109, 151, 152, 159
NUT 117, 159

O

Office of Fair Trading 323
Office of Population Censuses and Surveys
156
Office of Public Service 266–7
Office of Technology Assessment 442
Official Monster Raving Loony Party 83
Official Secrets Acts
1911 131, 290, 425
1989 131, 378
Ofgas 320, 322
Ofsted 355
Oftel 320, 322, 323
Ofwat 322
Ombudsman 131, 296–7, 379, 387–9
European 377
'Operation Countryman' 383
opinion polls 155–6, 159–60, 186, 187
Opposition parties 293, 430, 437,
composition of 211, 214
functions 224–5, 225–6

Treaty of Accession (1972)   11, 181, 401
Treaty of Berlin (1878)   239
Treaty of Paris   406
Treaty of Rome   400, 405–6
Treaty of Utrecht   179
tribunals   366, 370, 386–7
Tribunals and Inquiries Acts   386, 387
Trosa Report (1993)   300
TUC   102, 104, 108, 110
Two-Ballot System   36

U

UK Permanent Delegation in Brussels   410
Ulster Popular Unionists   81
Ulster Unionist Party   81, 452
ultra vires doctrine   296, 389
Uniform Business Rate   25, 350–1, 353, 356, 357, 361, 362, 363
Unitary Authorities   339–40, 345, 358
unitary state   4–5
United Nations   182
   Declaration of Human Rights   376
United States   4, 400, 442
Urban Development Corporations   354, 358
Urban Priority Areas   156

V

Van Gend en Loos case   404
'virtual representatives'   211
voting behaviour   45–65, 149
   age-based   49–50
   class-based   47–9, 51, 61–2
   electoral groups   46–54
   floaters and abstainers   46–7
   gender-based   49–50, 62
   influences   54–9
   party loyalists   46
   sectional cleavages   50–4
   uncertainties   59–65

see also electorate
voting power (of pressure groups)   112–13
voting procedures   30–3

W

Wales   198
   devolution   23, 154–5, 361
   local government   338–40, 341, 343, 361
   Plaid Cymru   6, 81, 361, 422
   union with England   4
War Crimes Act (1991)   198
War Damage Act (1965)   374
Water Authorities   321, 332
Welsh Church Act (1914)   198
West Germany   4, 36, 41, 303
West Midlands Serious Crime Squad   383
Western European Union   400
Westland affair   58, 150, 229, 256, 272
'Wets' (in Conservative Party)   164, 257, 436
Whips   218, 219–22
Whitehall
   Cabinet support in   245–7
   conventions   287–8
   Department structure   264–71
   special advisers   441
   structural change   442
   see also Civil Service
Widdicombe Committee   342
Wilson Committee on Financial Institutions   327
Windsor Castle fire (1992)   186
Wing Airport Resistance Association   105
'Witan'   171–2, 190
Workers' Revolutionary P)arty   82
working class voters   51–3, 61

Z

Zimbabwe Independence Act (1980)   182